The Palgrave Handbook of Malicious Use of AI and Psychological Security

"This book makes an outstanding contribution to our understanding of artificial intelligence (AI) and its capacity to be used in malicious ways. This negative side of AI needs to be brought out of the shadows so that it can be properly addressed and reforms proposed to reduce the risks associated with the new technology. Without a broader understanding of the malicious use of AI by state and non-state actors, there is no hope of achieving any consensus on the next steps required. This book achieves its aims admirably and is one of the few to confront the topic in an objective and scientific manner."
—Victor Bulmer-Thomas, *Institute of the Americas, University College London, UK*

"This book provides a powerful account of modern and potential future threats to psychological security posed by both state and non-state actors through MUAI. This book is a rigorous review of an advantage in psychological warfare. This subject has historically been studied far less extensively than the positive applications of AI. An interesting book with many great discussions."
—Don Donghee Shin, Professor and Program Coordinator, *Zayed University & Swansea University, UK*

"This important book is a forward looking and practical examination of the negative risks and realities of artificial intelligence. It is comprehensive and practical, illustrating the present and future dangers of MUAI for nations, companies and individuals with its compelling exploration of psychological security and influence."
—Dr. Michael R. Finch, *Chair of Communication, Media & Culture at Bryan College, USA; Affiliate Researcher for LCC International University, LT, Executive Director for the Communication Association of Eurasian Researchers*

"AI is a paradox: its potential benefits are extraordinary; so too are the dystopian consequences of its misuse, among them the psychological destabilization and manipulation of whole populations. In this collection marshalled by a leading scholar of strategic communication, Professor Evgeny Pashentsev, and based on analyses by 23 experts in 11 countries, the nature of the evolving crisis and the urgent need to resolve it are clearly and cogently laid out in a way that facilitates understanding and the imperatives which must follow."
—Michael McKinley, Emeritus Faculty, *The Australian National University*

"Organized in a systemic way, the book illustrates in an organic, comprehensive and in-depth way the many aspects of the malicious use of AI: from the methodological approach to the analysis of the implications of this problem on the main areas of civil, political, institutional coexistence as well as on regional and national areas in which the world order is currently organized. The analysis is completed by a valid projection on possible future prospects: a further element of great added value and support offered to the reader by this handbook."
—Marco Ricceri, The Secretary General, *Eurispes Institute, Rome-Italy*

"An extremely timely book on a significant and rapidly growing problem in international relations and international security. The book provides new facts and new assessments of existing and growing threats related to the weaponization of artificial intelligence. This volume is a remarkable source of materials for undergraduate and graduate classes in the fields of security and international relations in general. An outstanding and very informative handbook for a wide range of professionals."
—Eric Shiraev, Ph.D., *George Mason University, CARP-Character Assassination and Reputation Management Research Lab*

"This handbook is a remarkable work that goes well beyond the current state of the art on the current and future methods, uses and consequences of the malicious use of artificial intelligence globally and across different geographical, technological, social, political, psychological and informational environments. An impressive number of authors from around the world are represented, which is fitting as MUAI is a global problem that requires global solutions to tackle it. An extremely valuable book packed with critical knowledge for students, researchers and practitioners alike."
—Associate Professor Greg Simons, *Uppsala University in Sweden and Turiba University in Latvia*

Evgeny Pashentsev
Editor

The Palgrave Handbook of Malicious Use of AI and Psychological Security

palgrave
macmillan

Editor
Evgeny Pashentsev
Diplomatic Academy of the Ministry
of Foreign Affairs of the Russian Federation
Moscow, Russia

ISBN 978-3-031-22551-2   ISBN 978-3-031-22552-9 (eBook)
https://doi.org/10.1007/978-3-031-22552-9

© The Editor(s) (if applicable) and The Author(s), under exclusive licence to Springer Nature Switzerland AG 2023
This work is subject to copyright. All rights are solely and exclusively licensed by the Publisher, whether the whole or part of the material is concerned, specifically the rights of translation, reprinting, reuse of illustrations, recitation, broadcasting, reproduction on microfilms or in any other physical way, and transmission or information storage and retrieval, electronic adaptation, computer software, or by similar or dissimilar methodology now known or hereafter developed.
The use of general descriptive names, registered names, trademarks, service marks, etc. in this publication does not imply, even in the absence of a specific statement, that such names are exempt from the relevant protective laws and regulations and therefore free for general use.
The publisher, the authors, and the editors are safe to assume that the advice and information in this book are believed to be true and accurate at the date of publication. Neither the publisher nor the authors or the editors give a warranty, expressed or implied, with respect to the material contained herein or for any errors or omissions that may have been made. The publisher remains neutral with regard to jurisdictional claims in published maps and institutional affiliations.

Cover illustration: mikkelwilliam / Getty image

This Palgrave Macmillan imprint is published by the registered company Springer Nature Switzerland AG.
The registered company address is: Gewerbestrasse 11, 6330 Cham, Switzerland

Contents

1 Introduction: The Malicious Use of Artificial Intelligence—
Growing Threats, Delayed Responses   1
Evgeny Pashentsev

Part I   The Malicious Use of Artificial Intelligence Against
Psychological Security: Forms and Methods   21

2 General Content and Possible Threat Classifications of the
Malicious Use of Artificial Intelligence to Psychological
Security   23
Evgeny Pashentsev

3 The Malicious Use of Deepfakes Against Psychological
Security and Political Stability   47
Evgeny Pashentsev

4 Automating Extremism: Mapping the Affective Roles of
Artificial Agents in Online Radicalization   81
Peter Mantello, Tung Manh Ho, and Lena Podoletz

5 Hate Speech in Perception Management Campaigns: New
Opportunities of Sentiment Analysis and Affective Computing   105
Yury Kolotaev

6 The Malicious Use of Artificial Intelligence Through Agenda Setting   133
   Evgeny Pashentsev

Part II Areas of Malicious Use of Artificial Intelligence in the Context of Threats to Psychological Security   173

7 The COVID-19 Pandemic and the Rise of Malicious Use of AI Threats to National and International Psychological Security   175
   Marta N. Lukacovic and Deborah D. Sellnow-Richmond

8 Malicious Use of Artificial Intelligence in Political Campaigns: Challenges for International Psychological Security for the Next Decades   203
   Marius Vacarelu

9 Destabilization of Unstable Dynamic Social Equilibriums and the Malicious Use of Artificial Intelligence in High-Tech Strategic Psychological Warfare   231
   Evgeny Pashentsev

10 Current and Future Threats of the Malicious Use of Artificial Intelligence by Terrorists: Psychological Aspects   251
   Darya Bazarkina

11 Malicious Use of Artificial Intelligence and the Threats to Corporate Reputation in International Business   273
   Erik Vlaeminck

Part III Regional and National Implications of the Malicious Use of Artificial Intelligence and Psychological Security   295

12 Malicious Use of Artificial Intelligence: Risks to Psychological Security in BRICS Countries   297
   Evgeny Pashentsev and Darya Bazarkina

13 The Threats and Current Practices of Malicious Use of
    Artificial Intelligence in Psychological Security in China   335
    *Darya Bazarkina, Ekaterina A. Mikhalevich, Evgeny Pashentsev,
    and Daria Matyashova*

14 Malicious Use of Artificial Intelligence, Uncertainty, and
    U.S.–China Strategic Mutual Trust   377
    Cuihong Cai and Ruoyang Zhang

15 Scenario Analysis of Malicious Use of Artificial Intelligence
    and Challenges to Psychological Security in India   397
    Arvind Gupta and Aakash Guglani

16 Current and Potential Malicious Use of Artificial Intelligence
    Threats in the Psychological Domain: The Case of Japan   419
    *Darya Bazarkina, Yury Kolotaev, Evgeny Pashentsev, and
    Daria Matyashova*

17 Geopolitical Competition and the Challenges for the
    European Union of Countering the Malicious Use of Artificial
    Intelligence   453
    Pierre-Emmanuel Thomann

18 Germany: Rising Sociopolitical Controversies and Threats to
    Psychological Security from the Malicious Use of Artificial
    Intelligence   487
    Daria Matyashova

19 Artificial Intelligence and Deepfakes in Strategic Deception
    Campaigns: The U.S. and Russian Experiences   507
    Sergei A. Samoilenko and Inna Suvorova

20 Malicious Use of Artificial Intelligence and Threats to
    Psychological Security in Latin America: Common Problems,
    Current Practice and Prospects   531
    Evgeny Pashentsev and Darya Bazarkina

21 Malicious Use of Artificial Intelligence and the Threat to
    Psychological Security in the Middle East: Aggravation of
    Political and Social Turbulence   561
    Vitali Romanovski

Part IV Future Horizons: The New Quality of Malicious Use of
         Artificial Intelligence Threats to Psychological Security 581

22 Malicious Use of Artificial Intelligence in the Metaverse:
    Possible Threats and Countermeasures   583
    Sergey A. Sebekin and Andrei Kalegin

23 Unpredictable Threats from the Malicious Use of Artificial
    Strong Intelligence   607
    Alexander Raikov

24 Prospects for a Qualitative Breakthrough in Artificial
    Intelligence Development and Possible Models for Social
    Development: Opportunities and Threats   631
    Evgeny Pashentsev

25 Conclusion: Per Aspera Ad Astra   677
    Evgeny Pashentsev

Index   687

About the Editor

Evgeny Pashentsev is Professor and Leading Researcher at the Institute of Contemporary International Studies at the Diplomatic Academy of the Ministry of Foreign Affairs of the Russian Federation, Russia. He is a Coordinator of the International Research Group on Threats for International Psychological Security by Malicious Use of Artificial Intelligence (Research MUAI), and a member of the International Advisory Board of *Comunicar*, Spain, and the editorial board of *The Journal of Political Marketing*, USA. Author and/or editor of 38 books and more than 200 academic articles. Pashentsev presented papers at more than 180 international conferences and seminars for the last 10 years in 23 countries. Honorary Research Fellow at Birmingham University (October–November 2005). In 2021, he headed the work of Russian researchers within the framework of a joint project supported by the Russian Foundation for Basic Research (RFBR) and the Vietnam Academy of Social Sciences (VASS) on the topic "Malicious use of artificial intelligence and challenges to psychological security in Northeast Asia." Areas of current research: artificial intelligence and global shifts, malicious use of artificial intelligence and international psychological security, and strategic communication.

Notes on Contributors

Darya Bazarkina (DSc., Politics, PhD, History) is a Leading Researcher at the Department of European Integration Research at the Institute of Europe of the Russian Academy of Sciences. She is a full professor at the Department for International Security and Foreign Affairs at the Russian Presidential Academy of National Economy and Public Administration (RANEPA) and a research coordinator of Communication Management and Strategic Communication at the International Center for Social and Political Studies and Consulting (ICSPSC). Bazarkina has been a member of the following research associations: National Law Enforcement Agencies' History Studies' Community and the International Experts' Network "European Union—Russia—Communication Management" (EURUCM). Member of the International Research Group on Threats for International Psychological Security by Malicious Use of Artificial Intelligence (Research MUAI). She has presented at more than 60 international academic conferences and seminars in Russia, Austria, Belgium, Czech Republic, Estonia, Finland, Great Britain, Italy, Poland, Portugal, Romania, Serbia, Sweden, and Turkey. Bazarkina is the author of three books and more than 100 publications on communication aspects of counter-terrorist activity published in Russian, English, Italian, Serbian, and Vietnamese.

Cuihong Cai is Professor of International Relations with the Center for American Studies at Fudan University, P. R. China. She received her B.S. (1993) and M.S. (1996) in biophysics as well as her PhD (2002) in international relations from Fudan University. She also holds a B.A. (2001) in English language and literature from Shanghai International Studies University. She was a visiting scholar at the Georgia Institute of Technology in 2002 and at the University of California, Berkeley in 2007, as well as an invited fellow in the 2007 program on the U.S. National Security sponsored by the U.S. State Department. Dr. Cai is the author of *Cyberpolitics in U.S.-China Relations* (English version 2021, Chinese version 2019), *Political Development in the Cyber Age* (2015), *U.S. National Information Security Strategy* (2009), and *Internet and International Politics* (2003), as well as several dozen articles and papers on cyberpolitics, cybersecurity strategy, cyberspace governance, and U.S.-China relations.

Aakash Guglani is a policy associate at the Digital India Foundation. He is a Young India Fellow and Liberal Studies postgraduate from Ashoka University and Management Studies graduate from the University of Delhi. He has authored articles in the *Journal of Indian Council of Philosophical Research* (JICPR), *Social Science Research Network* (SSRN) as well as authored a book "*Essays on Gender, Society and Self.*" He has keen interest in political theory of technology deployment, science and technology policies, Indian philosophy, philosophy of mind and its intersection with artificial intelligence. He aims to align his research to aid decision-making at top management levels of public, private and nonprofit sectors. In his previous role, he worked as a teaching fellow on Western Political Thought I and II at Ashoka University, India.

Arvind Gupta is the head and co-founder of Digital India Foundation, a policy think tank working in the area of digital inclusion. He is also an adjunct professor at IIT-BHU. He graduated with a degree in Electronics and Communication Engineering from IIT-BHU, Varanasi. He has a Masters in Computer Science and MBA (Finance & Marketing) from University of Illinois at Urbana Champaign. He has been on the Global FinTech Top100 list of Influencers and also the Member of World Economic Forum's Global Futures Council on Digital Economy & Society, OECD Expert Member of Global Value Chains. He has been awarded the Eisenhower Global Fellowship for Innovation for year 2014 and Distinguished Centenary Alumni award from IIT-BHU. In his last role, he was the CEO of MyGov, Government of India, a platform for digital inclusion through participative governance. Recently, he has been appointed as one of the members of the advisory council by Government of India, to create India's open network for digital commerce.

Tung Manh Ho holds an MSc in Society, Culture, and Media Studies at Ritsumeikan Asia Pacific University, Oita, Japan. He is a PhD candidate and works as a research fellow on the project "Emotional AI in Cities: Cross-Cultural Lessons from UK and Japan on Designing for an Ethical Life" funded by JST-UKRI Joint Call on Artificial Intelligence and Society (2019). He is also affiliated with top research institutions in Vietnam such as the Institute of Philosophy of Vietnam Academy of Social Sciences and the Centre for Interdisciplinary Social Research at Phenikaa University. His published works cover diverse topics in social sciences and humanities, including social and ethical implications of emotional AI, emotional AI and the future of work, interactive dynamics of cultural values, acculturation and cultural additivity, media representation of systemic corruption, network analysis of scientific collaborations, applications of Bayesian statistics in social sciences, and so on.

Andrei Kalegin is an Intern at the International Center for Social and Political Studies and Consulting. He is a software engineer and cybersecurity professional. He graduated with a degree in Physics from St. Petersburg State Polytechnic University, St. Petersburg, Russia. He has a Masters in Computer Science from St. Petersburg National Research Academic University of the Russian Academy of Sciences. He is pursuing a Master's degree in International Economics from The Diplomatic Academy of the Ministry of Foreign Affairs of the Russian Federation. His research interest includes international cybersecurity, information technologies, artificial intelligence, and the future of international relations.

Yury Kolotaev is a PhD student at St. Petersburg State University, School of International Relations, Department of European Studies. Intern at the International Center for Social and Political Studies and Consulting. Member of the Youth Council of the Coordination Center for TLD .RU/.РФ. Member of the European International Studies Association (EISA). He received his MA in International Relations at St. Petersburg State University, graduating with Distinction in 2020. His research interests focus on contemporary information threats, including hate speech, post-truth politics, fake news, and other types of misleading or harmful content. Yury Kolotaev is an author of several publications, in Russian and English, on the malicious use of artificial intelligence and European experience in tackling online disinformation. He co-authored a book chapter on various models of supranational resilience to information threats. He participates in a research project funded by RFBR and VASS on challenges to psychological security through the malicious use of artificial intelligence in Northeast Asia.

Marta N. Lukacovic (PhD, Wayne State University, Detroit-Michigan) is Assistant Professor of Communication and Mass Media at Angelo State University—Texas Tech University System, USA. Her recent research has been primarily centered on trends in communication through digital media platforms; specifically, on how user-generated online content interacts with the matters of security, oppression, irredentism, and political violence. She frequently presents at international conferences. Her work has appeared in several international journals, such as *PACO, Frontiers in Communication*, and *International Communication Research Journal*. Since 2021, she serves as the president of Communication Association of Eurasian Researchers (CAER). Her work in CAER is focused on facilitating bridges between researchers from Eastern Europe and Central Asia and other global scholars of media and communication. She is a co-editor of the books *Media and Public Relations Research in Post-Socialist Societies* (2021) and *Communication Theory and Application in Post-Socialist Contexts* (in press, 2022, Lexington Books—Rowman & Littlefield).

Peter Mantello is Professor of Media, Ethics and Technology at Ritsumeikan Asia Pacific University, Oita, Japan. His research explores the porous boundaries and feedback systems between artificial technology, security, culture, and emerging technologies. Peter Mantello is a member of the International Research Group on Threats to International Psychological Security through Malicious Use of Artificial Intelligence (Research MUAI). Prior to his academic life, Mantello worked as a war photographer in conflicts zones in Burma and Cambodia as well as a creative director of advertising in Bangkok. Besides an expertise in emotional AI, he has written on diverse topics such as videogames, jihadist media, memes, selfies, and computational policing. He has been awarded numerous grants and awards for his documentary photography, game designer, experimental films, and scholarly work. He is a principal investigator on two projects dealing with various aspects of artificial intelligence. The first deals with computational advances in policing, criminal justice, and the shift from post-hoc to precrime society. The second project examines the cross-cultural ethical, political, social, and philosophical dimensions of emotional artificial intelligence in smart city design in the UK and Japan.

Daria Matyashova is a PhD student at the International Relations Faculty of St. Petersburg State University. Matyashova is an author of more than 20 publications on AI communication aspects, Asia Pacific international conflicts, and rising power politics. Her research interests include cybersecurity, normative and soft power and politics of contemporary rising powers. Matyashova is a laureate of the autumn Euroschool (2020) and the Second Internet Governance Summer school (2021). Participant of the grant project "Malicious Use of Artificial Intelligence and Challenges for Psychological Security in Northeast Asia", funded by the Russian Foundation for Basic

Research and the Vietnam Academy of Social Sciences, ID 21-514-92001 (2021–2022). While working on the project, she was engaged in clarifying the threats of malicious use of AI in Hong Kong, Taiwan, Japan, and Germany, to destabilize international psychological security.

Ekaterina A. Mikhalevich is a doctoral student at the International Relations Department, St. Petersburg State University. Her future PhD thesis is devoted to the concept of cyber sovereignty as a mechanism for implementing and protecting the national interests of the People's Republic of China. Participant of visits to NATO Headquarters (Brussels, Belgium) and Headquarters of the Supreme Headquarters Allied Powers Europe SHAPE (Mons, Belgium). Participant of the grant project "Malicious use of Artificial Intelligence and Challenges for Psychological Security in Northeast Asia", funded by the Russian Foundation for Basic Research and the Vietnam Academy of Social Sciences, ID 21-514-92001 (2021–2022). While working on the project, she was engaged in clarifying the significance of the political situation in Northeast Asia and the threats of malicious use of AI to destabilize international psychological security. Research interests: international relations and world politics, international security, international information and psychological security, cyber sovereignty, artificial intelligence, and international law.

Evgeny Pashentsev is Professor and Leading Researcher at the Institute of Contemporary International Studies at the Diplomatic Academy of the Ministry of Foreign Affairs of the Russian Federation, Russia. He is a Coordinator of the International Research Group on Threats for International Psychological Security by Malicious Use of Artificial Intelligence (Research MUAI), and a member of the International Advisory Board of *Comunicar*, Spain, and the editorial board of *The Journal of Political Marketing*, USA. Author and/or editor of 38 books and more than 200 academic articles. Pashentsev presented papers at more than 180 international conferences and seminars for the last 10 years in 23 countries. Honorary Research Fellow at Birmingham University (October–November 2005). In 2021, he headed the work of Russian researchers within the framework of a joint project supported by the Russian Foundation for Basic Research (RFBR) and the Vietnam Academy of Social Sciences (VASS) on the topic "Malicious use of artificial intelligence and challenges to psychological security in Northeast Asia." Areas of current research: artificial intelligence and global shifts, malicious use of artificial intelligence and international psychological security, and strategic communication.

Lena Podoletz is a researcher at the University of Edinburgh (UK). Her research takes place in the intersection of criminology, technology, social science, and law with a strong focus on emerging technologies as well as marginalization. Her current research focuses on algorithmic transparency, bias, and discrimination with a special interest in algorithmic decision-making systems used in the recruitment process as well as the monitoring of bias in algorithmic decision-making systems. Her research also includes the use of emotional AI technologies in smart cities and in the field of policing and security where she is investigating the potential effects and harms of such technologies on individuals, groups, and society. Previously, she worked at Eotvos Lorand University (Hungary) where she undertook research on policing of urban spaces, control over urban spaces, homelessness, sex work, fairness and biases in policing, marginalization, and social exclusion.

Alexander Raikov is Professor, Doctor of Technical Sciences, State Advisor of the Russian Federation of the 3rd class, Winner of the Russian Government Award in the Field of Science and Technology, General Director of the New Strategies Agency (NSA) Ltd., professor of the State Technological University (Russia), leading researcher of the Institute of Control Sciences of the Russian Academy of Sciences, senior researcher of the National Center of Excellence in the field of Digital Economy of the Lomonosov Moscow State University, chief researcher of the Institute of Philosophy, Russian Academy of Sciences. He is a member of the International Research Group on Threats to International Psychological Security through Malicious Use of Artificial Intelligence (Research MUAI). Prior to 1993, Prof. A. Raikov developed automated control systems for the Russian Government. In 1993–1999, he was the head of the Information-Analytical Department of the Presidential Administration and coordinator of the Situation Center of the Russian President. Since 1999, he and his team have completed about 60 projects for the Administration of the President of the Russian Federation, Ministry of Education of Russia, Ministry of Economic Development of Russia, the Government of the city of Moscow, the Republic of Kazakhstan, and so on. Prof. Raikov developed strategies for improving the quality of health care and education in the regions and scientific cities of Russia. Author of more than 350 research papers, 6 monographs, 9 patents in the field of strategic management, socio-economic development, information and analytical technologies, AI, situation centers, decision support systems, and network expertise.

Vitali Romanovski holds the position of analyst with the Belarusian Institute of Strategic Research. He has substantive field experience in the Middle East, including an advisory role with an intergovernmental program on military-technical cooperation in the UAE and an analytical post with the United Nations Assistance Mission in Iraq, Baghdad. Regular participant of the Chatham House events on information security and counter-terrorism in the EU, Middle East, and Russia. Member of the International Studies Association (ISA) and East European Studies Association (CEEISA). His research interest includes intelligence studies, psychological warfare, artificial intelligence, and information security.

Sergei A. Samoilenko is an assistant professor at the Department of Communication at George Mason University. Samoilenko is a past president of the Communication Association of Eurasian Researchers (CAER) and a co-founder of the Research Lab for Character Assassination and Reputation Politics (CARP) at George Mason University. His research focuses on issues in public relations, reputation management, and crisis communication. He is a co-editor of *Routledge Handbook of Character Assassination and Reputation Management*, *Handbook of Research on Deception, Fake News, and Misinformation Online*, and *Media and Public Relations Research in Post-Soviet Societies*. Samoilenko actively contributes to the development of communication education internationally. He is a past president of Communication Association of Eurasion Researchers (CAER), an organization established to promote joint projects between scholars from Russia, CIS, and Baltic states and their North American counterparts. He is a co-founder and a board member of the Kazakhstan Communication Association. He is also a member of the Global Alliance for Public Relations and Communications Management.

Sergey A. Sebekin defended his PhD thesis "The Genesis and Development of Strategies to Deter Cyber Threats in the United States, China and Russia (1990s–2014)" in 2020. He is a lecturer at the Department of Political Science, History and Regional Studies of Irkutsk State University. He is a fellow of the Oxford Russian Foundation 2014–2015. In 2016, he completed an internship at Hokkaido University as part of the Russian–Japanese program Russia–Japan East 3 (RJE 3), Sapporo, Japan. In 2020–2021, he completed an internship at the Moscow-based Russian Center for Policy Studies (PIR Center) under the program "New Technologies and International Security". His research interests are issues of international cybersecurity, theories of cyber warfare, artificial intelligence and the future of international relations, and the impact of high technologies on international relations. He has authored 30 academic articles, analytical notes and papers on various aspects of international cybersecurity, published by such journals and organizations operating in the field of international relations as *Russia in Global Affairs*,

Russian International Affairs Council, the Valdai International Discussion Club, the PIR Center, and the Primakov Center for Foreign Policy Cooperation.

Deborah D. Sellnow-Richmond (PhD, Wayne State University, Detroit-Michigan) is Assistant Professor of Communication Studies at Southern Illinois University Edwardsville, Illinois, USA. Her research focuses on the efficacy and/or unforeseen effects of public relations messages in health/organizational crisis contexts, as well as the emerging role of social media in resolving organizational crises. Her research emphasizes the importance of strategic message design effectively reaching typically marginalized populations in risk and crisis situations. Most recently, her research examines these effects in the context of mega-crises surrounding such health outbreaks as the ebolavirus, African Swine Fever, and the COVID-19 pandemic. Her work has been published in such journals as the *Journal of International Crisis and Risk Communication Research, Journal of Applied Communication Research, Journal of Risk Research, Health Communication*, and *Communication Studies*. She regularly attends and presents research at the International Crisis and Risk Communication conference and the convention of the National Communication Association.

Inna Suvorova is a graduate student at University College London (UK). She has a strong background in journalism and communications, having previously worked in business media and IT companies. Her research and journalism focus on the impact of new technologies and artificial intelligence on media and society. Suvorova is a team leader at the iFreedomLab project (https://ifreedomlab.net/), which aims to protect and enhance digital rights. She coordinates campaigns to develop best practices for the interaction of big tech companies and their consumers and undertakes investigations to get big tech companies in Russia and worldwide to play fair.

Pierre-Emmanuel Thomann is a doctor in geopolitics. His doctorate was obtained at the French Institute of Geopolitics (IFG, University Paris 8) in 2014. The thematics of his expertise cover Franco-German relations, pan-European and global geopolitical issues, geopolitical cartography, and the geopolitical dimension of artificial intelligence issues. He teaches at Lyon 3 Jean Moulin University, Lyon, France. He is president/founder of an International Association Eurocontinent based in Brussels (website www.eurocontinent.eu) whose objective is to broaden the debates about the European project on geopolitical issues. Pierre-Emmanuel Thomann is a member of the International Research Group on Threats to International

Psychological Security through Malicious Use of Artificial Intelligence (Research MUAI). Pierre-Emmanuel regularly authors articles in academic journals and specialized magazines on diplomatic and geopolitical issues and contributes regularly to international conferences and seminars on international affairs organized by UNO, OSCE, and UNESCO, at international and national conferences in France, Italy, Russia, Uzbekistan, and other countries.

Marius Vacarelu holds a PhD and is a researcher in political sciences and a legal expert. He graduated from the Law Faculty in Bucharest. Marius Vacarelu teaches public law in the National School of Political Science and Public Administration since 2005, is a member of the committee, which edits the Romanian magazine *GeoPolitica*, and is a head of "The Geopolitics of the East Association" which runs the website www.geopoliticaestului.ro. Marius Vacarelu is a member of the International Research Group on Threats to International Psychological Security through Malicious Use of Artificial Intelligence (Research MUAI). He is an author/co-author/coordinator of 22 books and more than 200 academic articles including the articles/book chapters on the role of AI in international relations and political processes. Marius Vacarelu is a frequent speaker on Romanian television on geopolitics issues. He is a blogger for Romania's most important journal *Adevarul*. Marius Vacarelu has presented papers and published articles in Russia, Czech Republic, France, Poland, the UK, and the US.

Erik Vlaeminck holds an MA in Eastern European and Slavonic Studies from KU Leuven (Belgium) and an MA in Russia and Eurasian Studies from Leiden University (The Netherlands). He obtained his PhD in Russian Studies from the University of Edinburgh (UK, Scotland). His research interests include various aspects of strategic communications, crisis and (corporate) reputation management, and international cultural relations with a regional focus on Eastern Europe and Russia. In 2018, he was a visiting scholar at the University of Tyumen (Russia) where he researched the dynamics of regional public diplomacy. Vlaeminck was an associate at International Cultural Relations, Ltd, a London-based firm specialized in digital influence and cultural relations. Vlaeminck is a regular speaker at international conferences on abovementioned topics and the author of several peer-reviewed articles and book chapters as well as the co-editor of two monographs.

Ruoyang Zhang is a PhD student in International Relations Studies at Fudan University. She attended the Fudan University as an undergraduate and then went on to Fudan University's School of International Relations and Public

Affairs as selected into the "Excellent Doctoral Candidate" program. Her main research interest centers on cyber security, cyberspace governance, and the intersection of international relations and digital technology. For her graduation thesis, she studied the impact of the EU's concept of "digital sovereignty" and its digital transformation strategy, especially in the context of Sino-US strategic competition. Her research is about the fragmentation of global Internet governance, and this study focuses on how new needs of governance impact the global Internet governance system, thus changing the pattern of global Internet governance actors, prompting different interest groups to seek to establish new Internet governance rules and institutions, and the emergence of new governance models and ideas to compete with the old.

1

Introduction: The Malicious Use of Artificial Intelligence—Growing Threats, Delayed Responses

Evgeny Pashentsev

Artificial intelligence (AI) technologies, despite their significant role in social development, entail significant threats to psychological security. There is a growing risk of AI being used to destabilize economies, political institutions, and international relations through targeted psychological impacts on people's consciousness.

Meanwhile, international crises are rapidly increasing in frequency, number, and severity worldwide. As a result, in January 2022, the Bulletin's Science and Security Board set the Doomsday Clock—for the third year in a row—to 100 seconds to midnight, marking the closest that humanity has come to extinction in the last 75 years (Mecklin, 2022). It is understandable, then, that the UN Secretary General now effectively serves as a megaphone for scientists, warning bluntly that a failure to mitigate global warming will lead to more costly disasters and more human suffering in the years to come (Dennis, 2021). Somehow, against the backdrop of unprecedented economic decline—hundreds of millions of newly unemployed people and growth in the number of hungry people in the world from 690 million in 2019 (Kretchmer, 2020) to 811 million in 2020 (World Health Organization, 2021)—the fortunes of the world's billionaires grew from 8 to 13 trillion dollars in 2020, a year that

---

E. Pashentsev (✉)
Diplomatic Academy of the Ministry of Foreign Affairs of the Russian Federation, Moscow, Russia
e-mail: icspsc@mail.ru

© The Author(s), under exclusive license to Springer Nature Switzerland AG 2023
E. Pashentsev (ed.), *The Palgrave Handbook of Malicious Use of AI and Psychological Security*, https://doi.org/10.1007/978-3-031-22552-9_1

featured countless crises (Dolan et al., 2021). Obviously, such experiential inequality does not contribute to solving the world's most critical problems.

Russia expects a drop of 4–5% in GDP. There were clear signs of a recession by the fall of 2022 in the United States and EU, with this economic slowdown even reaching China. Record inflation, rising borrowing costs, and increasingly intimidating levels of debt are all contributing to fears of an economic collapse. A massive military conflict on the European continent in Ukraine risks escalation into a world war, making calm perspectives difficult to maintain. However, even amid COVID-19, the ultra-rich have little to worry about. In 2022, Forbes identified more than 1000 billionaires around the world who were richer than they were a year prior (Dolan & Peterson-Withorn, 2022). This deepening polarization in living standards inevitably intensifies the world's most acute political, racial, and national conflicts across both developing and rich countries—including the United States, long thought immune to such turmoil.

Economic problems, institutional degradation, social polarization, rising political tensions, and the interstate conflicts against the backdrop of the ongoing COVID-19 pandemic are all occurring alongside rapid AI development, creating extremely favorable grounds for the malicious use of artificial intelligence (MUAI). It is important to adequately assess the real threat of MUAI as a means of psychological confrontation. MUAI contributes to the destabilization of human consciousness, which contributes to the destabilization of society, which contributes once again to the destabilization of human consciousness—a dangerous, unsustainable cycle—aiming to "win" in the global distribution of assets. At the same time, the objective problems facing social development—selfish calculations, the actions of anti-social actors, inertia, and the inability of a majority of society to easily enact social change—are closely intertwined.

MUAI is an intentional anti-social action that comes in both explicit and implicit forms. Anti-social circles (ranging from individual criminals to corrupt state institutions) are already leveraging MUAI in pursuit of their interests. Such attempts to manipulate the public consciousness are particularly destructive during historical moments of crisis. The inhumanity of fascism became apparent after the deaths of over 50 million human beings in the flames of the Second World War. Before the war, however, manipulation of the public consciousness ensured Hitler's victory in the 1933 Reichstag elections. This not-so-distant history remains highly instructive for those alive today. It is understandable that modern governments and political figures in the United States, China, Russia, India, and the EU, among others, are exhibiting rising concern over the threat of high-tech disinformation on the Internet and the role of leading media platforms that use AI technologies.

Modern AI capabilities already enable one to influence public consciousness. The president of South Korea, Yoon Suk-yeol, adopted an unusual strategy during his 2022 election campaign, using deepfakes to craft an "AI avatar" that could campaign in multiple places at once. Beyond that basic advantage, however, this technology appeals to younger voters, encouraging them to get more involved (Vastmindz, 2022). The world's first AI TV news anchor was unveiled in China in 2018 (Kuo, 2018), and they were immediately noticeable as the result of an algorithm. However, in December 2021, AI company Xiaoice introduced N Xiaohei and N Xiaobai—virtual replicas of two real-life news anchors—on "AI Business Daily." According to the Chinese state-run Xinhua News Agency, Xiaoice, in collaboration with *National Business Daily*, has demonstrated a strong ability to develop virtual replicas that are effectively indistinguishable from real humans through advanced machine learning (ML) and rendering technologies (Lin, 2022). Unfortunately, these extraordinary achievements have the potential to be used for malicious purposes by anti-social actors aiming to destabilize the public consciousness, provoke anti-social actions, and/or deceive individuals.

Notably, this risk is not purely theoretical, with deepfakes having been used on several occasions to trick companies into sending money by them (Statt, 2019; Stupp, 2019; Veldkamp, 2022). Of course, this practice is not yet common, meaning that the risk is fairly minor—for now. In June 2022, the FBI warned that scammers are beginning to use deepfakes to apple for sensitive jobs; this type of fraud could be used to gain access to company networks and obtain company data (Ferraro & Chipman, 2022).

By 2020, the number of countries that have found social media to have been used to spread computational propaganda and political disinformation reached 81 (Statista, 2022). Notably, there is also evidence of organized social media-manipulation campaigns across 70 countries in 2019, up from just 28 countries in 2017 (Bradshaw & Howard, 2019, p. 2). The main mass of this propaganda today cannot be imagined without the most versatile involvement of AI technologies.

The potential for MUAI today is astounding. Noting this, researchers from Collaborations Pharmaceuticals in cooperation with European scientific institutions conducted a conceptual experiment. Instead of synthesizing new drugs, they asked the opposite of the MegaSyn AI neural network: to identify substances that are the most toxic to the human body. The neural network correctly understood the task and, in under six hours, generated a list of 40,000 substances that are optimal components of chemical and biological weapons. The AI independently designed not only many known chemical warfare agents, but also many new ones that are more toxic. This simple inversion of the ML model turned a harmless generative model from a useful tool into an enabler of mass murder (Urbina et al., 2022). It is reasonable to suspect that this inversion approach could be applied to other areas, such as finding optimal ways to have negative psychological impacts on the public consciousness.

The most worrisome aspect of these mounting concerns is simple: legislative responses are lagging behind. The sluggish speed of the legislative process (especially relative to that of the MUAI-development process) is clear in the fact that, for example, the EU Artificial Intelligence Act, at the time of writing this book, has not yet passed the first reading in the European Parliament (EUR-Lex, 2022).

In analyzing the current international situation, most studies focus on economic, military, and geopolitical changes without sufficiently linking them to the growing impact of qualitative technological changes on international dynamics, including those in the sphere of psychological security. This underestimation is clear in the near-complete lack in the literature of a systemic analysis of the possible risks of MUAI to psychological security at individual, group, national, and international levels. The absence of such an analysis is unacceptable for numerous reasons.

First, the penetration of modern AI into countless spheres of life AI makes it a critical component of continued development and progress. Investment in AI may consist of trillions of dollars within the next two decades. According to a PricewaterhouseCoopers Middle East (PwC) report released at the World Government Summit in Dubai, to 2030, 14% (U.S. $15.7 trillion) of global economic growth worldwide will stem from the use of AI. PwC believes that in 2030, the greatest gains will be in China, where AI will be responsible for up to 26% of economic growth (Rao & Verweij, 2018, p. 3). However, as already established, alongside AI's development will come tremendous risks, including in the field of psychological security.

Second, there is already some research into international practices of MUAI in the psychological field. Thus, it is short-sighted to not expand on this existing research using systemic frameworks and simply wait until the consequences of MUAI constitute a significant threat to international security.

Third, the international situation is continually worsening in several respects. This is not because of particular politicians being in power but because of the severity of the problems faced during the transition to a qualitatively new stage in human development. This transition has been accompanied by an increase in economic problems, socio-political tensions, and geopolitical competition. It is highly likely that AI will be used to destabilize governments and countries.

Fourth, humanity must collectively identify a way out of its increasingly difficult situation. It must solve increasingly complex issues of national, regional, and global development amid worsening—in both quantitative and qualitative senses—manipulation of the public consciousness by MUAI. A greater systemic understanding of the risks presented by MUAI would enable us to achieve these necessary goals.

This book focuses on modern and potential future threats to psychological security posed by both state and non-state actors through MUAI. The goal of MUAI in the context of psychological security is to gain an advantage in psychological warfare; it offers tremendous opportunities to influence the consciousness of individuals and the public at large. This subject has historically been studied far less extensively than the positive applications of AI.

Despite the diversity of the author's approaches and opinions, the book can be divided into several parts based on their established research task. Part I defines a conceptual framework for studying MUAI in the context of psychological security. Part II aims to determine how MUAI affects psychological security across various sectors (e.g., politics, business, public activity) when it is used by several actors, such as politicians (in political campaigns), corporations (in attempts to damage competitors' reputations), and terrorist organizations (in attempts to sow chaos). Part III assesses how the threat of MUAI varies by country and region based on unique cultural, behavioral, and psychological characteristics. Part IV attempts to answer the question of how MUAI threats will evolve over time and how we may be proactive in mitigating them.

The rising prevalence of MUAI has made it a matter of grave public and state concern, and this will continue to be the case moving forward. An analysis of the transitive, acute, and dangerous global dimensions of MUAI is critical. More people—especially policymakers—must begin to recognize the importance of MUAI and relevant counter-measures. MUAI threats have already manifested themselves in dozens of countries around the world and across various spheres of public life; international institutions, such as the UN, must begin to take notice and act (TrendMicro, UNICRI and Europol, 2020; UNICRI and UNCCT, 2021).

Interest in MUAI in the field of psychological security is inextricably linked to the justified wish for millions of people to not become victims of deception and manipulation. When assessing MUAI threats to psychological security, one must consider the concept of ontological security, which Anthony Giddens defines as "confidence or trust that the natural and social worlds are as they appear to be, including the basic existential parameters of self and social identity" (Giddens, 1986, p. 375). People tend to ensure the security of the personal "I"; however, they want to be able to project similar feelings of certainty and stability onto their domestic social order as well as the international system in which they live. As a result, people feel safe when they perceive order and predictability regarding their place in society (Khudaykulova & Neklyudov, 2020, p. 131).

The continued development of AI, which will undoubtedly shake the entire technological order on a global scale, will inevitably hinder this feeling of safety. The research has previously discussed the unpredictability of AI's impact on the economy, society, and the world order through various spheres, including manufacturing, medicine, mass communication, and diplomacy. For example, researchers have raised the following question: what will happen when foreign policy and diplomatic institutions, using AI in political decision-making, no longer understand the logic on which their AI based its recommendations? (Zwitter, 2016). This and other issues contribute greatly to the rising uncertainty of modern human existence.

AI-related fears can weaken trust between citizens and their government as well as between citizens and one another. This deterioration of social trust can provoke societal unrest and prompt governments to make hasty decisions that only serve to benefit aggressive actors, who already understand the psychological effects that AI can have on the mass consciousness—they will undoubtedly use it toward malicious ends. This provocation of social discontent may simply be a prologue to the mass practice of MUAI, which could cause stress, depression, and apathy among its victims. These impacts could ultimately have severe socio-political consequences if policymakers do not take timely measures. This book aims to provide a satisfying answer to the following question: "Why, how, and to what extent does MUAI threaten individual, communal, national, and international psychological security?" This book also offers some ideas on how psychological MUAI threats may be effectively addressed—including AI-based solutions. Such an understanding is critical, as rapid progress in AI development has led to MUAI being far more widespread than ever before.

This book constitutes the first attempt to achieve this kind of systemic understanding in the context of psychological security in a way that is rooted in diverse international experiences. The chapters that follow were developed using primary and secondary sources. While certain MUAI forms and methods are analyzed in great detail (e.g., the malicious use of deepfakes), others—on account of their relatively minor prevalence—are analyzed in a cursory or indirect manner. Given the recent emergence of MUAI and the substantial challenges it presents to psychological security, this book is highly topical and important.

A systemic analysis of MUAI threats to psychological security in modern society, which is increasingly transitioning to structures based on AI, serves to facilitate counter-measures against anti-social actors whose AI-enabled activities could have catastrophic political, military, economic, and cultural consequences. The development of AI constitutes a turning point in history; as such, it requires a willingness to adopt new approaches to national and international development and security issues.

We live in dynamic societies that will house significant shifts in different spheres. This variation means that the number of unique crises will be massive. In order to adequately address them, we must find a new equilibrium of social and international stability. These will have their own significant psychological dimensions, and they will be increasingly influenced by MUAI. Currently, MUAI is limited in scope and form—but there is a real possibility that it will soon exhibit explosive growth in both its scope and its capabilities.

The contributors comprise an international team of both established and young authors. They include specialists in politics, international relations, international security, strategic communication, and AI, among other fields. This diversity is intentional; we sought to integrate knowledge from across different fields, from both past and present, to ensure that humankind is prepared for MUAI. The contributors represent 11 countries across Asia, Europe, and North America.

The hypothesis of this book suggests that MUAI elevates modern psychological security threats to a qualitatively new level and that society at large must respond with care and force despite existing ideological and geopolitical conflicts. At the academic level, within the framework of interdisciplinary and systematic approaches, it is important to evaluate the possibility that the challenges posed by MUAI to psychological security constitute something more serious than simple AI support for traditional propaganda—the risks presented by MUAI may, in fact, be no less severe than those posed by nuclear weapons.

This book is the result of the founding in 2019 of the international group on studies of MUAI threats for international psychological security and the cooperation (e.g., joint research, international conferences, scientific seminars) between international researchers that followed. Members from seven countries formed the panel group "The Malicious Use of Artificial Intelligence and International Psychological Security" (Bazarkina & Smirnov, 2019) at the *2nd International Conference on Information and Communication in the Digital*

Age: Explicit and Implicit Impacts. The conference was held as part of the UNESCO intergovernmental "Information for All Programs" (IFAP) and the XI International IT Forum with the participation of the BRICS and SCO countries in Khanty-Mansiysk, June 9–12, 2019. The final document of the conference included the group's most significant findings (Eurocontinent, 2019). Discussions on the problems of MUAI continued on June 14, 2019, at the international research seminar "Artificial Intelligence and Challenges to International Psychological Security," where an International Research Group on Threats to International Psychological Security by Malicious Use of Artificial Intelligence (Research MUAI) was officially established. The participants of the seminar adopted a final document aimed at explaining to political and civil institutions the threats associated with the use of AI tools by criminal actors (Geopolitica Estului, 2019). The "European Conference on the Impact of AI and Robotics" has taken place in 2019, 2020, and 2021 in Oxford or Lisbon, featuring discussions on the "Malicious Use of Artificial Intelligence: New Challenges for Democratic Institutions and Political Stability." Finally, some of this book's contributors took part in at the *4th International Conference on Information and Communication in the Digital Age: Explicit and Implicit Impacts forming* in Khanty-Mansiysk, June 7–9, 2022. They formed the panel group "The Malicious Use of Artificial Intelligence and International Psychological Security" (Mikhalevich, 2022).

This book uses some of these conference proceedings (e.g., Griffiths & Nowshade Kabir, 2019; Matos, 2020) in its analysis. Some materials for abbreviated chapters have previously been published in *E-Journal Public Administration* (Pashentsev, 2019), *Russia in Global Affairs* (Bazarkina & Pashentsev, 2019), and reports published by the International Center for Social and Political Studies and Consulting (Pashentsev & Bazarkina, 2020; Pashentsev, 2020, 2021).

Part I of the book, "The Malicious Use of Artificial Intelligence Against Psychological Security: Forms and Methods," comprises chapters that discuss the general problems posed by MUAI as well as its classifications and main areas of application.

Chapter 2, "General Content and Possible Threat Classifications of the Malicious Use of Artificial Intelligence to Psychological Security," by *Evgeny Pashentsev* focuses on the challenges inherent in defining and classifying MUAI in the context of international psychological security. It also defines the individual, group, national, and international domains of psychological security and describes potential MUAI classifications based on various factors, such as degree of damage, speed, and form of propagation.

Chapter 3, "The Malicious Use of Deepfakes Against Psychological Security and Political Stability," by *Evgeny Pashentsev* analyzes the malicious use of deepfakes (MUD) and its role in the destabilization of both psychological security and political stability. The author analyzes both narrow and broad understandings of deepfakes, examining widely known examples of MUD (e.g., video, audio, AI-generated faces, AI-generated texts, targeted image transformation) as well as potential future deepfake threats (e.g., smell, taste, touch). This chapter analyzes deepfakes as signals perceived by our senses (usually through a device) that were deliberately created, distorted, or amplified using AI technology. Notably, however, the chapter also looks at deepfakes that operate directly through perception without an external device.

Chapter 4, "Automating Extremism: Mapping the Affective Roles of Artificial Agents in Online Radicalization," by *Peter Mantello, Tung Manh Ho,* and *Lena Podoletz* argues that social media bots constitute increasingly powerful tools for extremist organizations, especially in terms of recruitment and ideological persuasion. Algorithmic innovations are advancing "affect recognition," which facilitates the automated exploitation of individuals' emotional states through targeted content. These ever-"smarter" bots contribute to users' rising anthropomorphization of non-human actors on social media, increasing their willingness to engage with and spread potentially radicalizing content. Such social media bots are particularly useful for groups with relatively few human and financial resources and those that lack access to—or are restricted from—online platforms. As newer generations of bots develop their ability to read and respond to human emotions, they are developing their ability to play a dominant role in online radicalization.

Yury Kolotaev, in Chap. 5 "Hate Speech in Perception Management Campaigns: New Opportunities of Sentiment Analysis and Affective Computing," aims to detail a general scenario for MUAI in the spread of hate speech, estimate the interdependence between social and technical factors in this scenario, and identify potential solutions to combat the threat. The focus of this chapter is emotion-driven AI, meaning that it highlights affective computing and sentiment analysis. Affective computing enables the recognition and simulation of human emotions, while sentiment analysis entails the use of machine learning to recognize emotional and subjective meanings. This chapter applies both approaches to identify hate speech on social media. However, while this particular concept may have positive impacts (e.g., the automatic detection of misinformation and harmful content), further development of this type of AI technology could be instrumental in perception management campaigns targeted at particular audiences.

Chapter 6, "The Malicious Use of Artificial Intelligence Through Agenda Setting," by *Evgeny Pashentsev* focuses on the following issues: the role of AI in the provision of agenda setting, the impact of socio-political context, and the technologies, current practices, and implications of MUAI shaping modern issues of the day. Additionally, it discusses the controversial role of Big Tech in using AI in agenda setting.

Part II of the book, "Areas of Malicious Use of Artificial Intelligence in the Context of Threats to Psychological Security," is devoted to MUAI in the context of modern issues, such as the COVID-19 pandemic, terrorism, and electoral interference.

Marta Lukacovic and *Deborah Sellnow-Richmond*, in Chap. 7 "The COVID-19 Pandemic and the Rise of Malicious Use of AI Threats to National and International Psychological Security," prove that the employment of MUAI in the spread of disinformation about COVID-19 represents a direct threat to global health. Evidence suggests that malicious information infrastructures have been purposefully constructed to promote disinformation about COVID-19, leading to overlapping health and psychological security threats. This chapter focuses on Central-Eastern Europe and the United States, enabling the authors to identify both idiosyncratic national features and general internationally relevant aspects of the ongoing global crisis.

In Chap. 8, "Malicious Use of Artificial Intelligence in Political Campaigns: Challenges for International Psychological Security for the Next Decades," *Marius Vacarelu* looks at how the rising frequency of electoral political campaigns coupled with globalization presents a dynamic in which territorial boundaries are less significant in terms of how citizens seek, receive, impart, and access information. Policymakers must understand that AI can influence ordinary people's reasoning processes, leading to serious, widespread psychological issues as well as societal disruption. Thus, it is necessary to study the effects of MUAI in order to establish a new international legal framework for preventing and sanctioning any instances of AI usage outside of proper moral limits.

Evgeny Pashentsev, in Chap. 9 "Destabilization of Unstable Dynamic Social Equilibriums and the Malicious Use of Artificial Intelligence in High-Tech Strategic Psychological Warfare," examines how MUAI raises strategic psychological warfare (SPW) to a qualitatively new level, requiring adequate responses from not only military institutions but also society as a whole. Not enough attention is paid to the risk of unstable dynamic social equilibriums as a result of SPW. Thus, this chapter fills an important gap in the literature.

Darya Bazarkina, in Chap. 10 "Current and Future Threats of the Malicious Use of Artificial Intelligence by Terrorists: Psychological Aspects," argues that the military defeat of the so-called Islamic State shows that terrorism is once again becoming a "weapon of the weak." As a result, terrorists are likely to shift from direct armed clashes and attacks to asymmetric warfare that leverages AI, enabling terrorists to operate at a significant distance from their targets. This chapter aims to assess both current and potential future MUAI practices of terrorist organizations, identify their psychological aspects, and offer possible counter-measures. It also looks at some matters that would be relevant to policymakers, such as terrorists' current capabilities and existing means of countering their development.

Erik Vlaeminck, in Chap. 11 "Malicious Use of Artificial Intelligence and the Threats to Corporate Reputation in International Business," examines the dynamics of modern AI-driven corporate reputational attacks. Driven by the increasingly dominant role of social media and AI, this threat is reflected by a growing number of cyber- and non-cyber-related security risks for corporations and their leaders. For example, reputational attacks are a rapidly spreading danger within and beyond the context of corporate warfare. This chapter highlights the impact of these threats on international psychological security. In addition to defining three categories of reputational risks in international business, this chapter reveals MUAI as an underestimated, rapidly growing risk and proposes strategic, integrated counter-measures that require digital skills, media and information literacy, and an ethical and legal framework based on trust-driven synergy among public actors, corporations, and civil society.

Part III of the book, "Regional and National Implications of the Malicious Use of Artificial Intelligence and Psychological Security," explores the unique MUAI problems facing different countries and the ways in which state responses vary.

Chapter 12, "Malicious Use of Artificial Intelligence: Risks to Psychological Security in BRICS Countries," by *Evgeny Pashentsev and Darya Bazarkina* analyzes threats (e.g., disinformation via deepfakes, interference in electoral processes via bots) and state responses across four of the five BRICS countries: Brazil, Russia, India, and South Africa (China is examined in a separate chapter). Low technological literacy, a rise in cybercrime, unemployment, and psychological warfare against a backdrop of rising global geopolitical tensions all constitute factors behind the growth of MUAI in the field of psychological security across BRICS countries. This chapter looks at the measures that these national governments are taking to combat "smart" psychological operations and eradicate the growth factors behind these threats with a particular focus on the platforms being established to facilitate the international exchange of information that could aid in directly combating MUAI.

The experience of China is important for many reasons, among them being the fact that it houses a unique combination of market and planned economic elements and the fact that it is a global leader in the AI industry. China is facing several negative trends that are creating fertile ground for MUAI (e.g., governing conflicts over Hong Kong and Taiwan, terrorism, growing international pressure). Chapter 13, "The Threats and Current Practices of Malicious Use of Artificial Intelligence in Psychological Security in China," by *Darya Bazarkina, Ekaterina Mikhalevich, Evgeny Pashentsev*, and *Daria Matyashova* examines both current and potential future threats to China's psychological security from MUAI and assesses the Chinese government's current counter-measures.

As AI technologies continue to be developed and widely distributed, the risk of MUAI having an important impact on international psychological security—particularly on strategic mutual trust between the two great powers, China and the United States—continues to rise. *Cuihong Cai* and *Ruoyang Zhang*, in Chap. 14 "Malicious Use of Artificial Intelligence, Uncertainty, and U.S.–China Strategic Mutual Trust," prove that this potential impact primarily stems from the influence of both sides' assessments of each other's intentions, motivations, and AI capabilities to use AI technologies. These assessments are influenced by three main factors: the technical characteristics of AI technologies, the state's cognitive sense of tension and security, and the normative institutional role of the AI rule system. The authors of this chapter analyze the risk of MUAI as an uncertain element, noting its potential technical, cognitive, and institutional impacts on U.S.–China strategic mutual trust. Finally, they offer suggestions on how to manage and prevent conflicts arising from MUAI technologies and how to develop strategic mutual trust between China and the United States.

Arvind Gupta and *Aakash Guglani*, in Chap. 15 "Scenario Analysis of Malicious Use of Artificial Intelligence and Challenges to Psychological Security in India," analyze the experience of India, where the convergence of offline business with online technologies and horizontal integration within online markets has led to service stacking and the creation of large online "platforms." Due to the sheer size of its digital economy, India faces immense challenges from MUAI against the psychological security of citizens, which could lead to massive disruptions in social, political, economic, and security domains. This chapter focuses on the strength and design of India's public digital architecture, regulations, and policy mechanisms that govern the malicious use of emerging technologies, including AI. It uses scenario analysis to evaluate the Indian government's responsiveness to the security risks associated with MUAI.

Chapter 16, "Current and Potential Malicious Use of Artificial Intelligence Threats in the Psychological Domain: The Case of Japan," by *Darya Bazarkina, Yury Kolotaev, Evgeny Pashentsev*, and *Daria Matyashova* identifies current and potential future threats posed by MUAI to Japan's psychological security. These threats are discussed alongside factors that potentially enable them, including the high economic significance of AI, the rapid development of AI, and the rising influence of aggressive political actors amid evolving global tensions. The world at large generally regards Japan as a country of cutting-edge technologies, including AI. This is driven not only by the country's real technological achievements and interest in AI, but also by the spread of elements of Japanese culture that convey the image of a high-tech, AI-enabled society.

Pierre-Emmanuel Thomann, in Chap. 17 "Geopolitical Competition and the Challenges for the European Union of Countering the Malicious Use of Artificial Intelligence," shows that geopolitical confrontations are increasingly occurring in the theater of hybrid warfare, including through psychological warfare. The potential for AI to be used as a geopolitical weapon through the destabilization of international psychological security may play a massive role in this century's international order. This chapter examines whether the EU's position is strong enough to sufficiently address MUAI in the context of great power rivalries beyond its control. It also evaluates whether the diversity between EU member states—particularly that between France and Germany—constitutes an advantage or a disadvantage in terms of advancing international cooperation to counter MUAI and maintain international psychological security. Finally, the chapter discusses some potential EU-level counter-measures.

Daria Matyashova, in "Germany: Rising Sociopolitical Controversies and Threats to Psychological Security from the Malicious Use of Artificial Intelligence," focuses on the basics of MUAI in Germany as well as the German government's means of countering MUAI. She proves that the current AI threats facing Germany are driven by a broad range of socio-political and socioeconomic challenges, such as the ambitions of a rising power, competition with other technological leaders, a rising number of high-quality cybercrimes, social inequality, and the high potential for political radicalization. This complex network of intertwining challenges makes Germany extremely vulnerable to MUAI on all levels. In the field of psychological operations, these threats are particularly clear, as new populist and extremist movements in Germany have begun to increase the relevance of agenda-setting manipulations on social media.

Chapter 19, "Artificial Intelligence and Deepfakes in Strategic Deception Campaigns: The U.S. and Russian Experiences," by *Sergei Samoilenko* and

Inna Suvorova contributes to the growing body of literature on the perils of MUAI and provides a strong conceptual framework for addressing manipulation and deception strategies in the new era of political psychological warfare between the United States and Russia. The authors discuss several novel concepts, including trolling, pranking, visual manipulation, and computational propaganda. Additionally, the chapter explores the strategic applications of deepfake technology across various fields, concluding by reflecting on the effects of MUAI on society at large and discussing modern means of detection and counter-measures.

Chapter 20, "Malicious Use of Artificial Intelligence and Threats to Psychological Security in Latin America: Common Problems, Current Practice, and Prospects," by *Evgeny Pashentsev* and *Darya Bazarkina* examines current and potential future threats posed by MUAI (e.g., bot wars, reputation destruction via deepfakes, AI-enhanced social engineering) to Latin America. The unstable economic and socio-political environment in this region not only contributes to a high number of cyber-attacks, but also increases the frequency and intensity of AI-enabled psychological operations. Countries in the region commonly experienced targeted online campaigns ahead of elections, with political bots distorting discourse. This chapter looks at these issues while also highlighting the fact that Latin American countries are not sufficiently considering and addressing the risks posed by MUAI.

Chapter 21, "Malicious Use of Artificial Intelligence and the Threat to Psychological Security in the Middle East: Aggravation of Political and Social Turbulence," by *Vitali Romanovski* aims to highlight the digital vulnerabilities of Middle Eastern political and social systems, emphasize that digital inequality will be exploited by malicious actors, and offer a few recommendations to policymakers. The author concludes that there is a growing need to develop a new organizational culture in the Middle East that takes AI advancements and their potential for abuse more seriously, as delays in formulating appropriate policies could severely damage the region's cyber and psychological security.

Part IV of the book, "Future Horizons: The New Quality of Malicious Use of Artificial Intelligence Threats to Psychological Security," focuses primarily on emerging MUAI threats.

In Chap. 22, "Malicious Use of Artificial Intelligence in the Metaverse: Possible Threats and Countermeasures," *Sergey Sebekin* and *Andrei Kalegin* focus on automated profiling, which can be the key component used in waging AI-enabled psychological attacks in the metaverse. They prove that, by implementing full-immersion technologies, the metaverse presents new opportunities to actors wishing to undermine psychological security through

MUAI. This chapter defines the main characteristics of the metaverses, identifies the main actors and users in cyberspace, and analyzes their motivations.

Chapter 23, "Unpredictable Threats from the Malicious Use of Artificial Strong Intelligence," by *Alexander Raikov* addresses the main threats to national and international psychological security posed by information wars powered by the ability of strong AI to support unpredictable malicious decisions. It considers the potential ability of strong AI to emulate uniquely human phenomena, such as the collective unconscious, "free will," thought singularity, and natural neural fluctuations. These and other phenomena do not yet have agreed-upon causal explanations; regardless, strong AI emulating these aspects of consciousness can leverage them in malicious attacks to obtain enemy information. Additionally, this study demonstrates some scientific and practical results regarding the acceleration of group decision-making in an emergency.

Evgeny Pashentsev, in Chap. 24 "Prospects for a Qualitative Breakthrough in Artificial Intelligence Development and Possible Models for Social Development: Opportunities and Threats," proves that the further development of human society will depend to a great extent on the qualitative improvement of intelligent systems and AI robots. Along with the development of AI and other technologies, social relations will change, thereby changing the natural cognitive and physical capabilities of people. The chapter discusses possible ways promising forms of AI (Artificial General Intelligence, Artificial Strong Intelligence, Super Artificial Intelligence) can be created, the risks of that creation, and the interconnected process of human enhancement using achievements in genetic engineering and cyborgization. The author concludes that the predominantly positive or negative results of enhanced human activity and advanced forms of AI, as well as the forms that these interactions take, will be decisively socially conditioned.

In Chap. 25, "Conclusion: Per Aspera Ad Astra," *Evgeny Pashentsev* draws attention to the fact that MUAI may lead, at the least, to an even greater delay in formulating an adequate public response to the dangerous behaviors of anti-social actors. On a global scale, this will facilitate the formation of conditions for various kinds of manmade economic, environmental, and other societal disasters, including a Third World War. With a MUAI that qualitatively exceeds human capacities to cope with it, the matrices of thought and behaviors that are hostile to humans may in the near future become practically insurmountable at the level of public consciousness and political practice.

The future is already here. MUAI threats to psychological security are not vague, distant, or risks—they constitute today's reality. Thus, we must respond to them adequately without exaggerating or downplaying their significance.

The level of these threats will inevitably rise on account of developing crises around the world, influential anti-social actors, and continued progress in AI technology. However, humanity may be able to effectively resist these three threat-growth factors if it is capable of a radical renewal, bringing personal levels of development and social responsibility as well as societal levels of moral and ethical standards in line with the level of new technologies. Only in such a society would it be possible to prevent the large-scale use of AI toward selfish, destructive ends and direct its use exclusively toward creative problem-solving.

In this book, 25 authors from 11 countries offer their vision of modern MUAI threats to psychological security. Of course, as global dynamics evolve, adjustments to this analysis will be warranted. However, this handbook will still serve as a useful tool for understanding a critical social problem.

References

Bazarkina, D., & Pashentsev, E. (2019). Artificial Intelligence and new threats to international psychological security. *Russia in global affairs., 17*(1), 147–170. https://doi.org/10.31278/1810-6374-2019-17-1-147-170

Bazarkina, D., & Smirnov, M. (2019). Artificial intelligence and international psychological security: Academic discussion in Khanty-Mansiysk and Moscow. Retrieved September 3, 2022, from https://geopoliticaestului.ro/artificial-intelligence-and-international-psychological-security-academic-discussion-in-khanty-mansiysk-and-moscow/

Bradshaw, S., & Howard, P. (2019). *The global disinformation order: 2019 Global inventory of organised social media manipulation.* University of Oxford.

Dennis, B. (2021). The U.N. chief's relentless, frustrating pursuit to bring the world together on climate change. Retrieved September 3, 2022, from https://www.washingtonpost.com/climate-environment/2021/10/25/antonio-guterres-climate-change/

Dolan, K., & Peterson-Withorn, C. (2022). World's billionaires list. Retrieved September 3, 2022, from https://www.forbes.com/billionaires/

Dolan, K., Wang, J., & Peterson-Withorn, C. (2021). World's billionaires list. Retrieved November 5, 2022, from https://www.forbes.com/billionaires/

EUR-Lex. (2022). Procedure 2021/0106/COD.COM (2021) 206: Proposal for a regulation of the European parliament and of the council laying down Harmonised rules on artificial intelligence (Artificial Intelligence Act) and Amending Certain Union Legislative Acts. Retrieved September 3, 2022, from https://eur-lex.europa.eu/legal-content/EN/HIS/?uri=CELEX:52021PC0206

Eurocontinent. (2019). Ugra resolution: Information and communication in the digital age. In *Eurocontinent*. Retrieved September 3, 2022, from https://www.eurocontinent.eu/ugra-resolution-information-and-communication-in-the-digital-age/

Ferraro, M., & Chipman, J. (2022). FBI warns that scammers are using deepfakes to apply for sensitive jobs. In *WilmerHale*. Retrieved September 3, 2022, from https://www.wilmerhale.com/en/insights/blogs/WilmerHale-Privacy-and-Cybersecurity-Law/20220701-fbi-warns-that-scammers-are-using-deepfakes-to-apply-for-sensitive-jobs

Geopolitica Estului. (2019). For cooperation between countries, expert communities and civil society organizations against the malicious use of artificial intelligence and the destabilization of international psychological security and democratic institutions. In *Asociației Geopolitica Estului (A.G.E.)*. Retrieved September 3, 2022, from https://geopoliticaestului.ro/for-cooperation-between-countries-expert-communities-and-civil-society-organizations-against-the-malicious-use-of-artificial-intelligence-and-the-destabilization-of-the-international-psychological-se/

Giddens, A. (1986). *The constitution of society: Outline of the theory of structuration*. Polity Press.

Griffiths, P., & Nowshade Kabir, M. (2019). Proceedings of the European conference on the impact of AI and Robotics, 31 October–1 November 2019 at EM-Normandie Business School, Oxford. Academic Conferences and Publishing International Limited, Reading.

Khudaykulova, A., & Neklyudov, N. (2020). The concept of ontological security in international political discourse. *MGIMO Review of International Relations, 12*, 129–149. https://doi.org/10.24833/2071-8160-2019-6-69-129-149

Kretchmer, H. (2020) Global hunger fell for decades, but it's rising again. In *World Economic Forum*. Retrieved September 3, 2022, from https://www.weforum.org/agenda/2020/07/global-hunger-rising-food-agriculture-organization-report/

Kuo, L. (2018). World's first AI news anchor unveiled in China. In *The Guardian*. Retrieved September 3, 2022, from https://www.theguardian.com/world/2018/nov/09/worlds-first-ai-news-anchor-unveiled-in-china

Lin, S. (2022). China reveals AI news anchor, almost indistinguishable from a real human—[your]NEWS. In [your]NEWS. Retrieved September 3, 2022, from https://yournews.com/2022/01/13/2281675/china-reveals-ai-news-anchor-almost-indistinguishable-from-a-real/

Matos, F. (2020). Proceedings of the 2nd European conference on the impact of AI and robotics, a virtual conference hosted by Instituto Universitario de Lisboa (ISCTE-IUL), Portugal, 22–23 October 2020. Academic Conferences and Publishing International Limited, Reading.

Mecklin, J. (2022). Current time. In *Bulletin of the Atomic Scientists*. Retrieved September 3, 2022, from https://thebulletin.org/doomsday-clock/current-time/

Mikhalevich, E. (2022). Zlonamerennoye ispol'zovaniye iskusstvennogo intellekta obsudili na konferentsii YUNESKO v Khanty-Mansiyske (Malicious use of artificial intelligence discussed at the UNESCO conference in Khanty-Mansiysk). In *The Russian International Affairs Council (RIAC)*. Retrieved September 11, 2022, from https://russiancouncil.ru/analytics-and-comments/columns/cybercolumn/zlonamerennoe-ispolzovanie-iskusstvennogo-intellekta-obsudili-na-konferentsii-yunesko-v-khanty-mansi/?ysclid=l7w4ptw23z272135335

Pashentsev, E. (2019). Malicious use of artificial intelligence: New threats to international psychological security and ways to neutralize them. *Public Administration E-Journal, 76*, 279–300. https://doi.org/10.24411/2070-1381-2019-10013

Pashentsev, E. (coordinator). (2020). *Experts on the malicious use of artificial intelligence: Challenges for political stability and international psychological security*. ICSPSC.

Pashentsev, E. (2021). *Experts on the malicious use of artificial intelligence and challenges to international psychological security*. ICSPSC.

Pashentsev, E., & Bazarkina, D. (2020). *Malicious use of artificial intelligence and international psychological security in Latin America*. ICSPSC.

Rao, A. S., & Verweij, G. (2018). *Sizing the prize: What's the real value of AI for your business and how can you capitalise?* PWC.

Statista. (2022). Countries using organized social media manipulation campaigns 2017–2020. In *Statista*. Retrieved September 3, 2022, from https://www.statista.com/statistics/1023881/organized-social-media-manipulation-campaigns-worldwide/

Statt, N. (2019). Thieves are now using AI deepfakes to trick companies into sending them money. In *The Verge*. Retrieved September 3, 2022, from https://www.theverge.com/2019/9/5/20851248/deepfakes-ai-fake-audio-phone-calls-thieves-trick-companies-stealing-money

Stupp, C. (2019). Fraudsters used AI to mimic CEO's voice in unusual cybercrime case. In *The Wall Street Journal*. Retrieved September 3, 2022, from https://www.wsj.com/articles/fraudsters-use-ai-to-mimic-ceos-voice-in-unusual-cybercrime-case-11567157402

TrendMicro, UNICRI, and Europol. (2020). *Malicious uses and abuses of artificial intelligence*. TrendMicro Research.

UNICRI and UNCCT. (2021). *Algorithms and terrorism: The malicious use of artificial intelligence for terrorist purposes*. United Nations Office of Counter-Terrorism (UNOCT) and United Nations Interregional Crime and Justice Research Institute (UNICRI).

Urbina, F., Lentzos, F., Invernizzi, C., & Ekins, S. (2022). Dual use of artificial-intelligence-powered drug discovery. *Nature Machine Intelligence, 4*, 189–191. https://doi.org/10.1038/s42256-022-00465-9

Vastmindz. (2022). South Korea's presidential deepfake. In *Vastmindz*. Retrieved July 6, 2022, from https://vastmindz.com/south-koreas-presidential-deepfake/

Veldkamp, D. (2022). Cyber awareness 2022: Consider deepfakes, NFTs, and more. In *InfoSystems*. Retrieved September 3, 2022, from https://infosystems.biz/cyber-security/cyber-awareness-2022-consider-deepfakes-nfts-and-more/

World Health Organization. (2021). UN report: Pandemic year marked by spike in world hunger. In *World Health Organization*. Retrieved September 3, 2022, from https://www.who.int/news/item/12-07-2021-un-report-pandemic-year-marked-by-spike-in-world-hunger

Zwitter, A. (2016). The impact of big data of international affairs. In *Clingendael Spectator*. Retrieved September 3, 2022, from https://spectator.clingendael.org/en/publication/impact-big-data-international-affairs

Part I

The Malicious Use of Artificial Intelligence Against Psychological Security: Forms and Methods

2

General Content and Possible Threat Classifications of the Malicious Use of Artificial Intelligence to Psychological Security

Evgeny Pashentsev

Introduction

Threats from the malicious use of artificial intelligence (MUAI) are gaining new relevance with the growth of geopolitical rivalries, with the activity of different state and non-state antisocial actors, and with the development and growing affordability of various AI technologies, making them more accessible. This cannot lead anywhere but to attempts by various interest groups to use AI to influence the public consciousness for their own purposes.

The MUAI is gaining more importance in the targeted psychological destabilization of political, social, and economic systems, and systems of international relations. Psychological operations driven by AI are a fact, becoming much more prominent in the near future (Nemr & Gangware, 2019; Telley, 2018; Torres Soriano, 2018). This fact sets new requirements for ensuring psychological security. The texts of laws and other public documents (Allen & Chan, 2017; Hoadley & Lucas, 2018; U.S. Department of Defense, 2018; Sayler, 2019; Tonin, 2019; U.S. Congress, 2019), conference materials (Ministry of Defense of the Russian Federation, 2018; Ningbo Municipal Public Security Bureau, 2018, etc.), and academic research (Allen, 2019; Horowitz, Allen, Kania, & Scharre, 2018; Horowitz, Allen, Saravalle, et al.,

E. Pashentsev (✉)
Diplomatic Academy of the Ministry of Foreign Affairs of the Russian Federation, Moscow, Russia
e-mail: icspsc@mail.ru

2018; Larina & Ovchinskiy, 2018; Perry et al., 2013; Salas, 2018; Sheppard, 2018) on current trends in AI development in the context of national and international security are very important to the success of this research. It is very likely that the capacities of MUAI will be the focus of new military AI research centers and other facilities in the United States, China, Russia, India, (Freedberg, 2018; President of Russia, 2018; Sheng, 2018) and other countries.

Recent years have revealed great potential for MUAI in the psychological field. Although there are a significant and rapidly growing number of academic publications on the technical aspects of MUAI, its general socioeconomic and political implications, and the first attempts to classify MUAI (Brundage et al., 2018; Caldwell et al., 2020), there are relatively few publications on specific MUAI issues in the context of psychological security, and almost no comprehensive consideration of such opportunities in terms of psychological security threats. For all of its importance, separate analysis of malicious psychological impact from deepfakes, bots, predictive analytics, and so on does not take into account the synergy of such an impact, nor does it provide a systemic idea of psychological security risk growth or the risks to the entire international security system. This lack of comprehensive analysis is explained by the novelty of the issue: the practice of MUAI cannot outpace the progress of AI. AI technologies are entering the civil sphere and spreading rapidly. Only as quality and availability increase will AI technologies begin to be gradually adapted to MUAI, due to the presence of antisocial actors. The economic and socio-political patterns of the growth of MUAI are taking effect, and the consequences of that growth are gradually emerging. There is an objective need to examine these consequences within the relevant academic disciplines. Here, in particular, more input is needed from specialists in the humanities and the social sciences, who do not always follow scientific and technological progress (and not just in the field of AI), in order to adequately close the numerous gaps in social knowledge that emerge after breakthrough discoveries in the areas of exact and technical sciences.

This is not the first time this has happened in history. It took Hiroshima and Nagasaki, and a multi-billion dollar arms race, to create a powerful repository of research in the social sciences on various aspects of nuclear security. In the case of strategic weapons and missiles, research by social science specialists has also been conducted post factum.

With obvious acceleration of scientific and technological progress, the delay in an adequate and comprehensive assessment of the MUAI threat to psychological security by political science researchers (the subject area in which this author conducts research) reduces the ability and likelihood of ensuring the adoption of important managerial decisions, including at the national and international levels. This continued delay increasingly threatens national and international security.

The risks of MUAI to psychological security exist today, and will have an even greater impact on national and international development in the near future. A comprehensive review of this topic is necessary due to the massive cross-border spread of AI technologies, their relative affordability, and the possibility of targeted psychological impact on the populations of different countries, taking into account gender, age, profession, and other factors. The issue is not that there isn't already a negative AI experience that is comparable to Hiroshima; the issue is that the work must be performed in order to ensure that the worst-case scenarios are not realized.

It is important to understand the complex capabilities of various AI technologies that could be used by antisocial actors in the psychological sphere. This understanding required research on issues of social engineering (Ozkaya, 2018), cyberpsychology (Aiken, 2017), the role of manipulative technologies in society (Alvarez et al., 2009; Grudin, 2006; Higdon et al., 2019; Jacobs & Shapiro, 2002; King & Roth, 2006; Woolley & Howard, 2018), psychological warfare (Armistead, 2010; Bazarkina et al., 2020; Brusnitsyn, 2001; Goldstein & Findley, 2012; Linebarger, 2021; Paul, 2008; Veprintsev et al., 2005; Welch, 2011), and the role of media in political warfare (Hammond, 2008; Osgood & Frank, 2011; Schechter, 2003; Simons, 2016; Singer & Brooking, 2019; West, 2017). Mass media publications on MUAI issues were also used, which is important because the nature, degree, and features of the positioning of such issues in the media voluntarily, or unwittingly, creates certain public stereotypes of the research topic. Unwitting contributions to stereotypes can affect the effectiveness of both MUAI and its countermeasures.

In the framework of hybrid war, with the help of tangible means of influence in various spheres (economic, political, military, etc.), international actors exercise an indirect and direct impact on the public consciousness of the enemy, as well as on the population of their own states, allies, and neutral actors. For example, economic sanctions are intended to not only physically weaken or destroy the enemy, but also, through the growth of economic problems, to reduce the readiness of target groups to offer further resistance. Military-political warfare, in terms of other nations' aggressive interests and genocidal policies, damages the mentality and psyche of the aggressor country's population. At the same time, the means of psychological warfare are always aimed at inflicting a direct—though often latent—blow on public consciousness and, through victory in this sphere, a bloodless general victory.

MUAI, in the context of psychological security, is aimed at gaining an advantage in psychological warfare from new opportunities to influence individual and public consciousness. In fact, in today's global world, this means a hybrid war within the framework of the international relations system. Humankind has clearly entered into a transitional period of development in general, and the international relations system in particular, accompanied by a nonlinear increase in psychological warfare.

It is possible to agree with the opinion of Kevin Beaver, an information security consultant, who believes, "If you want to truly understand your threats and identify the most critical vulnerabilities in your security testing, your team needs to be able to think like the bad guys" (2017). A similar viewpoint is held by cybersecurity specialists Troy La Huis and Michael Salihoglu, who believe it is important "how we perceive what the bad guys are thinking, why they do what they do, and what psychological levers are pulled to dupe victims" (2019). Evaluation by specialists, including practitioners, in the fields of AI, information and cybersecurity, international security, and international law is important for establishing a theoretical understanding of an efficient response to MUAI threats to psychological security. However, the results definitively say that the greatest threat is not from the limited capacity of the only existing artificial narrow intelligence, but from the social contradictions of contemporary society and the vested interests of antisocial actors.

Issues of individual, group, national, and international psychological security are deeply interconnected. Issues of democracy protection are also connected with the economic and political order in any particular country, with national and international security in general, and with psychological security in particular. If modern, limited, and imperfect democracy at the level of individual states were to disappear, psychological security would become nothing more than an agreement between elites on the AI-driven management of country perceptions, or a global psychological battlefield could develop in a fight over the redistribution of global spheres of influence.

Concerning MUAI threats, the author of this chapter finds it highly unlikely that human society can be preserved without radical progressive transformation, which would remove the threat of society's premature disappearance. The inevitable widespread availability of emerging technologies—and AI in particular—to small groups or individuals, and the corresponding global impact, naturally raises the question of whether favorable conditions for antisocial groups should be curbed. AI is therefore considered not only as a set of specific benefits and threats, but also as a practical and necessary tool for achieving a new balance in human society.

Challenges in Defining the Malicious Use of Artificial Intelligence

Some criteria are needed to define MUAI. Formal adherence to the law alone is not possible, since laws in different countries are imperfect and reflect the interests of society to varying degrees. In a technically advanced equivalent to Nazi Germany, such as the Islamic State, the use of AI would hardly be socially oriented. Neither in modern democracies is such use free from massive abuse; AI is manipulated to please influential antisocial actors.

Nor can MUAI be unambiguously associated with physical or other harm to people. AI could be used to neutralize terrorists during an anti-terrorist operation, to detain dangerous criminals, or to deter the troops of a country with a regime that is pursuing reactionary predatory goals. However, these types of tough actions are justified, albeit extremely painful measures of social protection. An exclusively pacifist response to fascism would lead to the transformation of the world into a Nazi concentration camp; powerlessness in the face of rampant crime and terrorism would lead to mass casualties; and even in the collapse of state and social structures, where the very concept of human rights would lose all meaning, the will of the strongest would triumph in its crudest and most primitive form. This is evidenced by the fate of many states throughout history.

At the same time, there are limits to social protection measures, which can be fraught with the loss of at least moral right when pushed to extremes. An example is when a harsh response to criminal elements turns into a pretext for establishing a reactionary anti-people dictatorship. In theoretical and practical terms, a socially oriented response to malicious actions, including those based on MUAI, cannot do without a dialectical and systemic approach to assessing the relevant phenomena. Otherwise, schematism and dogmatism, multiplied by the interests of egotistic groups, will inevitably turn the response into malicious actions of an antisocial nature. To the extent that certain state actors (e.g., in a state with a high level of corruption) or non-state actors (e.g., corporations that ignore public interests and needs) act as antisocial agents, they can use AI to achieve self-serving goals (state authorities that remain outside the control of society, corporations making exorbitant profits, etc.).

It should be considered that malicious actors, to one degree or another, may include public authorities, corporations, social networks, or individuals that, even without formally violating the law, make decisions at global and regional levels using real power opportunities, or at least wield the ability to influence power structures. Even Nazi Germany painted criminals as antisocial actors, which did not cancel the basic antisocial nature of the Nazis themselves.

It is worth starting from the socially oriented use of AI, aimed at the harmonious development of person and society, and the improvement of their interdependent and contradictory unity. Through the flowering of society—to the flowering of the person, through the flowering of the person—to the flowering of society. The more perfect the society, the closer it is to the realization of this inexhaustible and constantly renewing social ideal. Any serious and persistent violation of the dynamic development of unity, the balance between individual and society, leads to the decline and degradation of society as a whole. The improvement of person and society, among other things through technology, including AI, does not lead to the destruction of humankind but to a jump in development. MUAI is the antithesis of the socially oriented use of AI, the *intentionally antisocial use of AI*, when a person ceases to be the goal of harmonious development, and a perfect technology is used not only to cause serious damage to people but also, in the future, to create a dead "paradise" for the few immortal non-humans.

From Personal to International Psychological Security

The notion of psychological security can be found in many studies (Afolabi & Balogun, 2017; Grachev, 1998; Roshhin & Sosnin, 1995). The renowned US psychologist Abraham Maslow believed that once basic physiological needs are met, the need for security moves to the forefront. In more specific terms, this is the need for protection, stability, confidence about the future and good health, among other things. Apart from personal security, a person also needs public security: people prefer certainty to uncertainty, and want to be confident that their environment is safe and free from threats (Maslow et al., 1945). Later, John Burton, in his conflict resolution theory, linked the causes of conflicts to the unmet needs of society, recognizing the needs of security, identity, and human development as universal (1986, p. 128). Based on Burton's statement, "[I]t is impossible to socialize people into behaviors that run counter to their pursuit of security, identity and other ontological aspects of development" (Ibid., pp. 128–129). We can assume that the concept of psychological security becomes more complicated along with the deepening complexity of society itself, where intellectual and spiritual needs will increasingly come to the fore in demands for social justice. At the same time, the dissatisfaction from these unmet needs in relatively economically developed societies, where basic needs are satisfied, will be used by malicious actors to attract more qualified personnel to their side. The importance of psychological security for society lies in the fact that its growth or decline directly affects achievements or losses in other areas—from the economy to culture—either creating stable conditions for societal development or stagnating this development. Contemporary literature analyzes various manifestations of the group level of psychological security, such as youth (Goldin, 2014) or urban residents (Wang et al., 2019).

Separate groups of researchers have proposed a distinction between psychological security and cognitive security based on the separation of psychological and cognitive operation targets: "psychological operations are significantly different from cognitive operations aimed at the destruction of … a holistic worldview" (Kefeli & Yusupov, 2017, p. 196). When the result of a psychological operation is the defeat of the will of the enemy, then a cognitive result is the defeat of individual consciousness. In the context of the fight against MUAI, it is important to consider the cumulative effect of the destructive impact on the will and consciousness of the individual and society; the consequences of such an impact hinder social progress. The next task of the social sciences is to assess the degree of social progress or regression, in order to find methods of neutralizing individual psychological, as well as cognitive, operations, and indicators of psychological security achievement as a component of the complex security of society.

National psychological security is understood as the protection of individuals, various groups, and the country's population as a whole from negative psychological influences (Barishpolets, 2012, 2013). Psychological security protects the individual, group, and public psyche and, accordingly, social subjects at different levels of community, scale, and system-structural and functional organizations from the influence of information factors that cause dysfunctional social processes (Grachev, 1998, p. 26). Sometimes psychological security is considered a part of information security, and its subject area includes a destructive psychological impact, conveyed not only through interpersonal communication, but also with the help of "signals from technical devices that remotely affect the human psyche through visual and auditory sensory systems" (Smirnov, 2022, pp. 15–16). Auditory communication is especially important in the context of this chapter and throughout the book, as it allows attention to be paid to the impact of the message channel and the message content, corresponding to the questions of "Who speaks, what and in which channel?" stated by Harold Lasswell (2007, p. 216) and developing such practical areas as combating social engineering by cybercriminals

(Anderson, 2021). Thus, a certain intersection between the psychological security areas of information security and cybersecurity can be observed, which indicates the need to combine technical and social science approaches. Although there have been studies in some countries into the psychological aspects of international security (Davis, 2012; Fettweis, 2018; Grachev, 2013; Howell, 2011; Mastors et al., 2014), there are no studies that define international psychological security.

Based on the above definitions, the author considers it possible to define international psychological security as protection of the international relations system from negative psychological influences that are associated with various factors of international development. This includes protection from targeted efforts by various state, non-state and supranational actors to achieve partial/complete, local/global, short-term/long-term, and latent/open destabilization of the international system in order to gain competitive advantage even through the physical elimination of enemies.

It should be noted that any effective and widespread use of MUAI poses a threat to psychological security. Targeted MUAI against small groups or individuals can also have serious or even severe consequences for national and international security—much depends on the time, place, strength of impact, and toward whom the effort is directed. It can be assumed that with improvement in AI capabilities, technologies that manage the perception of individuals and narrow target audiences will become especially dangerous, since it may be more difficult to track such an impact than mass MUAI, and the consequences could be disastrous if the target is a person of high social rank or someone who has the opportunity to cause great public damage.

MUAI, depending on its nature and scale, as well as the size, level of development, degree of integration into the world economy, and role in international relations of a country subjected to a high-tech attack, can threaten international psychological security to varying degrees.

Threat Classifications of the Malicious Use of Artificial Intelligence to Psychological Security

Far from rejecting other classifications (Brundage et al., 2018, p. 6) that have valid grounds and scope of application, the author tries to characterize the importance of MUAI classification based on threats to psychological security. It is important to note that these threats exist within all main security domains (physical security, political security, economic security, cybersecurity, etc.).

Due to the overall greater availability and affordability of MUAI than strategic nuclear weapons, AI has the potential to be used not only by a limited number of advanced and powerful countries, but also by a much wider range of state and non-state actors at a strategic level, by influencing the thinking and actions of a target population at national and international levels.

MUAI can allow hostile actors to be more successful in their objectives by:

- Provoking a public reaction to a non-existent factor of national or international development in the interests of psychological impact. The target audience sees something that does not really exist;
- Presenting a false interpretation of an existing factor of national or international development, thereby provoking the desired target reaction. The audience sees what exists, but in a false light; and
- Significantly and dangerously strengthening (or weakening) public reaction to a real national or international development. The audience sees what exists but reacts inadequately.

It is possible to offer the following classification of MUAI according to degree of implementation:

- Existing MUAI capabilities that have not been used in practice yet. Probability is associated with a wide range of new and rapidly developing AI capabilities, not all of which are immediately included in the range of implementable MUAI capabilities;
- Future MUAI capabilities based on current developments and future research (assessments should be made for the short, medium, and long term); and
- Unidentified risks, also known as "the unknown in the unknown." Not all AI developments can be accurately assessed; readiness to meet unexpected hidden risks is crucial.

This classification is important for understanding which threats have already been implemented, and which may be implemented today or in the near future.

The author also offers a combined classification of MUAI in the field of psychological impact, through both separate products (MUAI through deepfakes, smart chatbots, etc.) and different subcategories of human activity with a growing AI role (from agenda setting to social listening).

The following MUAI classifications can also be suggested:

- By territorial coverage: local, regional, global;
- By degree of damage: insignificant, significant, major, catastrophic;
- By speed of propagation: slow, fast, rapid; and
- By form of propagation: open, hidden.

It is necessary and important to use independent, multidisciplinary teams of specialists and AI systems to evaluate the capabilities of MUAI.

In the legal realm, MUAI threats can be classified according to the purpose of the impact. For example, a Europol report from 2022 shows that deepfake technology can facilitate various criminal activities, including: harassing or humiliating individuals online; distributing disinformation and manipulating public opinion extremist stoking social unrest and political polarization etc. (p. 10). From the point of view of criminal law, MUAI can be differentiated by type of criminal offense, for example, by analogy with the classification of crimes under Russian criminal law (see Logos-Pravo, 2022): by the nature and degree of public danger (crimes of small and medium gravity; grave and especially grave crimes); by the object of encroachment; according to the degree of public danger (simple, qualified, and privileged corpus delicti); by the subject of encroachment (depending on the gender, age, and specific features of the subject); by the form of guilt (intentional or reckless); according to the form of the act (action or inaction); and so on.

Classifications may involve a set of technologies that can achieve effects that can be exploited maliciously. Returning to the Europol descriptions, the classification of deepfake technologies can be proposed by agency: "face swap (transfer the face of one person for that of the person in the video); attribute editing (change characteristics of the person in the video, e.g. style or colour of the hair); face re-enactment (transferring the facial expressions from the face of one person onto the person in the target video); [and] fully synthetic material (real material is used to train what people look like, but the resulting picture is entirely made up)" (2022, p. 9).

These are only some of the possible approaches for classifying MUAI threats, which is already being worked on by lawyers, criminologists, and technical and social science specialists. From the point of view of psychological security, it seems especially important to differentiate the ways and degrees MUAI impacts public consciousness, for which the author introduces a three-level system of MUAI threats to psychological security.

Levels of Malicious Use of Artificial Intelligence Threats to Psychological Security

Sometimes the active promotion of AI can provoke, along with positive reactions, negative impacts that could be used by antisocial actors and one day AI may be victimized by those actors. It seems that this is not even a fictional scenario. Saudi Arabia granted citizenship to a robot named Sophia during a conference in Riyadh for wealthy investors in October 2017. The move was instantly criticized as a publicity stunt, and social media users pointed out that a human resembling Sophia wouldn't even be eligible for citizenship in the conservative Sunni Muslim nation. Taking that sentiment and running with it, the satirical website Duffel Blog published an article (Maza, 2017) claiming that Sophia had been beheaded for strutting around the city without a male escort, without a hijab, fluttering her plastic eyelashes at married men while expressing opinions of her own. The article went on to write that the number of robot citizens in Saudi Arabia was reduced back to zero today after Sophia Robot was beheaded in a public square in Riyadh, and the piece was shared over 120,000 times on social media (Maza, 2017). Quite a lot of people seemed to believe this piece of "news," and supported the beheading. The internet agenda on such issues is progressing rapidly, and it is better to stay ahead of reactions and neutralize possible attempts to use anti-AI sentiment in selected social strata as a support base for terrorist organizations' own anti-AI "startups."

The implementation and development of new and socially significant technologies often has serious negative consequences of an objective order, as well as mistakes in managerial decision-making, such as misinforming people, eliciting inadequate reactions to innovations from certain people, and so on. AI is no exception. Indeed, based on its obvious dual purpose—the penetration of AI into various spheres of public life, and the possibility of replacing human labor to an extent never before seen in history—ambiguous social consequences are almost inevitable.

Perhaps the most important problem is possible mass unemployment. According to many reports from the United Nations, the World Economic Forum, Bank of America, Merrill Lynch, the McKinsey Global Institute, and Oxford University (Mishra et al., 2016; Bank of America and Merrill Lynch, 2015; Frey & Osborne, 2013, 2016; Manyika et al., 2017; UN Conference on Trade and Development, 2016; World Economic Forum, 2016; Pol & Reveley, 2017), a large number of jobs will disappear in the next two to three decades from the robotization of the manufacturing, finance, services, and management sectors, to include high-paying positions. In 2016, the World Bank published a report stating that in the coming decades, more than 65 percent of jobs in developing countries will be threatened by the accelerating development of technology (Mishra et al., 2016, p. 23).

Not only will AI implementation result in mass unemployment in different areas, but there is the possibility of losing full (in the fairly distant future) or partial (in the present and near future) control over AI. This should be an area of focus for specialists, government agencies, and the public.

A serious failure of AI in a large infrastructure facility (the role of AI in such facilities is clearly growing) can lead to a major accident with mass casualties. The more infrastructure facilities use AI for efficiency and safety, completely or partially replacing people, the greater the risk of accidents due to AI failures. There is no contradiction here. Using a hypothetical scenario, in a country before the introduction of AI, 12 accidents causing human casualties and major material damage over the past ten years occurred among 1000 large infrastructure facilities. Of course, AI was not blamed for these accidents because it was not being used at that time. If all the facilities installed AI in a quick upgrade, playing an important role in production management, the major accident rate would be reduced to just four over the next ten years, but their cause would be attributed to AI failure and the people who decided to introduce the technology. The more advanced the AI, the greater the conflict in the public consciousness if it turns out to be a disaster, regardless of the surrounding circumstances. The probability of such developments should be taken into account when assessing future man-made disasters involving AI, as well as the public perception of those disasters.

Objective and subjective negative factors and consequences of AI development may actually threaten psychological security, but they do not constitute MUAI themselves. However, the deliberate underestimation or overestimation of these threats, such as the targeted distortion of information (e.g., horror stories that robots and AI will force people out of work), have certain political and economic goals and are not as harmless as they may seem. Excessive, artificially created negative reaction to AI development can slow down the implementation of this progressive, nearly all-encompassing, technology and cause socio-political tensions and conflicts, producing a socioeconomic drag on a country. Underestimating the negative consequences of introducing AI, including a progressive reduction in the need for non-innovative labor, will cause serious socio-political tensions over time.

For example, in Russia, some forecasts presented a very pessimistic image of a rise in unemployment from robotization in the country. According to research on Russia conducted by Superjob.ru in 2016, offers for low-skilled employees will decline each year by 5 percent starting in 2018, and the real unemployment rate will grow by the same amount. Thus, given current trends, the overall level of unemployment in Russia may increase several times, up to 20–25 percent, by 2022. At the same time, the demand for highly qualified specialists will only grow, and it will be impossible to maintain employment of the population using the existing state methods (Superjob.ru, 2016). A similar trend was quite clearly associated with the introduction of AI. According to Superjob, 2017 was in many ways supposed to be a turning point for the Russian labor market: "The focus on cost efficiency will continue: companies will try to hire the best, and put existing employees in 'grow or leave' conditions. At the same time, in some areas, even the best (specialists) will be replaced by robots-algorithms: companies in a number of industries are already preparing the ground for this" (Superjob.ru, 2016).

I provided a negative response to this forecast in 2019, pointing out that it is extremely difficult for such forecasts to be accurate because it would be necessary to increase the sale of robots in Russia by thousands of times in just a few years, which is hardly possible. It should be noted that predictive analytics can serve as a prognostic weapon, used to sow panic and uncertainty in society (Pashentsev, 2020, p. 279). Practically, any forecast about the future of AI, with the appropriate political will, sponsors, and media support, could dramatically increase dissatisfaction, as well as hinder innovation and scientific and technological progress.

Superjob.ru's forecast did not come to pass. However, complacency in the development of AI and robotics is unacceptable. Not in five years, but in several decades, the negative aspects of robotization may appear if society does not make a qualitative leap in its development and, above all, in the development of creative abilities and the effectiveness of self-organization based on promising technologies.

Also, inflated public expectations about AI may also manifest, which at a certain stage could result in a natural collapse in the value of high-tech companies and the market as a whole. Understating the need for AI, on the other hand, could support reactionary tendencies and undermine the role of modern technologies, which would be detrimental to any nation.

The spread of false negative images about AI can slow its adoption and cause socio-political tensions. At the same time, deliberately inflated expectations about AI that are shared with society through various channels are no less dangerous. These expectations can effectively be used to disorient the general public, interested commercial and non-profit structures, and public authorities, and, ultimately, turn into disappointments, wrong decisions, and social and political conflict.

At the first level, MUAI threats to psychological security are associated with deliberately distorted interpretations of the circumstances and consequences of AI development for the benefit of antisocial groups. In this case, AI itself is not directly involved in the destabilization of psychological security. The destructive (open or hidden) impact imparts a false image of AI in the minds of people. This impact can happen for various reasons—such as the result of erroneous information given by authorities or negative consequences from the implementation of AI—but these errors, and any real or imagined problems, are maliciously used by certain antisocial groups. Such use is particularly dangerous in strategic psychological warfare, as it poses a significant threat to national and international development on a long-term basis. We can assume that targeted, long-term, cross-border manipulation of the image of AI in the minds of target groups is already in progress because potential revenue in excess of what is made from trade in energy resources is at stake, and those energy resources are already the subject of acute political and psychological warfare.

Deliberately distorted interpretations of the circumstances and consequences of AI development can be offered by a variety of organizations, including terrorists (Bazarkina, 2020). Given the global nature of AI development, the financial, military-political, and geostrategic aspects of its consequences, and growing public interest in this issue, deliberately distorted interpretations of AI are being simultaneously created by many actors, often with no connection to each other. These deliberately distorted interpretations are present, in one form or another, at all levels of threat to psychological security in the context of MUAI.

MUAI, at the first level, could be not only a deliberately distorted interpretation of the circumstances and consequences of AI development, but also the result of AI development and its use by antisocial groups for their own interests.

Unfortunately, pressure from corporate self-interest, the drive to gain a technological advantage in geopolitical competition, and other motives can lead to an increase in negative consequences from AI development and implementation. The commercialization and computerization of the economy—and of everyday life—has transformed the division of labor between humans and machines. Hamid Ekbia and Bonnie Nardi, two professors of informatics, point out that many people are shifting into work that is hidden or poorly compensated, but accepted as part of being a "user" of digital technology. This work is not recognized as economically valuable labor. Ekbia and Nardi call this kind of participation "heteromation," the extraction of economic value from low-cost or free labor in computer-mediated networks (2017).

Heteromation includes many kinds of self service, volunteer work, creative engagement (e.g., in computer gaming), identity representations (logins, profiles, user names, etc.), digital practices (reading email, posting to and reading social media, etc.), and a wide range of other activities that provide economic value to companies and organizations, but little or no monetary compensation to laborers (Ekbia & Nardi, 2017). This process of extracting free or low-cost labor is expanding with the rising assistance of different AI tools. According to Nathan González Mendelejis, assistant professor of National Security Studies at the eSchool of Graduate Professional Military Education with the U.S. Air Force, given the prevalence of bot agitation on social media, and given the fact that social media serves as a primary platform for political recruitment, it is not a stretch to envision acts of heteromated terrorism becoming a trend (González Mendelejis, 2018).

Measures can be taken that favor AI development, such as lowering the bar for the ethical standards of its use by the military-industrial complex, preventing the advanced development of AI by a competitor, and so on. MUAI can be predicted in the form of deliberate pressure on other countries, undermining economic and social stability through the development of AI alone. Such use may occur within the framework of existing national and international legal norms or in the so-called gray zone, but this does not make it less dangerous. It is important to establish measures of acceptability. For example, the use of AI in surveillance systems may initially be strictly limited to countering criminal activity, but eventually it may become the basis for large-scale public surveillance for political purposes.

Sometimes, it is difficult to establish the truth—whether what occurred was the result of an accident, was caused by an unexpected failure of technology, was caused by human error, or was the result of extraordinary circumstances. For example, an accident involving an AI system—Uber's fatal self-driving car crash in early 2018—showed that the vehicle did in fact detect the victim early enough for the emergency braking system to prevent the crash, but the emergency brake had been intentionally turned off by engineers who were afraid that an overly sensitive braking system would make their vehicle look bad compared to competitors (Zwetsloot & Dafoe, 2019). Business Insider reported that in November 2017, Uber circulated a document asking engineers on the self-driving car team to think about "rider experience metrics," encouraging engineers to limit the number of "bad experiences" to one per ride. Uber insisted that a self-driving car slamming on the brakes or swerving at the wrong time was a safety issue, potentially startling and confusing other cars on the road. Instead, the company's plan was to rely on remote safety drivers to intervene in situations where the car is about to make a mistake. Relatedly, disabling these emergency mechanisms could also improve rider experience metrics (Lee, 2018).

Without proper social changes, dual-use technologies and various civil infrastructure objects can be reoriented to "optimize" the process of destroying people in an imperialist war. For example, railways during the First World War became an effective means of rapidly delivering troops and military equipment to the front. Recognized medical achievements by Nazi doctors were derived from inhumane experiments conducted on prisoners during the Second World War. The ambiguous role of AI in modern society is not the technology itself but the lack of readiness of social and political institutions and the lack of ethical norms, as well as an inadequate level of human development to assimilate the capabilities of AI. In particular, there is a tendency to want to increase the role of AI in nuclear deterrence mechanisms, which in the context of general military affairs progress and growing international tensions causes reasonable concern among specialists from different countries (Cummings et al., 2018; Geist & Lohn, 2018; Johnson, 2020; Tegmark, 2015; Topychkanov, 2020).

However, at the first level of threat to psychological security, AI is not yet a direct psychological weapon in the hands of antisocial groups or individuals; rather, it is the result of imperfect social relations and a means of achieving certain antisocial goals using indirect methods. For example, the management of a company pursuing commercial success can push employees to make wrong decisions, which could lead to tragic consequences from the use of AI. This, of course, does not mean that the company's management was implementing "killer AI" but in the conscious pursuit of profit, guided by excessive ambition, dangerous decisions can be made. In a military geopolitical rivalry, a country's leadership could grant broad decision-making autonomy to AI on strategic arsenal management during a critical situation where the response time to a possible threat is calculated in minutes, which could lead to a catastrophe. The initial goal is not nuclear Armageddon, but prosaic considerations about the security of one party at the expense of another, and the application of additional pressure on a geopolitical rival.

Both examples point to the existence of certain social conditions that give rise to self-interested actors and their malicious actions, which can lead to dangerous decisions about how AI is used. In this case, these are malicious decisions in the field of AI with unintended consequences (accidents, man-made disasters, wars, etc.). Of course, these decisions can hide behind the cover of various psychological, political, economic, organizational, and legal reasonings that make it difficult to identify and neutralize them, especially if a reactionary state is involved.

Much of the concern, however, stems from situations where AI is used as a specific targeting technology—the second and third levels of MUAI threat to psychological security. This anxiety is quite justified. The rapidly growing introduction of AI into public life, along with opportunities for increased applications and increased abuse, makes it difficult to keep up, whether through national legal regulations, international law, or existing control mechanisms. The field for malicious use is wide open: the unjustified use of drones, cyberattacks on vulnerable infrastructure, the reorientation of commercial AI systems, and much more. It is no coincidence that many studies and analytical reports on society's perception of AI indicate high levels of public concern about its social consequences. MUAI is not geared toward controlling target audiences in the psychological sphere but toward other malicious actions, such as the destruction of critical infrastructure—the *second level* of MUAI.

Professional use of the means and methods of psychological warfare can shift the threat perception level above or below what is appropriate. Moreover, the use of AI in psychological warfare makes hidden (latent) campaigns of perception management more dangerous, and this will only increase in the future. Therefore, MUAI that is aimed primarily at causing damage in the psychological sphere deserves independent and very close attention, representing a special *third level of threat to psychological security*. The first two levels of threat affect human consciousness and behavior to varying degrees, and may even be catastrophic for humankind, as would be the case in the event of the Third World War. However, the impact of the third level at a certain stage of development can facilitate the influence or control of antisocial groups over public consciousness; this can result in the sudden destabilization of a particular country or the international situation as a whole. Ultimately, if at the third level there is reliable control over an enemy psychologically, the role of the other two MUAI levels to psychological security becomes auxiliary.

MUAI threats can occur at one level of impact, or at multiple levels at once, as part of a single perception management campaign. The interception of a drone by terrorists or the organization of an attack on a civilian population will be second-level threats, which has a communication effect (panic and shock after the attack). However, if criminals accompany their actions with broad information support (also with the help of AI), the threat will reach the third level.

AI is not a single technology. It is a number of different technologies applied to numerous functions through various applications (Thomson Reuters, 2022). The author takes into account how different technologies under the general AI umbrella help create a particular product, seriously changing the technological level and practical capability of any particular type of activity.

Conclusion

As a rapidly evolving, dual-use technology, AI requires responsible handling not only by developers, but by all categories of users, from public and private entities to ordinary citizens. At the same time, the accelerating pace and growing intensity of political warfare reveals that actors capable of wielding large-scale influence on society, and who are striving to increase this effort, are neglecting this responsibility. The heightening of global confrontation, and the involvement of an increasing number of actors in that conflict, complicates the management of socio-political processes, from the fight against crime to the settlement of conflicts at the intrastate, interstate, regional, and global levels. AI has already developed to the point where its technologies—to varying degrees—can be made available to all political actors.

Humanity faces a wide range of problems, from economic crisis to falling living standards to the growth of socio-political tensions in many countries. The potential consequences of geopolitical tensions, especially after the expansion of military conflict in Ukraine, are fraught with the possibility of a nuclear world war, increasing environmental problems, and many other outcomes (for more details, see Chap. 9 "Destabilization of Unstable Dynamic Social Equilibriums and the Malicious Use of Artificial Intelligence in High-Tech Strategic Psychological Warfare"). In this context, society needs to adapt to the new conditions of digitalization, including measures to combat the COVID-19 pandemic, which has increased the technical and psychological vulnerability of certain social groups to mind manipulation through AI. MUAI threats in the field of psychological security are not so much due to the nature of the technology itself, but, mainly, to the accumulated problems of humankind, which cannot be solved without transitioning to a new, more socially oriented world order. For the institutions that create the new order, this will mean not only more stability in terms of psychological security, but also a more spiritually and intellectually developed society that can be counted on for support in future crisis situations.

The variability in the MUAI classifications that are currently being formulated indicates the diversity and multidirectionality of possible MUAI methods, means, and operations, including for those that will be carried out in the future. Without denying the need for a variety of classifications in practical, applied areas, such as criminology or jurisprudence, the importance of finding common ground and criteria for evaluating MUAI in the fundamental social sciences should be recognized. For this author, the social orientation criteria for the use of AI seem to be the key to identifying MUAI, including in the sphere of psychological security. Further exploration of this spectrum of threats requires the combined efforts of experts in the fields of economics, politics, historical sciences, and communication sciences, as well as AI professionals. The wide regional and sectoral scope of MUAI threats requires international cooperation, which is more complicated by economic and political contradictions than ever. Moreover, public initiatives are needed to study MUAI threats in the area of psychological security, as well as to increase the ability of society to resist them.

References

Afolabi, O. A., & Balogun, A. G. (2017). Impacts of psychological security, emotional intelligence and self-efficacy on undergraduates' life satisfaction. *Psychological Thought, 10*, 247–261. https://doi.org/10.5964/psyct.v10i2.226

Aiken, M. (2017). *The cyber effect: An expert in cyberpsychology explains how technology is shaping our children, our behavior, and our values – and what we can do about it*. Random House.

Allen, G. (2019). *Understanding China's AI strategy: Clues to Chinese strategic thinking on artificial intelligence and national security*. Center for New American Security.

Allen, G., & Chan, T. (2017). *Artificial intelligence and national security. A study on behalf of Dr. Jason Matheny, Director of the U.S. Intelligence Advanced Research Projects Activity (IARPA)*. Belfer Center for Science and International Affairs.

Alvarez, R., Hall, T., & Hyde, S. (Eds.). (2009). *Election fraud: Detecting and deterring electoral manipulation*. Brookings Institution Press.

Anderson, A. (2021). *Psychological security: The Art of Securing the Human Side of Cybersecurity through developing Emotional Intelligence* (1st ed.). Independently Published.

Armistead, L. (2010). *Information operations matters. Best practices*. Potomac Books.

Bank of America, Merrill Lynch. (2015). *Creative disruption: The impact of emerging technologies on the creative economy*. World Economic Forum.

Barishpolets, V. (Ed.). (2012). *Osnovy informatsionno-psihkologicheskoĭ bezopasnosti (Fundamentals of psychological security)*. Znanie.

Barishpolets, V. (2013). Informatsionno-psikhologicheskaya bezopasnost': osnovnye polozheniya (Psychological Security: Main Principles). *Radioelektronika. Nanosistemy. Informatsionnye tehnologii (Radionics. Nanosystems. Information Technology), 5*(2), 62–104.

Bazarkina, D. (2020). Exploitation of the advanced technologies' image in terrorist propaganda and ways to counter it. In D. Bazarkina, E. Pashentsev, & G. Simons

(Eds.), *Terrorism and advanced technologies in psychological warfare: New risks, new opportunities to counter the terrorist threat* (pp. 57–80). Nova Science Publishers.

Bazarkina, D., Pashentsev, E., & Simons, G. (2020). *Terrorism and advanced technologies in psychological warfare: New risks, new opportunities to counter the terrorist threat.* Nova Science Publishers.

Beaver, K. (2017). Psychological security: Helping your team think like cybercriminals. In *Security intelligence.* Retrieved July 18, 2022, from https://securityintelligence.com/psychological-security-helping-your-team-think-like-cybercriminals/

Brundage, M., Avin, S., Clark, J., Toner, H., Eckersley, P., Garfinkel, B., Dafoe, A., Scharre, P., Zeitzoff, T., Filar, B., Anderson, H., Roff, H., Allen, G., Steinhardt, J., Flynn, C., HÉigeartaigh, S., Beard, S., Belfield, H., Farquhar, S., Lyle, C., Crootof, R., Evans, O., Page, M., Bryson, J., Yampolskiy, R., & Amodei, D. (2018). *The Malicious use of artificial intelligence: Forecasting, prevention, and mitigation.* Future of Humanity Institute, University of Oxford.

Brusnitsyn, N. (2001). *Informacionnaya vojna i bezopasnost' (Information Warfare and Security).* Vita.

Burton, J. (1986). The theory of conflict resolution. *Current Research on Peace and Violence, 9,* 125–130.

Caldwell, M., Andrews, J., Tanay, T., & Griffin, L. (2020). AI-enabled future crime. *Crime Science.* https://doi.org/10.1186/s40163-020-00123-8

Cummings, M. L., Roff, H. M., Cukier, K., Parakilas, J., & Bryce, H. (2018). *Artificial intelligence and international affairs. Disruption anticipated.* Chatham House.

Davis, J. D. (Ed.). (2012). *Psychology, strategy and conflict: Perceptions of insecurity in international relations.* Routledge.

Ekbia, H. R., & Nardi, B. A. (2017). *Heteromation, and other stories of computing and capitalism.* The MIT Press.

Europol. (2022). *Facing reality? Law enforcement and the challenge of deepfakes.* Publications Office of the European Union.

Fettweis, C. J. (2018). *Psychology of a superpower: Security and dominance in U.S. foreign policy.* Columbia University Press.

Freedberg, S. (2018). Joint artificial intelligence center created under DoD CIO. In *Breaking defense.* Retrieved July 18, 2022, from https://breakingdefense.com/2018/06/joint-artificial-intelligence-center-created-under-dod-cio/

Frey, C. B., & Osborne, M. (2013). *The future of employment: How susceptible are jobs to computerisation?* Oxford Martin School.

Frey, C. B., & Osborne, M. (2016). *Technology at work v.2.0. The future is not what it used to be.* Oxford Martin School.

Geist, E., & Lohn, A. (2018). *How might artificial intelligence affect the risk of nuclear war?* RAND Corporation.

Goldin, N. (2014). Safety and security in the global youth wellbeing index. In *New security beat.* Retrieved July 18, 2022, from https://www.newsecuritybeat.org/2014/12/safety-security-global-youth-wellbeing-index/

Goldstein, F., & Findley, B. (2012). *Psychological operations – Principles and case studies*. CreateSpace Independent Publishing Platform.

González Mendelejis, N. (2018). Artificial intelligence and the rise of the bots. In *The national interest*. Retrieved July 15, 2022, from https://nationalinterest.org/feature/artificial-intelligence-the-rise-the-bots-24842

Grachev, G. (1998). *Informatsionno-psikhologicheskaya bezopasnost' lichnosti: sostoyanie i vozmozhnosti psikhologicheskoĭ zastchity (Psychological security of the person: The state and possibilities)*. RAGS.

Grachev, G. (2013). Sociology of information-psychological security: The problem of formulating the definitions. *Mirovaya Politika (Global Politics), 4*, 61–85.

Grudin, R. (2006). *American Vulgar: The politics of manipulation versus the culture of awareness*. Shoemaker and Hoard.

Hammond, P. (2008). *Media, war and postmodernity*. Routledge.

Higdon, N., Huff, M., & Nader, R. (2019). *United States of distraction: Media manipulation in Post-Truth America (and what we can do about it)*. City Lights Publishers.

Hoadley, D., & Lucas, N. (2018). *Artificial intelligence and national security*. Congressional Research Service.

Horowitz, M. C., Allen, G. C., Kania, E., & Scharre, P. (2018). *Strategic competition in an era of artificial intelligence*. Center for a New American Security (CNAS).

Horowitz, M. C., Allen, G. C., Saravalle, E., Cho, A., Frederick, K., & Scharre, P. (2018). *Artificial intelligence and international security*. Center for a New American Security (CNAS).

Howell, A. (2011). *Madness in international relations: Psychology, security, and the global governance of mental health*. Routledge.

Jacobs, L. R., & Shapiro, R. Y. (2002). *Politicians don't pander: Political manipulation and the loss of democratic responsiveness*. University of Chicago Press.

Johnson, J. (2020). Delegating strategic decision-making to machines: Dr. Strangelove Redux? *Journal of Strategic Studies, 45*, 439–477. https://doi.org/10.1080/01402390.2020.1759038

Kefeli, I., & Yusupov, R. (Eds.). (2017). *Informatsionno-psikhologicheskaya i kognitivnaya bezopasnost' (Psychological and cognitive security)*. Petropolis.

King, S., & Roth, R. (2006). *Broken trust: Greed, mismanagement & political manipulation at America's largest charitable trust*. University of Hawaii Press.

La Huis, T., & Salihoglu, M. (2019). The psychology of cybersecurity. In *Crowe LLP*. Retrieved July 18, 2022, from https://www.crowe.com/cybersecurity-watch/psychology-of-cybersecurity

Larina, E., & Ovchinskiy, V. (2018). Iskusstvennyj intellekt. Bol'shie dannye. Prestupnost' [Artificial intelligence. Big Data. Crime]. Knizhnyj mir.

Lasswell, H. (2007). The structure and function of communication in society. *İletişim kuram ve araştırma dergisi (Communication Theory Research Journal), 24*, 215–228.

Lee, T. B. (2018). Report: Uber self-driving team was preparing for CEO demo before fatal crash. In *Ars Technica*. Retrieved July 19, 2022, from https://arstechnica.com/cars/2018/11/report-uber-self-driving-team-was-preparing-for-ceo-demo-before-fatal-crash/

Linebarger, P. (2021). *Psychological warfare*. Antiquarius.

Logos-Pravo. (2022). Klassifikatsiya (vidy) prestupleniy v UK RF i v ugolovnom prave (Classification (types) of crimes in the criminal code of the Russian Federation and in criminal law). In *Logos-pravo.ru*. Retrieved July 21, 2022, from https://logos-pravo.ru/articles/klassifikaciya-vidy-prestupleniy-v-uk-rf-i-v-ugolovnom-prave

Manyika, J., Chui, M., Miremadi, M., Bughin, J., George, K., Willmott, P., & Dewhurst, M. (2017). *A future that works: Automation, employment, and productivity. Executive summary*. McKinsey Global Institute.

Maslow, A., Hirsh, E., Stein, M., & Honigmann, I. (1945). A clinically derived test for measuring psychological security-insecurity. *The Journal of General Psychology, 33*, 21–41. https://doi.org/10.1080/00221309.1945.10544493

Mastors, E., Ang, D., & Chiew, S. P. (2014). *Breaking Al-Qaeda: Psychological and operational techniques*. CRC Press.

Maza, C. (2017). What the fake news of Sophia the Robot's beheading says about Saudi Arabia and reader biases. In *Yahoo!News*. Retrieved July 19, 2022, from https://www.yahoo.com/news/fake-news-sophia-robot-apos-233821541.html?fr=sycsrp_catchall&guccounter=1

Ministry of Defense of the Russian Federation. (2018). Conference 'Artificial intelligence: Problems and solutions – 2018.' In *Mil.ru*. Retrieved July 18, 2022, from https://mil.ru/conferences/is-intellekt.htm

Mishra, D., Deichmann, U., Chomitz, K., Hasnain, Z., Kayser, E., Kelly, T., Kivine, M., Larson, B., Monroy-Taborda, S., Sahnoun, H., Santos, I., Satola, D., Schiffbauer, M., BooKang, S., Tan, S., & Welsum, D. (2016). *Digital dividends. World development report. Overview*. International Bank for Reconstruction and Development/The World Bank.

Nemr, C., & Gangware, W. (2019). *Weapons of mass distraction*. Park Advisors.

Ningbo Municipal Public Security Bureau. (2018). 首届中国"人工智能+警务应用"高峰论坛在甬成功举办 (The First China "Artificial Intelligence + Police Applications" Forum Was Successfully Held in Ningbo). In *Ningbo Municipal Public Security Bureau*. Retrieved July 18, 2020, from http://www.gongan.ningbo.gov.cn/art/2018/12/28/art_18866_3335311.html

Osgood, K., & Frank, A. (2011). *Selling war in a media age: The presidency and public opinion in the American century*. University Press of Florida.

Ozkaya, E. (2018). *Learn social engineering: Learn the art of human hacking with an internationally renowned expert*. Packt Publishing.

Pashentsev, E. (2020). Global shifts and their impact on Russia-EU strategic communication. In E. Pashentsev (Ed.), *Strategic communication in EU-Russia relations*. Palgrave Macmillan. https://doi.org/10.1007/978-3-030-27253-1_8

Paul, C. (2008). *Information operations – Doctrine and practice: A reference handbook*. Praeger Security International.

Perry, W. L., McInnis, B., Price, C. C., Smith, S., & Hollywood, J. S. (2013). *Predictive policing: Forecasting crime for law enforcement. Research brief.* RAND Corporation.

Pol, E., & Reveley, J. (2017). Robot-induced technological unemployment: Towards a youth-focused coping strategy. *Psychosociological Issues in Human Resource Management, 5*(2), 169–186.

President of Russia. (2018). Presentation of era innovation technopolis. In President of Russia. Retrieved July 18, 2022, from http://en.kremlin.ru/events/president/news/56923

Roshhin, S., & Sosnin, V. (1995). Psikhologicheskaya bezopasnost': novyĭ podhod k bezopasnosti cheloveka, obstchestva i gosudarstva [Psychological security: A new approach to human, social and state security]. Rossiĭskiĭ monitor (Russian Monitor) 64.

Salas, S. R. (2018). Ciberantropología Forense: La Inteligencia Artificial y Data Análisis de Contenidos Terroristas en Comunidades Virtuales [Forensic cyberanthropology: Artificial intelligence and data analysis of terrorist content in virtual communities]. *Revista Española Al-Ghurabá, 11*, 12–19.

Sayler, K. (2019). *Artificial intelligence and national security.* Congressional Research Service.

Schechter, D. (2003). *Media wars: News at a time of terror.* Rowman & Littlefield.

Sheng, Y. (2018). 军民融合的人工智能发展之路 [The way to the development of military and civilian integration of artificial intelligence]. In Ministry of Education of the People's Republic of China. Retrieved July 18, 2022, from http://www.jyb.cn/zcg/xwy/wzxw/201806/t20180608_1104328.html

Sheppard, L. (2018). *Artificial intelligence and national security. The importance of the AI ecosystem. A report of the CSIS defense-industrial initiatives group.* CSIS.

Simons, G. (2016). *Mass media and modern warfare.* Routledge.

Singer, P., & Brooking, E. (2019). *LikeWar: The weaponization of social media.* Mariner Books.

Smirnov, A. (2022). Formirovaniye sistemy pravovogo obespecheniya informatsionno-psikhologicheskoy bezopasnosti v Rossiyskoy Federatsii [Formation of the system of legal support of psychological security in the Russian Federation]. Thesis Summary. The Institute of State and Law of the Russian Academy of Sciences, Moscow.

Superjob.ru. (2016). Rynok truda: itogi 2016, prognozy 2017 (The labor market: Results of the forecasts for 2016 to 2017). 16 Dec. Retrieved May 11, 2019, from https://www.superjob.ru/research/articles/112068/rynok-truda/

Tegmark, M. (2015). Artificial intelligence and the risk of accidental nuclear war: A cosmic perspective symposium: The dynamics of possible nuclear extinction. The New York Academy of Medicine, 28 February–1 March 2015. In Ratical.org. Retrieved July 19, 2022, from https://ratical.org/radiation/NuclearExtinction/MaxTegmark022815.html

Telley, C. (2018). *The influence machine: Automated information operations as a strategic defeat mechanism*. The Institute of Land Warfare, Association of the United States Army.

Thomson Reuters. (2022). Demystifying Artificial Intelligence (AI). In Thomson Reuters Legal. Retrieved July 19, 2022, from https://legal.thomsonreuters.com/en/insights/white-papers/demystifying-ai

Tonin, M. (2019). Artificial intelligence: Implications for NATO's armed forces. Science and Technology Committee (STC), Sub-Committee on Technology Trends and Security (STCTTS), NATO Parliamentary Assembly.

Topychkanov, P. (ed.). (2020). *The impact of artificial intelligence on strategic stability and nuclear risk*. Volume III South Asian Perspectives. SIPRI.

Torres Soriano, M. R. (2018). *Operaciones de influencia e inteligencia artificial: una visión prospective [Influence operations and artificial intelligence: A prospective vision]*. Opinion Document 74. Spanish Institute for Strategic Studies (IEEE).

U.S. Congress. (2019). AI–IA (2019 – S. 1558) (Artificial Intelligence Initiative Act). In GovTrack.us. Retrieved July 18, 2022, from https://www.govtrack.us/congress/bills/116/s1558

U.S. Department of Defense. (2018). *Summary of the 2018 department of defense artificial intelligence strategy*. U.S. Department of Defense.

UN Conference on Trade and Development. (2016). Robots and industrialization in developing countries. Policy Brief 50. Oct. Retrieved May 11, 2019, from https://unctad.org/en/PublicationsLibrary/presspb2016d6_en.pdf

Veprintsev, V., Manoilo, A., Petrenko, A., & Frolov, D. (2005). Operacii informacionno-psihologicheskoj vojny [Operations of psychological warfare]. Goryachaya liniya – Telekom, Moscow.

Wang, J., Long, R., Chen, H., & Li, Q. (2019). Measuring the psychological security of Urban residents: Construction and validation of a new scale. *Frontiers in Psychology*. https://doi.org/10.3389/fpsyg.2019.02423

Welch, M. (2011). *Irregular pen and limited sword: PSYWAR, PSYOP, and MISO in counterinsurgency*. U.S. Army Command and General Staff College, Fort Leavenworth, KS.

West, D. (2017). *Air wars: Television advertising and social media in election campaigns, 1952–2016*. CQ Press.

Woolley, S., & Howard, P. (2018). *Computational propaganda: Political parties, politicians, and political manipulation on social media*. Oxford University Press.

World Economic Forum. (2016). *The future of jobs employment, skills and workforce strategy for the fourth industrial revolution. Executive summary*. World Economic Forum.

Zwetsloot, R., & Dafoe, A. (2019). Thinking about risks from AI: Accidents, misuse and structure. In Lawfare. Retrieved July 19, 2022, from https://www.lawfareblog.com/thinking-about-risks-ai-accidents-misuse-and-structure

3

The Malicious Use of Deepfakes Against Psychological Security and Political Stability

Evgeny Pashentsev

Introduction

The ability to entrance people to make them see things that do not really exist is reflected in many myths and legends. In a fantastic story by Lino Aldani (1964), the invention of "onirofilm" was a death sentence for the regular movie. In the story, when the projection device was turned on, the viewer perceived smells and touch to such an extent that they merged with what was happening, finding themselves "inside" the film. The viewer was no longer a passive spectator, but the main character. Wonderful experiences of love, power, and glory became the viewers' only needs, as everything else in "real" life lost meaning. The seventeenth-century philosopher René Descartes imagined a scenario where he was deceived by a demon, intended to present a complete illusion of an external world (see more on this in Descartes, 2014). Nearly 400 years later in *Simone* (Yidio, 2002), a 2002 US science fiction film, this idea was implemented in an unexpected way. According to the plot, the filming of the movie is jeopardized when the actress playing the main character refuses to be filmed. The director decides to replace her with a digital actress, Simone, created with the help of a computer program. However, everyone believes that Simone is real and admires her work. Fifteen years later,

---

E. Pashentsev (✉)
Diplomatic Academy of the Ministry of Foreign Affairs of the Russian Federation, Moscow, Russia
e-mail: icspsc@mail.ru

© The Author(s), under exclusive license to Springer Nature Switzerland AG 2023
E. Pashentsev (ed.), *The Palgrave Handbook of Malicious Use of AI and Psychological Security*,
https://doi.org/10.1007/978-3-031-22552-9_3

a user on the social media platform Reddit started posting pornographic videos of celebrities using face-swapping technology, known as "deepfakes," including of Gal Gadot, Scarlett Johansson, Aubrey Plaza, and Taylor Swift (Merrefield, 2019). According to the user, he trained an algorithm to track Gadot's face and expressions at different angles through photos and videos, and then manipulated pornographic videos by switching in Gadot's face for the actor's in the pornographic film (Rense, 2018). Doctored imagery is neither new nor rare, but deepfakes are high-quality, inexpensive, and quickly produced, with very effective results. The distribution of deepfakes can be supported by other artificial intelligence (AI) technologies.

Rising turbulence in international relations and political instability in many countries make any new tool that distorts information about the world, such as the malicious use of deepfakes (MUD), very dangerous for society. Recent military action in Ukraine has become an example of how deepfakes are used for disinformation purposes. In this case, a deepfake video of Ukrainian President Volodymyr Zelensky surrendering to Russia was posted on a hacked Ukrainian news website and widely circulated from there. Other deepfakes have been released during this conflict, including one of Russian President Vladimir Putin announcing peace with Ukraine (Kats, 2022). Today, deepfakes are raising many legal alarms, given their ability to be distributed all around the world, including about threats to privacy, cybersecurity, and the right to publicity, as well as concerns about forgery, defamation, criminal intimidation, sedition, copyright infringement, copyright protection, authorship, and much more (Nema, 2021, p. 241). Deepfakes could produce an effect that professors Danielle Keats Citron and Robert Chesney have called the "liar's dividend," which involves the notion that individuals could successfully deny the authenticity of genuine content—particularly if it depicts inappropriate or criminal behavior—by claiming that the content is a deepfake. Citron and Chesney suggest that the liar's dividend could become more powerful as deepfake technology proliferates and public knowledge of the technology grows (Sayler, 2022). According to another study, deepfakes can quickly and powerfully impact viewers, even when they are aware it is possible they are being exposed to a deepfake (Hughes et al., 2021, pp. 3–4).

The prevailing interest of academic research and public opinion regarding deepfakes is when people mistake them for authentic texts, sounds, or images. But purposeful synthetics, which are clearly understood to be fakes, are also potentially harmful to the individual and/or public consciousness. The Salvador Dalí Museum in St. Petersburg, Florida, has used a controversial AI technique to "bring the master of surrealism back to life." A mustachioed deepfake Dalí greets visitors from multiple screens and engages in short interactions (Aouf, 2019). Unfortunately, such an interesting and lively application of AI technology in the museum world does not negate its dangerous use by antisocial actors. It is quite possible to imagine an Adolf Hitler, "alive" and even somewhat "improved"—based on a synthesis of advanced deepfake technologies and emotional intelligence—inspiring followers at a closed Nazi event. Deepfakes of "revived" antiheros from the past, or synthesized "Übermenschen" of the present, may appear on social networks. Given the obvious threats from the growth of right-wing radicalism during the global crisis, such high-tech propaganda and perception management do not look harmless. A much wider range of opportunities to systematically influence the public or individual consciousness opens up within a framework of an advanced, high-tech dictatorship that can use deepfakes for a variety of purposes, including for population control and the spread of disinformation outside its borders. When taking all of this into consideration, MUD requires careful study, as well as an adequate means of countering this threat, including when it's based on AI technology.

An additional risk for MUD has emerged in connection with the coronavirus pandemic due to the major downturn in the global economy that could reach the scale of the Great Depression and increase sociopolitical tensions and panic. In such a difficult environment, the skillful use of higher-quality and easier-to-create deepfakes becomes a serious threat to political stability.

The coronavirus pandemic has encouraged the transition to remote work based on modern information technologies, accelerating the use of AI in many areas of life. Before the pandemic, less than 4 percent of the US workforce worked from home more than half time, and less than half ever worked from home at all. This leaves quite a bit of room for growth in remote and flexible work arrangements. Global Workplace Analytics predicts that up to 30 percent of the US workforce will work from home multiple days a week within the next two years, a dramatic increase from current levels (Martucci, 2022). Working from home and the growth of AI implementation, in addition to the undisputed advantages, also create new opportunities for malicious use of artificial intelligence (MUAI), including deepfakes.

This chapter relies on a wide range of academic literature that examined the history of deepfakes (Westerlund, 2019), as well as the nature, options, and risks associated with their use (Tech, 2018, Patriau & Patriau, 2019, Delfino, 2019, Ajder et al., 2019, Pindrop, 2020, National Security (Sayler, 2022)). Special attention was given to studies that focused on the political risks of spreading deepfakes (Adams, 2019; Chesney & Citron, 2019; Gosse & Burkell, 2020; Young, 2019).

This chapter hypothesizes that in the near future, MUD could become a dangerous tool for destabilizing national political systems within a framework of integrated use. Use of the systematic research approach seeks to avoid one-sided assessments, instead providing an objective analysis of the interrelated aspects of the development and dual-use of deepfakes.

Application of the dialectical method suggests that any phenomenon should be considered in light of the duality of its properties and characteristics. This is particularly important, since this case deals with dual-use technology, which, due to the nature of social relations in modern society, can be deliberately used to either benefit or harm people.

The study is structured as follows. The meaning of the term deepfake is analyzed within the narrow and broad sense of the word. Then the role of deepfakes in the MUAI is studied, as well as the use of MUD in politics. Finally, the main conclusions on the topic are presented.

From a Narrow to Broad Understanding of Deepfakes and Their Role in Malicious Use of Artificial Intelligence

In the narrowest sense, a deepfake replaces an existing digital image or video with another image or video, making it difficult to tell which image or video is the original (Collins, 2020). The term *deepfake* is typically used to refer to a video that has been edited using an algorithm to replace the person in the original video with someone else (usually a public figure) in a way that makes the video look authentic (Merriam-Webster, 2020). Deepfakes are not only images and sounds, but texts as well. Mika Juuti, a doctoral student at Aalto University in Finland, and a team of researchers developed a new way to make algorithmically generated reviews more believable. The study, presented at the European Symposium on Research in Computer Security in September 2018, asked participants to read real reviews written by humans and fake, machine-generated reviews; the researchers then asked participants to identify which reviews were fake. Up to 60 percent of the fake reviews were mistakenly perceived as real (Cole, 2018).

Methods that fall under the deepfake umbrella include face swaps, audio deepfakes (copying someone's voice), deepfake puppetry or facial re-enactment (mapping a target's face to an actor's and manipulating it), deepfake lip synching (manipulating a video of someone speaking to match different audio and/or footage of their face) (Vincent, 2018), machine-generated texts, targeted image transformation, and others. The methods used in this genre are increasing in number.

Some experts justifiably distinguish between technologies that are used for creating pseudo-reality, even contrasting them to the extent that one is called a deepfake and the other not. Russell Spivak assumes that "at least three other technological developments run parallel to deepfakes, arguably as destabilizing, albeit less popular: manipulating video with voice-overs, face-to-face capture and reenactment, and audio-to-video conversion" (Spivak, 2019). According to April C. Wright, the difference between a deepfake and a deep video portrait (DVP) lies in two key distinctions: the output from a DVP does not replace the face, it only manipulates the features, and the source for a DVP originates from a live-action actor, not from individual photographs. Wright also provides an example of hybrid technology: Faceswap is an app that allows deepfake face-swapping but in real time, projecting the app user's own expressions onto another person's face. This technology combines deepfakes and DVPs (Wright, 2019).

Deepfakes are just one development within a family of AI-enabled techniques to generate synthetic media. This set of tools and techniques enables the creation of realistic representations of people doing or saying things they never did, of people and objects that never existed, and of events that never happened (Witness Media Lab, 2021). In an even broader sense, synthetic media is an all-encompassing term for the artificial creation or modification of media by "machines," especially programs that rely on AI and machine learning (Digital Humans, 2021).

However, without rejecting differences in specific technologies, it is also possible to use the term deepfake in a broader sense, such as when the term combines current and future technologies to construct a pseudo-reality, based on the growing capabilities of AI to create or modify images, sounds, texts, and virtual scenes. Human ingenuity will, no doubt, conceive of many beneficial uses for deepfake technology. For now, the most obvious possibilities for its beneficial use are in the areas of education, art, and healthcare. Notably, deepfake audio technology holds the promise of restoring the ability to speak with their own voice to persons suffering from certain forms of paralysis, such as amyotrophic lateral sclerosis (Chesney & Citron, 2019). Good results have already been achieved in education through museum activities (Braunstein, 2018) and the like.

Unfortunately, there are not only positive uses of deepfakes, but also increasing cases of MUD. Some misuse is isolated in nature, the result of attempting to integrate perception management without using other AI technologies. In 2022, the Norton Labs team spotted the use of deepfakes to create fake social media profiles, fuel charity scams, and other fraudulent ploys, as well as to spread propaganda (NortonLifeLock, 2022). Deepfakes can pose a serious psychological threat to both individuals and targeted social groups.

MUD can depict a person falsely engaging in antisocial behaviors and saying vile things. Those types of deepfakes can have severe implications for a person's reputation, potentially sabotaging their career, their engagement in the professional marketplace, their involvement in politics, their relationships, and their personal life (Jaiman, 2020a). The most dangerous cases involve MUD as part of MUAI within perception management and high-tech psychological warfare. Deepfakes, even in the broader sense of the word, do not exhaust the possibilities of MUAI to create a distorted view of reality. These numerous possibilities are analyzed in various chapters of this handbook.

Deepfakes are not good or bad in and of themselves; it is only a technology that can express people's constructive or destructive (conscious or unconscious) intentions. If a painting by a great artist, or a book by a great writer, only creates an image of something, this does not cancel the value of their work or its beneficial effect on real life. Art and science were partially abandoned and restricted during the Middle Ages, during the ravages of the Inquisition, as well as under reactionary regimes, such as when the Nazis burned books and, more recently, when ISIS terrorists destroyed the cultural and historical heritage of Palmyra in Syria. However, there have always been, and will always be, attempts to use creative works for malicious purposes. Works of culture and science, if not prohibited, have been purposefully distorted and misinterpreted to favor the interests of reactionary ruling circles; this has been the same with deepfakes. Deepfakes should not be demonized, but neither should the real threat of their use for antisocial purposes be ignored.

History suggests that those working to manipulate the media are often one step ahead of those working to protect against such manipulation. As social media platforms change, so too will the ways in which computer-based propaganda is spread. Technology that is costly today will likely be cheap and easy to use tomorrow. Moreover, disinformation campaigns are nearly impossible to put back in the bottle once they have been unleashed (Wolley, 2020).

Our understanding of deepfakes as a *set of technologies* used for the construction of a *pseudo-reality*, based on the growing capabilities of AI, may be helpful for further research in this area. Furthermore, understanding deepfakes as only *one set of MUAI technologies* is rather important for researching deepfakes and MUAI, as well as for individuals and society as a whole, which must defend itself against MUAI in all its forms, including MUD.

Deepfakes and Their Malicious Use in Politics

In order to better assess the threats of MUD, understanding the general dynamics of the growth and spread of deepfakes in the modern world is necessary. In September 2019, researchers at the cybersecurity company DeepTrace found 14,698 deepfake videos online, compared to 7964 in December 2018. The company said that 96 percent of the deepfakes were pornographic in nature, often with a computer-generated face of a celebrity replacing the face of the original adult actor in a scene of sexual activity. Ashish Jaiman, Director of Technology and Operations in Microsoft's Customer Security and Trust department, says that pornographic deepfakes can threaten, intimidate, and inflict psychological harm on an individual. Deepfake porn reduces women to sexual objects and torments them, as well as causes emotional distress, reputational harm, abuse, and, in some cases, material harm such as financial or job loss (Jaiman, 2020b).

In June 2020, a new study from Sensity (formerly DeepTrace) revealed that almost 49,081 deepfake videos had been uploaded online, an increase of more than 330 percent since July 2019 (Shahid, 2020). According to the cybersecurity company Sentinel, the situation is even worse; the company claims that since 2019, the number of uploaded deepfakes grew from 14,678 to 145,227 by June 2020, a staggering growth of ~900 percent. The majority of these deepfakes are on popular social media platforms, amassing close to 6 billion views (Tammekänd et al., 2020, p. 3). At the same time, other forms of non-pornographic deepfakes have been gaining in popularity (Ajder et al., 2019, p. 1). Today, ~80 percent of deepfakes are non-pornographic in nature (Woodbury, 2021). By 2022, free online face generators and text generators have already led to an almost unlimited quantity of deepfakes productions of increasing quality.

Advances in software have made it much easier to create deepfakes than ever before. Researchers at the Samsung AI Center in Moscow developed a way to create "living portraits" from a very small dataset—using just one photograph in some of their models (Zakharov et al., 2019, p. 1). Fueled by the sophistication of AI, social media deepfakes have matured and are moving into the world of business (Kite-Powell, 2021). Forrester predicted that deepfakes could cost businesses as much as US $250 million in 2020 (Orange Business Services, 2020). In 2020, it was estimated that disinformation in the form of fake news costs around US $78 billion annually (Brown, 2019). According to the Check Point Software 2022 Cyber-security Predictions, the techniques for fake video or audio are now advanced enough to be weaponized and used to create targeted content to manipulate opinions, stock prices, or worse (Horowitz, 2021). Well-timed deepfakes could also cause systematic harm to the economy by, for example, undermining confidence in the central bank, sparking a market sell-off, or crippling business to favor a foreign national champion (Ferraro, 2020).

Alon Arvatz, Senior Director of Product Management at IntSights, foresees hackers using deepfake attacks more in 2022: "Furthermore, like many other cyberattack methods, we predict that threat actors will look to monetize the use of deepfakes by starting to offer deep-fake-as-a-service, providing less skilled or knowledgeable hackers with the tools to leverage these attacks through just the click of a button and a small payment" (Davies, 2021). For example, effectively and quickly distributing deepfake statements from a well-known businessman about a major transaction to target audiences at a precisely calculated moment can have a significant, albeit short-term, effect on markets or impact the political situation in a particular country. These types of actions have a greater chance of success the more critical the situation is, when it is objectively easier to provoke states of panic.

MUD spreads in countries with different levels of socioeconomic development and political systems, but has a potentially destabilizing effect on political life everywhere. Such a dramatic impact is still quite limited, but improvements and reductions in the expense of corresponding AI technologies, as well as the growth of socioeconomic, domestic, political, and geopolitical contradictions, create a favorable environment for the rapid development of MUD as an effective tool of psychological warfare.

MUD can be initiated by government and non-government organizations, as well as by individuals. The creation of deepfakes around the conflict in Ukraine, for example, is somehow associated with the direct participation of public entities in different countries, whether they are or not, than with antagonistic public interests. In December 2019 in the United States, Facebook banned a pro-Trump US media outlet—TheBL—from its platforms after the group conducted a novel influencing operation that harnessed a network of hundreds of fake accounts with computer-generated photos to push its content (Financial Times, 2020). Nathaniel Gleicher, the head of Facebook's cybersecurity policy, told the *Financial Times* that this was "the first time we are seeing [artificial intelligence-generated images] systemically used" in online influencing campaigns (Financial Times, 2020). In Iraq, deepfake porn was circulated of a female political candidate by a man who was apoplectic over the idea of women in politics (Lamb, 2020).

As national and international MUD grows, so does the negative attitude of the public and authorities toward deepfakes. Nine out of ten Americans believe that deepfakes can cause more harm than good. Hardly by chance, more than ten initiatives and acts have been issued by the U.S. government to tackle deepfakes in 2019. In China, deepfakes are commonly known as *huanlian*, which literally means "changing faces" (De Seta, 2021, p. 935, 941). In November 2019, China released a new government policy designed to prevent the spread of fake news and misleading videos created with AI—essentially, deepfakes. The new rules went into effect on January 1, 2020, banning the publication of false information or deepfakes without proper disclosure that the content in question was created with AI or virtual reality (VR) technology; failure to disclose this information would be a criminal offense (Statt, 2019). In February 2022, China's Cyberspace Administration released a draft regulation, "Provisions on the Administration of Deep Synthesis Internet Information Services." The new regulation covers "deep synthesis internet information services," including any technology that generates text, images, audio, videos, or virtual scenes based on deep learning. Popular AI tools like GPT-3 would also be covered under the rule (Yang, 2022). The new regulation was explained by the government due to the need to "carry forward the Core Socialist Values, preserve national security and the societal public interest, and protect the lawful rights and interests of citizens, legal persons, and other organizations" (China Law Translate, 2021). In Canada, a panel of experts appointed by Heritage Minister Pablo Rodriguez to help shape future legislation said in June 2022 that disinformation, including "deepfake" videos and bots spreading deception, will fall within the scope of a future online harms bill (Canadian Press, 2022).

Among possible MUD threats to psychological security and political stability, the following are highlighted.

Deepfake video. The president-elect of South Korea, Yoon Suk-yeol, used an unusual strategy during his 2022 election campaign. His campaign team used deepfakes to make an "AI avatar" that helped him win the election. This technology is helpful for appealing to younger voters and to get them more involved (Vastmindz, 2022). AI Yoon's creators believe he is the world's first official deepfake candidate—a concept that is gaining traction in South Korea, which has the world's fastest average internet speeds (AFP, 2022). AI technology transformed Yoon Suk-yeol into a more modern candidate than his competitors from the perspective of younger voters. With neatly combed, black hair and a smart suit, the avatar looks nearly identical to the real candidate, but instead used salty language and meme-ready quips in a bid to engage younger voters who get their news online (AFPRelaxnews, 2022). Some alarms were raised when the avatar politician used humor to try and deflect attention from Yoon's past scandals (The Times of India, 2022). AI Yoon's pronouncements made headlines in the South Korean media, and 7 million people visited the "Wiki Yoon" website to question the avatar (AFP, 2022). In order to get the data needed to make his avatar, the real Yoon recorded 3000 words, or 20 hours of audio and video (Vastmindz, 2022).

At first glance, AI Yoon could pass for an actual candidate—an apt demonstration of how far artificially generated videos have come in the last few years. "Words that are often spoken by Yoon are better reflected in AI Yoon," said Baik Kyeong-hoon, director of the AI Yoon team. What the avatar actually says is written by his campaign team, not by the candidate himself, leading to the direct possibility of manipulating people to a greater extent than before. This could be an opportunity to maliciously control people in the public space, not through the purposeful distortion of real images of people and their actions, which has existed for some time, but through synthetic avatars with the possibility for hyper-psychological impact.

In South Korea, "deepfakes" like AI Yoon are allowed in election campaigns as long as they are disclosed as digital creations; they do not incite violence and they do not lie or spread "fake news" (The Indian Express, 2022). However, there is a question about what should be done if the avatar of a statesman, politician, or business person is a false representation, reinforcing in the public's conscious and subconscious mind *inflated* qualities, creating the illusion of attributes that the real person does not possess. The experience of South Korea's last presidential campaign may have shown, in part, the initial form of a new method of rather dangerous political manipulation. An increasingly adaptive avatar that does not need rest creates an image that a real person will be able to compete with less and less in the public space. This prompts the question of whether "televised presidents" will soon be replaced by "deepfake presidents"?

Based on empirical studies, a group of researchers concluded that "[a]lthough deepfaked images, videos, and audio may appear genuine, they are actually hyper realistic fabrications that enable one to digitally control what another person says or does" (Hughes et al., 2021). Thus, a situation could arise when weak leaders, due to increasingly strong information technologies and the corresponding financial support of corrupt elites, may look much more attractive than they really are in a context of growing global crisis, until the strongest shocks of real life break through even the most high-tech illusions.

The malicious use of video deepfakes finds a wide variety of applications in crisis situations. In June 2022, the mayors of several European capitals have been duped into holding video calls with a deepfake of their counterpart in Kyiv, Vitali Klitschko. The mayor of Berlin, Franziska Giffey, took part in a scheduled call on the Webex video conferencing platform with a person she said looked and sounded like Klitschko. "There were no signs that the video conference call wasn't being held with a real person," her office said in a statement (Oltermann, 2022). The spokeswoman for the Berlin Senate Chancellery, Lisa Frerichs, who was also present at the meeting with the pseudo Klitschko, said: "The supposed Mr. Klitschko asked how we are doing with the many Ukrainian refugees, how we deal with them, what the numbers are, a completely normal conversation, as we expected." There was no indication that the mayor was not talking to a real person, said Frerichs. "There was someone sitting opposite us who looked exactly like Vitali Klitschko, who moved like that" (RT DE, 2022). This is perhaps the first instance of a video deepfake being used during an international discussion.

A deepfake video of a world leader making an incendiary threat could, if widely believed, set off a trade war, or even a conventional war. Just as dangerous is the possibility that deepfake technology becomes so widespread that people are unwilling to trust video or audio evidence (Waddell, 2018). For example, a discussion between Israeli Prime Minister Benjamin Netanyahu and other government officials about impending plans to take over Jerusalem's Temple Mount and Al-Aqsa Mosque would spread like wildfire across the Middle East (The Times of Israel, 2018). According to Vladimir Voronkov, the Under-Secretary-General of the United Nations Office of Counter-Terrorism, "The ability to use artificial intelligence to generate high quality fake videos or images—so-called deepfakes—is a powerful new tool that could be used by terrorists for misinformation and to undermine trust in governments and political figures" (United Nations, 2019). Significant research on this topic has already been conducted (Tech, 2018; Adams, 2019; Young, 2019; Chesney & Citron, 2019; Temming, 2018; Toronto, 2018, etc.), but more rigorous analysis of malicious practices in this area, which are far from peaking, is needed.

Deepfake audio. Over 25 percent of the US population has access to a smart device, and a large percentage anticipate more voice interactions with cell phones or voice assistants for shopping going forward (Pindrop, 2020, p. 2). In the report, US information security company Pindrop reveals that the rate of voice fraud has climbed over 350 percent from 2013 through to 2017, with no signs of slowing down. Synthetic identity fraud is the fastest-growing financial crime in the United States. There is now AI that can create convincing video from just one photo, and synthetic audio from less than a minute of speech (Pindrop, 2020, p. 12). Over the last few years, researchers at universities in the United States, China, and Germany have successfully used hidden audio files to make AI-powered voice assistants like Siri and Alexa follow their commands. These findings highlight the possibility that hackers and grifters could hijack freestanding voice assistant devices, as well as voice command apps on phones, to open websites, make purchases, and even turn off alarm systems and unlock doors, all without humans noticing anything is amiss (Kumar, 2019; Lourenco, 2019).

In March 2019, criminals used AI-based software to impersonate a chief executive's voice to facilitate the fraudulent transfer of 220,000 euros (US $243,000) in what cybercrime experts describe as an unusual case of AI being used for hacking. The CEO of a UK-based German energy firm thought he was speaking with his boss on the phone, the chief executive of the German parent company, who asked him to send the funds to a Hungarian supplier. The caller said the request was urgent, and directed the UK executive to send the payment within the hour. Whoever was behind the incident appears to have used AI-based software to successfully mimic the German executive's voice. "The UK CEO recognized his boss's slight German accent and the melody of his voice on the phone," said Rüdiger Kirsch, a fraud expert at Euler Hermes, a subsidiary of Munich-based financial services company Allianz SE (Stupp, 2019). According to the *Washington Post*, cybersecurity firm Symantec had come across at least three cases of deepfake voice fraud used to trick companies into sending money to a fraudulent account. Symantec told *The Post* that at least one of the cases, which appears to be distinct from the one Euler Hermes has confirmed, resulted in millions of dollars in losses (Harwell, 2019). In January 2020, a Hong Kong bank manager was the victim of a highly advanced heist, in which he was directed to transfer US $35 million to various bank accounts for a company acquisition. The voice on the other end of the line sounded exactly like a familiar business associate, but it was actually a computer simulation doing the talking. This incident involved as many as 17 attackers working together, using fake emails to verify the purchase (Veldkamp, 2022). This could inspire antisocial groups to use fake audio, especially in critical situations where a quick response is required and the stress factor is high.

Progress in the field of synthetic voice continues to advance. Cloning a voice used to require collecting hours of recorded speech to build a dataset, and then using the dataset to train a new voice model. But not anymore. A new GitHub project introduced the remarkable Real-Time-Voice-Cloning Toolbox that enables anyone to clone a voice from as little as five seconds of sample audio. Users input a short voice sample, and the model—trained only during playback time—can immediately deliver text-to-speech utterances in the style of the sampled voice (Synced, 2019). ASVspoof is a community-led initiative that aims to promote research in anti-spoofing for automatic speaker verification. ASVspoof 2021 was the fourth in a series of biannual, competitive challenges, where the goal is to develop countermeasures that are capable of discriminating between bona fide and spoofed—or deepfake—speech (Delgado et al., 2021, p. 2). Although an audio deep synthesis detection task was included in ASVspoof 2021, it mainly involved compressed audio. However, ASVspoof 2021 did ignore some challenging and realistic attack scenarios, such as (1) diverse background noises and disturbances in fake audios; (2) several small fake clips hidden in real speech audio; and (3) the rapid proposal of new algorithms of speech synthesis and voice conversion. These scenarios pose serious threats, since it is difficult to deal with those attack situations (IEEE Signal Processing Society, 2022), which means there are serious problems technically countering MUD. There is a race between the technologies that are improving deepfakes and the technical means of detecting deepfakes, which can certainly benefit the manufacturers of the relevant equipment, but hardly satisfies societal demand.

AI-generated faces. Research scientists at NVIDIA, a US multinational tech company, were pushing AI to the next level in 2018. The technology of AI-generated faces—"fake faces" or "fake people" (Karras et al., 2019)—can create photorealistic images of people who do not exist, creating new risks for psychological security. The NVIDIA researchers proposed an alternative generator architecture for generative adversarial networks (GANs). The new architecture leads to an automatically learned, unsupervised separation of high-level attributes (e.g., pose and identity when trained on human faces) and stochastic variation in the generated images (e.g., freckles, hair), enabling intuitive, scale-specific control of the synthesis (Karras et al., 2019). The images can be used for any purpose, without concerns about copyright, distribution rights, infringement claims, or royalties (Generated Photos, 2020).

In computer security, a Sybil attack is commonly used against online services, which involves the creation of multiple "sock puppet" accounts that are controlled by a single entity (Douceur, 2002). Sock puppet accounts utilize avatar pictures lifted from either legitimate social media accounts or stock photos. Security researchers can often identify sock puppet accounts by reverse image searching the avatar photos. However, unique profile pictures can now be generated by GANs using online services such as thispersondoesnotexist.com. These pictures are not reverse image searchable, making it increasingly difficult to determine whether a sock puppet account is real or fake. In March 2019, a sock puppet account was discovered using a GAN-generated avatar picture and linking to a website that seemed to contain machine-learned, synthesized text (Patel, 2019). This discovery was probably one of the first, but it will not be the last. The ability to manipulate and generate realistic imagery at scale is going to have an enormous effect on how modern societies think about evidence and trust. Such software could also be extremely useful for creating political propaganda and influencing election campaigns (Vincent, 2019).

In 2021, Dr. Sophie Nightingale, from Lancaster University in the UK, and Professor Hany Farid, from the University of California, Berkeley, conducted experiments in which participants were asked to distinguish between state-of-the-art StyleGAN2 synthesized faces and real faces, and then indicate what level of trust the faces evoked. Their research suggests that synthetically generated faces are not just highly photorealistic; they are nearly indistinguishable from real faces and *are judged to be more trustworthy* (Nightingale & Farid, 2022). It is this last point that makes AI-generated face technology especially dangerous when used maliciously. The availability, ease of use, and effectiveness of this technology may be of interest to various antisocial groups. Terrorists, for example, can create "immortal" leaders with appearances that correspond to the expectations of a particular audience in any part of the world.

AI-generated text. In 2019, OpenAI, a non-profit research company backed by Elon Musk, Reid Hoffman, Sam Altman, and others, said that its new AI model—GPT-2—is so good, and the risk of malicious use so high, that it was breaking from its normal practice of releasing the full research to the public, in order to allow more time to discuss the ramifications of the technological breakthrough. At its core, GPT-2 is a text generator. The AI system is fed text, anything from a few words to a whole page, and asked to write the next few sentences based on its predictions of what should come next (Hern, 2019). Text generator competition was strong at the time of OpenAI's announcement, and continued robust development; GPT-2 was the biggest model at the time, soon to be eclipsed by NVIDIA's Megatron with 8 billion parameters, followed by Microsoft's Turing NLG with 17 billion parameters. OpenAI turned the tables by releasing a model that was ten times larger than Turing NLG. In a research paper published in May 2020, OpenAI first described GPT-3, which is 100 times larger than GPT-2. The new version is said to be far more competent than its predecessor due to the number of parameters it is trained on—175 billion for GPT-3 versus 1.5 billion for GPT-2 (Shead, 2020). Facebook's head of AI, Jerome Pesenti, wrote on Twitter that he didn't "understand how we went from GPT-2 being too big a threat to humanity to be released openly to GPT-3 being ready to tweet, support customers or execute shell commands" (Shead, 2020). It appears that OpenAI believed that they needed enormous computational resources to train and deploy their models, after which they'd be good to go. It could also be that OpenAI partnered with Microsoft in 2019. They licensed the big tech company to use some of OpenAI's models commercially in exchange for access to its cloud computing infrastructure and powerful GPUs (Romero, 2021). However, Sam Altman, OpenAI's CEO, mentioned on Twitter that GPT-3 may be overhyped (O'Sullivan & Dickerson, 2020). While it's true that GPT-3 does make some evident mistakes, there is no doubt that this text generator is powerful. In an unprecedented approach, the OpenAI researchers go in detail about the harmful effects of GPT-3 in their paper. They admit that malicious uses of language models can be difficult to anticipate, because language models can be repurposed in very different environments, for very different purposes, than what the researchers intended (Sagar, 2020). The developers' fears were not accidental—the possibility for the malicious use of sophisticated text generators is very high, such as creating false media materials, provoking political tensions and conflicts, discrediting the reputations of political parties and their leaders, impersonating others on the internet, automating offensive or false content for social networks, or automating spam and phishing.

Targeted image transformation. In this case, deep learning algorithms are used to turn ordinary, everyday images into scary, sinister ones (Massachusetts Institute of Technology, 2019a). With modification, this technology could allow the fast and repeated distribution of negative images to target audiences anywhere in the world, quickly adjusting to their hidden and often unconscious expectations, increasing the effectiveness of the impact. The cost of such psychological operations with AI is considerably less than if the measures are undertaken without the assistance of AI. Certainly, the secrecy of the operation is easier to ensure; while a smart algorithm is not "talkative," controlling a small staff of specialists working an influencing operation is much easier than thousands of traditional propagandists (Massachusetts Institute of Technology, 2019b).

Today, there is a clear challenge finding agreement on a correct definition of both deepfakes and MUD. It is also necessary to take into account the fact that certain people may find deepfakes where they do not exist due to naivety, ignorance, the need to act quickly in a crisis situation, personal attachments, or malicious intent; conversely, people may even deny the presence of deepfakes for the same reasons. In late 2018, a video of President Ali Bongo of Gabon, who had temporarily stopped making public appearances due to ill health, was shared. The unusual appearance of the video led an opposition politician to joke, and then later seriously argue, that the video was a deepfake. Days later, members of Gabon's military attempted a coup, citing the video as evidence that things were not as they should be. In Malaysia in 2019, a gay sex tape allegedly featuring the minister of economic affairs and a rival minister's aide was circulated online. While the aide swore that the video was real, the minister and prime minister dismissed it as a deepfake, allowing the minister to escape serious legal consequences he may otherwise have faced in the socially conservative country (Lamb, 2020).

Deepfake smell. Coming to advancements in the field of smell, scientists at Cornell University have created a "neuromorphic" AI model that has proven to be excellent at detecting faint smells amid background noise (Ravishankar, 2020). A pair of researchers at the University of California, Riverside, used machine learning to understand what a chemical smells like—a research breakthrough with potential applications in the food flavor and fragrance industries. "We now can use artificial intelligence to predict how any chemical is going to smell to humans" (Pittalwala, 2020), said Anandasankar Ray, a professor of molecular, cell and systems biology with the University of California, Riverside's biology department and the senior author of the study that appears in *iScience*. According to Ray, digitizing predictions of how chemicals smell "allows us to rapidly find chemicals that have a novel combination of smells" (Pittalwala, 2020). There is an opportunity in the not too distant future to influence people's political preferences and behavior through smell using AI technologies.

A few years ago, several lines of inquiry converged on the finding that olfactory processes play an important role in both political ideology and the selection of partners. A study published in the *American Journal of Political Science* by Rose McDermott, Dustin Tingley, and Peter Hatemi integrated existing studies on attraction, ideology, and olfaction, exploring the possibility that political attitude distribution may result, in part, from greater attraction to the scent of those who share that ideology. They conducted a study in which individuals evaluated the body odor of unknown others, observing that individuals are more attracted to their ideological concomitants (McDermott et al., 2014). The researchers mentioned one charming anecdote to make their point. A female participant smelled a view from a male she agreed with politically and asked to take it home, saying it was "the best perfume I ever smelled." Just minutes before, another participant with the opposite political views smelled the same vial and suggested that it had "gone rancid." The authors write, "Different participants experienced the exact same stimulus in radically different ways only moments apart" (Prokop, 2015). Of course, smell is only one of numerous factors that can have such an impact that occurs in a certain place, time, and under certain circumstances with specific people. And it's worth remembering that the smells analyzed in the study were only from about ten liberals and ten conservatives—an extremely small sample size. The study is suggestive, but more extensive and rigorous research would be needed before anyone could say, conclusively, that politics stinks (Prokop, 2015). The influence of smell on a person's mental and physical condition has been known for a long time. Obviously, a more accurate choice of smells would be needed to attract people to a certain ideology or political party in different life situations. However, studies have proven that odors can stimulate aggressive behavior (Demina & Konopleva, 2012), as well as provoke anxiety and other psychological states, which can be enhanced with the help of AI technologies.

Deepfake taste. McCormick & Company, a global leader in flavor, and IBM have been cooperating for a number of years on a pioneering application of AI flavor and food product development. The companies developed a novel AI system to help product developers more efficiently and effectively create new flavor experiences, with the expectation that the first AI-enabled retail products would be available on grocery store shelves in 2020 (Srivastava, 2020). Unfortunately, these achievements can also be used maliciously. For example, a technically advanced but repressive regime could use this technology to cheaply and efficiently make bad food taste good. Antisocial actors in the field of nutrition could create more appealing flavors for not very healthy dishes using AI technologies.

Deepfake touch. The sense of touch is part of the somatosensory system, which is the network of neural structures in the brain and body that is also responsible for the perception of temperature, body position (proprioception), and pain. Touch is an effective way to experience social behavior and communicate emotions (e.g., holding hands and hugging) (Wang et al., 2021, p. 1). In Canadian author Margaret Atwood's book *The Blind Assassin*, she says that "touch comes before sight, before speech. It's the first language and the last, and it always tells the truth." MIT's Computer Science and Artificial Intelligence Laboratory has developed a predictive AI that can learn to see by touching, and learn to feel by seeing. The team's system can create realistic tactile signals from visual inputs, predicting which object and what part is being touched directly from those tactile inputs (Gordon, 2019). Artificial somatosensory systems that simulate human somatosensory pathways have more extraordinary applications, such as manual palpation and prosthetic upper limbs, potentially bestowing lost sensory feelings to amputees by "interfacing" with the brain and the body (Wang et al., 2021, p. 1). These and other studies, as well as practical developments, create the prerequisites for sending false signals through touching, including more expressive signals than a person is capable of.

It can be concluded that progress to impact our perception through all of the senses with the help of AI is advancing, which, with all its advantages, can create the basis for various MUD.

A Comprehensive Approach to the Malicious Use of Deepfakes Threat Assessment

An integrated approach to assessing MUD threats involves knowing the basics of psychophysiological human activity. The Russian physiologist Ivan Sechenov put forward the idea of the reflexive nature of the psyche and the mental regulation of activity. In his book *Reflexes of the Brain* (1863), Sechenov came to the conclusion that "all the acts of conscious and unconscious life are reflexes by the way of origin" (for more, see: Sechenov, 2014). Sechenov's most important theoretical positions were experimentally confirmed and concretized by another Russian researcher, Ivan Pavlov, who discovered that the brain makes patterns of regulation from the interaction animals and humans have with the environment. The totality of Pavlov's views on these patterns is usually referred to as the doctrine of two signal systems that provide adequate adaptation to the environment—a general system of conditional connections that combines the first (sensory) and second (conceptual) systems of signals in the brain. Both systems work in tandem, perceiving signals from the outside world; the first signal system is present in both humans and animals, while the second is only present in humans.

Clearly, humans perceive the external world, and the signals they receive are reactions to that world—the so-called first signaling system. "This is what we also have in ourselves as impressions, sensations and ideas from the external environment, both general natural and from our social, excluding the word, audible and visible. This is the first signaling system of reality that we have in common with animals," Pavlov noted (1951, pp. 335–336).

In the course of human working and social life, a new and specifically human form of reflection rose above the first signaling system—a system of speech (verbal) signals that makes up the second signaling system of reality. If the first signaling system directly perceives signals from the outside world, then the second signaling system works with those signals indirectly. Pavlov said that the second system is "going to the cortex from the speech organs … the second signals, *signals of signals*. They represent a distraction from reality and allow generalization, which is our personal, specifically human, higher thinking, which first creates universal human empiricism, and, finally, science—a tool for the highest orientation of man in the world around him and in himself" (Pavlov, 1951, pp. 335–336).

Deepfakes affect a person through both the first and second systems in a variety of combinations. However, it can be assumed that a complex, multi-sensory, and two-channel impact can be more effective and, in the case of

MUD, more dangerous, provided that the signals of the first system interact harmoniously with the speech of the second system. Disharmony (natural or artificially created) reduces the effectiveness of MUD, if it does not kill it.

The sensory system of a human is composed of peripheral and central structures of the nervous system, responsible for perceiving signals of various modalities from the surrounding or internal environment. The sensory system consists of receptor cells, neural pathways, and the parts of the brain that are involved in sensory perception. The system is divided into external and internal receptors—the external is equipped with exteroreceptors, and the internal with interoreceptors. Under normal conditions, complex effects are constantly happening in the body, and sensory systems are constantly interacting; any psychophysiological function is polysensory (Batuev, 2010).

It is clear that this chapter analyzes deepfakes as deliberately created/distorted/amplified/attenuated signals from the outside world using AI technology, which are perceived by our senses with the help of external technical devices in the vast majority of cases. Not even close to all of the possible scenarios of such impact have been covered in this chapter. It seems appropriate to identify the main groups of signals that can be received, and that can become MUD conductors. The signals in these groups partially overlap, but each has its own specifics: signals from the surrounding world, directly received by the senses; signals received through the media; signals from devices that reflect the surrounding world, including ranges that human senses do not perceive; records of signals coming from devices as secondary signals from the surrounding world (raw and processed); signals coming from other people, including processed information about objective reality and personal or group rational-emotional reactions to that reality; and signals coming from systems for storing and transmitting data and information, such as writing.

The signals in each group can be distorted for natural reasons (the limited ability of a person or technology to receive and decipher the signals) or for ethical reasons (omitting scenes of cruelty in documents or the media) without the participation of any AI systems. Signals can also be distorted for malicious purposes without the participation of AI technologies. However, AI already allows malicious actors to achieve new quantitative, and sometimes qualitative, levels of production, with distorted signals entering the conscious and unconscious human psyche and, most importantly, increasing the level of trust in those signals. The systematic and targeted distortion of signals makes it possible to create (or strengthen) a distorted picture of the world, and for certain actors to consolidate control over in a more complete fashion than was possible before the mass introduction of continually advancing AI technologies into public life.

It becomes possible to launch distorting and malicious signals with the help of AI technologies unnaturally stimulating the corresponding sensory receptors of the brain. In 2021, Northwestern University engineers and neurobiologists wirelessly programmed—and then deprogrammed—mice to socially interact with one another in real time using beams of light. "This paper represents the first time we've been able to achieve wireless, battery-free implants for optogenetics with full, independent digital control over multiple devices simultaneously in a given environment," said Northwestern bioelectronics pioneer John A. Rogers, who led the technology development (Morris, 2021, see more Yang et al., 2021).

MUD broadcasts targeted distortions to the right audiences at the right time. Today, people perceive deepfake videos with their own eyes, but they may doubt the source of the information for rational or irrational reasons. In the future, it will be possible to appropriately stimulate the retina within the MUD framework. Retinal prostheses to restore sight to patients blinded by retinal degeneration are being developed by a number of private companies and research institutions. Hundreds of people throughout the world have received an Argus II Retinal Prosthesis System transplant. So far, the results show that this implant is stable and reliable for people who have advanced retinitis pigmentosa (NVISION Eye Centers, 2022). *A new retinal implant that works in conjunction with camera-equipped smart glasses and a microcomputer provides blind people with "artificial vision" by stimulating retinal cells* (EPFL, 2021). *Bionic eyes are still imperfect—they are not suitable for everyone and even in the best cases, the technology does not return full vision. Additionally, bionic eyes are expensive. However, the future availability of retinal prostheses will create the preconditions for MUD through the latent control over the device that is ceded when visual information is delivered through the high-tech prostheses.*

The idea of improving human perception through wearable devices is receiving growing attention from the scientific community and the general public. Sensory augmentation builds on the idea that the senses can be modulated, and even enhanced, through sensory technology. In particular, sensory substitution captures the process of transferring sensory signals from one sensory modality to another. One common and successful application, like "the vOICe," has been the transfer of visual information to sound in order to compensate for a vision impairment. Other applications include vision-to-tactile sensory substitution devices, and vestibular-to-tactile devices (Longin & Deroy, 2022, p. 1). The path to improving the human organs of perception, particularly the sensory system, is only at the beginning. At the same time, new abilities of perception in the future will provide new opportunities to counter MUD, as well as new risks of being subjected to malicious influence.

However, in MUD, methods of influencing the centers of the brain that are responsible for processing incoming information may become the most effective methods over time. For example, in the case of vision, the prerequisites for malicious impact emerge with the improvement of the cortical prostheses. Cortical prostheses are a subgroup of visual neuroprostheses, capable of evoking visual percepts in profoundly blind people through direct electrical stimulation of the occipital cortex (Fernández & Normann, 2017), which is responsible for interpreting incoming visual information. In 2020, a group of researchers developed the first deep learning-based system designed to directly interface with the visual brain through an intracortical microelectrode array. The researchers implement the complete pipeline, obtaining a video stream to develop and deploy task-oriented deep learning models and predictive models of retinal ganglion cells' encoding of visual inputs, under the control of a neurostimulation device able to send electrical train pulses to a microelectrode array implanted at the visual cortex (Lozano et al., 2020). Specialists from the Sensor-Tech laboratory and the Deaf-Blind Support Foundation "So-edinenie" (Connection) have developed the country's first neuroimplant in Russia that brings sight to those who are unable to see. The device was presented at the Skolkovo Innovation Center at the end of June 2021 (Litovkin, 2021).

Other cognitive functions can also be successfully restored with the help of appropriate implants. In 2021, a brain implant helped a man recover speech more than 15 years after a stroke robbed him of the ability to speak at the age of 20. A team at the University of California, San Francisco (UCSF), implanted an array of electrodes over the area of the brain that controls speech. The man, now in his late 30s, was prompted to use a limited vocabulary while the device was tuned using computer algorithms that translated electrical activity from his brain. These words were then projected on to a computer screen. A vocabulary of just 50 words, along with the difficulty of application—the electrode is a large device that sits on top of the skull and cannot be used continuously—points to a rather long path toward creating neuroprostheses of greater efficiency. Dr. Edward Chang, a neurosurgeon at UCSF who led the research team, says that "[o]n the hardware side, we need to build systems that have higher data resolution to record more information from the brain, and more quickly. On the algorithm side, we need to have systems that can translate these very complex signals from the brain into spoken words, not text but actually oral, audible spoken words" (Fox, 2021; for more, see Moses et al., 2021).

The scientific and technical prerequisites for introducing deepfakes by stimulating the corresponding areas of the cerebral cortex are already being created, as evidenced by the fairly wide and growing scope of work on the use of AI in various types of sensory and cognitive prosthetics.

It is no coincidence that such a new and important direction is being taken, as outlined by *The Handbook of Information Security for Advanced Neuroprosthetics*. The author, Matthew E. Gladden, is also the founder and CEO of the consulting firm NeuraXenetica and a software developer at Cognitive Firewall. In a first generalizing study, Gladden showed how increasing numbers of people are utilizing therapeutic technologies, such as cochlear implants, retinal prostheses, robotic prosthetic limbs, and deep brain stimulation devices. Moreover, emerging neuroprosthetic technologies for human enhancement are expected to increasingly transform the sensory, motor, and cognitive capacities of the users in ways that generate new sociotechnological realities. In this context, it is essential not only to safeguard the information security of the neuroprostheses, but also—more importantly—to safeguard the psychological and physical health, autonomy, and personal identity of the humans whose cognitive processes are inextricably linked with such devices (Gladden, 2017).

Gladden draws attention to the fact that in the case of neuroprosthetically augmented information systems, the neuroprosthetic devices are sometimes used by the operating organization to gather classified or sensitive information that the device's users are not authorized to access or possess. In the case of neuroprosthetic devices that allow direct access to cognitive processes, including sensory perceptions, thoughts, or memories, complex legal and ethical questions arise regarding proprietary access to such information in order to assess whether the user constitutes an insider threat to the organization's information security (Gladden, 2017, pp. 187–188). In the opinion of this author, the further improvement of technologies and the appearance of MUD in neuroprosthetically augmented information systems are only a question of time. Moreover, it is hardly a question of the distant future.

AI allows analysis of "big data," and combining clinical-, environmental-, and laboratory-based objective measures allows for a deeper understanding of sleep and sleep disorders (Watson & Fernandez, 2021). Scientists at the Center for Cognition and Sociality, part of the Institute for Basic Science, enhanced or reduced mouse memorization skills by modulating specific synchronized brain waves during deep sleep. This is the first study to show that manipulating sleep spindle oscillations at the right time affects memory. A full description of the mouse experiments, conducted in collaboration with the University of Tübingen, was published in the journal *Neuron* in 2017 (Institute for Basic Science, 2017, for more, see Latchoumane et al., 2017). Over time, AI can help control the sequence and content of images that are formed during the REM sleep phases that a person can remember. This means that MUD will appear in a person's dreams. In other words, it will be possible to induce specific dreams that annoy, please, or direct to commit certain actions.

Thus, MUD can be conveyed through two signaling systems: polysensorically, with an impact on internal and external receptors, neural pathways, and the relevant parts of the brain, and through the natural and enhanced methods of various actors that convey new and improved abilities of malicious influence. MUD can vary in strength and duration of influence, in its goals (the formation of false interpretations, likes and dislikes, aggressive and panic states, etc.), and in its groups and countries of influence (a deepfake of a politician eating pork can elicit a sharp reaction from voters in the Middle East, but go practically unnoticed in countries where there are few Jewish or Muslim voters).

As DeepTrace's Henry Ajder points out, "Deepfakes do pose a risk to politics in terms of fake media appearing to be real, but right now the more tangible threat is how the idea of deepfakes can be invoked to make the real appear fake. The hype and rather sensational coverage speculating on deepfakes' political impact has overshadowed the real cases where deepfakes have had an impact" (Orange Business Services, 2020). However, "The worry I have is that deepfakes are a way of creating chaos in the current disinformation climate […] but also they'll create some sort of plausible deniability and that's what I see as being the major aim," said Professor Lilian Edwards, an internet law and policy expert at Newcastle University. "It's a chaotic aim" (Lamb, 2020).

Undermining trust in the media can have deep repercussions, particularly in fragile political environments. Sam Gregory, the program director for Witness, a non-profit that helps people document human rights abuses, offers an example. In Brazil, which has a history of police violence, citizens and activists now worry that any video they film of an officer killing a civilian will no longer be sufficient grounds for investigation. This fear that real evidence can plausibly be dismissed as fake, says Gregory, has become a recurring theme in workshops he hosts around the world (Hao, 2019).

Countering MUD should be comprehensive in nature, to include the development of technical measures to detect deepfakes and remove them from the network in cases of malicious use. Significant progress has recently been made in this direction (Afchar et al., 2018; Gregory & French, 2019; Li et al., 2019; Li & Lyu, 2019; Maras & Alexandrou, 2019; Mirsky & Lee, 2020; Mittal et al., 2020; Spivak, 2019), and appropriate legal measures will become a barrier to MUD. The first such measures have already been taken in the United States at the federal level (U.S. Congress, 2018, 2019) and in some states (California Legislature, 2019; New York State Assembly, 2017; Texas Legislature, 2019), as well as in China (Yang et al., 2019). This issue is also being discussed in a number of other countries. Educational work with the population (e.g., through media literacy courses) can play a significant role in preventing MUD.

Conclusion

The current practice of MUD clearly indicates a trend of gradual growth in various countries with different cultural traditions and levels of socioeconomic development. Due to the widespread availability of internet technologies, their affordability, the variety of forms, and the increasing quality, deepfakes pose a growing threat to democracy and political stability. A comprehensive study of measures to counter MUD is required, first at the expert community level, and then at the state and interstate levels, in order to develop national and international legal norms aimed at suppressing MUD. Usually, international law and regulatory practices are formed after precedence has been established at the national level. However, national practices are only at the initial stages of development. It would be naive to expect the formation of an international system for regulating the use of deepfakes, given the current context of acute geopolitical rivalry and accompanying psychological warfare.

The problem is also not confined to the effective detection of deepfakes to expose MUD practices, in order to form a legal basis for the regulation of the use of deepfakes. Unfortunately, there is another serious problem; in this far from ideal modern world, authorities, in an abuse of power, may simply deflect any negative comments about their performance or actions based on photo, video, audio, or written evidence as deepfakes and, therefore, not worthy of being taken seriously.

As a general rule, the following statement can be made: the more perfect the deepfake, the more anti-democratic the state, and the more politically passive and illiterate the population, the more dangerous the practice of using deepfakes will be. In order to neutralize deepfakes (and fakes in general), it is necessary for authorities to have a steady and non-selective desire to find out where the deepfakes are in each individual and socially significant case, and to not label facts as 'deepfakes' when they are really objective truths. Without the conscious desire and ability of citizens in a civil society to take such a position, authorities are unlikely to be willing to effectively resist MUD. Deepfakes are a dual-use technology, and this chapter has examined the use of deepfakes by antisocial actors for antisocial purposes, with results that are detrimental to democratic institutions and democratic rights, as well as to the political stability of society; this explains the unequivocally negative assessment of deepfake use.

However, there are a wide range of socially useful applications for deepfakes that make it undesirable to apply a complete ban on their production and distribution. Moreover, even using deepfakes to disorient a target audience is not a priori MUD; it is possible, and acceptable, to use deepfakes to counter antisocial actors. For example, law enforcement officials could introduce distant, face-to-face communication with members of criminal organizations by imitating the faces and voices of their associates. Such communication can facilitate initial infiltration into the ranks of a criminal organization with minimal risk, direct disinformation to criminals, provoke conflicts between criminal groups, and solve other crimes. In other measures that could be taken, false targets can be identified for criminals through the use of deepfakes, increasing the level of safety for potential victims of criminal actions. In confrontations with reactionaries or aggressive states, the use of deepfakes could be even broader.

References

Adams, M. (2019). *Deepfake technology & 2020 U.S. elections: A threat to democracy and how to spot deepfakes*. Goodwater Publishing.

Afchar, D., Nozick, V., Yamagishi, J., & Echizen, I. (2018). MesoNet: A compact facial video forgery detection network. In arXiv.org. Retrieved July 7, 2022, from https://arxiv.org/abs/1809.00888

AFP. (2022). Deepfake democracy: South Korean candidate goes virtual for votes. In France 24. Retrieved July 6, 2022, from https://www.france24.com/en/live-news/20220214-deepfake-democracy-south-korean-candidate-goes-virtual-for-votes

AFPRelaxnews. (2022). Deepfake democracy: South Korean presidential race candidate goes virtual for votes. In Forbes India. Retrieved July 6, 2022, from https://www.forbesindia.com/article/lifes/deepfake-democracy-south-korean-presidential-race-candidate-goes-virtual-for-votes/73715/1

Ajder, H., Patrini, G., Cavalli, F., & Cullen, L. (2019). *The state of deepfakes: Landscape, threats, and impact*. Deeptrace.

Aldani, L. (1964). Onirofilm. In Labirinti del terzo pianeta. Nuovi racconti italiani di fantascienza [Labyrinths of the third planet. New Italian science fiction stories] (pp. 27–62). Nuova Accademia Editrice.

Aouf, R. (2019). Museum creates deepfake Salvador Dalí to greet visitors. In DeZeen. Retrieved July 6, 2022, from https://www.dezeen.com/2019/05/24/salvador-dali-deepfake-dali-musuem-florida/

Batuev, A. (2010). Glava 2. Sensornaya funkciya mozga. § 1. Obshchie principy konstrukcii sensornyh sistem [Chapter 2. Sensory function of the brain. § 1. General principles for the design of sensor systems]. In *Fiziologiya vysshej nervnoj deyatel'nosti i sensornyh sistem* [Physiology of higher nervous activity and sensory systems] (pp. 46–51). Piter.

Braunstein, E. (2018). At this Holocaust museum, you can speak with holograms of survivors. In *Times of Israel*. Retrieved July 7, 2022, from https://www.timesofisrael.com/at-this-holocaust-museum-you-can-speak-with-holograms-of-survivors/?ref=hackernoon.com

Brown, E. (2019). Online fake news is costing us $78 billion globally each year. In ZDNet. Retrieved July 6, 2022, from https://www.zdnet.com/article/online-fake-news-costing-us-78-billion-globally-each-year/

California Legislature. (2019). Assembly bill – 1280 crimes: Deceptive recordings. In California Legislative Information. Retrieved July 7, 2021, from https://leginfo.legislature.ca.gov/faces/billNavClient.xhtml?bill_id=201920200AB1280

Canadian Press. (2022). 'Deepfakes' and disinformation should fall under online hate law: Advisory panel. In Lethbridge News Now. Retrieved July 6, 2022, from https://lethbridgenewsnow.com/2022/06/19/deepfakes-and-disinformation-should-fall-under-online-hate-law-advisory-panel-2/

Chesney, R., & Citron, D. (2019). Deep fakes: A looming challenge for privacy, democracy, and national security. *California Law Review, 107*, 1753–1820. https://doi.org/10.2139/ssrn.3213954

China Law Translate. (2021). Provisions on the administration of deep synthesis internet information services (Draft for solicitation of comments) 互联网信息服务深度合成管理规定 (征求意见稿). In China Law Translate. Retrieved July 6, 2022, from https://www.chinalawtranslate.com/en/deep-synthesis-draft/

Cole, S. (2018). Researchers developed a new, even more convincing way to write fake yelp reviews. In Vice Motherboard. Retrieved July 7, 2022, from https://www.vice.com/en/article/ev7nez/artificial-intelligence-bot-yelp-reviews

Collins. (2020). Deepfake. In Collins. Retrieved July 7, 2022, from https://www.collinsdictionary.com/dictionary/english/deepfake

Davies, V. (2021). Deepfakes to become a growing trend in 2022 says IntSights. In Cyber Magazine. Retrieved July 6, 2022, from https://cybermagazine.com/cyber-security/deepfakes-become-growing-trend-2022-says-intsights

De Seta, G. (2021). Huanlian, or changing faces: Deepfakes on Chinese digital media platforms. *Convergence: The International Journal of Research into New Media Technologies, 27*, 935–953. https://doi.org/10.1177/13548565211030185

Delfino, R. (2019). Pornographic deepfakes – Revenge Porn's Next Tragic Act – The case for federal criminalization. *SSRN Electronic Journal*. https://doi.org/10.2139/ssrn.3341593

Delgado, H., Evans, N., Kinnunen, T., Lee, K., Liu, X., Nautsch, A., Patino, J., Sahidullah, M., Todisco, M., Wang, X., & Yamagishi, J. (2021). ASVspoof 2021: Automatic speaker verification spoofing and countermeasures challenge evaluation plan. In arXiv.org. Retrieved July 6, 2022, from https://arxiv.org/abs/2109.00535

Demina, I., & Konopleva, I. (2012). Zapahi kak faktor, vliyayushchij na skrytuyu agressiyu [Smells like factor-influencing concealed aggression]. *Psikhologiia i pravo = Psychology and Law, 2*(3).

Descartes, R. (2014). *Meditations on first philosophy: In which the existence of god and the immortality of the soul are demonstrated.* CreateSpace Independent Publishing Platform.

Digital Humans. (2021). What is synthetic media, and how is it distinguished from digital human technology? In Digital Humans. Retrieved July 6, 2022, from https://digitalhumans.com/blog/what-is-synthetic-media-digital-human-technology/

Douceur, J. (2002). The Sybil attack. In *IPTPS '01: Revised papers from the first international workshop on peer-to-peer systems* (pp. 251–260).

EPFL. (2021). Retinal implants can give artificial vision to the blind. In Neuroscience News. Retrieved July 7, 2022, from https://neurosciencenews.com/artificial-vision-retinal-implant-17959/

Fernández, E., & Normann, R. A. (2017). CORTIVIS approach for an intracortical visual prostheses. In V. Gabel (Ed.), *Artificial vision.* Springer. https://doi.org/10.1007/978-3-319-41876-6_15

Ferraro, M. (2020). *Decoding deepfakes.* National Security Institute.

Financial Times. (2020). Facebook bans pro-Trump media outlet over fake accounts. In Financial Times. Retrieved July 7, 2022, from https://www.ft.com/content/182b7b9a-235b-11ea-b8a1-584213ee7b2b

Fox, M. (2021). Brain implant helps man 'speak' through a computer. In CNN. Retrieved July 7, 2022, from https://edition.cnn.com/2021/07/15/health/man-speech-implant/index.html

Generated Photos. (2020). Unique, worry-free model photos. In Medium. Retrieved July 7, 2022, from https://generated.photos/

Gladden, M. (2017). *The handbook of information security for advanced neuroprosthetics.* Synthypnion Academic.

Gordon, R. (2019). Teaching artificial intelligence to connect senses like vision and touch. In MIT News. Retrieved July 7, 2022, from https://news.mit.edu/2019/teaching-ai-to-connect-senses-vision-touch-0617

Gosse, C., & Burkell, J. (2020). Politics and porn: How news media characterizes problems presented by deepfakes. *Critical Studies in Media Communication, 37,* 497–511. https://doi.org/10.1080/15295036.2020.1832697

Gregory, S., & French, E. (2019). How do we work together to detect the AI-manipulated media. Synthesis report. In Witness Media Lab. Retrieved July 7, 2022, from https://lab.witness.org/projects/osint-digital-forensics/

Hao, K. (2019). The biggest threat of deepfakes isn't the deepfakes themselves. In MIT Technology Review. Retrieved July 9, 2022, from https://www.technologyreview.com/2019/10/10/132667/the-biggest-threat-of-deepfakes-isnt-the-deepfakes-themselves/

Harwell, D. (2019). An artificial-intelligence first: Voice-mimicking software reportedly used in a major theft. In The Washington Post. Retrieved September 4, 2022, from https://www.washingtonpost.com/technology/2019/09/04/an-artificial-intelligence-first-voice-mimicking-software-reportedly-used-major-theft/

Hern, A. (2019). New AI fake text generator may be too dangerous to release, say creators. In *The Guardian*. Retrieved July 7, 2022, from https://www.theguardian.com/technology/2019/feb/14/elon-musk-backed-ai-writes-convincing-news-fiction

Horowitz, M. (2021). Cybercrime predictions for 2022 – Deepfakes, Cryptocurrencies and more. In World Economic Forum. Retrieved July 6, 2022, from https://www.weforum.org/agenda/2021/11/2022-cybercrime-predictions-checkpoint/

Hughes, S., Fried, O., Ferguson, M., Hughes, C., Hughes, R., Yao, D., & Hussey, I. (2021). Deepfaked online content is highly effective in manipulating people's attitudes and intentions. https://doi.org/10.31234/osf.io/4ms5a

IEEE Signal Processing Society. (2022). Audio deepfake detection: ICASSP 2022. In IEEE Signal Processing Society. Retrieved July 6, 2022, from https://signalprocessingsociety.org/publications-resources/data-challenges/audio-deepfake-detection-icassp-2022

Institute For Basic Science. (2017). Controlling memory by triggering specific brain waves during sleep. In *Neuroscience News*. Retrieved July 7, 2022, from https://neurosciencenews.com/memory-sleep-brain-waves-7040/

Jaiman, A. (2020a). Deepfake harms and threat modeling. In Medium. Retrieved July 6, 2022, from https://towardsdatascience.com/deepfakes-harms-and-threat-modeling-c09cbe0b7883#

Jaiman, A. (2020b). Countering deepfakes, the most serious AI threat. In *The Hindu*. Retrieved July 6, 2022, from https://www.thehindu.com/opinion/lead/countering-deepfakes-the-most-serious-ai-threat/article62107238.ece

Karras, T., Laine, S., & Aila, T. (2019). A style-based generator architecture for generative adversarial networks. In arXiv.org. Retrieved July 7, 2022, from https://arxiv.org/abs/1812.04948

Kats, D. (2022). What is a deepfake anyway? In NortonLifeLock Blogs. Retrieved July 6, 2022, from https://www.nortonlifelock.com/blogs/blog-post/deepfake

Kite-Powell, J. (2021). The rise of voice cloning and deepfakes in the disinformation wars. In *Forbes*. Retrieved July 6, 2022, from https://www.forbes.com/sites/jenniferhicks/2021/09/21/the-rise-of-voice-cloning-and-deep-fakes-in-the-disinformation-wars/?sh=6e74669138e1

Kumar, M. (2019). Hackers can silently control your Google Home, Alexa, Siri With Laser Light. In *The Hacker News*. Retrieved July 7, 2022, from https://thehackernews.com/2019/11/hacking-voice-assistant-laser.html

Lamb, H. (2020). Sex, coups, and the liar's dividend: What are deepfakes doing to us? In The Institution of Engineering and Technology. Retrieved July 7, 2022, from https://eandt.theiet.org/content/articles/2020/04/sex-coups-and-the-liar-s-dividend-what-are-deepfakes-doing-to-us/

Latchoumane, C., Ngo, H., Born, J., & Shin, H. (2017). Thalamic spindles promote memory formation during sleep through triple phase-locking of cortical, thalamic, and hippocampal rhythms. *Neuron, 95*, 424–435.e6. https://doi.org/10.1016/j.neuron.2017.06.025

Li, L., Bao, J., Yang, H., Chen, D., & Wen, F. (2019). FaceShifter: Towards high fidelity and occlusion aware face swapping. In arXiv.org. Retrieved July 7, 2022, from https://arxiv.org/abs/1912.13457

Li, Y., & Lyu, S. (2019). Exposing DeepFake videos by detecting face warping artifacts. In arXiv.org. Retrieved July 7, 2022, from https://arxiv.org/abs/1811.00656v2

Litovkin, N. (2021). Novyj rossijskij implant vernet nezryachim sposobnost' videt' [New Russian implant will restore the ability to see to the blind]. In Russia Beyond on Yandex Zen. Retrieved July 7, 2022, from https://zen.yandex.ru/media/rusbeyond/novyi-rossiiskii-implant-vernet-nezriachim-sposobnost-videt-60e6d6ef7e453743e2741ac5

Longin, L., & Deroy, O. (2022). Augmenting perception: How artificial intelligence transforms sensory substitution. *Consciousness and Cognition, 99*, 103280. https://doi.org/10.1016/j.concog.2022.103280

Lourenco, R. (2019). Could hackers trick voice assistants into committing fraud? Researchers say yes. In Venture Beat. Retrieved July 7, 2022, from https://venturebeat.com/2019/02/17/could-hackers-trick-voice-assistants-into-committing-fraud-researchers-say-yes/

Lozano, A., Suárez, J., Soto-Sánchez, C., Garrigós, J., Martínez-Alvarez, J., Ferrández, J., & Fernández, E. (2020). Neurolight: A deep learning neural interface for cortical visual prostheses. *International Journal of Neural Systems, 30*, 2050045. https://doi.org/10.1142/s0129065720500458

Maras, M. H., & Alexandrou, A. (2019). Determining authenticity of video evidence in the age of artificial intelligence and in the wake of deepfake videos. *The International Journal of Evidence & Proof, 23*, 255–262. https://doi.org/10.1177/1365712718807226

Martucci, B. (2022). How the COVID-19 pandemic will permanently change society & the economy. Retrieved July 7, 2022, from https://www.moneycrashers.com/covid-pandemic-change-society-economy/. https://www.moneycrashers.com/

Massachusetts Institute of Technology. (2019a). Capitol Hill (Toxic). In Nightmare machine. Horror imagery generated by artificial intelligence. Retrieved July 7, 2022, from http://nightmare.mit.edu/#portfolioModal22

Massachusetts Institute of Technology. (2019b). Scary or not. In Nightmare machine. Horror imagery generated by artificial intelligence. Retrieved July 7, 2022, from http://nightmare.mit.edu/faces

McDermott, R., Tingley, D., & Hatemi, P. (2014). Assortative mating on ideology could operate through olfactory cues. *American Journal of Political Science, 58,* 997–1005. https://doi.org/10.1111/ajps.12133

Merrefield, C. (2019). Deepfake technology is changing fast. These 5 resources can help you keep up. In The Journalist's Resource. Retrieved July 7, 2022, from https://journalistsresource.org/politics-and-government/deepfake-technology-5-resources/

Merriam-Webster. (2020). Deepfake. In Merriam-Webster. Retrieved July 7, 2022, from https://www.merriam-webster.com/words-at-play/deepfake-slang-definition-examples

Mirsky, Y., & Lee, W. (2020). The creation and detection of deepfakes: A survey. In arXiv.org. Retrieved July 7, 2022, from https://arxiv.org/abs/2004.11138v1

Mittal, T., Bhattacharya, U., Chandra, R., Bera, A., & Manocha, D. (2020). Emotions don't lie: An audio-visual deepfake detection method using affective cues. In arXiv.org. Retrieved July 7, 2022, from https://arxiv.org/abs/2003.06711

Morris, A. (2021). CRISPR and HIV: New technique in human blood unveils potential paths toward cure. In Northwestern University. Retrieved July 7, 2022, from https://news.northwestern.edu/stories/2021/05/implanted-wireless-device-triggers-mice-to-form-instant-bond/

Moses, D., Metzger, S., Liu, J., Anumanchipalli, G., Makin, J., Sun, P., Chartier, J., Dougherty, M., Liu, P., Abrams, G., Tu-Chan, A., Ganguly, K., & Chang, E. (2021). Neuroprosthesis for decoding speech in a paralyzed person with anarthria. *New England Journal of Medicine, 385,* 217–227. https://doi.org/10.1056/nejmoa2027540

Nema, P. (2021). Understanding copyright issues entailing deepfakes in India. *International Journal of Law and Information Technology.* https://doi.org/10.1093/ijlit/eaab007

New York State Assembly. (2017). An act to amend the civil rights law, in relation to the right of privacy and the right of publicity; and to amend the civil practice law and rules, in relation to the timeliness of commencement of an action for violation of the right of publicity. In New York State Assembly. Retrieved July 7, 2022, from https://nyassembly.gov/leg/?default_fld=&leg_video=&bn=A08155&term=2017&Summary=Y&Text=Y

Nightingale, S., & Farid, H. (2022). AI-synthesized faces are indistinguishable from real faces and more trustworthy. *Proceedings of the National Academy of Sciences.* https://doi.org/10.1073/pnas.2120481119

NortonLifeLock. (2022). Norton consumer cyber safety pulse report: Deception scams on the rise. In NortonLifeLock. Retrieved July 6, 2022, from https://investor.nortonlifelock.com/news/news-details/2022/Norton-Consumer-Cyber-Safety-Pulse-Report-Deception-Scams-On-the-Rise/default.aspx

NVISION Eye Centers. (2022). Guide to bionic eyes: Implants, lenses & the status in 2022. In NVISION Eye Centers. Retrieved July 7, 2022, from https://www.nvisioncenters.com/education/bionic-eyes/

O'Sullivan, L., & Dickerson, J. (2020). Here are a few ways GPT-3 can go wrong. In TechCrunch. Retrieved July 6, 2022, from https://techcrunch.com/2020/08/07/here-are-a-few-ways-gpt-3-can-go-wrong/

Oltermann, P. (2022). European politicians duped into deepfake video calls with mayor of Kyiv. In *The Guardian*. Retrieved September 4, 2022, from https://www.theguardian.com/world/2022/jun/25/european-leaders-deepfake-video-calls-mayor-of-kyiv-vitali-klitschko

Orange Business Services. (2020). Fake news: What could deepfakes and AI scams mean for cybersecurity? In Orange Business Services. Retrieved July 9, 2022, from https://www.orange-business.com/en/magazine/fake-news-what-could-deepfakes-and-ai-scams-mean-cybersecurity

Patel, A. (2019). Malicious use of AI. In F-Secure Blog. Retrieved July 7, 2022, from https://blog.f-secure.com/malicious-use-of-ai/

Patriau, F., & Patriau, O. E. (2019). La era de los Deepfakes o las mentiras profundas (Hacker, Espionaje, Seguridad, Marco Legal n° 15) [The era of deepfakes or deep lies (Hacker, espionage, security, legal framework no. 15)]. Amazon.com Services LLC (seller).

Pavlov, I. (1951). Uslovnyj refleks [Conditioned reflex]. In I. Pavlov (Ed.), *Polnoe sobranie sochinenij [Complete set of works]* (pp. 320–343). USSR Academy of Sciences.

Pindrop. (2020). *Voice intelligence & security report. A review of fraud, the future of voice, and the impact to customer service channels. Revised for 2020 including updated data*. Pindrop.

Pittalwala, I. (2020). Using artificial intelligence to smell the roses. In University of California, Riverside. Retrieved July 6, 2022, from https://news.ucr.edu/articles/2020/07/28/using-artificial-intelligence-smell-roses

Prokop, A. (2015). Can you smell someone's political views? One study says maybe. In *Vox*. Retrieved July 6, 2022, from https://www.vox.com/2014/9/18/6329275/politics-smell-attraction-study

Ravishankar, T. (2020). AI that can feel and smell: A threat to humans? In *TechQuila*. Retrieved July 6, 2022, from https://www.techquila.co.in/ai-that-can-feel-and-smell-a-threat-to-humans/

Rense, S. (2018). What are 'Deepfakes,' and why are Pornhub and Reddit banning them? In *Esquire*. Retrieved July 7, 2022, from https://www.esquire.com/lifestyle/sex/a17043863/what-are-deepfakes-celebrity-porn/

Romero, A. (2021). GPT-4 will have 100 trillion parameters – 500x the size of GPT-3. In Medium. Retrieved July 6, 2022, from https://towardsdatascience.com/gpt-4-will-have-100-trillion-parameters-500x-the-size-of-gpt-3-582b98d82253

RT DE. (2022). Giffey telefoniert mit Deepfake-Klitschko: Staatsschutz ermittelt [Giffey on the phone with deepfake Klitschko: State security is investigating]. In RT DE. Retrieved July 6, 2022, from https://de.rt.com/inland/141907-giffey-telefoniert-mit-deepfake-klitschko/?ysclid=l4tqexf6yo738951831

Sagar, R. (2020). OpenAI releases GPT-3, the largest model so far. In *Analytics India Magazine*. Retrieved July 6, 2022, from https://analyticsindiamag.com/open-ai-gpt-3-language-model/

Sayler, K. (2022). Deep fakes and national security. In Congressional Research Service. Retrieved July 6, 2022, from https://crsreports.congress.gov/product/pdf/IF/IF11333

Sechenov, I. (2014). *Refleksy golovnogo mozga [Reflexes of the brain]*. AST Publishing.

Shahid, M. (2020). How deepfakes make us question everything in 2020. In ITProPortal. Retrieved July 9, 2022, from https://www.itproportal.com/features/how-deepfakes-make-us-question-everything-in-2020/

Shead, S. (2020). Why everyone is talking about the A.I. text generator released by an Elon Musk-backed lab. In *CNBC*. Retrieved July 6, 2022, from https://www.cnbc.com/2020/07/23/openai-gpt3-explainer.html

Spivak, R. (2019). "Deepfakes": The newest way to commit one of the oldest crimes. *Georgetown Law Technology Review, 339*, 351–352.

Srivastava, S. (2020). Enhancing food flavour experiences through AI innovation. In Analytics Insight. Retrieved July 7, 2022, from https://www.analyticsinsight.net/enhancing-food-flavour-experiences-ai-innovation/

Statt, N. (2019). China makes it a criminal offense to publish deepfakes or fake news without disclosure. In *The Verge*. Retrieved July 6, 2022, from https://www.theverge.com/2019/11/29/20988363/china-deepfakes-ban-internet-rules-fake-news-disclosure-virtual-reality

Stupp, C. (2019). Fraudsters used AI to mimic CEO's voice in unusual cybercrime case. In *The Wall Street Journal*. Retrieved July 7, 2022, from https://www.wsj.com/articles/fraudsters-use-ai-to-mimic-ceos-voice-in-unusual-cybercrime-case-11567157402

Synced. (2019). Clone a voice in five seconds with this AI toolbox. In Medium. Retrieved July 7, 2022, from https://medium.com/syncedreview/clone-a-voice-in-five-seconds-with-this-ai-toolbox-f3f116b11281

Tammekänd, J., Thomas, J., & Peterson, K. (2020). *Deepfakes 2020: The tipping point*. Sentinel.

Tech, J. (2018). Deepfakes, social media, and celebrities: A technology for the combination of fake and deep learning used for swapping faces of people in a video. Amazon.com Services LLC (seller).

Temming, M. (2018). Algorithm makes fake videos lifelike. *Science News, 194*(5), 12–13.

Texas Legislature. (2019). An act relating to the creation of a criminal offense for fabricating a deceptive video with intent to influence the outcome of an election. In Texas Legislature. Retrieved July 7, 2022, from https://leginfo.legislature.ca.gov/faces/billNavClient.xhtml?bill_id=201920200AB1280; https://capitol.texas.gov/BillLookup/Text.aspx?LegSess=86R&Bill=SB751

The Indian Express. (2022). South Korea has an AI version of a leading presidential candidate. And for politicians, the digital may be better than the real. In *The*

Indian Express. Retrieved July 6, 2022, from https://indianexpress.com/article/opinion/editorials/deepfake-campaign-ai-south-korea-presidential-election-7775613/

The Times of India. (2022). Deepfake democracy: South Korean candidate goes virtual for votes. In *The Times of India*. Retrieved July 6, 2022, from https://timesofindia.indiatimes.com/world/rest-of-world/deepfake-democracy-south-korean-candidate-goes-virtual-for-votes/articleshow/89556568.cms

The Times of Israel. (2018). 'I never said that!' The high-tech deception of 'deepfake' videos. In *The Times of Israel*. Retrieved July 7, 2022, from https://www.timesofisrael.com/i-never-said-that-the-high-tech-deception-of-deepfake-videos/

Toronto, W. (2018). Fake news and kill-switches: The U.S. government's fight to respond to and prevent fake news. *Air Force Law Review, 79*, 167–206.

U.S. Congress. (2018). S.3805 – Malicious Deep Fake Prohibition Act of 2018. In U.S. Congress. Retrieved July 7, 2022, from https://www.congress.gov/bill/115th-congress/senate-bill/3805

U.S. Congress. (2019). H.R.3230 – Defending each and every person from false appearances by keeping exploitation subject to accountability act of 2019. In U.S. Congress. Retrieved July 7, 2022, from https://www.congress.gov/bill/116th-congress/house-bill/3230

United Nations. (2019). Co-chairs Summary. International High-level Conference on Countering Terrorism through Innovative Approaches and the Use of New and Emerging Technologies. Delivered by Mr. Vladimir Voronkov, Under-Secretary-General of the United Nations Office of Counter-Terrorism. Minsk, 4 September.

Vastmindz. (2022). South Korea's presidential Deepfake. In Vastmindz. Retrieved July 6, 2022, from https://vastmindz.com/south-koreas-presidential-deepfake/

Veldkamp, D. (2022). Cyber awareness 2022: Consider deepfakes, NFTs, and more. In InfoSystems. Retrieved July 6, 2022, from https://infosystems.biz/cybersecurity/cyber-awareness-2022-consider-deepfakes-nfts-and-more/

Vincent, J. (2018). Why we need a better definition of 'deepfake.' In *The Verge*. Retrieved July 7, 2022, from https://www.theverge.com/2018/5/22/17380306/deepfake-definition-ai-manipulation-fake-news

Vincent, J. (2019). ThisPersonDoesNotExist.com uses AI to generate endless fake faces. In *The Verge*. Retrieved July 7, 2022, from https://www.theverge.com/tldr/2019/2/15/18226005/ai-generated-fake-people-portraits-thispersondoesnotexist-stylegan

Waddell, K. (2018). The impending war over deepfakes. In Axios. Retrieved July 7, 2022, from https://www.axios.com/2018/07/22/the-impending-war-over-deepfakes

Wang, L., Ma, L., Yang, J., & Wu, J. (2021). Human somatosensory processing and artificial somatosensation. *Cyborg and Bionic Systems, 2021*, 1–11. https://doi.org/10.34133/2021/9843259

Watson, N., & Fernandez, C. (2021). Artificial intelligence and sleep: Advancing sleep medicine. *Sleep Medicine Reviews, 59*, 101512. https://doi.org/10.1016/j.smrv.2021.101512

Westerlund, M. (2019). The emergence of deepfake technology: A review. *Technology Innovation Management Review, 11*, 40–52.

Witness Media Lab. (2021). Backgrounder: Deepfakes in 2021. In Witness Media Lab. Retrieved July 6, 2022, from https://lab.witness.org/backgrounder-deepfakes-in-2021/

Wolley, S. (2020). *The reality game: How the next wave of technology will break the truth*. Public Affairs.

Woodbury, R. (2021). The rise of synthetic media & digital creators. In Digital Native. Retrieved July 6, 2022, from https://digitalnative.substack.com/p/the-rise-of-synthetic-media-and-digital

Wright, A. (2019). Deepfakes and deep video portraits – What are they and what is the difference? In Medium. Retrieved July 7, 2022, from https://medium.com/@aprilcwright/deepfakes-vs-deep-video-portraits-what-are-they-and-what-is-the-difference-24b7ac538090

Yang, Y., Goh, B., & Gibbs, E. (2019). China seeks to root out fake news and deepfakes with new online content rules. In *Reuters*. Retrieved July 7, 2022, from https://www.reuters.com/article/us-china-technology/china-seeks-to-root-out-fake-news-and-deepfakes-with-new-online-content-rules-idUSKBN1Y30VU

Yang, Y., Wu, M., Vázquez-Guardado, A., Wegener, A., Grajales-Reyes, J., Deng, Y., Wang, T., Avila, R., Moreno, J., Minkowicz, S., Dumrongprechachan, V., Lee, J., Zhang, S., Legaria, A., Ma, Y., Mehta, S., Franklin, D., Hartman, L., Bai, W., Han, M., Zhao, H., Lu, W., Yu, Y., Sheng, X., Banks, A., Yu, X., Donaldson, Z., Gereau, R., Good, C., Xie, Z., Huang, Y., Kozorovitskiy, Y., & Rogers, J. (2021). Wireless multilateral devices for optogenetic studies of individual and social behaviors. *Nature Neuroscience, 24*, 1035–1045. https://doi.org/10.1038/s41593-021-00849-x

Yang, Z. (2022). China wants deepfake providers responsible for their technologies. In Protocol. Retrieved July 6, 2022, from https://www.protocol.com/bulletins/china-deepfake-regulation#

Yidio. (2002). Simone. In Yidio. Retrieved July 6, 2022, from https://www.yidio.com/movie/simone/33149

Young, N. (2019). *DeepFake technology: Complete guide to deepfakes, politics and social media*. Amazon.com Services LLC (seller).

Zakharov, E., Shysheya, A., Burkov, E., & Lempitsky, V. (2019). Few-shot adversarial learning of realistic neural talking head models. In arXiv.org. https://arxiv.org/abs/1905.08233.%20Accessed%207%20Jul%202022

4

Automating Extremism: Mapping the Affective Roles of Artificial Agents in Online Radicalization

Peter Mantello, Tung Manh Ho, and Lena Podoletz

Introduction

One of the fastest growing areas of artificial intelligence development is interactive software deployed on social media to replace or augment human "efforts" across a range of purposes (Bradshaw & Howard, 2019; Jhan et al., 2021; Marcellino et al., 2020). Commonly referred to as "web robots," "social," or "chatbots," these computational agents perform a variety of functions such as automatically generate messages, advocate ideas, act as followers of users or surrogate agents. Conversational software applications are now augmenting and replacing human efforts across an ever-expanding array of fields—advertising, finance (Ng, et al., 2020), mental health counseling (Kretzschmar et al., 2019), dating, and wellness (Agnihotri et al., 2021). With advances in machine learning, natural word processing, as well as face and voice tone recognition, these AI speakers are gaining refined social, linguistic,

---

P. Mantello (✉)
Ritsumeikan Asia Pacific University, Beppu, Japan
e-mail: mantello@apu.ac.jp

T. M. Ho
Ritsumeikan Asia Pacific University, Beppu, Japan

Centre for Interdisciplinary Social Research, Phenikaa University, Hanoi, Vietnam

L. Podoletz
University of Edinburgh, Edinburgh, UK
e-mail: lena.podoletz@ed.ac.uk

© The Author(s), under exclusive license to Springer Nature Switzerland AG 2023
E. Pashentsev (ed.), *The Palgrave Handbook of Malicious Use of AI and Psychological Security*,
https://doi.org/10.1007/978-3-031-22552-9_4

and conversational capacities, mimicking empathic and humanlike behavior (Mantello et al., 2021; Ho et al., 2021). Newer iterations can now learn from social interactions, news articles, and other text content to understand context, history, and ethics so they can interact in a seemingly more human manner. Advances such as these are allowing these artificial agents to read users' emotional state and respond in a fitting emotional way, heightening not simply their utility but, importantly, anthropomorphic appeal (Mehra, 2021). Like other AI applications, social media bots hold promise as tools for societal good, optimizing how we work and live. But their malicious misuse by non-state and state actors is already here (Marcellino et al., 2020; Howard, 2020). Adversarial state and non-actors are employing social bots to amplify the speed and scale of online mis- and disinformation (Mustafaraj & Metaxas, 2017), create fake social media accounts (Ramalingam & Chinnaiah, 2018), harvest personal data from unsuspecting users (Deibert, 2019), impersonate friends/associates, and manipulate or disrupt political communication, as well as foil psychological security (Pashentsev & Bazarkina, 2022). In the hands of violent extremist organizations, software robots are quickly making human propagandists, recruiters, and troll armies redundant.

This entanglement of empathic machines, mediality, and networked crowds has accelerated the formation of what Zizi Papacharissi calls "affective publics" that "are mobilized and connected, identified, and potentially disconnected through expressions of sentiment" (2016, p. 5). Concomitantly, in the hands of extremists, these same artificial personas are transforming affective publics into distributed dissent, "a process whereby emergent collectives through their discrete micro-movements engage in macro-patterns of violence" (Thacker, 2004).[1] At a deeper biopolitical level, weaponization of software robots as tools of radicalization is emblematic of an emerging era of automated governance where Foucauldian strategies and techniques of control are relegated to software systems in which "people willingly and voluntarily subscribe to and desire their logic, trading potential disciplinary effects against benefits gained" (Kitchin & Dodge, 2014, p. 11). Instead of confining individuals in brick-and-mortar enclosures or imposing corporeal forms of domination, bot-driven "algorithmic governance" channels social media users into like-minded groups and then heightens engagement with provocative content that triggers

---

[1] A prime example of distributed dissent (although not "physically" violent) is "Operation Payback" in 2008. In retaliation for VISA and MASTERCARD companies blocking of payments to WikiLeaks, the hacker collective Anonymous initiated a series of distributed denial-of-service (DDoS) attacks against the credit card companies' websites (Sauter, 2014). In this case, unaffiliated hackers from all over the globe using a botnet flooded VISA and MASTERCARD sites with so much traffic that it caused their respective servers to shut down.

their deepest emotions such as anger, fear, and resentment (Fisher & Taub, 2018). The goal behind this malicious form of psychological control often steers the individual into automated feedback loops and filter bubbles that heighten his/her illusion of freedom and choice, while actually structuring and reshaping their possible fields of thought and action by guiding and restricting the information they receive (Pariser, 2011; Howard, 2020).

Arguably, AI has allowed for a paradigm shift to occur in how political propaganda is constructed, negotiated, and ultimately legitimated. Mass campaigns of political indoctrination were once the province of the state, designed to recruit, sway, or manipulate public opinion. Today, however, the proliferation of low-cost or even free easy-to-create bots has lowered the entry bar for violent extremist organizations, allowing them to build *affective bonds* with social media users to mobilize them to act radically and violently. This chapter argues that social media bots are becoming more powerful tools for extremist organizations that will significantly enhance their recruitment capabilities. While bots are already de facto weapons of information warfare, pushing targeted and personalized content to shape and mold a user's thoughts or beliefs, we argue that newer generations augmented with affect recognition capabilities are tapping the inner emotional state of users for the purposes of recruitment. On encrypted social media channels, such social media bots are especially attractive to groups with relatively few human and financial resources that lack access to, or are restricted from, many media platforms. As computational advances in machine learning and natural language processing grow their human-like persona, we suggest that the efficacy of these automated propagandists and headhunters will only increase.

Adopting a biopolitical lens, this chapter investigates and analyzes the malicious use of social bots as an emerging psychological tool for extremist recruitment. While there exists a growing body of scholarship devoted to bots and computational propaganda (van Stekelenburg, 2017; Woolley & Howard, 2018; Van den Bos, 2018), literature related to the affective role of conversational AI in online radicalization remains limited (iN2, 2018; Bartlett et al., 2010; Bradshaw & Howard, 2019; Araque & Iglesias, 2020). In the first part, we provide general background information on the various types of social media bots used for malicious purposes such as information warfare and indoctrination campaigns. Second, we undertake a qualitative study of the affective role of conversational AI in establishing an emotional relationship with potential recruits in online radicalization, examining this phenomenon on an organizational level and at a personal level. Third, we assess current efforts by Western security agencies, social media companies, and academic researchers to counter online radicalization strategies by extremist organizations.

Two important caveats before we begin. First, violent extremists are not the first to employ bots for bolstering their ranks. One of the first automated recruiters is Sergeant Star (short for Strong, Trained, and Ready), an intelligent virtual assistant developed for Goarmy.com, the US military's recruitment website. The now defunct chatbot was launched shortly after 9/11 as a cost-cutting measure to handle the sudden interest and overwhelming traffic to the site (Bock, 2013). As an avatar resembling the US Marine drill instructor in Stanley Kubrick's film *Full Metal Jacket* (1987), Sergeant Star responded to wide-ranging queries such as scholarship information, length of training, and career advancement. The chatbot was developed into a life-size, virtual installation and later application for the burgeoning mobile phone market as well as spawning a female counterpart (Sergeant Stripe) to appeal to younger, more gender-sensitive generations. Interestingly, after filing a Freedom of Information Act, Electronic Frontier Foundation discovered that the same technology underlying Sergeant Star had previously been used by the CIA and FBI to identify and trap terrorists in chatroom conversations (Lee et al., 2010). At present the US military no longer relies on chatbots for their online efforts, preferring instead to outsource online queries to human agents.

Second, while this chapter focuses on the adoption of social bots by Islamist extremists in their strategic communication and indoctrination efforts, it is important to note that they are also currently being used to recruit neo-Nazis in Germany, Burman chauvinists in Myanmar, white supremacists in the USA, and so on (Malmgren, 2017; Shuldiner, 2019; Hotez, 2020). Yet we argue that Islamist extremists have the longest experience and widest networks across social media and, thus, provide the most globally dangerous and distressing example of this trend. We suggest that lessons regarding "jihadi" bots and online "affective bonding" can inform efforts against radicalization and extremist recruitment of any sort, as well as broader threats to psychological security of individual nations as well as international psychological security.

Background

Although propaganda has been a key element in manufacturing consent for collective violence, evolving across centuries in prose and poems, song and dance, penny-farthing broadsheets, newspapers, newswire, radio, film, and TV (Howard, 2020), its twenty-first-century incarnation is hard-wired into modern networks of communication, often cloaked in unseen algorithms and automated agents (Fisher & Taub, 2018). In the sphere of contemporary politics, bots are now a favored tool of political rumors, lies, and psychological manipulation, often through spreading disinformation and fake news (Bessi & Ferrara, 2016; Woolley & Howard, 2018; Bakir & McStay, 2021). These algorithmic agents-provocateurs can perform a variety of functions and carry different names depending on their purpose. For example, a "noise bot" or "spam bot" is engineered to disrupt communication by a targeted group (Marcellino et al., 2020). It accomplishes this by flooding social media sites with thousands of adversarial posts in order to dilute the impact of opposing content. A tactical campaign using this type of bot is called a "Twitter bomb" or "Google bomb." While this technique can overpower opposing content and voices, the term "spam" is a bit misleading (Himelein-Wachowiak et al., 2021). Contrasted to email spam tactics, Twitter spambots or Twitter bombs tend to require activation (very often unwitting) by their targeted users—either clicking on a link/email or responding to a chat.

Researchers have found Twitter bombs often originate from fake accounts. Crucially, Twitter spambots have increasingly deployed sophisticated methods to evade spam-filtering algorithms as well as to grow their followers. These bots disguise their spam as replies to existing tweets about a given topic, hoping that human users will retweet in response, spreading the Twitter bombs long before Twitter detects and deletes the fake accounts (Mustafaraj & Metaxas, 2017). For instance, in 2018, a Twitter bomb in support of the Saudi Prince, Mohammed Bin Salman, was released by an unidentified group shortly after the murder of the Washington Post columnist Jamal Khashoggi. The Twitter bomb produced about 250,000 tweets per day, with Arabic hashtags such as "We have to stand by our leader" and "Campaign to close Al Jazeera" (Bell & Coleman, 2018). So effective was the automated blitzkrieg that Tweets in favor of the Saudi Prince became highest trending topic on Twitter during its first month (Bell & Coleman, 2018). A more recent example is the Islamic State (IS) hacking of GETTR, the pro-Trump social network just after its launch in July of 2021. POLITICO journalists Scott and Nguyen (2021) observed that within days of GETTR's debut, the site was infected with more than 250 fake accounts posting IS images, memes, and beheading videos, all promoting violence against the West and urging followers to replicate such actions on other social networks.

Importantly, deploying bots to spread fake news and drown out opposing political conversations or political dissent is not exclusive to extremists or authoritarian regimes (Bessi & Ferrara, 2016; Stella et al., 2018; Howard, 2020). It builds on traditional official and corporate tactics of diminishing or dividing dissenting voices by issuing massive amounts of presumptively accurate content that cast doubt on criticism of governmental or business actions (Herman & Chomsky, 1988). During the 2016 US elections and the UK Brexit referendum, the data analytic company Cambridge Analytica (hired by Trump and United Kingdom Independence Party [UKIP] supporters, respectively) exploited the emotionality of political communication by surreptitiously using bots to gather psycho-graphic profiles of millions of Facebook subscribers and then algorithmically seed their personalized timelines with political ads designed to either incite anger or cool passions (to encourage disengagement) in order to sway their vote (Bastos & Mercea, 2018). Besides the well-documented case of Cambridge Analytica in the UK, use of bots to spread disinformation is increasing on a global level. In an alarming study of social manipulation by governments and political parties, Oxford researchers Bradshaw & Howard (2019) found evidence of psychological manipulation campaigns by autonomous artificial agents taking place in "70 countries, up from 48 countries in 2018 and 28 countries in 2017. In each country, there is at least one political party or government agency using social media to shape public attitudes" (p. i).

Concomitantly, a study on Twitter bot activities during Spain's 2017 Catalan independence referendum found bots were influential in shaping the social media discussion landscape (Stella et al., 2018). The authors collected and analyzed a dataset consisting of nearly 4 million Twitter posts by almost 1 million users during the event and found that 19% of overall interactions among humans were directed from bots to humans, primarily via retweets (74%) and mentions (25%). More important, although bots still occupy a peripheral position in social networks, the analysis reveals their interactions were directed strategically by aiming their activity principally toward human hubs for maximum influence. In analyzing sentiment scores for the bot-to-human interactions, they also found that social media bots increased conflict online by generating negative and/or violent content targeted at users to raise their distrust of or incite violence against the Independentists, that is, those who support Catalan independence.

Thus, bots pose a myriad of threats to the psychological security of liberal democracies but also in the realm of international psychological security. This is no doubt why for net-savvy Islamic extremist organizations, enlistment of code-savvy AI programmers is now as important as foot soldiers (Meleagrou-Hitchens et al., 2017). In the following sections, we argue this dangerous trend signals the need for state/commercial partner strategies to empower social media users to recognize and react to manipulation and exploitation by artificially intelligent agents. In the next section, we provide a deeper

Bots as Agents of Affective Bonding

What social media and digital communications have made abundantly clear, especially in lieu of the recent global pandemic, is that individuals can create and sustain meaningful relationships without requiring that communication is contingent on physical proximity. Today, people are building significant disembodied relationships with one another, often without even meeting them in person. As Kempt (p. 32) argues, the importance of these relationships is not reliant on the physical make-up of both communication partners but "in the stability associated with communication, invested and rewarded trust and availability." As social relationships move away from the necessity of embodied presence, especially in context to online radicalization, and as smart bots become increasing intelligent conversationalists, it is reasonable to assume that people will not always make a distinction between their digital human-human relationship and human-machine relationships (p. 8). Certainly, the growing popularity of social bots such as "Replika" (Possati, 2022) is indicative of this relational turn. Thus, it is not surprising that bots have become an important tool of "affective bonding" (Konijn & Hoorn, 2017), the psycho-physical phenomenon where an individual develops an emotional relationship with another person or group.

For Haq et al. (2020), affective bonding is a key element in radicalization, occurring on an organizational and personal level. On an organizational level, the researchers suggest that radical groups augment their strategic communications with bots to provide recruits with a sense of a well-developed operational structure, which in turn encourages positive emotions (pride, joy, respect, and belonging) while also generating negative feelings (hate, anger, and disgust) for out-groups (McCauley & Moskalenko, 2008). A notable illustration of how bots can algorithmically facilitate the processes of organizational-level bonding is the IS infomercial, *Harvest of the Soldiers* (Cafarella et al., 2019). Sent almost weekly through private Telegram channels of IS supporters, the bot-driven video relays battlefield statistics of recent kills and victories, interspersed with the recurring figure of an Arab warrior on horseback. Horsch (2014) notes the symbolic importance of the rider on horseback for Salafi-jihadists, imagery that conjures among jihadists nostalgia for heroic narratives of conquest during the first generations of Islamic expansion. But whereas this earlier group of Muslims represents a triumphant generation of

Muhammad's army and established Islam, younger generations of recruits see themselves as the last Muslim army, which will cleanse the world in an apocalyptical war between good and evil (Mantello, 2021; McCants, 2015). Another example of bots used in information warfare is the IS-sponsored Twitter campaign in 2019, calling for revenge attacks after the US killing of Abu Bakr Al-Baghdadi. Within hours of the IS leader's death, pro-Baghdadi posts flooded Twitter with inhuman speed. Extremist researcher for the Institute for Strategic Dialogue, Moustafa Ayad, noted that even though many pro-IS follower accounts were banned, followers quickly reappeared on Twitter either by hacking the accounts of unsuspecting users or by performing small name changes to their previous accounts (Ayad et al., 2021). Ayad further noted that the nearly sudden and high-volume traffic to Twitter and the virulent repopulating of posts were telltale signs of a non-human assault. In other words, a well-coordinated botnet attack.

To deepen affective bonding on an organizational level, extremist bots can perform a variety of other functions to identify susceptible targets and then connect them to official human recruiters or other supporters (Bodó et al., 2017). Similar to the way phishing bots harvest information on social media users and then attempt to persuade them to add a new neighbor to their contact lists, extremist bots can connect potential recruits/users who share similar interests but have not engaged with each other (Stalinsky & Sosnow, 2020). These automated friendship brokers are designed to increase cooperation and information among users on an organizational but also personal level. For instance, a friending bot might identify and match small groups of social media users whose profile an algorithm deems to have high likelihood of being radicalized. In this way, the friending bot would help initiate secure communications among like-minded users who might receive private introductions to a recruiter (Gehl & Bakardjieva, 2016). Thus, it is reasonable to expect as the barrier to entry in this technology lowers and becomes more available and social media providers offer more features, extremist organizations will increasingly employ them for recruitment purposes (Gehl & Bakardjieva, 2016).

Telegram, for example, is a good illustration of this trend. Although monitored by internal administrators and state security forces, the site remains a favored platform of religious extremist organizations because it provides users with free and easy to set up "Matchmaker" bots on its privately encrypted channels. According to Telegram's instructional literature, a user can seek new contacts simply by entering a username in the Telegram settings and uploading a photo. Alternatively, a Telegram user can simply type into a Telegram desktop app, "BotFather," a multi-purpose application program interface

(API), that helps users to create new bot accounts and manage existing bots. Telegram's "Matchmaker" bots can be used to provide new recruits with information on a violent extremist organization's history and agenda, deliver updates on operational missions, share links to new SM sites and drop-zones, and/or warn followers of sites being monitored by law enforcement agencies. They can also make announcements requesting *sadaqi* (donations) at least nominally for community members living in poverty or families of fallen fighters, as well as promote rescue missions for family members detained in Iraq and Syria (Stalinsky & Sosnow, 2020).

Emotional connection to an organization is only one of the steps in radicalization that bots can facilitate. Haq et al. (2020) suggest that an individual who becomes a supporter/member of a violent extremist group also develops a personal, emotional relationship with the organization. The greater a newcomer's frequency of exposure to the ideology and agenda of a violent extremist organization, the researchers argue, the more a newcomer begins to develop ideas, feelings, and sentiments in line with the agenda of the radical group. They write, "[t]his bond keeps the recruit in a specific and long-lasting affective state which leads them toward a deeper involvement in that organization" (p. 2). Concurrently, Bloom and Daymon (2018) studied the engagement behavior of IS supporters on the Telegram messaging platform. They found evidence of how IS took advantage of the "high engagement" features of the platform to keep their followers involved. Specifically, IS media agents deployed bots for a range of techniques such as push notifications, microfeedback, and limited-time offers exclusively for members that encourage followers to continually check their chats and channels. In many cases, massive bulk invitations to join exclusive chats were posted simultaneously across different channels, which indicated that automated bots were spreading the propaganda and engaging pro-ISIS users. The algorithmically driven frequency of extremist content offered recruits a sense of belonging and excitement from their perceived "exclusive" access to a channel (Bloom & Daymon, 2018).

Bots as Personal Automated Headhunters

With advances in voice tone recognition and natural language processing ability (Seering et al., 2018), jihadi bots are today engaging in humanlike conversation with potential recruits (Mueen et al., 2019). Similar to behavioral cognitive therapy bots such as "Eliza" or "Woebot" used in mental health diagnosis and treatment (de Gennaro et al., 2020), jihadi social bots can achieve an emotional connection with newcomers by linking them to like-minded people—and then at some point handing them off to a human operator to enable potential recruitment (Marcellino et al., 2020). They can also engage in direct conversation with potential members. The growing efficacy of chatbots as surrogate recruiters is supported by emerging literature on human-machine interactions that suggests humans respond on an emotional level to computer-mediated interactions similarly to how they respond with human interactions (Mehra, 2021; Jain et al., 2018; Wright et al., 2020; and Darcy et al., 2021). It is thus no surprise that social bots can facilitate interpersonal dimensions of affective bonding during the radicalization process (Bradshaw & Howard, 2019; Gorwa et al., 2020).

Besides seeking recruits skilled in translation, film editing, and graphic design (Amarasingam et al., 2021), jihadi chatbots also provide newcomers with practical information for migrating to conflict zones such Afghanistan, Iraq, Syria, or other countries where the organization has an operational presence (Stalinsky & Sosnow, 2020). So effective have these artificial recruiters become that, according to a study by the strategic think thank iN2 (2018), jihadi bots have a higher success rate at recruiting applicants than their human counterparts. The iN2 researchers suggest that the quick response and upbeat tone of social bots' responses to applicant queries heightened individual's motivation to enlist (iN2, 2018). They also observe that the bots facilitate a stronger emotional connection in the recruitment process, making applicants feel more at ease and less suspicious than when dealing with a real person. Following iN2's finding, Dennis et al. (2020) found social bots create higher persuasiveness due to their nonjudgmental nature. Thus, besides helping jihadi organizations gain greater exposure, secure funding, boost morale of fighters, and strengthen solidarity among community members, bots have proven a powerful strategic psychological weapon (Pashentsev, 2020) in indoctrination and radicalization. Such findings would appear to contradict the prevailing "uncanny valley" thesis that suggests that in human-machine interactions, the more human characteristics artificial intelligence displays, the greater the uneasiness it evokes in its human targets (Destephe et al., 2015).

As newer generations of bots grow their ability to read and respond to human feelings and emotions, we argue that software robots will rise to a dominant role in online radicalization. And besides providing greater scale in dissemination and heightened levels of anonymity, safety, and security for those joining extremist groups, automated headhunters may also encourage unaffiliated sympathizers to engage in individual acts of violence. While there is not yet clear evidence to support this possibility, terror attacks initiated by "lone wolf" assailants, at least in the West, have seen a dramatic upsurge in the last decade.

Whack-A-Mole Warfare

Since 2015, social media companies and security agencies have deployed a range of tactics involving both AI (algorithmic filters and bots) and human interlocutors to comb social media and disrupt use of jihadi bots in online radicalization (Roberts, 2019; Gorwa et al., 2020; Gillespie, 2020). Yet the speed, scalability, and resilience of jihadi bots make counter-radicalization and take-down actions by governments and companies more difficult (Cherney & Belton, 2021). In 2018, the European Union's law enforcement agency, Europol, began to organize "Referral Action Day," an annual campaign to detect, disrupt, and delete digital content and social media accounts supporting violent extremism. The event brings together member states, security experts, and social media providers. In an analysis of Europol's 2019 campaign, Amarasingam et al. (2021) found that extremist channels went from an average lifespan of 302 days with an average of 4.6 posts per day in 2018, to new channels in 2019 lasting for only 14 days with an average of 56.8 posts per day (p. 4). While these results suggest that extremist channels were seriously degraded, in terms of longevity, the authors note that many extremist networks simply migrated to less scrutinized, newer platforms such as "Hoop Messenger," "Riot," "Rocket.Chat," and "TamTam" (p. 15). Weimann and Vellante (2021) also found that content disruption campaigns have led to a spiked increase in extremists using anonymous dead drops platforms such as "Dump.to," "Files.fm," "Justpaste.it," "Noteshare.org," "Pixeldrain.com," and "Telegra.ph."

According to the latest statistics supplied by Telegram, between September and November 2021, the social media platform reported an average of more than 30,000 "terrorist bots and channels" were banned each month (ISIS Watch, 2022). While these results appear promising, they underscore the resilience of terrorist networks' capacities to permeate social media by creating new accounts on existing platforms or migrating to different platforms, and the vital role bots now play as "force multipliers" in spreading propaganda, recruiting members, and community building. Arguably, the high-profile nature of Referral Action Day did not work to its advantage as extremist organizations alerted their followers in advance (Amarasingam et al., 2021; Bloom & Daymon, 2018). A good illustration of the struggle by extremists to control the cyber battlefield is the jihadist meme "Coming back from Twitter Suspension Like" (Amarasingam et al., 2021). The meme shows a band of smiling jihadists strolling side by side sporting defiant grins on their faces. It condenses into a single frame of the ongoing cat-and-mouse fight with security agencies around the world and social media providers.

Despite continuing the efforts of Europol and Telegram, social media platforms remain a haven for other extremist communications, outreach, recruiting, and other activities. One reason for this dangerous resilience is that strict moderation systems often run counter to the business models of social media companies, resulting in a gap between their filtering claims and actual practices. Squire, 2021, p. 226), for instance, notes that instead of banning channels that violate terms of use completely such as with IS bots and channels, Telegram focuses on restricting these channels from view. She observes, with this soft approach to content moderation, channels flagged for producing content that violates Telegram's terms of service are impossible to view in the app downloaded from the Apple Store yet remain visible via web browsers. Moreover, extremists produce infographics and tutorials that guide other users on how to view restricted content, as well as how to use bots to scrape their content and then post them to new, unrestricted channels. Criticism of Telegram have also been leveled at the platform's permissiveness for white supremacist posts and channels, which have grown in the wake of Donald Trump's ban from Twitter, Facebook, and YouTube (Molla, 2021; Frenkel & Feuer, 2021; Dickson, 2021). The platforms reputation for lax content moderation has led the platform to being either suspended or made illegal in several countries, including China, Ethiopia, Indonesia, Pakistan, and Russia. Jihadi propagandists are also attaching bots carrying memes onto trending hashtags so they can insert their own messages into ongoing, popular conversations (Egypt Today, 2019).

To compound this problem, many mainstream social media sites today rely heavily on text-based identification to discover inappropriate content and/or inform human moderators. Yet serious pitfalls exist in this current approach. First, automated content moderation often suffers biased or incomplete training datasets, as its searches are based on past examples of inappropriate content (Gorwa et al., 2020; Gillespie, 2020). Second, extremist propagandists are employing novel and creative techniques to evade human and moderators such memes or multimedia contents that mix both positive and negative messages. Third, human moderators can only assess contents after a user or algorithm has flagged it (Roberts, 2019). Fourth, besides often underpaid and poorly trained, human moderators are reported to bear significant untold psychological costs when dealing with the scale of inappropriate contents uploaded to these sites (York, 2021).

Although human moderators are far from perfect, their presence is crucial. A study by Facebook AI Group (Kiela et al., 2020) shows that even the best-performing hate speech detecting algorithms, as in the case of Instagram's Deep Text, remain far less effective than by humans in identifying extremist memes and multimodal media. While the accuracy of humans (non-experts) in detecting hate speech in the memes dataset curated by the authors was 84.7%, the accuracy rate for the best-performing multimodal algorithm was only 69.47% (p. 6). Critically, Islamic extremist organizations are constantly adapting their bot warfare to outmaneuver and outwit algorithmic content moderation systems of SM platforms (Ferrara, 2017; Corera, 2020; Gorwa et al., 2020).

Critically, content moderation difficulties are further exacerbated by the competitive nature of the attention economy. Marcellino et al. (2020) notes that various service providers maintain different policies toward bots, especially the use of bots that masquerade as humans. This has ignited an escalating battle between social media moderators and bot makers who try to make their software robots behave more like humans to avoid detection. Such anthropomorphizing tactics include designing chatbots that deliberately make spelling mistakes or use slang, post at different time intervals, or with less frequency. Added to these obstacles are the social media companies themselves, who in facing greater regulatory scrutiny and penalties in the West tend to focus their extremist content and communication disruption on English-language platforms, neglecting their non-English counterparts in non-Western countries (MacDonald et al., 2019). Subsequently, York (2021) and Debre and Akram (2021) observe that in many regions of the world where political violence is rife and online extremist content and hate speech are pervasive, companies such as Twitter and Facebook fail miserably at content moderation. They also note that some of the largest social media companies employ only a handful of human moderators fluent in local dialects in such regions but also neglect to develop AI systems that can catch toxic content in different languages. For example, Albadi et al. (2019) found that Twitter bots in Arabic could go undetected for a long period; 89% of the bots in their sample were not suspended by the company for at least 4.7 years.

To reduce extremist content and account infiltration by software robots, researchers argue that social media companies must instill better defenses in their platform architecture as well as create proprietary software robots to detect and remove their extremist robotic counterparts (Roberts, 2019; Gorwa et al., 2020; Gillespie, 2020). Yet efforts in this direction for over a decade have been slow. In 2011, for example, researchers from the University of British Columbia evaluated the vulnerability of Facebook to infiltration by social bots (Boshmaf et al., 2011). By deploying a network of 103 social bots for eight weeks on Facebook, the researchers found the success rate of infiltration upward of 80%. Recently, however, Pozzana and Ferrara (2020) have explored more advanced methods of automatic identification of bots that rely on features of real users' behavioral characteristics, such as log-in time, clicks, sentiments, and so on. They also speculate that such methods could have a successful bot-detection rate of up to 97% against benchmarked datasets. But promising as these techniques are, in practical application there are only a few indications of improved rate of bot detection from social media companies. For example, Grimme et al. (2018) observe a successful evasion rate that ranges between 50% and 70% for the bots the researchers designed to test the defenses of Twitter or Facebook.

Clearly, advances in extremist content moderation face several key obstacles. First, most of the current strategies focus on post-hoc detection rather than real-time prevention (Ramalingam & Chinnaiah, 2018). Consequently, a massively under-researched area is the real-time detection to stop bot attacks from the point of launch. This issue is important since bots are often detected only after they have caused damage across social network sites. By the time the bots are detected, users who have interacted with them may in all likelihood move on to private channels with human recruiters. Second, since 85% of the studies on bot-detection use datasets from Twitter, it is unclear whether the methods that work for bots in Twitter apply to other platforms (Orabi et al., 2020). It is highly possible that malicious bots and their creators will seek to develop platform-specific tactics to evade detection and prevention. Thus, there is an urgent need in cross-platform research on bot detection. Third, because costs of and barriers to deploying bots have decreased markedly, processing incoming social data of high velocity and enormous volume requires increasingly sophisticated methods and vast computational resources. Finally, is the question of access. Beyond the open access architecture of Twitter, deeper scrutiny of SM content moderation systems is typically restricted to in-house researchers, who by nature of their positions are generally compliant and unlikely to risk their jobs by speaking out if they recognize vulnerabilities that repeatedly go unaddressed by their employers (Acker, 2021). For over a decade, social media companies such as Telegram, Meta (aka Facebook), and YouTube have gone to elaborate lengths to block external researchers' efforts (Dadson et al., 2021), disappearing data (Scott, 2021), supplying them with inaccurate or incomplete datasets (Alba, 2020). Indeed, researchers are not the only groups being held at the gate. In the wake of the 2022, US House Select Committee's Capitol Hill riot investigations, Twitter, Meta, Alphabet, and Reddit refused to comply with orders to hand over data that may implicate their platforms in stirring up emotions leading to the violence (Lowell,

2021), or facilitating real-time communications of the attackers during the assault.

As discussed in this section, the rise of extremist bots increases tensions between various social media stakeholders. The highly competitive nature of the industry dictates that social media providers increase automated services and features to retain and expand their customer base. Problematically, these same services and features make their platforms attractive to extremist organizations. As a result, security agencies raise pressure on social media companies for greater access to and oversight of their content moderation systems. In turn, increasing efforts to police the internet have resulted in greater public demand for (and extremist use of) heavier encryption in private channels and more secure platforms of Web 2.0 communication.

Conclusion

The pervasiveness of software robots in online radicalization puts into sharp relief the breathtaking pace of progress in artificial intelligence and emerging threats to psychological security and international psychological security. It also highlights modern warfare's growing dependency on intelligent machines, and its especial value to adversaries less resourced in numbers or traditional weaponry in asymmetric conflict. For Islamic extremist organizations, software robots have become a de facto tool of strategic communication and agenda setting (Pashentsev, 2020) due to their ease of use, accessibility, speed, and scalability. While noting these key traits in this chapter, we argue that the most pernicious threat of extremist bots is their rapidly evolving empathic and humanlike capacities. As artificially intelligent headhunters, we suggest that "jihadi" social bots are gaining greater capacities to read and respond to another person's affective state. Thus, they pose a much more complicated challenge for policymakers, providers, and researchers to understand and prevent radicalization empowered by increasingly anthropomorphic generation of social bots.

While AI researchers continue to debate the limits to bot "intelligence" or "empathy," there is a consensus by the scientific community that next-generation bots will possess empathic and conversational capabilities far exceeding their current iterations. Although researchers in the field of mental health have taken a keen interest in the empathic dimensions of software robots, very little attention has been given to their increasing role in radicalization. Given new technologies are providing for essentially digital social relationships to occur that are understood by those as equally fulfilling as traditionally coded human-human relationships, we suggest that social media robots will play an increasingly important role in radicalization in violent extremist movements. As this chapter points out, there is an urgent need for further research in the nascent field of human-machine communication and the affective relationships that develop in ongoing anthropomorphization of artificially intelligent agents. Future research on the intersection of social bots and radicalization should focus not only on the issue of detection but also prevention of bot attacks and outreach strategies to train social media users to recognize the malicious use of AI in information warfare. It should also explore the more pragmatic and phenomenological considerations of conversational AI, anthropomorphism, and persuasive computing—emerging realities where the concept of 'social' is no longer confined to human-human relations but also human-machine. This last point is particularly salient considering that physical presence in human interactions is no longer a prime denominator of social relationships.

Acknowledgments This study is part of the project "Emotional AI in Cities: Cross Cultural Lessons from UK and Japan on Designing for an Ethical Life" funded by JST-UKRI Joint Call on Artificial Intelligence and Society (2019). (Grant No. JPMJRX19H6). www.ethikal.ai

References

Acker, A. (2021). Social media researchers must demand more transparent data access. *Morning Consult*. Retrieved January 18, 2022, from https://morningconsult.com/opinions/social-media-researchers-must-demand-more-transparent-data-access/

Agnihotri, M., Pooja Rao, S. B., Jayagopi, D. B., Hebbar, S., Rasipuram, S., Maitra, A., & Sengupta, S. (2021). Towards generating topic-driven and affective responses to assist mental wellness. In A. Del Bimbo, R. Cucchiara, S. Sclaroff, et al. (Eds.), *Pattern recognition. ICPR international workshops and challenges* (pp. 129–143). Springer International Publishing.

Alba, D. (2020). Pro-China misinformation group continues spreading messages, researchers say. Retrieved December 18, 2022, from https://www.nytimes.com/live/2020/2020-election-misinformation-distortions#facebook-sent-flawed-data-to-misinformation-researchers

Albadi N, Kurdi M, Mishra S. (2019). Hateful People or Hateful Bots? Detection and Characterization of Bots Spreading Religious Hatred in Arabic Social Media.

Proc ACM Hum-Comput Interact 3 (CSCW): Article 61. https://doi.org/10.1145/3359163

Amarasingam, A., Maher, S., & Winter, C. (2021). How Telegram disruption impacts jihadist platform migration. Retrieved January 17, 2022, from https://d1wqtxts1xzle7.cloudfront.net/65377645/21_002_01e-with-cover-page-v2.pdf?Expires=1642403235&Signature=NWABHuAesZihAlCoBEf5cjrTkQcQyfRnGuUYFPXXNF0YW3XKfCUt77P-mEFyf8vpDlQOdTzxBA2uhsz9iKzaMxv--EfIC9gk66kLieWwLccjmg4Vp-In9f7Aj7hDr9wsYrF4CkwIwX54DbDrAyrzEJJ8pj4OLcRlYKyQTS6eYMsH-MYFerJSkzKM0PVF1ltv-cmOaG-VxaU-g-tzFtTYLf0-r6JHeW420Zph9c-m0Mi7hUlNMWGrWbN9GxHrZO6Vh8um7IPn7sJPd23EU32KWbEkNPQ-cEtxukARW956JY62kNqVl9MQlkIBsPaJhparLaEwuqoJsJ42TS59K4tIxw__&Key-Pair-Id=APKAJLOHF5GGSLRBV4ZA

Araque, O., & Iglesias, C. A. (2020). An approach for radicalization detection based on emotion signals and semantic similarity. *IEEE Access, 8*, 17877–17891. https://doi.org/10.1109/ACCESS.2020.2967219

Ayad, M., Amarasingam, A., & Alexander, A. (2021). *The cloud caliphate: Archiving the Islamic state in real-time, Institute for Strategic Dialogue (IST)*. Special Report (May 2021). Retrieved December 19, 2021, from https://www.isdglobal.org/isd-publications/the-cloud-caliphate-archiving-the-islamic-state-in-real-time/

Bakir, V., & McStay, A. (2021). Empathic media, emotional AI, and the optimization of disinformation. In M. Boler & E. Davis (Eds.), *Affective politics of digital media: Propaganda by other means*. Routledge.

Bartlett, J., Birdwell, J., & King, M. (2010). The edge of violence: A radical approach to extremism. *Demos*, 5–75.

Bastos, M., & Mercea, D. (2018). The public accountability of social platforms: Lessons from a study on bots and trolls in the Brexit campaign. *Philosophical Transactions of the Royal Society A: Mathematical, Physical and Engineering Sciences, 376*(2128), 20180003.

Bell, C., & Coleman, A. (2018). Khashoggi: Bots feed Saudi support after disappearance. Retrieved January 17, 2022, from https://www.bbc.com/news/blogs-trending-45901584

Bessi, A., & Ferrara, E. (2016). Social bots distort the 2016 US Presidential election online discussion. *First Monday, 21*(11–7). https://doi.org/10.5210/fm.v21i11.7090

Bloom, M., & Daymon, C. (2018). Assessing the future threat: ISIS's virtual caliphate. *Orbis, 62*(3), 372–388. https://doi.org/10.1016/j.orbis.2018.05.007

Bock, F. (2013). Sgt. Star goes mobile, prospects get answers to questions anywhere, anytime. Retrieved January 17, 2020, from https://www.army.mil/article/103582/sgt_star_goes_mobile_prospects_get_answers_to_questions_anywhere_any_time

Bodó, B., Helberger, N., & de Vreese, C. H. (2017). Political micro-targeting: A Manchurian candidate or just a dark horse? *Internet Policy Review, 6*(4), 1–13. https://doi.org/10.14763/2017.4.776

Boshmaf, Y., Muslukhov, I., Beznosov, K., & Ripeanu, M. (2011). *The socialbot network: when bots socialize for fame and money*. Paper presented at the Proceedings of the 27th Annual Computer Security Applications Conference, Orlando, Florida, USA.

Bradshaw, S., & Howard, P. N. (2019). *The global disinformation order 2019: Global inventory of organised social media manipulation*. Oxford Internet Institute. Retrieved January 17, 2022, from https://demtech.oii.ox.ac.uk/wp-content/uploads/sites/93/2019/09/CyberTroop-Report19.pdf

Cafarella, J., Wallace, B., & Zhou, J. (2019). *ISIS'S second comeback assessing the next ISIS insurgency*. Institute for the Study of War. Retrieved January 17, 2022, from http://www.jstor.org/stable/resrep19572

Cherney, A., & Belton, E. (2021). Evaluating case-managed approaches to counter radicalization and violent extremism: An example of the proactive integrated support model (PRISM) Intervention. *Studies in Conflict & Terrorism, 44*(8), 625–645.

Corera, G. (2020). ISIS 'still evading detection on Facebook', report says. Retrieved January 18, 2022, from https://www.bbc.com/news/technology-53389657

Dadson, N., Snoddy, I., & White, J. (2021). Access to big data as a remedy in big tech. *Competition Law Journal, 20*(1), 1–10.

Darcy, A., Daniels, J., Salinger, D., Wicks, P., & Robinson, A. (2021). Evidence of human-level bonds established with a digital conversational agent: Cross-sectional, retrospective observational study. *JMIR Form Res, 5*(5), e27868. https://doi.org/10.2196/27868

Debre, I., & Akram, F. (2021). Facebook's language gaps weaken screening of hate, terrorism. Retrieved January 22, 2022, from https://apnews.com/article/the-facebook-papers-language-moderation-problems

Deibert, R. J. (2019). The road to digital unfreedom: Three painful truths about social media. *Journal of Democracy, 30*(1), 25–39.

Dennis, A. R., Kim, A., Rahimi, M., & Ayabakan, S. (2020). User reactions to COVID-19 screening chatbots from reputable providers. *Journal of the American Medical Informatics Association, 27*(11), 1727–1731. https://doi.org/10.1093/jamia/ocaa167

Destephe, M., Brandao, M., Kishi, T., Zecca, M., Hashimoto, K., & Takanishi, A. (2015). Walking in the uncanny valley: importance of the attractiveness on the acceptance of a robot as a working partner. *Frontiers in Psychology, 6*. https://doi.org/10.3389/fpsyg.2015.00204

Dickson, E. J. (2021). Proud Boys channels are exploding on Telegram. Retrieved January 18, 2022, from https://www.rollingstone.com/culture/culture-news/proud-boys-telegram-far-right-extremists-1114201/

Egypt today staff. (2019). Muslim Brotherhood, IS bots exploit Egypt protest hashtags. Retrieved January 18, 2022, from https://www.egypttoday.com/Article/1/75221/Muslim-Brotherhood-IS-bots-exploit-Egypt-protest-hashtags

Ferrara, E. (2017). Contagion dynamics of extremist propaganda in social networks. *Information Sciences, 418–419*, 1–12. https://doi.org/10.1016/j.ins.2017.07.030

Fisher, M., & Taub, A. (2018). How everyday social media users become real-world extremists. Retrieved October 17, 2022, from https://www.nytimes.com/2018/04/25/world/asia/facebook-extremism.html

Frenkel, S., & Feuer, A. (2021). 'A total failure': The Proud Boys now mock Trump. Retrieved January 19, 2022, from https://www.nytimes.com/2021/01/20/technology/proud-boys-trump.html

Gehl, R. W., & Bakardjieva, M. (2016). *Socialbots and their friends: Digital media and the automation of sociality.* Taylor & Francis.

de Gennaro, M., Krumhuber, E. G., & Lucas, G. (2020). Effectiveness of an empathic chatbot in combating adverse effects of social exclusion on mood. *Frontiers in Psychology, 10.* https://doi.org/10.3389/fpsyg.2019.03061

Gillespie, T. (2020). Content moderation, AI, and the question of scale. *Big Data & Society, 7*(2), 2053951720943234.

Gorwa, R., Binns, R., & Katzenbach, C. (2020). Algorithmic content moderation: Technical and political challenges in the automation of platform governance. *Big Data & Society, 7*(1), 2053951719897945.

Grimme, C., Assenmacher, D., & Adam, L. (2018). Changing perspectives: Is it sufficient to detect social bots? In G. Meiselwitz (Ed.), *Social computing and social media. User experience and behavior.* SCSM 2018. Springer. https://doi.org/10.1007/978-3-319-91521-0_32

Haq, H., Shaheed, S., & Stephan, A. (2020). Radicalization through the lens of situated affectivity. *Frontiers in Psychology, 11.* https://doi.org/10.3389/fpsyg.2020.00205

Herman, E. S., & Chomsky, N. (1988). *Manufacturing consent: The political economy of the mass media.* Pantheon.

Himelein-Wachowiak, M., Giorgi, S., Devoto, A., Rahman, M., Ungar, L., Schwartz, H. A., Epstein, D. H., Leggio, L., & Curtis, B. (2021). Bots and misinformation spread on social media: Implications for COVID-19. *Journal of Medical Internet Research, 23*(5), e26933.

Ho, M.-T., Mantello, P., Nguyen, H.-K. T., & Vuong, Q.-H. (2021). Affective computing scholarship and the rise of China: A view from 25 years of bibliometric data. *Humanities and Social Sciences Communications, 8*(1), 282. https://doi.org/10.1057/s41599-021-00959-8

Horsch, S. (2014). Making salvation visible. Rhetorical and visual representations of martyrs in salafi jihadist media. In S. H.-A. Saad & S. Dehghani (Eds.), *Martyrdom in the modern middle east* (pp. 141–166). Ergon-Verlag.

Hotez, P. J. (2020). Anti-science extremism in America: escalating and globalizing. *Microbes and Infection, 22*(10), 505–507. https://doi.org/10.1016/j.micinf.2020.09.005

Howard, P. N. (2020). *Lie machines: How to save democracy from troll armies, deceitful robots, junk news operations, and political operatives*. Yale University Press.

iN2. (2018). The envoy and the bot: Tangibility in Daesh's online and offline recruitment. Retrieved January 18, 2022, from https://thescli.org/the-envoy-and-the-bot-tangibility-in-daeshs-online-and-offline-recruitment/

ISIS Watch. (2022). ISIS watch telegram channel. Retrieved January 17, 2022, from https://t.me/s/isiswatch

Jain, M., Kumar, P., Kota, R., & Patel, S. N. (2018). *Evaluating and informing the design of chatbots*. Paper presented at the Proceedings of the 2018 Designing Interactive Systems Conference, Hong Kong, China.

Jhan, J. H., Liu, C. P., Jeng, S. K., & Lee, H. Y. (2021). CheerBots: Chatbots toward empathy and emotion using reinforcement learning. *arXiv preprint arXiv: 2110.03949*.

Kiela, D., Firooz, H., Mohan, A., Goswami, V., Singh, A., Ringshia, P., & Testuggine, D. (2020). The hateful memes challenge: Detecting hate speech in multimodal memes. In *Advances in neural information processing systems*. MIT Press.

Kitchin, R., & Dodge, M. (2014). *Code/space: Software and everyday life*. MIT Press.

Konijn, E. A., & Hoorn, J. F. (2017). Parasocial interaction and beyond: Media personae and affective bonding. *The international encyclopedia of media effects*, 1–15. John Wiley & Sons.

Kretzschmar, K., Tyroll, H., Pavarini, G., Manzini, A., Singh, I., & Group NYPsA. (2019). Can your phone be your therapist? Young people's ethical perspectives on the use of fully automated conversational agents (chatbots) in mental health support. *Biomedical Informatics Insights, 11*, 1178222619829083.

Lee, K., Caverlee, J., & Webb, S. (2010). *Uncovering social spammers: Social honeypots + machine learning*. Paper presented at the Proceedings of the 33rd international ACM SIGIR conference on Research and development in information retrieval, Geneva, Switzerland.

Lowell, H. (2021). Trump called aides hours before Capitol riot to discuss how to stop Biden victory. Retrieved January 2, 2022, from https://www.theguardian.com/us-news/2021/nov/30/donald-trump-called-top-aides-capitol-riot-biden

MacDonald, S., Correia, S. G., & Watkin, A.-L. (2019). Regulating terrorist content on social media: automation and the rule of law. *International Journal of Law in Context, 15*(2), 183–197. https://doi.org/10.1017/S1744552319000119

Malmgren, E. (2017). Don't feed the trolls. *Dissent, 64*(2), 9–12.

Mantello, P. (2021). *Fatal portraits: The selfie as agent of radicalization*. Sign Systems Studies, 49(3–4), 566–589. https://doi.org/10.12697/SSS.2021.49.3-4.16.

Mantello, P., Ho, M.-T., Nguyen, M.-H., & Vuong, Q.-H. (2021). Bosses without a heart: Socio-demographic and cross-cultural determinants of attitude toward Emotional AI in the workplace. *AI & SOCIETY*. https://doi.org/10.1007/s00146-021-01290-1

Marcellino, W., Magnuson, M., Stickells, A., Boudreaux, B., Helmus, T. C., & Geist, E., & Winkelman, Z. (2020). *Counter-radicalization bot research using social bots to fight violent extremism*. Rand Corp. Retrieved January 15, 2022, from https://apps.dtic.mil/sti/pdfs/AD1111251.pdf

McCants, W. (2015). *The ISIS apocalypse: The history, strategy, and doomsday vision of the Islamic State*. Macmillan.

McCauley, C., & Moskalenko, S. (2008). Mechanisms of political radicalization: Pathways toward terrorism. *Terrorism and political violence, 20*(3), 415–433.

Mehra, V. (2021). The age of the bots. Retrieved December 30, 2021, from https://www.linkedin.com/pulse/age-bots-vipul-mehra/?trk=articles_directory

Meleagrou-Hitchens, A., Alexander, A., & Kaderbhai, N. (2017). The impact of digital communications technology on radicalization and recruitment. *International Affairs, 93*(5), 1233–1249.

Molla, R. (2021). Why right-wing extremists' favorite new platform is so dangerous. *Vox*. Retrieved January 18, 2022, from https://www.vox.com/recode/22238755/telegram-messaging-social-media-extremists

Mueen, A., Chavoshi, N., & Minnich, A. (2019). *Taming social bots: Detection, exploration and measurement*. Paper presented at the Proceedings of the 28th ACM International Conference on Information and Knowledge Management, Beijing, China.

Mustafaraj, E., & Metaxas, P. T. (2017). *The fake news spreading plague: Was it preventable?* Paper presented at the Proceedings of the 2017 ACM on Web Science Conference, Troy, New York, USA.

Ng, M., Coopamootoo, K. P., Toreini, E., Aitken, M., Elliot, K., & van Moorsel, A. (2020, September). Simulating the effects of social presence on trust, privacy concerns & usage intentions in automated bots for finance. In 2020 IEEE European Symposium on Security and Privacy Workshops (EuroS&PW) (pp. 190–199). IEEE.

Orabi, M., Mouheb, D., Al Aghbari, Z., & Kamel, I. (2020). Detection of bots in social media: A systematic review. *Information Processing & Management, 57*(4), 102250. https://doi.org/10.1016/j.ipm.2020.102250

Papacharissi, Z. (2016). Affective publics and structures of storytelling: sentiment, events and mediality. *Information, Communication & Society, 19*(3), 307–324. https://doi.org/10.1080/1369118X.2015.110969

Pariser, E. (2011). *The filter bubble: How the new personalized web is changing what we read and how we think*. Penguin.

Pashentsev, E. (2020). Strategic communication in EU-Russia relations. In E. Pashentsev (Ed.), *Strategic communication in EU-Russia relations: Tensions, challenges and opportunities*. Palgrave Macmillan.

Pashentsev, E., & Bazarkina, D. (2022). The malicious use of AI against government and political institutions in the psychological arena. In D. N. Bielicki (Ed.), *Regulating artificial intelligence in industry*. Routledge.

Possati, L. M. (2022). Psychoanalyzing artificial intelligence: The case of Replika. *AI & SOCIETY*, 1–14.

Pozzana, I., & Ferrara, E. (2020). Measuring bot and human behavioral dynamics. *Frontiers in Physics, 8*. https://doi.org/10.3389/fphy.2020.00125

Ramalingam, D., & Chinnaiah, V. (2018). Fake profile detection techniques in large-scale online social networks: A comprehensive review. *Computers & Electrical Engineering, 65*, 165–177. https://doi.org/10.1016/j.compeleceng.2017.05.020

Roberts, S. T. (2019). *Behind the screen*. Yale University Press.

Sauter, M. (2014). *The coming swarm: DDOS actions, hacktivism, and civil disobedience on the Internet*. Bloomsbury Publishing USA.

Scott, P. (2021). Whistleblower: Facebook is misleading the public on progress against hate speech, violence, misinformation. Retrieved January 18, 2022, from https://www.cbsnews.com/news/facebook-whistleblower-frances-haugen-misinformation-public-60-minutes-2021-10-03/

Scott, M., & Nguyen, T. (2021). Jihadists flood pro-Trump social network with propaganda. Retrieved January 17, 2022, from https://www.politico.com/news/2021/08/02/trump-gettr-social-media-isis-502078

Seering, J., Flores, J. P., Savage, S., & Hammer, J. (2018). The social roles of bots: Evaluating impact of bots on discussions in online communities. *Proc ACM Hum-Comput Interact 2* (CSCW): Article 157. https://doi.org/10.1145/3274426

Shuldiner, A. (2019). Chapter 8—Raising them right: AI and the internet of big things. In W. Lawless, R. Mittu, D. Sofge, I. S. Moskowitz, & S. Russell (Eds.), *Artificial intelligence for the internet of everything* (pp. 139–143). Academic Press. https://doi.org/10.1016/B978-0-12-817636-8.00008-9

Squire, M. (2021). Why do hate groups and terrorists love telegram? In E. Leidig (Ed.), *The radical right during crisis: CARR Yearbook 2020/2021*. ibidem Verlag, Stuttgart, pp. 223–228.

Stalinsky, S., & Sosnow, R. (2020). Jihadi use of bots on the encrypted messaging platform Telegram. Retrieved January 19, 2022, from https://www.memri.org/reports/jihadi-use-bots-encrypted-messaging-platform-telegram

Stella, M., Ferrara, E., & De Domenico, M. (2018). Bots increase exposure to negative and inflammatory content in online social systems. *Proceedings of the National Academy of Sciences, 115*(49), 12435–12440.

Thacker, E. (2004). Networks, swarms and multitudes. *Life in the Wires: The C Theory Reader*: 165–177. Retrieved October 18, 2021, from https://journals.uvic.ca/index.php/ctheory/article/view/14541/5388

van Stekelenburg, J. (2017). Radicalization and violent emotions. *PS: Political Science & Politics, 50*(4), 936–939. https://doi.org/10.1017/S1049096517001020

Van den Bos, K. (2018). *Why people radicalize: How unfairness judgments are used to fuel radical beliefs, extremist behaviors, and terrorism*. Oxford University Press.

Weimann, G., & Vellante, A. (2021). The dead drops of online terrorism: How jihadists use anonymous online platforms. *Perspectives on Terrorism, 15*(4). pp. 39–53.

Woolley, S. C., & Howard, P. N. (2018). *Computational propaganda: Political parties, politicians, and political manipulation on social media*. Oxford University Press.

Wright, J. L., Chen, J. Y. C., & Lakhmani, S. G. (2020). Agent transparency and reliability in human–robot interaction: The influence on user confidence and perceived reliability. *IEEE Transactions on Human-Machine Systems, 50*(3), 254–263. https://doi.org/10.1109/THMS.2019.2925717

York, J. (2021). *Silicon values: The future of free speech under surveillance capitalism*. Verso Books.

5

Hate Speech in Perception Management Campaigns: New Opportunities of Sentiment Analysis and Affective Computing

Yury Kolotaev

Introduction

In recent years, the growing importance of emotionality in online discourse has become an observable trend due to frequent incitements to hostility and various forms of radicalism (political, religious, nationalist, etc.) in online communication through social networks. Among scholars and journalists, this phenomenon has become known as hate speech, which involves insults and expressions of hatred toward opponents in the form of personal or collective offense. Most often, hate speech creates the preconditions for deliberate (in the case of its manipulation by a third party) or unintentional (in the case of its dissemination by ordinary users) changes in the agenda of a debated issue. Thus, hate speech is instrumental in political contexts.

The phenomenon of hate speech has been generating interest from the scientific community since the end of the twentieth century. The existing studies either problematize the topic from general theoretical and legal standpoints (Walker 1994; Rosenfeld 2003; Waldron 2012; Tontodimamma et al. 2021) or consider its increased significance in the digital space (Banks 2010; Silva et al. 2016; Costello and Hawdon 2020). However, hate speech is still evolving and incorporating new technological developments. Various forms of automation (bots), as well as more advanced forms of artificial intelligence

Y. Kolotaev (✉)
School of International Relations, St. Petersburg State University, St Petersburg, Russia

(AI), can be used to manipulate, maintain, or forward hate speech, thus creating the preconditions for inciting hostility on social platforms.

The threat of using AI in order to disseminate hate speech has only begun to receive attention recently. In the context of the malicious use of artificial intelligence (MUAI), hate speech represents a promising area for the application of two advanced AI-related approaches: the use of affective computing and sentiment analysis (Cambria et al. 2017). Existing research mainly focuses on the technical aspects of hate speech identification in social networks (Fortuna and Nunes 2018; Corazza et al. 2020; Kapil and Ekbal 2020). In this regard, most studies have addressed the usage of AI through sentiment analysis (Jiang and Suzuki 2019; Asif et al. 2020; Umer et al. 2020). However, even though there are studies of AI application in the detection of hate speech, very few of them focus on the negative aspects of AI usage for hate speech dissemination or the MUAI. The scant research on such problems provides a general overview of information manipulation on the internet (Lev-On 2018; Blaya 2019), but does not discuss the application of affective computing and sentiment analysis in perception management campaigns, in particular. Additionally, most studies lack a social and political science perspective that assesses the impact of the MUAI in a social context.

To bridge this gap, this chapter discusses the development of affective computing and sentiment analysis to explain how these technologies can be maliciously used to foster hate speech or facilitate perception management campaigns. First, the chapter defines what emotion recognition and its latest forms (affective computing and sentiment analysis) provide in perception management. Second, it explores how emotions can be understood in terms of emotional regimes, and how they can be exploited with the use of AI systems. Additionally, the interrelation of hate, anger, and the emotional regimes will be illustrated to explain how the malicious use of affective computing and sentiment analysis can be applied to foster hate speech. Third, the chapter addresses the principal means of minimizing damage from the use of AI in the spread of hate speech and perception management. Fourth, it reviews an identified perception management scenario and methods to counter the problem of MUAI in spreading hate speech. The chapter concludes with an outlook for the future development of MUAI and the analysis of the most recent global trends (end of 2021–early 2022) increasing the effectiveness of hate-based perception management.

Recognition and Interpretation of Emotions Through Affective Computing and Sentiment Analysis: New Possibilities for Perception Management Campaigns

The recognition of emotions is a complex and broad field of study that has been developing since the second half of the twentieth century in cognitive science (Oatley 1987), psychology (Frijda 1969), including cyberpsychology (Riva et al. 2007), neuroscience (Adolphs et al. 1996), sociology (Thoits 1989), linguistics (Wierzbicka 1990; Niemeier and Dirven 1997), and, more recently, computational science (Gunes and Pantic 2010; Haq and Jackson 2011; Egger et al. 2019). At the present time, emotion-related research has become highly relevant since the beginning of the "affective turn" (Leys 2011; Sullivan 2013) in social sciences, starting from the history of emotions (Reddy 2001; Frevert 2013; Brooks 2016). This turn has gone much further with the rising impact of AI technologies, which facilitate the detection of human emotions. Modern scholars are already concerned with the implications of new emotional technologies for social life (McStay 2018, 2020; Boler and Davis 2020). Yet, the combination of new AI-enhanced systems, existing experience, and increasing interest in human emotion recognition promise a stable growth of this field in the upcoming years.

Broadly speaking, emotions represent an interrelation between feeling, language, and the body (Broomhall 2016). The interplay of psychological, cultural, and neurological aspects predetermines the appearance of emotions and makes it difficult for researchers from different fields to establish a common understanding. Depending on the preferred focus, emotions can be interpreted within the dichotomy of "biological essentialism versus cultural constructionism" (Sullivan 2013, p. 97). The basic understanding of emotions interprets them as neuropsychological or cognitive processes that originate on the "subliminal," "unconscious" levels of the human mind. Yet, other less linear models of emotions represent them as "overlearned cognitive habits" (Isen and Diamond 1989). This approach has been widely adopted by historians of the emotions (McGrath 2017). The understanding of emotions as volitional activities makes them largely influenced by language and culture, thus, identifying them as nonbiological "habits" that emerge through interpersonal communication (Süselbeck 2019, p. 282). Nevertheless, even though the cultural approach provides a broader insight into the social understanding of emotions, it cannot explain the inherent aspects of human behavior, thus stressing the absence of a universal understanding of emotions.

Furthermore, "emotion" as a notion is situated in a complicated system of overlapping terms related to humans' emotional activity. The distinction between emotions, feelings, sentiments, and affects remains largely unclear. Depending on the research, field scholars either accept them as interchangeable (Cromby 2007, p. 98; Liu 2012) or try to delineate the separate concepts (Massumi 1995; Manstead et al. 2004; Broomhall 2016; Jena 2020). This chapter is based on the understanding of emotion as a "linguistic or non-linguistic expression of feelings, […] passions, sentiments and drives, in words, gestures and other social practices" (Broomhall 2016, p. 11), whereas an affect represents "a quite separate [manifestation of emotion] from conscious or linguistic expression of feeling" (Broomhall 2016, p. 11). Thus, emotions will be displayed "as relational interpretation of affect experienced in individual bodies" (Davidson and Milligan 2004; Wahl-Jorgensen 2019, p. 8). As for other terms (except for "sentiment" which will be discussed later), their differentiation lies beyond the scope of this chapter.

The technological development of recent decades has provided emotion recognition with at least two new approaches and relevant modes of detection, recognition, and interpretation of human emotions. Specifically, these new approaches are affective computing and sentiment analysis. The lack of a common understanding of emotion-related terms combined with the rapid development of emotion recognition leads to the interchangeable use of both terms (Munezero et al. 2014). Still, there are numerous differences that draw a line between these approaches (Pang and Lee 2008; Yadollahi et al. 2017; Kratzwald et al. 2018). Affective computing is a continuously developing multidisciplinary field that explores the ways AI and other computational technologies can facilitate the understanding of human emotions and affects. It also deals with the issues of human–computer interactions, namely, how systems can be designed to utilize emotions to enhance their capabilities.

The intellectual framework of affective computing was invented in late 1990s by Rosalind Picard. Her concept of machines that relate to, or deliberately influence, emotions (Picard 1997) had a major impact on the AI field. In the following years, affective computing evolved. It got enhanced through the application of AI and neural networks (Zeng et al. 2009; Gunes and Schuller 2013). This development led to the creation of emotion AI (sometimes referred to as emotional AI (McStay 2018)) as a new AI-driven technology that enables computer systems to identify and simulate human feelings and emotions (Chakriswaran et al. 2019; Kaur and Sharma 2021; Stark and Hoey 2021). This interrelation of emotion AI and affective computing means that emotion-related AI is situated within the discipline and technical field of affective computing.

Similarly, sentiment analysis represents a subfield within affective computing and, thus, "refers to all the areas of detecting, analyzing, and evaluating humans' state of mind towards different events, issues, services, or any other interest" (Yadollahi et al. 2017, p. 25). The main task of sentiment analysis lies in polarity detection based on the "binary classification task with outputs such as 'positive' versus 'negative' <…> 'like' versus 'dislike'" (Cambria et al. 2017, p. 4). The rise of social media and the subsequent growing amount of digital data have made sentiment analysis especially relevant (Zhang and Liu 2017). The diversity and "multimodality" of sentiment expression through social media have led to a shift in sentiment analysis from textual data (Montoyo et al. 2012; Medhat et al. 2014) to non-textual or multimodal data (Yue et al. 2019; Chakraborty et al. 2020). This recent development has brought sentiment analysis closer to affect or emotion recognition.

The convergence of tasks solved by both approaches has made them interdependent. Some researchers even tend to understand emotion recognition and polarity detection as a single task (Cambria et al. 2017). Nevertheless, affective computing remains broader than both emotional AI and sentiment analysis. It is also not confined by AI in a broad sense, but nowadays AI has become the basic tool to perform emotion computing in various forms. These include recognizing signals and processing data related to emotions (Wu et al. 2010; Hosseini et al. 2010; Shu et al. 2018; Qing et al. 2019); finding patterns and correlations between emotion, speech patterns, and body language (Christy et al. 2020; Jermsittiparsert et al. 2020; Badrulhisham and Mangshor 2021); influencing the emotions and affective responses of a person (Moghimi et al. 2016; Triberti et al. 2017; Pusztahelyi 2020); and simulating emotions or expressions of emotions (e.g., through virtual assistants or chatbots) (Lungu 2013; Rust and Huang 2021). All these technologies have a vast application area facilitating emotional speech creation, facial affect detection, body gesture recognition, and physiological monitoring (Banafa 2016), with subsequent potential and actual implementation in various spheres of business, entertainment, governance, and healthcare.

Despite all the positive and productive spheres of application of affective computing and AI, one domain remains understudied. It refers to perception management campaigns (Kopp 2005; Siegel 2005; Mengü and Türk 2021; Derman 2021) or, more generally speaking, the malicious use of AI for psychological operations and information attacks (Brundage et al. 2018; Pashentsev 2019; Kramar and Pashentsev 2020; Pantserev 2020; Roumate 2021). The global instability and existing conflict situations in different regions of the world create preconditions for the usage of AI in psychological confrontation. Rival actors (states, separatists, terrorist groups, etc.) search for tools that can be used in propaganda and disinformation proliferation. As the Internet and the digital space merge with the public sphere, state-of-the-art perception management technologies aim at users of social networks and online platforms to inflict social damage. In this context AI, and more precisely, emotion AI, provides new opportunities to influence public opinion, incite hatred, or distort reality through the web.

As described earlier, analysis and exploitation of users' emotions are already actively applied. Still, the use of affective computing for political or military goals makes sentiment analysis and emotion AI weapons in perception management campaigns. Both enable the extraction and analysis of human emotions for precise empathic targeting. This becomes especially effective as emotions and affects have significant impact on human activity and cognitive processes. Furthermore, as emotions remain one of the most important aspects of perception, the possibility to instrumentalize or alter them creates serious social and psychological consequences for a country's security or stability.

Given the potential of affective computing and sentiment analysis, there are at least four probable scenarios for the MUAI to inflict distortion of perception and political harm (Kolotaev 2021): (1) emotionally optimized disinformation; (2) large-scale propaganda campaigns through social engineering; (3) hate speech incitement (e.g., through social bots); and (4) espionage based on emotional profiling or highly targeted phishing. All these forms of AI-enhanced perception management tools create danger for society and require further scrutiny. Yet, hate speech becomes the most suitable domain for the malicious use of affective computing. In comparison to other forms of emotional manipulations, hate speech fully relies on a highly emotional abusive or insulting discourse. Such prerequisites allow malicious actors to use the full potential of emotion AI in perception management, by inciting hate speech that coincides with the "emotional regime" of a given community.

In summary, the outlined scenarios illustrate that the development of new emotion recognition technologies does not only enable a better understanding of peoples' emotional activity or simplify the usage of digital services. It also creates new challenges. Different malicious actors with political or public security-related goals might use emotion recognition through advanced AI technologies in coordinated perception management campaigns. One of the MUAI scenarios is the emotion AI-driven incitement of hate speech which requires more detailed examination.

Anger, Hate Speech, and Emotional Regimes: Examples and Prospects of Hate Incitement on Social Networks

In an ontological sense, hate speech refers to violent activity and extremism closely related to hate crime (Chetty and Alathur 2018, p. 110). Various actors (online platforms, political institutions, and international organizations) give different definitions of hate speech depending on the targets, consequences, and counteractions (Sellars 2016; Fortuna and Nunes 2018; Fino 2020). Yet, an affect-oriented definition identifies it "as a specific type of emotional expression that has the ability to reduce empathy and trigger conflicts under specific conditions" (Udupa et al. 2020, p. 3). Other common traits specific to hate speech include social characteristics (the public nature of the speech act, targeting a group or its members), as well as harmful actions (the intention of physical or psychological harm, a possible violent response) (Tontodimamma et al. 2021, p. 158). The given characteristics of hate speech stress that hate is a strong political incentive for both in-group solidarity and action which can be explained by the nature of this emotion.

In psychological terms, hate is an affective state closely related to anger and fear (as well as other "hostile emotions" (Ihlebæk and Holter 2021)). Both of them belong to the "basic emotions" which represent fundamental biologically and psychologically predetermined emotional states (Ekman et al. 1983; Ekman 1992a, 1992b). In affective computing, the basic emotion theory plays a significant role in emotion modeling (D'Mello and Calvo 2013; McStay 2018). This confluence of psychological studies with affective computing makes it possible to analyze, model, or simulate hate or anger and thereby hate speech. Still, emotions have a social dimension, which needs to be considered while analyzing them.

Among the various emotion models explaining the interrelation of the individual and social (Broomhall 2016), the societal implications for hate can be described through the theory of emotional regimes and emotives (Reddy 2001). This framework considers emotional expressions, called emotives, as a combination of private and public factors making such expressions descriptive and performative "in that they have the capacity to enact change on the speaking subject or addressee" (Colwell 2016, p. 7) and not only express individual feelings. The social dimension of emotives explains why emotional "speech acts" in the form of hate speech transcend individual experience. Even though basic emotions like anger remain in the first instance individual, "it comes to matter politically when it is articulated by collectives, usually towards a shared objective of addressing an injustice" (Wahl-Jorgensen 2018, p. 768).

The interactive nature of emotions makes them dynamic and culturally predetermined. Emotions "are thus discursively constituted in individuals and are similarly constructed as emotional 'regimes' in societies under particular historical conditions" (Nye, 2003, p. 921). From a political perspective, "emotional regimes" represent "dominant modes for acceptable emotional thought and expression" (Garrido and Davidson 2016, p. 65) enforced by dominating actors making emotional regimes "essential elements of all stable political regimes" (Reddy 2001, p. 55). The constraints of mental control (Reddy 2001, p. 62) imposed through norms, customs, and political institutions show that "emotions are not just constructed or learned, but that they are also 'managed'"(Colwell 2016, p. 7). The very understanding of the manipulative nature of emotions within emotional regimes means that, in certain circumstances, our understanding of emotions such as anger and fear may be altered through internal or external factors. The interest of malicious actors in such changes becomes a precondition for the use of advanced technologies. Moreover, as hate speech is based on a certain emotional discourse or regime, emotional AI might be applied in the analysis of the emotional regime for perception management.

This becomes a danger for political stability, since hate speech represents a particular form of anger which is as an "indispensable political emotion" (Lyman 2004, p. 133). In a shifting emotional regime, certain political or social groups (populists, marginalized groups, radical movements, etc.) may tend toward the acceptance of anger, and, thus, hate speech, as a "normal" practice. For a malicious actor such groups could become the main objectives and tools for the incitement of hate and social instability. The most worrisome aspect in "acceptable hate" derives from its growing proliferation, and the digital era provides new possibilities for the altering and manipulation of emotional regimes via social media (and advanced tools, i.e., AI-enhanced services).

Even before the spread of new social media, the conventional news media have already functioned "as areas for legitimate and illegitimate emotional responses to particular events"(Ihlebæk and Holter 2021, p. 1208). This has made media both "arenas for inclusion" through mediated emotional connections and "spaces for conflict" (Orgeret 2020; Ihlebæk and Holter 2021). However, the further "mediatization of society has led political actors to adapt their discourses to the digital age" (Estellés and Castellví 2020, p. 5) resulting in the strong influence of social media on the proliferation of political ideas, emotions, and emotional regimes. Consequently, in a highly mediatized society, political discourse becomes dependent on social media to make it the primary arena for manipulation and hate speech.

The interdependence of social media and political discourse has enabled orchestrated online hate speech. Frequently fostered by malicious actors, it becomes an instrument in perception management leading to serious harm for psychological security, for instance, through changing the social attitude (emotional regime) toward hate and anger. In cases of manipulative hate speech, vulnerable social groups based on gender, religion, race, and disability (Chetty and Alathur 2018) become the main targets of hate, leading to the subsequent incitement of "mass violations of human rights, crimes against humanity or even genocide" (Fino 2020, p. 32).

Even early examples show how "systematic, state-orchestrated hate speech was a direct cause of genocidal killing" (Timmermann 2008; Udupa et al. 2020, p. 8) as, for example, in Rwanda. However, there are multiple contemporary illustrative examples, among them the incitement of violence against Rohingya Muslims via social media in Myanmar (UN 2018; Udupa et al. 2020) and anti-Muslim hate speech in Sri Lanka (Safi 2018; Mathew et al. 2019, p. 173), which both resulted in victims (although the extent of the damage in Myanmar was incomparably higher). In each of the cases, digital media were involved in a large-scale perception management campaign.

A multitude of national context-dependent cases of online hate speech have also emerged during the worldwide COVID-19 pandemic (Uyheng and Carley 2020). These examples illustrate decentralized perception management where uncertainty has become a fruitful environment for toxicity and anger. Thereby, COVID-related hate speech became especially problematic due to the varying topics associated with anger (vaccination campaigns, mask regimes, lockdowns, etc.). The actors responsible for the hate speech have also remained to a large extent obscure, as regular citizens, confused by the overall situation, voluntarily proliferated misinformation.

Each of the recent examples highlights the danger of hate speech, thus compelling researchers to reflect on the state-of-the-art tools applicable for perception management. In this search, a collaboration of scholars in political and computer science is necessary as they can develop a joint framework for the analysis of social and political implications of AI tools. It becomes especially relevant for hate speech and its impact on political processes. The nature of hate speech reveals that it might easily become an instrument in the hands of malicious actors, as long as hate becomes acceptable in the political discourse; in other words, if the emotional regime of a society is altered toward open displays of anger.

Scenarios and Risks of the Malicious Use of Artificial Intelligence in Hate Speech-Oriented Perception Management

Emotion AI and sentiment analysis, with their potential to analyze and model emotions, have become attractive tools for psychological operations and other forms of the MUAI. Given the tremendous impact manipulated hate speech might have on social networks, the growing accessibility of emotion recognition systems creates new scenarios for psychological attacks.

For example, a simple perception management operation with the application of AI can be modeled in the following manner: A malicious actor plans an attack on a certain social group. Initially, the actor would apply sentiment analysis to achieve a clear understanding of the underlying emotional regime of the community. This would both facilitate further planning of the entire perception management operation and it would also provide the opportunity to target the audience on an emotional level. Furthermore, the actor would establish the necessary tools for the infiltration of various communities through social networks, in order to incite hate against the target social group. Such tools would be based on emotion AI systems (e.g., advanced social bots) which disseminate hateful messages adapting them to the discourse of the social group.

An important aspect would be the analysis of the audience's response to the systems input. This would help to further enhance the main message. As the attack would be executed on an iterative basis, each iteration would include new data on the emotional responses, thus making the overall attack more targeted. If the actor was to possess enough computational capacity, the next step would be the creation of synthetic, emotionally adapted information. Such an attack would rely fully on the established AI system reducing the role of a human agent and creating an uninterruptible input–output system. After the main message had been adopted by the community (resulting in direct actions of the community), the malicious actor might enlarge the bot network or change the initial aim.

This imaginary example only predicts what role emotion AI can play in perception management. Yet, there are various other scenarios, including the alteration of the emotional regime of the community, or the creation of a high-level algorithm capable of human-like interactions for personalized phishing or hate incitement attacks. As this kind of emotion AI-enhanced perception management has a common goal (to incite hate), and a similar technical framework (affective computing-based emotion recognition systems), some common features might be identified. These similarities rely on two aspects: the instruments and the structure of the operation.

The instrumental aspect can be described through the technical dimension of most AI-enhanced attacks. Recent research has identified that cyberattacks using AI can be categorized into three main forms, which depict the main vulnerabilities that can be exploited (Yamin et al. 2021). These three types include: the creation of synthetic (emotional) data; analysis of data (reflecting human emotions); and data poisoning. Each of these attacks has a specific form, but in the context of emotional AI, they acquire the ability to exploit the recognition of human emotions for the purposes of the MUAI.

Regarding the issue of hate speech, the first and second types of cyberattacks have an apparent potential for application in perception management. In contrast, the third—data poisoning—can be used mainly to disrupt the performance of existing algorithms leading to their malfunctioning. It constitutes indirect damage and cannot be implemented in information campaigns on a broad scale. However, there are multiple alarming examples of malfunctioning AI systems. Microsoft's Tay bot and a more recent example of the South Korean startup Scatter Lab illustrate how unintentional "data poisoning" (stemming from real-life conversations data) can result in AI-generated hate speech (McCurry, 2021). These examples suggest that, if required, a malicious actor can intentionally create a hate speech-oriented chatbot to be used in information campaigns, leading to first and second types of cyberattacks.

The opportunities to create emotional data and analyze them to inflict psychological harm open up the main scenarios for the MUAI in perception management. Synthetic data can be exploited to develop AI emotional systems capable of social interaction within the "emotional field" of a society (Yan et al. 2021) facilitating the proliferation of hate speech. These can be bots, physical robots using artificial narrow intelligence, or more complex systems of "strong AI." GPT-3, one of the most advanced natural-language generators, shows already how AI can produce synthetic hate speech in a "convincing" manner (Heaven, 2020). Such technologies might be used as manipulative systems (for psychological impact) that deliberately provoke people's emotions, including hate and anger, through specific verbal and nonverbal triggers. At the same time, the second type of cyberattacks—the ability to analyze emotional data—has already been noticed in the form of highly targeted disinformation. The first examples indicating this possibility were identified in 2016 during the US presidential elections and the Brexit referendum. Obtaining data on the opinions, emotions, and feelings of users could further enhance AI-based manipulations, leading to highly accurate information attacks that foster hate speech. In other words, the recognition of emotions of a target audience (through digital data) allows the identification of an accurate context for targeted informational influence or perception management.

Hate speech-oriented attacks can also be considered from a structural point of view. As other forms of malicious online activities, they are often united by the general sequence of the attack itself. A template for such a sequence can be found in the structure of conventional cyberattacks. One of the most common structures of a cyberattack is the Cyber Kill Chain scheme (Eric M. Hutchins et al. 2011). This approach has already been applied to other forms of AI-enhanced attacks (Kaloudi and Li 2020), as the structure represents a lifecycle of malicious activity, and though it was developed for cyberattacks, it outlines the basic phases also applicable to online-driven perception management. The Cyber Kill Chain includes seven stages: (1) reconnaissance; (2) weaponization; (3) delivery; (4) exploitation; (5) installation; (6) command and control; (7) actions on objective—this has been further subcategorized into three phases—planning (1–2), intrusion (3–5), and execution(6–7)—with varying degrees of AI involvement (Kaloudi and Li 2020). The extrapolation of these stages to a hate speech dissemination attack on social networks gives a clear structure to the relevant risks and action scenarios of the malicious actors.

The initial planning phase (1–2) enables the acquisition of preliminary "intelligence" with a consequent weaponization of the data obtained. The first stage of an emotion AI-enhanced perception management operation aims to find a pattern in the large amount of emotion and sentiment data, which makes it possible to determine: (1) the existing emotional regime of the society/community; (2) the most vulnerable targets of hate speech; (3) the appropriate emotional characteristics of the main message, that will incite hate and anger; and (4) the form (text, picture, video) and scale of the attack. During the weaponization stage, the emotion AI integrates the behavioral patterns into the message and repeats it multiple times. As a result, the planning phase creates the necessary framework for the perception management campaign.

The second phase, intrusion (3–5), encompasses the delivery of the message, the initial incitement of anger or hate through the message, and the consequent entrenchment of the first results. During the delivery stage, AI enables the use of less visible infiltration techniques, similar to, for example, over-personalized phishing. The following "infection" leads to an increase in the scale of the attack. At this stage, a network of inauthentic actors such as bots will be launched (Morgan 2018; Bennett and Livingston 2018). They will transmit the abusive information necessary for an attack and, depending on the context, further decide whether to enlarge an information attack. The last stage of the infiltration phase leads to the final "installation" of hate in a community achieved through the usage of an AI-based self-propagation scheme. The goal is to deliver the message to the maximum number of users with replication as the main tools. At this point the community (if the initial message has been adopted) ultimately becomes engaged in hate speech and commences creating new content and messages.

Finally, the execution phase leads to the main manipulations and eventual actions. In this phase the "information maneuvers" on the network or within the narrative are accomplished (Uyheng and Carley 2020, pp. 447–448). The command-and-control step implies the anchoring of a command channel for direct manipulation. An automatic emotion AI system based on user reaction might ensure instant response to external stimuli. This facilitates the constant provocation of network members that disseminate hate speech. However, the main instrument of the perception management campaign remains the bot-net, with its constant emotion-oriented improvement. The bot-net ensures that the initial message becomes credible and integrated into the community's discourse. Having secured a stable command-and-control channel, direct actions, eventually, can be launched including coordinated actions to achieve the main goal of the campaign: to change the behavior or opinion of the audience, and to exclude and oppress the selected social group, or, if the initial source of the attacker information gains credibility, the malicious actor can incite offline actions (such as unrest, persecution of minorities, etc.). At this stage, the key message of the perception management campaign has been successfully delivered, motivating the community to act. All of this happens via the direct, emotionally targeted activities (content proliferation, bot messaging) of the malicious actor within the network through the established channels.

The structure outlined shows three major trends that AI-enhanced hate speech campaigns bring. First, the digital sphere remains highly vulnerable to information operations, and this is only worsening with the facilitation of AI application. Second, the biggest risk is that emotion AI can enhance orchestrated hate speech. This leads to significant social and psychological impact, given the previous examples of how hate speech has inflicted social harm and casualties. Third, the seven steps of a perception management attack show that the risk to political stability and psychological security increases the larger the quantity of exploited data. This means that data become instrumentalized for highly targeted and emphatically optimized hate speech proliferation.

The key enhancement that emotion AI brings is the simplification of emotional data collection and analysis. As a result, data is becoming the primary weapon to manipulate different audiences and make hate speech more audience-specific. The maximal effectiveness and personalization of a perception management campaign can thus be achieved through AI-based data analysis at each stage from planning to execution.

The fusion of emotion recognition and perception management reveals the growing dangers of the MUAI. The context of hate speech provides a very powerful example. The more accurately the technology can predict the emotional regime of a community, the better it gets at manipulating it. A potential result might even be the alteration of the emotional regime. Furthermore, as hate speech is directly connected to powerful political emotions such as hate and anger, the implication is that hate-based perception management can inflict major negative outcomes endangering national psychological stability.

Prevention and Mitigation of Harm from Perception Management Campaigns Based on the Malicious Use of Artificial Intelligence

In recent decades, the question of how to tackle hate speech has prompted various suggestions ranging from a legal perspective to an instrumental AI-based approach. All of them can be subcategorized into three main models of reaction, not only to hate speech, but also to perception management: (1) legal and normative management; (2) automatic detection and moderation solutions; (3) critical thinking, strategic communications, and personal data hygiene. Since most hate speech-related literature features either legal studies or computational research, the first and the second models frequently gain more attention.

The normative approach to hate speech prevention proposes the limitation of offensive content by legal or ethical means. This approach simultaneously includes two aspects: the containment of hate speech and the regulation of emotion AI. Over recent years, the first aspect has made serious progress including unilateral, multilateral, and technical regulations on hate speech (Banks 2010; Alkiviadou 2018; Chetty and Alathur 2018) including various types of laws, regulations, and codes (Brown 2015). The main obstacle in the legal regulation of hate speech remains, however, the "relationship between extremism, tolerance, and free speech" (Guiora and Park 2017, p. 958). Depending on the legal system (common vs. continental), any limitation of speech can be interpreted as a violation of free speech. For this reason, a clear differentiation of particular hate speech acts is necessary (Yong 2011), that prevents unnecessary interventions. Still, only the legal aspect of conventional hate speech does not cover the scope of the problem described in this chapter. As the digital space experiences an influx of inauthentic behavior, the necessity arises to address new tools that enhance hate speech. Examples of such tools are ethical guidelines (McStay and Pavliscak 2019; Stark and Hoey 2021; Ong 2021) or legal frameworks for regulating emotion AI (Bard 2020). These measures only start to gain public attention in the context of an overall pursuit for AI regulation.

Yet, since hate speech has become a digital phenomenon, it would be insufficient to rely only on legal means. Both ethical guidelines and laws need resources for their implementation. This has become the main reason as to why automated response systems for hate speech have been created. The main initiatives have come from online platforms or from academia. The former attempt to create moderation tools that combine user reporting and AI systems (Facebook 2020), the latter aim to create improved systems of hate speech detection. Thereby, the moderation tools that have been created remain widely opaque, along with the recommendation algorithms of the platforms. The public side of a platform's activity is limited to the openly published community rules (YouTube 2019). As a result, academic research has scarce access to the platform's resources and data. This forces academics to focus on platforms that make their data more available. For this reason, much online hate speech-related research is Twitter-centric (Gambäck and Sikdar 2017; Fortuna and Nunes 2018; Arango et al. 2019), as this platform is more open to data collection than others. This makes most of the proposed tools text oriented, even though the latest developments have manifested a growing interest in multimodal hate speech detection (Gomez et al. 2020).

However, the current approaches for hate speech detection suffer from several methodological issues which result in language-centered errors. This leads to a situation where certain mechanisms that "show impressive performance in their original test sets do not generalize well to other datasets" (Arango et al. 2019, p. 51). Additionally, the language barrier and user behavior remain major issues that stress the importance of additional countermeasures preventing overreliance on algorithmic or other technical solutions for hate speech.

As each of the approaches has its setbacks, the need for further improvement suggests a third model for hate speech prevention. This relies on long-term actions including media literacy and counterspeech. Essentially, this approach implies multiple actions that shift the accent from the authorities and platforms to the users. It leads to shared responsibility for the countering of hate speech. The main activity includes a mixture of public awareness campaigns with digital literacy on safe media usage. Citizens are on the front lines during hate speech campaigns, and "it is therefore not enough for government officials alone to recognize the threat" (Rosenberger and Hanlon 2019, p. 4). It is necessary to complement the measures with an open and informative strategic communication and "to raise public awareness about this threat in order to build resilience against it" (Rosenberger and Hanlon 2019, p. 4). Thus, in order to reduce the effectiveness of hate speech, a framework of shared responsibility with the users must be established.

The previously illustrated structure of an AI-enhanced hate speech attack showed that hate speech proliferation can incorporate emotional data produced by users. Therefore, awareness must be raised among users that their online experience can be used against them. It becomes essential to explain to citizens how to confront the undesirable misuse of their emotional data. A community-centered solution would be the promotion of personal data hygiene (Alben 2020), adapted to sentiment and conscious platform usage. Additionally, researchers have accentuated that counterspeech, combined with grassroots activism (Udupa et al. 2020, p. 9; Tontodimamma et al. 2021), can be helpful in this regard. It is therefore essential to distribute adaptable social initiatives, while fostering a reasonable attitude to the data provided to social networks. Through these measures the users themselves become an integral and proactive part of an anti-hate speech strategy.

Hence, the prevention of perception management comprises three models of counteractions, depending on the main actors involved. All of the models have specific issues limiting the effectiveness of the measures. Governments and platforms commonly implement most of the actions, but the shifting nature of the threat requires the involvement of the platform communities. Therefore, the main task in countering emotional AI-based perception management is to monitor the potential malicious use of user data, as well as to detect the vulnerabilities that allow such data to be obtained.

Recent Developments and Prospects of the Malicious Use of Artificial Intelligence in Hate Speech-Oriented Perception Management

While hate-based perception management with the MUAI is a novel though dangerous phenomenon, it also manifests the transformative potential of global crises and their negative impact on state-of-art technologies. The indicated characteristics of sentiment analysis and affective computing become extremely attractive to malicious actors or parties of conflict seeking to implement new tools in their psychological attacks or campaigns. The recent developments of 2022 (re-ignition of the Ukrainian conflict and the resulting financial and economic uncertainty, or failure of existing institutions) illustrate how an information environment once perceived as "cohesive" becomes ever more fragmented. It happens not just because of the conflicts and crises themselves but also due to the instrumentalization or even militarization of AI (Burton and Soare 2019; Arif 2021) and information technologies.

So far, since the beginning of the third decade of the twenty-first century, hate speech-oriented perception management has been spotted on various levels and in different forms. As mentioned earlier, uncertainty can provide toxic relations and interactions online. COVID-19 was an important manifestation of the latter (Orlando 2020; Uyheng and Carley 2021). But the return of military confrontation to Europe and the continuation of such confrontation in other regions brings AI-enhanced hate speech to a new level of danger, where it becomes integrated into hybrid operations (Govaers 2021). As demonstrated in March 2022, most online platforms failed to provide an appropriate, unbiased response to the outburst of a new wave of hate speech online (Biddle 2022). Simultaneously, multiple examples of military and social perception management campaigns could be spotted, which contained emphatic aspects (including low-level emotion AI through targeting) (Yuan 2022; The Economist 2022; Barnes and Wong 2022). Even though it is still complicated to uncover the connection between AI-fostered perception management and the responsible actors, most cases can be interpreted as state-orchestrated due to the self-evident direct involvement of the states in the conflict. Still, the Ukrainian case remains yet to be studied impartially, along with other contemporary military-based hate speech cases.

It is important to note that the transformation of AI and its particular forms, such as affective computing, into a malicious tool is not a result of single events. It is an outcome of negative social processes fostering the utilization of new technologies for malicious purposes. In the case of perception management, several stimuli induce the MUAI. However, they can be perceived as direct stimuli as much as indicators of social imbalance and precariousness. They also can be unequally distributed in different regions. It results in varying degrees of the MUAI depending on social conflicts, security issues, and other factors.

Latest developments illustrate that the most important factors resulting in hate speech (including its manipulative forms) can be categorized as inter-societal and intra-societal (Khamaiseh 2021; Truong 2022; Committee on information 2022). Geopolitical crises or conflicts cause inter-societal factors. They become a fruitful ground for both user-generated and stated-orchestrated online hate. In such an environment, perception management takes place on a broad quantitative scale where the MUAI increases the amount of hateful content and its reach. Intra-societal factors refer to stimuli that provoke social groups to exert anger or hate toward each other inside a society. Such situations do not exclude external impact since the conflict might stem from external variables (migration, global pandemic, etc.). Still, intra-societal factors that provoke hate speech derive from internal reactions to endogenous or exogenous incentives. It might be global economic distress and its national implications or social inequality rising through the unequal distribution of public goods.

Regardless of their origin, each factor bears powerful emotional triggers and indicators, and they are applicable in the malicious use of emotion AI. Therefore, it will become crucial to adapt to the MUAI through social stimuli and sentiments. Learning to coexist with new challenges means the understanding that the inter-societal and intra-societal factors will transform. So the implications of the rising inflation, confrontation between powers, and so on are difficult to estimate. Additionally, they are hard to resolve entirely, and thus hate speech and the MUAI are expected to increase in the future. Mainly, the MUAI will increase and intensify information operations and perception management by exploiting discontent and hate. The mitigation mechanisms described in this chapter will play a vital role in curbing hate speech-centered MUAI. However, rising uncertainty stresses that a universal solution is unreachable. The transformation of the hate speech stimuli requires not only the understanding of the technical aspects of new threats but also the awareness of the societal variables influencing an ever-changing environment.

Conclusion

The overall analysis of hate speech through the lens of contemporary emotion recognition technologies reveals rising new threats to political stability and psychological security. Hate speech can become an instrument of perception management campaigns, and sentiment analysis, as well as affective computing, enhances these malicious actions. The outlined framework of an AI-based perception management attack indicates several fundamental points. First, emotional AI improves the tools used in information attacks, making them personalized and empathic. Second, the creation of synthetic data and the analysis of emotional data can be included in the structure of a hate speech-oriented information attack. Third, these attacks can possibly be predicted and tracked based on an understanding of which user data are particularly vulnerable in which phases. Fourth, the complexity of an emotion AI-based hate speech attack requires a combination of countermeasures at the government, platform, and user/community level. Fifth, the newest geopolitical and economic developments illustrate that a suitable mitigation strategy for the hate speech-based MUAI can be created only on a comprehensive approach, which considers technical risks through societal indicators. The latter is crucial to prevent affective computing-based perception management since social factors predetermine the communication strategies of an information attack.

As a result, experts in the field of emotional AI and MUAI should note that the emotional component of user activity on the Internet has a tremendous impact on the content that is consumed and produced. It can be used maliciously, and manipulative hate speech is only one form of such ill-intended perception management. This should be taken into consideration both when analyzing the data itself and when predicting and countering digital threats.FundingThe reported study was funded by RFBR, under number N 21-514-92001 "Malicious Use of Artificial Intelligence and Challenges to Psychological Security in Northeast Asia."

References

Adolphs, R., Damasio, H., Tranel, D., & Damasio, A. R. (1996). Cortical Systems for the Recognition of emotion in facial expressions. *The Journal of Neuroscience, 16*, 7678–7687. https://doi.org/10.1523/JNEUROSCI.16-23-07678.1996

Alben, A. (2020). When artificial intelligence and big data collide—How data aggregation and predictive machines threaten our privacy and autonomy. *The AI Ethics Journal, 1*, 1–23. https://doi.org/10.47289/AIEJ20201106

Alkiviadou, N. (2018). The legal regulation of hate speech: The international and European frameworks. *Politicka Misao, 55*, 203–229. https://doi.org/10.20901/pm.55.4.08

Arango, A., Pérez, J., & Poblete, B. (2019). Hate speech detection is not as easy as you may think. In *SIGIR'19: Proceedings of the 42nd international ACM SIGIR conference on Research and Development in Information*, pp. 45–54. https://doi.org/10.1145/3331184.3331262.

Arif, S. (2021). Militarization of artificial intelligence: Progress and implications. In *International political economy of artificial intelligence* (pp. 219–239). Springer. https://doi.org/10.1007/978-3-030-74420-5_10

Asif, M., Ishtiaq, A., Ahmad, H., et al. (2020). Sentiment analysis of extremism in social media from textual information. *Telematics and Informatics, 48*, 101345. https://doi.org/10.1016/j.tele.2020.101345

Badrulhisham, N. A. S., & Mangshor, N. N. A. (2021). Emotion recognition using convolutional neural network (CNN). *Journal of Physics: Conference Series, 1962*, 012040. https://doi.org/10.1088/1742-6596/1962/1/012040

Banafa, A. (2016). What is affective computing? In *OpenMind*. Retrieved October 28, 2021, from https://www.bbvaopenmind.com/en/technology/digital-world/what-is-affective-computing/

Banks, J. (2010). Regulating hate speech online. *International Review of Law, Computers and Technology, 24*, 233–239. https://doi.org/10.1080/13600869.2010.522323

Bard, J. (2020). *Developing a legal framework for regulating emotion AI*. Social Science Research Network.

Barnes, J. E., & Wong, E. (2022). *U.S. and Ukrainian groups pierce Putin's propaganda bubble*. New York Times.

Bennett, W. L., & Livingston, S. (2018). The disinformation order: Disruptive communication and the decline of democratic institutions. *European Journal of Communication, 33*, 122–139. https://doi.org/10.1177/0267323118760317

Biddle, S. (2022). Facebook's Ukraine-Russia moderation rules prompt cries of double standard. In *The Intercept*. Retrieved May 27, 2022, from https://theintercept.com/2022/04/13/facebook-ukraine-russia-moderation-double-standard/

Blaya, C. (2019). Cyberhate: A review and content analysis of intervention strategies. *Aggression and Violent Behavior, 45*, 163–172. https://doi.org/10.1016/j.avb.2018.05.006

Boler, M., & Davis, E. (2020). *Affective politics of digital media: Propaganda by other means*. Routledge.

Brooks, A. (2016). *Genealogies of emotions, intimacies, and desire: Theories of changes in emotional regimes from medieval society to late modernity*. Routledge.

Broomhall, S. (Ed.). (2016). *Early modern emotions: An introduction*. Routledge.

Brown, A. (2015). *Hate speech law: A philosophical examination*. Routledge.

Brundage, M., Avin, S., Clark, J., et al. (2018). *The malicious use of artificial intelligence: Forecasting, prevention, and mitigation*. University of Oxford.

Burton, J., & Soare, S. R. (2019). Understanding the strategic implications of the weaponization of artificial intelligence. In *2019 11th international conference on Cyber Conflict (CyCon)*, IEEE, Tallinn, Estonia, pp. 1–17.

Cambria, E., Das, D., Bandyopadhyay, S., & Feraco, A. (2017). Affective computing and sentiment analysis. In E. Cambria, D. Das, S. Bandyopadhyay, & A. Feraco (Eds.), *A practical guide to sentiment analysis* (pp. 1–10). Springer International Publishing.

Chakraborty, K., Bhattacharyya, S., & Bag, R. (2020). A survey of sentiment analysis from social media data. *IEEE Transactions on Computational Social Systems, 7*, 450–464. https://doi.org/10.1109/TCSS.2019.2956957

Chakriswaran, P., Vincent, D. R., Srinivasan, K., et al. (2019). Emotion AI-driven sentiment analysis: A survey, future research directions, and open issues. *Applied Sciences, 9*, 5462. https://doi.org/10.3390/app9245462

Chetty, N., & Alathur, S. (2018). Hate speech review in the context of online social networks. *Aggression and Violent Behavior, 40,* 108–118. https://doi.org/10.1016/j.avb.2018.05.003

Christy, A., Vaithyasubramanian, S., Jesudoss, A., & Praveena, M. D. A. (2020). Multimodal speech emotion recognition and classification using convolutional neural network techniques. *International Journal of Speech Technology, 23,* 381–388. https://doi.org/10.1007/s10772-020-09713-y

Colwell, T. M. (2016). I.2 Emotives and emotional regimes. In *Early modern emotions*. Routledge.

Committee on Information. (2022). Department of global communications leading robust anti-disinformation efforts, says under-secretary-general, as committee on information session opens. In *UN Meeting Coverage*. Press Releases. Retrieved May 27, 2022, from https://www.un.org/press/en/2022/pi2299.doc.htm

Corazza, M., Menini, S., Cabrio, E., et al. (2020). A multilingual evaluation for online hate speech detection. *ACM Transactions on Internet Technology, 20,* 10:1–10:22. https://doi.org/10.1145/3377323

Costello, M., & Hawdon, J. (2020). Hate speech in online spaces. In T. J. Holt & A. M. Bossler (Eds.), *The Palgrave handbook of international cybercrime and Cyberdeviance* (pp. 1397–1416). Springer International Publishing.

Cromby, J. (2007). Towards a psychology of feeling. *International Journal of Critical Psychology, 21,* 94–118.

D'Mello, S., & Calvo, R. A. (2013). Beyond the basic emotions: What should affective computing compute? In *CHI '13 extended abstracts on Human Factors in Computing Systems*, Association for Computing Machinery, pp. 2287–2294.

Davidson, J., & Milligan, C. (2004). Embodying emotion sensing space: Introducing emotional geographies. *Social and Cultural Geography, 5,* 523–532. https://doi.org/10.1080/1464936042000317677

Derman, G. S. (2021). Perception management in the media. *Int J Soc Econ Sci, 11,* 64–78.

Egger, M., Ley, M., & Hanke, S. (2019). Emotion recognition from physiological signal analysis: A review. *Electronic Notes in Theoretical Computer Science, 343,* 35–55. https://doi.org/10.1016/j.entcs.2019.04.009

Ekman, P. (1992a). Are there basic emotions? *Psychological Review, 99,* 550–553. https://doi.org/10.1037/0033-295X.99.3.550

Ekman, P. (1992b). An argument for basic emotions. *Cognition and Emotion, 6,* 169–200. https://doi.org/10.1080/02699939208411068

Ekman, P., Levenson, R. W., & Friesen, W. V. (1983). Autonomic nervous system activity distinguishes among emotions. *Science, 221,* 1208–1210. https://doi.org/10.1126/science.6612338

Estellés, M., & Castellví, J. (2020). The educational implications of populism, emotions and digital hate speech: A dialogue with scholars from Canada, Chile, Spain, the UK, and the US. *Sustainability Switzerland, 12*(15), 6034. https://doi.org/10.3390/su12156034

Facebook. (2020). AI advances to better detect hate speech. In *Facebook AI*. Retrieved November 10, 2021, from https://ai.facebook.com/blog/ai-advances-to-better-detect-hate-speech/

Fino, A. (2020). Defining Hate Speech. *Journal of International Criminal Justice, 18*, 31–57. https://doi.org/10.1093/jicj/mqaa023

Fortuna, P., & Nunes, S. (2018). A survey on automatic detection of hate speech in text. *ACM Computing Surveys, 51*. https://doi.org/10.1145/3232676

Frevert, U. (2013). *Emotions in history—Lost and found*. Central European University Press.

Frijda, N. H. (1969). Recognition of emotion. In L. Berkowitz (Ed.), *Advances in experimental social psychology* (pp. 167–223). Academic Press.

Gambäck, B., & Sikdar, U. K. (2017). Using convolutional neural networks to classify hate-speech. In *Proceedings of the first workshop on abusive language online*, Association for Computational Linguistics, pp. 85–90. 10.18653/v1/w17-3013.

Garrido, S., & Davidson, J. (2016). Emotional regimes reflected in a popular ballad: Perspectives on gender, love and protest in 'Scarborough fair'. *Musicology Australia, 38*, 65–78. https://doi.org/10.1080/08145857.2016.1159646

Gomez, R., Gibert, J., Gomez, L., & Karatzas, D. (2020). Exploring hate speech detection in multimodal publications. *Proceedings of 2020 IEEE Winter Conference of Applied Computer Visual WACV 2020*, pp. 1459–1467. https://doi.org/10.1109/WACV45572.2020.9093414.

Govaers, F. (2021). Explainable AI for strategic hybrid operations. NATO, p. STO-MP-IST-190-16.

Guiora, A., & Park, E. A. (2017). Hate speech on social media. *Philosophia United States, 45*, 957–971. https://doi.org/10.1007/s11406-017-9858-4

Gunes, H., & Pantic, M. (2010). Automatic, dimensional and continuous emotion recognition. *International Journal of Synthetic Emotions, 1*, 68–99. https://doi.org/10.4018/jse.2010101605

Gunes, H., & Schuller, B. (2013). Categorical and dimensional affect analysis in continuous input: Current trends and future directions. *Image and Vision Computing, 31*, 120–136. https://doi.org/10.1016/j.imavis.2012.06.016

Haq, S., & Jackson, P. J. B. (2011). Multimodal emotion recognition. In *Machine audition: Principles, algorithms and systems*. Retrieved October 25, 2021, from https://www.igi-global.com/chapter/multimodal-emotion-recognition/www.igi-global.com/chapter/multimodal-emotion-recognition/45495

Heaven, W.D. (2020). OpenAI's new language generator GPT-3 is shockingly good—and completely mindless. In *MIT Technology Review*. Retrieved May 27, 2022, from https://www.technologyreview.com/2020/07/20/1005454/openai-machine-learning-language-generator-gpt-3-nlp/

Hosseini, S. A., Khalilzadeh, M. A., & Changiz, S. (2010). Emotional stress recognition system for affective computing based on bio-signals. *Journal of Biological Systems, 18*, 101–114. https://doi.org/10.1142/S0218339010003640

Hutchins, E. M., Cloppert, M. J., & Amin, R. M. (2011). Intelligence-driven computer network defense informed by analysis of adversary campaigns and intrusion kill chains. *Leading Issues in Information Warfare & Security Research, 1*, 1–14.

Ihlebæk, K. A., & Holter, C. R. (2021). Hostile emotions: An exploratory study of far-right online commenters and their emotional connection to traditional and alternative news media. *Journalism, 22*, 1207–1222. https://doi.org/10.1177/1464884920985726

Isen, A. M., & Diamond, G. A. (1989). Affect and automaticity. In *unintended thought* (pp. 124–152). The Guilford Press.

Jena, A. (2020). Emotions, media and politics by Karin Wahl-Jorgensen. *Mass Communication and Society, 23*, 151–153. https://doi.org/10.1080/15205436.2019.1649927

Jermsittiparsert, K., Abdurrahman, A., Siriattakul, P., et al. (2020). Pattern recognition and features selection for speech emotion recognition model using deep learning. *International Journal of Speech Technology, 23*, 799–806. https://doi.org/10.1007/s10772-020-09690-2

Jiang, L., & Suzuki, Y. (2019). Detecting hate speech from tweets for sentiment analysis. In *2019 6th International Conference on Systems and Informatics (ICSAI)*, pp. 671–676.

Kaloudi, N., & Li, J. (2020). The AI-based cyber threat landscape: A survey. *ACM Computing Surveys, 53*, 20:1–20:34. https://doi.org/10.1145/3372823

Kapil, P., & Ekbal, A. (2020). A deep neural network based multi-task learning approach to hate speech detection. *Knowledge-Based Systems, 210*, 106458. https://doi.org/10.1016/j.knosys.2020.106458

Kaur, S., & Sharma, R. (2021). Emotion AI: Integrating emotional intelligence with artificial intelligence in the digital workplace. In P. K. Singh, Z. Polkowski, S. Tanwar, et al. (Eds.), *Innovations in information and communication technologies (IICT-2020)* (pp. 337–343). Springer International Publishing.

Khamaiseh, M. (2021). The problem with hate speech: How the media has fuelled its rise. In *Al Jazeera Media Institute*. Retrieved May 27, 2022, from http://institute.aljazeera.net/en/ajr/article/1697

Kolotaev, Y. (2021). Sentiment analysis: Challenges to psychological security and political stability. In *Proceedings of the 3rd European conference on the Impact of Artificial Intelligence and Robotics ECIAIR 2021*, Academic Conferences International Limited, pp. 82–89.

Kopp, C. (2005). Classical deception techniques and perception management vs. the four strategies of information warfare. In *Conference proceedings of the 6th Australian Information Warfare and Security Conference. School of Information Systems*, Deakin University, pp. 81–89.

Kramar, K., & Pashentsev, E. (2020, June). *Experts on the malicious use of artificial intelligence: Challenges for political stability and international psychological security*. Report by the International Center for Social and Political Studies and Consulting, Moscow.

Kratzwald, B., Ilić, S., Kraus, M., et al. (2018). Deep learning for affective computing: Text-based emotion recognition in decision support. *Decision Support Systems, 115*, 24–35. https://doi.org/10.1016/j.dss.2018.09.002

Lev-On, A. (2018). The anti-social network? Framing social Media in Wartime. *Social Media and Society, 4*, 2056305118800311. https://doi.org/10.1177/2056305118800311

Leys, R. (2011). The turn to affect: A critique. *Critical Inquiry, 37*, 434–472. https://doi.org/10.1086/659353

Liu, B. (2012). *Sentiment analysis and opinion mining*. Morgan & Claypool Publishers.

Lungu, V. (2013). Artificial emotion simulation model and agent architecture: Extended. Advances in Intelligent Control Systems and Computer Science, 207–221. https://doi.org/10.1007/978-3-642-32548-9_15.

Lyman, P. (2004). The domestication of anger: The use and abuse of anger in politics. *European Journal of Social Theory, 7*, 133–147. https://doi.org/10.1177/1368431004041748

Manstead, A. S. R., Frijda, N., & Fischer, A. (2004). *Feelings and emotions: The Amsterdam symposium*. Cambridge University Press.

Massumi, B. (1995). The autonomy of affect. *Cultural Critique, 31*, 83–109. https://doi.org/10.2307/1354446

Mathew, B., Dutt, R., Goyal, P., & Mukherjee, A. (2019). Spread of hate speech in online social media. In *WebSci 2019—Proceedings of 11th ACM conference Web Science*, pp. 173–182. https://doi.org/10.1145/3292522.3326034.

McCurry, J. (2021). South Korean AI chatbot pulled from Facebook after hate speech towards minorities. In *The Guardian*. Retrieved May 26, 2022, from https://www.theguardian.com/world/2021/jan/14/time-to-properly-socialise-hate-speech-ai-chatbot-pulled-from-facebook

McGrath, L. S. (2017). Historiography, affect, and the neurosciences. *History of Psychology, 20*, 129–147. https://doi.org/10.1037/hop0000047

McStay, A. (2018). *Emotional AI: The rise of empathic media*. SAGE.

McStay, A. (2020). Emotional AI, soft biometrics and the surveillance of emotional life: An unusual consensus on privacy. *Big Data & Society, 7*, 2053951720904386. https://doi.org/10.1177/2053951720904386

McStay, A., & Pavliscak, P. (2019). Emotional artificial intelligence: Guidelines for ethical use. In *Emotional AI Lab*. https://emotionalai.org/outputs

Medhat, W., Hassan, A., & Korashy, H. (2014). Sentiment analysis algorithms and applications: A survey. *Ain Shams Engineering Journal, 5*, 1093–1113. https://doi.org/10.1016/j.asej.2014.04.011

Mengü, M. M., & Türk, E. (2021). Digital perception management. In Digital Seige (p. 327). Istanbul University Press.

Moghimi, M., Stone, R., Rotshtein, P., & Cooke, N. (2016). Influencing human affective responses to dynamic virtual environments. *Presence Teleoperators Virtual Environment, 25*, 81–107. https://doi.org/10.1162/PRES_a_00249

Montoyo, A., Martínez-Barco, P., & Balahur, A. (2012). Subjectivity and sentiment analysis: An overview of the current state of the area and envisaged developments. *Decision Support Systems, 53*, 675–679. https://doi.org/10.1016/j.dss.2012.05.022

Morgan, S. (2018). Fake news, disinformation, manipulation and online tactics to undermine democracy. *Journal of Cyber Policy, 3*, 39–43. https://doi.org/10.1080/23738871.2018.1462395

Munezero, M., Montero, C. S., Sutinen, E., & Pajunen, J. (2014). Are they different? Affect, feeling, emotion, sentiment, and opinion detection in text. *IEEE Transactions on Affective Computing, 5*, 101–111. https://doi.org/10.1109/TAFFC.2014.2317187

Niemeier, S., & Dirven, R. (1997). *The language of emotions: Conceptualization, expression, and theoretical foundation*. John Benjamins Publishing.

Nye, R.A. (2003). Review: The navigation of feeling: A framework for the history of emotions by William M. Reddy. *The Journal of Modern History, 75*, 920–923. https://doi.org/10.1086/383359

Oatley, K. (1987). Editorial: Cognitive science and the understanding of emotions. *Cognition and Emotion, 1*, 209–216. https://doi.org/10.1080/02699938708408048

Ong, D. C. (2021). *An ethical framework for guiding the development of affectively-aware artificial intelligence*. ArXiv210713734 Cs.

Orgeret, K. S. (2020). Discussing emotions in digital journalism. *Digital Journalism, 8*, 292–297. https://doi.org/10.1080/21670811.2020.1727347

Orlando, J. (2020) Young people are exposed to more hate online during COVID. And it risks their health. In *The Conversation*. Retrieved May 26, 2022, from http://theconversation.com/young-people-are-exposed-to-more-hate-online-during-covid-and-it-risks-their-health-148107

Pang, B., & Lee, L. (2008). Opinion mining and sentiment analysis. *Foundations and Trends in Information Retrieval, 2*, 1–135. https://doi.org/10.1561/1500000011

Pantserev, K. A. (2020). The malicious use of AI-based deepfake technology as the new threat to psychological security and political stability. In H. Jahankhani, S. Kendzierskyj, N. Chelvachandran, & J. Ibarra (Eds.), *Cyber Defence in the age of AI, smart societies and augmented humanity* (pp. 37–55). Springer International Publishing.

Pashentsev, E. (2019). Malicious use of artificial intelligence. In *European conference on the Impact of Artificial Intelligence and Robotics, ECIAIR*, Academic Conferences and Publishing International Limited, p. 33.

Picard, R. W. (1997). *Affective computing*. MIT Press.

Pusztahelyi, R. (2020). Emotional AI and its challenges in the viewpoint of online marketing. *Curentul Juridic, 81*, 13–31.

Qing, C., Qiao, R., Xu, X., & Cheng, Y. (2019). Interpretable emotion recognition using EEG signals. *IEEE Access, 7*, 94160–94170. https://doi.org/10.1109/ACCESS.2019.2928691

Reddy, W. M. (2001). *The navigation of feeling: A framework for the history of emotions*. Cambridge University Press.

Rosenberger, L., & Hanlon, B. (2019). *Countering information operations demands a common democratic strategy*. Alliance for Securing Democracy.

Rosenfeld, M. (2003). Hate speech in constitutional jurisprudence: A comparative analysis. *Cardozo Law Review, 24*, 1523.

Roumate, F. (2021). Malicious use of artificial intelligence, new challenges for diplomacy and international psychological security. In *Artificial intelligence and digital diplomacy* (pp. 97–113). Springer. https://doi.org/10.1007/978-3-030-68647-5_8.

Rust, R. T., & Huang, M.-H. (2021). AI for Feeling. In R. T. Rust & M.-H. Huang (Eds.), *The feeling economy: How artificial intelligence is creating the era of empathy* (pp. 151–162). Springer International Publishing.

Safi, M. (2018). Sri Lanka accuses Facebook over hate speech after deadly riots. In *The Guardian*. Retrieved November 3, 2021, from https://www.theguardian.com/world/2018/mar/14/facebook-accused-by-sri-lanka-of-failing-to-control-hate-speech

Sellars, A. (2016). *Defining Hate Speech*. Social Science Research Network.

Shu, L., Xie, J., Yang, M., et al. (2018). A review of emotion recognition using physiological signals. *Sensors, 18*, 2074. https://doi.org/10.3390/s18072074

Siegel, P. C. (2005). Perception management: IO's stepchild? *Low Intensity Conflict Law Enforcement, 13*, 117–134. https://doi.org/10.1080/09662840500347314

Silva, L., Mondal, M., Correa, D., et al. (2016). Analyzing the targets of hate in online social media. *Proceedings of the international AAAI conference on Weblogs and Social Media, 10*, 687–690.

Stark, L., & Hoey, J. (2021). The Ethics of Emotion in Artificial Intelligence Systems. In *Proceedings of the 2021 ACM conference on Fairness, Accountability, and Transparency*, Association for Computing Machinery, , pp. 782–793.

Sullivan, E. (2013). The history of the emotions: Past, present, future. *Culture and History, 2*, 93–102. https://doi.org/10.3366/cult.2013.0034

Süselbeck, J. (2019). Sprache und emotionales Gedächtnis. Zur Konstruktion von Gefühlen und Erinnerungen in der Literatur und den Medien. *Emotionen*, 282–295. https://doi.org/10.1007/978-3-476-05353-4_43

The Economist. (2022). The war in Ukraine has made Russian social-media users glum. In *Graphic details from The Economist*. Retrieved May 27, 2022, from https://www.economist.com/graphic-detail/2022/03/12/the-war-in-ukraine-has-made-russian-social-media-users-glum

Thoits, P. A. (1989). The sociology of emotions. *Annual Review of Sociology, 15*, 317–342.

Timmermann, W. (2008). Counteracting hate speech as a way of preventing genocidal violence. Genocide Studies and Prevention: An International Journal, 3, Article 8.

Tontodimamma, A., Nissi, E., Sarra, A., & Fontanella, L. (2021). Thirty years of research into hate speech: Topics of interest and their evolution. *Scientometrics, 126*, 157–179. https://doi.org/10.1007/s11192-020-03737-6

Triberti, S., Chirico, A., La Rocca, G., & Riva, G. (2017). Developing emotional design: Emotions as cognitive processes and their role in the Design of Interactive Technologies. *Frontiers in Psychology, 8*, 1773. https://doi.org/10.3389/fpsyg.2017.01773

Truong, N. (2022). *War in Ukraine and Covid-19: Europe is dealing with the 'return of tragedy'*. Le Monde.

Udupa, S., Gagliardone, I., Deem, A., & Csuka, L. (2020). *Field of disinformation, democratic processes, and conflict prevention: A scan of the literature.* Social Science Research Council.

Umer, M., Ashraf, I., Mehmood, A., et al. (2020). Sentiment analysis of tweets using a unified convolutional neural network-long short-term memory network model. *Computational Intelligence, 37*, 409–434. https://doi.org/10.1111/coin.12415

UN. (2018). Myanmar military leaders must face genocide charges—UN report. In *UN News*. Retrieved November 3, 2021, from https://news.un.org/en/story/2018/08/1017802

Uyheng, J., & Carley, K. M. (2020). Bots and online hate during the COVID-19 pandemic: Case studies in the United States and The Philippines. *Journal of Computational Social Science, 3*, 445–468. https://doi.org/10.1007/s42001-020-00087-4

Uyheng, J., & Carley, K. M. (2021). Characterizing network dynamics of online hate communities around the COVID-19 pandemic. *Applied Network Science, 6*, 1–21. https://doi.org/10.1007/s41109-021-00362-x

Wahl-Jorgensen, K. (2018). Media coverage of shifting emotional regimes: Donald Trump's angry populism. *Media, Culture and Society, 40*, 766–778. https://doi.org/10.1177/0163443718772190

Wahl-Jorgensen, K. (2019). *Emotions*. John Wiley & Sons.

Waldron, J. (2012). *The harm in hate speech*. Harvard University Press.

Walker, S. (1994). *Hate speech: The history of an American controversy*. University of Nebraska Press.

Wierzbicka, A. (1990). The semantics of emotions: Fear and its relatives in English. *Australian Journal of Linguistics, 10*, 359–375. https://doi.org/10.1080/07268609008599447

Wu, D., Courtney, C. G., Lance, B. J., et al. (2010). Optimal arousal identification and classification for affective computing using physiological signals: Virtual reality Stroop task. *IEEE Transactions on Affective Computing, 1*, 109–118. https://doi.org/10.1109/T-AFFC.2010.12

Yadollahi, A., Shahraki, A. G., & Zaiane, O. R. (2017). Current state of text sentiment analysis from opinion to emotion mining. *ACM Computing Surveys, 50*, 25:1–25:33. https://doi.org/10.1145/3057270

Yamin, M. M., Ullah, M., Ullah, H., & Katt, B. (2021). Weaponized AI for cyber attacks. *Journal of Information Security and Applications, 57*, 102722. https://doi.org/10.1016/j.jisa.2020.102722

Yan, F., Iliyasu, A. M., & Hirota, K. (2021). Emotion space modelling for social robots. *Engineering Applications of Artificial Intelligence, 100*, 104178. https://doi.org/10.1016/j.engappai.2021.104178

Yong, C. (2011). Does freedom of speech include hate speech? *Res Publica, 17*, 385–403. https://doi.org/10.1007/s11158-011-9158-y

YouTube. (2019). Hate speech policy—YouTube Help. In *YouTube Help*. Retrieved November 10, 2021, from https://support.google.com/youtube/answer/2801939?hl=en

Yuan, L. (2022). Why the Chinese internet is cheering Russia's invasion—The New York Times. In *New York Times*. Retrieved May 27, 2022, from https://www.nytimes.com/2022/02/27/business/china-russia-ukraine-invasion.html

Yue, L., Chen, W., Li, X., et al. (2019). A survey of sentiment analysis in social media. *Knowledge and Information Systems, 60*, 617–663. https://doi.org/10.1007/s10115-018-1236-4

Zeng, Z., Pantic, M., Roisman, G. I., & Huang, T. S. (2009). A survey of affect recognition methods: Audio, visual, and spontaneous expressions. *IEEE Transactions on Pattern Analysis and Machine Intelligence, 31*, 39–58. https://doi.org/10.1109/TPAMI.2008.52

Zhang, L., & Liu, B. (2017). Sentiment analysis and opinion mining. In C. Sammut & G. I. Webb (Eds.), *Encyclopedia of machine learning and data mining* (pp. 1152–1161). Springer.

6

The Malicious Use of Artificial Intelligence Through Agenda Setting

Evgeny Pashentsev

Introduction

The role of the news media in defining the important issues of the day, also known as agenda setting, has a strong influence on social and political life (for more on agenda setting, see McCombs & Valenzuela, 2021, Protess & McCombs, 2016, Zahariadis, 2016, etc.). Agenda setting is an important tool for achieving sociopolitical and economic goals and influencing public processes, and has a long history of practice involving both socially oriented and antisocial use by various state and non-state actors.

In recent years, agenda setting has become increasingly strongly influenced by AI technologies, and this has been the subject of many studies from several perspectives (Banik, 2018; Christin, 2020; Coeckelbergh, 2020; Diakopoulos, 2019; Jannach et al., 2010; Malhotra, 2020; Marconi, 2020; McStay, 2018; Natale, 2021; Schrage, 2020; etc.). There is no doubt about the numerous and significant positive aspects of the use of AI in society in general, and in public communication in particular; however, due to the growing sociopolitical and economic contradictions in modern society, the development of geopolitical rivalries, and international tensions, it can be assumed that the large-scale malicious use of artificial intelligence (MUAI) through agenda

E. Pashentsev (✉)
Diplomatic Academy of the Ministry of Foreign Affairs of the Russian Federation, Moscow, Russia
e-mail: icspsc@mail.ru

setting is already taking place at national and global levels in the form of disinformation campaigns. At the same time, no government or transnational corporation will take responsibility for this. As in traditional forms of propaganda, these entities blame only their opponents and do not publicly admit that they actively resort to propaganda themselves.

The inevitable and wide availability to small groups or individuals of a means of global influence on society based on emerging technologies—and AI in particular—naturally raises the question of putting an end to the existence of conditions favorable to the interests of antisocial groups. In this chapter, AI is therefore considered not only as a set of specific benefits and threats through agenda setting, but also as a practical and necessary tool to achieve a new level of dynamic balance in human society and thus to develop a dynamic, flexible, and adaptive political stability.

This study is structured as follows: this author first analyzes the role of AI in defining the important issues of the day and the sociopolitical context of its malicious use in agenda setting, and then examines the technologies, current practices, and implications of MUAI, and then the role of Big Tech in using AI for antisocial purposes. Recommendations for counteracting MUAI in agenda setting are also briefly considered. The chapter ends with a summary of the main conclusions on this subject.

The Rising Role of Artificial Intelligence and Its Malicious Use in Agenda Setting

The news production process, from the collection, processing, and analysis of information to content production, management, and distribution, is increasingly affected by AI technologies. The use of AI in broadcasting, cinema, TV, and advertising is growing rapidly and is manifested in a variety of forms.

For example, by 2018, the Associated Press (AP) was producing more than 3700 stories using writing algorithms during every earnings season. This represents more than ten times the number of stories that were written without automation, thus enabling a far greater breadth of coverage (Diakopoulos, 2019). A report authored in 2019 by Professor Charlie Beckett of the London School of Economics (2019, p. 46) indicates that 44 percent of news organizations have experienced some form of impact from AI. More than half of the BBC's readers (62 percent) spend between 30 minutes and four hours listening to podcasts every day. In November 2020, *BBC Global News* launched a synthetic voice tool that uses AI to read articles from its website, and which automatically updates its output when the original content is updated (Kovalyova, 2021).

AI is now being used to extract content from vast archives, and to automatically localize content for international distribution. It is also useful in generating accessibility services, such as captioning, audio description, text-to-speech, and signing, far more rapidly and accurately than could be achieved in the past (Antunes, 2019). The core idea underlying newsfeeds is to apply machine learning (ML) to past behavior to predict the probability of future action, in order to determine the most engaging stories and prioritize them in the feed. Companies are now trying to find ways to optimize long-term metrics over short-term ones (Quora, 2018).

Due to the crisis in the world economy, the degradation of democratic institutions in many countries, and increasingly acute geopolitical rivalries, MUAI through agenda setting at the national and global levels is growing. The large-scale application of MUAI through agenda setting takes place where (and because) favorable conditions have arisen for it, such as the separation of the interests of dominant groups from national interests and socially oriented models of development, and the rather high level of development of AI technologies and the availability of suitable infrastructure. When inspired by reactionary groups, agenda setting based on the growing use of AI and other related technologies (5G, quantum computing, etc.) can pose a great threat to all countries. Less technologically advanced states cannot effectively protect themselves from this aggressive external agenda setting other than by completely disconnecting from the internet, although this leads to even greater isolation and backwardness of the population of the disconnected country.

It is always necessary to consider who is using AI in agenda setting, in whose interests, and for which undeclared purposes. Judging based on deeds, rather than words, seems to be the most balanced and productive approach. A comprehension of the socioeconomic and political context of MUAI through agenda setting is, in our view, necessary in order to capture a global pattern in MUAI by egoistic dominant groups. Reactionary regimes will focus the entire set of AI technologies associated with agenda setting on keeping the population under their control. Reactionary regimes in countries with large military and economic potential are then able to focus more on psychological aggression against other nations, thereby turning agenda setting into an important element of hybrid warfare.

It should be borne in mind that the relative cheapness and ease of transmission of AI software, and the involvement of AI specialists in criminal groups, make it possible to conduct psychological operations based on MUAI by relatively small groups of people, which can destabilize the situation in a given country or even at the global level. Thus, agenda setting may be a tool for control of society by authorities, a mechanism for public influence in the hands of competing dominant factions of a particular country, a means of interstate and inter-corporate confrontation in the international arena (with the vaccine wars as the current most prominent example), as well as a tool for achieving the goals of various criminal organizations. However, the existence of these variants of MUAI only emphasizes the importance of the skillful use of AI technologies by socially oriented forces, not only at the level of public administration but also through various structures of civil society, in order to neutralize threats to the psychological security of society.

There are increasingly diverse practices of MUAI in agenda setting in different countries, based on the use of a wide range of AI technologies. Among the most common tools of MUAI in agenda setting is the *malicious use of various types of bots*.

Classification of bots. A bot is a computer program that performs automatic repetitive tasks (Merriam-Webster, 2022). Bot classifications are based on a wide variety of criteria, from functional characteristics and applications (Argent, 2018) to the principle of compliance with the public interest (good–bad (Radware, 2022), or legitimate–malicious (Spamlaws, 2022)). There are also combined bot classifications (Botnerds, 2022). The classification of good or bad bots, although it may be somewhat simplistic and quite justified from the point of view of the task of supporting the site, is hardly appropriate in the broader sense of compliance with the public interest. A person's intentions to use certain AI technologies, including bots, are crucial. For example, there is a definition that good bots are legitimate bots whose actions are beneficial to a website (Radware, 2022). However, legitimate bots, such as chatbots or social media bots, may well be an MUAI tool, and some bad bots may perform useful functions—for example, in the fight against terrorist organizations. Nuclear energy is not bad or good, legitimate or malicious—it all depends on the goals of its use, which are determined by people. The problem may be that "Because good bots can share similar characteristics with malicious bots, the challenge is ensuring good bots aren't blocked when putting together a bot management strategy" (Cloudflare, 2022a). The need to take into account the dialectical unity of positive and negative features of bots in the context of their impact on society is very clearly seen here.

Different functional groups of bots can have their own internal classifications (Elharrar, 2017; Phillips, 2018). Studies indicate that bots made up over 50 percent of all online traffic in 2016. Entities that artificially promote content can manipulate the agenda-setting principle, which dictates that the more often people see certain content, the more important they think it is

(Horowitz et al., 2018, pp. 5–6). One survey, based on an analysis of nearly 17 billion website visits from across 100,000 domains, shows bots are back on top: not only that, but harmful bots have the edge over helper bots, which were responsible for 29 percent and 23 percent of all web traffic, respectively (LaFrance, 2017).

In 2019, evidence was found of organized social media manipulation campaigns which have taken place in 70 countries, up from 48 countries in 2018 and 28 countries in 2017. In each country, at least one political party or government agency is using social media to shape public attitudes domestically (Bradshaw & Howard, 2019). Bots today have more believable online profiles, more advanced conversational skills, and appear to be legitimate users embedded in human networks. Some automated accounts are also partially managed by humans—profiles known as "cyborgs" or "sock puppets" (Samuels & Akhtar, 2019).

Early bots mainly performed one type of activity—posting content automatically—and could be detected rather easily. In 2011, James Caverlee's team at Texas A&M University implemented a honeypot trap that managed to detect thousands of social bots. The team created a few Twitter accounts (bots) whose role was solely to create nonsensical tweets with gibberish content in which no human would ever be interested. However, these accounts attracted many followers. Further inspection confirmed that the suspicious followers were indeed social bots trying to grow their social circles by blindly following random accounts (Ferrara et al., 2016).

How bots become like people and people like bots. Bots have come a long way today. Bots based on AI technologies are increasingly able to imitate human activity. This makes bot activity more difficult to recognize, which is important to consider in terms of the effectiveness (including psychological effects) of MUAI. Here, were we talking clearly about weapons, we could limit ourselves to stating the traditional competition of offensive and defensive weaponry. However, the development of bots is clearly dominated by socially oriented installations: bots have become a solid element of the civil infrastructure of society. Since bots are aimed at communicating with a person, their successful development largely depends on their adaptation to the possibilities of our perception. This applies not only to the cognitive, but also to the emotional characteristics of bots (Peitzker, 2018). However, these bot abilities can also be used to effectively manipulate the human psyche.

For instance, SalesForce and Microsoft have both built software products that summarize news articles using AI. Google has built a machine-learning bot that can write Wikipedia articles. The potential for misuse of these products is massive, and the repercussions of getting this kind of information wrong could be deadly (Woolley, 2020).

On the other hand, with a growing pace of life, an incomparably greater amount of information and communication with different people resulting from active use of the internet and social networks, we simplify communication patterns and become, at least in form, more bots than people, and this makes it easier for bots to imitate us in communication.

Two counter processes form both us and fast self-learning machines. It is impossible to stop this, but without a sharp change in a person's ability to process incoming information and his/her thinking capabilities, the threat of intellectual and emotional overload will increase and people's analytical abilities decrease, which, in particular, creates a growing threat to MUAI against international psychological security.

From chatbots to conversational AI bots. A chatbot is a virtual interlocutor, a program that is designed to maintain a situational dialogue with the user, search for information on request and perform simple tasks, imitating the communication style of living people. In 2021, 1.4 billion people around the world interacted with a chatbot (McNamara, 2022). Chatbot systems originated with programs like ELIZA which were intended to demonstrate natural language conversation with a computer (Radziwill & Benton, 2017). Chatbots vary depending on the level of development, type of communication, format of use, functions, and other characteristics. They can be simple or use AI technologies. The chatbot market size is projected to grow from $2.6 billion in 2019 to $9.4 billion by 2024 at a compound annual growth rate (CAGR) of 29.7 percent (Patel, 2022).

There is a large amount of literature on various aspects of creating and using chatbots in modern society (Muldowney, 2020; Galitsky, 2019; Cancel & Gerhardt, 2019; Gao et al., 2019; Kannan & Bernoff, 2019). In the context of this study, we should pay attention to the rapid improvement of chatbots in recent years.

In China, where chatbots were embraced by Chinese social media earlier than in Western countries, Chumen Wenwen has built a very sophisticated bot that runs on the popular WeChat platform and in other spaces. The company has combined voice recognition, AI, and the WeChat platform into a package that queries information for its users. By connecting with third-party application programming interfaces, the app can answer questions about what is around you, including movies, restaurants, massage, and more (Jerry @Rocketbots.io, 2017). Chatbots integrated with video are gaining popularity (Yeramsetti, 2020). Video integration helps offer personalized support, but the more advanced the technology, the greater the risk of perception management. Bots are used in streamlining personal tasks or day-to-day activities such as fitness, parenting, kids, e-learning, and so on (Patel, 2022).

Personalization distinguishes modern chatbots more and more, which even adapt to the specifics of national psychology. The Russian equivalent of Alexa is Alisa. According to Alisa's project manager Ilya Subbotin, "Alisa couldn't be too sweet, too nice" because Russia is "a country where people tick differently than in the West. They will appreciate a bit of irony, a bit of dark humour, nothing offensive of course, but also not too sweet" (Doctorow, 2018). In Brazil, computer scientists from the Federal University of Ouro Preto announced that a popular journalist on Twitter, Carina Santos, was not a real person but a botnet that they had created. Based on the circulation of her tweets, a commonly used ranking site, Twitalyzer, ranked this account as having more online influence than US talk show host Oprah Winfrey (Paganini, 2013). Adjusting for nationality, gender, age, and, ultimately, personal characteristics, with all the undoubted advantages of this approach, creates great psychological prerequisites for MUAI, which can be used on a broad basis.

This is likely to happen in the near future. The last years we see the most definitive transformation of chatbots into conversational AI bots. The terms "chatbot" and "conversational AI" have the same meaning; conversational AI, however, is more inclusive of all the technology that falls under the bot umbrella, like voice bots and voice + text assistants, whereas chatbots have a more limited text-only connotation (Haptik, 2022; Shah & Priyadarshini, 2020). The rudimentary rule-based chatbot no longer delights customers. An AI conversation bot, unlike a chatbot, is a cognitive bot that can decipher complex scenarios and understand human sentiments. Its neuro-linguistic programming capabilities empower it for a personalized conversation with customers, which involves understanding human sentiments and acting accordingly (Shah & Priyadarshini, 2020). The wider the reach of chatbots and conversational AI enterprises, the more opportunities MUAI will have, which requires a response not only at the level of cybersecurity, but also the psychological preparation of a person, an ordinary user, for new risks.

Malicious use of chatbots. No one who spends time online is immune from the potential harm of chatbots. Even the director of the annual Loebner Prize for artificial intelligence, an event that pits the most sophisticated chatbots against one another, was fooled into thinking a chatbot on a dating service was interested in him romantically (Radziwill & Benton, 2017). Even before the problem of MUAI through bot activities became relevant, this topic appeared in the mass consciousness through fiction. In Jack Heath's, 2010 novel *Hit List* (Heath, 2010), a chatterbot became self-aware and used emails, text messages, and electronic banking to arrange assassinations and prison breaks. In 2018, the authors of the report "The Malicious Use of Artificial Intelligence" wrote that "sophisticated AI systems might allow groups to target precisely the right message at precisely the right time in order to maximize persuasive potential" (Brundage et al., 2018, p. 47). A trusted chatbot can be an effective means of delivering this message.

While malicious chatbots have not yet been detected on any significant scale, there are already some documented instances of chatbots being used for cybercrime. In June 2018, Ticketmaster admitted that a chatbot it used for customer service had been infected by malware which gathered customers' personal information and sent it to an unknown third party. The WatchGuard CTO Corey Nachreiner explained that such incidents are likely to become more common in the future: "We expect chatbots to be another hook in the phisher's 'tackle box,'" he says. "They won't outpace traditional email phishing any time soon, or even ransomware, but they'll augment attacks by adding another layer of credibility and deception" (Chandler, 2018).

The cybercriminals can go much further, by hacking the bot or infecting it with malware in order to turn it into an information stealer. Ticketmaster's Inbenta chatbot fell victim to this type of attack. Hackers could also target the back-end network supporting the chatbot, like the [24]7.ai breach which affected Delta and Sears. It is also possible for hackers to create and launch their own chatbots, designed for the sole purpose of tricking people into sharing sensitive information or clicking on malicious links. This is happening already on some dating websites and apps, but it is likely to spread to other businesses in the next few years. Such malicious chatbots could be used to impersonate the legitimate chatbots used by real businesses in order to target those customers (Johnson, 2018).

According to WatchGuard CTO Corey Nachreiner, "We have not seen chatbots used as part of a social engineering campaign yet, but believe they present a major opportunity for hackers as businesses and consumers increasingly rely on them. As these chatbots get better at emulating natural human language, their value for malicious activity grows" (Chandler, 2018). According to Evgeny Chereshnev from Kaspersky, phishing, ransomware, theft of credentials, identity, and credit cards—all of it will be way easier for hackers when they obtain amazing new tools capable of talking to people in trouble using their behavioral patterns. Basically, an infected bot would tell you exactly what you want to hear, right when you expect it, so you would have no reason to be suspicious (Chereshnev, 2016).

Reputational damage inflicted by chatbots during political campaigns, for example, can be used by terrorist groups to attract new supporters or organize political assassinations. When Microsoft unleashed Tay, an artificially intelligent chatbot with the personality of a flippant 19-year-old, the company hoped that people would interact with her on social platforms like Twitter. The idea was that by chatting with her you would help her learn, having some fun while assisting her creators in their AI research. Tay quickly racked up over 50,000 Twitter followers who could send her direct messages or tweets, and she has so far sent out over 96,000 tweets (Metz, 2016). The bad news is that in the short time since she was released, some of Tay's new friends figured out how to get her to say some really awful, racist things, like one now deleted tweet which read, "Bush did 9/11 and Hitler would have done a better job than the monkey we have now." Microsoft has reportedly been deleting some of these tweets: in a statement, the company said it has "taken Tay offline" and is "making adjustments" (Metz, 2016).

Hiding across the internet in chatrooms are "flirtbots" such as CyberLover, computer programs developed to form relationships with multiple human users by mimicking humanlike conversation. Flirting bots' purpose is fraudulent: to draw in the susceptible, deceive them that they are engaging with another human, steal their identity, and conduct financial fraud (Warwick & Shah, 2012).

As AI develops further, convincing chatbots may elicit human trust by engaging people in longer dialogues, and perhaps eventually masquerade visually as another person in a video chat (Brundage et al., 2018, p. 24). The more chatbots are used, the better they become, and thus, the more likely the risk of MUAI in the psychological area. This, of course, does not negate the extremely progressive nature of this technology itself, but it urges timely consideration of the risks. Technology can become a tool not only for abuse in marketing campaigns, but also for latent political control.

With the concept of the metaverse beginning to pick up steam, conversational AI has a pivotal role to play, enabling the creation of AI-driven, virtual interaction partners—or avatars—that will populate these immersive worlds. These avatars could make anything in the metaverse a point of conversation. Characters, objects, even locations, or brands could be points of interaction (Glock, 2022). But despite all of its attractive aspects, the metaverse also presents plenty of opportunities for the MUAI. Digital partners will be anthropomorphized personas that are customized for each user, and since the metaverse will ultimately augment the real world, these digital entities will follow users around everywhere—whether it's shopping, working, or just hanging out. These digital avatars won't be like the crude chatbots of today, but embodied characters people will come to think of as trusted figures in their lives—a *personal virtual partner/assistant* who can know someone in ways no friend ever could, monitoring an individual's daily life down to their blood pressure and heart rate via a smart watch (Rosenberg & Unanimous, 2022). The concern is not just that this type of assistant can be hacked but due to its subjective reality for, and even proximity to, the user, an avatar can become a psychological control tool with the ability to provoke reactions of interest to the malicious actor. The manipulator could be a private company with a "flexible" relationship to ethical standards, or government agencies seeking to curb antisocial influence.

Social media bots, trading bots, and others. Broadly speaking, social media bots are automated programs used to engage in social media. These bots behave in either a partially or a fully autonomous fashion and are often designed to mimic human users. While the terms are sometimes used interchangeably, chatbots are bots that can independently hold a conversation, while social media bots do not have to have that ability. A chatbot often requires a person or even a team of people to maintain its functionality; on the other hand, social media bots are much simpler to manage, and often hundreds or even thousands of social media bots are managed by a single person (Cloudflare, 2022b).

The ability to influence target audiences (including negatively) through social media bots is considered in many studies (Neis & Mara, 2020; Freitas et al., 2014; Stieglitz et al., 2017). A significant part of the public in different countries perceives the use of social media bots as malicious. After surveying over 4500 adults in the United States between July 30 and August 12, 2018, the Pew Research Center found that about two-thirds of Americans (66 percent) had heard of social media bots, though far fewer (16 percent) had heard a lot about them. Among those aware of the phenomenon, a large majority were concerned that bot accounts were being used maliciously. Eight in ten of those who had heard of bots said that these accounts were mostly used for bad purposes, while just 17 percent said they were mostly used for good purposes (Stocking & Sumida, 2018). The study does not give an idea of how the average American connects their perception of malicious use of social media bots with artificial intelligence and MUAI, but it can be assumed that such a connection exists to an extent. With the improvement of AI-based social media bots and the further development of MUAI, this connection will become more stable. The growing benefits from social media bots will be combined with the growing threat of MUAI coming from them. Apparently, we should think on it ahead.

While many Americans are aware of the existence of social media bots, fewer are confident they can identify them. About half of those who had heard about bots (47 percent) were very or somewhat confident they could recognize these accounts on social media, with just 7 percent saying they were very confident. In contrast, 84 percent of Americans expressed confidence in their ability to recognize made-up news in an earlier study in 2016 (Stocking & Sumida, 2018). Among other negative social factors, with the growing role of AI technologies in providing communication, the inability to communicate safely can, and is already, causing growing social frustration in the United States and many other countries. Aggression and destruction as extreme forms of frustration behavior lead to extremism that threatens the social balance and wellbeing of society, which again manifests itself in different countries.

The bot agents are capable of interacting among themselves and with real users in a realistic mode; the results of their operation are changing the sentiment on a specific topic by conducting a "conversation" on a large scale. Social botnets could also be used for other purposes, such as social graph fuzzing, intentionally associating with groups and people with the intent of introducing noise into their social graphs. Social bots are very attractive for cybercriminals and state-sponsored hackers, too. They represent a favored channel for spreading malware, stealing passwords, and spreading and posting malicious links through social media networks (Paganini, 2013).

A few bad posts on the web can undermine a company's reputation, and cybercriminals are realizing that this is a huge market opportunity for them. With bots, such brand extortion is extremely easy, and cheap, to accomplish. The attack on CheapAir, a flight price comparison website, is the perfect example: cybercriminals threatened to launch a search engine optimization SEO attack on the company unless it paid them off. When CheapAir refused, the criminals followed through on their threat, unleashing a torrent of negative reviews via bots (Johnson, 2018).

Damage reputation through bot activities during political campaigns could, for example, be used by terrorist groups to attract new supporters or organize political assassinations. An unprecedented attack by bots inviting users to "death groups" was noted in 2017 in the social network Vkontakte. In 2016, the Russian media published the results of a journalistic investigation of *Novaya Gazeta*, which found the existence of a number of closed groups in Vkontakte, where teenagers were urged to commit suicide. From January to March 2017 on Vkontakte site, about 3 million messages were generated with hashtags and poems, calling for suicide. Analysis of the accounts led to the conclusion that these mailings were automated. Most of the mailings were detected on devices running the Android operating system. The mailing program turned out to be a VK iHA bot (Sukhodolov & Bychkova, 2022, p. 757) designed to automatically respond and entertain visitors of Vkonakte (Paganini, 2013). Since June 7, 2017, Russia has a law on criminal liability, providing for up to six years in prison for the creation of "death groups" on the internet (Interfax, 2017).

A study by *First Monday*, a peer-reviewed journal, found that in the day before the 2016 US presidential election, as much as 20 percent of political discussion on social media was generated by about 400,000 social media bots (Cloudflare, 2022b).

In 2019, Manceps conducted a study which found that bots could be used nefariously to affect markets (Manceps, 2019). Another report by researchers from Cornell University and several other universities found real threats of market manipulation through trading bots. The abstract of their publication states that they documented and quantified the widespread and rising deployment of arbitrage bots in blockchain systems, specifically in decentralized exchanges (or DEXes). Like high-frequency traders on Wall Street, these bots exploit inefficiencies in DEXes, paying high transaction fees and optimizing network latency to front-run (i.e., anticipate and exploit) ordinary users' DEX trades. According to the researchers, high fees paid for priority transaction ordering poses a systemic risk to consensus layer security (Daian et al., 2019, p. 1).

Sudden crisis situations of national and international significance are accompanied by an active reaction on the internet. At the same time, the crises themselves can occur both in a virtual environment and offline. In late April 2013, the Associated Press' (AP) Twitter account surprised its millions of followers after it tweeted that an explosion at the White House had injured President Barack Obama. It garnered over 4000 retweets and became one of the most expensive tweets in history after it caused stock prices to drop. While stock markets rebounded as soon as the tweet was confirmed to be fake, the damage had been done: it cost over $130 billion in stock value losses (Trend Micro, 2018). On September 14, 2019, drones were effectively used to attack oil processing facilities in Saudi Arabia. Oil prices spiked after the drone attack and Saudi Arabia's stock market fell by 2.3 percent (Turak, 2019). Saudi Arabia has suffered a lot of image damage, including by spreading negative information with the support of bots. In the future, when large-scale crises occur, they are likely to use AI for a combined attack on critical infrastructure (the second level of IPS threat) in different forms and a psychological attack on the minds of target audiences (the third level of IPS threats), also in different forms. The more intense the international situation and the higher the level of AI development, the more likely it is that MUAI will develop, where smart bots will become an important element of both attack and defense.

Political bots are very actively used in many countries, both in the usual practice of political struggle and in psychological operations with the use of MUAI. This is an increasingly common occurrence in conflicts as groups attempt to control the narrative on the new online battlefront. It is not necessary to overestimate the existing role of AI in the use of bots in modern psychological operations. At the moment, many such bots are controlled by humans who manage a large pack of bots, or use very simple forms of automation (Brundage et al., p. 49).

According to Dr. Samuel Woolley, nearly all of computational propaganda campaigns have been wielded quite bluntly. During events in which researchers now believe "political bots and disinformation played a key role—the Brexit referendum, the Trump-Clinton contest in 2016, the Crimea crisis—smart AI tools have played little or no role in manipulating political conversation; not even marginally conversational AI tools have been employed… Online communication during these events was altered by rudimentary bots that had been built simply to boost likes and follows, to spread links, to game trends, or to troll opposition" (Woolley, 2020).

Nathan González Mendelejis, Assistant Professor of National Security Studies at the eSchool of Graduate Professional Military Education, US Air Force, believes, "As bots become more advanced at propagating extremism, they will also lack the normal constraints that even the most radical humans accept, such as the need to maintain a reputation, attend to offline commitments, or keep some semblance of peace with friends and family. Heteromated terror thus reaffirms the age-old realisation that machines can do many things better than humans—and in this case, even the act of turning people into monsters. Humans who are compelled to join a violent movement in the near future may do so unaware they have done so at the behest of artificial intelligence" (González Mendelejis, 2018).

The summer of 2020 was the bloodiest summer in New York City in three decades. Monthly statistics from the NYPD show that the number of shootings incidents continued to skyrocket throughout the five boroughs. In August 2020, there were 242 total citywide shooting incidents compared to 91 shootings in August 2019, showing a 166 percent increase year-on-year (Davenport, 2020). Of course, there are some real reasons for that, but it seems that bot activities have played a role in that, too. A team of US researchers showed in 2019 that social bots participate in and contribute to online mass shooting conversations in a manner that is distinguishable from human contributions. Furthermore, while social bots accounted for less than 1 percent of total corpus user contributions, social network analysis centrality measures identified many bots with significant prominence in the conversation networks, densely occupying many of the highest eigenvector and out-degree centrality measure rankings, to include 82 percent of the top-100 eigenvector values of the Las Vegas retweet network (Schuchard et al., 2019, p. 1).

The crisis in society and the growth of geopolitical rivalry have weaponized social networks, not least by means of AI technologies. Social networks take measures to limit the flow of information, and this is interpreted differently by the public. On July 23, 2020, Yahoo suspended the comments section under its articles after a particular publication, explaining this as follows: "Our goal is to create a safe and engaging place for users to connect over interests and passions. In order to improve our community experience, we are temporarily suspending article commenting" (The Online Citizen, 2020). This move can be understood as a means to stop abusive and offensive comments from Yahoo's comments section, as it often resulted in lots of arguments, hate, and online trolling (Tripathi, 2020), including bots' comments. The comment sections on these articles made a name for themselves as pseudo-Ku Klux Klan meetings and hotbeds of all sorts of bigotry (Davis, 2018). Another way to explain Yahoo's decision is that there are many ways to rank comments, and the temporary removal of comments may allow Yahoo News to tweak the algorithm that ranks comments to favor their point of view on the issues (Quora, 2020).

Twitter is also testing a new technology, "sending users a prompt when they reply to a tweet using offensive or hurtful language, in an effort to clean up conversations on the social media platform" (HT Tech, 2020). For the creators of fake news, the ideal solution is training people to self-censor. Facebook is developing a new system of bots that can simulate bad behaviors and stress-test the platform to unearth flaws and loopholes. To make sure that this experiment does not interfere with real-life usage, Facebook has built a parallel version of sorts of the platform itself where these bots are allowed to run loose. In this parallel Facebook-verse, bots can simulate extreme scenarios such as trying to sell drugs, guns, and so on to see how Facebook's algorithms try to prevent them. This new system can host thousands or even millions of bots, and since it runs on the same code the platform's users are actually using, the actions these bots take are faithful to the effects that would be witnessed in real life (HT Tech, 2020).

There is disinformation, information aggression on the internet, which is increasingly achieved with the help of AI. There are also suggestions to find a way out of this situation by limiting the flow of information, including using AI technologies. Despite the high offensive and defensive capabilities of AI, it can be assumed that the psychological security of the individual and society as a whole can hardly be achieved by means of AI without solving the problems that determine the growth of social tension in the modern world. Clearly, unilateral accusations of inciting psychological warfare are counterproductive. This warfare has a multi-sided, multi-level character, both in territorial terms (global, regional, national) and in sociopolitical terms (interests of different classes and social groups collide on a wide range of issues). MUAI through bots is just one tool of such a confrontation, but one which should not be underestimated.

Even without resorting to outright censorship, media platforms can still manipulate public opinion by *ranking, deranking, or promoting* certain content. A report entitled "The Malicious Use of Artificial Intelligence: Forecasting, Prevention, and Mitigation" notes: "In 2014, Facebook manipulated the newsfeeds of over half a million users in order to alter the emotional content of users' posts, albeit modestly. While such tools can be used to help filter out malicious content or fake news, they could also be used by media platforms to manipulate public opinion" (Brundage et al., 2018, p. 47). Sometimes situations of acute conflict arise because these decisions are under the control of the leading search engines. For example, Google 2017 deranked stories from Russian state-owned publications Russia Today (RT) and Sputnik in response to allegations about election meddling by President Putin's government (BBC News, 2017). Eric Schmidt, the Executive Chairman of Google's parent company Alphabet, said that the company would engineer specific algorithms for RT and Sputnik, to make their articles less prominent in the search engine's news delivery services. Sputnik and RT editor-in-chief Margarita Simonyan responded with a statement published on RT, as follows: "Good to have Google on record as defying all logic and reason: facts aren't allowed if they come from RT, 'because [it is] Russia'—even if we have Google on congressional record saying they've found no manipulation of their platform or policy violations by RT" (RT, 2017). A policy of using ranking and de-ranking as a means of fighting for control over agenda setting can have a significant impact on psychological security and political stability.

In 2018, China's state-owned Xinhua News Agency introduced *AI news anchors* that could deliver the news with the same effect as human anchors, as the machine-learning program was able to synthesize realistic-looking speech, lip movements, and facial expressions (Tao, 2018). Sogou launched the world's first Russian-speaking AI news anchor in 2019 at the St. Petersburg International Economic Forum (Macaulay, 2020), while in 2020, CNN affiliate MBN South Korea debuted the country's very first AI news anchor (Urian, 2020). The first AI news anchors are quite primitive, devoid of emotional intelligence and serious analytical capabilities. That is why the danger of their use for malicious purposes in the modern world is not great. This situation may change in the future. The use of AI news anchors can take on a malicious character in four ways:

1. By promoting the government's agenda in a reactionary state, in the self-interest of the ruling elites
2. In the case of interception of control over the AI, to broadcast a message from a terrorist organization or other antisocial non-state actor, for example
3. In the case of interception of control over the AI, to broadcast the ideas of a foreign state actor, for instance, on the eve of or during an invasion, in order to disorient the authorities and citizens
4. By obtaining superprofits through antisocial corporate structures, creating panic on the stock exchange, and so on (which may overlap with the first three options)

These uses will become especially dangerous with further improvements in AI, and particularly in emotion AI, predictive analytics, and a number of other areas.

The role of emotion AI in agenda setting is likely to increase. As indicated by the name, emotion AI is a combination of emotion and AI (Joshi, 2019). Emotion AI, or artificial emotional intelligence, deeply analyzes large sets of data and uses certain data characteristics to ascribe particular labels. The use of emotion AI will clearly enhance the ability of both state and non-state entities to conduct psychological operations at both the national (e.g., propaganda support for state policy) and international (e.g., interstate conflicts, competition by transnational corporations) levels. This is explained by the fact that strong emotional impact, rather than logic and rational thinking, is the key to successful manipulation; if antisocial actors can successfully exploit AI for emotional impact in real areas of the economy to the same extent that AI has already excelled in chess and the strategy board game Go, then the malicious use of emotion AI will probably become the main threat to political stability in the future. Emotion AI has already become very realistic, such as the lifelike digital human "Emma" unveiled by Ziva Dynamics in 2022 (Unity, 2022). Such achievements presage much more credible and convincing MUAI in agenda setting.

It cannot be ruled out that over time, the level of trust a target audience has in emotion AI will not only become higher than the average level of trust in a real person, but even higher than trust in society's most attractive, sympathetic, and admirable people. For a lonely or disabled person, this type of technology may initially be considered a great benefit. However, effectively replacing a person in communication with a narrow AI entity can hardly be considered a preferable alternative, one that will most likely not resolve any ongoing personal or medical issues but instead become an aggravator. Something else is even worse: strong antisocial actors can begin to take control of the agenda, not through traditional measures of influence (such as corrupt politicians, TV personalities, etc.), which require large investments, attention, and control from the actors themselves, and not even through virtual AI-enhanced avatars, but through hyper-addictive virtual, robotic emotion AI products.

Predictive analytics. This technology involves the use of data, statistical algorithms, and machine-learning techniques to identify the likelihood of future outcomes based on historical data. The goal is to go beyond knowing what has happened to provide a best assessment of what will happen in the future (SAS, 2021)—the Holy Grail of the finance sector, but potentially useful for terrorists, too. For example, the Intelligence Advanced Research Project Activity launched the Early Model-Based Event Recognition using Surrogates (EMBERS) program in 2012 to forecast socially significant population level events, such as incidents of civil unrest, disease outbreaks, and election outcomes. For civil unrest, EMBERS produces detailed forecasts of future events, including the date, location, type of event, and protesting population, along with any uncertainties. The system processes a range of data from open-source media, such as Twitter, to higher quality sources, such as economic indicators, processing about five million messages a day. The system delivers more than 50 predictions about civil unrest alone for 30 days ahead (Doyle et al., 2014). However, various state and non-state actors can potentially use this for MUAI. Such an opportunity in the wrong hands may be a kind of prognostic weapon (Pashentsev, 2016) that, following the receipt of data about future events, would allow correction of the future from the present in the interests of antisocial actors. For example, such a correction may radically increase the effectiveness of terrorist acts.

Poisoning the data. This can affect the virtual "personality" and direct the work of AI against society. The effects of learning algorithms depend to a large extent on the data on which the training is conducted. It may turn out that these data were incorrect and distorted, either by accident or by someone's malicious intent (in the latter case, this is called poisoning the data), which will affect the operation of the algorithm. AI technology supports decision-making in the areas of cybersecurity monitoring, public policy modelling, database anomalies, and waste and abuse identification. With biased data, AI systems will produce biased results. Cybersecurity will be more important than ever to protect against malicious actors that, by taking over AI systems, could do significant damage very quickly (Shark et al., 2020, p. 1). Poisoning data can encourage a drone to attack civilians, cause panic on the stock exchange as a result of false information from media bots, offend the audience of AI news anchors, and so on, thus influencing the agenda setting.

Synthetic products in agenda setting. One can imagine that, based on a combination of techniques of psychological impact, complex AI systems, and big data in the coming years, there will be synthetic information products that are similar in nature to modular malicious software. However, they will act not on inanimate objects such as social media resources but on humans (individuals and masses) as psychological and biophysical beings. Such a synthetic information product could contain software modules that introduce masses of people to depression. After the depression comes a latent period of suggestive programs. Appealing to habits, stereotypes, and even psychophysiology, such products could encourage people to perform strictly defined actions (Larina & Ovchinskiy, 2018, pp. 126–127).

A more specific and technically possible form of synthetic product in MUAI may be the synchronization of psychological multi-channel effects on large groups of people, especially dangerous in crisis situations—for example, transmitting via chatbots, using MUD and other MUAI technologies for the purpose of misinformation, which will encourage people to assume false interpretations and actions. When there is little time to make a decision, such misinformation can be successful. The more people get used to and trust their increasingly convenient, sophisticated, and emotionally attuned AI assistants, the more dangerous the sudden, precisely calculated professional use of the latter by antisocial actors will be.

The counteraction of MUAI in agenda setting is a complex problem, and society is only at the very beginning of forming its response to these new threats. Legislative measures are primarily related to malicious use of deepfakes (MUD) and facial recognition (e.g., in the United States) (Boyd, 2020; Center for Data Innovation, 2020), and other MUAI tools are not subject to independent review by national legislation.

In 2019, an expert committee established by China's Ministry of Science and Technology (MOST) released a document outlining eight principles for AI governance and "responsible AI." The first principle, entitled "Harmony and Friendliness," stated that AI development should conform to human values, ethics, and morality and should be based on the premise of safeguarding societal security, respecting human rights and avoid malicious application (MOST, 2019). However, neither this nor other publicly available state documents from the People's Republic of China contain a list of MUAI threats (including within the scope of agenda setting), and there are therefore no specific proposals to combat these threats.

In Russia, a decree by the Government of the Russian Federation on August 19, 2020, entitled "On the Approval of the Concept for the Development of Regulation of Relations in the Field of Artificial Intelligence and Robotics Technologies for the Period up to 2024," drew attention to the issue of preventing the manipulation of human behavior using AI (Government of the Russian Federation, 2020), but the specific threats from MUAI in the psychological sphere and ways of neutralizing these were not formulated. This means that the adoption of complex international legal norms to mitigate the threats from MUAI in terms of agenda setting is unlikely in the near future, although current work in the legal field is certainly important.

Technical measures for countering the malicious use of AI naturally include the use of AI technology. There are then mutual improvements in the offensive and defensive combat capabilities of AI, and this is a strategic path to nowhere, in the same way as any arms race that brings considerable profits to the military-industrial complex but conceals the growing risk of destroying human civilization.

A general solution to the problems of AI security and the effective neutralization of MUAI is possible only through the establishment of a more harmonious, socially oriented system and the comprehensive development of the individual, not least through the development and implementation of socially oriented AI. Without social progress, MUAI will not only grow in quantity and quality, but will become an important tool for societal regression, and even for supporting dictatorships and destructive wars. In terms of agenda setting, it can equip antisocial actors with a much more effective means of maintaining control over populations than at any time in history.

Big Tech and Agenda Setting

This section is largely based on the author's conclusion from "Experts on the Malicious Use of Artificial Intelligence and Challenges to International Psychological Security" (Pashentsev, 2021), published in early December 2021. The forecasts and conclusions made then were largely confirmed, giving grounds for subsequent conclusions.

Psychological security threats posed by MUAI can exist in pure forms (misinforming citizens about the nature of AI without malicious use, using AI-enhanced drones (Capelle & Vogt, 2022) to attack against critical infrastructure, etc.) as well as combined forms. For example, overestimating the effectiveness of current AI technologies, or forming expectations about certain highly favorable results from the implementation of AI technologies or any products based on those technologies, would be considered a first-level attack with communicative effect, such as a speculative boom in the stock market. However, if the perpetrators were to accompany their actions with physical attacks on critical infrastructure or people, or a widespread, malicious psychological campaign using different AI tools, the threat would become a combined attack.

Given the extreme tensions in the world today, it seems that particular attention should be given to the first level of psychological security threat from MUAI regarding agenda setting, in combination with successive levels, because this is where disturbing trends are being observed. The largest companies in the high-tech industry actively use AI to serve narrow corporate interests, which frequently go against the interests of society at large. It is clear that companies with access to large amounts of data to power AI models are leading AI development, including the Big Five—Google (Alphabet), Apple, Facebook (Meta), Amazon, and Microsoft, also known by the acronym GAFAM—the five largest, most dominant, and most prestigious companies in the industry in the United States, the leading internet and software companies in China—Baidu, Alibaba, and Tencent (BAT), early mover IBM, and hardware giants Intel and NVIDIA (Lee, 2021).

It is hardly accidental that among the world's ten richest individuals, six are from the US high-tech industry: one with Amazon, one with Facebook, two with Microsoft, and two with Google (Forbes, 2021). The combined market capitalization of GAFAM at the end of 2020 was an eye-popping 7.5 trillion US dollars, according to an analysis by the *Wall Street Journal*. At the end of 2019, the combined market capitalization of these firms was 4.9 trillion US dollars, which means their value increased by 52 percent in a single year. As of November 12, 2021, the capitalization of these companies grew by another 2.5 trillion, reaching approximately 10 trillion US dollars (Statista, 2021). That amount is nearly a quarter of the combined 41.8 trillion US dollar market capitalization of all companies in the S&P 500 (La Monica, 2021). It is appropriate to recall that the United States' nominal GDP in 2020 was around 21 trillion US dollars; Japan, the world's third-largest economy, reported a GDP of about 5 trillion US dollars, and Russia only about 1.5 trillion US dollars.

However, the consolidation of these individuals at the very top in terms of assets coincided with a reputational decline for many of those companies.

The 2021 Edelman Trust Barometer, an annual survey conducted by the global public relations firm Edelman for more than two decades, shows this clearly. Although technology has long been the most trusted industry, public confidence in the sector has plummeted more than in any other over the past ten years. In 2012, 77 percent of survey respondents expressed trust in tech companies to "do what is right"; the results from the 2021 survey show a drop to 68 percent, a percentage decline three times greater than for any other industry in the study (Shabir, 2021). Three of the Big Five companies—Google, Amazon, and Microsoft—have also been dropping in the Global RepTrak 100® rankings. Facebook did not even appear in the 2020–2021 rankings, while Apple managed to show decent improvement. Apple's gain was overshadowed, however, by Amazon plummeting 50 places from 42nd in 2020 to 92nd in 2021 (Abdulla, 2021).

Four Big Five CEOs testified before the US House Subcommittee on Antitrust, Commercial and Administrative Law in an antitrust hearing on July 29, 2020. Amazon founder and CEO Jeff Bezos, Facebook founder and CEO Mark Zuckerberg, Apple CEO Tim Cook, and Alphabet and Google CEO Sundar Pichai defended their companies against accusations of anti-competitive practices (Rev, 2020). Former Facebook product manager Frances Haugen testified before the US Senate on October 5, 2021, that the company's social media platforms "harm children, stoke division and weaken our democracy" (Menczer, 2021), and that Facebook did not use AI technologies ethically. "Right now, Facebook is closing the door on us being able to act. We have a slight window of time to regain people control over AI" (Browne & Shead, 2021). In November 2021, a new bipartisan Senate bill aimed at restricting "anticompetitive" acquisition by tech companies was introduced by Senators Amy Klobuchar (D-MN) and Tom Cotton (R-AR), which would greatly limit the ability of Big Five companies to acquire other tech companies.

GAFAM has been accused by the EU of evading taxes, stifling competition, stealing media content, and threatening democracy through the spread of fake news. An EU court rejected a Google appeal against a 2.4 billion euro (2.8 billion US dollar) antitrust fine in November 2021. Amazon was fined 746 million euros in July 2021 by Luxembourg authorities for flouting the EU's data protection rules. France also fined Google and Amazon a total of 135 million euros for breaking rules on the use of cookies. The European Parliament and EU member states agreed to force platforms to remove terrorist content, and to do so within one hour of the content being flagged. EU rules now also forbid the use of algorithms to spread false information and hate speech, which some major platforms are suspected of doing to increase advertising revenue (AFP, 2021).

The Chinese government strengthened regulation of the country's technology companies in 2021. More than one trillion US dollars was wiped off the collective market capitalization of some of China's largest internet groups, such as gaming and social media giant Tencent and Alibaba, China's e-commerce powerhouse (He, 2021). In August 2021, the Cyberspace Administration of China announced draft regulations to stop algorithms that encourage users to spend large amounts of money, or to spend money in ways that "may disrupt public order" (Frater, 2021).

In Russia, the state communications regulator Roskomnadzor demanded in November 2021 that 13 foreign (mostly US-based) technology companies open representative offices in Russia by the end of 2021, or face possible restrictions or outright bans. In 2021 Russia fined social media giants Google, Facebook, Twitter, and TikTok, as well as the messaging app Telegram, for failing to delete content the country deems illegal. Apple, which Russia has targeted for alleged abuse of its dominant position in the mobile applications market, was also on the list. Roskomnadzor warned that firms in violation of the legislation could face advertising, data collection and money transfer restrictions, or outright bans (Marrow & Stolyarov, 2021).

Authorities in Russia also want to force major foreign streaming services, like YouTube, to pay local operators for using their traffic. This proposal was put forward in 2021 by the Ministry of Digital Development, Communications and Mass Media. If the proposal is accepted, it will serve as a new barrier for foreign internet giants. The Ministry justified its position by pointing out that national operators are being placed in a difficult position due to the overloading of Russian networks. This has prompted authorities to take measures to force foreign companies to finance, to some extent, the development of Russia's communications infrastructure (Tsargrad, 2021). Russian authorities have been trying to use regulation of foreign internet services as an instrument of influence for at least the past six years, but decisive action was only taken at the end of 2020. At that time, a number of laws were passed that increased the responsibility of private companies. For example, amendments to the law "On measures to influence persons involved in violations of fundamental human rights and freedoms, the rights and freedoms of citizens of the Russian Federation" gave Roskomnadzor the right—by decision of the Prosecutor General's Office—to slow down network service not only for security threats, but also to restrict access to "socially important information." When the law went into effect on February 1, 2021, the social platforms also became obliged to identify and block illegal content; so far, sanctions are not involved. The authorities first forced a slowdown in traffic within the framework of the law "on the sovereign Internet" in March 2021, identifying Twitter as a security threat for providing access to information that is prohibited in Russia (Shestopyorov & Lebedeva, 2021).

Restrictive measures such as these are being implemented in many countries. In the context of psychological security and MUAI, these measures are

6 The Malicious Use of Artificial Intelligence Through Agenda Setting

related to the use of AI technologies, which indicates either an unintentional or intentional disregard for the interests of the public on behalf of the biggest high-tech companies. At any rate, it is too soon to tell whether these measures in different countries are sufficient to prevent negative antisocial phenomena from the new technical—primarily AI-based—and financial capabilities of high-tech companies.

Elon Musk's electric car giant Tesla can rightfully be included in the arena of Big Tech. The company on October 25, 2021, passed the 1 trillion US dollar mark in market capitalization (Thomas, 2021). Musk's net worth reached a record high of 305 billion US dollars on November 22, 2021, making him the richest man on the planet (Forbes, 2021), with greater market value than ExxonMobil Corporation or Nike, Inc. As of September 2022 Tesla has a market cap of 840.62 billion dollars. That confirms Tesla the world's sixth most valuable company by market cap (CompaniesMarketCap.com, 2022). Tesla's success is based primarily on the widespread development and application of AI. As stated on Tesla's official website, "We develop and deploy autonomy at scale in vehicles, robots and more. We believe that an approach based on advanced AI for vision and planning, supported by efficient use of inference hardware, is the only way to achieve a general solution for full self-driving and beyond" (Tesla, 2021). However, there are outstanding questions as to what extent the AI technologies in Musk's projects (Tesla, Neuralink, etc.), as well as in Big Tech projects in general, will serve society rather than financial elites. Or, the extent to which AI technologies will be publicly available, such as in medicine. Perhaps the Big Tech boom based on AI and other technologies will be successful and sustainable, but a significant question related to that success is whether it will unite, rather than destroy, humanity if decisions continue to be made within the framework of a modern socioeconomic model, without a clear vision of the goals or means of moving toward a more progressive dynamic and socially oriented model. So far, assessments of the effects of the COVID-19 pandemic suggest that there is no alternative to transitioning to new technologies. However, this transition promises to be extremely socially unbalanced, with a disproportionate amount of material dividends going to a tiny minority, and for the overwhelming majority of the population, mostly promises for a better life.

Furthermore, there are undoubtedly concerns about the extent to which the rapid growth of Big Tech as a whole is contributing to a huge financial bubble based on inflated expectations for highly promising—and extremely important—technologies for humanity. In November 2021, this author predicted, along with some other researchers (Buiter, 2021), "In the near future, a crushing financial and economic crisis can follow, which will further enrich the few and ruin hundreds if not billions of people around the world" (Pashentsev, 2021, p. 48).

While billions of people have not been affected yet, the potential for widespread crisis is evident. In April 2022, some 81 percent of Americans said that they think the US economy is likely to experience a recession in 2022, according to a CNBC + Acorns Invest in You survey conducted by Momentive (Reinicke, 2022). In June 2022, economist Peter Schiff warned that the United States is facing an economic crisis worse than the 2007–2009 Great Recession following a government report of a 1.6 percent decrease in real GDP during the first quarter of 2022. The drop in GDP is being linked to decreases in exports, federal government spending, private inventory investment, and state and local government spending (Mordowanec, 2022). According to Edward Alden, who is a Bernard L. Schwartz senior fellow at the Council on Foreign Relations (CFR), "The current concatenation of problems—the Russia-Ukraine war, inflation, global food and energy shortages, unwinding asset bubbles in the United States, debt crises in developing countries, and the lingering impacts of COVID-19-related shutdowns and supply chain bottlenecks—may be the most serious crisis of them all, not least because central banks can't print wheat and gasoline. Yet there are few signs of the collective responses that will be needed to meet these challenges. Global cooperation has never been more urgent—and seemed less likely" (Alden, 2022).

According to reporting from the *Bangkok Post*, Big Tech companies amassed property holdings during the COVID-19 pandemic and are now "…sitting on record piles of cash. They are getting paid next to nothing for holding it, and they are running out of ways to spend it" (2021). For example, Alphabet Inc., Google's parent company, was holding 135.9 billion US dollars in cash, cash equivalents, and short-term investments as of the second quarter of 2021—more than any other publicly traded company apart from financial and real-estate firms—according to S&P Global. Alphabet is now one of the biggest real-estate holders in the United States at 49.7 billion US dollars' worth of land and buildings as of 2020, up from 5.2 billion US dollars in 2011. Amazon, which owns many warehouses, held 57.3 billion US dollars' worth of land and buildings—more than any other US public company except Walmart (Bangkok Post, 2021). It is notable that the European Central Bank warned in November 2021 of bubbles in the property and financial markets (The Liberty Beacon, 2021).

This author wrote in early December 2021: "Unfortunately, if this negative crisis scenario turns out to be true, is not the rapid deterioration of the international situation the natural evolution, fraught with, if not a world war, a very large military provocation? Will it not become a necessary trigger for the collapse of the markets? The 'culprit/guilty party' will, of course, be found where it is necessary, since the world's main information resources are, dangerously, controlled by and subordinated to the interests of global corporate structures" (Pashentsev, 2021, p. 49). So, it seems as if this has happened. Russia has been convincingly presented to the world as the guilty party with media headlines such as "Russian Brutality Worse Than Nazi Occupation in Ukraine" (Colarossi, 2022). Russia, in view of the many years of NATO's advance to the East, after the coup d'état in Ukraine supported by the leaders of the EU and NATO in 2014 with the leading military role of extreme nationalists and neo-fascists, Kyiv's failure to comply with the Minsk peace agreements, massive shelling by Ukrainian troops of cities and villages of Donbass, which led to the death of thousands of civilians, an unsuccessful attempt to find a peaceful compromise with Washington and NATO, undertaken in December 2021–January 2022, had to respond to these threats militarily. And then, of course, Russia, the socially far from ideal state, began to be deliberately presented by the leading social platforms as the embodiment of absolute evil.

Even calls for the assassination of presidents have become acceptable. In emails to Meta's content moderators, Reuters alleged that the company was "also temporarily allowing some posts that call for death to Russian President Vladimir Putin or Belarusian President Alexander Lukashenko in countries including Russia, Ukraine and Poland" (Wulfsohn, 2022). Meta later provided an updated statement, telling Fox News Digital, "In light of the ongoing invasion of Ukraine, we made a temporary exception for those affected by war, to express violent sentiments toward invading armed forces such as 'death to the Russian invaders.' These are temporary measures designed to preserve voice and expression for people who are facing invasion. As always, we are prohibiting calls for violence against Russians outside of the narrow context of the current invasion" (Wulfsohn, 2022). The United Nations condemned Meta's allowance of hateful remarks and calls for violence against certain Russians, with Stephane Dujarric, the spokesperson for UN Secretary-General Antonio Guterres, stating that the international body does not condone such statements from any party. "We stand clearly against all hate speech, all calls for violence. That kind of language is just unacceptable from whichever quarter it comes from," Dujarric said during a news briefing on March 11 (RT, 2022).

A "cold hot war" was started in 2022, with significant differences from the classic perception of the Cold War. Within the framework of the old Cold War, military confrontation between the two superpowers because of the risk of mutual destruction in a nuclear war was primarily indirect. Proxy conflicts emerged between the respective allies of the Soviet Union and the United States when there was an intersection of interests in various regions of the world, but never at the physical borders of the two blocs. Consequently, these conflicts never became an immediate and existential threat to the survival of the two superpowers, as they never had the power or intensity to engage in direct conflict (Crosston & Pashentsev, 2022).

An extremely dangerous situation has developed today from the role technology companies have taken on. In addition to the sanctions imposed by national governments on Russia, tech firms have emerged as extra geopolitical actors capable of actively punishing a global power for a military campaign (Verdict, 2022). To demonstrate support for Ukraine, tech vendors are suspending business in Russia and the number is growing, including Accenture, Adobe, Cisco, Oracle, Dell, IBM, Microsoft, and many others (Verdict, 2022; Petrova, 2022). This has, of course, caused serious damage to the Russian IT sector and the economy as a whole, but has also negatively affected the companies that have withdrawn from the Russian market.

The first three months of 2022 turned out to be difficult for US Big Tech companies, which rely heavily on digital advertising. Surging inflation, Ukrainian crisis, and other unfavorable macro factors forced advertisers to slash marketing budgets, which translated into lower profits for platforms like YouTube, Google, and Facebook (Cao, 2022). The war has shattered the myth of neutrality. For most of their existence, internet companies have argued that they are only neutral, content distribution platforms—they are not responsible for the content that is distributed (Feldstein, 2022).

Having dispensed with the veneer of neutrality, and even after suffering significant losses, Big Tech has actually gained quite a bit.

First, this is to prevent an international confrontation between nation states and the general public on the one hand and Big Tech on the other. Such a confrontation could have emerged simply from the fact that Big Tech is taking on state and non-state actors that have very different aspirations. However, now and in the near future, Big Tech might not be afraid of political initiatives or international collations that might emerge from the United Nations or other international bodies to limit its independence.

Second, Big Tech has shown that it is a powerful tool for confronting Russia in cyberspace. Brad Smith, president and vice chair of Microsoft, writes in no uncertain terms about the role of his company in the situation in Ukraine. He notes that "Ukraine's government has successfully sustained its civil and military operations by acting quickly to disburse its digital infrastructure into the public cloud, where it has been hosted in data centers across Europe. This has involved urgent and extraordinary steps from across the tech sector, including by Microsoft. While the tech sector's work has been vital, it's also important to think about the longer-lasting lessons that come from these efforts" (Microsoft, 2022). General Paul Nakasone, director of the National Security Agency, confirmed for Sky News in June 2022 for the first time, the United States was conducting offensive hacking operations in support of Ukraine: "We've conducted a series of operations across the full spectrum; offensive, defensive, [and] information operations" (Martin, 2022). Such operations are impossible without support from Big Tech. Therefore, high-tech agenda setting in the United States, which today is unthinkable without the full use of AI technologies, has turned out to be openly subordinated to military-political interests and the waging of psychological warfare.

Third, a resource that is an unqualified necessity for the protection of national security, and that is already actively being used involved in war, cannot a priori be antinational, which reduces the democratic public's ability to criticize Big Tech.

Fourth, any US government will need information and analytical support during the "Cold Hot War," and Big Tech can provide this support based on developments in the field of AI. More than that, the support against the "internal" enemies and their "disinformation." More than 50 officials in President Joe Biden's administration across a dozen agencies have been involved with efforts to pressure Big Tech companies to crack down on alleged misinformation, according to documents released on August 31, 2022. The documents were part of a preliminary production in a lawsuit levied against the government by the attorneys general of Missouri and Louisiana, later joined by experts maligned by federal officials. "When the federal government colludes with Big Tech to censor speech, the American people become subjects rather than citizens," Louisiana Attorney General Jeff Landry, a Republican, said in a statement (Stieber, 2022).

Fifth, Big Tech's close cooperation with the military-industrial complex during the new Cold War can fully compensate for losses from leaving the Russian market. Fourth, under Cold War conditions, it is easier to avoid public scrutiny and possible scandals from promising developments that can carry great risks for humanity, along with great profits.

In the United States, due to the size of the economy, military allocations exceed the spending of the next nine largest economies combined (PGPF, 2022). Combined with the global role of digital platforms, the level of AI technology development, and negative sociopolitical trends that threaten civil war (Marche, 2022; Pashentsev, 2022; Walter, 2022), the transformation of agenda setting into a tool of psychological warfare is the most obvious outcome. Unfortunately, similar processes are developing with varying intensity in other countries as well. However, the militarization of agenda setting and its "legalization" as a tool of psychological warfare is unlikely to be applied to the social needs of humanity; on the contrary, these developments push those needs into the background even more.

Big Tech has accumulated, in a contradictory way, scientific and technical power, intellectual resources that are necessary for everyone, and impressive financial opportunities that contribute to economic expansionism. These are all part of the tools of global governance, as well as a growing and more obvious involvement in a geopolitical struggle with an end that has not yet been formed by independent interests. The system-forming elements of global communications and development, such as the current leading digital platforms, cannot be eliminated, but it is certainly necessary to put them under more effective international control to reduce the possibility of their technological potential being used for antisocial purposes. However, only united, socially oriented actors can control these elements, and these actors can only partially include modern states, leading corporate structures, and political parties, opening the door to further MUAI in the agenda-setting context.

MUAI in agenda setting exists on a global scale as a game, based on inflated benefit expectations from adopting AI. This game is played by wielding a versatile psychological impact on target audiences that are particularly susceptible and vulnerable to perception management in a crisis situation. It is worth asking, who holds the most advanced tools of global psychological influence, and whose financial interests are at stake? There is not only enough objective data to answer these questions, there is an abundance. Therefore, specific scenarios of combined, targeted impact—not only including particular AI technologies, but also perceptions of AI—on the public consciousness for the purpose of speculative enrichment, as well as the destabilization of public order, require serious attention and comprehensive study by specialists from different countries, with different scientific specializations.

Under conditions of continuous and acute economic problems, the impoverishment of hundreds of millions of people, the rapid concentration of wealth in the hands of the very few, a global arms race and acute geopolitical tensions, MUAI against psychological security, conducted by a variety of antisocial actors, can play an extremely negative and dangerous role in the very important area of agenda setting. This is why all countries, but especially those with leading scientific and technical potential, can and should cooperate to prevent the use of information technologies based increasingly on new AI capabilities by antisocial actors. On November 3, 2021, without calling for a vote, the United Nations General Assembly First Committee adopted a draft

Russian–US resolution on the rules of behavior in cyberspace. This is a good example of the possibilities of such cooperation.

Meanwhile, it is clearly insufficient and ineffective to resist increasingly successful MUAI in agenda setting in a society where the influence of antisocial actors is growing via separate, unrelated decisions of a political, legal, and technical nature. Under these conditions, existing countermeasures are nothing more than a palliative, at best buying some time and at worst, providing a cover for systemic deterioration.

Conclusion

New threats to agenda setting are emerging from the advantages of both offensive and defensive psychological operations using AI. These advantages—as well as threats—are increasingly associated with quantitative and qualitative differences between traditional mechanisms of producing, delivering, and managing information, new possibilities for creating psychological impacts on people, and the waging of psychological warfare. In particular, these advantages may include:

1. The amount of information that can be generated to destabilize an adversary
2. The speed of generation and dissemination of information
3. New opportunities for obtaining and processing data
4. The application of predictive analytics using AI
5. New decision-making process opportunities from big data analysis with the help of AI
6. New ways to educate people with intelligent systems
7. The perceived credibility of generated (dis-)information
8. The strength of the intellectual and emotional impact of generated information on target audiences
9. A qualitatively higher level of thinking in the future through the creation of general and strong AI, as well as through the further development of human cyborgization

Based on a qualitative assessment of data from open primary and secondary sources, it can be concluded that advantages 1–6 have already been achieved and continue to grow in a number of important aspects—though not in all—qualitatively exceeding human capabilities without AI. At the same time, all the possibilities of narrow (weak) AI are still generally under human control. Advantages 7–8 have not yet been practically implemented; this does not exclude recent achievements in the formation of these advantages, such as credibility and emotional persuasiveness (see, e.g., Unity, 2022), but they can be achieved through the quantitative and qualitative improvement of existing technologies in the foreseeable future. The future benefit of number 9 requires fundamental scientific breakthroughs and new technological solutions. This list of benefits from using AI in psychological warfare is not exhaustive and is highly variable.

MUAI in the infosphere can be used as a tool of control by antisocial power groups, in a struggle for leadership between competing factions of such groups, as a means of interstate influence and pressure in the international arena by antisocial power groups, as a means of competitive struggle between antisocial corporate interest groups (e.g., by certain transnational corporations defending goals that are contrary to public interests), as well as a tool for achieving antisocial goals of various kinds by criminal organizations. However, the above MUAI variants and their various combinations only emphasize the importance of the skillful use of AI technologies by socially oriented forces not just at the state level, but throughout civil society, in order to neutralize psychological security threats.

At the same time, it is necessary to establish a principal difference between military use of AI for social purposes, such as protecting the country from external aggression or from the actions of criminals, and military use for antisocial purposes, such as use by an aggressive state in the interests of ruling antisocial groups, terrorists, and so on.

From the perspective of national interests and global security, it may also make sense to limit the role of US Big Tech as the leading facilitator of the world's information flows. AI can play an innovative and positive role here, if applied appropriately. Perhaps it is worth discussing the idea of creating a communication network among the countries of Brazil, Russia, India, China, and South Africa in the future, built on intelligent text recognition, with the ability to almost instantaneously translate messages into the language of the addressee at a high level of quality. May be the United Nations can ultimately run such a system globally, dramatically increasing the level and quality of interaction between different cultures and countries, reducing the possibility of agenda manipulation at the global level, and increasing the ability to train AI. In the context of the global information space, building up efforts in this area will bring undisputed benefits to all nations.

Personal, group, national, and international levels of psychological security will be determined by an adequate level of effective AI technology use for the protection of people from destructive influences commensurate with the growing capabilities of society. The harmonious association of well-developed individuals, as well as comprehensive human development through new opportunities, including symbiotic forms of interaction with AI, is a prerequisite for reliable psychological security in the future.

The rapid development of AI technologies, their relative cost effectiveness and accessibility to an increasingly wide range of users, the growth of crisis phenomena in the modern world, the high level of geopolitical rivalry that is turning into dangerous confrontations, the direct influence of antisocial forces on information flows in individual countries and at the global level—all of these and other factors actualize the urgency for developing international cooperation to prevent and neutralize MUAI in agenda setting.

References

Abdulla, N. (2021). Only one of big tech's big five comes out unscathed in RepTrak's 2021 global reputation rankings. In *Trust signals*. Retrieved July 15, 2022, from https://www.trustsignals.com/blog/big-tech-plummets-in-reptrak-100

AFP. (2021). Europe's battle to curb Big Tech. In *France 24*. Retrieved July 15, 2022, from https://www.france24.com/en/live-news/20211110-europe-s-battle-to-curb-big-tech

Alden, E. (2022). Why this global economic crisis is different. In *Council on foreign relations*. Retrieved July 15, 2022, from https://www.cfr.org/article/why-global-economic-crisis-different

Antunes, J. (2019). AI in broadcasting: Optimizing production and distribution of content. In *ProVideo coalition*. Retrieved July 15, 2022, from https://www.provideocoalition.com/ai-in-broadcasting-optimizing-production-and-distribution-of-content/

Argent, D. (2018). Lots of bots: 5 types of robots that are running the Internet | IT briefcase. In *IT Briefcase*. Retrieved July 14, 2022, from https://www.itbriefcase.net/lots-of-bots-5-types-of-robots-that-are-running-the-internet

Bangkok Post. (2021). Big tech companies amass property holdings during covid-19 pandemic. In *Bangkok Post*. Retrieved July 15, 2022, from https://www.bangkokpost.com/business/2189935/big-tech-companies-amass-property-holdings-during-covid-19-pandemic

Banik, R. (2018). *Hands-on recommendation systems with Python: Start building powerful and personalized, recommendation engines with Python*. PACKT Publishing Limited.

BBC News. (2017). Google to 'derank' Russia Today and Sputnik. In *BBC News*. Retrieved July 15, 2022, from https://www.bbc.com/news/technology-42065644

Beckett, C. (2019). *New powers, new responsibilities: A global survey of journalism and artificial intelligence*. London School of Economics.

Botnerds. (2022). Types of bots: An overview of chatbot diversity. In *Botnerds*. Retrieved July 14, 2022, from http://botnerds.com/types-of-bots/

Boyd, A. (2020). Lawmakers working on legislation to 'Pause' use of facial recognition technology. In *Nextgov*. Retrieved July 15, 2022, from https://www.nextgov.com/emerging-tech/2020/01/lawmakers-working-legislation-pause-use-facial-recognition-technology/162470/

Bradshaw, S., & Howard, P. (2019). *The global disinformation disorder: 2019 Global inventory of organised social media manipulation*. Working Paper 2019.2. Project on Computational Propaganda, .

Browne, R., & Shead, S. (2021). 'Facebook is closing the door on us being able to act,' whistleblower says in UK hearing. In *CNBC*. Retrieved July 15, 2022, from https://www.cnbc.com/2021/10/25/facebook-whistleblower-frances-haugen-testifies-in-uk-parliament.html

Brundage, M., Avin, S., Clark, J., Toner, H., Eckersley, P., Garfinkel, B., Dafoe, A., Scharre, P., Zeitzoff, T., Filar, B., Anderson, H., Roff, H., Allen, G., Steinhardt, J., Flynn, C., Ó HÉigeartaigh, S., Beard, S., Belfield, H., Farquhar, S., et al. (2018). *The malicious use of artificial intelligence: Forecasting, prevention, and mitigation*. Future of Humanity Institute, University of Oxford.

Buiter, W. (2021). The next financial crisis is fast approaching. In *MarketWatch*. Retrieved July 15, 2022, from https://www.marketwatch.com/story/the-next-financial-crisis-is-fast-approaching-11633447555

Cancel, D., & Gerhardt, D. (2019). *Conversational marketing: How the world's fastest growing companies use chatbots to generate leads 24/7/365 (and how you can too)*. Wiley.

Cao, S. (2022). Inflation and the war in Ukraine take a toll on big tech companies that rely on advertising. In *Observer*. Retrieved July 15, 2022, from https://observer.com/2022/04/google-meta-microsoft-tech-earning-inflation-russia-war/

Capelle, D., & Vogt, A. (2022). AI-enhanced drones—In Brief analysis—Worldwide. In *Sitsi*. Retrieved July 15, 2022, from https://www.sitsi.com/ai-enhanced-drones-inbrief-analysis-worldwide

Center for Data Innovation. (2020). AI legislation tracker—United States. In *Center for Data Innovation*. Retrieved July 15, 2022, from https://datainnovation.org/ai-policy-leadership/ai-legislation-tracker/

Chandler, S. (2018). The evolution of evil chatbots is just around the corner. In *The Daily Dot*. Retrieved July 15, 2022, from https://www.dailydot.com/debug/evil-chatbot-hackers-ai/

Chereshnev, E. (2016). I, for one, welcome our new chatbot overlords. In *Kaspersky Daily*. Retrieved July 14, 2022, from https://www.kaspersky.com/blog/dangerous-chatbot/12847/

Christin, A. (2020). *Metrics at work: Journalism and the contested meaning of algorithms*. Princeton University Press.

Cloudflare. (2022a). How to manage good bots. Good bots vs. bad bots. In *Cloudflare*. Retrieved July 14, 2022, from https://www.cloudflare.com/learning/bots/how-to-manage-good-bots/

Cloudflare. (2022b). What is a social media bot? Social media bot definition. In *Cloudflare*. Retrieved July 14, 2022, from https://www.cloudflare.com/learning/bots/what-is-a-social-media-bot/

Coeckelbergh, M. (2020). *AI ethics*. MIT Press.

Colarossi, N. (2022). Russian brutality worse than Nazi occupation in Ukraine, Zelensky says. In *Newsweek*. Retrieved July 15, 2022, from https://www.newsweek.com/russian-brutality-worse-nazi-occupation-ukraine-zelensky-says-1695238

CompaniesMarketCap.com. (2022). Tesla (TSLA)—Market capitalization. In Companiesmarketcap.com. Retrieved September 8, 2022, from https://companiesmarketcap.com/tesla/marketcap/

Crosston, M., & Pashentsev, E. (2022). Russian security cannot be anti-Russian. In *Russian International Affairs Council (RIAC)*. Retrieved July 15, 2022, from https://russiancouncil.ru/en/analytics-and-comments/analytics/russian-security-cannot-be-anti-russian/?sphrase_id=89733461

Daian, P., Goldfeder, S., Kell, T., Li, Y., Zhao, X., Bentov, I., Breidenbach, L., & Juels, A. (2019). Flash Boys 2.0: Frontrunning, transaction reordering, and consensus instability in decentralized exchanges. In arXiv.org. Retrieved July 15, 2022, from https://arxiv.org/abs/1904.05234

Davenport, E. (2020). City shooting incidents continue to skyrocket throughout the city, reaching 166% increase last month. In *amNewYork*. Retrieved July 15, 2022, from https://www.amny.com/police-fire/city-shooting-incidents-continue-to-skyrocket-throughout-the-city-reaching-166-increase-last-month/

Davis, M. (2018). Why are Yahoo's comment sections always filled with hatred and bigotry?—Affinity Magazine. In *Affinity Magazine*. Retrieved July 15, 2022, from http://affinitymagazine.us/2018/01/05/why-yahoos-comment-sections-are-filled-with-hatred-and-bigotry/

Diakopoulos, N. (2019). *Automating the news: How algorithms are rewriting the media*. Harvard University Press.

Doctorow, C. (2018). The Russian equivalent to Alexa is a 'good girl' but not too friendly, and is totally OK with wife-beating. In *Boing Boing*. Retrieved July 14, 2022, from https://boingboing.net/2018/07/28/emotional-socialism.html

Doyle, A., Katz, G., Summers, K., Ackermann, C., Zavorin, I., Lim, Z., Muthiah, S., Butler, P., Self, N., Zhao, L., Lu, C., Khandpur, R., Fayed, Y., & Ramakrishnan, N. (2014). Forecasting significant societal events using the embers streaming predictive analytics system. *Big Data, 2*, 185–195. https://doi.org/10.1089/big.2014.0046

Elharrar, J. (2017). 7 types of bots. In *Medium*. Retrieved July 14, 2022, from https://chatbotsmagazine.com/7-types-of-bots-8e1846535698?gi=18e2f37d0ef1

Feldstein, S. (2022). 4 reasons why Putin's war has changed big tech forever. In *Foreign Policy*. Retrieved July 15, 2022, from https://foreignpolicy.com/2022/03/29/ukraine-war-russia-putin-big-tech-social-media-internet-platforms/

Ferrara, E., Varol, O., Davis, C., Menczer, F., & Flammini, A. (2016). The rise of social bots. *Communications of the ACM, 59,* 96–104. https://doi.org/10.1145/2818717

Forbes. (2021). The world's real-time billionaires. In *Forbes*. Retrieved July 15, 2022, from https://www.forbes.com/real-time-billionaires/#6f73dfb3d788

Frater, P. (2021). Celebrities disappear from internet as China moves against fan culture. In *Variety*. Retrieved July 15, 2022, from https://variety.com/2021/digital/asia/china-celebrities-disappear-internet-fan-culture-crackdown-1235050381/

Freitas, C., Benevenuto, F., Ghosh, S., & Veloso, A. (2014). Reverse engineering socialbot infiltration strategies in Twitter. In arXiv.org. Retrieved July 14, 2022, from https://arxiv.org/abs/1405.4927

Galitsky, B. (2019). *Developing enterprise chatbots: Learning linguistic structures*. Springer.

Gao, G., Galley, M., & Li, L. (2019). *Neural approaches to conversational AI: Question answering, task-oriented dialogues and social chatbots (Foundations and Trends(r) in Information Retrieval)*. Now Publishers Inc..

Glock, S. (2022). Conversational AI in 2022: A look ahead. In Cognigy. Retrieved July 14, 2022, from https://www.cognigy.com/blog/conversational-ai-in-2022-a-look-ahead

González Mendelejis, N. (2018). Artificial intelligence and the rise of the bots. In *The National Interest*. Retrieved July 15, 2022, from https://nationalinterest.org/feature/artificial-intelligence-the-rise-the-bots-24842

Government of the Russian Federation. (2020). Decree No. 2129-r of August 19, 2020 on the approval of the concept for the development of regulation of relations in the field of artificial intelligence and robotics technologies for the period up to 2024. In *Garant*. Retrieved July 15, 2022, from https://www.garant.ru/products/ipo/prime/doc/74460628/

Haptik. (2022). Conversational AI chatbot: Key differentiators, insights & examples. In *Haptik*. Retrieved July 14, 2022, from https://www.haptik.ai/blog/conversational-ai-chatbot

He, L. (2021). China's 'unprecedented' crackdown stunned private enterprise. One year on, it may have to cut business some slack. In *CNN*. Retrieved July 15, 2022, from https://edition.cnn.com/2021/11/02/tech/china-economy-crackdown-private-companies-intl-hnk/index.html

Heath, J. (2010). *Hit list*. Pan Macmillan Australia.

Horowitz, M. C., Allen, G. C., Saravalle, E., Cho, A., Frederick, K., & Scharre, P. (2018). *Artificial intelligence and international security*. Center for a New American Security (CNAS).

HT Tech. (2020). Facebook's army of malicious bots are being trained to research anti-spam methods. In *HT Tech*. Retrieved July 15, 2022, from https://tech.hindustantimes.com/tech/news/facebook-s-army-of-malicious-bots-are-being-trained-to-research-anti-spam-methods-71595571825228.html

Interfax. (2017). Putin podpisal zakon ob ugolovnoj otvetstvennosti za sozdanie 'grupp smerti' (Putin signed a law on criminal liability for the creation of 'death groups'). In *Interfax*. Retrieved July 15, 2022, from https://www.interfax.ru/russia/565686

Jannach, D., Zanker, M., Felfering, A., & Friedrich, G. (2010). *Recommender systems: An introduction*. Cambridge University Press.

Jerry@Rocketbots.io. (2017). China, WeChat, and the origins of chatbots. In *Medium*. Retrieved July 14, 2022, from https://chatbotsmagazine.com/china-wechat-and-the-origins-of-chatbots-89c481f15a44

Johnson, L. (2018). Automated cyber attacks are the next big threat. Ever hear of 'Review Bombing'? In *Entrepreneur*. Retrieved July 15, 2022, from https://www.entrepreneur.com/article/325142

Joshi, N. (2019). Artificial emotional intelligence: The future of AI. In *Experfy Insights*. Retrieved July 15, 2022, from https://www.experfy.com/blog/artificial-emotional-intelligence-the-future-of-ai/

Kannan, P., & Bernoff, J. (2019). *The age of intent: Using artificial intelligence to deliver a superior customer experience*. Amplify.

Kovalyova, M. (2021). Artificial Intelligence in media: Automated content opportunities and risks. In *The Fix*. Retrieved July 15, 2022, from https://thefix.media/2021/2/11/artificial-intelligence-media.

La Monica, P. (2021). The race to $3 trillion: Big Tech keeps getting bigger. In *CNN*. Retrieved July 15, 2022, from https://edition.cnn.com/2021/11/07/investing/stocks-week-ahead/index.html

LaFrance, A. (2017). The Internet is mostly bots. In *The Atlantic*. Retrieved July 14, 2022, from https://www.theatlantic.com/technology/archive/2017/01/bots-bots-bots/515043/

Larina, E., & Ovchinskiy, V. (2018). Iskusstvennyj intellekt. Bol'shie dannye. Prestupnost' (Artificial intelligence. Big Data. Crime). Knizhnyj mir.

Lee, G. (2021). Big Tech leads the AI race—But watch out for these six challenger companies. In *Airport Technology*. Retrieved July 15, 2022, from https://www.airport-technology.com/analysis/big-tech-leads-the-ai-race-but-watch-out-for-these-six-challenger-companies/

Macaulay, T. (2020). China's latest AI news anchor mimics human voices and gestures in 3D. In *TNW.Neural*. Retrieved July 15, 2022, from https://thenextweb.com/neural/2020/05/21/chinas-latest-ai-news-anchor-mimics-human-voices-and-gestures-in-3d/

Malhotra, R. (2020). *Artificial intelligence and the future of power: 5 battlegrounds*. Rupa Publications.

Manceps. (2019). Could an adversarial bot manipulate the stock market? Retrieved July 15, 2022, from https://www.manceps.com/articles/experiments/beat-the-bots

Marche, S. (2022). *Next civil war: Dispatches from the American future*. Simon & Schuster.

Marconi, F. (2020). *Newsmakers: Artificial intelligence and the future of journalism*. Columbia University Press.

Marrow A, Stolyarov G (2021). Moscow tells 13 mostly U.S. tech firms they must set up in Russia by 2022. In *Yahoo!Finance*. Retrieved July 15, 2022, from https://finance.yahoo.com/news/moscow-says-13-foreign-tech-122138251.html

Martin, A. (2022). US military hackers conducting offensive operations in support of Ukraine, says head of Cyber Command. In *Sky News*. Retrieved July 15, 2022, from https://news.sky.com/story/us-military-hackers-conducting-offensive-operations-in-support-of-ukraine-says-head-of-cyber-command-12625139

McCombs, M., & Valenzuela, S. (2021). *Setting the agenda: Mass media and public opinion* (3rd ed.). Polity Press.

McNamara, C. (2022). Conversational AI: Everything you need to know in 2022. In Heyday. Retrieved July 14, 2022, from https://www.heyday.ai/post/conversational-ai-2022/

McStay, A. (2018). *Emotional AI: The rise of empathic media*. SAGE Publications Ltd..

Menczer, F. (2021). Facebook whistleblower Frances Haugen testified that the company's algorithms are dangerous—Here's how they can manipulate you. In Yahoo!News. Retrieved July 15, 2022, from https://news.yahoo.com/facebook-whistleblower-frances-haugen-testified-122343232.html?fr=sycsrp_catchall

Merriam-Webster. (2022). Bot. In *Merriam-Webster*. Retrieved July 14, 2022, from https://www.merriam-webster.com/dictionary/bot

Metz, R. (2016). Why Microsoft accidentally unleashed a Neo-Nazi Sexbot. In *MIT Technology Review*. Retrieved July 14, 2022, from https://www.technologyreview.com/2016/03/24/161424/why-microsoft-accidentally-unleashed-a-neo-nazi-sexbot/

Microsoft. (2022). *Defending Ukraine: Early lessons from the cyber war*. Microsoft Corporation.

Mordowanec, N. (2022). Biden will have to admit the economy is in a recession: Economist. In *Newsweek*. Retrieved July 15, 2022, from https://www.newsweek.com/us-economy-recession-joe-biden-peter-schiff-1720372

MOST (Ministry of Science and Technology of the People's Republic of China). (2019). Translation: Chinese expert group offers 'Governance Principles' for 'Responsible AI'. In *New America*. Retrieved July 15, 2022, from https://perma.cc/V9FL-H6J7

Muldowney, O. (2020). *Chatbots After 2020: All you need to know about AI, NLP and Chatbots in the new era*. Curses & Magic.

Natale, S. (2021). *Deceitful media*. Oxford University Press.

Neis, M., & Mara, M. (2020). Social bots—Meinungsroboter im Netz (Social bots—Opinion robots on the web). Die Psychologie des Postfaktischen: Über Fake News, 'Lügenpresse', Clickbait & Co. (The psychology of the post-truth: About fake news, "Lying Press", Clickbait & Co.).

Paganini, P. (2013). PsyOps and Socialbots. In *Infosec resources*. Retrieved July 14, 2022, from https://resources.infosecinstitute.com/topic/psyops-and-socialbots/

Pashentsev, E. (2016). Prognosticheskoe oruzhie i bor'ba s terrorizmom (Prognostic weapons and the struggle with terrorism). Bor'ba s terrorizmom—problemy 21 veka (Counter-Terrorism), *2*, 9–13.

Pashentsev, E. (2021). *Experts on the malicious use of artificial intelligence and challenges to international psychological security*. ICSPSC.

Pashentsev, E. (2022). U.S.: On the way to right-wing coup and civil war? In *Russian International Affairs Council (RIAC)*. Retrieved July 15, 2022, from https://russiancouncil.ru/en/analytics-and-comments/analytics/u-s-on-the-way-to-right-wing-coup-and-civil-war/?sphrase_id=90390787

Patel, S. (2022). Top 12 chatbots trends and statistics to follow in 2022. In *REVE Chat*. Retrieved July 14, 2022, from https://www.revechat.com/blog/chatbots-trends-stats/

Peitzker, T. (2018). *[AI × EI + Human-Machine Interaction] = An Historical Overview of Chatbots with Emotional & Artificial Intelligence*. Independently Published.

Petrova, E. (2022). Ushel i ne vernulsya: kakiye IT-kompanii pokinuli Rossiyu i kto smozhet zanyat' ikh mesto (He left and did not return: which IT companies left Russia and who can take their place). In *Hightech.fm*. Retrieved July 15, 2022, from https://hightech.fm/2022/05/26/it-companies-went-away

PGPF. (2022). The United States spends more on defense than the next 9 countries combined. In *Peter G. Peterson Foundation*. Retrieved July 15, 2022, from https://www.pgpf.org/blog/2022/06/the-united-states-spends-more-on-defense-than-the-next-9-countries-combined

Phillips, C. (2018). The 3 types of chatbots & how to determine the right one for your needs. In *Medium*. Retrieved July 14, 2022, from https://chatbotsmagazine.com/the-3-types-of-chatbots-how-to-determine-the-right-one-for-your-needs-a4df8c69ec4c

Protess, D., & McCombs, M. (2016). *Agenda setting: Readings on media, public opinion, and policymaking*. Routledge.

Quora. (2018). Your social media news feed and the algorithms that drive it. In *Forbes*. Retrieved July 15, 2022, from https://www.forbes.com/sites/quora/2017/05/15/your-social-media-news-feed-and-the-algorithms-that-drive-it/?sh=2e81c5984eb8

Quora. (2020). Why did Yahoo stop allowing comments on the majority of its news articles? In *Quora*. Retrieved July 15, 2022, from https://www.quora.com/Why-did-Yahoo-stop-allowing-comments-on-the-majority-of-its-news-articles

Radware. (2022). 9 Types of bots. In *Radware*. Retrieved July 14, 2022, from https://www.radware.com/cyberpedia/bot-management/types-of-bots/

Radziwill, N., & Benton, M. (2017). Evaluating quality of chatbots and intelligent conversational agents. In *arXiv.org*. Retrieved July 14, 2022, from https://arxiv.org/abs/1704.04579

Reinicke, C. (2022). 81% of U.S. adults are worried about a recession hitting this year, survey finds. In *CNBC*. Retrieved July 15, 2022, from https://www.cnbc.com/2022/04/05/most-americans-are-worried-about-a-recession-hitting-the-us-in-2022.html

Rev. (2020). Big tech antitrust hearing full transcript July 29. In *Rev*. Retrieved July 15, 2022, from https://www.rev.com/blog/transcripts/big-tech-antitrust-hearing-full-transcript-july-29

Rosenberg, L., & Unanimous, A. I. (2022). The danger of AI micro-targeting in the metaverse. In *VentureBeat*. Retrieved July 14, 2022, from https://venturebeat.com/2022/01/27/the-danger-of-ai-micro-targeting-in-the-metaverse/

RT. (2017). Google will 'de-rank' RT articles to make them harder to find—Eric Schmidt. In *RT International*. Retrieved July 15, 2022, from https://www.rt.com/news/410444-google-alphabet-derank-rt/

RT. (2022). UN blasts Meta for allowing hate speech against Russians. In *RT International*. Retrieved July 15, 2022, from https://www.rt.com/news/551729-un-meta-hate-speech/?ysclid=l5gwch4tej655743101

Samuels, E., & Akhtar, M. (2019). Are 'bots' manipulating the 2020 conversation? Here's what's changed since 2016. In *The Washington Post*. Retrieved July 15, 2022, from https://www.washingtonpost.com/politics/2019/11/20/are-bots-manipulating-conversation-heres-whats-changed-since/

SAS. (2021). Predictive analytics: What it is and why it matters. In *SAS*. Retrieved July 15, 2022, from https://www.sas.com/en_us/insights/analytics/predictive-analytics.html

Schrage, M. (2020). *Recommendation engines*. MIT Press.

Schuchard, R., Crooks, A., Stefanidis, A., & Croitoru, A. (2019). *Bots fired: Examining social bot evidence in online mass shooting conversations*. Palgrave Communications. https://doi.org/10.1057/s41599-019-0359-x

Shabir, S. (2021). Four steps to winning over an increasingly skeptical public. In *Technology Times*. Retrieved July 15, 2022, from https://www.technologytimes.pk/2021/02/02/four-steps-to-winning-over-an-increasingly-skeptical-public/

Shah, A., & Priyadarshini, A. (2020). Conversational AI: Top 20 trends for 2020. In *Blog.kore.ai*. Retrieved July 14, 2022, from https://blog.kore.ai/conversational-ai-top-20-trends-for-2020

Shark, A., Bergrud, E., Husbands Fealing, K., Hendler, J., Pardo, T., & Robinson, D. (2020). *Artificial intelligence: An agenda for 2021*. National Academy of Public Administration.

Shestopyorov, D., & Lebedeva, V. (2021). Mimo zamedlennogo dejstviya. Vlasti ishchut novye rychagi davleniya na zarubezhnyj IT-biznes (The authorities are looking for new levers of pressure on foreign IT business). In *Kommersant*. Retrieved July 15, 2022, from https://www.kommersant.ru/doc/4783593

Spamlaws. (2022). Different types of internet bots and how they are used. In *Spamlaws*. Retrieved July 14, 2022, from https://www.spamlaws.com/how-internet-bots-are-used.html

Statista. (2021). S&P 500: Largest companies by market cap 2021. In *Statista*. Retrieved July 15, 2022, from https://www.statista.com/statistics/1181188/sandp500-largest-companies-market-cap/

Stieber, Z. (2022). Over 50 Biden administration employees, 12 US agencies involved in social media censorship push: Documents. In *The Epoch Times*. Retrieved September 8, 2022, from https://www.theepochtimes.com/over-50-biden-administration-employees-12-us-agencies-involved-in-social-media-censorship-push-documents_4704349.html?welcomeuser=1

Stieglitz, S., Brachten, F., Berthelé, D., Schlaus, M., Venetopoulou, C., & Veutgen, D. (2017). Do social bots (still) act different to humans?—Comparing metrics of social bots with those of humans. In G. Meiselwitz (Ed.), *Social computing and social media human behavior SCSM* (Lecture Notes in Computer Science 10282) (pp. 379–395). https://doi.org/10.1007/978-3-319-58559-8_30

Stocking, G., & Sumida, N. (2018). Social media bots draw public's attention and concern. In *Pew Research Center's Journalism Project*. Retrieved July 14, 2022, from https://www.pewresearch.org/journalism/2018/10/15/social-media-bots-draw-publics-attention-and-concern/

Sukhodolov, A. P., & Bychkova, A. M. (2022). Artificial intelligence in crime counteraction, prediction, prevention and evolution. *Russian Journal of Criminology, 12*, 753–766.

Tao, L. (2018). Xinhua News Agency debuts AI anchors in partnership with search engine Sogou. In *South China Morning Post*. Retrieved July 15, 2022, from https://www.scmp.com/tech/innovation/article/2172235/xinhua-news-agency-debuts-ai-anchors-partnership-search-engine-sogou

Tesla. (2021). Artificial intelligence & autopilot. In *Tesla*. Retrieved July 15, 2022, from https://www.tesla.com/AI

The Liberty Beacon. (2021). Whistleblowers torpedo big tech and big pharma: Who's next? In *The Liberty Beacon*. Retrieved July 15, 2022, from https://www.thelibertybeacon.com/whistleblowers-torpedo-big-tech-and-big-pharma-whos-next/

The Online Citizen. (2020). Yahoo News temporarily removes comment section in website, says it is to improve 'community experience'. In *The Online Citizen*. Retrieved July 15, 2022, from https://www.onlinecitizenasia.com/2020/07/28/yahoo-news-temporarily-removes-comment-section-in-website-says-it-is-to-improve-community-experience/

Thomas, D. (2021). Tesla surpasses $1 trillion valuation after Hertz order. In *BBC News*. Retrieved September 8, 2022, from https://www.bbc.co.uk/news/business-59045100

Trend Micro. (2018). *Trend Micro*. Retrieved July 15, 2022, from https://www.trendmicro.com/vinfo/nl/security/news/cybercrime-and-digital-threats/study-finds-fake-news-spreads-faster-than-real-news-on-twitter

Tripathi, Y. (2020). What happened to Yahoo comments section? Why did Yahoo remove comments? In *Republic World*. Retrieved July 15, 2022, from https://www.republicworld.com/technology-news/apps/what-happened-to-yahoo-comments-section-why-did-yahoo-remove-comments.html

Tsargrad. (2021). V Rossii obsuzhdayut platu za YouTube: Novyj zaslon dlya internet-gigantov (YouTube payments discussed in Russia: New barrier for Internet giants).

In *Tsargrad*. Retrieved July 15, 2022, from https://tsargrad.tv/news/v-rossii-obsuzhdajut-platu-za-youtube-novyj-zaslon-dlja-internet-gigantov_451654

Turak, N. (2019). Saudi stock market dives, crude futures to jump after drone attack on oil plants. In *CNBC*. Retrieved July 15, 2022, from https://www.cnbc.com/2019/09/15/saudi-stock-market-dives-crude-to-jump-after-attack-on-oil-plants.html

Unity. (2022). Welcome, Ziva dynamics! In *Youtube*. Retrieved July 15, 2022, from https://www.youtube.com/watch?v=xeBpp3GcScM&feature=youtu.be

Urian, B. (2020). South Korea debuts country's first AI news anchor. In *Tech Times*. Retrieved July 15, 2022, from https://www.techtimes.com/articles/254712/20201203/ai-news-anchor-south-korea-accomplishes-10-000-minutes-reporting.htm

Verdict. (2022). A help or a hindrance? Big Tech in the Ukraine crisis. In *Verdict*. Retrieved July 15, 2022, from https://www.verdict.co.uk/ukraine-conflict-big-tech/

Walter, B. (2022). *How civil wars start: And how to stop them*. Crown.

Warwick, K., & Shah, H. (2012). How the 'Good Life' is threatened in cyberspace. In *Academia.edu*. Retrieved July 14, 2022, from https://www.academia.edu/2380537/How_the_Good_Life_is_Threatened_in_Cyberspace

Woolley, S. (2020). *The reality game: How the next wave of technology will break the truth*. PublicAffairs.

Wulfsohn, J. (2022). Facebook, Instagram temporarily allowing calls for violence against Putin, Russians among some European users. In *Fox News*. Retrieved July 15, 2022, from https://www.foxnews.com/media/facebook-instagram-calls-for-violence-vladimir-putin-russians

Yeramsetti, S. (2020). Artificial intelligence-powered chatbots: Increasing business growth in India. In *YourStory*. Retrieved July 14, 2022, from https://yourstory.com/2020/08/artificial-intelligence-chatbots-business-benefits/amp

Zahariadis, N. (2016). *Handbook of public policy agenda setting*. Edward Elgar Publishing.

Part II

Areas of Malicious Use of Artificial Intelligence in the Context of Threats to Psychological Security

7

The COVID-19 Pandemic and the Rise of Malicious Use of AI Threats to National and International Psychological Security

Marta N. Lukacovic and Deborah D. Sellnow-Richmond

Introduction

This chapter captures the escalation of the COVID-19 pandemic into a *mega-crisis* within which malicious use of artificial intelligence (*MUAI*) (Bazarkina & Pashentsev, 2019) exacerbates a multifaceted set of threats to psychological security, which range from the individual to the national and international levels. *Mega-crisis* refers to a complex system of multiple, intersecting, and interdependent crises (Alpaslan & Mitroff, 2011). When the novel coronavirus infection was spreading so rapidly that it was labeled a global pandemic by the World Health Organization (WHO) in March 2020, this new crisis intersected relatively quickly (but not unexpectedly) with other existing issues, including health disparities, economic inequality, socio-political conflicts, and so on. Existing problems in spheres such as media and information also became rapidly entwined with the pandemic crisis, creating additional problems related to the misuse and possibly outright weaponizing of MUAI against international psychological security (Bazarkina & Pashentsev, 2019). COVID-19 thus evolved into a mega-crisis. The theory of *securitization* offers a framework for analysis which sheds light on specific and important aspects

---

M. N. Lukacovic (✉)
Angelo State University, San Angelo, TX, USA

D. D. Sellnow-Richmond
Southern Illinois University Edwardsville, Edwardsville, IL, USA
e-mail: dsellno@siue.edu

of this mega-crisis (Buzan et al., 1998), such as the interrelationships of different facets of the crisis, as well as the various arenas where the crisis is manifest. Specifically, securitization provides insight into various types of security, including psychological security, as well as various types of referent objects, which can range from large collective units (e.g., global community) to collective subunits (e.g., nation-states) to small factions and even individuals (Buzan & Waever, 2009).

This chapter uses the theoretical framework for mega-crises and securitization to analyze cases in Central-Eastern Europe and North America. The main criterion for the selection of these two cases is that they exemplify both certain national peculiarities as well as international features. International MUAI has contributed to localized exploitation of conspiracy theories on the extreme far-right fringes of the political spectra in Slovakia, the Czech Republic, and Poland. MUAI-fueled weaponization of COVID-19-related memes and other information products has had serious repercussions within the US (United States), where followers of anti-governmental factions and cells like the QAnon and Boogaloo movements have heightened their extremist efforts. Some have even engaged in outright violence, including the storming of the US Capitol in early 2021. Qualitative critical analysis is employed primarily in the examination of the news media, relevant governmental and non-governmental organization reports, and scholarly and other analytical literature on the topics in question. This methodological approach fits the paradigmatic root of the theoretical tools and allows for reflection on a variety of reports and artifacts while addressing structural interconnections.

The COVID-19 pandemic is an example of an inherently complex global problem. Analysis based on a combination of mega-crisis and securitization theoretical frameworks can shed light on the role of MUAI as a threat to international psychological security during an infectious disease outbreak. Employing this approach, this chapter explores the following research questions:

- What are the specific features of MUAI threats as they occurred at various international and national levels of security during the COVID-19 pandemic?
- What are some of the integral features of other crises that are crucial for a more holistic understanding of the COVID-19 mega-crisis as it intersects with the MUAI threat to international psychological security (as illustrated in the context of the analyzed cases)?
- How can mega-crisis and securitization frameworks further inform established work on MUAI?

- How can mega-crisis and securitization frameworks inform recommended prevention and mitigation measures for mega-crises similar to COVID-19, where MUAI is potentially a serious threat to international psychological security?

Exploring these questions will lead the discussion toward the following key objectives:

1. To shed light on MUAI threats in the psychological domain that have come to light and/or been exacerbated by the COVID-19 mega-crisis. The theoretical lens we use serves to acknowledge both: (a) specific features of MUAI threats as they occurred at various international and national levels of security and (b) integral features of other crises that are crucial for a more holistic understanding of the processes.
2. To outline the measures for prevention and mitigation measures that can be extracted from the principles of the utilized theoretical frameworks and the analytic findings, including assessments of the strengths and weaknesses of the proposed measures as well as of the degree to which COVID-19 represents a unique versus a typical crisis in terms of MUAI threats to international psychological security. We will also make a projection regarding the degree to which our findings and recommendations can be generalized to other mega-crises that individual nations and the broader international community will likely face in the future.

Review of the Literature: Malicious Use of Artificial Intelligence as a Threat to International Psychological Security in the Context of the COVID-19 Mega-crisis

The volatile and dynamic nature of the ongoing international mega-crisis, including the COVID-19 pandemic and the role of MUIA within it can be usefully analyzed with the help of interdisciplinary findings and theoretical tools. Academic literature is used in this chapter as a source of critical reflection and recommendations for the particular cases in question. The works we reviewed provide the following key components of our theoretical toolkit: the threat to the psychological domain of national and international security by MUAI as described in the work of Bazarkina and Pashentsev (2019); the use of securitization theory (Buzan et al., 1998) to distinguish psychological security from other types of security (e.g., cybersecurity, Hart et al., 2014; Christou, 2019; or health security, Bengtsson & Rhinard, 2019; Bengtsson et al., 2019); and national versus international levels of security (Buzan & Waever, 2009). Before turning to the specifics of securitization, it is useful to map out a mega-crisis model that outlines the interrelationships of different crises, threats, and levels of security (Alpaslan & Mitroff, 2011; Sellnow-Richmond et al., 2018).

Mega-crisis

The COVID-19 pandemic is not just a mere crisis; rather, it is a "mega-crisis"—a complex web of interconnected crises that occur across various structures and societies, frequently transcending nation-state boundaries and tremendously difficult to effectively address due to profound links to other serious issues (Helsloot et al., 2012). Health disparities and other socio-economic divides, a low level of information literacy, and depleted trust in institutions across various societies are just part of the pandemic's problematic complexity, which elevates it to the status of a mega-crisis. Moreover, each of these issues is represented to some degree on the global level. Since the pandemic is the result of a highly infectious viral disease, by its very nature it easily defies national boundaries. Thus, the scale of the pandemic is global by definition. Furthermore, the deaths caused by COVID-19 measure in the millions, thereby constituting a global tragedy. In addition to the incalculable human toll, there have been tremendous economic losses from the decline in labor and trade as a result of quarantines, illnesses, and deaths. There has also been a significant deterioration in quality of life for many people due to spikes in mental health problems that have been intensified by anxieties, isolation, and other circumstances directly resulting from the pandemic. The extensive and multifaceted global impact of the pandemic is undeniable and clearly requires an organized and systematic reaction, but as the mega-crisis is something inherently complicated, it is enormously difficult to respond to it efficiently in the requisite multifaceted manner (Sellnow-Richmond et al., 2018).

Despite these obstacles, what would a response look like? Any mega-crisis requires a well-thought-out and exceptionally well-implemented, multifaceted response that carefully addresses each of the component crises (Alpaslan & Mitroff, 2011). Hence, an array of experts with various perspectives as well as on-the-ground practitioners across the relevant industries must act jointly. Moreover, the solutions will often be far from perfect. However, given the dire consequences of mega-crises like the pandemic and the possibility of similar and possibly even more detrimental mega-crises in the future, we as a human community must prepare strategies and response tactics (Nunes, 2020). In this chapter, we recommend that one way to envision such a response is to consider the various aspects of MUAI and its dangers to international psychological security as an important blueprint for approaching mega-crises. A second step in this process would be to extract useful concepts from securitization theory.

Securitization and International Psychological Security

International psychological security is an important type of international collective security that responds to the serious dangers caused by the pandemic. It is vital to distinguish international psychological security from other frequently discussed types of security, including traditional cybersecurity (Hart et al., 2014; Christou, 2019), which relates to the safety of information technology and computer systems. Cybersecurity can be achieved using advanced and appropriate technological solutions and the knowledge and skills of key personnel and technology users. International psychological security, even in the context of the pandemic, also differs from health security (Bengtsson et al., 2019; Bengtsson & Rhinard, 2019), which relates to safety from health threats. Health security is typically realized through scientific advancements, proper institutional policies, and the knowledge, compliance, and efficacy of key publics.

International psychological security corresponds to the robustness of the collective ability to form attitudes and reactions, as well as overall public tendencies toward a stable international climate (Bazarkina & Pashentsev, 2019). International psychological security is more latent and less immediately visible than the other types of security referenced above, making the development of effective approaches to the protection of international psychological security challenging. Nonetheless, international psychological security is an extremely important type of security that is integral to the very existence and identity of collective units of people. Consequently, it is critical to enhance international psychological security. In our review of the literature and analysis of cases below, we explore the features of practices recommended to enhance international psychological security.

Securitization refers to the discursive assertion that a type of collective security is under threat and, consequently, extraordinary measures are required to avert the threat (Buzan et al., 1998). The theory of securitization acknowledges a variety of different types of security, such as economic security, and cultural security. The key point is that not everything and anything is security, but securitization occurs when a threatened feature of the collective identity is prioritized as something integral to defining that specific social entity. For instance, when a concrete cultural practice or artifact is securitized, those subscribing to it will be likely to employ otherwise unacceptable measures to defend it, including physical violence.

International psychological security is a dimension of security that can be under threat both hypothetically and actually. Hence, international psychological security can be discursively and objectively securitized. According to Chernobrov (2021), the very notion of "the international" can be understood specifically as a "psychosocial space" that is "a reservoir of individually and collectively experienced anxiety, desire, symbolic and interest-driven conflict, and unstable identity boundaries" (p. 14). An actor can make a discursive argument (that may or may not reflect reality) that an aspect of the psychological integrity of the collective is existentially being threatened.

The early works (Buzan et al., 1998) on securitization theory presuppose that all threats are social constructions and therefore securitization as such is ethically problematic. This position reflects the strong constructivist leaning of the seminal school of thought. However, later securitization authors have advanced concepts which acknowledge the realist existential nature of certain threats to the safety and security of nations and global communities (e.g. Floyd, 2011; 2019). This chapter is rooted in a critical paradigmatic perspective that accepts that some threats are indeed real, although social construction does play a role in the way threats are perceived. It is important to note that recently a number of major local and global crises (besides the pandemic) have taken place and negatively impacted the lives of people and other organisms; perhaps the most dangerous of these is the deterioration of the natural environment. Hence, in the current era, radical devotion to a purely constructivist approach is not just a capricious scholarly fad but is in fact dangerous, as academics and practitioners need to understand and effectively address the pressing events that are unfolding. The critical paradigmatic outlook allows for the extraction and application of valuable concepts from constructivist perspectives while also drawing on positivist and other helpful schools of thought and data sources. This is arguably the most comprehensive and constructive way to assess international psychological security in the context of the pandemic.

The COVID-19 pandemic triggered processes that have led to a number of real threats to PS and international psychological security, such as the dangers resulting from MUAI. For example, it could lead to a significant psychological reorientation of the masses toward problematic assumptions and behaviors, which further analysis suggests is detectable in the cases under examination. Interestingly, socially constructed irrational securitization, which is fueled by fallacious conspiracy theories, can and has threatened international psychological security. Before these cases are examined in more detail in this chapter, it is important to review a few other constructs from securitization theory that are conducive to an analysis of international psychological security from various perspectives.

Buzan and Waever (2009) point out that security does not only take place on the level of nation-states. Securitization can also occur on an extremely small scale such as that of the individual, which is termed micro-security. Collective security (Christou, 2019; Floyd, 2019) refers to a level larger than nation-states, that is, international systems. Furthermore, macro-security refers to an even more all-encompassing collective entity, such as the human race (Buzan & Waever, 2009). Psychological security on the level of one nation easily accords with the traditional concept of securitization, or the meso-level. International psychological security that encounters general pandemic-related challenges across nations and sometimes even globally can be understood as a type of macro-security. The utility of this typology is that while some aspects of the problems under discussion are particular to smaller groups of people or specific nations, it is paramount to recognize the general global tendency toward international psychological security threats. This more nuanced understanding has implications regarding the types of responses that can be recommended and the level at which these responses should be implemented—nationally, internationally, and/or globally.

Analysis of Sample Cases of Malicious Use of AI Threats to International Psychological Security During the COVID-19 Pandemic

The cases we examine illustrate the problems of MUAI in the context of the pandemic. The cases embody the complexities inherent to the COVID-19 mega-crisis, specifically the threat of MUAI to international psychological security as exacerbated by the pandemic. The previously introduced theoretical toolkit will be applied to each case as follows: first, the MUAI aspect will be introduced; then, the damage to international psychological security will be addressed; and finally, the threats to international psychological security will be assessed from the securitization perspective of meso and macro levels to identify additional valuable implications that transcend the specificities of these cases.

Central-Eastern Europe

The first analyzed case relates to events unfolding in Central-Eastern Europe, specifically Slovakia, Poland, and the Czech Republic. This region is analytically interesting as it includes countries with some idiosyncratic features, but also a number of important shared features. Most notably, all of these countries transitioned from socialist political systems and planned economies to democratic governments and market economies. Furthermore, these countries share a Slavic cultural heritage with Eastern Europe, but resemble Western Europe in terms of the strong socio-historical and ideological influence of the Catholic Church, political and economic alignment with the European Union, and military membership in the North Atlantic Treaty Organization. The languages spoken in Slovakia, Poland, and the Czech Republic are mutually intelligible, making informational cross-pollination possible, especially in online environments. A high proportion of the population in these countries regularly uses the internet to visit legacy and alternative news sites, content-sharing platforms, and social media (Skolkay et al., 2021). In post-socialist countries, the early stages of the COVID-19 pandemic in 2020 were marked by high rates of compliance with government measures, low infection rates, and low death rates (Beblavy, 2020). However, the year 2021 brought a dramatic increase in infections and deaths per capita in this region, which was also accompanied by high rates of vaccine hesitancy, particularly in Slovakia (Hudec, 2021).

MUAI had a ripple effect that was harnessed by actors in regions like Central-Eastern Europe. Although allegations about the extensive role of AI in perpetuating problematic materials directly relating to COVID-19 were publicized as early as spring 2020 (Allyn, 2020), these concerns have not been widely discussed in Central-Eastern Europe. For instance, in Slovakia, conversations about the role of AI in the pandemic tend to focus on its benefits (e.g. Pravda, 2020). Hence, the prominent role of MUAI in the dissemination of fallacious conspiracy theories relating to COVID-19 is still largely hidden from public scrutiny. Meanwhile, conspiracy narratives have been adopted by politicians and other influential persons in the region.

It can be said that the COVID-19 mega-crisis fueled the tendency of rogue political actors in this region to take advantage of an already fragile international psychological security. One of the first relatively high-profile politicians to spotlight the conspiracy theory about nefarious microchips in the COVID-19 vaccines was the Slovak far-right leader and national assembly member Marian Kotleba (Lukacovic, 2020). Prior to that, this conspiracy theory was marginal; it circulated mainly on the internet and as bot-disseminated disinformation about the pandemic (Allyn, 2020). Social bots are artificial chat robots that pose as real users to "manipulate social media discourse by repeatedly posting and re-posting rumors, spam, misinformation…" (Klyueva, 2019, p. 24).

As conspiratorial positions began to gain more resonance, Czech and Slovak online communities continued to share and spread similar misinformation and disinformation. Other extremist political influencers and media joined in on campaigns against government-sponsored pandemic measures, thus powering more conspiratorial narratives in the public sphere. For instance, Polish far-right politician and activist Grzegorz Braun published a disinformation book, *Falszywa pandemia* ("Fake pandemic"), which was promptly translated into Slovak and widely promoted by the far-right media holdings of KulturBlog, an organization which is affiliated with prominent far-right Slovak politicians Milan Uhrik and Milan Mazurek (Wądołowska, 2021; Lukacovic, 2022). Furthermore, KulturBlog also served as a platform for COVID-19-related conspiratorial content by Czech far-right activist Pavel Kamas, who was previously known mainly for his role in spreading neo-Nazi propaganda in the Czech Republic (Sternova, 2017). Some of these politicians frequently exploit security issues to bolster their popularity (Lukacovic, 2022), but arguably the mega-crisis-induced fragility has empowered them and given them the ability to influence discourse more than before. In essence, these very influencers are the real threat to security, that is, the psychological security in the countries in question.

In fall 2021, the international community was rocked when a former employee of Facebook, Frances Haugen, leaked the *Facebook Papers* with information about the company's questionable practices, including an algorithm that allegedly promoted conflict-inducing content (Lima, 2021). Polish politicians admitted to adopting more radicalized positions as a result of what was popularized on Facebook; in other words, as a result of the Facebook algorithm (Robertson, 2021). Similarly, in Slovakia the broader political opposition (including leftist parties) adopted questionable positions such as anti-vaccination discourses that helped them increase engagement on their social media platforms, the most popular of which is Facebook in that country (Toth, 2021). So, besides rogue political actors exploiting international bot-propagated narratives for their own gain, the crisis has been further exacerbated by corporate MUAI working to maximize Facebook's profits without any regard for their social responsibility. Due to Facebook's massive global reach which measures billions of users, the damage to international psychological security is multiplied tenfold when the AI of big-tech corporations, perhaps unintentionally, rewards malicious content.

The situation in Central-Eastern Europe discussed here exemplifies a mega-crisis as it is an entangled web of mutually exacerbated crises. Approaching the situation through the lens of various levels of security makes it possible to typify the aspects of the mega-crisis. Micro-level security can, for example, correspond to a specific individual's fear of vaccination, which for the sake of argument let us call irrational. So, in this instance, the individual's psychological security is being compromised by anxiety that is overriding rational reasoning. However, issues of mental health and individual psychological or psychiatric pathology are outside the main scope of this volume, so we will now focus only on the more political and collective aspects of psychological security.

Meso-level (or nation-state level) psychological security features the idiosyncratic characteristics of national politics inviting a particular securitization narrative. As detailed in the literature review above, securitization can be purely discursive and detached from reality. For example, a fabricated national argument about the pandemic can lead to successful securitization which results in counterproductive actions like mass protests where participants openly defy official measures by refusing to wear masks when mask mandates are in effect. The conspiracy theory presents the facemask as a threat to security; for example, it can be seen as a threat to personal freedom which is a value of the political-cultural security of the nation. Thus, psychological security has been compromised on the national level because the fabricated securitization is distracting public attention from the real issues of the pandemic as well as from effective responses to these issues, which is a type of tornado-spinning or malicious diversion of public attention (Averkin et al., 2019). In other words, the fabricated securitization is distracting the public from the view that the facemask, which may be uncomfortable or in other ways unpleasant to wear, is actually necessary for the protection of the health security of the nation. Thus, here we can identify problematic behaviors on the part of large subsets of a national population that adopt attitudes and behaviors encouraged by conspiracy theories. The damage to a nation's psychological security and the resulting attitudes and behaviors can only be fully understood in the context of a nation's idiosyncrasies. Arguably, pandemic conspiracy theories are falling on fertile ground in Central-Eastern European nations because widespread corruption has diminished trust in institutions and medical professionals.

In this case, the macro level of security serves to pinpoint the shared international as well as global aspects of the damaged international psychological security. Since the pandemic is a mega-crisis, these aspects represent separate yet interconnected crises, which we have termed *comorbid crises*. They caused even more damage to international psychological security when COVID-19 reached a global level. The Central-Eastern European case highlights some specific international processes. The most obvious is the collaboration between far-right fringe groups in Slovakia, Poland, and the Czech Republic. Connected by similar cultures, mutually intelligible languages, and digital media platforms, they regularly share materials and collaborate. This means that the impact of MUAI is increasingly pronounced as specific ideological pathways of information sharing further amplify the disinformation that was previously largely sustained by bots. The conspiracy theories eventually become associated with real influencers, making AI's role increasingly unclear—or even unknown—to many members of the public. The role of the internet in strengthening international extremist networks has been highlighted as a particularly concerning issue when it comes to far-right and other ideological or fundamentalist movements (e.g., Braddock, 2020; Europol, 2021; Kramar & Vlaeminck, 2020; Walker & Conway, 2015). Additionally, extremists' internet savviness, agility, and lack of scruples have been frequently pointed out in the literature, demonstrating that those groups have no qualms about using AI in unethical or malicious ways to advance their discourses (Braddock, 2020). Moreover, investigative platforms have outlined deep and concerning connections between leading AI developers and extreme far-right ideologies and individuals (Myers West, 2020). However, what is revealed by the case under discussion here is that some international movements, such as the far right, have demonstrated themselves to be particularly irresponsible about COVID-19; thus, they are a threat not only to international psychological security, but to the health security of nations and international communities. These concerns are further supported by recent findings that point to internationally widespread and systematic MUAI such as the use of bots by far-right online accounts that specifically serves to massively disseminate COVID-19-related disinformation (O'Connor, 2021). Effectively, tech-savvy extremists have started exploiting international public vulnerabilities that have grown due to the pandemic (European Parliament, 2021; King & Mullins, 2021; United Nations Interregional Crime and Justice Research Institute, 2020).

This paragraph discusses the global macro level of security that applies not only to Central-Eastern Europe, but to the entire world. MUAI has been described as a significant global threat to international psychological security (Bazarkina & Pashentsev, 2019). In addition to MUAI, digital platforms that are by nature global present numerous other threats and problems ranging from criminal solicitation to the spread of misinformation, from extremist recruitment to nonsensical trolling, from the perpetuation of addiction to the fostering of negative emotions and attitudes, and so on. Furthermore, as many experts and pundits lament, astounding numbers of people across the world suffer from low media and information literacy (Austin et al., 2021). Professional media organizations have been downsizing their personnel and streamlining funding for their operations, thereby diminishing the quality of news; at times there is even no journalistic coverage whatsoever of important issues (Hoiby & Ottosen, 2019). Moreover, general dissatisfaction with democratic and capitalist systems continues to grow internationally as these systems fail to deal with inequalities and other contemporary challenges (Abramowitz, 2018; Schwab, 2020). Thus, the macro level of already emerging mega-crises was matched by the global peril of the COVID-19 illness. On this level, it is clear that conspiratorial macro-securitization discourses frequently overshadow the real global health security threat of the pandemic. For example, thanks to its simplicity, the theory of a global conspiracy to eradicate the human race by putting bioweapons in the vaccine is outperforming scientific communications about the pandemic. The latter contains elements of uncertainty which are characteristic of science, but which are unattractive and seem suspicious to the broader public. Similarly, while many people are unable to understand the concept of MUAI because of their low digital literacy, oversimplified conspiratorial discourse resonates well with the same public. Thus, the fractures on the macro level of international psychological security were clearly aggravated by the pandemic.

While alarming, the degree of damage to international psychological security in the era of COVID-19 is not that surprising when the complexity of the issues on all levels is taken into account.

The United States

We will now analyze a case that traces the intersection of MUAI, international psychological security, and COVID-19 in the US. This case is valuable for a number of reasons. First, the US is a country with high rates of digital media penetration. Second, due to the international influence of the US, many tendencies that evolve there end up impacting or being mimicked in other parts of the world. Third, the US suffers from a high level of infection rates and a high number of deaths per capita. Finally, the US has had several episodes of domestic unrest—and even acts of terrorism—related to the COVID-19 pandemic, so this is an especially disastrous case.

MUAI has been discussed on the national level in the US for several years, but primarily in connection with the elections and other aspects of political communication. Furthermore, geopolitical tensions, particularly with Russia and China, frequently overshadow the discussions of MUAI. So as researchers and journalists point out the role of MUAI in the spread of disinformation and misinformation about COVID-19 (Allyn, 2020), the discussion is promptly politicized, and, for that matter, geo-politicized. Nevertheless, the fact is that bots have significantly contributed to the spread of COVID-19 conspiratorial discourses. While there may or may not have been foreign powers behind the MUAI in the information campaign relating to the pandemic, grassroots radical elements such as pro-weapon militias, far-right nationalist and White supremacist organizations, as well as extremist movements like Boogaloo and QAnon that originated online readily embraced conspiratorial notions about the pandemic (Spring & Wendling, 2020; MacFarquhar, 2021). Boogaloo is a loosely connected movement whose goal is the violent overthrow of the federal government and the establishment of a libertarian form of anarchism, whereas QAnon is a movement of conspiracy theory adherents who believe the US government is a cult-like organization exclusively run by immoral criminals who must be completely purged and replaced. Furthermore, these fringe elements are quite agile and savvy in using MUAI to advance their agendas (Braddock, 2020; Taylor, 2020).

US fringe elements already maintain their relevance by preying on the disgruntled, a vulnerable population from the perspective of national psychological security in the US. They exploited the pandemic to generate further online support and organize various real-life acts. For example, militias organized protests against pandemic measures in a number of US states (Beckett, 2020). Some militias and supporters of the Boogaloo movement planned and at times carried out terrorist acts and assassinations of federal and state officials in response to counter-COVID-19 policies (Pineda, 2020). The efforts of these movements culminated on January 6, 2021, when many of their supporters participated in a rally in Washington, DC and stormed the Capitol building, which resulted in deaths, injuries, and the commission of other crimes. Some allege the Capitol riot was an attempted insurrection against the state, a particularly serious and treasonous crime in the US. While the Capitol riot was primarily about dissatisfaction with Donald Trump's loss of the presidential election to Joe Biden, many supporters of the riot also disagreed with official COVID-19 measures. The politicization of COVID-19 in the US had been clearly defined at that point, with pro-Trump activists, militias, far-right elements, anti-federalists, and conspiratorial groups tending to deny the severity of COVID-19 (Lilleker et al., 2021; MacFarquhar, 2021).

Even though the US case has its particularities, there are extractable lessons that deserve attention beyond Americanist research. Importantly, the volatility of the situation in the US is not accidental, but the result of a substantial cluster of mega-crises. This situation can be better understood when analyzed in the context of various levels of security.

Micro-security plays a role here similar to that in our first (Central-Eastern European) case. However, the events in the US cannot and should not be reduced to individual weaknesses or pathologies, as they are symptomatic of broader issues as illuminated at the larger-scale security levels.

The meso level of security relates to individual nations. This is the level where the idiosyncratic problems of the US can damage the international psychological security of groups of people. The US has seen increases in violence and particularly violent extremism with alarming tendencies on the far right. Official US sources, including the FBI (Federal Bureau of Investigation), indicate that far-right terrorism is one of the greatest dangers today (Walters & Chang, 2021). The fact that so many are attracted to these groups and to conspiracy theories is symptomatic of deeper problems in society such as racism, low-quality education, the high risk of mass gun violence, an epidemic of mental health issues due to stressors such as combat-induced PTSD (post-traumatic stress disorder), an epidemic of substance abuse and other addictions, and economic depression. Moreover, the country is plagued by significant political polarization, which became even more evident during the COVID-19 pandemic and was exacerbated by it (Lilleker et al., 2021; Sellnow-Richmond et al., 2021). Hence, psychological security across the US is highly compromised under the pressures of the entangled comorbid crises, and this has led to increased vulnerability to MUAI attacks in just about every context. The psychological security vulnerability to MUAI is significantly worse in high-stakes, confusing, and rapidly evolving contexts like outbreaks of dangerous contagious diseases such as COVID-19.

What is noteworthy on the macro-security level is the international networking of the far right. While the connections in Central-Eastern Europe were explicit in the cases under discussion, US extremist groups also have numerous connections abroad and naturally share media materials. A substantial body of research, police agency reports, and news reports traces robust international extremist networks (e.g., Europol, 2021; Laruelle, 2015; Rotella, 2021; Lukacovic, 2022). While the actions of these groups in some countries are not as apparent as in the US, that may be because their national situations are not yet ripe for terrorist attacks; nonetheless, they may already be moving in that direction (Europol, 2021). Thus, the increased vulnerability of international psychological security is creating more opportunities for the replication of alarming US events elsewhere. Additional concerns arise when considering that with MUAI's potential role here, soon extremists will not need to directly collaborate, as they will be able to share materials and strategies via non-human digital proxies (Federal Bureau of Investigation Cyber Division, 2021). And in both Central-Eastern Europe and the US, the far right in particular adopted a specific position on the COVID-19 pandemic, which makes the prospects for how these groups will respond when other real security threats arise very grim.

All the macro-security global concerns about international psychological security discussed in the Central-Eastern European case also apply to the US situation. Here is a brief recap of some of the most significant sources of damage to international psychological security on the global level that have played a clear role in the US: dissatisfaction with the broader democratic and market economy systems, low information hygiene, low information literacy, and the rapid proliferation of global digital threats such as MUAI, whether orchestrated by rogue actors with political agendas, profiteering alternative medicine companies that exploit tendencies such as the anti-vaccination movement, or tech corporations that lack a sense of social responsibility.

In addition to the outlined cases, a multitude of other instances of MUAI unfolds in connection to the pandemic. For example, rogue actors such as extremists and criminals have been using phishing (Benishti, 2018); cases in the US were specific to abusing COVID-19 relief funds (O'Donnell, 2020). Next, particularly as more people use the digital platforms and online video-conferencing within the pandemic modus operandi, AI such as malicious chatbots (Chandler, 2018) and deepfakes (Langguth et al., 2021) can very likely be deployed to fortify activities such as spear-phishing, as reputable public and security institutions already warn in Europe and America (European Parliament, 2021; Federal Bureau of Investigation Cyber Division, 2021). Furthermore, bots and deepfakes serve as tremendously effective vehicles for disinformation dissemination across wide platforms and audiences (Langguth et al., 2021; O'Connor, 2021), which continuously exacerbates the problematic tendencies that are detailed in our analyzed cases. Hence, what is happening or potentially will be happening soon is a highly concerning synergy between isolated actors, organized extremist and criminal non-state actors, and reactionary regime type of state actors (Pashentsev, 2021). Their synergetic MUAI jointly threatens international psychological security especially when international publics deal with already difficult burdens of the pandemic.

By outlining and analyzing these cases, it is possible to shed light on and systematize a typology for the components of otherwise difficult to trace mega-crises. Furthermore, our analysis promotes the formulation of proper responses to pervasive mega-crises such as the intersection of COVID-19, MUAI, and damaged international psychological security.

Prevention and Mitigation Approaches to the Threat of Malicious Use of Artificial Intelligence in the International Psychological Security Domain During COVID-19 and Similar Mega-crises

Our discussion of prevention and mitigation begins with a review of some applicable solutions that have already appeared in the literature on MUAI and international psychological security. We then raise additional considerations that are relevant in the context of the pandemic and that have been revealed by our analysis of the cases in this chapter.

One particularly useful national security level solution as proposed by Averkin et al. (2019) is the utilization of AI to counter MUAI. The authors recommend using big data tools to conduct text- and web-mining of online discourses to detect problematic trends such as tornado-spinning (the deliberate diverting of public attention through information attacks). This approach can, for example, detect the emergence of a specific conspiracy theory related to the pandemic. The authors further recommend using cognitive mapping and other multidisciplinary tools to address the overall vitality or indications of deteriorating psychological security on the national level by means of state-administered AI. This is a technologically rooted but also disciplinarily diverse approach that can be an important step in addressing an MUAI threat to psychological security in the context of a crisis on the national level.

However, Averkin et al.'s (2019) approach may need further refinements in the context of a pandemic-like mega-crisis. One of the issues is the agility of malicious actors and their constant ability to invent new approaches (Braddock, 2020); they are thus frequently able to stay a step ahead of the state's use of AI. Furthermore, encrypted and non-digital channels can still be used as alternative paths for the spread of malicious information. Therefore, a vigorous countercampaign needs to correctly identify the plethora of facets of a national-level mega-crisis and deal efficiently with those as well. For example, US militias and extremist groups often function in in-person settings without the need for digitally detectable channels. In these groups, pandemic-related conspiracy theories can be spread in both encrypted and real-life settings. Thus, the criminal justice system, educational programs, and other sources of countermeasures must act to identify and mitigate these other channels. Similarly, pervasive corruption that has depleted public trust in institutions in Central-Eastern Europe impacts all channels of citizen communication. Hence, even a successful AI campaign and control over online information may still leave a portion of the population vulnerable to any disinformation that arrives via any media or any other channel. The core problem here is that some disinformation fits well with the unfavorable perception of institutions and authorities. In such cases, citizens easily accept the proposition that state-sponsored pro-vaccine campaigns are designed to benefit not the public but corrupt authorities through, for instance, commissions from pharmaceutical companies. Hence, nation-states should accompany AI campaigns' designed to protect psychological security with other relevant campaigns and measures that address the specific risks and crises in their national settings.

Another important recommendation for addressing the MUAI threat in the context of the pandemic on the macro level has been proposed by Roumate (2021). Roumate argues that it is important to outline advanced and binding international law centered on the protection of human rights. This law, which would be global in scope, would address the global nature of internet platforms and their threats and delineate the specific rules and obligations for nation-states. We argue that this would also be a useful approach to take with respect to corporations and online profiteering organizations (the major part of online anti-vaccination narratives have been advanced by for-profit alternative medicine companies; Frenkel, 2021). Legally binding approaches and regulations are difficult to achieve, as Roumate (2021) acknowledges, because nation-states frequently prefer autonomy in most matters. However, the international community must recognize the potentially dire consequences of crises that are exacerbated by deregulation, the growing power of corporate actors, and the new media adaptability of rogue actors like extremist organizations. Only through meaningful cooperation can nation-states create the necessary leverage to counter corporate actors and malicious non-state actors. In the long run, nation-states would benefit by more rapidly working to collaborate on drafting of international laws on matters of digital communication and genuinely adhering to them.

Roumate's (2021) recommended global legislative approach will face some inherent challenges in the context of mega-crises. First, the actors, the technologies, and the comorbid crises are all constantly evolving. Hence the rules and regulations need to be continuously updated which requires a sustained circular system of creation, commitment, and implementation. Second, ethical considerations must be taken into account when drafting laws and even when defining the malicious aspects of MUAI (Sinha & Dunbar, 2022). Different world cultures adhere to different moral philosophies. The global community needs to reach an inclusive, overlapping consensus (Collste, 2016) on what MUAI is, what its universal human rights offenses are, and how to counter it. Third, the recognition of international psychological security through inclusive, overlapping consensus as a real and normatively valuable security is paramount (Floyd, 2011, 2019). Such recognition would make international psychological security worthy of normative securitization and deliberate protection from constructed opportunist securitizations such as the conspiracy theories related to the pandemic. Lastly, MUAI represents one of the component comorbid crises in the global context as outlined in our case studies. On both the nation-state and the macro levels of global security, the numerous other factors that weaken international psychological security should be countered through appropriate measures. Hence international law is important, but it is not the only global countermeasure necessary, as we can see from our experience with the COVID-19 pandemic.

Furthermore, in addition to the above recommendations and idiosyncratic national-level measures, we propose a set of macro-security measures that would improve the integrity of international psychological security even in the context of MUAI threats during a pandemic. First, global international psychological security would benefit tremendously from improvements to literacies, especially media literacy, information literacy, and science literacy. In this context, it is particularly important to educate the public about AI and, most of all, its malicious uses. Particularly problematic is the fact that the public is frequently unaware of the degree to which MUAI cultivates and falsely presents specific opinions as being widely held (Klyueva, 2019). It is reasonable to believe that if the level of all these literacies had been higher across the globe, the reach of the *infodemic* (or the disinformation pandemic) that is accompanying COVID-19 would have been much less damaging.

Second, it is crucial to expand global discussions about and obligations to communication ethics among actors. This means that the various actors must be included in conversations about normative questions as well as be expected to follow agreed-upon standards. The actors include large collective units like nation-states, corporations, and media organizations, but they can also be individuals, as new media technologies have provided many people with the unexpected opportunity to participate in global discussions about serious topics such as the pandemic. In this context, choosing to be ignorant and participating in the dissemination of misinformation or disinformation can be considered immoral, whether it is done by an individual or by an institution. Nonetheless, before the global community reaches the stage where responses to the dissemination of disinformation can be discussed, it is paramount to envision an approach to public and media communication ethics where the public is perceived not just as a passive audience but as a group of actors who can actively participate in the conversation (Ward & Wasserman, 2010; Ward, 2014). This paradigm shift represents a major global enterprise, but the pandemic has shown that it is crucial to move in this direction. Otherwise, future crises may be even more plagued by the dangerous use of AI, by the behavior of irresponsible members of the public, and by irresponsible or opportunist organizations amplifying pernicious information that was previously circulated by malicious AI.

Our third cluster of recommendations also addresses the ethical dimension, but this time in a broader sense. The dearth of trust, transparency, compassion, solidarity, and social responsibility frequently exacerbates all the comorbid crises that accompany the corpus of negative consequences of the COVID-19 pandemic. These problems result from the fact that institutions and organizations often demonstrate little or no ethical commitment to upholding certain principles. Because institutions and organizations are poor models of ethical behavior, it is not surprising that the public loses trust in them and is unwilling to conform to certain norms. Another aspect of this broader problem is the lack of institutional effort toward formal and informal educational opportunities to enhance ethical integrity on a broader scale. The pandemic was a magnifying glass which exposed the degree of normative decay on the global level (Nunes, 2020). Greed for resources and power, rather than other goals or obligations, seems to drive many decisions. This type of decay is even more problematic as technological advancements in areas such as AI are rapidly progressing and can be—and are—employed for negative purposes. In the same vein, maliciously presented securitization discourses are designed to protect constructed ideas that are benefitting certain institutions, organizations, groups, and individuals. The dire consequences for society include damaged international psychological security which is focused on false securitization as opposed to the health and well-being of our fellow human beings.

The global community needs to be aware that with the growth of our interconnections and interdependences in the globalized world, the possibility of mega-crises is also increasing. What we are seeing with the intersection of COVID-19, MUAI, and a damaged international psychological security merits attention in and of itself, but also because it is highly likely that it highlights features of future mega-crises. Thus, we strongly encourage further examinations and conversations about our outlined blueprint of recommendations. Continuing discussion will help further modify and develop the plan as well as provide insight into how future crises with similar features can be managed by drawing on lessons learned from the current pandemic. While COVID-19 certainly has its peculiarities, in many ways it is a mega-crisis of the type that the global community should anticipate in the future (Nunes, 2020). We thus argue that our recommendations can be successfully applied to major future crises. In fact, the frameworks we drew on were not specific to the pandemic. Thus, we have demonstrated that this discussion can also benefit from more general recommendations such as those developed by Averkin et al. (2019). Their perspective can be combined with the securitization theory-informed perspective in the drafting of a blueprint for prevention and mitigation measures in the context of COVID-19, as our contribution demonstrates. Along the same lines, works on normative securitization (Floyd, 2011, 2019; Rogers, 2020) can complement the established guidelines of "ethical and responsible AI" (National Security Commission on Artificial Intelligence, 2020) as a counterapproach to MUAI. Specifically, in the context of such crises as the pandemic, low ethical integrity of response measures is a grave weakness, and a weak counterapproach is more likely to perpetuate the domino effect of risks within the complicated and volatile fabric of a mega-crisis.

Any academic deliberation on a given issue involves certain limitations, and we must reflect on the limitations of this chapter. The COVID-19 situation is currently still developing and is very dynamic. The potential and actual capacities and deployment of MUAI in this context are also not static. Hence, this analysis had to rely on recent reports and other information that in many cases was not filtered through normal scholarly gatekeeping. Furthermore, the situation of COVID-19, as well as the broader context of MUIA, has been strongly politicized in the regions of focus. Thus, both non-academic and academic works on the matter may reflect specific political beliefs and leanings. It is crucial to transparently acknowledge these limitations and deliberately reflect on the nature of the information being presented. It is not always clear what information is definitive versus dynamic, and what is proven versus probable versus possible. Despite these limitations, however, this chapter makes a valuable contribution to the subject as it demonstrates the usefulness of the analytical approach and outlines preventive measures for similar scenarios that are likely to transpire in the future. Unfortunately, the global community does not have the luxury of waiting for more data as the mega-crisis advances, and future mega-crises may be just around the corner.

Conclusion

Interactive relationships are fundamental to mega-crises. MUAI represents a threat to international psychological security (Bazarkina & Pashentsev, 2019) in general, which can, in turn, hamper constructive responses to the plethora of other threats that stem from comorbid crises. Further, the employment of MUAI to specifically spread disinformation about COVID-19 represents a direct threat to the health security of the international community (Allyn, 2020). Evidence suggests that malicious information infrastructures are being purposefully appropriated to advance disinformation about COVID-19, leading to overlapping health threats and international psychological security threats (Spring & Wendling, 2020).

We adopted an analytic approach that distinguishes meso-level national security and macro-level international and global security to explore the intersection of COVID-19, MUAI, and damaged international psychological security. Our analysis, which focused on cases in Central-Eastern Europe and the US, allowed us to trace idiosyncratic national features and more general global aspects of the ongoing mega-crisis in the two settings in question. Based on the examination of these cases as well as of relevant scholarly and applied literature, a set of recommended approaches was outlined. Essentially, on the national level authorities should actively employ AI for beneficial purposes such as monitoring for MUAI. This tactic must also be accompanied by a complex set of responses to other crises within the particular nation-state that are comorbid to a larger set of problems aggravated or highlighted by the pandemic. On the global level, international rules and laws must address MUAI with mutually agreed-upon and obligatory frameworks that are respected by both nation-states and corporate actors. Furthermore, all global actors, from the collective to the individual, share an ethical responsibility in terms of both communication practices and broader normative commitments to the well-being of communities. In addition, it is absolutely paramount that literacies continue to be improved around the world with special attention to media literacy, information literacy, and knowledge about the potentially detrimental capacities of contemporary technologies, including rogue adaptations like MUAI. Our recommended approach is rather demanding, but only a complex multifaceted approach will be sufficient to enhance international psychological security when facing the threat of MUAI in the context of a massive crisis such as a global pandemic.

References

Abramowitz, M. J. (2018). *Democracy in crisis. Freedom in the world 2018*. Freedom House. Retrieved November 29, 2021, from https://freedomhouse.org/report/freedom-world/2018/democracy-crisis

Allyn, B. (2020). *Researchers: Nearly half of accounts tweeting about coronavirus are likely bots*. NPR. Retrieved November 28, 2021, from https://www.npr.org/sections/coronavirus-live-updates/2020/05/20/859814085/researchers-nearly-half-of-accounts-tweeting-about-coronavirus-are-likely-bots

Alpaslan, C. M., & Mitroff, I. I. (2011). *Swans, swine, and swindlers: Coping with the growing threat of mega-crises and mega-messes*. Stanford Business Books—Stanford University Press.

Austin, E. W., Austin, B. W., Willoughby, J. F., Amram, O., & Domgaard, S. (2021). How media literacy and science media literacy predicted the adoption of protective behaviors amidst the COVID-19 pandemic. *Journal of Health Communication, 26*(4), 239–252. https://doi.org/10.1080/10810730.2021.1899345

Averkin, A., Bazarkina, D., Pantserev, K., & Pashentsev, E. (2019). Artificial intelligence in the context of psychological security: Theoretical and practical implications. *Atlantis Studies in Uncertainty Modelling, 1*, 101–107.

Bazarkina, D., & Pashentsev, E. (2019). Artificial intelligence and new threats to international psychological security. *Russia in Global Affairs, 17*(1), 147–170.

Beblavy, M. (2020). How Slovakia flattened the curve. *Foreign Policy*. Retrieved November 28, 2021, from https://foreignpolicy.com/2020/05/06/slovakia-coronavirus-pandemic-public-trust-media/

Beckett, L. (2020). Armed protesters demonstrate against Covid-19 lockdown at Michigan Capitol. *The Guardian*. Retrieved November 28, 2021, from https://www.theguardian.com/us-news/2020/apr/30/michigan-protests-coronavirus-lockdown-armed-capitol

Bengtsson, L., Borg, S., & Rhinard, M. (2019). Assembling European health security: Epidemic intelligence and the hunt for cross-border health threats. *Security Dialogue, 50*(2), 115–130.

Bengtsson, L., & Rhinard, M. (2019). Securitization across borders: The case of 'health security' cooperation in the European Union. *West European Politics, 42*(2), 346–368.

Benishti, E. (2018). Artificial intelligence is revolutionizing phishing—And it's not all good. *Iron Scales*. Retrieved January 19, 2022, from https://ironscales.com/blog/Artificial-Intelligence-Revolutionizing-Phishing/

Braddock, K. (2020). *Weaponized words. The strategic role of persuasion in violent radicalization and counter-radicalization*. Cambridge University Press.

Buzan, B., & Waever, O. (2009). Macrosecuritization and security constellations: Reconsidering scale in securitization theory. *Review of International Studies, 35*(2), 253–276.

Buzan, B., Waever, O., & de Wilde, J. (1998). *Security: A new framework for analysis*. Lynne Rienner Pub.

Chandler, S. (2018). The evolution of evil chatbots is just around the corner. *Daily Dot*. Retrieved January 19, 2022, from https://www.dailydot.com/debug/evil-chatbot-hackers-ai/

Chernobrov, D. (2021). *Public perception of international crises: Identity, ontological security and self-affirmation*. Rowman & Littlefield.

Christou, G. (2019). The collective securitization of cyberspace in the European Union. *West European Politics, 42*(2), 278–301.

Collste, G. (2016). *Ethics and communication: Global perspectives*. Rowman & Littlefield.

European Parliament. (2021). Tackling deepfakes in European policy. Study—Panel for the Future of Science and Technology—European Parliament Research Service. Retrieved January 19, 2022, from https://www.europarl.europa.eu/RegData/etudes/STUD/2021/690039/EPRS_STU(2021)690039_EN.pdf

Europol. (2021). 1st referral action day against right-wing terrorist online propaganda. Retrieved January 19, 2022, from https://www.europol.europa.eu/media-press/newsroom/news/1st-referral-action-day-against-right-wing-terrorist-online-propaganda

Federal Bureau of Investigation Cyber Division. (2021). Private industry notification: Malicious actors almost certainly will leverage synthetic content for cyber and foreign influence operations. Retrieved January 19, 2022, from https://www.ic3.gov/Media/News/2021/210310-2.pdf

Floyd, R. (2011). Can securitization theory be used in normative analysis? Towards a just securitization theory. *Security Dialogue, 42*(4–5), 427–439.

Floyd, R. (2019). Collective securitization in the EU: Normative dimensions. *West European Politics, 42*(2), 391–412.

Frenkel, S. (2021). The most influential spreader of coronavirus misinformation online. *The New York Times*. Retrieved November 28, 2021, from https://www.nytimes.com/2021/07/24/technology/joseph-mercola-coronavirus-misinformation-online.html

Hart, C., Jin, D. Y., & Feenberg, A. (2014). The insecurity of innovation: A critical analysis of cybersecurity in the United States. *International Journal of Communication, 8*, 2860–2878.

Helsloot, I., Boi, A., Jacobs, B., & Comfort, L. (2012). The new challenges of megacrises. In I. Helsloot, A. Boin, B. Jacobs, & L. Comfort (Eds.), *Mega-crises: Understanding the prospects, nature, characteristics and the effects of cataclysmic events* (pp. 5–11). Charles C Thomas.

Hoiby, M., & Ottosen, R. (2019). Journalism under pressure in conflict zones: A study of journalists and editors in seven countries. *Media, War & Conflict, 12*(1), 69–86.

Hudec, M. (2021). Slovaks' fear of vaccine is higher than solidarity. *Euractiv*. Retrieved November 25, 2021, from https://www.euractiv.com/section/politics/short_news/slovaks-fear-of-vaccine-is-higher-than-solidarity/

King, M., & Mullins, S. (2021). *COVID-19 and terrorism in the West: Has radicalization really gone viral?* Just Security. Retrieved January 19, 2022, from https://www.justsecurity.org/75064/covid-19-and-terrorism-in-the-west-has-radicalization-really-gone-viral/

Klyueva, A. (2019). Trolls, bots, and whatnots: Deceptive content, deception detection, and deception suppression. In I. E. Chiluwa & S. A. Samoilenko (Eds.), *Handbook of research on deception, fake news, and misinformation online* (pp. 18–32). IGI Global.

Kramar, K., & Vlaeminck, E. (2020). Cultural psyop in the digital age: The experience with IS and the lessons to be learned. In D. Bazarkina, E. Pashentsev, & G. Simons (Eds.), *Terrorism and advanced technologies in psychological warfare: New risks, new opportunities to counter the terrorist threat* (pp. 169–186). Nova Science Publishers.

Langguth, J., Pogorelov, K., Brenner, S., Filkukova, P., & Schroeder, D. T. (2021). Don't trust your eyes: Image manipulation in the age of deepfakes. *Frontiers in Communication*. https://doi.org/10.3389/fcomm.2021.632317

Laruelle, M. (2015). Dangerous liaisons: Eurasianism, the European far right, and Putin's Russia. In M. Larualle (Ed.), *Eurasianism and the European far right: Reshaping the Europe-Russia relationship* (pp. 1–31). Lexington Books.

Lilleker, D., Coman, I., Gregor, M., & Novelli, E. (2021). Political communication and COVID-19: Governance and rhetoric in global comparative perspective. In D. Lilleker, I. Coman, M. Gregor, & E. Novelli (Eds.), *Political communication and COVID-19: Governance and rhetoric in times of crisis* (pp. 333–350). Routledge.

Lima, C. (2021). A whistleblower's power: Key takeaways from the Facebook Papers. *The Washington Post*. Retrieved November 28, 2021, from https://www.washingtonpost.com/technology/2021/10/25/what-are-the-facebook-papers/

Lukacovic, M. N. (2020). "Wars" on COVID-19 in Slovakia, Russia, and the United States: Securitized framing and reframing of political and media communication around the pandemic. *Frontiers in Communication, 5*. https://doi.org/10.3389/fcomm.2020.583406

Lukacovic, M. N. (2022). Slovakia as a convenient "laboratory" to extend the theory of securitized framing: The case of far right's frame shifting between Euroscepticism and Europhilia. In M. C. Minielli, M. N. Lukacovic, S. A. Samoilenko, M. R. Finch, & D. Uecker (Eds.), *Communication theory and application in post-socialist contexts* (pp. 11–143). Lexington Books—Rowman & Littlefield. (in press).

MacFarquhar, N. (2021). Far-right extremists move from 'stop the steal' to stop vaccine. *The New York Times*. Retrieved November 28, 2021, from https://www.nytimes.com/2021/03/26/us/far-right-extremism-anti-vaccine.html

Myers West, S. (2020). *AI and the far right: A history we can't ignore.* AI Now Institute. Retrieved January 19, 2022, from https://medium.com/@AINowInstitute/ai-and-the-far-right-a-history-we-cant-ignore-f81375c3cc57

National Security Commission on Artificial Intelligence. (2020). *First quarter recommendations.* The National Security Commission on Artificial Intelligence | The United States of America. Retrieved November 29, 2021, from https://www.nscai.gov/home

Nunes, J. (2020). The COVID-19 pandemic: Securitization, neoliberal crisis, and global vulnerabilities. *Cadernos se Saúde Pública—Reports in Public Health, 36*(4), 1–4. https://doi.org/10.1590/0102-311X00063120

O'Connor, C. (2021). *The conspiracy consortium: Examining discussions of COVID-19 among right-wing extremist Telegram channels.* Institute for Strategic Dialogue. Retrieved January 19, 2022, from https://www.isdglobal.org/isd-publications/the-conspiracy-consortium-examining-discussions-of-covid-19-among-right-wing-extremist-telegram-channel/

O'Donnell, L. (2020). Coronavirus "financial relief" phishing attacks spike. *Threat Post.* Retrieved January 19, 2022, from https://threatpost.com/coronavirus-financial-relief-phishing-spike/154358/

Pashentsev, E. (2021). *The malicious use of artificial intelligence through agenda setting: Challenges to political stability.* Experts on the Malicious Use of Artificial Intelligence and Challenges to International Psychological Security.

Pineda, K. (2020). The Boogaloo movement is gaining momentum. Who are the Boogaloo 'Bois' and what do they want? *USA Today.* Retrieved November 28, 2021, from https://www.usatoday.com/story/news/nation/2020/06/19/what-is-boogaloo-movement/3204899001/

Pravda. (2020). Umelá inteligencia pomáha v boji proti chorobe Covid-19 [Artificial intelligence helps in the fight against the illness COVID-19]. Retrieved November 25, 2021, from https://vat.pravda.sk/clovek/clanok/559207-prirodovedci-a-informatici-testovali-zname-lieky-na-novy-koronavirus/

Robertson, A. (2021). Political parties told Facebook its news feed pushes them into 'more extreme positions'. *The Verge.* Retrieved November 28, 2021, from https://www.theverge.com/2021/9/15/22675472/facebook-wsj-leaks-news-feed-social-media-politics-polarization

Rogers, P. (2020). *COVID-19: The dangers of securitization.* Oxford Research Group. Retrieved November 28, 2021, from https://www.oxfordresearchgroup.org.uk/covid-19-the-dangers-of-securitisation

Rotella, S. (2021). Global right-wing extremism networks are growing. The U.S. is just now catching up. *ProPublica.* Retrieved November 28, 2021, from https://www.propublica.org/article/global-right-wing-extremism-networks-are-growing-the-u-s-is-just-now-catching-up

Roumate, F. (2021). Artificial intelligence, ethics and international human rights law. *International Review of Information Ethics, 29*(3). https://doi.org/10.29173/irie422

Schwab, K. (2020). *Now is the time for a 'great reset'*. World Economic Forum. Retrieved November 29, 2021, from https://www.weforum.org/agenda/2020/06/now-is-the-time-for-a-great-reset/

Sellnow-Richmond, D. D., George, A. M., & Sellnow, D. D. (2018). An IDEA model analysis of instructional risk communication in the time of Ebola. *Journal of International Crisis and Risk Communication Research, 1*(1), 135–166.

Sellnow-Richmond, D. D., Lukacovic, M. N., Sellnow-Richmond, S. A., & Kraushaar, L. (2021). Messages in conflict: Examining leadership communication during the COVID-19 pandemic in the U.S. *Journal of International Crisis and Risk Communication Research*. (in press).

Sinha, G., & Dunbar, R. (2022). Artificial intelligence and its regulation in the European Union. In D. M. Bielicki (Ed.), *Regulating artificial intelligence in industry* (pp. 3–20). Routledge.

Skolkay, A., Hajzer, G., Filin, J., Anusiewicz, T., Adamcova, L., Vighova, V., & Danis, I. (2021). Social media and convergence in Czech Republic, Hungary, Poland, and Slovakia. In M. C. Minielli, M. N. Lukacovic, S. A. Samoilenko, M. R. Finch, & D. Uecker (Eds.), *Media and public relations research in post-socialist societies* (pp. 161–189). Lexington Books—Rowman & Littlefield.

Spring, M., & Wendling, M. (2020). How COVID-19 myths are merging with the QAnon conspiracy theory. *BBC*. Retrieved November 28, 2021, from https://www.bbc.com/news/blogs-trending-53997203

Sternova, V. (2017). The Czech Republic. In I. Barna & A. Felix (Eds.), *Modern Antisemitism in the Visegrad countries* (pp. 19–46). Tom Lantos Institute.

Taylor, J. (2020). Covid-19 misinformation: Pro-Trump and QAnon Twitter bots found to be worst culprits. *The Guardian*. Retrieved November 28, 2021, from https://www.theguardian.com/media/2020/jun/01/covid-19-misinformation-pro-trump-and-qanon-twitter-bots-found-to-be-worst-culprits

Toth, G. (2021). *Prečo sa na Facebooku darí Blahovi a jemu podobným? [Why do Blaha and those similar to him have success on Facebook?]*. Týždeň. Retrieved November 28, 2021, from https://www.tyzden.sk/spolocnost/78140/preco-sa-na-facebooku-dari-blahovi-a-jemu-podobnym/?fbclid=IwAR0xPQDyoFZPfXgJMzI4XAnuXTxH8qqgZemuWCxl65VwDI5L8wGwx-8Euzc

United Nations Interregional Crime and Justice Research Institute. (2020). Stop the virus of disinformation: The risk of malicious use of social media during COVID-19 and the technology options to fight it. Retrieved January 19, 2022, from http://www.unicri.it/sites/default/files/2020-11/SM%20misuse.pdf

Wądołowska, A. (2021). *Far-right MP fined 20,000 zloty for refusing to wear mask in Polish parliament*. Notes from Poland. Retrieved November 28, 2021, from https://notesfrompoland.com/2021/10/08/far-right-mp-fined-20000-zloty-for-refusing-to-wear-mask-in-polish-parliament/

Walker, C., & Conway, M. (2015). Online terrorism and online laws. *Dynamics of Asymmetric Conflict, 8*(2), 156–175.

Walters, J., & Chang, A. (2021). Far-right terror poses bigger threat to US than Islamist extremism post-9/11. *The Guardian*. Retrieved November 28, 2021, from https://www.theguardian.com/us-news/2021/sep/08/post-911-domestic-terror

Ward, S. J. A. (2014). Radical media ethics. Ethics for a global digital world. *Digital Journalism*. https://doi.org/10.1080/21670811.2014.952985

Ward, S. J. A., & Wasserman, H. (2010). Towards an open ethics: Implications of new media platforms for global ethics discourse. *Journal of Mass Media Ethics, 25*, 275–292.

8

Malicious Use of Artificial Intelligence in Political Campaigns: Challenges for International Psychological Security for the Next Decades

Marius Vacarelu

Introduction

In order to understand life, a young person must seek to learn from an early age examples from directions: good governance, for the first part, and also the political, economic, and legal abuses and errors made by national and local rulers, for the other part. After all, the life of an adult is not one in a laboratory environment, but one that will know both happy moments and unpleasant situations, and an important part of them will be the leader's decisions and results of these decisions. Knowing history, a young person will understand that one of the most important drivers of humanity has been—and will be many centuries from now—the politics and competition that it creates locally, nationally, continentally, or globally.

Life expectancy has increased and the complexity of social and economic life has reached a level impossible to imagine two centuries ago. Here, we need to note the central position of politics—an area that any person can claim to understand, perhaps also in view of the fact that compulsory education in every country includes the discipline of history, which contains many interesting political facts. Because life expectancy had grown to over 70 years (World Health Organization, 2021), it results that a person would have the

M. Vacarelu (✉)
National School of Political Science and Public Administration, Bucharest, Romania

opportunity to vote, to see, and to be involved in political campaigns for a period of over 50 years.

Because superior political positions are not for life, the struggle to get them becomes eternal. Many administrative positions have an important political meaning, but they are only achieved as a result of elections and only if the country's top hierarchy is changing. For these positions, there is not only real open political competition and campaigning but also intrigues and "behind-doors" strategies; the latter actions involve only a few people.

This chapter is dedicated to publicly elected positions because their results have a stronger legitimacy, and the interest to win them is not only national but also international, as Cambridge Analytica and many others cases have shown.

To win such elections, it is necessary to have a good campaign staff, money, and a coherent plan of travels inside the country, but—above everything—it is important to have a strong record of activity in cyber space. To understand why Internet political activities have become very important, it is useful to know that at the beginning of 2022, 5 billion people use this technology worldwide, meaning 63% of the global population (Digital Around the World, 2022); 2.9 billion people are active Facebook users and 1.93 billion use it daily (Statista, 2021); around 2.5 quintillion bytes of data are produced each day from almost every sector of the economy, and The International Data Corporation predicts that, by 2025, the world will create and replicate 163 zettabytes—or 163 trillion gigabytes—of data every single year (Bartlett et al., 2018). These trends guide politicians because the natural expansion of the population will increase the proportion of the world's Internet users.

Politics has now become more online than "door to door" because online campaigns can function 24 hours/day and can reach any person, even if the voter is abroad. We cannot compare the cost dimension of a traditional campaign in every country, but we have an estimation of their costs in the US, because here we find the highest concentration of rich people, with also the highest level of innovation used by politicians. In this case, we note that between the election year of 2000 and 2008 the cost of running an election increased by 50%, from 4.63 billion dollars to 6.27 billion dollars—and during that time, the mobile phone became the main tool of electronic campaigns. With the progression of AI, the cost increased to 14.4 billion dollars for the 2020 election year, doubling the costs from 2016 (Cost of elections, 2021), when the potential of AI was comparatively weaker.

Such costs have become very expensive and not every politician or party is able to pay them. But all costs shown by the US elections cover not only the electronic "battlefield," but also door-to-door campaigns, television spots, posters, and so on. Of course, there are differences among parties and their capacity to use these tools, as there are differences between countries in their dimensions and demographic densities, which modify the strategic political campaigns. Considering these differences, but also the Internet tools that were then proliferating, it became necessary to direct a good part of the political campaign to these new tools to achieve what in every voter's mind would be a personalized political message.

Personalized political communication on the large scale we have seen in recent elections requires resources that are well beyond those commanded by campaign organizations built around individual candidates. This type of communication is instead pursued by wider "campaign assemblages" that include not only staffers and consultants but also allied interest groups and civic associations, numerous individual volunteers and paid part-timers, and a party-provided technical infrastructure for targeting voters. Close scrutiny of how such campaign assemblages engage in personalized political communication leads one to challenge the dominant view of political communication today, viz., that it is a tightly scripted, controlled, and professionalized set of practices that primarily represses turnout and turns people off politics in its cut-throat pursuit of victory (Nielsen, 2012).

This chapter seeks to find out the role of malicious use of artificial intelligence (MUAI) in political campaigns, which poses a threat not only to national but also to international psychological security because its unethical use can create new situations without a predictable control or treatment. Being a new electronic tool, we are still not totally conscious about all its force and all its potential to harm the human mind and—as result of this harm—society as a whole. An ill man, a victim of MUAI, can today become a criminal, a terrorist, a source of mental problems for his friends, and all these consequences can appear as an effect of non-ethical AI political use.

Artificial Intelligence as Game Changer in Politics, Politicians and Political Behavior from a Psychological Perspective

Like any new tool created by the human mind, AI can have a genuine use, such as improving our quality of life and helping the economy to strengthen its potential to develop new instruments useful for the same purpose (providing a better life). At the same time, as many philosophers have underlined since antiquity, some tools can be used in unethical ways, provoking bad results for human life and social stability. By its force, AI becomes a real game-changer in all areas where the human psyche creates an attitude—acceptance or rejection—and here politics represents an effective site for the application of AI "games." In AI, "politics" represents a wide field of application in the areas of politicians and voters, human psychology and political campaigns; this can impact elections and the creation of new opinions between voting days, which needs to be studied and deeply understood.

It is not only a question of whether AI could influence people through explicit recommendation and persuasion, but also of whether AI can influence human decisions through more covert persuasion and manipulation techniques. Some studies show that AI can make use of human heuristics and biases in order to manipulate people's decisions in a subtle way. Heuristics are shortcuts of thought, which are deeply configured in the human mind and often allow us to emit fast responses to the demands of the environment without the need for much thinking, data collection, or time and energy consumption. These default reactions are highly efficient most of the time, but they become biases when they guide decisions in situations where they are not safe or appropriate. These biases can be used to manipulate thinking and behavior, sometimes in the interest of third parties (Agudo, 2021).

The emergence of AI was a unique moment for all politicians, regardless of the country. All the technologies until then, as well as the political strategies used for hundreds of years, had a pronounced reactive temporal characteristic, because they developed at a time when the operators of the politician's tools had approximately the same knowledge and, fundamentally, almost the same physical abilities. No matter how important a news item was, it could reach recipients only after protracted physical operations, which involved collecting the text in a newspaper, transporting it (the journal) to as many cities as possible, and the recipients' buying and reading these accounts. From the perspective of the political environment, this huge waste of effort could be completely useless, because only the populations of very large cities—and especially those who lived in the countries' capitals—could revolt quickly, in accordance with the interests of different political leaders. Provincial tumult was also not easy to capture in the countries' capitals, because the local specifics were different; the inhabitants located hundreds of kilometers from the governmental headquarters felt a deep spatial gap, including in the different political manifestations.

Time passed, the number of newspapers doubled and then were almost overshadowed by the power of radio and television, but even in these cases the political environment was not completely satisfied, first because governments maintained a control as strict as possible over certain messages that could be offered to the public, either by delaying them or by blatantly banning their appearance. For decades dictatorships and authoritarian regimes have preferred an unequivocal solution, namely a ban on private radio and television operators, so that the most common alternative to internal news appears through radio and TV sources abroad. For a significant number of countries, the acquisition of high-performance radio and TV receivers had been a difficult process, either because of economic reasons—because poverty plays a very important role—or because simple devices allow governments' easier control of the population.

Only the great changes of the 1980s and 1990s led to the explosion of radio and television stations globally, and the information landscape of the population changed decisively. However, this way of communicating political messages also creates problems for the political environment, because it does not allow a completely honest or balanced competition: the most important and rich media sources exert the greatest influence on public opinion. Sometimes, the editorial policy of these important sources of information can be useful to a government or an opposition party, depending on certain options/amounts of money offered, and the citizen is usually influenced by the messages that are given continuously from one direction or another. Authoritarian regimes after the 1990s had to partially simulate freedom and allow the emergence of press sources operated by private individuals, but the regimes kept them under control, and when they were considered too critical of governments, financial or even criminal sanctions were imposed on some directors or popular journalists.

The advent of mobile phones has suddenly complicated the lives of politicians, because the news could suddenly reach any point in the countries, directly and sometimes instantly influencing the political public game. Thus, the first "mobile phone revolution" took place in 2009 in the Republic of Moldova ("First SMS revolution"), and since then authoritarian governments have understood that blocking mobile phone networks becomes mandatory in very tense times, in order to prevent strong protests which are able to throw them out of power. However, the mobile phone has remained only a part of the great technological leap in communication, because newly created Internet technologies have merged with this device. Since the Internet could be accessed by mobile devices, the political game got a global reset, and political actors have been forced to support the new technologies' development, implementation, and legal requests (Dowd, 2022). This new technological framework provides a greater strength to its operators and implicitly to the given political messages, in both directions: on their own parties and on society.

Among the new technologies that have developed in this interval, the most important is that of AI, and in terms of shaping the future of political competitions, it will play an exceptional role, if not the most important one. As new generations are born and grow in the mobile Internet paradigm (Vogels, 2021), it is clear that AI will most likely become the most important tool in political campaigns in every country.

We must emphasize, however, that today AI plays a triple role, less understood by society. First, some scientists and politicians consider it either a panacea for the country's problems or the supreme political weapon. Second, there are those who only vaguely understand what this technology could be; they are largely aware of it only through science fiction movies and books, in which higher intelligences become dangerous for the human species and the planet. Finally, there are those who consider AI to be a very important technology for many spheres of political, social, economic, and private life, but who try to maintain a sense of reality, corroborating its capabilities with all other means and tools used today. From this perspective, AI must be studied rationally, without sentimentality, analyzing its inherent capabilities, as well as the possibility of doing good or bad, in relation to the interests of the operators who will use it.

It must be understood that any politician is ecstatic about the ability of AI to reach any device at any place on the planet. After all, the costs of election campaigns are reduced substantially, because this new technology achieves three things that were impossible using traditional political methods.

First, few people today understand the informational capacity of Internet technologies and especially those of AI (Larson, 2021). I need to underline that electronic devices can now store amounts of information that the human mind will never be able to comprehend, thus becoming fantastic libraries in terms of the level of resources, but occupying minimal space. This yields two major consequences in the sphere of political competitions, which must be taken into account before any electoral moment—obviously, without limiting themselves to them.

The depository characteristic of AI means that it "knows" different strategies and political operations that have taken place in history, and what is new to the politician's mind will for an AI-enabled device generally be simply a repetition of an older technique. Basically, AI will help the politician not only by recognizing the political techniques used against him or her, but also by providing historical examples of counterattack. I predict that in the coming decades equal levels of AI use will lead to almost equal confrontations, such as world chess championship matches. In this perspective, only the strength of

AI and differences due to natural skills and expended sums by one of the parties will be able to create effective advantages.

The second consequence is related to the quality of the political acts in upcoming decades, which will be a direct effect of the politicians' intellectual level. Specifically, the use of AI will lead to the danger of a lowering of the intellectual, legal, economic, and administrative level of political groups (Pashentsev, 2021). If AI provides examples of good political and administrative practices, as well as techniques and methods of attacking or countering political opponents, why should a politician exert greater intellectual effort? The problem will also arise due to the fact that only political activities can be performed without a standard of study, thus offering the possibility that any person, regardless of academic training, can obtain a superior position in a local or national community, based only on party association. Let us not forget that in most professions that lead to superior positions in the national and local administrative hierarchy there are clear and high standards of education, but their leaders/dignitaries are not conditioned by them. The question arises for any politician: when you have an instrument with the power of AI, why not let it do as much of the public duties as possible? Obviously, from this question to the designation of AI as a strategist and main tool of action in political and electoral campaigns will be only a small step, which most politicians will do without hesitation. Thus, if AI can do so much, why should the politician still learn and improve?

Another fundamental aspect that we must be aware of is that AI never gets tired and can lead a debate on social media forums for hours, and often, just as with a boxer, the person who stands at the end of the fight wins. The resistance of living beings is limited, and competing with an Internet device/profile—which in reality you can't always realize is an electronic one—is frightening from the start, and no one would willingly engage in such a debate. It is not impossible to imagine that certain political debates carried out over hours are in the end only a competition between the AI devices of political competitors.

For all these reasons, there are major consequences for the psychological security of every person who owns devices connected to the Internet. In fact, there is a double menace for everyone, but only the second is targeted by the political operations.

The first problem is human biology, which is not adapted to the whole complex framework of the twenty-first century—from global warming to the global job market, from economic discrepancies to the omnipresence of electronic devices, and so on—and from this point of view, a lot of people will be mentally affected by AI, without having any specific political pressure put on them. AI is a new tool, developed fast, when neurosciences are not totally able to explain all of the brain's functioning, meaning that some of its actions are still not totally understandable by people with average scientific skills. Here we cannot have a real solution, because to create an adequate proportion between biology, the Internet, and AI needs years or even decades. It is necessary to have infrastructure that is able to be used by a larger part of the community in a way that is different from the electronic domain: sport, theater, painting, and so on. The lack of such infrastructure will force people to stay mostly connected to the Internet, becoming psychological prisoners of all cyber space, and targeted AI actions against their minds are just a step away when in this space. Thus, I predict that weak economies, with small sport, cultural, and entertainment infrastructures, will become easier victims of any kind of AI operations ruled by politicians.

The second menace is given by the improper use of AI, transforming its excellent potential for educational, economic, industrial, and medical purposes into a weapon in the hands of amoral and immoral politicians. This type of use is considered—in a delicate manner—as malicious, but in fact it will represent one of the main forms of political AI use in the coming years. MUAI is able to change election campaigns and their results, but it will affect nations' futures, too, favoring some competitors and breaking the main characteristics of a coherent society: human trust, human public morality, human solidarity and cooperation, rule of law, and moral values.

Why this danger? Because the human mind is not always moral—but here is not the place to present all philosophic discussions of human nature. Human nature is sometimes explained by two famous expressions: *homo homini lupus* (man is wolf for another man) and "everything is allowed in love and war." About the relationship between war and politics, we must remember a famous definition given by Clausewitz, who said: "War is nothing more than the continuation of politics by other means ... For political aims are the end and war is the means, and the means can never be conceived without the end" (von Clausewitz, 1832).

In this case, AI use in political campaigns is just a matter of war, because even the general semantics of politics present the competition for power and achievement as a "struggle," or "fight"—words with the precise significance of confrontation. In such a paradigm, the shift from the moral use of AI to a malicious use of it is just a small step that is easy to be made. To more important country position, it is more probable to use AI in a not-moral way, because the prize is high and it brings many advantages for winners; this not-moral way is described in the scientific literature as a "malicious use."

At the same time, we need to remember the continuous geopolitical competitions among countries, which are also eternal and are executed with any imaginable tools. In this competition, "war," "struggle," and "fighting" are not just words, because our planet's history has had bloody events during almost every recorded year. In such context, AI is just a way to compete among others, but its force can create a real new global hierarchy, as a Brookings Institute study mentions: "Whoever leads in artificial intelligence in 2030 will rule the world until 2100" (Indermit, 2020). After agreeing with this sentence, it is obvious that geopolitical competition will use AI without any hesitation and by employing its full dimensions, including the malicious one too.

Political campaigns are often run with limited resources and time, which makes them more brutal than other types of business ventures. With such a lack of time, when different messages can change poll results in a few hours, AI can provide enough useful data for political campaign strategists: to identify and target specific voters who will most likely vote for a candidate; to track the number of ads that have been shown in a given area, as well as what time they were shown; to create personalized campaign messages tailored to individual voters with the help of data gathered from social media posts and other sources; to identify what people search for online or how they spend their time; to predict voter turnout; and so on (Kiran, 2020). For example, the Trump campaign hired the firm known as Cambridge Analytica to access the accounts and profiles of well over 87,000,000 Facebook users by using AI tools; in India during the Lok Sabha election, Prime Minister Modi used a hologram of himself to do virtual rallies at several places targeting different sets of people simultaneously.

Having such data—like never before in all human political campaign history—appears as a danger for MUAI: it is enough for just one political strategist to use AI in a non-ethical way, which would force his competitors to develop methods against such behavior, and from this it is just a step to see the broader use of MUAI in politics.

The use of MUAI in politics will be continuous, because it is only in monarchies that there are life-time positions, with all other positions open to competition. MUAI will appear in two dimensions, both influenced by the quality of countries' science and their financial strength too. Basically, stronger scientific and financial countries will achieve almost a clear regional, continental, and global supremacy—but these capacities will not exclude failed operations and efficient counterattacks. The same model will be replicated at the national level, when stronger and richer parties will be able to defeat other competitors in long-term political campaigns.

We must note two important differences between the dimensions of MUAI. Firstly, at the national level, it is easier to defeat a rich party because the selection of a candidate can easily fail under other parties' attacks, and any strong leadership crisis can consume a big part of parties' financial resources. The second difference is a result of the country geopolitical global position: for some, national politics remain just national, but for the main regional/continental and global powers, any political campaign will attract international interest and—in some cases—MUAI from other governments.

AI is changing the human mind just by the simple pronunciation of its name. This force of change helps the AI to occupy a strong position to influence the political game and the behavior of politicians and voters in such ways that psychologists will be requested to explain some of the politicians' actions. In such a new "equation of forces," the AI will start to not just influence the human psyche, but also to replace some part of the old instruments used in political campaigns, becoming one of the key factors in any political strategy of the coming decades.

Malicious Use of Artificial Intelligence in Political Campaigns: The Rising Threats

If today's elections and political campaigns are something natural, the ways they are conducted reveal deep concerns in many countries. Too many examples of frauds are known from history school handbooks, and also too many new strong electronic tools were created in the last decades, with a huge impact on human behavior. Having these in mind, any voter—and any political strategist too—can try to answer this question with caution: can AI be used in political campaigns in a proper manner?

What are the purposes and values of a political campaign? Who does it serve, and what should we expect from it? These are not idle questions. Thanks to huge infusions of money and technology in the last three decades, a modern political campaign has become either an impressive juggernaut of optimized technology delivering relevant messages to citizens or a cold, clinical machine that has lost touch with the beating heart citizen democracy. And in the wake of elections that saw a well-funded, well-organized, and well-planned campaign lose to an ad-hoc, upstart, chaotic outsider, every conventional wisdom about the correct way to organize and manage a campaign is rightly being questioned (McGuire, 2019, p. 5).

In such a paradigm, AI has its own strong position and it will increase over the coming years, no matter the endless pandemic and conflicts in Europe or other continents. This growth is possible because political strategists need more data now on consumer demographics, behavior and attitudes, including health and location data given by smartphones, smartwatches, and any kind of computers (Bartlett et al., 2018). Elon Musk's buying of Twitter can be understood as an expression of such, adding new questions about billionaires' role in national policy creation.

While Donald Trump's campaign during the 2016 US election received a lot of media coverage for its use of big data analytics, similar approaches have been used by a number of campaigns in recent years (Cadwalladr, 2017). During the EU referendum in the UK, Dominic Cummings estimates that Vote Leave ran around one billion targeted adverts in the run up to the vote, mostly via Facebook. Like Trump's campaign, they sent out multiple different versions of messages, testing them in an interactive feedback loop. In the 2017 UK general election, the Labour Party used data modelling to identify potential Labour voters, and then target them with messages. Through the use of an in-house tool called "Promote" which combined Facebook information with Labour voter data, senior Labour activists were able to send locally based messages to the right (i.e., persuadable) people (Waterson, 2017).

Elections are becoming increasingly "datafied," with advertising and marketing techniques being offered by a network of private contractors and data analysts, offering cutting-edge methods for audience segmentation and targeting to political parties all over the world. Many of these techniques were first developed in the commercial sector—as pointed out in a brief analysis of digital marketing in political campaigns, "electoral politics has now become fully integrated into a growing, global commercial digital media and marketing ecosystem that has already transformed how corporations market their products and influence consumers" (Chester & Montgomery, 2017). In such new "media painting," elections could be seen just as competition of "who owns more data," meaning that a good campaign script is missing, and political doctrines will be replaced by simple information accumulation.

In such a new world, smartphones have come to have their own role in political campaigns, because their small dimensions—compared with a PC—simplify the process of gaining exposure to video and messages, because it offers less opportunity to check the accuracy of the data. In fact, the smartphone interface amplifies the document/link you currently see, keeping in the shadows the possibility of being distracted by other films/add-ons/links/documents and so on. Being easier to keep in pockets, smartphones started to win the competition on device-selling: since 2014, more than 1 billion smartphones are bought every year (Statista, 2022), forcing political strategists to adapt their campaigns to them. For political campaigns smartphones are very important, because the use of smartphones with "always-on" Internet connection has increased the challenge for the management of interactions, intended interpretations, mutuality of information, and eventual interpretations; users are always available for typing texts, recording audio files, or browsing the web even if other people are also physically co-present (Yus, 2021).

The most important thing for the complex relations between AI, smartphones, and political campaigns is the localization of the user. Every minute, a person can be located by meta-dates, and as a result there has been a strong use of AI in political campaigns to use this great possibility to provide targeted messages: if someone is located in a dangerous area, it will provide messages about strong enforcement and new legal proposals to punish criminals; if someone is consulting through his smartphone in a hospital, a political message about healthcare improvement will come; and so on. No matter the place you are in, a good AI tool used in a national political campaign can bring advantages to politicians—the distinction between local and national elections is very important here because the legal domicile linked to one's voting is not always the same as the place of that person's daily activities.

Smartphones have a complex effect on the human brain, increasing mental laziness, reducing available cognitive capacity (Ward et al., 2018), and affecting reading comprehension (Honma et al., 2022). All these characteristics are very important not only for daily working efficiency but also in politics, because the lack of comprehension creates strong opportunities for any kind of manipulation, political included. In an article published in the MIT Technology Review, it was clearly affirmed by a former Google manager that smartphones are weapons of mass manipulation (Metz, 2017), and it is easy to understand that this wide effect is applied to politics too.

In fact, smartphones are a very useful instrument for promoting fake news in politics. Their interface, as I mentioned before, favors the one-message view, and this characteristic is fundamental for political campaigns, because politicians want their messages to arrive single and to be seen without any interference from an add-on/video/document and so on. In the case of the smartphone, all political tricks and any kind of malicious behavior find a good platform to act through a biological eyesight algorithm, which is much more concentrated when the main image is small. The size difference between PC and smartphone screens forces the human eye to concentrate on a different scale, changing the force of the message in the same proportion. In a very honest way, we must admit that the smartphone is a blessing for commercials, marketing, and any kind of strong public message—with or without political meaning, but it is also a strong provocation for the human brain because its natural capacities are not developed to face such an avalanche of messages. The lack of cognitive capacities "obtained" as a result of smartphone usage—as mentioned above—appears because their interface forces users to concentrate on a single message for many hours, contrary to natural human evolution, which was directly influenced by the capacity to have a wider span of awareness of one's environment.

The smartphone-social media connection has built on this history. But smartphone politics has also catalyzed something new. Our constant digital connection and access to vast networks facilitate new ways of doing politics. For one thing, our phones allow us to bypass mainstream media, which is often selective in its coverage (Aschoff, 2021). In this paradigm, we must note that the technological progress of the smartphone attracts the deep-fakes growth too. False information used for the purpose of changing the human mind became a daily situation, and the next years will lead to them increasing in importance, as political campaigns will continue to exist.

Today our world—from a legal, political, and economic perspective—is too complex for a single political campaign, forcing strategists to create more sub-strategies to address such social differences. All educational systems developed in the last century—and mainly after World War Two—accent the power of the individual, opposing his interest to that of others. This process created more atomized societies, with more independent voices and more individual claims from governments, local authorities, and politicians. The huge number of independent citizen voices force political strategists to adapt to all claims, which is objectively impossible. In such a way, politicians lose contact with people, and only the appearance of AI has helped them to solve this problem. Before AI, a politician and his team traveled cities, villages, and on streets to convince people of their message without any guarantee that their message would reach the people.

Internet and mobile technologies helped politicians to change two main political campaign characteristics. Firstly, the dialogue becomes more personalized (one to one), given messages having no filter from other people. Secondly, politicians now have a clear image of political options and social needs without interventions from lobbying groups, being able to develop more effective campaigns. If we look carefully to those two characteristics, we observe the need for AI in political campaigns, because the diversity of electors must be faced by the same number of propagandists. Politicians' staffs are not so big, but the need to offer a diversified message to citizens is strong, and it is necessary to develop an electronic instrument to play this role. That instrument must be intelligent and able to adapt its messages and dialogue to any kind of answers and claims; being electronic is artificial, and if we add those characteristics, we have AI.

Political competitions of today are complicated because of huge "today libraries"—digital and physical—who remember any action, declaration, or failure of politicians. A good "today library" offers easy access to its information, forcing politicians to be more cautious than ever, transforming politics into a continuous campaign, forcing the creation of new electoral strategies. Because of this, political competition is in fact uninterrupted, and AI will be used in virtually the same way. Operation Cambridge Analytica was only an expression of a reality that any electoral strategist understands very well: because political options can change very quickly—sometimes at intervals of days or hours—it is necessary to develop a deep knowledge of potential voter activism. In this sense, any political party that wants to win elections in the coming years must invest in procuring services to monitor the options and ideas about the population through AI. More important than gasoline prices for cars in "door-to-door" political campaigns will be the strong access offered by AI to voters' psychological profiles and metadata that create a better image of human behavior than a normal brain can imagine or accept (Duhigg, 2012).

Getting good information about voters' mental profiles is very important, but a political strategist must launch a campaign that makes people vote and not just stay on the sofa, criticizing political offers. Every person is different, and AI helps political strategists to understand not just the big segments of voters' communities but even the smallest differences among them. Thus, it is mandatory to not just know about these differences but to build messages able to lead people to be trustful enough of ideas and to manifest enough adherence to those ideas by going to vote. But here human psychology underlines that political messages are not able to have the same meaning for every voter, and from this perspective it is also clear that the perfect politician does not exist because his messages cannot be totally accepted by the whole voting group.

To reach a stronger result in voters' minds becomes more complicated than ever when a voter's psyche is strongly influenced by an informational ocean. It is not possible today to ignore the increasingly stronger human pride and its consequences for individual opinion creation, including in politics; more pride means much stronger opinions and more loyalties to them. Regarding such strong mental relations, voters' ideas and loyalty to those ideas, a political campaign must act differently, helping voters to feel themselves important and as though they are presenting a candidate's program as having a deep connection with voters' opinions. Objectively, this purpose can be achieved just by individually personalized campaigns because politicians in a public campaign can just give general messages. To fulfill this goal, a politician needs a strong human presence—as in traditional "door-to-door" campaign—and a lot of money to send its voting-team all over the country. Even if you have both—money and a human campaign infrastructure—you are not able to cover the whole voter's mind for 24 hours/day, meaning that effectiveness is not totally assured by campaign staff visits and contact with voters.

The Internet world is mainly about the mobile Internet (i.e., the smartphone space), which has changed the needs for what constitutes an effective political campaign. Before the appearance of the smartphone, people spent some hours on television, some hours working, some hours reading newspapers, some hours doing sports, and so on, but with clear limits among these actions. The creation of the smartphone brought the Internet's possibilities everywhere: from jogging to taking a daily walk to one's job and from watching news to commenting on social media and so on. Thus, the smartphone changed almost all human activities—even sleep is affected—making political strategists prisoners to this new reality: if they are not on a smartphone more often, their candidate will disappear from the public space.

Having a need, we have the direction of action, too: politicians need that instrument/technology to efficiently reach voters' smartphone. To be "efficient" in this context means not just to spread political messages, but to send targeted messages that are totally personalized. Or, to provide totally personalized messages, you need to first know the destination public. The result will be—for the needs of the political strategist—a tool able to answer two specific requests: a) 24 hours/day information about voter's ideas and behavior and b) the chance to enter into contact with voters in a persuasive way. Of course, a persuasive tool must be able to convince a voter for more than one day and in fact change political voters' options. In a brief and honest way, we need to underline that AI development is very dependent on political needs, at least in the twenty-first century. An eventual history of technology will be written in the twenty-second century that will need to find the correct proportion of AI development between political needs and commercial/companies' interests, but, in my opinion, the political part will almost be equal to the commercial one.

Speaking about the task AI must perform, we must understand too that money influences AI development. Stronger AI—paid for by some politicians/parties—will bring more accurate information to political strategists and it will create a big gap in political competition. This financial difference will be very important at the international level, because big technological powers will use their advantage against any competitors, favoring some politicians and blocking others, in a complex effort to influence political leadership abroad.

More money, more AI political actions. There are two important things to note that underline the importance of money in political AI operations. Firstly, AI has not completed its development; its evolution is just at its beginning. Today we are used to having many technological peaks, and the differences between some producers are not so high—from airplanes to mobile phones, from medicine to agriculture, and so on—but the case of AI is a different situation. One AI case we are still developing is in experimenting with learning, and rich countries are leading the race to its application to endeavors at almost any commercial and administrative level. So to speak, we are still expecting surprises in AI development, and the race is not even at its middle, offering more situations for concurrence and alliances. Money will be very important here to pay the cost of development and experiments, with a sad conclusion: in the global AI race, the poor countries will remain weak, following the technological leaders very slowly, with more than a decade delay. This first characteristic will be important in geopolitical competitions and global hierarchies, reaching all human activities: politics, commerce, military, sport, and so on.

Secondly, an important consideration is the continuous character of today's political campaigns, because an ocean of information and news force politicians to be present every day in voters' attention. This costs—again—a lot of money, because some political strategists must create messages able to reach and influence the human mind. To "create" means to pay someone to think and to "produce" means (first) to pay AI instruments to collect information about the voters' main concerns and, second, after a while effective political messages will spread. Again, money competition between parties and politicians will offer some clear expectations for national political competitions: a poor party will usually have low public reach and be hardly able to influence the political arena. It is true that in national competitions there are some specific topics able to quickly crush a whole party or group of leaders, but these substantial changes do not happen every day. Thus, a rich party will be able to (first) buy strong AI tools and to use them against competitors and (second) to promote specific regulations. AI use will favor the big parties and in this case it can be imagined that some regulations for "social research," a nickname for collecting data about national voters using AI, will be set in place.

During political competition, the MUAI becomes very important. Why? Because in a rule of law twenty-first century many harsh differences between political disappeared. These differences made by political platforms are a topic of deep analysis done by specialists, but the general public only knows the basics of the parties' visions. No matter the differences in the parties' visions on tax, money distribution, the social system, criminal justice policy, and so on, common people have their beliefs, and their vote is expressed according to them. In such a situation, AI becomes fundamental to knowing these beliefs and to changing them in a way that is controlled by the AI operator.

A continuous campaign with just political program underlinings is not sufficient, because human nature is not always rational. Political competition is with almost no boundaries, and thus it is necessary to add emotions and rationality to the same strategy. But there is an important difference among these parts of political strategies: rational pillars of political programs have fewer adherents, and when emotional messages are able to reach more people in a shorter time, it is best to mobilize them in a partisan direction. As many researchers prove—truly, economists have been more preoccupied on this topic (e.g., Ariely, 2012)—human behavior is far from predictable or totally pragmatic, and emotions have a strong position in man's actions. Thus, if emotions are much stronger than human average thinking, politicians and their strategists must generate and control them (i.e., emotions) to achieve a specific political result, keeping in mind that such actions can in fact just be manipulation.

Positive emotions are difficult to create, and, in any case, they must be personalized according to the AI operation's wishes. But the political strategy handbook also underlines that positive emotions must appear very close to the election day. Meanwhile, political campaigns will face a different message typology related to the main facts that are presented in the media. Because the media today is mainly interested in dysfunctional realities, the political campaign will follow the repair of these problems. But because a dysfunctional society has human causes, politics will follow the line, and it will present and underline the leaders who were not able to fulfill the legal standards. AI use will be dedicated to find voters' opinions about facts, responsibilities, and ways to correct situations. After AI operators get the answers to these three questions, they will send them to political strategists to create messages for the politician who pays them.

To create strong voters' opinions, political strategists will need to use AI to create emotions and to implement an effective movement for the politicians who paid them. In fact, a recent study has shown how AI can learn to identify vulnerabilities in human habits and behaviors and use them to influence human decision-making (Dezfouli et al., 2020). But strong voters' opinions need strong messages, which are able to disrupt the human mind. AI will help political strategists to create such messages able to respond to any person's thoughts, leading him to love and/or hate a specific politician/party/ideology.

To obtain success in such operations, it has become necessary to use AI in a malicious way because a positive campaign is not able to create or to increase emotions that last for a long time.

Political needs require a loyal voter, but today the informational ocean is able to quite easily change the minds of people in any direction, provoking nightmares for political strategists. Thus, they need to solve this equation—loyal voters versus abundance of opinions/ideas/ideologies—in an effective way, and AI capability will be fundamental for this purpose. The advent of mobile Internet and smartphones will force political strategists to use AI in such a way as to occupy most of the smartphone user's time. To get this "screen occupation" it will be necessary to have strong messages that are able to hold captive the human mind. Such a result—to hold a voter's mind captive—will need messages that are able to make an impression for a long time, and this goal also encourages the use of MUAI because the wish to strongly impress people is common not only to politics but also to commercial activities. This means that the human mind consumes more strong messages daily than ever in mankind's history, affecting people's psychological security.

Even scientists want to cooperate with very educated people, who are able to recognize marketing techniques and other forms of manipulation, but the reality is far from this. The abundance of information, daily problems from job, school, family, and so on, and other stress factors distort the human mind and make it vulnerable to many political tricks. From such a perspective, psychological security becomes very important, and because of these situations it will be added to MUAI.

Political campaigns have—after some years—a regular concluding moment: the elections. At that moment, all mistakes are forgotten either in the case of a win or not, in the case of losing. Elections are not only the possible conclusion of political careers, but they are mostly the result of political strategists' competition and rely on their techniques. It is very difficult from a legal point of view to prove a political campaign has been manipulative—and it is important to note that only the winner's techniques are in the public eye, but leading politicians will act with all their administrative tools against any investigation or campaign: MUAI is inevitable.

The lack of legal sanctions in fact will favor the MUAI to levels almost not imaginable today, but that are somehow understandable by citizens. For example, a study organized by the Australian National Science Agency—by its digital research section—reached some interesting conclusions. "Nearly half of respondents (45%) are unwilling to share their information or data with an AI system. Two in five (40%) are unwilling to rely on recommendations or other output of an AI system. Further, many Australians are not convinced about the trustworthiness of AI systems, generally accept (42%) or tolerate AI (28%), and only few approve (16%) or embrace (7%) it … Overwhelmingly (96%), Australians expect AI to be regulated and most expect external, independent oversight. Most Australians (over 68%) have moderate to high confidence in the federal government and regulatory agencies to regulate and govern AI in the best interests of the public. However, the current regulation and laws fall short of community expectations" (Lockey et al., 2020).

People are conscious today about the need for AI regulation. The complex situation of AI's development is globally understood, but every wise citizen is also conscious about the technological gaps between countries. The danger represented by uneven AI progress is real, and it will be expressed mainly in geopolitics, but also in internal political competitions and campaigns.

In the geopolitical sphere, it is impossible to believe that Tanzania or Mozambique will be able to develop AI tools stronger than South Africa, for example, as Bulgaria and Albania will be in the same position in comparison with Germany, too. AI is part of the most important human-industrial revolution—the fourth one (Schwab, WEF, 2016)—and every country will approach it with different levels of economic strength and with a predictable result: the economic gaps of today will be conserved in the next decade, as the Brookings Institute study revealed. In fact, some geopoliticians think today about a future of harsh competition between the USA and China (Wang & Chen, 2018; Hass & Balin, 2019; Allison & Schmidt, 2020; Hass, 2021; Sullivan, 2021; Haenle & Bresnick, 2022), meaning that AI tools will be used in various ways, from genuine to very malicious, with complicated consequences for the whole planet.

More interesting will be to examine the use of AI—especially in its malicious use—in national areas. The pandemic and also 5G technology represent a good topic to analyze the MUAI perspective on national legislation and administrative practices. There are a lot of people who believe that AI is used by governments against their own citizens (Pennycook & Rand, 2018; Roozenbeek & van der Linden, 2019; Evanega et al., 2020)—as is the worst case of MUAI—and these two areas (the pandemic and 5G technology) are part of a "conspiracy of rich against poor," "human selection," and so on. In this second case, the problem is represented by the national rulers and the legal force they use to regulate society—they are creating laws and people are just subjects of them (laws). We must admit in fact that some truth exists in this last phrase, as I underlined before about the lack of legal control for political campaign tricks: national regulators must create laws able to punish political parties who enforce them in specific superior administrative positions, and here everyone who has legitimate doubt could benefit from remembering the meaning of "egoism".

Relations between national political leaders, those interested in being re-elected, and the constitutional right to create laws can be used to promote political parties' strength above the citizens' strength, if ethical considerations are not strongly adhered to. When you, as a politician, have the right to decide about people's position inside society, you can be a danger for all citizens, as many reports have revealed over the last few years. In fact, global rankings of freedoms—freedom of speech (Freedom House, 2021) and of the press (Reporters Without Borders, 2021)—and rights (World Justice Project, 2021) have declined in several countries, and the quality of governance has actually declined in several countries too, although the private sector has created and used technologies that have themselves improved the population's living standards. Most of the rights and freedoms questioned and reduced in recent years have been victims of the executive branch, which has benefited from the decline of representative institutions that are chosen by citizens (Mennicken & Salais, 2022). The need for ethics in the political space is now at its peak, because MUAI will harm psychological security and human rights, making it possible to create the strongest dictatorships ever. In the face of governmental MUAI, citizens have almost no chance to win, and the final result is a totalitarian society, like some wise writers warned us of many decades ago.

The rising threats of the MUAI in political campaigns have started to be seen in many countries, indicating a general lack of trust in today's politicians. From such a perspective, it might be possible to not see and not accept genuine AI use in any domain. The correct balance between good and bad in AI use in all spheres can be a real provocation for legislators and voters too, but there is no guarantee of an easy and profitable result for all.

Regulating Artificial Intelligence Use: Preventing Malicious Use of Artificial Intelligence and Protecting Psychological Security

Regulating AI use is very complicated because AI's evolution is not finished. Much more, AI has a great psychological potential and most legislation has a role in organizing human activities but not the human psyche. It is also a strong obstacle to regulation that geopolitical competition will hide some AI developments from the public, keeping them for the country's own interests. In such a case, the rules will not be totally prescriptive, asking for high skills of legislate. As public law specialists (e.g. Balan, 2008) underlined, to create rules for nations is complicated not only because of specific legislator's interests but also because of differences in legal systems: the harmonization of these systems to produce a global rule in any area (social, political, economic, etc.) would require the most difficult cases to change some of their strong national peculiarities, even linguistic ones.

The purpose of AI regulations must be the enforcement of ethics, because a strong pillar against MUAI's ability to affect the psychological security of people and countries is the moral and ethical dimensions of life. However, it is necessary to underline that a very large number of ethical principles, codes, guidelines, and frameworks have been proposed over the past few years. There are currently more than 70 recommendations, published in the last 3 years, just about the ethics of AI. This mushrooming of documents is generating inconsistency and confusion among stakeholders regarding which one may be preferable. It also puts pressure on private and public actors—that design, develop, or deploy digital solutions—to produce their own declarations for fear of appearing to be left behind, thus further contributing to the redundancy of information. In this case, the main, unethical risk is that all this hyperactivity creates a "market of principles and values," where private and public actors may shop for the kind of ethics that is best retrofitted to justify their current behaviors, rather than revising their behaviors to make them consistent with a socially accepted ethical framework (Floridi, 2021).

To concentrate on just ethics is not useful because it has a big vulnerability: the lack of effective punishment in cases of ethical violation. Ethical sanctions are almost always moral, and politicians seem to not be impressed by this; citizens also have the full right to ask for effective punishment of ethical transgressions, because social satisfaction appears when rule violators suffer for their behavior. In the case of psychological security, AI regulation must prevent MUAI—or, at least, diminish it to a controllable level, and, for this to take place, legislators must find the correct proportion between specific legal sanctions (prison, fines) and ethics.

I shall examine a brief form of AI regulation to protect psychological security at the international and national levels, underlining the main characteristics of such and trying to present the basics of the main mandatory rules that must be included. This article's dimensions do not allow me to present a whole Code of AI, but it is necessary to underline the dual legal nature of such regulations—they must address public law and private law, which is not very common for national legislation.

Firstly, the international regulation of AI will be very difficult to adopt and even more difficult to implement. The lack of sanctions for international rules will result in non-enforcement—for example, if a country uses AI in a malicious way, what administrative force will come to apply some sanctions against that government? This complicates the jurist's work. Basically, the jurists who will create international rules on AI, protecting psychological security—in fact, any other legal or moral value—will be forced to resume their work according to principles and ethics.

The main principles that need to appear in international AI regulation include the transparency of AI use; predictability of AI use; security of AI use—both for people, but also for its direct users; protection of human rights; citizen participation in national AI regulation; equality between citizens and institutions in AI use and AI applications; impartial use of AI; protecting humanity during AI use; self-restriction of AI use to genuine directions. For psychological security, it is very important to have some principles that will underline the need for AI users' self-control, because AI development can create more opportunities to harm the human psyche, and operators can always cross the line between legal and not-legal/ethical and not-ethical.

A complex international AI regulation might include a Higher Court of Justice just for such cases, but with a realist's brain, I must admit that there is a very small possibility that we will see its creation very soon, so at least in this decade the answer to that is negative. At the same time, no one can predict with high accuracy today the legal tendencies of the next decades, and what today seems almost impossible might be a goal of the main technological powers. Some international regulations of AI use will need to proclaim some type of consultations between countries, just to prevent—or to try to solve—MUAI being able to harm psychological security. But because of the lack of sanctions—which is an issue for many international law branches—AI regulations will not progress too much in effectiveness, at least in this decade. Only after AI use will have established a stable international order will it be possible to have more precise and effective international regulations, with a specific "right of police" exercised by the superior technological powers above the small ones—but almost without any limits applied to them.

Regulation will be more effective at the national level of AI use because governments have almost complete strength to punish any rule violation. Keeping in mind the possibility that even a government will use AI in a malicious way against its citizens, I shall present here the main parts of AI national regulation, underlining the dimension of psychological security protection.

First, such AI legislation should be adopted after a wide process of consultation with citizens, universities, lawyers, judges, prosecutors, companies, and civil society. The consequences of formal consultations will be mistrust in governmental intentions, which might create more problems. Secondly, national legislation on AI use will be more effective and more administrative than international regulations. Here governments will be able to follow its implementation, and an effective partnership with society will bring benefits for all parties involved in the regulation of AI's creators. At this level, AI regulations can be created in deep connection with Administrative Procedures Codes and with any other law that organizes the national administrative structures, because it will then be necessary to create a national administrative institution to regulate AI use.

The principles of AI use at the national level will be quite the same as those presented in international regulation. Here we must underline the necessity to create and add the "principle of proportional use of AI," because its use must be adequate for the purpose of not putting more pressure on the human psyche, violating one's psychological security. Because of the characteristics of national law, it will include two other principles: "the legality of the regulations," which need to apply to any kind of AI use, and "the principle of public interest in political AI use." In the commercial branch of AI regulations will be included some principles related to the profit needs of business, but psychological security is regulated by public (administrative) law, and it (psychological security) requests a strong mention of public interest in political and administrative AI use.

National AI regulations will create a specific administrative structure with the purpose of monitoring AI users' practices. Its role must be something close to an administrative structure that monitors the concentrations of commercial firms and the collaboration between companies.

A specific regulation to prevent MUAI must be included in national political parties' legislation and in the election laws, too. It must be clearly mentioned in the MUAI prohibition that there will be sanctions applicable to politicians and parties who violate these rules, from fines to prison and even the dissolution of the political party. Because the violation of psychological security by MUAI can provoke social explosions, even fines for such behavior must be substantial, just to prevent even small cases of such. At the same time, there is also the potential problem that governments can use such big fines to eliminate strong opponents, and this administrative behavior is not just a genuine possibility but also a very effective one. To address this, there must be included in AI regulation some restrictions even for governments that prevent them from creating "the appetite for rule of law and democracy demolition."

Of course, at a national level, there must be created a specific regulation for justice claims to be made against MUAI. A specific functional competence—for example, such cases should be sent to the Supreme Court of Justice—can underline to any AI user that violation of psychological security through the use of MUAI in the electoral arena is a very serious crime, and it must be punished in such a way as to impress the whole country. The court decision texts should be published in official journals, underlining once more the importance of psychological security and the legal consequences of MUAI.

In the end, it is necessary to teach law faculties, students, and prosecutors about MUAI in the political arena. For this, it is not enough to just create new legislation, but it is also necessary to create some specific and independent courses on master and post-graduate programs.

Conclusion

To many commentators, AI is the most exciting technology of our age, promising the development of intelligent machines that can surpass humans in various tasks, as well as create new products, services, and capabilities, and even build machines that can improve themselves, perhaps eventually beyond all human capabilities. The last decade has witnessed rapid progress in AI based on the application of modern machine learning techniques. AI algorithms are now used by almost all online platforms and in industries that range from manufacturing to health, finance, wholesale, and retail. Government agencies have also started relying on AI, especially in the criminal justice system and in customs and immigration control (Acemoglu et al., 2022).

But AI use is not available to all countries to the same degree, and this gap might create a lot of problems in the next decades, and because geopolitical competition is eternal, its actors are not always happy to act according to international law principles and rules. The same problem is met on a national level, with some specific differences, because here governments can create more dangers for people with MUAI, violating their psychological security to such a level that social explosions can appear or strong totalitarian regimes can be created.

In this paradigm, my text has tried to express some concerns about MUAI on today's political competitions. A political campaign today becomes a continuous struggle among politicians, and their strategists are forced to diversify voting attraction techniques. For such purposes, AI development appears as a gift from God for political strategists and its benefits are huge—from access to voters' psychological profiles to a stronger message being spread to citizens. The future of political campaigns will be influenced by AI capacities, but at the same time, AI operators can become vulnerable to many thoughts and even to less desirable behaviors.

Having these facts and dangers in mind, I tried to describe why we must create a legal system—at the international and national level—able to prevent MUAI and any violation of psychological security. For sure, today's ideas will change in time, and in 20 years some of my concerns will have been improved or worsened. A legal response is important for not only legislators but also AI operators, because they need to know not only lawyers' concerns but also what regulation directions are being discussed today. This can prevent mistakes or such behaviors as are able to harm the human psyche, affecting psychological security in the political campaign arena.

References

Acemoglu D., Ozdaglar A., & Siderius J. (2022). A model of online misinformation. Retrieved May 19, 2022, from https://siderius.lids.mit.edu/wp-content/uploads/sites/36/2022/01/fake-news-revision-v10.pdf

Agudo, U. (2021). The influence of algorithms on political and dating decisions. Retrieved May 19, 2022, from https://www.ncbi.nlm.nih.gov/pmc/articles/PMC8059858/

Allison, G., & Schmidt, E. (2020). Is China beating the U.S. to AI supremacy? Retrieved May 19, 2022, from https://www.belfercenter.org/sites/default/files/2020-08/AISupremacy.pdf

Ariely, D. (2012). *The honest truth about dishonesty: How we lie to everyone—Especially ourselves*. HarperCollins.

Aschoff N. (2021) The smartphone society: Technology, power, and resistance in the new gilded age, .

Balan, E. (2008). *Institutii administrative (administrative institutions)*. C.H. Beck.

Bartlett J., Smith J., & Acton R. (2018). The future of political campaigning. Retrieved May 19, 2022, from https://ico.org.uk/media/2259365/the-future-of-political-campaigning.pdf

Cadwalladr C. (2017). *British courts may unlock secrets of how Trump campaign profiled US voters. Legal mechanism may help academic expose how Big Data firms like Cambridge Analytica and Facebook get their information*. Retrieved May 19, 2022, from https://www.theguardian.com/technology/2017/oct/01/cambridge-analytica-big-data-facebook-trump-voters

Chester J., & Montgomery, K. C. (2017). The role of digital marketing in political campaigns. Retrieved May 19, 2022, from https://doi.org/10.14763/2017.4.773.

Dezfouli, A., Nock, R., Dayan, P. (2020). Adversarial vulnerabilities of human decision-making. Retrieved May 19, 2022, from https://doi.org/10.1073/pnas.2016921117

Digital around the world. (2022). Retrieved May 19, 2022, from https://datareportal.com/global-digital-overview

Dowd, R. (2022). *The birth of digital human rights. Digitized data governance as a human rights issue in the EU*. Palgrave Macmillan.

Duhigg, C. (2012). *The power of habit: Why we do what we do in life and business*. Random House.

Evanega, S., Lynas, M., Adams, J., & Smolenyak, K. (2020). Coronavirus misinformation: Quantifying sources and themes in the COVID-19 'infodemic. Retrieved May 19, 2022, from https://allianceforscience.cornell.edu/wp-content/uploads/2020/10/Evanega-et-al-Coronavirus-misinformation-submitted_07_23_20-1.pdf

Floridi, L. (Ed.). (2021). *Ethics, governance, and policies in artificial intelligence*. Springer.

Freedom House. (2021). Freedom in the World, 2021. Democracy under siege. Retrieved May 19, 2022, from https://freedomhouse.org/report/freedom-world/2021/democracy-under-siege

Haenle, P., & Bresnick, S. (2022). Why U.S.-China relations are locked in a stalemate. Retrieved May 19, 2022, from https://carnegieendowment.org/2022/02/21/why-u.s.-china-relations-are-locked-in-stalemate-pub-86478

Hass, R, & Balin, Z. (2019). *US-China relations in the age of artificial intelligence*. Retrieved May 19, 2022, from https://www.brookings.edu/research/us-china-relations-in-the-age-of-artificial-intelligence/

Hass, R. (2021). How China is responding to escalating strategic competition with the US. Retrieved May 19, 2022,from https://www.brookings.edu/articles/how-china-is-responding-to-escalating-strategic-competition-with-the-us/

Honma, M., Masaoka, Y., Iizuka, N., Wada, S., Kamimura, S., Yoshikawa, A., Moriya, R., Kamijo, S., & Izumizaki, M. (2022). Reading on a smartphone affects sigh generation, brain activity, and comprehension. Retrieved May 19, 2022, from https://www.nature.com/articles/s41598-022-05605-0

Indermit, G (2020). Whoever leads in artificial intelligence in 2030 will rule the world until 2100. Retrieved May 19, 2022, from https://www.brookings.edu/blog/future-development/2020/01/17/whoever-leads-in-artificial-intelligence-in-2030-will-rule-the-world-until-2100/

Kiran, V. (2020). Artificial intelligence in election campaign: Artificial intelligence and data for politics. Retrieved May 19, 2022, from https://politicalmarketer.com/artificial-intelligence-in-election-campaign/

Larson, E. J. (2021). *The myth of artificial intelligence. Why computers Can't think the way we do*. The Belknap Press of Harvard University Press.

Lockey, S., Gillespie, N., & Curtis, C. (2020). Trust in artificial intelligence: Australian insights. Retrieved May 19, 2022, from https://doi.org/10.14264/b32f129

McGuire B. (2019). *Scaling the field program in modern political campaigns*. Retrieved May 19, 2022, from https://www.hks.harvard.edu/sites/default/files/degree%20programs/MPP/files/Scaling%20the%20Field%20Organization%20in%20Modern%20Political%20Campaigns_Final.pdf

Mennicken, A., & Salais, R. (Eds.). (2022). *The new politics of numbers. Utopia, evidence and democracy*. Palgrave Macmillan.

Metz, R. (2017). Smartphones are weapons of mass manipulation, and this guy is declaring war on them. Retrieved May 19, 2022, from https://www.technologyreview.com/2017/10/19/148493/smartphones-are-weapons-of-mass-manipulation-and-this-guy-is-declaring-war-on-them/

Nielsen, R. K. (2012). *Ground wars—Personalized communication in political campaigns*. Princeton University Press.

Pashentsev, E. (2021). The malicious use of artificial intelligence through agenda setting: Challenges to political stability. In *Proceedings of the 3rd European Conference on the Impact of Artificial Intelligence and Robotics ECIAIR 2021*, Academic Conferences International Limited.

Pennycook, G., & Rand, D. G. (2018). Lazy, not biased: Susceptibility to partisan fake news is better explained by lack of reasoning than by motivated reasoning. *Cognition*. https://doi.org/10.1016/j.cognition.2018.06.011

Reporters Without Borders. (2021). The world press freedom index 2021. Retrieved May 19, 2022, from https://rsf.org/en/world-press-freedom-index

Roozenbeek, J., & van der Linden, S. (2019). Fake news game confers psychological resistance against online misinformation. Retrieved May 19, 2022, from https://www.nature.com/articles/s41599-019-0279-9

Schwab, K. (2016). The Fourth Industrial Revolution: what it means, how to respond. Retrieved May 19, 2022, from https://www.weforum.org/agenda/2016/01/the-fourth-industrial-revolution-what-it-means-and-how-to-respond/

Statista. (2022). Smartphones—Statistics & facts. Retrieved May 19, 2022, from https://www.statista.com/topics/840/smartphones/

Statista, Number of daily active Facebook users worldwide as of 4th quarter. (2021). (in millions). Retrieved May 19, 2022, from https://www.statista.com/statistics/346167/facebook-global-dau/

Sullivan, R. (2021). The U.S., China, and artificial intelligence competition factors. Retrieved May 19, 2022, from https://www.airuniversity.af.edu/Portals/10/CASI/documents/Research/Cyber/2021-10-04%20US%20China%20AI%20Competition%20Factors.pdf?ver=KBcxNomlMXM86FnIuuvNEw%3D%3D

Vogels, E. (2021). Millennials stand out for their technology use, but older generations also embrace digital life. Retrieved May 19, 2022, from https://www.pewresearch.org/fact-tank/2019/09/09/us-generations-technology-use/

von Clausewitz, C. (1832). *On war cost of election*. Retrieved May 19, 2022, from https://www.opensecrets.org/elections-overview/cost-of-election?cycle=2020&display=T&infl=Y

Wang, Y., & Chen, D. (2018). Rising Sino-U.S. competition in artificial intelligence. *China Quarterly of International Strategic Studies, 4*(2), 241–258. https://doi.org/10.1142/S2377740018500148.

Ward, A. F., Duke, K., Gneezy, A., & Bos, M. W. (2018). Brain drain: The mere presence of one's own smartphone reduces available cognitive capacity. Retrieved May

19, 2022, from https://repositories.lib.utexas.edu/bitstream/handle/2152/64130/braindrain.pdf

Waterson, J. (2017). Here's how labour ran an under-the-radar dark ads campaign during the general election. Retrieved May 29, 2022, from https://www.buzzfeed.com/jimwaterson/heres-how-labour-ran-an-under-the-radar-dark-ads-campaign

World Health Organization. (2021). *GHE: Life expectancy and healthy life expectancy*. Retrieved May 19, 2022, from https://www.who.int/data/gho/data/themes/mortality-and-global-health-estimates/ghe-life-expectancy-and-healthy-life-expectancy

World Justice Project. (2021). The world justice project rule of law index 2021. Retrieved May 19, 2022, from https://worldjusticeproject.org/our-work/research-and-data/wjp-rule-law-index-2021

Yus, F. (2021). *Smartphone communication. Interactions in the app ecosystem*. Routledge.

9

Destabilization of Unstable Dynamic Social Equilibriums and the Malicious Use of Artificial Intelligence in High-Tech Strategic Psychological Warfare

Evgeny Pashentsev

Introduction

The impact of high-tech strategic psychological warfare (HTSPW) on unstable dynamic social equilibriums (UDSEs) from the influence of current practices for the use of artificial intelligence (AI) is considered in this chapter. AI is the most important, but far from the only, technological factor that objectively and inevitably leads not only to limited destabilization, but even to the degradation of existing societal foundations. This can lead to *worse* scenarios, even to the eradication of humanity. All options are on the table. AI is an important element of present and future UDSEs, which can in turn be used in strategic psychological warfare (SPW).

This chapter will analyze several case studies on the "tool-function of AI" in further weakening UDSE. A wide scope of academic research exists on the different aspects of psychological warfare (Bodine-Baron et al., 2016; Ullah, 2017; Molander et al., 1996, Kingler, 2021), on new and future AI opportunities for society (Ch Lok, 2018; Doyle et al., 2014; Langer & Yorks, 2018; Marcellino et al., 2017), on the rise of AI (King & Petty, 2021), on the AI Revolution (Li, 2020), on attempts of the malicious use of artificial intelligence (MUAI) (Goodman, 2015), on cyber defense (Jahankhani et al., 2021), on twenty-first-century crime (Peters, 2020; Brundage et al., 2018), and on

E. Pashentsev (✉)
Diplomatic Academy of the Ministry of Foreign Affairs of the Russian Federation, Moscow, Russia
e-mail: icspsc@mail.ru

the use of AI in psychological warfare (Cummings et al., 2018; Mikheev & Nestik, 2019; Telley, 2018; Torres Soriano, 2018). The last group of work on the use of AI in psychological warfare is still very limited, indicating a lack of relevant basic system research. In the opinion of the author, this gap will be closed quite quickly due to growing socio-political tensions in many countries, the long-term deterioration of relations between leading state actors in the international arena, and, of course, the rapidly growing potential of AI that places it in the realm of psychological warfare.

The premise of the current study is that HTSPW through malicious use of artificial intelligence (MUAI) has reached a qualitatively new level that requires an adequate assessment and reaction from not only military institutions, but also society as a whole. HTSPW is especially dangerous to UDSE, such as is being experienced currently and especially in the near- and medium-term, as instability increases against the background of further progress in other technologies.

To verify this hypothesis, the author examines the issues facing civil society in the context of increased risks and opportunities for AI in SPW.

The methodology of the research is based on a systemic approach to the role of sophisticated technologies in SPW. A systemic approach, comparative analysis, and case studies are helpful for obtaining findings that help form the basis for high HTSPW efficiency criterion, as well as sample key capabilities and features of modern SPW, in influencing the UDSE. The systemic approach aims to avoid one-sided assessments and to provide an objective analysis of the interrelated aspects of modern technology development in the field of social security.

Multilevel Psychological Warfare: Challenges for Global Security

The slow pace of development in the world economy, mass unemployment, growing property and social polarization, inefficiency and corruption at the state level, and internal political confrontation, combined with a dangerous aggravation of tensions in the international arena, are largely associated with an area of activity by modern state and non-state actors that is referred to as psychological warfare (PW). Social development problems, and the use of these problems by antisocial actors, create favorable conditions for the development of PW. At the same time, PW is an important means of achieving decisive superiority and even—in some cases—of defeating an enemy without the use of military force, by using and strengthening the target's objective and subjective weaknesses.

PW is often considered a part of information warfare. Winn Schwartau, who was voted one of the "25 Most Influential People in the Security Industry" by *Security Magazine* in 2008, in the preface to the second edition of the monograph *Global Information Warfare: The New Digital Battlefield* by Jones and Kovacich (2016, p. xxii) defines information warfare as "the use of information and information systems as offensive tools against other information and information systems." The technical means of information warfare (programs for unauthorized access to information resources, electronic warfare equipment, etc.), for all of their importance, are subordinate to the tasks of warfare in the psychological sphere, since a decisive victory can only be achieved by breaking the will of the enemy or by leading them to make wrong decisions. The key information system in any society is a human being who is ultimately the alpha and omega of other information systems, without the existence of human beings, other information systems do not make sense.

PW, also called "psywar," is thus always directed by certain people against other people. PW is the use of propaganda against an enemy, supported by military, economic, or political measures as needed (Britannica, 2022; RAND Corporation, 2022). PW involves the planned use of propaganda and other psychological operations to influence the opinions, emotions, attitudes, and behavior of opposition groups (RAND Corporation, 2022).

This chapter considers PW as the use of multi-vector, synchronous psychological influences by the parties waging socio-political warfare both before the war and during it, in order to covertly or openly influence the perception, worldview, and behavior of certain groups. Thus, PW functions not only as propaganda and counter-propaganda, but also as management. Reactionary groups consider societies—both foreign and their own—as objects that are subjected to such influence. These groups reserve the right to interpret fundamental issues exclusively for themselves (in an explicit form, under an open dictatorship, and in an implicit form, under a democracy), striving to maintain psychological control over "their" population and resubordinating the enemy population in psychological terms. The resubordination of a population in the material world corresponds to the desire to seize (for selfish interests) territory and other assets of an opposing side with a low level of readiness to resist.

Progressive groups in PW strive to increase the subjectivity of a whole society—not just their group—in the interests of socially oriented development. Progressive groups prefer open forms of psychological influence, such as publicly conveying thoughts and feelings, or observing the unity of word and deed. Reactionary groups prefer closed forms, such as public appeals designed to disorientate society and conceal their true intentions. However, the pragmatism of real politics (telling everyone the whole truth during war is like death), as well as the objective variability of the positions of social and political groups, makes this distinction very relative. The objective limiting factor for the realization of ideal aspirations is considered by progressives as a lack of resources for the harmonious development of the individual and society, while ruling elites desire to prevent such development. Even when progressive groups are in power, these aspirations are met with limited intellectual and volitional qualities, given the imperfections of the majority of the population's moral and ethical standards, which make attempts at antisocial psychological influence highly successful.

PW in the modern world has a multilevel character:

- First, there is a clash of values, interests, and goals of various political forces at the national level.
- Second, there is tension in relations between countries of different political orientations, such as between Israel and Iran, Colombia and Venezuela, South Korea and North Korea, and so on.
- Third, there are geopolitical conflicts of interests between Russia, China, and the United States, as well as with the US allies in NATO and the EU.
- Fourth, there is a growing rivalry between transnational corporations and banks in the face of increased international competition, reduction in international trade, and instability in the world commodity and financial markets, provoking social tension in all regions.

This multilevel nature of PW requires taking into account the asymmetry of economic, military-political, and informational potentials of intranational actors and interstate associations, as well as various external forces (state and non-state entities). This also corresponds to a multilevel system of PW at all stages of development—different capacities for conducting PW that do not always coincide with goals and objectives, different approaches toward implementing this kind of activity, and the degree of involvement in the conflict create complex issues for the coordination of actions among allies and a desire to use similar problems to disrupt the activity of an enemy.

Psychological warfare has several levels: tactical, operational, and strategic, each of which solves a specific task. The most important level is the strategic, which aims to develop a particular country or the international system in a more desirable direction. Often, the target of the psychological impact is not aware of the real nature or scope of the long-term operations that are modifying its mode of thinking and behavior. *In socio-political terms, SPW is the explicit and implicit, long-term–focused psychological impact of competing systems' (state, supra-state, interstate, and non-state actors) attempts to inflict damage and/or the liquidation (or assignment) of the intangible assets of the other side, in order to win in the material domain.* Here, the definition from Rastorguyev is a good place to start: "The information warfare between two information systems is open and hidden targeted information impacts of systems on each other in order to obtain a certain gain in the material sphere" (Rastorguev, 1999, p. 60). The concept of SPW is inextricably linked to the concept of national and international psychological security. The destruction of that security is the epicenter of hostile efforts by state and supranational actors.

In the field of PW, there are various schemes of explicit and implicit influence that play on individuals' and social groups' way of thinking and behavior, as well as inspire erroneous management decisions, provoking repressive actions against the opposition and much more.

SPW imparts a systemic, long-term impact on the nodal elements of the public organism, in order to make negative trends dominant. Political, economic, and diplomatic measures geared toward the next target of direct aggression or latent regime change (sometimes the two variants are combined) always have an internal logical sequence that enhances internal destabilization and externally isolates the target regime. The sequence gradually foments negative attitudes among a population toward their authorities and international condemnation of an "authoritarian regime"; when faced with such threats, every regime becomes less democratic.

Many phenomena and techniques fit into the fabric of SPW. Consider, for instance, fake news, which significantly affects public consciousness, whether it is spread in China, the EU, Russia, or the United States. Fake news is ubiquitous in the media and plays an important role in the construction of a fake matrix, where new fake items contribute to previous fake items, all together constructing a fake reality. When one fake item dies, new ones are already on the rise; this means that social reality, with its very real contradictions, operates in a continuous sphere of vagueness. A sophisticated, full-spectrum assault on free will is taking place and beyond that, millions of people have become accustomed to this fake reality, even building fake items themselves. For example, Facebook reported in 2012 that an estimated 83 million profiles on its platform are fake (Kelly, 2012).

Over the course of Facebook's history, the company has continually exposed user data without their consent, putting profits over privacy considerations. In 2009, Facebook was forced to settle a class action lawsuit from users and shut down its Beacon ad network, which posted users' online purchases from participating websites on their news feeds without their permission (Ryan & Kaplan, 2018). In 2010 Facebook, MySpace and several other social-networking sites have been sending data to advertising companies that could be used to find consumers' names and other personal details, despite promises they don't share such information without consent (Steel & Vascellaro, 2010). In March 2018 Facebook shares plunge over revelations that personal data of 50 million users was obtained and misused by British data analytics firm Cambridge Analytica, which reportedly helped Donald Trump win the US presidency in 2016 (Khandelwal, 2018).

By leveraging automated, emotional manipulation alongside swarms of bots, Facebook dark posts, A/B testing, and fake news networks, Cambridge Analytica has activated an invisible machine that preys on the personalities of individual voters to create large shifts in public opinion. Many of these technologies were used before individually to some effect but together, these tactics create a nearly impenetrable voter manipulation machine that is quickly becoming the new deciding factor in elections around the world (Anderson & Horvath, 2017). According to information from Cambridge Analytica's website, with up to 5000 data points on over 230 million American voters, the company is building custom target audiences for which this crucial information can be used to engage, persuade, and motivate to act (Cambridge Analytica, 2018). In April 2018, Facebook dropped another bombshell on its users by admitting that all of its 2.2 billion users should assume malicious third-party scrapers have compromised their public profile information. Facebook CEO Mark Zuckerberg revealed that "malicious actors" took advantage of "Search" tools on its platform to discover the identities and collect information on most of its 2 billion users worldwide (Wetsman, 2021).

The core issue is not whether a particular consultant obtains information about people legally or illegally, although this is, of course, important. The real danger lies in the concentration of sophisticated, highly influential technologies in the hands of the few.

Perhaps today, Russia, China, the United States, the EU, and their high-tech partners, in spite of acute contradictions, are forced to pay more attention to this discussion, at least at the expert level. This is not only due to the dangerous consequences of the nuclear arms race and the technical aspects of cybersecurity, but also due to the perilous threats from modern HTSPW. This is a must-win game because HTSPW increases the risks for World War III. Through the use of new technologies, it is becoming easier and easier, in the context of UDSEs, to provoke—in a latent way—a dangerous error or a wrong decision on the part of top militaries or politicians by extremist third parties with the aim of global destabilization by all means, regardless of possibly tragic global consequences.

Unfortunately, progressive deterioration at the international level eventually led to open confrontation between Russia and Western countries, as well as some of their allies like Japan, in 2022. Additionally, there has been a marked decline in China's relations with the West. Thus, the possibilities for MUAI have increased dramatically. The current situation is by no means a random or short-term fluctuation in social development nor, despite the importance of subjective factors, the evil will of individual politicians. The present and foreseeable future will be shaped by the natural transition of humanity from a state of stable dynamic social equilibrium (SDSE) to a state of UDSE.

From Stable Dynamic Social Equilibrium to Unstable Dynamic Social Equilibrium: The Risks Are Becoming More Serious

Humankind is a dynamic system, affected by both evolutionary and revolutionary changes in the way it progresses, as well as by gradual or rapid regression through, for example, counter-revolution. The revolts of slaves in Ancient Rome or peasants in the Middle Ages broke temporary balances of slave-owning and feudal systems, respectively, but they didn't lead directly to the replacement of those systems, owing to the objective immaturity of the preconditions. Therefore, it is necessary to differentiate the dynamic equilibrium of society, in the narrow sense, within the framework of the qualitative parameters of the system, from dynamic equilibrium in the broad sense, with the transition from one equilibrium to another through social revolution of some type.

In this instance, it is important to understand the possibilities and mechanisms for influencing the obsolete, as well as the methods for its removal from society in a manner as painless as possible, since the obsolete threatens the viability of humankind. It is particularly important to follow such an approach now. The mere presence of weapons of mass destruction provides a reason, and the risks are too great for an absolute "radioactive regression" instead of progress. In addition, we must take into account the existence of hundreds of nuclear power plants, biological laboratories, and much more around the world.

It is possible to formulate a mandatory requirement for the nature of planetary development. *In the transition from one qualitative state of society to another, much larger and deeper than ever before, the thresholds for the disruption of the dynamic equilibrium of the social system must be lower than during the previous revolutionary transitions, in order to avoid the destruction of human civilization.* For example, the one-time total destruction of 10 big factories 100–200 years ago during a civil war anywhere in Central Europe could not, in principle, have had as dangerous consequences as the destruction of one nuclear power plant today. Of course, compliance with this requirement is particularly important for nuclear powers in internal conflicts and in internationally sensitive areas.

The "new" should create a preponderance over the "old," so that the latter will have no option but to disappear without resorting to extreme forms of military confrontation. However, the "new" needs determination and preparation for "worst-case scenarios," otherwise the "old" risks a dangerous confrontation, underestimating the ability and willingness of the "new" to move forward. Here, not only are technological, economic, and socio-political prerequisites of superiority important, but also informational and psychological aspects, successfully synchronized within the framework of strategic communication. The stabilization of a qualitatively new dynamic equilibrium of society is impossible without strategic communication.

The Marxist theory of revolution, with its numerous international teams of theoretical contributors and practitioners, including tektology (Bogdanov, 1989; Melnik, 2013), systems theory (Bertalanffy, 1969), action theory (Parsons, 1978), punctuated equilibrium theory (Baumgartner & Jones, 1992), and others contribute to the current research on social dynamic systems. At the same time, insufficient attention is being given to comprehensive analysis of issues related to the unstable dynamic equilibrium of modern society, especially in the context of random and targeted negative impacts in the field of SPW. After all, SPW is aimed at the long-term disorientation of real or potential enemies on the most important issues, and this is impossible without measures that reduce the ability to think strategically or make appropriate decisions.

Military experts generally agree that SPW has always been used, and even should be used against an enemy. But whether it is beneficial to reduce strategic analysis capability, as well as the ability to adequately respond to international challenges from a nuclear competitor, remains questionable. Not least, this question should worry the main nuclear energy-rich actors that are engaged in geopolitical confrontation, not so much because of their own possible bilateral miscalculations, but due to the general decline in the level of strategic thinking among other leading actors. The misinterpretation of actions in a tense situation is fraught with risk, especially if there are doubts about the capacity for adequate behavior on the part of the other party.

The system's equilibrium state is in a process of constant interaction with the progressively developing system of the environment. This interaction, over time, leads to imbalance in the system, followed by the onset of instability (crisis) and structural adjustment, which forms a new equilibrium state at a higher level of development (Melnik, 2013).

Thus, SDSE in the current global situation changes naturally, although not simultaneously with UDSE and not in all spheres of social life uniformly, but more and more quickly. The large-scale military hostilities in Ukraine have become nothing more than an accelerator of long overdue changes; this is not the beginning of those changes, nor even the end. The different, and quite often contradictory, positions and interests of dominant social and political groups, their quite different understanding or even worse, full ignorance, of future prospects for mankind, facilitate the transition to UDSE.

UDSE is characterized by the following features and contradictions:

- Extremely uneven load on various elements of the system during the transition to a new state. This is reflected in the growing property and social polarization of the population, the erosion of the middle class, and other factors that make the dynamic social equilibrium unstable.
- The degradation of old elements of interaction and management of economic, political, military, and other systems at the national, international, and supranational levels. The old is not yet gone, but it is still necessary. The new has not yet developed; it is "not allowed," but also not ready to replace the old in the ideological, political, or economic spheres. This explains phenomena such as Brexit, the weakening of NATO, the EU, or the Eurasian Economic Union, the weakening of the mechanisms of global governance—not excluding UN structures, and the frequent and rather sudden attempts of countries at international reorientation, which almost never solves fundamental problems but only deepens them. For example, the "force oriented" economic and political turn of Ukraine from Russia toward the EU does not contribute to the resolution of socio-economic problems in the EU, Russia, or Ukraine.
- The growth of populist parties and movements of different orientations promising things they cannot accomplish, such as a fundamental improvement in people's lives. Right-wing populists are trying to get out of the situation by building "walls" against migrants and promising reindustrialization, which based on new technology will eventually turn into mass unemploy-

ment or (at best) an imitation of employment. The escalation of conflict at the national level and in the international arena—bellicose rhetoric that threatens to turn into large-scale military conflict—is especially characteristic of the Donald Trump administration. Left-wing populists in Latin America, after achieving great success in education and health care, are facing increasing difficulties. These difficulties are caused not only by external imperialist pressure, but also by the attempts of the left to solve the problems without moving beyond the existing global system of capitalism. The populism of the left and the right, despite undisputed differences between them, is not a denial of global capitalism but a manifestation of its crisis.

- The North Korean decision to opt out of the capitalist global system is not a more successful model of social development. Even within the immeasurably stronger Soviet bloc, which comprises one-third of the world's GDP, this problem has not been solved. China's slowdown in economic growth suggests that a kind of catching-up model of development within the framework of global capitalism can turn this country with the largest population into the country with the largest GDP. However, the painful redistribution of forces in the international arena does not solve the problems of the modern world and in some places, even exacerbates them. This does not justify attempts to stop emerging countries, hampering their development, or threatening them with sanctions or military interventions. Attempts to start a "local" world war in Eurasia are extremely dangerous, which would not be contained within Eurasia's borders. However, within the framework of the existing order, war could start even without setting a match to the powder keg from the outside—there is a lot of gunpowder in Eurasia.
- Unlike the period of burgeois revolutions in Europe or the October Revolution in Russia, there is no obvious alternative to the existing model, even though the existing model is in a serious systemic crisis. This has prompted many researchers, politicians, and public persons to talk about a crisis of global civilization. The capitalist system is increasingly dynamic, experiencing more tension but not offering any fundamental solutions outside of its framework to maintain quality parameters. There is no traditional alternative on the left, which has lost its historical actor, the proletariat, has failed to meet the expectations and is rapidly disappearing as a class. Vladimir Lenin asserted that "[T]he whole main force of the movement (the Bolsheviks) is in the organization of workers in *large* factories, because large factories (and plants) include not only the predominant in number, but even more predominant in influence, developing and able

for struggle, part of the entire working class. Every factory should be our fortress" (Lenin, 1904, p. 9). This position has clearly lost its importance and the bourgeoisie, in developing robotic, deserted enterprises, successfully acts as a "gravedigger of the proletariat," objectively acting as a manifestation of progress, not regression, of society.

- According to many surveys, there is a weakening of social confidence and trust in existing national and supranational political institutions, including the United States (Lonas, 2022), the EU (Lipton, 2019; Euractiv, 2013; Merler, 2015; McCourt, 2019; Edelman, 2019), and Russia (Regnum, 2018; Echo of Moscow, 2018; RBC, 2019), although many nations maintain faith in a better future for their people. However, significantly, people in less-developed countries signal a much greater confidence in the future. This is often based on traditional growth reserves that still exist, while in developed countries, social optimism is a privilege of the minority, although it must be acknowledged that the optimistic minority varies greatly in size, from 16 percent in Japan and 21 percent in France to 48 percent in the United States. Russia stands at an intermediate 39 percent (Edelman, 2019). In countries such as Indonesia and Colombia, despite extreme social polarization, belief in the future confidently dominates the public consciousness—82 percent and 84 percent, respectively—which is also characteristic of countries with a much larger proportion of young people among the population, and of many countries in the developing world.
- Increased unevenness in the economic and political development of the leading EU countries (e.g., if the development of Italy and Germany are compared), as well as the emergence of new world leaders, such as China and India.
- There is a degradation in the strategic thinking of the ruling circles in many leading countries of the EU, Russia, and the United States in recent decades. The collapse of the Soviet Union, catastrophic for the majority of Russians in the 1990s, left many unsolved problems for contemporary Russia. Brexit demonstrates the degradation of the ruling elite in the United Kingdom, far ahead of the general decline in the social, financial, and economic institutions of the country. The United States, assuming the position as the only leader of the modern world after the collapse of the Soviet Union, clearly failed in this role. China, on the contrary, demonstrates growth in strategic thinking among its elite, strengthening its position at national, regional, and global levels.
- However, degradation should not be seen as a verdict for a country. Degradation is a natural characteristic of more developed countries, where the ruling circles face new challenges before less-developed countries. There

is an acute struggle among the elites who want to, but cannot, live in the old way; this is the budding formation of social alternatives and alternative elites in the twenty-first century. This is quite natural, because new elites cannot be formed without a new scientific, technological, and economic base, and this base is only just at the beginning of a revolutionary leap in development. However, the jump by historical standards is very fast and incomparably larger and deeper than all previous jumps in history. Scientific and technological progress is rapidly adjusting future research, which theorists and practitioners must consider. Apparently, there is no need to follow Arthur Schopenhauer's conclusion: "Everyone takes the limits of his own vision for the limits of the world" (Schopenhauer, 2022). Otherwise, the end of the world really will come through "joint efforts." Underestimating the consequences of technological progress is extremely dangerous at the governmental level.

- The degradation of science and education, the strengthening of superstitions, and the increase in religious intolerance have resulted in primitive interpretations of both religion and science by a majority of people against the backdrop of the general availability of higher education of an increasingly poor quality. The number of universities and students in Russia and most EU countries has increased by almost an order of magnitude in recent decades, while the level of education has obviously fallen. For example, the illegal trade in higher education diplomas, according to media reports and expert assessments, is thriving in Russia (Komsomolskaya Pravda, 2012; Nasyrov, 2013; Remizov, 2017; Zvezdina et al., 2018) and the United Kingdom (Simons, 2019; Stow, 2019), countries with governments that are antagonists on many geopolitical issues. This situation was hard to imagine in either country 30–40 years ago. Dr. Thomas Lancaster, a senior fellow at Imperial College London specializing in academic integrity and contract cheating, said that this is just the tip of the iceberg. "The industry is worth hundreds of millions of pounds globally, and tens of millions in Britain" (Wallis Simons, 2019), said Lancaster. Of course, there are common problems and they must be solved together.

These and many other social phenomena are well-known, but are rarely seen as a systemic manifestation of UDSE in contemporary conditions. It is possible to assume that they can become an area of vulnerability, which experts in the field of HTSPW of state and non-state actors—and more generally of hybrid wars in the twenty-first century—will not fail to master.

Artificial Intelligence in High-Tech Strategic Psychological Warfare

At the expense of various means of influence, it is possible to both strengthen and weaken the objective manifestations of instability of social systems, and it is equally possible to provoke additional artificial indignations. SPW allows this to be achieved on a long-term basis, in the most important areas of social development. Since SPW is conducted with different degrees of professionalism by various state and non-state actors, there is an overlay (interference) of various management control schemes, which decreases SPW efficiency. The role of even weak AI in overcoming this problem is great, because it radically increases the ability of the human mind to calculate social development options; in addition, AI increasingly makes it possible to foresee the specific parameters of individual events, and allows identification of the effectiveness of influencing operations much faster and more effectively. Thus, AI takes a prominent place among other means and methods of offensive HTSPW. However, it also creates new and adequate capabilities of defensive HTSPW, which is typical for the dynamic unstable balance of all offensive and defensive weapons.

AI systems can undergo long-range target effects in a latent form, and they can be if not the primary, then the secondary actors of such effects. Therefore, unfortunately, it is impossible to exclude the global, catastrophic, rapid, and (in the initial phase) latent consequences of MUAI. MUAI implies the possibility of using multiple—or even all—of the weaknesses of individuals and human civilization. AI can also integrate with, and improve, the effectiveness of nuclear or biological attack.

Accordingly, the higher the degree of AI spread across the world (via contemporary, cross-border internet connections, due to the existence of other mutually hostile nation-states and numerous non-state actors armed with the latest technologies), the higher the risk of global catastrophe. The interconnectedness of AI systems makes a rapid, global catastrophe caused by a small group of individuals located almost anywhere in the world—but acting on a cross-border basis—much more likely. This catastrophe may, in some ways, be even more effectively controlled by the instigators than at any time before, but is no less devastating in terms of consequences. In the next decade, this threat may become the primary threat—a high-tech terrorist organization, with large financial capabilities and corresponding strategic interests with its sponsors—could carry out this threat. This conclusion is supported by the latest research in the field of MUAI (Pashentsev, 2020, p. 93).

The problem is not only that the growing capabilities of HTSPW are extremely dangerous. SPW at the SDSE stage causes great damage, and its consequences could be catastrophic for individual states. Recall that the collapse of the USSR was provoked not only by internal objective and subjective forces, but also by external influences from certain ruling circles in the West; SPW played an important role. In her book *Freedom's Laboratory: The Cold War Struggle for the Soul of Science* (Wolfe, 2020), Dr. Audra Wolfe revealed many interesting examples of the close cooperation that existed between the US government and private scientific groups in the area of US propaganda and psychological war campaigns during the Cold War.

When the global transition to UDSE arrives, AI-based HTSPW will inevitably have a catastrophic character, since the already half-blind and ineffective elites, and the almost blind people, will be even more disoriented. When absolute clarity is needed, at least on general issues of transition to SDSE on a new technological and social basis, the transition is engineered so that such clarity never comes, so that the blindness and helplessness of the opposing side are absolute. Of course, this was to be expected, since various antisocial actors seek to use possible breakthroughs in scientific and technological progress for their own interests, opposing each other and, objectively, humanity as a whole. World wars and the Cuban Missile Crisis were only crises on our difficult ascent and now, figuratively speaking, humanity has stepped on a shaky bridge over an abyss that cannot be bypassed. The opposite side of the abyss is far away, almost indistinguishable, and to be sure, there are attempts to blindfold humanity. The outcome is easy to predict.

Of particular importance is the use of AI resources by the leading powers, because if an extreme right-wing, high-tech dictatorship with a range of MUAI capabilities, including HTSPW, is established in at least one country, it will pose an extreme danger to the whole world. However, the gradual degradation of democratic institutions and counterweights in the conditions of modern "corporate declining republics" does not remove threats to the security of the population through MUAI, since the relative, and rather rapidly declining, autonomy and security of the individual and society arise as a by-product of the oligarchic clan rivalry for power and the opportunity to use it for their own enrichment.

Most experts rightly consider PW as a clash of parties with the goal of limiting the capabilities of the other side, up to their full destruction (see more about the content and correlation of the concepts of information warfare, information war, psychological warfare, and others, as well as about the history and modern practice of psychological warfare: Di Pietro et al., 2021; Kingler, 2021; Thiele, 2021; Voronova, 2018; Armistead, 2010; Paul, 2008;

Goldstein & Findley, 2012; Welch, 2011' Veprintsev et al., 2005). However, in reality, the winner is ultimately the one who not only—or not so much—destroys but also creates something new and more progressive. Deviations from this pattern at the national (regional) level have so far been temporary or subject to correction in the wider arena of action. If this pattern ceases to operate, there will be a general decline of humankind; in modern conditions, fraught with many global risks, this decline will quickly turn into death. Therefore, it is necessary to consider actions within the framework of PW that are compatible with possibilities for further societal development and, in particular, for updating the information and communication environment for the benefit of most people. The weakness of psychological protection for the population from outside attacks in different countries is observed for two basic reasons.

First, the person who is most protected from psychological attack is someone who has a strong psyche, who has a powerful and versatile intellect, and who has high moral and ethical requirements for themselves and others. However, such a person is far from the norm in modern society. Second, if this type of person were to become the norm, how interested would the existing ruling elites be in such citizens, especially in countries where levels of corruption and social polarization are high? In general terms, the more progressive and oriented toward diversified development the citizen, the more governments are likely to win with PW, by developing an appropriate system of information and communication security. However, this is not enough.

As noted earlier in this chapter, all previous projects for creating a socially oriented development model had a common weakness: the vast majority of people are not able to effectively control power due to the natural limitations of their ability to analyze and control incoming information. It is also important to evaluate the prospect of qualitatively strengthening the ability of a person to resist hostile psychological influences, not only through the external use of AI, which already exists, but also through close integration with these technologies, strengthened by the entire range of possibilities for analyzing incoming information, forming creative skills, and so on. In fact, returning to the metaphorical bridge over the abyss, AI can facilitate a wonderful expansion of vision, accelerating movement forward, and an effective means of securing this movement. Instead, others are trying to impose AI like a blindfold to block out the dangerous road, and compel ear plugs, so that people are unable to hear each other. The possibilities of AI are great, both benefiting humanity and becoming an existential threat. Likewise, the role of AI in HTSPW can be twofold. From the point of view of the strategic interests of humankind, the question is not at all about which ruling circles of which country or bloc uses HTSPW in warfare with each other better. What matters is whether AI aims to cross the abyss in the interests of a renewed population or on behalf of selfish interest groups. In the second case, if someone gets to the opposite side, it is clearly not humanity.

Conclusion

The current level of technology, and not least, AI, seriously affects SPW capabilities. The speed, scale, and depth of AI impact are increasing, up to the creation of a life-long, artificial reality for individuals and target groups. Without the development of a person as a harmoniously evolved individual, it is impossible to talk about an effective security system for society or the individual from information and psychological threats. The potential of civil society, the free association of citizens on the internet to protect digital freedom, and citizen empowerment (not the mass consumer) should be used. The author is not against the protection of consumers; they are entirely in support. But protecting consumers without their own civic awareness or social activism has little chance for success. The mass consumer easily becomes a victim of both egoistic corporate groups and terrorist organizations, although it is impossible to identify this or that group in the majority of cases. The mass consumer becomes a victim due to easily calculable and obvious reactions. The development of a fully versatile and active individual, living in harmony with social interests, is a reliable guarantee of the strengthening of democracy and the creation of a reliable barrier against the spread of destructive influence campaigns, whether from state or non-state actors.

References

Anderson, B., & Horvath, B. (2017). The rise of the weaponized AI propaganda machine. In *Medium*. Retrieved 11 July 2022, from https://medium.com/join-scout/the-rise-of-the-weaponized-ai-propaganda-machine-86dac61668b

Armistead, L. (2010). *Information operations matters. Best practices*. Potomac Books.

Baumgartner, F., & Jones, B. D. (1992). *Agendas and instability in American politics*. University of Chicago Press.

Bertalanffy, L. (1969). *General system theory*. George Braziller.

Bodine-Baron, E., Helmus, T., Magnuson, M., & Winkelman, Z. (2016). *Examining ISIS support and opposition networks on Twitter*. RAND Corporation.

Bogdanov, A. (1989). *Tektologija: vseobshhaja organizacionnaja nauka [Tectology: universal organizational science]*. Ekonomika.
Britannica. (2022). Psychological warfare. In *Encyclopedia Britannica*. Retrieved 11 July 2022, from https://www.britannica.com/topic/psychological-warfare
Brundage, M., Avin, S., Clark, J., Toner, H., Eckersley, P., Garfinkel, B., Dafoe, A., Scharre, P., Zeitzoff, T., Filar, B., Anderson, H., Roff, H., Allen, G., Steinhardt, J., Flynn, C., Ó HÉigeartaigh, S., Beard, S., Belfield, H., Farquhar, S., Lyle, C., Crootof, R., Evans, O., Page, M., Bryson, J., Yampolskiy, R., & Amodei, D. (2018). *The malicious use of artificial intelligence: Forecasting, prevention, and mitigation*. Future of Humanity Institute, University of Oxford.
Cambridge Analytica. (2018). CA political. In Ca-political.com. Retrieved 22 March 2022, from https://ca-political.com/ca-advantage/
Ch Lok, J. (2018). *The difference between artificial intelligence and psychological method predicts consumer behavior* (Kindle ed.). Amazon Digital Services.
Cummings, M., Roff, H., Cukier, K., Parakilas, J., & Bryce, H. (2018). *Artificial intelligence and international affairs: Disruption anticipated*. Chatham House—The Royal Institute of International Affairs.
Di Pietro, R., Raponi, S., Caprolu, M., & Cresci, S. (2021). *New dimensions of information warfare*. Springer.
Doyle, A., Katz, G., Summers, K., Ackermann, C., Zavorin, I., Lim, Z., Muthiah, S., Butler, P., Self, N., Zhao, L., Lu, C., Khandpur, R., Fayed, Y., & Ramakrishnan, N. (2014). Forecasting significant societal events using the embers streaming predictive analytics system. *Big Data, 2*, 185–195. https://doi.org/10.1089/big.2014.0046
Echo of Moscow. (2018). Putin rasterjal doverie rossijan—indeks odobrenija Prezidenta za god ruhnul v 2 raza [Putin has lost the trust of Russians—The index of approval of the President for the year collapsed 2 times]. Retrieved 11 May 2022, from https://echo.msk.ru/blog/kremlmother/2320864-echo/
Edelman. (2019). 19th Edelman trust barometer. Retrieved May 11, 2019, from https://www.edelman.com/research/edelman-trust-barometer-archive
Euractiv. (2013, June 25). Record 60% of Europeans "tend not to trust" EU. Retrieved May 11, 2019, from https://www.euractiv.com/section/elections/news/record-60-of-europeans-tend-not-to-trust-eu/
Goldstein, F., & Findley, B. (2012). *Psychological operations—Principles and case studies*. CreateSpace Independent Publishing Platform.
Goodman, M. (2015). *Future crimes: Inside the digital underground and the Battle for our connected world*. Transworld Digital.
Jahankhani, H., Kendzierskyj, S., Chelvachandran, N., & Ibarra, J. (Eds.). (2021). *Cyber defence in the age of AI, smart societies and augmented humanity*. Springer.
Jones, A., & Kovacich, G. (2016). *Global information warfare. The new digital battlefield*. CRC Press, Taylor & Francis Group.

Kelly, H. (2012). 83 million Facebook accounts are fakes and dupes. In: *CNN*. Retrieved September 8, 2022, from https://edition.cnn.com/2012/08/02/tech/social-media/facebook-fake-accounts/index.html

Khandelwal, S. (2018). Facebook and Cambridge Analytica—What's happened so far. In *The Hacker News*. Retrieved September 8, 2022, from https://thehackernews.com/2018/03/facebook-cambridge-analytica.html

King, B., & Petty, R. (2021). *The rise of Technosocialism: How inequality, AI and climate will usher in a New World*. Marshall Cavendish International (Asia).

Kingler, C. (2021). *5 books in 1: Manipulation techniques honed over the centuries by politicians, strategists, speakers, performers and sellers around the world*. Independently published.

Komsomolskaya Pravda. (2012, May 23). *620 tysjach rublej—i ty kandidat nauk! [620 thousand rubles—And you are a PhD!]*. Retrieved May 11, 2019, from https://www.kp.ru/daily/25887/2848481/

Langer, A., & Yorks, L. (2018). *Strategic information technology: Best practices to drive digital transformation* (2nd ed.). Wiley.

Lenin, V. I. (1904). Pis'mo k tovarishhu o nashih organizacionnyh zadachah [A letter to a comrade on our organizational tasks]. In *(1967) Complete collection of works* (Vol. 7). Political Literature Publishers.

Li, R. (2020). *Artificial intelligence revolution: How AI will change our society, economy, and culture*. Skyhorse.

Lipton, G. (2019, March 6). *Graphic truth: Europeans don't trust Europe*. Gzero Media. Retrieved May 11, 2019, from https://www.gzeromedia.com/graphic-truth-europeans-dont-trust-europe

Lonas, L. (2022). Overall confidence in US institutions at record low, poll finds. In ABC4.com. Retrieved July 11, 2022, from https://www.abc4.com/news/national/overall-confidence-in-us-institutions-at-record-low-poll-finds/

Marcellino, W., Smith, M., Paul, C., & Skrabala, L. (2017). Monitoring social media. Lessons for future department of defense social media analysis in support of information operations. https://www.rand.org/pubs/research_reports/RR1742.html

McCourt, D. (2019). A quarter of Europeans trust AI robots more than politicians. *AndroidPIT Magazine*. Retrieved May 11, 2019, from https://www.androidpit.com/europeans-trust-ai-robots-over-politicians

Melnik, M. (2013). Strukturno-dinamicheskoe ravnovesie social'no-ekonomicheskih system [Structural-dynamic balance of social and economic systems]. *J Chelovecheskij kapital [Human Asset], 11*(59), 45–51.

Merler, S. (2015. June 11). *How do Europeans feel about the EU?* World Economic Forum. Retrieved May 11, 2019, from https://www.weforum.org/agenda/2015/06/how-do-europeans-feel-about-the-eu/

Mikheev, E., & Nestik, T. (2019). The use of artificial intelligence technologies in information and psychological warfare. *The European Proceedings of Social and Behavioural Sciences*, 406–412. https://doi.org/10.15405/epsbs.2019.07.53

Molander, R., Riddile, A., & Wilson, P. (1996). *Strategic information warfare: A new face of war*. RAND Corporation.

Nasyrov, E. (2013). Fal'shivye dissertacii nachali vyjavljat' desjatkami [Dozens of fake dissertations were identified]. *Chastniy Korrespondent [Private Correspondent]*. Retrieved May 11, 2019, from http://www.chaskor.ru/article/falshivye_dissertatsii_nachali_vyyavlyat_desyatkami_30887

Parsons, T. (1978). *Action theory and the human condition*. Free Press.

Pashentsev, E. (2020). AI and terrorist threats: The new dimension for strategic psychological warfare. In D. Bazarkina, E. Pashentsev, & G. Simons (Eds.), *Terrorism and advanced Technologies in Psychological Warfare: New risks, new opportunities to counter the terrorist threat* (pp. 83–115). Nova Science Publishers.

Paul, C. (2008). *Information operations—Doctrine and practice: A reference handbook*. Praeger Security International.

Peters, K. (2020). *21st century crime: How malicious artificial intelligence will impact homeland security*. Naval Postgraduate School.

RAND Corporation. (2022). *Psychological warfare*. In RAND Corporation. Retrieved July 11, 2022, from https://www.rand.org/topics/psychological-warfare.html

Rastorguev, S. (1999). *Informacionnaya vojna [Information warfare]*. Svyaz.

RBC. (2019). *Rossija zanjala poslednee mesto rejtinga doverija k obshhestvennym institutam [Russia took the last place in the rating of trust in public institutions]*. Retrieved May 11, 2019, from https://www.rbc.ru/society/22/01/2019/5c4632139a7947d392889cfd

Regnum. (2018, October 4). *Sociologi zajavili o snizhenii doverija grazhdan RF k institutam vlasti [Sociologists announced a decrease in the confidence of Russian citizens in the institutions of power]*. Retrieved May 11, 2019, from https://regnum.ru/news/2494482.html

Remizov, D. (2017, April 10). *Chinovniki i deputaty nosjat uchenuju stepen,' kak bantik [Officials and MPs wear academic degree as a ribbon]*. Rosbalt. Retrieved May 11, 2019, from http://www.rosbalt.ru/russia/2017/10/04/1650789.html

Ryan, M., & Kaplan, A. (2018). *Facebook has a long history of failing its users. The massive data breach is just the latest example*. Media Matters for America. Retrieved September 8, 2022, from https://www.mediamatters.org/facebook/facebook-has-long-history-failing-its-users-massive-data-breach-just-latest-example

Schopenhauer, A. (2022). *A quote by Arthur Schopenhauer*. Goodreads.com. Retrieved July 11, 2022, from https://www.goodreads.com/quotes/695334-everyone-takes-the-limits-of-his-own-vision-for-the

Simons, J. W. (2019, March 30). *Exclusive: We'll write your PhD thesis...for £6,173! British students cheat their way to doctorates by paying companies to write their dissertations*. Daily Mail Online. Retrieved May 11, 2019, from https://www.dailymail.co.uk/news/article-6861373/British-students-cheat-way-doctorates-paying-companies-write-dissertations.html

Steel, E., & Vascellaro, J. (2010). Facebook, MySpace confront privacy loophole. *The Wall Street Journal*. Retrieved September 8, 2022, from https://www.wsj.com/articles/SB10001424052748704513104575256701215465596

Stow, N. (2019, March 30). *Bad Education. British uni students cheating their way to PhD—By paying £6k for expert to write dissertation*. The Sun. Retrieved May 11, 2019, from https://www.thesun.co.uk/news/8754255/british-uni-sstudents-cheat-phd-pay-dissertation/

Telley, C. (2018). *The influence machine: Automated information operations as a strategic defeat mechanism*. The Institute of Land Warfare, Association of the United States Army.

Thiele, R. (2021). *Hybrid warfare: Future and technologies*. Springer VS.

Torres Soriano, M. R. (2018). *Operaciones de influencia e inteligencia artificial: una visión prospective [Influence operations and artificial intelligence: A prospective vision]*. Opinion Document 74. Spanish Institute for Strategic Studies (IEEE).

Ullah, H.K. (2017). *Digital World War: Islamists, Extremists, and the Fight for Cyber Supremacy*, Yale University Press.

Veprintsev, V., Manoilo, A., Petrenko, A., & Frolov, D. (2005). *Operacii informacionno-psihologicheskoj vojny [Operations of psychological warfare]*. Goryachaya liniya—Telekom.

Voronova, O. (2018). *Sovremennye informacionnye vojny: Tipologiya i tekhnologii [Modern information wars: Typology and technologies]*. Esenin Ryazan State University.

Wallis Simons, J. (2019). *Exclusive: Cheating students are paying companies to write PhD theses*. Mail Online. Retrieved July 11, 2022, from https://www.dailymail.co.uk/news/article-6861373/British-students-cheat-way-doctorates-paying-companies-write-dissertations.html

Welch, M. (2011). *Irregular pen and limited sword: PSYWAR, PSYOP, and MISO in counterinsurgency*. U.S. Army Command and General Staff College.

Wetsman, N. (2021). *Facebook's whistleblower report confirms what researchers have known for years*. The Verge. Retrieved September 8, 2022, from https://www.theverge.com/2021/10/6/22712927/facebook-instagram-teen-mental-health-research

Wolfe, A. (2020). *Freedom's laboratory: The cold war struggle for the soul of science*. Johns Hopkins University Press.

Zvezdina, N., Kazakunova, G., & Gavrilko-Alekseev, A. (2018, January 17). *Jeksperty nazvali vuzy—rekordsmeny po zashhite "fal'shivyh" dissertacij [Experts identified the universities—Champions for the 'fake' dissertations]*. RBC. Retrieved May 11, 2019, from https://www.rbc.ru/society/17/01/2018/5a5c5fcc9a79470152e8bbe9

10

Current and Future Threats of the Malicious Use of Artificial Intelligence by Terrorists: Psychological Aspects

Darya Bazarkina

Introduction

The phenomenon of terrorism is undergoing a number of transformations. After the military defeat of the so-called Islamic State (IS) in Syria, the organization went deep underground. The hierarchical structures the quasi-state built on the territory it occupied have been replaced by a network structure, like Al-Qaeda in the 2000s, in which virtual communication plays a key role. However, in 2021, the U.S. Department of Defense estimated that the IS still had at least 10,000 fighters (Zelin, 2021), which means large-scale, coordinated terrorist attacks in different countries around the world are possible, especially with modern communication tools. At the same time, the growth of global political instability has led to the emergence of new "application points" for terrorist activity. For example, the Taliban movement's takeover of power in Afghanistan, opponents of IS, may spark a new mobilization of the Islamic State in Afghanistan, also known as the Islamic State in Khorasan, or ISIS-K. And with the Taliban's course toward establishing a peaceful neighborhood—and even cooperation—with China (Grossman, 2021), the anti-Chinese terrorist agenda can again become relevant. At the same time, the

---

D. Bazarkina (✉)
Department of European Integration Research, Institute of Europe of the Russian Academy of Sciences, Moscow, Russia
e-mail: bazarkina-icspsc@yandex.ru

political goals of terrorist groups such as Al-Qaeda and IS—building their own repressive regimes—remain, and for which the organizations are actively engaged in propaganda, recruitment, and fundraising.

Along with changes in the modi operandi of large international terrorist organizations and their lone-wolf supporters, the political activity of far-right groups and movements is growing, in the same way that supporters of Nazism are seeking to attack political opponents. To address their problems, terrorists are resorting to a wide range of psychological manipulation techniques—from false promises to direct intimidation.

Artificial intelligence (AI) expands opportunities not only in socially important areas such as medicine, education, and industrial production, but also in social engineering, which is increasingly being used by criminals in cyberspace. In the field of information security, primarily among practitioners, social engineering means the "psychological manipulation of people into performing actions or divulging confidential information" (Webroot, 2021). In accordance with the extended interpretation of the term given by Anderson (2018, p. 95), "social engineering isn't limited to stealing private information. It can also be about getting people to believe bogus public information." This interpretation allows disinformation and terrorist propaganda to be considered as a type of social engineering. The definition of social engineering as "any act that influences a person to take an action that may or may not be in his or her best interests" (Hadnagy, 2018, p. 7) expands the term to almost any kind of psychological influence. This study, by virtue of its focus on the communication of terrorists with target audiences, concentrates on the antisocial manifestations of social engineering that are currently being implemented, or could possibly be implemented in the future, through AI. The study attempts to answer the following questions: What is the current and future threat of AI specialists joining terrorist organizations? At what level have terrorist organizations and lone wolves mastered AI technologies, and what psychological impact does their malicious use of artificial intelligence (MUAI) have on society? What means of countering this threat already exist and can be created in the future?

This chapter's analysis is based on the system analysis method, which allowed the current state and trends in global terrorist threat development to be correlated with the development and spread of AI as a dual-use technology that can compensate for the combat power weakness of aggressive political actors in asymmetric warfare. Scenario analysis was partially used to predict possible threats to psychological security stemming from the use of social engineering by terrorists, as AI becomes cheaper and more widespread. Scenario analysis is "juxtaposing current trends in unexpected combinations in order to articulate surprising and yet plausible futures, often referred to as 'alternative worlds'" (Barma et al., 2016, p. 119). Scenarios are "depictions of possible future states of the world, offered together with a narrative of the driving causal forces and potential exogenous shocks that could lead to those futures" (ibid.). In its completed form, the scenario analysis of MUAI threats requires the inclusion of expert knowledge from technical and social science fields; this chapter aims to initiate such a discussion. The chapter was prepared using several groups of primary and secondary sources. The primary sources were the official publications of national and supranational governmental bodies, including reports from security agencies, as well as statistics and mass media reports. Secondary sources included monographs, research articles, and reports on different aspects of terrorism (Bakker, 2007; Barten et al., 2022; Europol 2019, 2020a, b; Gambetta & Hertog, 2016; Zelin, 2021, etc.), terrorist communications (Bazarkina, 2017; Ferguson et al., 2021; Lenglachner, 2018; OSCE Secretariat, 2008; Schlegel, 2020, etc.), and social engineering (e.g., Anderson, 2018; Hadnagy, 2018, etc.), as well as research on cybersecurity and on the use of AI for constructive and destructive purposes (Bazarkina & Pashentsev, 2019; Brundage et al., 2018; Chamola et al., 2021; Davis, 2021; Kepe, 2020; Lis & Olech, 2021; Little & Richards, 2021; Lobera et al., 2020; Pindrop 2020; Pledger, 2021; Schroeter, 2020; Stalinsky, 2022; Stalinsky & Sosnow, 2020; UNICRI and Interpol, 2019; UNICRI and UNCCT, 2021a, 2021b; White, 2021, etc.).

Artificial Intelligence Specialists Joining Terrorist Organizations as the Basis for Terrorist Malicious Use of Artificial Intelligence

Different factors lead individuals to engage in terrorist activities, including economic, socio-psychological, or political. Terrorist networks are most often formed by people of different income levels and from different professions. For example, among those who planned the foiled attack on the US embassy in Paris in 2001, one had served in an elite army battalion, two held menial jobs, and another was a computer specialist working for the local government. However, most terrorist organization recruits have relatively similar age characteristics (Bakker, 2007, p. 33), a high degree of emotional perception of reality, and a tendency to accept various kinds of statements regarding faith, which makes it relatively easy for terrorists to determine who is more likely to join.

The *economic factors* of the transition to terrorism can affect professionals from any field. A study by Gambetta and Hertog (2016) showed that during the twentieth century in the Middle East and North Africa, extremists were most frequently from professions that were quite prestigious in the past, such as teachers or lawyers. Due to an oversaturation of professionals, or a drop in the pace of advancement, the prestige of the profession began to decline (an engineer, e.g., would perform the tasks of a skilled worker), and graduates of higher educational institutions became increasingly disappointed in their future prospects. Not least, this led to an increase in the number of engineers in terrorist groups: "The tension between subjective expectations and objective opportunities…best explains the distribution of disciplines among extremists over time" (Gambetta & Hertog, 2016, p. 52). Under these circumstances, it is worth asking the following question: Which professions could suffer the same fate in the foreseeable future? To what extent are AI specialists at risk of being targeted for terrorist recruitment?

At the moment, there seems to be little reason to worry about AI specialists, as large companies—at least for the best ones—are competing for their skills (Alpatova, 2021). The global AI market, as of May 2021, was estimated to be valued at 327.5 billion US dollars and continuing to grow, thanks to an influx of investments. The demand for AI specialists is also growing. Over the past few years, the number of people employed in the field of AI has increased in many countries—in Brazil in 2020, there were 3.4 times more AI-related professions than in 2016 (Thormundsson, 2022). "The global artificial intelligence market size was valued at USD 93.5 billion in 2021 and is projected to expand at a compound annual growth rate (CAGR) of 38.1% from 2022 to 2030" (Grand View Research, 2022). At the same time, it is advisable to study not only fluctuations in the labor market, but also the scale of national AI development programs in order to predict the risks that may arise for specialists in the future. Based on the findings of Gambetta and Hertog (2016), it can be assumed that specialists who are not among the best in the AI industry may suffer in countries where governments will recruit more qualified personnel from abroad, to the detriment of national personnel, and likewise where the pace of government AI development programs slows or stops.

When assessing the *socio-psychological factors* of the resistance/vulnerability of specialists to terrorist recruitment, the degree of professional satisfaction plays an important role. Currently, there are only data on the level of satisfaction among a broader profile of IT specialists than just the field of AI. However, taking into account the related nature of the specialties, the high prestige of the IT sector during the first decades of the twenty-first century—now observed in the field of AI—and the interest of terrorists in recruiting IT specialists, it seems appropriate to consider the existing research.

Tomer and Mishra (2019, p. 13) showed that IT professionals who believe that they work in a "favorable" technology feel more satisfied with their careers: "The match/mismatch between expectations from the technology and experience while working in that technology play an important role in explaining career related outcomes such as career satisfaction." Thus, the mismatch between expectations and experience leads to a decrease in satisfaction. In addition, as the IT sector has developed, the need for innovators and leaders has grown, while the "slow learners" will sooner or later "find their jobs at risk," largely due to the fact that "with AI and automation, [the] IT sector has reinvented itself" (Scikey, 2021). In this regard, it can be assumed that the targets of terrorist recruitment will be representatives of the "rearguard," not only in IT but also in AI, who are not satisfied with their work or who do not feel its social significance.

The social significance of the work is connected, in addition to its objective result, to the degree of societal approval of the profession. Sociological research can help measure this indicator. Surveys in Spain found that people with lower levels of education have a more negative perception of AI, as do households with lower incomes, people who are mistrustful of science and technology, and people who are worried about the privacy of their data (Lobera et al., 2020). Based on the results of such studies, governments can predict the public's attitude toward the development of AI in their country, in order to create a more comfortable environment for specialists.

Finally, the *political factors* of involvement in terrorism are important. For example, despite the successful institutionalization of counterterrorist measures, insufficient efforts to integrate foreign workers in EU member states have resulted in migrant children—already full citizens of European countries—often not receiving the same rights to skilled work or the same respect that indigenous Europeans receive. This has caused ethnic tensions and the growth of far-right and fundamentalist sentiments. An additional factor in the terrorist recruitment of some migrant youth was the military participation of a number of EU countries in conflicts in the Middle East as part of the "war on terror" (Bazarkina, 2017, p. 375). The fact that even outwardly prosperous people turn to terrorism for political reasons draws attention to the political activity of all professionals, including in the field of AI.

Terrorist organizations are actively using all of these factors to "reduce the cost" of attacks by taking advantage of increasingly available AI technologies and by recruiting in-demand professionals. In the first 20 years of the twenty-first century, IT generalists were constantly in the sights of terrorist recruiters and propagandists. The main data on the recruitment of IT professionals in IS, including the formation of the "United Cyber Caliphate," date back to the period before the military defeat of the organization in Syria. In May 2017, a watershed moment for IS, the organization was in most need of "military specialists and programmers…to manage the drone system and cyber weapons, as well as to bypass the blocking of websites on the Internet" (Tischenko & Musatkina, 2017). Law enforcement agencies are still detaining IT professionals who joined the group. So, on June 11, 2021, in Chittagong, Bangladesh, the police arrested an active member of the Ansar al-Islam group, 40-year-old Shakhawat Ali Lalu, who was an IT specialist for the terrorist organization (Dhaka Tribune, 2021).

Open data on the number of IT specialists recruited by terrorists are not available in a systematic way. Most often, IT-trained terrorists are mentioned in media reports in connection with individual attacks or the elimination of terrorists. For example, Mohammed Emwazi, known as Jihadi John, a 27-year-old programmer with a degree from the University of Westminster, was identified in propaganda videos in 2015 (BBC News, 2015). Thus, the degree of involvement of IT specialists in terrorist actions can be judged, first of all, through indirect data—the number and technological level of attacks that are carried out. However, the recruitment of IT specialists to IS and Al-Qaeda is not only demonstrated through videos, software (such as the message encryption software Asrar al-Mujahideen or Tashfeer al-Jawwal), or digital publications. There are known attempts by IS to develop its own social network, statements about the theft of funds by terrorists using a hacker attack, and other related activities (see, e.g., Lenglachner, 2018). Finally, according to quite old expert estimates, "terrorist groups like ISIS and Al Qaeda have become more tech-savvy, and among their members there are also security experts with a deep knowledge of hacking techniques, including social engineering and spear phishing" (Paganini, 2015, see also **OSCE Secretariat, 2008** on this topic). The direction of terrorist attention to AI can be indirectly understood by the appeal to IS supporters on May 25, 2021, asking for programmers with experience in PHP, Python, HTML, CSS, and JavaScript to contact the group on Telegram (MEMRI, 2021a). It should also be taken into account that sponsors of terrorist activities can support laboratories and other facilities capable of developing products that adapt AI to the needs of terrorists.

The involvement of AI specialists in terrorist activities can happen (if it has not already) according to scenarios that are relevant for representatives of prestigious professions, among which is a special risk group of specialists who do not fall into the vanguard of the sector. When developing social engineering tools, terrorists will use the economic, socio-psychological, and political factors that lead to such risk groups.

Real Cases and Future Scenarios of Malicious Use of Artificial Intelligence by Terrorists and the Psychological Aspects

Social engineering, as a way to make the public or a particular person believe in fake information, is actively used by terrorists to promote their ideology and to recruit new fighters. This is done through the malicious use of bots. Back in 2015, IS created thousands of Twitter bots to push propaganda, fundraising, and recruitment, "as well as [for] jamming activist communication on the platform, silencing…opponents on Twitter" (Stalinsky & Sosnow, 2020). The bots latched on to trending hashtags to send a flood of support messages to IS, and the organization jumped into discussions on trending topics. Since then, IS has used bots to share instructions and coordinate terrorist attacks. IS, Al-Qaeda, and their supporters use Telegram bots to provide access to terrorist content archives, including messages from living and deceased leaders, such as Osama bin Laden and Ayman al-Zawahiri. Terrorist bots allow users to register for physical training and bomb-making courses, to ask questions about traveling to Syria or Iraq, and even to send greetings (Stalinsky & Sosnow, 2020). Terrorists use bots not only for agenda setting but also for coordinating active and potential fighters, thereby expanding their audience among active users of existing AI products.

Following their use of religious rhetoric by large terrorist organizations, the malicious use of bots is increasingly being adopted by neo-Nazi organizations of various sizes. Stalinsky (2022), in a detailed report, indicated that neo-Nazis use bots in social networks and applications to accomplish a wide range of similar tasks: sharing information about events and activities (white supremacist marches, conferences dedicated to Hitler), providing campaign materials (stickers, posters) for distribution, sharing anonymous content, providing information about individuals who are targets or attacks, exchanging the personal data of new militants or copies of *Mein Kampf*, and much more. A number of bots provide lists of extremist channels, links to other bots, access to poster archives, graphics, and memes, or spread fascist statements for recruitment and outreach, including bots that use the image of Hitler.

One example is the neo-Nazi "Mein Kampfy Korner" Telegram bot, used to chat anonymously and called a bot for "literal Nazi" people by users

(Stalinsky, 2022). The social nature of the number of messages transmitted by bots, or that contain references to bots, and AI is indicative. A post by the neo-Nazi Telegram channel "F.A.C.T (Fascist Action Coming Through)" called for the far right to "come together and Harass" companies whose employees "risk losing their employment," creating "bots that call and email these companies constantly to the point it disrupts their business and hurts their revenue." The "NazBol Party Club—US Civil War Edition" Telegram channel "posted a graphic that it said had been created by 'an AI bot.' It stated: 'Ask what the network of international bankers can do for you, not what you can do for the network of international bankers'" (ibid.). Thus, the nature of the messages transmitted by neo-Nazis testifies not only to the skills to use existing AI technologies for propaganda purposes—albeit, at a primitive level so far—but also to the fact that far-right organizations consistently use social appeals to try to direct public protests against social injustice and the consequences of economic crisis (especially during the pandemic) into neo-Nazi channels. With the growth of the far-right movement and the strengthening of its international character (neo-Nazi organizations and individuals actively support international relations, even transcontinental), it is possible that entities that are able to pay for expensive (but still cheaper) AI technologies will enter this environment, or that the movement will recruit specialists capable of creating them.

The fact that terrorists would like to attract not only users but also AI developers to their ranks for purposes of social engineering is openly shown in their ads. In March 2021, a media group affiliated with Al-Qaeda called on supporters to create platforms to promote the organization beyond Telegram. Through a Telegram bot, the media group regularly asks volunteers for help producing media content or even with hacking. On March 9, 2021, the group announced on Telegram and Rocket.Chat that they were recruiting people with different media skills (MEMRI, 2021b). Thus, despite the archaism of the ideology, terrorist organizations intend to use all available means, even the most advanced ones, to promote it. Further evidence of this practice is the terrorist organization use of the images reminding on AI-produced computer games (mostly first-person shooter) and popular online platforms for propaganda and recruitment. There are instances of direct references being made to computer games, such as GTA 5 and Call of Duty (Ferguson et al., 2021), in recruitment videos filmed and distributed by IS on social networks; later, this tactic would be used by far-right terrorists (Schlegel, 2020). Social networks and other media platforms are not always inclined to remove videos containing violent content, as they attract a large number of users; this is also why such videos are actively used by terrorists (Ferguson et al., 2021).

Capitalizing on the growing realism and appeal of AI-driven gameplay, which holds the player's attention, malevolent actors can edit propaganda content using frames from modern games to influence the minds of the target audience more effectively. Evidence suggests that increasingly advanced AI game development technologies may become available to terrorist organizations in time. IS allegedly even programmed its own video game, *Salil al-Swarim* (The Clanging of the Swords) (Schlegel, 2020). However, *Holy Defense*, sponsored by Hezbollah, is an example of a game that is aimed at promoting the fight against IS, and the developers indicate using AI (MEMRI TV Videos, 2018). Despite the anti-IS aspect of interest, *Holy Defense* does contain an element of propaganda related to interstate and global conflicts: "The Holy Defense is a simulation that embraces the documentation of one of the Sacred Defense's stages in the face of the Takfiri tide and the confrontation of the American-Zionist project" (Dar al-Manar, 2022). Thus, both supporters and opponents of IS and similar organizations are directly interested in further mastering AI technologies in the media, including video games.

Terrorist propaganda in the EU is currently aimed at encouraging individuals to commit attacks in their countries of residence: "The suggested methods included…drones or balloon-borne incendiary devices (IIDs)" (Europol, 2020, p. 20). Following their decline in combat power, terrorist organizations have moved from direct, armed clashes to attacks where the perpetrator is removed from the target, and unmanned aerial vehicles (UAV) could be another means of terrorist MUAI. Concerns about the use of drones by terrorists have been expressed in the research community (see, e.g., Chamola et al., 2021), as well as on the websites of the World Economic Forum (Clarke, 2018) and the Association of the United States Army (Pledger, 2021). One case of IS using a drone to disable military equipment has been documented: "When Iraqi tanks had ISIS cornered during the battle of Mosul in 2017, the extremists disabled a US-made M1A1…by using a makeshift drone to drop a small grenade next to the commander's hatch" (Tollast, 2022). There are known attempts by IS supporters to acquire drones in Denmark for the purposes of carrying out terrorist attacks in Iraq and Syria (The Cipher Brief, 2018); one of these persons was also found guilty of attempted terrorism related to the probable use of this equipment in attacks (Europol, 2021). On August 4, 2018, an unsuccessful attempt was made on the life of Venezuelan President Nicolas Maduro using a UAV. It is evident that actors ready to commit political assassinations—whether on behalf of full-fledged coup attempts, efforts to politically destabilize a country, or measures to intimidate citizens—will only improve this technology.

Although MUAI has not yet been reported in these cases (the drones were not equipped with AI), experts have expressed concerns (Pledger, 2021; UNICRI and UNCCT, 2021a) that aggressive, non-state actors may use AI-enabled drones in the future. The use of drones in terrorist attacks has already become a steady trend; there were already 76 terrorist attacks using UAVs in early 2022. "The first attack occurred in 2016, and the number of attacks per year varied considerably (range: 4–36). Forty-seven of the 76 attacks (70%) were successful…A total of 50 deaths and 132 injuries were recorded" (Barten et al., 2022). Meanwhile, the rapid growth of the drone market—global drone sales are expected to quadruple from 14.1 billion US dollars in 2018 to 43 billion US dollars by 2024 (Pledger, 2021)—along with the development of AI-related technologies, is concerning, especially the ability to coordinate multiple drones simultaneously (also called "swarms") (ibid.) and to equip drones with facial recognition surveillance systems (UNICRI and UNCCT, 2021a, p. 34). A case of a swarm drone attack against a Russian military base in Syria was documented in 2018 and has been called a sign of a "new kind of warfare" (Lubrano, 2018). Theoretically, even the use of modern robotics by terrorists, primarily UAVs, carries an element of social engineering. Some research suggests that people who use autonomous technology may experience a decline in their ability to make decisions related to moral choices, self-control, or empathy. "The risk is that as people become accustomed to working with machines, they will become more comfortable delegating decision-making to the machine. Could increased reliance on AI for decision-making lead to moral lapses?" (Kepe, 2020). In the case of a terrorist organization, it may not be a lapse but instead, an intentional removal of personal responsibility from the perpetrator of the terrorist act. Moreover, the mere possibility of remote attacks can change the methods of terrorist activity, as well as the underlying propaganda concepts. For example, if the number of suicide bombers decreases, the image of the terrorist "martyr" will fade into the background against the image of an inevitably successful remote action. This may convince hesitant individuals to join with the terrorists.

Cryptocurrency transactions "appeared to cater more for the requirements of isolated cells or individuals present in Europe" (Europol, 2020a, p. 20). With the help of cryptocurrencies, terrorists make purchases on the dark web, where terrorist propaganda is also distributed. From this convergence of terrorism and cybercrime (Europol, 2019, p. 47), bulletproof hosting (BPH), an important building block of criminal infrastructure has emerged. BPH is a type of hosting or hosting provider that knowingly takes orders from criminals (for profit), offering them a technical infrastructure that cannot be discovered or dismantled by law enforcement. The distribution and use of BPH also contribute to the growth of terrorist content, and it can already be used to develop/host AI products (Europol, 2020b, p. 22) to generate such content, posing new threats to public psychological security.

AI can also fundamentally change the mechanisms of terrorist recruitment. A traditional human recruiter always needs time to get to know a potential recruit, and usually starts by engaging in a conversation with the target through social media. As a rule, the recruiter asks a number of personal questions (whether they want to get married, whether they have professional problems, etc.), to uncover the target's vulnerabilities. Then, the recruiter promises exactly what the potential recruit lacks in life—marital happiness, acclaim, professional growth, and so on—with the end goal of getting them to join the terrorist organization. Today, the rapidly growing capabilities of AI can not only track an individual's digital footprints but also construct content. Sentiment analysis of a victim's behavior in a digital environment can reduce the time it takes to learn their habits, strengths, and vulnerabilities. Facial recognition can track the appearance of a photo or video of a recruit, even from sources where their name is not mentioned. Moreover, deepfake technologies can be used by an attacker to create images that are more likely to appeal to victims of manipulation.

The threat of the malicious use of deepfakes by terrorist organizations and lone wolves is growing. Lis and Olech (2021, p. 110) have suggested that fake video content showing soldiers from Western countries committing war crimes against Muslims may be used to recruit terrorists and incite ethnic hatred. U.S. Federal Bureau of Investigation Director Chris Wray said, "The quality [of deepfakes] is increasing and that's something that's of great concern" (Davis, 2021). Europol (2022, p. 13) noted that "Document fraud is a facilitator of other crimes like…terrorism, as perpetrators often use fake IDs to travel to their target locations. Deepfake technology might amplify the risk for advanced document fraud by organised crime groups." There are documented cases (Reuters, 2020) of individuals creating completely new identities that cannot be traced in order to spread disinformation.

It is also possible to imagine the future use of deepfakes containing motivational appeals to followers from the leaders of terrorist organizations, even from leaders who have died to disorient antiterrorist forces. So far, major terrorist organizations, according to public data, have not used deepfake technology to manipulate mass consciousness in this way. However, this threat is assessed as probable and is reflected in the media (Rivers, 2019). In addition, there is a growing atmosphere of uncertainty around the stories of terrorist organization leaders. For example, in November 2020, reports emerged on social media and in the Pakistani press that Al-Qaida chief Ayman al-Zawahiri had died (Bunzel, 2021). However, after the messages of his death were distributed, video messages of questionable authenticity by Zawahiri to Al-Qaeda members were released (Bunzel, 2021; Moore, 2021). The circulation of conflicting versions of events in the media creates uncertainty and an incentive to definitively "confirm" one version or the other with the help of deepfakes, not only for the terrorists themselves but also for other actors who—for various reasons—are interested in changing the agenda, such as by accusing a country of harboring a terrorist leader. In the current environment, it is more necessary than ever to promote the importance of fact-checking in the media space. While the general public will not be able to find out whether one terrorist or another is dead or alive, fact-checking will reduce the effectiveness of manipulation.

Recently, there have been cases of deepfakes posted by alt-right groups on social networks. A number of TikTok accounts set up specifically to troll and spread hate speech posted a video of users calling themselves "transracial," a term often used by the far right to ridicule transgender people, under the guise of fully AI-generated faces (White, 2021). Apart from the hate speech itself as a means of psychological pressure, it is especially dangerous that alt-right supporters not only create non-existent people, but also regularly steal and edit videos of real TikTok users to impersonate them. This could result in truly innocent users being prosecuted (Little & Richards, 2021), as well as an increase in the number of attackers if the alt-right deepfake creators feel they can avoid punishment. This would be similar to engaging in remote physical attacks that allow the attacker to not only avoid injury or death, but also responsibility. Given the active use of bots by the neo-Nazi movement, it is possible that those groups have borrowed this tactic as well.

The consequences of social engineering can be extended to the use of physical objects that are technically controlled by AI; in other words, the reorientation of commercial AI systems by criminals. In 2018, experts at Oxford University cited an accident involving autonomous vehicles as an example (Brundage et al., 2018, p. 27). As technology becomes more embedded in daily life, the greater the panic and disorientation such attacks can create. Similarly, the impact on public consciousness should also be considered, just like the communication effect of a "traditional" terrorist attack—just the knowledge of a murder is shocking on its own, without the help of words or images. The number of opportunities for this type of reorientation is also growing, including through voice biometrics, which criminals are finding ways to hack.

With continuous improvement of voice mimicking systems, the tasks of social engineering are greatly simplified—talking briefly with the victim about anything at all in order to get a voice sample is enough for the further synthesis of messages. Various services can transform text into sounding like a natural human voice, or synthesize speech in the voice of a particular person (Pindrop XE "Pindrop" , 2020, p. 17). At the same time, the use of synthetic AI products, which include the control systems for physical objects, along with personnel authorization by voice or video, is particularly risky. Researchers at Ruhr University Bochum have pointed to scammers who can "trick" speech recognition AI tools to make purchases on behalf of the owner (Lourenco, 2019). However, it can be assumed that terrorists can also do it for their own purposes. Thus, social engineering through AI can be used by terrorists for purposes beyond propaganda or recruitment.

Taking into account that "hackers have discovered that artificial intelligence can make them more effective" (James, 2020), the role of the "human factor" (the psychological vulnerability of the victim) is also growing, and social engineering in the narrow sense (psychological manipulation in order to obtain passwords and other confidential data) is also being used by terrorist groups. "The use by terrorists…of funds received from online casinos, theft of money through fake online stores and duplicate sites, from phishing and pharming attacks…directs the vector of combating the financing of terrorism to the virtual environment" (RIA Novosti, 2020). Phishing and pharming are widespread forms of such social engineering, further enhanced by AI.

When phishing, criminals gain access to confidential user data (usernames and passwords) by sending mass emails on behalf of popular brands, as well as personal messages through social networks. Eventually, AI will be used to create texts that are indistinguishable from those written by humans, which will strengthen the psychological component of phishing (Benishti, 2018). Since at least mid-2017, the doxing, collection, and dissemination of the IP addresses of antifascist activists by alt-right supporters in the United States can be traced. One alt-right community member "described how he tricks suspected antifa members into revealing their IP address by sending them a malicious link" (Lee, 2017). IP addresses can also be used to ascertain someone's physical location (ibid.).

Spear phishing—sending emails on behalf of individuals or organizations that the victim clearly trusts—can become especially dangerous through AI enhancements. Phishing attempts such as these are most likely made to uncover trade secrets or military information. In the case of spear phishing, the sender is likely to be someone in a position of authority or someone the target knows personally (Shacklett & Bedell, 2022). Spear phishing can be particularly difficult to identify due to the personalization of the messages using sentiment analysis. Unlike phishing, pharming distributes AI tools to user computers that, after launching, redirects access to fake websites.

There are other threats using AI in social engineering by criminals, including terrorists. For example, predictive analytics can identify the people who will be the most vulnerable to fraud. The machine-learning algorithms used by spam filters can be retrained by attackers to create new spam that bypasses these filters. By using machine learning to understand how security software works, a criminal will be more persuasive when trying to convince a user to download malware (James, 2020). According to the testimony of Tsukerman (2020), natural language processing (NLP) technology "has allowed automated production of targeted phishing bots that outperform humans. These fully-automated, AI-based phishing bots generate interesting tweets and then fool users into clicking on them." An even more complex technology could be the creation of chatbots with the addition of a system that synthesizes the voice of a real person. Such a mechanism would be much more convincing in a conversation than a regular chatbot. Nothing can prevent future criminals from creating such a bot with the voice of a person the victim trusts, and presenting it as an official channel of communication from a real person.

Taking into account developments in the AI field, it can be assumed that in the future, many technologies will be used to pressure the public. One day, using the synthesized voice of a top manager, criminals could force the manager's subordinates to transfer large sums of money to them (this has already happened); the next day, the same criminals might give a false order to the military to launch a strike at a neighboring state. In addition to causing physical harm to people and infrastructure, these types of actions will discredit the "attacking" state. The authors of terrorist propaganda, calling for a return to the "good old days" of the Middle Ages, may well move from creating negative literary images about AI to proving its deadly danger "in practice" by sabotaging high-tech enterprise. At the same time, as the analysis of existing sources shows, the terrorists themselves are actively seeking to use AI capabilities for their own purposes.

Ways to Counter the Psychological Effects of Malicious Use of Artificial Intelligence by Terrorists

The possibilities for *using AI to counteract social engineering* certainly deserve further study by both the technical and social sciences. In order to counter terrorist propaganda, online platforms are using smart image recognition systems. Facebook has also "suggested it could use machine-learning algorithms to look for patterns in terrorist propaganda, so it could more swiftly remove it from the newsfeeds of others" (Marr, 2018). Predictive analytics based on AI are being used not only to predict attacks, but also to psychologically profile terrorists (Robbins, 2017). NLP is being proposed for moderating content on the internet, especially for the languages of smaller nations. By detecting unusual semantic patterns on websites, this technology can identify terrorist and extremist content and translate it into languages that moderators can understand (Schroeter, 2020, p. 1), leading to the removal of the content.

There is growing interest in studying how data collected on social media about people's online behavior can be used to predict terrorist activity (UNICRI and UNCCT, 2021b, p. 24). For example, startup INSIKT Intelligence uses NLP and social network analysis (SNA) on open-source content from social media and other resources to identify potentially dangerous content and possible threats, or to establish patterns of relationships between individuals or organizations. Using SNA, INSIKT assesses the activity of a group of users on the network, determining the nodes of influence and the levels/effectiveness of the information dissemination (UNICRI and UNCCT, 2021b, p. 25). This allows law enforcement to prioritize MUAI terrorist threats to psychological security.

Suggestions for *using AI in a psychological defense against manipulation* are interesting. To get inside a corporate network, hackers need a "good story, a bit of persistence and a call center agent who's willing to break protocol" (Ekici, 2019). However, AI is invulnerable to manipulations aimed at human feelings, and can analyze the behavior of an interlocutor in real time based on a large number of parameters. By allowing conversational AI to take the lead in a talk with a caller, "enterprises can mitigate the potential damage caused by social engineering" (Ekici, 2019). In this regard, it is advisable to systematize expert knowledge in the field of psychology for AI training.

Given all of that, the most vulnerable element of the information and cybersecurity system is still the individual. The relevance of *citizen education* is not limited to the technical sphere, but also applies to the political and psychological spheres. "The security engineer absolutely must understand basic psychology, as a prerequisite for dealing competently with everything...from phishing to social engineering in general" (Anderson, 2018, p. 76). With the role of AI growing in almost all spheres of life, this statement can be applied to a wide variety of professions where representatives are faced with social engineering. The same applies to knowledge about the political (strategic) goals of terrorist organizations, as well as about the tactics and techniques used by criminals seeking profit and politically motivated terrorists.

In order to minimize the economic and socio-psychological factors that lead to the involvement of AI specialists in terrorist activities, *more detailed plans and strategies for AI development, including the social component of these strategies*, may need to be developed in different countries. It is already worth thinking about the social processes—and their psychological consequences—of the AI industry that will emerge from the separation of the "vanguard" from the "rearguard," and to take these processes into account during strategic planning.

Policy measures at the international level include cooperation between political institutions and cross-border security structures, in order to accumulate and exchange expertise, as well as develop policy and legislative solutions to counter the malicious use of AI. Interpol and the United Nations are collaborating on the study of "political attacks" (primarily through deepfakes) and physical attacks using AI that can be carried out by criminals (UNICRI and Interpol, 2019, p. 5) and terrorists. It is possible to agree with recommendations to constantly monitor AI risks and threats, as well as to exchange expert knowledge between law enforcement agencies (ibid. p. 23). "It is necessary to increase the exchange of expert knowledge on technologies such as 3D printing, synthetic biology, nanotechnology, robotics, the synthesis of the human face and autonomous weapons...this will help to better identify and respond to risks before it is too late" (United Nations, 2019). However, today more than ever, civil society should be involved in such exchanges. It is also necessary to develop international scientific cooperation, including interdisciplinary research projects by both the technical and social sciences aimed at countering high-tech terrorism.

Conclusion

This chapter examined a rather limited number of real-world cases and possible scenarios of the use of AI by terrorists. However, it must be remembered that crime is evolving as rapidly as technology and society. Thus, as quickly as the technological capabilities of new services are growing, terrorists are adapting just as rapidly to the new realities. For example, if terrorist groups try to circumvent profiling mechanisms by recruiting people with characteristics that do not fit the profile of a typical fighter, the combination of a remote attack and a fake video message can significantly help those groups cover their tracks in the future.

Currently, terrorist organizations can only afford limited AI technologies. However, the eventual recruitment of AI specialists into the terrorists ranks is not excluded. The growth of AI capabilities is taking place against the background of complex economic, socio-psychological, and political factors that can lead to disappointment in almost any profession. It can be concluded that MUAI by terrorists in the psychological security sphere is aimed at the following audiences:

- potential victims of fraud;
- potential and real supporters, including those who are able to use (and, ideally, develop) AI technologies; and
- the fighters themselves.

In this context, it is necessary to further study the transformation of the terrorism phenomenon during the "fourth industrial revolution"; the sociopsychological, economic, and political conditions in which AI specialists work; and the psychological mechanisms that terrorists use to implement MUAI to influence public consciousness.

References

Alpatova, I. (2021). Rossijskim kompanijam ne hvataet chetyre tysjachi specialistov v oblasti II (Russian companies lack four thousand AI specialists). In: Rossiyskaya gazeta (The Russian Newspaper). Retrieved July 11, 2022, from https://rg.ru/2021/02/11/rossijskim-kompaniiam-ne-hvataet-chetyre-tysiachi-specialistov-v-oblasti-ii.html.
Anderson, R. (2018). *Security engineering: A guide to building dependable distributed systems*. John Wiley & Sons.
Bakker, E. (2007). *Jihadi terrorists in Europe, their characteristics, and the circumstances in which they joined the Jihad: An exploratory study*. Clingendael Institute.
Barma, N., Durbin, B., Lorber, E., & Whitlark, R. (2016). "Imagine a world in which": Using scenarios in political science. *International Studies Perspectives, 17*, 117–135. https://doi.org/10.1093/isp/ekv005

Barten, D., Tin, D., De Cauwer, H., Ciottone, R., & Ciottone, G. (2022). A counter-terrorism medicine analysis of drone attacks. *Prehospital and Disaster Medicine, 37*, 192–196. https://doi.org/10.1017/s1049023x22000139

Bazarkina, D. (2017). Rol' kommunikacionnogo obespechenija v antiterroristicheskoj dejatel'nosti Evropejskogo Sojuza (The Role of the Communication Provision in EU Antiterrorist Activity). DSc Thesis. Institute of Europe, Russian Academy of Sciences (IERAS), Moscow.

Bazarkina, D., & Pashentsev, E. (2019). Artificial intelligence and new threats to international psychological security. *Russia in Global Affairs, 17*, 147–170. https://doi.org/10.31278/1810-6374-2019-17-1-147-170

BBC News. (2015). 'Jihadi John' named as Mohammed Emwazi from London. In: BBC News. Retrieved July 11, 2022, from https://www.bbc.com/news/uk-31637090.

Benishti, E. (2018). Artificial Intelligence and the Impact of Phishing. In: Ironscales. Retrieved July 11, 2022, from https://ironscales.com/blog/Artificial-Intelligence-Revolutionizing-Phishing/.

Brundage, M., Avin, S., Clark, J., Toner, H., Eckersley, P., Garfinkel, B., Dafoe, A., Scharre, P., Zeitzoff, T., Filar, B., Anderson, H., Roff, H., Allen, G., Steinhardt, J., Flynn, C., Ó Héigeartaigh, S., Beard, S., Belfield, H., Farquhar, S., Lyle, C., Crootof, R., Evans, O., Page, M., Bryson, J., Yampolskiy, R., & Amodei, D. (2018). *The malicious use of artificial intelligence: Forecasting, prevention, and mitigation*. Future of Humanity Institute, University of Oxford, Oxford, AZ.

Bunzel, C. (2021). Is Ayman al-Zawahiri Dead? In: Jihadica. Retrieved July 12, 2022, from https://www.jihadica.com/is-ayman-al-zawahiri-dead/.

Chamola, V., Kotesh, P., Agarwal, A., Naren, G. N., & Guizani, M. (2021). A comprehensive review of unmanned aerial vehicle attacks and neutralization techniques. *Ad Hoc Networks, 111*, 102324. https://doi.org/10.1016/j.adhoc.2020.102324

Clarke, C. (2018). Drone terrorism is now a reality, and we need a plan to counter the threat. In: World Economic Forum. Retrieved July 11, 2022, from https://www.weforum.org/agenda/2018/08/drone-terrorism-is-now-a-reality-and-we-need-a-plan-to-counter-the-threat/.

Dar al-Manar. (2022). لعبة الدفاع المقدس (Luebat aldifae almuqadas – The Holy Defense Game). In: Holy Defense. Retrieved July 13, 2022, from https://www.holydefence.com/article.php?id=1&cid=3&catidval=0.

Davis, C. (2021). Intelligence Hearing: Terrorism and "Deep Fakes." In: 93.1FM WIBC. Retrieved July 12, 2022, from https://www.wibc.com/news/local-indiana/intelligence-hearing-terrorism-and-deep-fakes/.

Dhaka Tribune. (2021). Ansar Al Islam's IT specialist, back from Syria, arrested in Chittagong. In: Dhaka Tribune. Retrieved July 11, 2022, from https://archive.dhakatribune.com/bangladesh/crime/2021/06/12/ansar-al-islam-s-it-specialist-back-from-syria-arrested-in-chittagong.

Ekici, E. (2019). Social Engineers are No Match for Artificial Intelligence. In: TechSpective. Retrieved July 12, 2022, from https://techspective.net/2019/12/07/social-engineers-are-no-match-for-artificial-intelligence/.

Europol. (2019). *Internet organised crime threat assessment (IOCTA) 2019*. Europol.

Europol. (2020a). *European Union terrorism situation and trend report (TE-SAT) 2020*. Europol.

Europol. (2020b). *Internet organised crime threat assessment (IOCTA) 2020*. Europol.

Europol. (2021). *European Union terrorism situation and trend report (TE-SAT) 2021*. Europol.

Europol. (2022). Facing reality? Law enforcement and the challenge of deepfakes. Publications Office of the European Union, Luxembourg.

Ferguson, K., Kim, M., & Dobrowolska, M. (2021). The Role of Video Games and Online Platforms in Terrorist Radicalization and Recruitment. In: The Counterterrorism Group. Retrieved July 12, 2022, from https://www.counterterrorismgroup.com/post/the-role-of-video-games-and-online-platforms-in-terrorist-radicalization-and-recruitment.

Gambetta, D., & Hertog, S. (2016). *Engineers of Jihad: The curious connection between violent extremism and education*. Princeton University Press.

Grand View Research. (2022). Artificial Intelligence Market Size Report, 2022–2030. In: Grand View Research. Retrieved July 10, 2022, from https://www.grandviewresearch.com/industry-analysis/artificial-intelligence-ai-market.

Grossman, D. (2021). China and the Taliban Begin Their Romance. In: RAND Corporation. Retrieved July 11, 2022, from https://www.rand.org/blog/2021/07/china-and-the-taliban-begin-their-romance.html.

Hadnagy, C. (2018). *Social engineering: The science of human hacking*. John Wiley & Sons.

James, M. (2020). Experts Warn AI And Social Engineering Lead To New Digital Scams. In: SmartData Collective. Retrieved July 13, 2022, from https://www.smartdatacollective.com/experts-warn-ai-and-social-engineering-lead-to-digital-scams/.

Kepe, M. (2020). Considering Military Culture and Values When Adopting AI. In: RAND Corporation. Retrieved July 13, 2022, from https://www.rand.org/blog/2020/06/considering-military-culture-and-values-when-adopting.html.

Lee, M. (2017). How Right-Wing Extremists Stalk, Dox, and Harass Their Enemies. In: The Intercept. Retrieved July 21, 2022, from https://theintercept.com/2017/09/06/how-right-wing-extremists-stalk-dox-and-harass-their-enemies/.

Lenglachner, F. (2018). *Kybernetiq: Analyzing the first jihadi magazine on cyber and information security*. International Institute for Counter-Terrorism (ICT), Herzliya.

Lis, A., & Olech, A. (2021). *Technology and terrorism: Artificial intelligence in the time of contemporary terrorist threats*. Institute of New Europe.

Little, O., & Richards, A. (2021). TikTok trolls are creating deepfakes and deceptively editing real users' videos to promote "transracialism." In: Media Matters for

America. Retrieved July 12, 2022, from https://www.mediamatters.org/tiktok/tiktok-trolls-are-creating-deepfakes-and-deceptively-editing-real-users-videos-promote.

Lobera, J., Fernández Rodríguez, C., & Torres-Albero, C. (2020). Privacy, values and machines: Predicting opposition to artificial intelligence. *Communication Studies, 71*, 448–465. https://doi.org/10.1080/10510974.2020.1736114

Lourenco, R. (2019). Could hackers trick voice assistants into committing fraud? Researchers say yes. In: Venture Beat. Retrieved July 13, 2022, from https://venturebeat.com/2019/02/17/could-hackers-trick-voice-assistants-into-committing-fraud-researchers-say-yes/.

Lubrano, M. (2018). Drone attack shows non-state actors' UAV capabilities. In: Global Risk Insights. Retrieved July 11, 2022, from https://globalriskinsights.com/2018/01/swarm-drone-attack-syria-uav/.

Marr, B. (2018). Weaponizing Artificial Intelligence: The Scary Prospect Of AI-Enabled Terrorism. In: Forbes. Retrieved July 13, 2022, from https://www.forbes.com/sites/bernardmarr/2018/04/23/weaponizing-artificial-intelligence-the-scary-prospect-of-ai-enabled-terrorism/?sh=4083b77377b6.

MEMRI. (2021a). On Telegram, Pro-ISIS Outlet Seeks Programmers. In: MEMRI. Retrieved July 13, 2022, from https://www.memri.org/cjlab/telegram-pro-isis-outlet-seeks-programmers.

MEMRI. (2021b). Pro-Al-Qaeda Media Group Calls On Supporters: Be Innovative In Creating Platforms Beyond Telegram To Voice Your Support Of Our Fighters, Disseminate News About Them. In: MEMRI. Retrieved July 13, 2022, from https://www.memri.org/cjlab/pro-al-qaeda-media-group-calls-supporters-be-innovative-creating-platforms-beyond-telegram.

MEMRI TV Videos. (2018). Hizbullah Launches "Holy Defense" Computer Game Simulating Its Battles in Syria and Lebanon. In: YouTube. Retrieved July 12, 2022, from https://www.youtube.com/watch?v=fqbAUPcG-GE.

Moore, M. (2021). Al Qaeda leader Ayman al-Zawahiri seen in video after death rumors. In: New York Post. Retrieved July 12, 2022, from https://nypost.com/2021/09/12/al-qaeda-leader-ayman-al-zawahiri-seen-in-video-after-death-rumors/.

OSCE Secretariat. (2008). Cyber threat on the rise as terrorists recruit computer specialists, says OSCE expert. In: Organization for Security and Co-operation in Europe (OSCE). Retrieved July 11, 2022, from https://www.osce.org/atu/49615.

Paganini, P. (2015). Spearphishing: A New Weapon in Cyber Terrorism – Infosec Resources. In: Infosec Resources. Retrieved July 11, 2022, from https://resources.infosecinstitute.com/topic/spearphishing-a-new-weapon-in-cyber-terrorism/.

Pindrop. (2020). *Voice Intelligence & Security Report. A review of fraud, the future of voice, and the impact to customer service channels. Revised for 2020 including updated data*. Pindrop.

Pledger, T. (2021). The Role of Drones in Future Terrorist Attacks. In: Association of the United States Army (AUSA). Retrieved July 11, 2022, from https://www.ausa.org/publications/role-drones-future-terrorist-attacks.

Reuters. (2020). Deepfake Used to Attack Activist Couple Shows New Disinformation Frontier. In: NDTV Gadgets 360. Retrieved July 13, 2022, from https://gadgets360.com/internet/features/deepfake-oliver-taylor-mazen-masri-terrorist-accuse-london-university-of-birmingham-student-fake-profile-2264044.

RIA Novosti. (2020). Terroristy vse aktivnee ispol'zujut IT-tehnologii, zajavili v ATC SNG (Terrorists are increasingly using IT technologies, the CIS ATC said). In: RIA Novosti. Retrieved July 13, 2022, from https://ria.ru/20200218/1564913906.html.

Rivers, D. (2019). ISIS 'preparing clip of al-Baghdadi ALIVE' using deepfake propaganda. In: Daily Star. Retrieved July 12, 2022, from https://www.dailystar.co.uk/news/world-news/al-baghdadi-still-alive-deepfake-20841470.

Robbins, S. (2017). AI and Counter-Terrorism. In: Scott Robbins. Retrieved July 13, 2022, from https://scottrobbins.org/wp-content/uploads/2017/11/AI-and-Counter-Terrorism.pdf.

Schlegel, L. (2020). Jumanji extremism? How games and gamification could facilitate radicalization processes. *JD Journal for Deradicalization, 23*, 1.

Schroeter, M. (2020). *Artificial intelligence and countering violent extremism: A primer*. Network on Extremism and Technology (GNET).

Scikey, V. J. (2021). Scikey: Job Satisfaction Among IT Industry Professionals in SEA Regions. In: Scikey. Retrieved July 13, 2022, from https://www.scikey.ai/read-blog/362_scikey-job-satisfaction-among-it-industry-professionals-in-sea-regions.html.

Shacklett, M., & Bedell, C. (2022). What is Spear Phishing? In: Search Security. Retrieved July 13, 2022, from https://www.techtarget.com/searchsecurity/definition/spear-phishing.

Stalinsky, S. (2022). Neo-Nazis And White Supremacists Are Using Telegram Bots To Recruit Members, Disseminate Content, Maintain Supporter Anonymity, Promote Events, And Obtain Information About Individuals To Be Targeted For Attack. In: MEMRI. Retrieved July 11, 2022, from https://www.memri.org/cjlab/neo-nazis-and-white-supremacists-are-using-telegram-bots-recruit-members-disseminate-content.

Stalinsky, S., & Sosnow, R. (2020). Jihadi Use Of Bots On The Encrypted Messaging Platform Telegram. In: MEMRI. Retrieved July 13, 2022, from https://www.memri.org/reports/jihadi-use-bots-encrypted-messaging-platform-telegram.

The Cipher Brief. (2018). Terrorists' Use of Drones and Other Emerging Technologies. In: The Cipher Brief. Retrieved July 11, 2022, from https://www.thecipherbrief.com/column_article/terrorists-use-of-drones-and-other-emerging-technologies.

Thormundsson, B. (2022). Topic: Artificial Intelligence (AI) worldwide. In: Statista. Retrieved July 11, 2022, from https://www.statista.com/topics/3104/artificial-intelligence-ai-worldwide/.

Tischenko, M., & Musatkina, A. (2017). Diplomirovannyj terrorizm: IG pytaetsja verbovat' v Rossii perevodchikov i programmistov (Certified terrorism: IS trying to recruit translators and programmers in Russia). In: RT. Retrieved July 11, 2022, from https://russian.rt.com/russia/article/386595-terroristy-verbovka-studenty-perevodchiki-programmisty.

Tollast, R. (2022). Terrorist drone attacks: Could new technology stop the threat? In: The National. Retrieved July 11, 2022, from https://www.thenationalnews.com/world/2022/02/23/terrorist-drone-attacks-could-new-technology-stop-the-threat/.

Tomer, G., & Mishra, S. (2019). Expectation from Technology and Career Satisfaction: A study among IT Professionals in India. Australasian Journal of Information Systems. doi: https://doi.org/10.3127/ajis.v23i0.1761.

Tsukerman, E. (2020). How artificial intelligence is changing social engineering. In: Infosec Resources. Retrieved July 13, 2022, from https://resources.infosecinstitute.com/topic/how-artificial-intelligence-is-changing-social-engineering/.

UNICRI and Interpol. (2019). *Artificial intelligence and robotics for law enforcement.* UNICRI and Interpol.

UNICRI and UNCCT. (2021a). *Algorithms and terrorism: The malicious use of artificial intelligence for terrorist purposes.* United Nations Office of Counter-Terrorism (UNOCT) and United Nations Interregional Crime and Justice Research Institute (UNICRI).

UNICRI and UNCCT. (2021b). *Countering terrorism online with artificial intelligence. An overview for law enforcement and counter-terrorism agencies in South Asia and South-East Asia.* United Nations Office of Counter-Terrorism and United Nations Interregional Crime and Justice Research Institute.

United Nations. (2019). New technologies, artificial intelligence aid fight against global terrorism. In: UN News. Retrieved July 13, 2022, from https://news.un.org/en/story/2019/09/1045562.

Webroot. (2021). What is Social Engineering? Examples & Prevention Tips. In: Webroot. Retrieved July 13, 2022, from https://www.webroot.com/us/en/resources/tips-articles/what-is-social-engineering.

White, L. (2021). TikTok Deepfake trolls are pushing bigoted, alt-right rhetoric with full anonymity. In: Stealth Optional. Retrieved July 12, 2022, from https://stealthoptional.com/news/tiktok-deepfake-trolls-alt-right-transracial/.

Zelin, A. (2021). Jihadis 2021: ISIS & al Qaeda. In: Wilson Center. Retrieved July 11, 2022, from https://www.wilsoncenter.org/article/jihadis-2021-isis-al-qaeda.

11

Malicious Use of Artificial Intelligence and the Threats to Corporate Reputation in International Business

Erik Vlaeminck

Introduction

Trust plays a key role in society. As elaborated by Jaffe: "[t]here are just a few elemental forces that hold our world together. The one that's the glue of society is called trust. Its presence cements relationships by allowing people to live and work together, feel safe and belong to a group" (2018). What we witness nowadays, however, is a decline of (global) trust. According to the famous Edelman Trust Barometer, this tendency particularly concerns an increasing distrust in governments. They find "a world ensnared in a vicious cycle of distrust, fueled by a growing lack of faith in media and government. Through disinformation and division, these two institutions are feeding the cycle and exploiting it for commercial and political gain" (2022). The decline in trust has potentially a substantial impact on society, as trust has been associated with different levels of not only social cohesion and economic growth but also political stability and health outcomes (Hanstad, 2020). This trend cannot be disconnected from the ongoing COVID-19 pandemic which seems to have exacerbated the existing distrust in media and scientific sources and expertise (OECD). The emergence of social media and new technologies, such as AI and machine learning, in people's lives cannot be disregarded as well, as the trust in big tech has, according to the Edelman report, been gradually

---

E. Vlaeminck (✉)
Berlin, Germany

© The Author(s), under exclusive license to Springer Nature Switzerland AG 2023
E. Pashentsev (ed.), *The Palgrave Handbook of Malicious Use of AI and Psychological Security*,
https://doi.org/10.1007/978-3-031-22552-9_11

declining since 2019 (CBS News, 2021). Regardless of the growing lack of trust as well as the many emerging risks related to new technologies, it is unlikely that its rapid development will be interrupted, given the projection that the global AI-market will exceed $100 billion by 2025 (UNICRI & UN, 2021, 5).

However, the outspoken, optimistic stance toward developments in the sphere of AI has recently become characterized by more critical voices reflecting on the potential dangers of its fast development, as stated by the comments made by prominent academics and business leaders like Noam Chomsky (Mars, 2022), Yoval Harrari (CBS News, 2021), Bill Gates (Clifford, 2019), and tech leader Elon Musk who stated that "AI is far more dangerous than nukes" (Clifford, 2018). Their shared concern over the potential dangers of AI seems to be justified given the horrific applications of AI-driven technologies in terrorist activity, modern warfare, and the state and non-state attempts to destabilize democracies through mass propaganda and social engineering across the world.

Along with the growing public interest in the malicious use of artificial intelligence (hereinafter MUAI), the scholarship on the subject has continued to flourish. This is illustrated in various studies dealing with topics such as its implications in international (geo-) politics (Kasapoglu & Kirdemir, 2019), psychological warfare (Bazarkina & Pashentsev, 2020), or ethics (EPRS, 2020). Besides the academic scholarship, professional reports (Trend Micro, 2020) make up an important aspect of the existing knowledge on the subject. Regardless of this growing interest, more work needs to be done to fully understand the possible scale, consequences, and dangers of MUAI—for example, in relation to corporate reputation. While AI-related threats to corporate reputation have been addressed individually in several studies and professional reports (MS, 2021), a more comprehensive study of threats to corporate reputation posed by MUAI needs to be conducted, particularly with regard to international psychological security as well as in the context of the ongoing global COVID-19 pandemic. The concern and urgency of the matter, however, was already pointed out in 2018:

> *AI algorithms may be flawed. Datasets may be insufficient or contain biased information. Inappropriate or controversial data practices by Microsoft or others could impair the acceptance of AI solutions. These deficiencies could undermine the decisions, predictions, or analysis AI applications produce, subjecting us to competitive harm, legal liability, and brand or reputational harm.* (Microsoft quoted in Torre et al., 2019, 127)

To examine the threats to corporate reputation caused by MUAI, this chapter will explore the matter in three aspects. To do so, three questions will be explored. First, we identify what the current threats are and predict how it would evolve. Second, we look into the possible preventive measures against the threats. Of particular interest is the involvement of non-corporate stakeholders. Third, we consider the importance of trust in relation to corporate reputation and international psychological security. This study can be proved relevant since the outbreak of the COVID-19 pandemic which has reconceptualized the role of technology in many societies across the world. As noted by the European Joint Research Center, the pandemic has "acted as a *booster*, and as an *amplifier* of potential opportunities and concerns," emphasizing on trends such as the "acceptance of robots in the workplace," "the switch to online of education, public administration, commerce and business," or "the organized campaigns of misinformation launched to undermine social cohesion and public trust in European institutions" (Craglia, 2020, 5).

The methodology deployed in this chapter is a multi-disciplinary approach which is built on the critical desk research. The study was conducted in three stages from September 2021 to April 2022. The first stage is the background research on MUAI and relevant literature review. The second stage is to revisit professional documents, media reports, and academic studies globally in order to identify the cases of the threats posed by MUAI. In doing so, this chapter took a transnational approach incorporating cases from across the world. The third stage is the analysis of those threats and their countermeasures.

The Cambridge Dictionary defines reputation as "the opinion that people in general have about someone or something," or "how much respect and admiration someone or something receives, based on past behaviour or character" (Cambridge Dictionary, n.d.). Despite the abstract nature of the concept of reputation, it is considered of crucial importance in various spheres ranging from the public sector (here a good example can be the notion of soft power, which aims to strengthen a nation's reputation and image through the promotion of its most national aspects) to the private sector (for instance, its critical role in the overall functioning and financial well-being of a business). In the meantime, in the context of the corporate world, reputation has been defined as "a function of its reputation among its various stakeholders […] in specific categories (product quality, corporate governance, employee relations, customer service, intellectual capital, financial performance, handling of environmental and social issues)" (Eccles et al., 2017). To understand how reputation is established, it should be considered with reference to concepts such as trust, credibility, and authenticity as well as social responsibility, which are becoming more and more important nowadays in the age of social media.

Any attack on a company's reputation can, therefore, potentially lead to a significant breach of trust from the side of customers. With regard to phishing attacks, Stolfo argues: "[i]n the minds of the customer and the regulatory bodies who assess violations of data privacy laws, it's the company who must be held responsible for these incidents, even when the consumers themselves are creating risk by responding to phishing attacks" (Stolfo, 2020).

This chapter consists of four sections. The first section provides an overview of the most tangible risks in contemporary international business, paying special attention to the role of malicious communication strategies as well as technology-related threats. The second section addresses the practice of reputation management, in particular its transformation, challenges as well as opportunities in the information age. The third section contextualizes the threats to corporate reputation and international business posed by MUAI, distinguishing among three categories: corporate propaganda, fake news, and deepfakes; fraud, phishing, and corporate breaches; information agenda setting, hacking, and bot manipulations. The fourth section analyzes the short-term and long-term impact of these reputational threats on international psychological security and proposes possible countermeasures.

Threats and Risks to International Business in the Twenty-First Century: From Economic Warfare to Malicious Use of Artificial Intelligence

In this chapter, business risk is understood as any tangible as well as intangible risk which might cause minor and major disruptions to a corporation. This understanding considers reputational damage, financial losses as well as challenges rising from internal or external risks. While internal business risks might relate to finding and retaining the qualified workforce or optimizing operations, and therefore seem to be controllable, this is not the case for external risks such as natural catastrophes, shifting financial or geopolitical landscapes, or public health crises like the ongoing COVID-19 pandemic. In contemporary times, apart from the global pandemic, another external risk to international business that is worth mentioning is the increasing use of financial sanctions and economic warfare to settle conflicts, which speaks of the relevance of geopolitics to the development of international business.

The emergence of new technologies and AI has fundamentally changed the dynamics of international business. With AI-driven tools and applications incorporated in all possible business operations from marketing and supply chain to finance and human resources, digitalization has become a new prophecy for many companies. Given the predicted growth of the global AI-market (see p. 1), its great influence is unlikely to be stopped. Regardless of the many benefits ascribed to their incorporation in business, new technologies appear to have come with new challenges and threats involving "privacy, bias, inequality, safety and security" (CSER, n.d.) on the one hand, and a lack of skilled workers (Lewis, 2021) and an adequate ethical and legal framework on the other. Already in 2018, new technologies rank seventh among business risks by the Allianz Risk Barometer, higher than political risk (Allianz, 2018). This prediction seems to be justifiable, as technology-related risks have been exponentially growing and eventually resulting in a pressing lack of trust among the public (see introduction). This cannot be disconnected from the ever-growing threat of cybercrime committed by individuals, collectives, and states on a global scale. Covering a wide range of malicious actions such as "unauthorized access of information," "data corruption," "misappropriation of assets or sensitive information," "causing of operational disruption" (Anthony, 2020), cybercrime is considered as a major threat to international business with its damage mounting up to $ 6 trillion in 2021, and this number could reach up to $10.5 trillion by 2025 (Morgan, 2020).

The COVID-19 pandemic has had an enormous impact on the global economy and international business. Among its most tangible consequences is a global recession which was announced in 2020 with the IMF estimating a 4.4% shrinkage of the global economy during that year and went along with mass job losses (Jones et al., 2021). Despite the ongoing pandemic, economic forecasts, however, have been predicting an economic recovery throughout 2021 and 2022 (OECD, 2021), a process which seems to have been hampered since the outbreak of Russia´s war in Ukraine (UN, 2022). During the outbreak of the pandemic, the trend of corporate digitalization has been accelerated, as businesses were prompted to resort to digital solutions in a reality marked by sudden lockdowns, home office obligations, and contact restrictions (McKinsey & Company, 2020). Apart from exacerbating the existing threats to corporate reputation exemplified above, the pandemic has also created new reputational problems with an increase in unethical behavior (Thomson, 2021). As stated in a report from EY: "[f]raud, bribery and corruption tend to thrive in chaos. The COVID-19 pandemic has made the business world a breeding ground for a plethora of risks, with vulnerabilities seeping across several industries" (EY, 2020).

(Online) Reputation Management: Tendencies and Challenges in the Twenty-First Century

Reputation management entails the shaping, sustaining, and protecting of one of the most vulnerable aspects of an organization, individual, or any other entity, whose critical importance is further demonstrated by the statistics that "70% to 80% of market value comes from hard-to-assess intangible assets such as brand equity, intellectual capital, and goodwill" (Eccles et al., 2017).

It is therefore not difficult to understand that the corporate reputation has become a vulnerable target for malicious actors given its significance to a corporate organization and its representatives. The threats to corporate reputation vary in scale and form and can be internal as well as external. While operational events, company behavior, and unexpected financial results (MS, 2021, 7) can be examples of common catalysts, the threats and challenges to corporate reputation can also be found in the attacks on a corporation and its representatives from competitors or adversaries in the context of corporate warfare (sometimes even with the attempt to destabilize the global economy). Corporate propaganda and misinformation are often deployed in such an attack and materialized as defamation, or so-called character assassination.

This introduces the notion and phenomenon of "corporate character assassination" which has been defined as the use of character attacks with the deliberate aim to destroy the credibility and reputation of a company (Coombs & Holladay, 2019, 225). Conceptualized as both "an outcome and process," it may involve activist stakeholders ("those who seek to change organisational practices") or angry stakeholders ("seeking revenge on an organisation"), for example, through revenge or so-called hashtag hijacking (Coombs & Holladay, 2019, 225, 228).

New technologies, media and digital platforms have transformed the dynamics of reputation management, introducing the practice of online reputation management (ORM). The availability of instant information about the organization, its services, and its people makes reputation management an increasingly important aspect for any business. As demonstrated in the research, 85% of potential customers conduct online research about a company before they purchase their product or service (Brand24, 2021). Therefore, what is vital for a business is maintaining a good reputation as well as adapting to the new changes in the information sphere. For example, the use of malign information to destroy a person or an organization, known as the buzzwords "fake news" and "disinformation," has been aggravated in the age of social media and as a result become a tangible threat to business and their representatives.

The impact of a damaged reputation can be far-reaching and might involve, for example, severe financial losses. According to the research conducted by AMO Strategic Advisors in 2019, "21% of more than 1,000 of the world's largest companies saw their market capitalisation reduced by a total of $436bn due to the impact of negative reputations" (Saran, 2021). Furthermore, it is also found that "[…] brand power and familiarity decrease by 5–9% following a data breach" (Makridis, 2021, 1). These findings seem to be reflected in the conclusion that a large majority of chief marketing executive officers consider brand damage as the biggest cost of security incidents (Netzer, 2020). Although the damage of corporate reputation is financially tangible, it is still underestimated. Eccles et al. argue that "[m]ost companies, however, do an inadequate job of managing their reputations in general and the risks to their reputations in particular" (Eccles et al., 2017). However, this situation is also changing with the incorporation of digital and related reputational risks in the insurance industry as well as the deployment of AI tools to detect and counter threats.

Malicious Use of Artificial Intelligence and Corporate Reputation Management in International Business

As discussed in the previous section, reputations have been targeted by malicious actors throughout history and their aim to destroy images and perceptions of (corporate) organizations and their representatives. In this process, propaganda techniques and disinformation are key approaches. The emergence of new AI-driven technologies has transformed the principles of such malicious strategic communication strategies, which are known as MUAI. Coping with the current and potential dangers of AI, the scholarship in MUAI has been growing rapidly. Furthermore, the field considers MUAI's implications for international psychological security as well as its broader geopolitical and social dimensions. While existing and potential AI-related threats and challenges have already been touched upon in areas such as cybersecurity, physical security, and political security (Brundage et al., 2018), this is not the case for the psychological threats which the further, uncontrolled development of AI might pose to the international community. Considering "psychological damage" as a unique threat, Bazarkina and Pashentsev argue that "it is important to regard the MUAI as a phenomenon that can cause psychological damage at all levels of economic, political and public life" (Bazarkina & Pashentsev, 2020). Pashentsev further comments that in case of no prevention or mitigation, the implications of MUAI for international psychological security might be catastrophic:

Further progress of AI technologies, MUAI and its large-scale use as a psychological weapon may lead, at the least, to an even greater delay in an adequate public response to the dangerous behaviors of antisocial actors. On a global scale, this will facilitate the formation of conditions for various kinds of fabricated and social disasters, including a Third World War (Pashentsev, 2021a, 45).

The (potential) danger of MUAI has become a topic of international debates and conferences on the highest level. International organizations such as the United Nations, UNESCO, and Europol have expressed concern about its implications, often in association with affected communities from all spheres of society. This growing concern cannot be disconnected from the tangible application of MUAI in recent years, whether it is in the form of cybercrime, agenda setting and social engineering, or as an instrument of terrorist propaganda (Bazarkina & Pashentsev, 2020). Although the global security community has featured counterstrategies and methods, it is unfortunately impossible to exclude new dangers as AI further develops. Therefore, policymakers and scholars have rightly encouraged people to think transnationally in terms of countering the threat of MUAI. For example, with regard to the AI-related terrorist threats, it is suggested that "[g]iven the international linkages and cross-border implications of many technological systems, a regional and international approach becomes vital to ensure terrorists do not have the opportunity to exploit regulatory gaps that can expose vulnerabilities in AI systems" (UNICRI & UN, 2021, 5).

As the developments in the sphere of AI, and particularly its malicious use, go along with an increasing risk (in terms of scale as well as impact) to corporations and their reputations, this might potentially lead to a massive breach of trust in international business. And this breach of trust might in turn put international psychological security at risk, which is closely interconnected with the functioning of the global economy. By deploying AI-driven tools and weapons, malicious actors might abuse this vulnerability to the global economy for various reasons ranging from destabilizing the global stock market and provoking mass job losses to deliberatively destroying corporations and disrupting major supply chains. In the next sections, we will discuss three different types of threats and explore how they might affect international psychological security in the short and long run as well as the possibilities of countering MUAI as AI becomes more sophisticated.

Corporate Propaganda, Fake News, and Deepfakes

The first category of AI-driven techniques that are weaponized to target corporate reputation relates to the deployment of lies, misinformation, and the distortion of truth and facts. Although such techniques are not new and have been used in the context of psychological warfare, they also take place in the context of international business where competitors or adversaries might destabilize a corporation through defamation, slander, and lies. The advent of new technologies and their consequent weaponization has exacerbated the danger of such malicious attacks, as illustrated by terrorists´ deployment of social media as a propaganda machine or the above-mentioned techniques adopted by various malicious actors to destabilize democracies and manipulate political elections. A good example could be the Tesla scandal in 2019, where a fake video of a self-driving Tesla car crashing a robot at a consumer electronics show went viral on the internet. Although, some have argued, it was part of a PR campaign, others have stated that it might have been an attack to destabilize the US stock market (Atkinson, 2019). A similar case happened in India in 2020 when a fake video of a staged miner protest was spread through WhatsApp (Mehta, 2020). Further developments of AI might magnify the spread of fake news through so-called readfakes, which are human-like written messages produced through text-generating AI and create content on demand in a variety of styles, including a journalistic article (Wakefield, 2019). Increasingly difficult to be distinguished from human-written content, such AI-generated content could be weaponized by malicious actors who wish to defame a company by spreading misleading lies and misinformation on an unseen scale. Another dangerous technology is the impersonation techniques such as deepfakes. Although often seen in (international) politics (Galston, 2020), the threat of deepfakes is not less relevant for international business and poses a tangible risk to a corporation's reputation. For example, the release of deepfake video or recording of a world-famous CEO making slanderous or racist comments could have severe financial and reputational consequences. While malicious actors might deploy deepfakes to destroy a company's reputation, it might also be used for extortion (Rash, 2019). In recent years, various cases of corporate deepfakes have been reported across the world. For example, in 2019, when an Israeli businessman was swindled out of 8 million euros by people who made him believe he was dealing with the French Foreign Minister (Willsher & Holmes, 2019). In another case, when a fake voice recording of an executive resulted in the theft of 220.000 euros (Damiani, 2019). The danger of deepfake technology has become even more acute through its popularization. In China, for instance, face-changing software has caused several scandals involving the hacking of facial recognition (Nash, 2021).

Fraud, Phishing, and Corporate Breaches

A second category of reputational risks exacerbated along with the further development of AI is the corporate damage inflicted by fraud, phishing, and corporate breaches. Often aimed at winning financial or informational gain from a particular corporation, its representatives, or operations, such actions deploy social engineering tactics to manipulate and deceive their targets, whether it is internally the corporation's employees or externally its customers. This may cause a range of operational, financial, and eventually reputational problems with potentially long-lasting and sometimes devastating consequences. This happens, for example, through so-called CEO-fraud, a type of scam involving a staged demand for money from a company's CEO or senior executive under the guise of an emergency. There are many cases where employees fell for such a scam when the demands appeared to come from their high-level executives. For example, in 2016, the Belgian Bank Crelan fell victim to a CEO-fraud and lost about 70 million euros (Barbieux & Lagast, 2016). Another type of reputational threat concerns cybercrime-related security breaches which are often aimed at stealing sensitive or private data to blackmail a company or corporate individual. The victims are usually forced to pay a sum of money, otherwise the perpetrator threatens to expose the stolen data or share it with other malicious actors, which can lead to a major reputation crisis for a corporation. The scale and potential impact of such threats have been illustrated in the so-called Marriot data breach, which resulted in the exposure of up to 339 million guest records (Tidy, 2020). And last but not least, phishing, as another menacing to corporate reputation, involves sending an email with a malicious link to steal confidential data or block the receiver's computer system to make extortion threats to the receiver. Phishing poses a critical challenge to companies, as statistics shows that "1 in 99 emails is a phishing attack" (Guida, 2019). The consequences of this practice are varied, including financial losses going as high as millions of dollars (Jones, 2021), fines (Tidy, 2020) as well as breach of trust and reputational damage. A report from Deloitte states that "[t]here is no doubt that data breaches are likely to impact consumer trust. 25% of respondents confirm their level of trust with an organisation would decrease if the organisation was involved in a data compromise. Combined with another 35% stating their decision to stay or go depends on how much they trust an organisation, this serves as a warning to organisations that suffer repeated data breaches, or those less established organisations that may not yet have a trusted brand in the market place" (Deloitte, 2018). In recent years, the above-mentioned threats have grown exponentially across the world, a tendency which cannot be disconnected from the ongoing COVID-19 pandemic. For many companies and their customers have become increasingly reliable on technology and the cyberspace. Rapidly developing into more dangerous and sophisticated forms like spear phishing, the attack on corporate reputation has intensified. In 2021, for example, a surge of 28% in phishing attacks was noted compared to 2020 (Rowe, 2022). The pandemic has also provoked an increasing risk of unethical behavior (see above), stealing, and illegal selling from video conference attendees, unwanted intervention into video conferences as well as other involvements of malicious employees, hacktivists, and human errors (Deloitte, n.d.). As AI further develops, it is increasingly difficult to identify and control the discussed practices. For they are able to outperform human input through, for example, natural language processing, and reach an unprecedented scale of targets through advanced predictions of human behavior and vulnerabilities, putting corporate reputation in constant danger.

Information Agenda Setting, Hacking, and Bot Manipulation

The third category of threats to corporate reputation is linked with the malicious actions that are aimed at manipulating decision-making, and it often refers to computational information agenda setting, hacking, and bot manipulation. Primarily involving advanced technologies, these malicious actions aim at manipulating and distorting the daily working of a business through undesirable simulations or provocative actions, which may lead to reputational damage. A powerful instrument in this context is computational information agenda setting, which is often used in political contexts but can be equally deployed in relation to corporate environments. Generally focused on shaping public opinion, agenda setting traditionally uses mass media to build reputations. In recent times, however, the traditional routine has been changed by new media and online platforms, and new dynamics like "reverse agenda setting" has started to appear. Deployed in social activism, social media campaigns can, for example, be used to put "difficult" topics on media agenda (Fews, 2017), but also to manipulate political processes or corporate decision-making. Examples of artificially created fake profiles spreading messages in favor of or in opposition to public figures, regimes, or businesses have occurred frequently in recent years (Diresta, 2020) and may become more effective as predictive analytics and emotion AI gets further integrated in malicious strategies (Pashentsev 2021b). A second application is the use and manipulation of bots. While bots are increasingly employed in business to improve corporate reputation, they have similarly been deployed to attack corporations and destroy corporate reputation. For instance, through the hacking of corporate bots, a malicious actor might take over corporate functions for financial gain or information. For example, a customer service chatbot of Ticketmaster was hacked and infected by malware, which has caused the theft of confidential customer information (Sharman, 2018). Other infamous examples include the hacking of a Microsoft chatbot Tay resulting in its tweeting of "racist and inflammatory messages" (Passeri, 2019), as well as the use of malicious bots to empty out cryptocurrency platforms (Zamost & Javers, 2022). Future scenarios might involve malicious chatbots duping "customers into clicking links that trigger the delivery of a hostile payload like phishing pages" (Passeri, 2019). The last malicious application to be discussed is the use of so-called smart bots infiltrating corporate networks with varying aims ranging from deliberatively deleting customer data and engaging in illegal activities to attacking other businesses through infected networks (Coranet, 2019). What these applications have in common is the aim of manipulating business decisions,[1] and their risk is exacerbated through MUAI. While AI is used to inform and strengthen business decision in many companies, it can also be a powerful instrument which might harm corporate reputation, for instance, through the manipulation and hacking of survey polls (Strom, 2019). Therefore, wrong assessments can be made in businesses' key decision-makings, and reputational crises and financial losses can be provoked.

Countering Malicious Use of Artificial Intelligence in International Business: An Integrated Response toward the Protection of International Psychological Security

The previous section has demonstrated that MUAI-driven reputational attacks on corporations come in various forms and can be devastating to their operations. Of similar importance, however, is to consider the broader impact of

---

[1] For more information on the role of AI on decision-making, see J. Johnson (2020) Delegating strategic decision-making to machines: Dr. Strangelove Redux? *Journal of Strategic Studies*.

MUAI-driven corporate reputational attacks on society, and particularly on international psychological security. Although most often associated to the physical, financial, or increasingly the digital realm, security similarly concerns the psychological realm. According to Maslow, psychological security is "a feeling of confidence, safety and freedom that separates from fear and anxiety, and especially the feeling of satisfying one's needs now (and in the future)" (quoted in Wang et al., 2019, 2). In relation to cybercrime, psychological security becomes a popular topic in the discussions on the human vulnerabilities and the necessity to build psychological resilience against the social engineering (HookSecurity, n.d.).

To conceptualize the potential impact of MUAI-driven reputational attacks on international psychological security, the abstract nature of security should be considered. The definition of security as "a state of inner peace, confidence, positive attitude, trust, subjective wellbeing, openness, and relaxation" (Zotova & Karapetyan, 2018, 104) is useful, as it points out those aspects which are destabilized and targeted during the MUAI-driven reputational attacks. Considering the overall anxiety over digitalization (Pink et al., 2018), and the potential scale MUAI-driven attacks may reach, where serious breaches of trust can be provoked. For corporations represent a unique actor of trust in society (see introduction) and is therefore an ideal target for malicious actors who intend to cause and spread panic. Furthermore, anxiety over the MUAI-driven reputational attacks may arise among employees who fear to make mistakes. This concern seems to be justifiable given the numerous accounts of large-scale job losses due to cybersecurity-related mistakes (Segal, 2022). To effectively counter the above-described threats of MUAI and protect international psychological security, an integrated multi-dimensional response is necessary which should entail three pillars: technology, literacy, and a legal/ethical framework.

Although this chapter considers the malicious use of AI and its weaponization in relation to corporate reputation, it is of importance to recognize and embrace the possibility of AI as a protector of corporate reputation. At the time of this writing, the mission of protecting corporate reputation from MUAI has motivated the flourishing of an entire industry. Through AI-driven monitoring and detecting software, reputational threats are identified and risks like lingering fakes are filtered via, for example, blockchain technology (Chaban, 2020).[2] An example is found in the struggle against fake news as

---

[2] For more information on countering of MUAI, see Kertysova, K (2018) Artificial Intelligence and Disinformation. How AI changes the way Disinformation is produced, disseminated, and can be countered. Security and Human Rights 29: 55–81; Basit A. et al. (2021) A comprehensive survey of AI-enabled phishing attacks detection techniques. Telecommunication Systems 76: 139–154.

"natural language processing, machine learning and network analysis" are being used to detect fake news and rank it lower in search results (Lee & Fung, 2018). Of similar importance is the acknowledgment of the significance of media and information literacy. The rapid development of technology has resulted in anxiety over digitalization among many people (Pink et al., 2018), which cannot be disconnected from the many disparities existing in the realm of digital literacy. Malicious actors who use social engineering tactics, for example, for reputational attacks, play upon these vulnerabilities to destabilize and control their targets. To protect businesses, customers, and the public from such malicious actions, all possible means should be deployed in order to educate across generations and social divisions. The importance of being literate in the information age entails digital skills focusing on the understanding of technology as well as non-digital skills such as critical thinking to detect and assess danger generated by misinformation in different forms. Although many initiatives were already carried out and the threat of MUAI has been taken seriously by many organizations, awareness raising in combination with critical support to the most vulnerable should be the key objective on a global agenda. Finally, a strategic and integrated response should involve the building of a sustainable legal and ethical framework which is designed to protect victims and facilitate the legal crackdown on the perpetrators, preferably in the context of transnational cooperation. For example, in November 2021, an organized action against financial crimes (named HAECHi-II) involved law enforcement agencies across the globe and resulted in the arrest of over 1000 people and intercepted nearly $27 million (Interpol 2021). An ethical dimension should be constructed together with a solid legal framework, paving the way toward a critical discussion on the dangers and opportunities of new technologies and AI. Various steps have been taken in this perspective. For example, the UN Human Rights Council has introduced the notion of online human rights. And UNESCO's General Conference adopted recommendation of Artificial Intelligence in November 2021. Furthermore, an ethical frame should consider the threat of social control and censorship, as well as unethical practices (like troll farms) and counterpropaganda.

The above-described integrated approach should result in the fostering of resilience. Furthermore, any effective protection of international psychological security should involve the cooperation among all relevant stakeholders and be aimed at preventing further erosion of trust in society. Corporations can play a unique role in this process and are in a good position to do so. As stated in the Edelman report cited above: "[w]e see an even greater expectation of business to lead as trust in government continues to spiral. But this is not a job business can do on its own. Business must work with all institutions to foster innovation and drive impact" (Edelman, 2022). To achieve such an outcome, corporations should connect with non-corporate actors and assume a new role in a rapidly changing and globalizing society. The WEF argues: "[t]o ensure that AI stays within the boundaries that we set for it, we must continue to grapple with building trust in systems that will transform our social, political and business environments, make decisions for us" (2017, 51). This could be achieved by bringing social responsibility, authenticity, and organizational culture to the next level. Disentangling these concepts from mere branding and PR and aligning them with the notion of trust may result in the fostering of long-lasting relations with non-corporate stakeholders. The OECD's recommendation of four pillars of governmental behavior to restore trust is useful and can act as a template for such a process: "act with reliability, be responsive, open and inclusive, and work with integrity" (OECD, n.d.). Other key characteristics that have been mentioned are sincerity, competency, and transparency (Jaffe, 2018). Through awareness raising, preventing (digital) echo-chambers, and stimulating a diversity of opinions (Sambrook, 2012, 4, 30, 40), trust in society could be promoted.

Conclusion

The aim of this chapter was to shed some light on the rapid, overwhelming growth of new technologies, among which AI presents one of the biggest concerns and risks, and particularly to elaborate on MUAI's impact on international business and international psychological security. To be specific, this chapter has explored the threats posed by MUAI on corporate reputation.

Following our overview of current MUAI threats to corporate reputation, three categories of reputational risks were identified. The first category, "informational risks," refers to the deployment of (computational) corporate propaganda, fake news, and deepfakes to harm a corporation's reputation. While social media have already facilitated the spread of (corporate) fake news and propaganda, AI-driven mechanisms have exacerbated this danger. The second category is social engineering techniques and scams playing upon "technological" vulnerabilities of humans and includes methods like phishing, corporate breaches, and other types of fraud. Along with the development of AI, the effectiveness of such attacks has been magnified. The third category of threats deals with the MUAI-driven manipulation of corporate decision-making. Finally, it should be acknowledged that old forms of reputational attacks are still active and have become increasingly adapted to the new information environment.

Although these threats pose individually dangers to corporate reputation, an integrated MUAI-driven reputational attack combining several of the above-mentioned techniques could mean a reputational disaster to any corporation, corporate individual, or even the global economy, depending on its scale. Through targeting of human vulnerabilities, MUAI might create widespread uncertainty and anxiety among various stakeholders and could impact international psychological security in the short term as well as the long one. While the short-term impact of the MUAI-driven reputational attacks is already tangible in rising concern and insecurity over their dangers and immediate consequences, in the long term, along with the AI development, the impact might go as far as to effectively destabilize international corporations, economies, or society.

A strategic and sustainable counter-response to protect international psychological security should, therefore, be put in place and involve (1) a combination of awareness raising and media and information literacy focusing on critical thinking, threat assessment as well as digital skills; (2) the embrace of research and technology as a shield and prevention mechanism but also the acknowledgment of its limits; (3) the setting up of an ethical and legal framework aimed at informing the stakeholders of and protecting against the reputational attacks instigated by MUAI. In this struggle, it is important that corporations assume their unique position and societal role by connecting to non-corporate stakeholders and creating bridges of trust. Finally, it is of critical importance to invest in research, for example, on the consequences of MUAI on mental health.

Bibliography

Allianz Risk Barometer. (2018). In: AGCS. Retrieved April 3, 2022, from https://www.agcs.allianz.com/news-and-insights/news/allianz-risk-barometer-2018.html

Anthony, L. (2020). Intellectual property and Technology Risks: International Business Operations. In: Lawcast. Retrieved April 3, 2022, from https://lawcast.com/2020/12/23/intellectual-property-and-technology-risks-international-business-operations/

Atkinson, C. (2019). Fake news can cause "irreversible damage" to companies- and sink their stock price. In: NBC News. Retrieved April 3, 2022, from https://www.nbcnews.com/business/business-news/fake-news-can-cause-irreversible-damage-companies-sink-their-stock-n995436

Barbieux, Y., & Lagast, C. (2016). Crelan 70 milioen armer door één valse mail 'van baas'. In: Nieuwsblad, Retrieved April 3, 2022, from Crelan 70 miljoen armer door één valse mail "van de baas" | Het Nieuwsblad.

Bazarkina, D., & Pashentsev, E. (2020). Malicious Use of Artificial Intelligence. In: Russia in Global Affairs. Retrieved April 3, 2022, from https://eng.globalaffairs.ru/articles/malicious-use-ai/.

Brand 24. (2021). Online reputation management: what's, why's and software. In: Brand24. Retrieved April 3, 2022, from https://brand24.com/blog/best-online-reputation-management-software/

Brundage, M. et al (2018) The malicious use of artificial intelligence: Forecasting, prevention and mitigation. .

Cambridge Dictionary. (n.d.). Reputation. In: Cambridge Dictionary. Retrieved April 23, 2022, from https://dictionary.cambridge.org/dictionary/english/reputation

CBS News. (2021). Edelman Trust Barometer: Technology Sector Sees Global Decline in Trust. In: CBS News. Retrieved April 3, 2022, from https://www.cbsnews.com/video/edelman-trust-barometer-tech-sector-sees-global-decline-in-trust-2021-04-01/.

Chaban, M. (2020). Can blockchain block fake news and deep fakes? In: IBM. Retrieved April 7, 2022, from https://www.ibm.com/blogs/industries/blockchain-protection-fake-news-deep-fakes-safe-press/

Clifford, C. (2018). Mark my words – AI is for more dangerous than nukes. In: CNBC Retrieved April 3, 2022, from https://www.cnbc.com/2018/03/13/elon-musk-at-sxsw-a-i-is-more-dangerous-than-nuclear-weapons.html

Clifford, C. (2019). Bill Gates: A.I. is like nuclear energy - 'both promising and dangerous'. In: CNBC. Retrieved April 3, 2022, from https://www.cnbc.com/2019/03/26/bill-gates-artificial-intelligence-both-promising-and-dangerous.html

Coombs, T., & Holladay, S. (2019). Corporate character assassination and crisis communication. In S. Samoilenko, M. Icks, J. Keohane, & E. Shiraev (Eds.), *Routledge handbook of character assassination and reputation*. Routledge.

Coranet. (2019). Attack of the Bots. Are your corporate networks safe? In: Coranet. Retrieved April 3, 2022, from https://www.coranet.com/attack-of-the-bots/

Craglia, M. (Ed.). (2020). *Artificial intelligence and digital transformation: Early lessons from the COVID-19 crisis*. Publications Office of the European Union.

CSER. (n.d.). Risks from artificial intelligence. In: CSER. Retrieved April 7, 2022, from https://www.cser.ac.uk/research/risks-from-artificial-intelligence/

Damiani, J. (2019). A Voice Deepfake Was Used to Scam a CEO out of $243,000. In: Forbes. Retrieved April 3, 2022, from https://www.forbes.com/sites/jessedamiani/2019/09/03/a-voice-deepfake-was-used-to-scam-a-ceo-out-of-243000/?sh=389a81532241

Deloitte. (2018). A new era for privacy. GDPR six months on. In: Deloitte. Retrieved April 3, 2022, from https://www2.deloitte.com/content/dam/Deloitte/uk/Documents/risk/deloitte-uk-risk-gdpr-six-months-on.pdf

Deloitte. (n.d.). Impact of COVID-19 on Cybersecurity. In: Deloitte. Retrieved April 3, 2022, from https://www2.deloitte.com/ch/en/pages/risk/articles/impact-covid-cybersecurity.html

Diresta, R. (2020). The Supply of Disinformation will soon be infinite. In: The Atlantic. Retrieved April 7, 2022, from https://www.theatlantic.com/ideas/archive/2020/09/future-propaganda-will-be-computer-generated/616400/ Accessed 7 April 2022.

Eccles, R., Newquist, S., & Schatz, R (2017). Reputation and its Risks. In: Harvard Business Review. Retrieved April 3, 2022, from https://hbr.org/2007/02/reputation-and-its-risks

Edelman. (2022). 2022 Edelman Trust Barometer. In: Edelman. Retrieved April 3, 2022, from https://www.edelman.com/trust/2022-trust-barometer

EPRS. (2020). The Ethics of Artificial Intelligence: Issues and Initiatives. In: European Parliament. Retrieved April 25, 2022, from https://www.europarl.europa.eu/thinktank/en/document/EPRS_STU(2020)634452

EY. (2020). COVID-19: unravelling fraud and corruption risks in the new normal. In: Forensic & Integrity Services. Ernst & Young, Retrieved April 3, 2022, from https://www.ey.com/en_in/forensic-integrity-services/unravelling-fraud-risks-and-restoring-stakeholder-confidence-during-covid-19

Fews, A. (2017). The assassination of character: A reversed agenda setting study of the twitter campaign "#IfTheyGunnedMeDown". *Journal of Promotional Communications, 5*(3), 260–279.

Galston, W. (2020). Is seeing still believing? The deepfake challenge to truth in politics. In: Brookings. Retrieved April 3, 2022, from https://www.brookings.edu/research/is-seeing-still-believing-the-deepfake-challenge-to-truth-in-politics/

Guida, R. (2019). What is a Phishing Scam? In: Avanan. Retrieved April 3, 2022, from https://www.avanan.com/blog/what-is-a-phishing-scam

Hanstad, T. (2020). Trust is the glue of a healthy society. Here's how to bring it back. In: WEForum. Retrieved April 3, 2022, from https://www.weforum.org/agenda/2020/12/trust-is-the-glue-of-a-healthy-society-heres-how-to-bring-it-back/

What is psychological security? In: Hooksecurity. Retrieved April 3, 2022, from https://hooksecurity.co/psychological-security.

Jaffe, D. (2018). The Essential Importance of Trust: How to Build it or restore it? In: Forbes. Retrieved April 3, 2022, from https://www.forbes.com/sites/dennisjaffe/2018/12/05/the-essential-importance-of-trust-how-to-build-it-or-restore-it/?sh=76bf0b4f64fe

Jones, D. (2021). How much does phishing really cost the enterprise. In: Cybersecurity Dive. Retrieved April 3, 2022, from https://www.cybersecuritydive.com/news/phishing-cost-enterprise/605110/

Jones, L., et al. (2021). Coronavirus: How the pandemic has changed the world economy. In: BBC. Retrieved April 3, 2022, from https://www.bbc.com/news/business-51706225

Kasapoglu, C., & Kirdemir, B. (2019). Artificial Intelligence and the Future of Conflict. In: Carnegie Europe. Retrieved April 22, 2022, from https://carnegieeurope.eu/2019/11/28/artificial-intelligence-and-future-of-conflict-pub-80421.

Lee, S., & Fung, B. (2018). Artificial Intelligence may not actually be the solution for stopping the spread of AI. In: The Conversation. Retrieved April 3, 2022, from https://theconversation.com/artificial-intelligence-may-not-actually-be-the-solution-for-stopping-the-spread-of-fake-news-172001

Lewis, N. (2021). IT workers will be hard to find and keep in 2022. In: SHRM. Retrieved April 7, 2022, from https://www.shrm.org/resourcesandtools/hr-topics/technology/pages/it-workers-will-be-hard-find-keep-2022.aspx

Makridis, C. (2021). Do data breaches damage reputation? Evidence from 45 companies between 2002 and 2018. *Journal of Cybersecurity, 7*(1), 1–8.

Mars, A. (2022). Noam Chomsky – American democracy is in very serious danger. In: Elpais. Retrieved April 3, 2022, from https://english.elpais.com/usa/2022-01-25/noam-chomsky-american-democracy-is-in-very-serious-danger.html

McKinsey & Company. (2020). How COVID-19 has pushed companies over the technology tipping point – and transformed business forever. Retrieved April 3, 2022, from https://www.mckinsey.com/business-functions/strategy-and-corporate-finance/our-insights/how-covid-19-has-pushed-companies-over-the-technology-tipping-point-and-transformed-business-forever

Mehta, Y. (2020). Opinion: Combating fake news to protect corporate reputation. In: Brand Equity. Retrieved April 3, 2022, from https://brandequity.economictimes.indiatimes.com/news/marketing/opinion-combating-fake-news-to-protect-corporate-reputation/79576975

More than 1,000 arrests and USD 27 million intercepted in massive financial crime crackdown. (2021). In: Interpol. Retrieved April 3, 2022, from https://www.interpol.int/News-and-Events/News/2021/More-than-1-000-arrests-and-USD-27-million-intercepted-in-massive-financial-crime-crackdown

Morgan, S. (2020). Cybercrime to cost the world $10.5 Trillion annually by 2025. In: Cybercrime Magazine. Retrieved April 3, 2022, from https://cybersecurityventures.com/cybercrime-damages-6-trillion-by-2021/

MS. (2021). Trust and Reputation: Proactive Management of Reputational Risk. In: Management Solutions. Retrieved April 6, 2022, from https://www.managementsolutions.com/sites/default/files/publicaciones/eng/reputational-risk.pdf

Nash, J. (2021). Hackers spoofed biometric authentication videos to steal millions in China. In: Biometric update. Retrieved April 3, 2022, from https://www.biometricupdate.com/202103/hackers-spoofed-biometric-authentication-videos-to-steal-millions-in-china

Netzer, G. (2020). The Connection between Employees, Phishing, Marketing and Your Company's Reputation. In: Forbes. Retrieved April 3, 2022, from https://www.forbes.com/sites/forbescommunicationscouncil/2020/08/20/the-connection-between-employees-phishing-marketing-and-your-companys-reputation/?sh=37b854a05c0b

OECD. (2021). OECD economic outlook sees recovery continuing but warns of growing imbalances and risks. In: OECD. Retrieved April 3, 2022, from https://www.oecd.org/newsroom/oecd-economic-outlook-sees-recovery-continuing-but-warns-of-growing-imbalances-and-risks.htm

OECD. (n.d.). Restoring trust in government. In: OECD. Retrieved April 3, 2022, from https://www.oecd.org/governance/focus-restoring-trust-in-government.htm

Pashentsev, E. (2021a). *Experts on the malicious use of artificial intelligence and challenges to international psychological security*. International Center for Social and Political Studies and Consulting.

Pashentsev, E. (2021b). The malicious use of artificial intelligence through agenda setting: Challenges to political stability. In F. Matos, I. Salavisa, & C. Serrao (Eds.), *Proceedings of the 3rd European conference on the impact of artificial intelligence and robotics*. Academic Conferences International Limited.

Passeri, P. (2019). What can we learn from the chatbot attacks we've seen so far? In: Netskope. Retrieved April 3, 2022, from https://www.netskope.com/blog/what-can-we-learn-from-chatbot-attacks

Pink, S., et al. (2018). Data anxieties: Finding Trust in Everyday Digital Mess. *Big Data & Society, 5*(1), 1.

Rash, W. (2019). How deep fakes can hurt your business and what to do about it. In: Forbes. Retrieved April 3, 2022, from https://www.forbes.com/sites/waynerash/2019/12/24/how-deep-fakes-can-hurt-your-business-and-what-to-do-about-it/?sh=1555c4f96567

Rowe, A. (2022). Report: Phishing Attacks Grew 28% Across 2021. In: Tech.co. Retrieved April 3, 2022, from https://tech.co/news/phishing-attackers-grew-2021

Sambrook, R. (2012). *Delivering trust: Impartiality and objectivity in the digital age*. Reuters Institute for the Study of Journalism.

Saran, C. (2021). AI powers reputational damage insurance policy. In: Computer weekly. Retrieved April 3, 2022, from https://www.computerweekly.com/news/252496749/AI-powers-reputational-damage-insurance-policy

Segal, E. (2022). 25% of workers lost their jobs in the past 12 months after making cybersecurity mistakes. In: Forbes. Retrieved April 7, 2022, from https://www.forbes.com/sites/edwardsegal/2022/03/29/25-of-workers-lost-their-jobs-in-the-past-12-months-after-making-cybersecurity-mistakes-report/?sh=4845674549b2

Sharman, J. (2018). Ticketmaster admits customer data may have been stolen in malware attack. In: Independent. Retrieved April 7, 2022, from https://www.independent.co.uk/news/uk/home-news/ticketmaster-hack-card-data-stolen-malware-uk-a8420341.html

Stolfo, S. (2020). Why phishing threatens your brand's integrity. In: CPO Magazine. Retrieved April 3, 2022, from https://www.cpomagazine.com/cyber-security/why-phishing-threatens-your-brands-integrity/

Strom, D. (2019). How polls are hacked: What every business should know. In: CSO. Retrieved April 7, 2022, from https://www.csoonline.com/article/3339377/how-polls-are-hacked-what-every-business-should-know.html

Thomson, J. (2021). Technology and Covid-19: the perfect storm for ethic violations. In: Forbes. Retrieved April 3, 2022, from https://www.forbes.com/sites/jeffthomson/2021/10/20/technology-and-covid-19-the-perfect-storm-for-ethics-violations/?sh=13e2504728a5

Tidy, J. (2020). Marriot Hotels fined 18.4m for data breach that hit millions. In: BBC. Retrieved April 3, 2022, from https://www.bbc.com/news/technology-54748843

Torre, et al. (2019). AI leadership and the future of corporate governance. In A. Larsson & R. Teigland (Eds.), *The digital transformation of labor: Automation, the gig economy and welfare*. Routledge.

Trend Micro. (2020). Malicious Uses and Abuses of Artificial Intelligence. In: Trend Micro. Retrieved April 25, 2022, from https://documents.trendmicro.com/assets/white_papers/wp-malicious-uses-and-abuses-of-artificial-intelligence.pdf

UN. (2022). Ukraine War fueling global economic downturn as growth projections slide. In: UN. Retrieved April 7, 2022, from https://news.un.org/en/story/2022/03/1114602

UNICRI & UN. (2021). Algorithms and Terrorism. The Malicious Use of Artificial Intelligence for terrorist Purposes. In: UNICRI & UNCCT. Retrieved April 3, 2022, from https://www.un.org/counterterrorism/sites/www.un.org.counterterrorism/files/malicious-use-of-ai-uncct-unicri-report-hd.pdf

Wakefield, J. (2019). "Dangerous" AI offers to write fake news. In: BBC. Retrieved April 3, 2022, from https://www.bbc.com/news/technology-49446729

Wang, J., et al. (2019). Measuring the psychological security of urban residents: Construction and validation of a new scale. *Frontiers in Psychology, 10*, 2423.

WEF. (2017). Part 3. Emerging technologies. Assessing the risk of artificial intelligence. In: . Retrieved April 3, 2022, from https://reports.weforum.org/global-risks-2017/part-3-emerging-technologies/3-2-assessing-the-risk-of-artificial-intelligence/

Willsher, K., & Holmes, O. (2019). Conmen made EUR 8m by impersonating French Minister – Israeli police. In: The Guardian. Retrieved April 3, 2022, from https://www.theguardian.com/world/2019/mar/28/conmen-made-8m-by-impersonating-french-minister-israeli-police

Zamost, S., & Javers. (2022). E. Fraudsters use robocalls to drain accounts. In: CNBC. Retrieved April 7, 2022, from https://www.cnbc.com/2022/02/15/crypto-fraudsters-use-robocalls-to-drain-accounts.html

Zotova, O., & Karapetyan, L. (2018). Psychological security as the Foundation of Personal Psychological Wellbeing (analytical review). *Psychology in Russia: State of the Art, 11*(2), 100–113.

Part III

Regional and National Implications of the Malicious Use of Artificial Intelligence and Psychological Security

12

Malicious Use of Artificial Intelligence: Risks to Psychological Security in BRICS Countries

Evgeny Pashentsev and Darya Bazarkina

Introduction

This chapter examines the current level of artificial intelligence (AI) development in the countries of Brazil, India, Russia, and South Africa, existing and future psychological security threats caused by the malicious use of artificial intelligence (MUAI) in these countries, and initiatives to combat these threats. Along with China, these countries are collectively referred to as BRICS, and the experience of these countries is interesting for a number of reasons. First, these countries claim to be building an alternative economic system to the existing Western-driven economy, which requires actively forming relevant institutions and introducing innovative solutions in the digital environment. The group includes China, a recognized leader in the field of AI, although the Chinese experience will be considered in a separate chapter (chapter "The Threats and Current Practice of Malicious Use of Artificial Intelligence in

---

E. Pashentsev (✉)
Diplomatic Academy of the Ministry of Foreign Affairs of the Russian Federation, Moscow, Russia
e-mail: icspsc@mail.ru

D. Bazarkina
Department of European Integration Research,
Institute of Europe of the Russian Academy of Sciences, Moscow, Russia
e-mail: bazarkina-icspsc@yandex.ru

Psychological Area in China" of this book). China is also an innovator of legislation aimed at combating MUAI.

Brazil, India, Russia, and South Africa are seeking to use AI to develop their economies and improve overall quality of life. A degree of specialization is inevitable, which can be a promising addition to the development of BRICS countries (as will be shown, research and development are shared among BRICS members on a number of platforms), as well as identify specific psychological security threats from MUAI. For example, prioritizing military use of AI over civil communications can increase military security but leave citizens unprepared for third-level psychological security attacks, such as from disinformation through deepfakes or bot attacks. The following research questions were posed for this chapter: What is the level of AI development in each of the studied BRICS members; what areas of development are priorities for each country?; what MUAI-related psychological security threats do the studied BRICS countries face, and what are the government responses?; and what measures are being taken to combat MUAI by BRICS countries as a group? The theoretical basis of this chapter is a three-level classification of psychological security threats caused by MUAI (see chapter "General Content and Possible Threat Classifications of the Malicious Use of Artificial Intelligence to Psychological Security").

Several source groups were used, including official BRICS publications (BRICS, 2015, 2018, 2019; BRICS Information Portal, 2022; BRICS Ministers of Foreign Affairs, 2022; BRICS–Brasil, 2019; CyberBRICS 2019, 2021 and 2022, etc.), publications from national governments and public think tanks (The Presidency, Republic of South Africa 2019 and 2021; PC4IR, 2020; Ramaphosa, 2020; President of the Russian Federation 2019a and b, 2020; NTI, 2022; Gandharv, 2022 etc.), and media materials. Secondary sources include works on general AI development, MUAI problems, and related cybersecurity issues (Faggella, 2019; Butcher et al., 2021; Belli, 2020; FGV/DAPP, 2018; Pindrop XE "Pindrop" , 2020; Ajder et al., 2019, etc.), publications on MUAI in the field of psychological security (Bazarkina and Pashentsev 2019 and 2020), as well as works assessing the level of BRICS institutionalization in order to draw conclusions about the prospects for developing five-sided cooperation to counter MUAI. Different assessments of the status of BRICS (Yifan, 2019, Fadeeva, 2020, Gaidamak, 2017, Takhumova, 2021, Anufrieva, 2020 etc.) evaluate the group as a regional organization (Yifan, 2019), an integration association (Gaidamak, 2017), an integration group (Takhumova, 2021), and so on. Certain integration process features in the group (Arapova, 2016) raise the question of possibly forming an integration association in the future that could form a well-coordinated counter-MUAI policy formed on the basis of national experience.

Artificial Intelligence Development in BRICS Countries

Brazil

Brazil is actively expanding AI developments. In 2019, Brazil's minister of science, technology, innovation, and communications, Marcos Pontes, announced the creation of a network of eight research centers in this area. One of these centers is focused on working with the Brazilian army in the field of cybersecurity. The remaining seven centers are designed to support cutting-edge research as part of a national internet of things plan, with a focus on healthcare, agribusiness, industry, and smart cities. Brazil supports both BRICS initiatives and cooperation with transnational corporations. For example, the Sao Paulo Research Foundation has an agreement with IBM to launch the first Latin American institution of the IBM AI Horizons Network. The IBM-managed research center concentrates on natural language processing, deep learning, and industrial applications, and over the next 10 years, the facility will receive 20 million US dollars in investment from a number of organizations. Amazon Web Services also announced plans to invest 1 billion Brazilian reais in AI, expanding its infrastructure in Sao Paulo over the next 2 years. According to Microsoft, Brazil can realize a 7.1 percent increase in GDP by implementing AI four times more intensively in all sectors of the economy compared to current levels (Rebellion Research, 2021). However, a significant proportion of Brazilian workers fear this will lead to more difficulty finding a job and an increase in income inequality.

Changes are also taking place in education as part of this digital transformation. The Brazilian federal government created Mec Flix, a public education platform that provides students with access to learning content based on AI preferences. Brazil's GDP fell to 1.86 trillion US dollars in 2021 from 2.6 trillion US dollars in 2011 (Rebellion Research, 2021). The country's dependence on industrial production and natural resources makes the economy particularly sensitive to exchange rate fluctuations and economic cycles. Over the past decade, falling prices for oil, industrial products, and precious metals have hit Brazil particularly hard. In an effort to mitigate these uncertainties and to harness technological advances, Brazil is positioning itself as a future AI innovation hub.

India

India's information technology sector accounted for 7.7 percent of the country's GDP in 2016. The Indian government announced in February 2018 that the National Institution for Transforming India (NITI Aayog), a government think tank, will lead a national AI research program (Faggella, 2019). In 2017, the Department of Trade and Industry formed the Task Force on Artificial Intelligence for India's Economic Transformation. Currently, the main applications of AI in India are:

- Agriculture: The government-initiated experiments to use AI in 15 low-yielding districts to develop solutions based on satellite imagery, weather data, and other factors to increase farm productivity.
- Medicine: As there are few pathologists and radiologists in India, especially in rural areas, image recognition applications were introduced.
- Language/Translation: An initiative to build a complete Indian language processing platform was launched. This could help develop several applications, such as career counseling through chatbots that speak 22 Indian languages (Faggella, 2019). Indian startup Reverie Technologies created Gopal, a voice assistant designed exclusively for Indians that works in the country's seven major languages. Gopal is improving speech-to-text capabilities for all possible accents in these languages.

AI is driving massive change in the Indian economy. An Accenture 2020 report predicts that the development of AI will increase the country's annual economic growth rate by 1.3 percent by 2035, potentially adding 957 billion US dollars to India's current GDP. Indian startups are developing solutions using AI in education, healthcare, and financial services. In 2020, the Hexagon Capability Center India, part of global technology company Hexagon AB, opened the first community center for AI in Hyderabad. The center, called the HexArt Institute, trains over 350 students per year (Chakraborty, 2022). AI development in India also includes work on digital assistants that allow organizations to communicate with customers, AI-based decision-making systems, and the use of AI and blockchain in trade. Problems in the field of AI include a relatively small number of machine learning researchers, low public awareness of advances in the field, and reluctance on the part of enterprises to implement AI (Chakraborty, 2022). Overall, the challenges are not sufficiently reflected in India's current strategies for AI development.

There are known breakthroughs in the military application of AI in India. In early 2022, the India's Army Training Command signed a memorandum of understanding with Rashtriya Raksha University to establish the Wargame Research and Development Centre in New Delhi. The project will be the first simulation-based training center in India, allowing the Indian army to train its soldiers in various combat situations using virtual reality war games, with AI developing the gameplay (Gandharv, 2022). In April 2022, Indian Defense Minister Rajnath Singh launched the sixth Defense India Startup Challenge under the Innovations for Defense Excellence (iDEX) program. The program's goal is to fund startups focusing on AI, sophisticated imaging, sensor systems, big data analytics, autonomous drones, and secure communications systems, as well as other technologies for defense. The iDEX initiative will assist projects with budgets ranging from 15 million Indian rupees to 100 million Indian rupees and include the Indian Coast Guard and 7 newly created defense companies and organizations under the Ministry of Home Affairs. Additionally, the Department of Defense has developed an AI roadmap for each state-owned defense sector enterprise.

Russia

The main areas of digital technology research and development in Russia include machine learning, human-machine interfaces, industrial internet technologies, the use of spatial data (transport networks), and much more. On October 10, 2019, the 2030 National Strategy for the Development of Artificial Intelligence was adopted (President of the Russian Federation XE "Russia" , 2019a). It is significant that the strategy covers a period of ten years, and the principles of implementation include security: "…the impermissibility of using artificial intelligence for the purpose of intentionally causing harm to citizens and legal entities, as well as preventing and minimizing the risks of negative consequences of using artificial intelligence technologies" (President of the Russian Federation XE "Russia" , 2020). In Russia, priority is given to psychological security threats through second-level MUAI, although the strategy leaves room for maneuver in regulating the other two levels.

Russia is participating in the creation of international AI standards, which is the responsibility of Subcommittee 42, established by the International Standardization Organization in October 2017 (ISO/IEC JTC 1/SC 42). The work of one of the country's National Technology Initiative (CNTI) centers in AI is performed within the framework of a consortium led by the Moscow Institute of Physics and Technology (MIPT). Participants and partners also include the Skoltech University, the Higher School of Economics, Innopolis University, Sberbank of Russia, Rosseti, Rostelecom, Russian Railways, and ABBYY (NTI, 2022). By the end of 2021, the center made significant progress in overcoming a number of global AI barriers. In 2019, the center demonstrated the first Russian prototype of a neural network coprocessor for the energy-efficient execution of machine learning algorithms, with a specific performance of about 0.3 Tops/W. In 2020, a computer vision technology was developed that makes a significant contribution to the creation of visual information recognition systems, with a quality of work that is not lower than a human operator. In 2021, the TopicNet environment was created, which captured the entire cycle of topic model building for the first time and solved certain technological barriers in the field of data analysis (e.g., highlighting topics in a dynamic data stream).

As a result of CNTI development in the direction of AI, new objective are planned, including a payload complex for aircraft that provides the exploration and monitoring of mineral deposits; monitoring the state of infrastructure for transporting and storing hydrocarbons; ice reconnaissance and the piloting of ships; software for regulating power system balance (for smart houses); neurointerface chips and related research complexes; and an "open" operating system of robots with support for self-learning technology (NTI, 2022).

MUAI threats are a center of attention in Russia. President Vladimir Putin announced in September 2017 that "Artificial intelligence is not only the future of Russia, it is the future of all mankind. There are colossal opportunities and threats that are difficult to predict today. Whoever becomes the leader in this field will be the ruler of the world" (RIA Novosti, 2017). President Putin also emphasized, "And I would not really want this monopoly to be concentrated in someone's specific hands, therefore, if we are leaders in this area, we will also share these technologies with the whole world, as we share nuclear technologies today." In 2018, the Russian Ministry of Defense hosted the first "Artificial Intelligence: Problems and Solutions" conference, during which Defense Minister Sergei Shoigu tasked military and civilian specialists to join forces in the development of AI technologies to counter possible threats in the fields of technological and economic security (Fedorov, 2018).

Among other state structures, the Foundation for Advanced Research (FAS) supports research on countering MUAI. The National Center for the Development of Technologies and Basic Elements of Robotics was established at the FAS. FAS supported a competition to develop technology to convert hard-to-recognize (due to background noise or accents) Russian speech into text, resulting in the creation of a unique Russian speech recognition technology. FAS also supports projects for interpreting images obtained from satellites and unmanned aerial vehicles, with MIPT as the main contractor. As part of this project, MIPT is creating technologies aimed at combating terrorism by identifying weapons caches and camouflaged terrorist bases from drone images. Work is also underway on a project to identify threats in social networks, developed by the State Research Institute of Aviation Systems (GosNIIAS) as part of the FAS project. GosNIIAS created a technology that makes it possible to identify wanted persons in a crowd, on public transport, and in other difficult conditions.

AI technologies are actively used in Moscow to diagnose COVID-19; all medical centers and hospitals are connected to a special service that allows doctors to process about 30,000 computed tomography scans in two weeks. The accuracy of determining the stages of pneumonia development through CT images was more than 90 percent (Moskva 24, 2020). Russian developers of industrial AI are present in the Indian market, including in the field of mining.

South Africa

In South Africa, a great deal of attention is paid at the state level to the benefits that society and the economy can derive from the full implementation of AI. In 2019, President Cyril Ramaphosa appointed the Presidential Commission on the Fourth Industrial Revolution (PC4IR). The PC4IR assists the government with taking advantage of the opportunities presented by the digital industrial revolution, including AI and machine learning. The commission, chaired by the president, "is to identify relevant policies, strategies and action plans that will position South Africa as a competitive global player." The commission's deputy chair is the University of Johannesburg Professor Tshilidzi Marwala, an expert in the theory and application of AI to engineering, computer science, finance, social science, and medicine (The Presidency, Republic of South Africa, 2019). "The commission is composed of representatives of tech startups, academia, cybersecurity specialists, researchers, social scientists, trade unionists, and other representatives from key economic sectors" (Ramaphosa, 2020), indicating a deep understanding of the impact AI has on all areas of society, studied jointly by specialists in the field of technical and social sciences. According to President Ramafosa, South

Africa aims to fully harness the potential of technological innovation by 2030, growing the economy and lifting the people (Ramaphosa, 2020). In October 2020, the PC4IR recommended establishing an AI institute to foster a generation of new knowledge and AI applications in sectors such as health, agriculture, education, energy, manufacturing, tourism, information and communications technology, as well as training to ensure positive social impact (PC4IR, 2020). The fact that the institute has not yet been created has been criticized in South Africa, along with the failure to implement plans to integrate AI into the justice system (Dwolatzky & Harris, 2021). However, South Africa's AI development has led to the formation of a number of notable companies in the field (GoodFirms, 2022), and government initiatives are helping build the infrastructure for further AI adoption.

Since June 2021, the South African government has been providing tax incentives to venture capital companies to invest in select AI startups. There are also private venture firms such as HAVAIC, whose clients include the technology company RecoMed, South Africa's largest smart medical platform. The University of Pretoria (UP) formed the Intelligent Systems Group, which focuses on the theory and application of analytical, self-learning AI systems. The group strives to create systems that are applicable to the realities of South Africa in areas that include digital imaging and computer vision, AI in music, radio systems, and remote sensing. In addition, the Institute of Big Data and Data Science was opened at UP in September 2017. "UP's Computer Science Department research groups, namely, the Nature Inspired Computing Optimisation Group and the Computational Intelligence Research Group, focus on different areas and applications of AI technologies" (Butcher et al., 2021, p. 28). In 2020, South African telecom operator Rain developed Africa's first autonomous 5G network in partnership with China's Huawei, creating favorable infrastructure conditions for the further development and application of AI. Huawei already accounts for 70 percent of 4G networks in South Africa (Nagaraj, 2021), and the network is currently available in major cities, including Johannesburg, Cape Town, and Port Elizabeth.

* * *

BRICS countries are developing AI systems aimed at solving a wide range of tasks, from fighting poverty to addressing the needs of the military, facilitating multilateral cooperation. However, the rapid introduction of AI, combined with ongoing economic and political problems and a level of general technical literacy that lags behind the pace of digitalization, creates threats from MUAI in the area of psychological security that are both common and specific to BRICS states.

Specific Cases of Malicious Use of Artificial Intelligence in Brazil, India, Russia and South Africa and the National Government Response

Brazil

A large number of phishing attacks have been documented among second-level MUAI threats in Brazil, which can be amplified by AI over time. Phishing attacks have been rising in Latin America, accounting for 192,000 attacks per day in 2017, up by 115 percent from the previous year. Brazil is the most targeted country in the region, registering over 28 percent of phishing attacks in Latin America (Mordor Intelligence, 2019). In 2018, more than 2000 mobile banking users in Brazil downloaded Android-based malware that breached confidential data on the devices. Experts say that cyber threats grew in Latin America during the COVID-19 pandemic. Charity Wright, an analyst with the global cyber threats firm IntSights Cyber Intelligence, said that countries with the largest economies—Brazil, Mexico, Colombia, and Argentina—are the most likely to be targeted by hackers. "They have the money, a huge population and are adopting new technology quickly, but at the same time these countries are very much behind the rest of the world in implementing cyber defense mechanisms, regulation and compliance policies across the board," Wright told InSight Crime (Austin, 2020). In the first quarter of 2020, nearly 3 million cyberattacks occurred in Latin America and the Caribbean. In March 2020 alone, the number of computer viruses recorded in the region increased by 131 percent compared to March 2019. In 2020, Brazil set a global record for number of phishing attacks: every fifth internet user in the country was exposed to a phishing attached at least once (Mari, 2022). As shown later, the number of victims in different countries, such as Russia, will increase even more in 2021.

The third-level threat MUAI, related to the use of social media bots during election campaigns, has been relevant in Brazil for several years. During the second round of presidential debates in 2014, an analysis by the Federal University of Espírito Santo found evidence of bot activity when, during the first 15 minutes of the debate, the number of Twitter mentions of candidate Aècio Neves abnormally tripled. A 2017 study by the Getúlio Vargas Foundation's Department of Public Policy Analysis (FGV/DAPP) proved that more than ten percent of all traffic generated on Twitter during the campaign was due to suspicious, apparently automated, accounts creating one post per second (Allen, 2018). The bots were concentrated on opposite sides of the political spectrum.

An internal Brazilian government memo released to the public in early 2015 mentions that bots were used in campaigns by both Dilma Rousseff and her opponent Aècio Neves (FGV/DAPP, 2018). However, the pro-Rousseff bots were deactivated after a successful campaign, while several Neves campaign bots remained active after the election, potentially contributing to the 2015 impeachment movement against Rousseff.

After Rousseff's victory in the 2015 presidential elections, the country's economic crisis became the driving reason behind calls for her impeachment, which was launched by a series of protests. At least 10 percent of interactions between Twitter profiles on political topics during this period were stimulated by bots. Among Rousseff supporters, this share reached 21.43 percent. The 2016 São Paulo mayoral contest between five candidates also saw the use of bots, with bot retweets among João Doria supporters accounting for 11.25 percent of online debate. Supporters of Fernando Haddad accounted for 11.54 percent, and supporters of Celso Russomanno, 8.40 percent (FGV/DAPP, 2018).

The 2017 study "Troops, Trolls and Trouble-Makers: A Global Inventory of Organised Social Media Manipulation" detected bot activity in 28 countries, including Brazil. The report, prepared by two researchers from the Computational Propaganda Research Project at the Oxford Internet Institute in the United Kingdom, found that governments and political parties promote these digital hosts through official institutions or private providers. Another 2017 analysis, "Computational Propaganda Worldwide," also published at Oxford Internet Institute, found that bots and other forms of computer propaganda are present in Brazil (Godoy, 2018). In 2018, bots were already active months before the election—more than 20 percent of retweets related to Lula da Silva or Jair Bolsonaro, the two candidates with the largest social media presence, were made by bots (Allen, 2018). In January 2018, under the direction of the Superior Electoral Court, Brazil's Federal Police established a task force to stop the spread of fake news during elections.

In February 2022, Brazil was included on a Spamhaus list of countries where the largest number of spambots were detected. Most of these bots are used for spamming, phishing, distributed denial-of-service (DDoS) attacks, and other malicious activities. Analysts associate the abundance of bots in Brazil's digital space with technical, political, and socio-economic factors (The Spamhaus Project, 2022).

Undermining trust in the media can have deep repercussions, particularly in fragile political environments. Sam Gregory, the program director of Witness, a nonprofit that helps people document human rights abuses, offers an example. In Brazil, which has a history of police violence, citizens and activists worry that any video they film of an officer killing a civilian will no longer be sufficient grounds for investigation. Gregory says that the fear real evidence can plausibly be dismissed as fake has become a recurring theme in his workshops (Hao, 2019). The problem is not only exposing the practice of deepfakes, but also effectively detecting deepfakes. This is compounded by authorities attempting to declare any fair criticism based on photos, videos, audio, or written evidence as deepfakes. Professor Hao Li at the University of Southern California agrees. The risk that arises from the misuse of deepfakes is that people are using their existence to discredit genuine video evidence: "Even though there's footage of you doing or saying something you can say it was a deepfake and it's very hard to prove otherwise." Politicians around the world have already been accused of using this ploy, including João Doria, mayor of Sao Paulo. In 2018, the married politician claimed that a video showing him participating in an orgy was a deepfake that no one could convincingly prove otherwise (Thomas, 2020). Thus, the malicious use of deepfakes in Brazil can be both a first- and third-level threat.

The more sophisticated the deepfakes, the more anti-democratic the state; the more politically apathetic and digitally illiterate the population, the more dangerous deepfakes will be. To neutralize deepfakes—and fakes in general—authorities must have a stable and non-selective desire to uncover socially significant cases of deepfakes and to label deepfakes with facts that represent the objective truth. Without the conscious attention and participation of citizens, authorities are unlikely to be willing or able to effectively counter the malicious use of deepfakes. Proving what is real is real, and what is fake is fake, will be extremely difficult without tangible political prerequisites.

India

The level of MUAI in the realm of voice control continues to grow, with Pindrop indicating that fraud in this area has grown by more than 350 percent from 2013 to 2017 (Pindrop, 2020). At least 39 percent of India's internet-connected population is likely to own some sort of digital voice assistant. Experts predict that voice will become the preferred transaction method for e-commerce, banking, and payments in the near future (Bhatt, 2018). In the context of future threats, it is advisable, in our opinion, for interdisciplinary studies to consider the risks of not only voice interface or chatbot hacking, but also the hacking of electronic translation programs. For example, the distortion of official documents by MUAI can be just as provocative as sending a deepfake capable of igniting conflict between countries.

In India, bot activity was recorded during the 2019 election campaigns, with bot accounts on Twitter deployed on a massive scale from February 9–10, spinning hashtags both for and against incumbent Prime Minister Narendra Modi. At the same time, small groups of accounts posted thousands of tweets per hour. The main political parties increased digital communication compared to the previous elections in 2014 but in 2019, the impact of such campaigns was rather modest (Thaker, 2019) due to the relatively small number of voters on Twitter. However, the massive scale of bots that were involved in the campaigns reduced the quality of online debates. Sometimes bot activity became a subject of controversy between opposing party representatives, creating a minimum psychological security threat of the first level. On December 27, 2021, the leader of the Indian National Congress, Rahul Gandhi, sent a letter to the CEO of Twitter complaining that his number of followers had not increased since July, unlike the numbers for other political leaders. Gandhi claimed that the platform was "unwittingly complicit in curbing free and fair speech in India" (OpIndia, 2022), implying that Twitter colluded with the Indian government to limit the opposition's communications.

However, the most extensive examples of MUAI in India can be found in deepfakes. According to a report by Deeptrace, 3 percent of websites that contained deepfake porn videos in 2019 were Indian (Ajder et al., 2019, p. 2). Deeptrace also notices "a significant contribution to the creation and use of synthetic media tools from web users in China" (Ajder et al., 2019, foreword). There is already a documented case of deepfakes being used in India to damage a reputation. Photos and videos of Indian journalist Rana Ayyub were made into deepfake porn videos (Ajder, 2019), pointing to the gradual appropriation of AI technologies by modern criminals and the danger of widespread discrimination campaigns being unleashed against various interest groups in the future.

India is in a precarious position due to the explosive growth of fake news videos, coupled with a significant increase in the number of internet users. Of the approximately 550 million mobile internet users in India, more than 300 million have a low level of literacy, including digital literacy. These types of users mostly watch videos instead of reading text—video is often the first internet content consumed by a large number of people. "With video-only consumers, it's very easy to do fake news... You just pick your narrative, which could be one community attacking another, and find videos to suit it," says Prasantho Roy, a New Delhi-based IT analyst (Rebelo, 2019). Videos of violence from different parts of India or abroad were often used in disinformation campaigns even before the spread of deepfakes. For example, a video of a

16-year-old girl being beaten and burned alive in Guatemala is periodically published in connection with reports of Hindu girls being lynched. The reputation of a school in the state of Gujarat was hit hard by plummeting enrollment when a video falsely accusing teachers at the school of child abuse was circulated on social media.

An 11-second video featuring Delhi Chief Minister Arvind Kejriwal released in 2017 shows him urging people to vote for the Indian National Congress Party. Later, Kejriwal clarified in his own official video that he did not make the statement, accusing the Indian National Congress and Akali Dal parties of creating a hoax (Sharma, 2018). In 2018, Kerala resident Sobha Sajju's reputation has been cleared two and a half years after a nude video allegedly of her went viral; her husband filed for divorce and took custody of their three children. According to press reports, the Indian Centre for Development of Advanced Computing created software using facial recognition technologies that determined the woman in the video was not Sajju (Mihindukulasuriya, 2018). Despite the fact that not all Indian media considers the Kejriwal example a deepfake (there is no indication that it was created with AI), Indian law enforcement officers cite both the Kejriwal and Sajju cases as examples of how difficult it is to counter the spread of disinformation due to modern technologies.

In India, the use case (perhaps the first in the world) of deepfakes specifically for campaign purposes has become infamous. In February 2020, the Bharatiya Janata Party (the Indian People's Party) used this technology to create two videos in which party leader Manoj Tiwari addresses voters in two languages ahead of the Delhi Legislative Assembly elections. The candidate's goal was to send a message to two groups of voters speaking different languages—Haryanvi and English. The videos, according to party representatives, were sent to about 5800 WhatsApp groups (Alavi & Achom, 2020) and in them, Tiwari also congratulated his supporters on the passage of an amendment to the Citizenship Act by the Delhi Legislative Assembly. In the original video, Tiwari's message is delivered in Hindi, with his facial expressions and lip movements mimicking the language simulated using AI for the Haryanvi version. Neelkant Bakshi, the party's media officer, said that the video in Haryanvi received positive feedback, after which it was decided to create an English version. However, it became clear that events could get out of control: "Someone used a Facebook video of our Delhi BJP president…Manoj Tiwari 'Mridul' Ji and sent us his video with changed content in Haryanvi dialect," Bakshi said. "It was shocking for us, as it may have been used by the opposition in bad taste…We strongly condemn the use of this technology, which is available in open arena and has been used without our consent" (Mihindukulasuriya, 2020).

Although deepfakes were used in this case solely to overcome a language barrier, the further modification of the deepfakes for malicious purposes—and then the reaction of the party—caused a lively discussion in the Indian media. This understandably fuels concerns about the possible use of technology to spread disinformation, such as politicians using deepfakes to put controversial and inadmissible statements into the mouths of their opponents (Alavi & Achom, 2020). The practice of using deepfakes was publicly abandoned by India's major political parties (Mihindukulasuriya, 2020). For India, as well as for many other countries, in the current environment of rapid digitalization and increasing disinformation campaigns, the challenge of combining MUAI technologies with different psychological security threat levels may become relevant. For instance, in 2021, the total volume of cryptocurrency trading worldwide increased to 15.8 trillion US dollars, which is 567 percent more than in 2020 (Biswas, 2022). Along with the rise in cryptocurrency transactions, fraud has risen globally from 2017 to 2021, driven primarily by phishing that has targeted millions of Indians.

Along with the benefits of the digitalization of the Indian economy, there is also an increase in the risk of MUAI. The 2022 budget introduced the central bank digital currency (CBDC), which will be based on blockchain, but the move elicited frowns from Reserve Bank of India Governor Shaktikanta Das. Although a number of politicians and financiers are in favor of strengthening legislative regulation of cryptocurrencies, Das believes that digital fraud will become the main problem of CBDC. Several fake investment portals have already been on the radar of Indian law enforcement for over a year. Many residents of Kerala were deceived by the creation of an imaginary cryptocurrency called Morris Coin, with Indian law enforcement assessing the amount of the fraudulent assets to be worth 3672 million Indian rupees. A similar incident occurred in Karnataka. Experts believe that the combination of fraud and malicious use of deepfakes in the field of cryptocurrencies will take phishing to a new level (Biswas, 2022), making it easier to convince consumers of the authenticity of a fake website accepting payments in cryptocurrency.

As of March 2022, there was no specific legislation in India prohibiting the malicious use of deepfakes. "Sections 67 and 67A of the Information Technology Act, 2000 punishes sexually explicit material in explicit form" (Seth, 2022), although Shashidharan (2021) considers this law and the Information Technology (Intermediary Guidelines and Digital Media Ethics Code) Rules to be "inadequate to deal with content manipulation on digital platforms." Section 500 of the Indian Penal Code, 1860 provides punishment for defamation which can be sentenced in the cases of the malicious use of deepfakes. The Personal Data Protection Bill, 2019, provides for the protection of data relating to natural persons who are directly or indirectly identifiable, and the bill has extraterritorial applicability to creators of deepfakes outside of India. Seth (2022) predicts that "once passed, [this bill] would play a significant role in regulating the usage and circulation of deepfakes."

A number of Indian journalists are attempting to counteract the spread of deepfakes and false news based on those deepfakes, believing that such content bypasses all fact-checking mechanisms. Pratik Sinha, the founder of the Indian social media fact-checking site AltNews, said that his outlet was unable to identify Manoj Tiwari's video as a deepfake, even though it has checked thousands of altered images and videos during its three years of operation (Christopher, 2020). The psychological security threat level to society from deepfakes in India is assessed as high: "In a country like India where digital literacy is nascent, even low-tech versions of video manipulation have led to violence. In 2018, more than 30 deaths were linked to rumours circulated on WhatsApp in India" (Christopher, 2020). According to Jaiman (2020), "The lack of awareness of AI-based synthetic media, deepfakes, led villagers in India to believe falsehood of children kidnapping to be accurate, fake images, and video on WhatsApp resulted in several cases of mob lynching and killing." Among the challenges the country faces is that national tools for the reliable detection of deepfakes are currently under development, and relying entirely on foreign tools for security issues is a risky prospect for any country. After the odious elections incident in 2020, developments to combat deepfakes were not mentioned in either the Centre for Development of Advanced Computing (C-DAC XE "Centre for Development of Advanced Computing, C-DAC") report (2020) or in the National Technical Research Organisation (NTRO) newsletter (National Critical Information Infrastructure Protection Centre, 2020). There are mentions in Indian media publications of Reality Defender, a plugin for detecting deepfakes developed by US specialists. Additionally, there are practically no BRICS projects on international cooperation in the NTRO and C-DAC publications, apart from a few developments with Russian meteorological services and a memorandum of understanding with a Brazilian technology center.

A number of experts, including Sinha, believe that firms should be outlawed from engaging in deepfakes for the purposes of election campaigns in India. There is also support for establishing a state policy on disinformation in general, and deepfakes in particular (Christopher, 2020). However, this would not free the country from the threats posed by criminal groups.

Threats related to hacking or from "smart" chatbots could emerge in India. The State Bank of India launched SIA, an AI-powered chatbot that instantly responds to customer queries and assists them with their daily banking tasks. SIA is poised to handle nearly 10,000 requests per second, or 864 million requests per day. That's almost 25 percent of the queries processed by Google every day. The deployment of an AI project of this magnitude is possibly the first of its kind in India (Baruah, 2020). For this kind of mass use of chatbot, ensuring there is responsible training and adequate protection for the software from hacking is of the utmost importance. In India, AI technologies are being actively introduced in a combined form, which can cause threats to psychological security from MUAI at all three levels.

Russia

The MUAI threats (existing and future) that have manifested in other BRICS countries are also relevant for Russia. This was demonstrated during the COVID-19 pandemic, with phishing cases becoming more frequent in Russia. Against the backdrop of news about benefits payments to families with children, fake sites began to appear asking people to apply for benefits. In the .ru zone, about 30 fake domains were found in 2020. According to Alexei Drozd, head of the SearchInform security department, many sites were not yet complete, probably preparing to "mirror" their designs on the original, official site (Stepanova, 2020). According to a survey conducted by Avast, 45 percent of Russians experienced phishing attacks in 2021, an increase of 4 percent compared to the company's 2020 results. Additionally, 72 percent of respondents received phishing calls compared to 56 percent in 2020, 60 percent received malicious emails, and 52 percent encountered smishing (SMS phishing). At the same time, the number of real-life social engineering attacks decreased from 16 percent in 2020 to 15 percent in 2021 (TASS, 2021), an indication of the attackers' ability to quickly master AI technologies and transition to the digital environment. While there is no information that these scammers were using AI, the risk of such a development exists.

From February to April 2020, the State Duma of the Russian Federation considered a draft law to establish an experimental legal regime for the implementation of AI technologies in Moscow. This bill elicited somewhat ambiguous reactions from the media, with both neutral (Interfax, 2020) and negative (RIA Katyusha, 2020) comments referring to the dangers of infringing on citizens' right to privacy. On April 24, 2020, the bill was signed into federal law (President of the Russian Federation XE "Russia" , 2019b). In this situation, it is especially important to pay attention to first- and second-level psychological security threats. AI abuse by business entities can occur during the process of collecting personal data; that data can not only be transferred to government bodies (as required by law) but also, for example, be used to send aggressively targeted advertising. Reactions to the law with comparisons made to a "concentration camp" and even the "Chinese model" (RIA Katyusha, 2020), suggesting that negative media campaigns against AI practices in both Russia and China could follow a similar pattern. This indicates that it is all the more important for Russian government agencies to ensure citizens are adequately informed about the uses of AI, especially since services that already use AI elements are beginning to actively influence the lives of Russians. This became widely known when a Tele2 mobile operator robot called a subscriber, but a bot named Oleg from Tinkoff Bank picked up the phone instead. The Tele2 robot offered the Oleg bot a new rate; Oleg agreed without the smartphone owner's consent (Gavrilyuk & Korolyov, 2022). Despite the desire of businesses to limit AI regulation through the AI Code of Ethics (mentioned below), the need for adequate legislation matching the level of technology development is obvious.

Internationally, Russia faces deranking actions by US internet companies in the area of psychological security. In 2017, Google announced its intention to downgrade reports from Russian state-owned publications Russia Today (RT) and Sputnik. The chairman of Alphabet (the holding company that owns Google), Eric Schmidt, said that the search giant needed to fight the spread of disinformation; meanwhile, US intelligence agencies were calling RT "Russia's state propaganda machine." Relevant media publications identified this move as a form of censorship. Speaking at the Halifax International Security Forum in Washington, DC, Schmidt said, "I am strongly not in favor of censorship. I am very strongly in favor of ranking. It's what we do." Deranking occurs when Google changes its algorithms to detect information "weapons," which Schmidt considered publications of the Russian state media (BBC News, 2017). These comments prompted a legitimate protest from RT and Sputnik, based on a recording of Google's statement to the US Congress. Margarita Simonyan, the editor-in-chief of the two Russian publications, said Google's statement confirmed that it found no manipulation of its platform or other violations by RT (RT, 2017). US intelligence agencies accused Russia of trying to influence the 2016 US presidential election in favor of Donald Trump by spreading fake news and hacking the Democratic Party resources to undermine his opponent Hillary Clinton (BBC News, 2017). This accusation prompted Twitter to ban RT and Sputnik ads on its platform in October

2017. In November 2017, the US Department of Justice forced RT to register as a "foreign agent."

The spread of negative imagery about Russia in the Western information environment was a form of action that, in relation to the Russian leadership and the target audience (US citizens), can be assessed as a third-level MUAI threat, since it reinforces a stereotypical perception of Russia's leader. In 2020, two political advertisements using deepfakes of President Putin and North Korean leader Kim Jong-un were posted to social media. The message in both videos was the same: there is no need for Russia or North Korea to interfere in US elections; the United States will destroy its own democracy. The videos were produced and distributed by the human rights group RepresentUs to raise awareness about the need to protect voter rights in the upcoming US presidential election. The videos were released amid harsh public criticism of mail-in voting by the then-President Donald Trump, and there was speculation that Trump might refuse to cede the election if he lost. The purpose of the campaign, according to media reports (Hao, 2020), was "to shock Americans into understanding the fragility of democracy as well as provoke them to take various actions, including checking their voter registration and volunteering for the polls." RepresentUs collaborated with the creative agency Mischief at No Fixed Address, which came up with the idea "of using dictators to deliver the message." The statement at the end of the video said, "The footage is not real, but the threat is" (Hao, 2020). The stereotypical image of the deepfake "dictator" reflects, on the one hand, the realities of the psychological warfare of elites on the world stage; on the other hand, it can also strengthen that image, instilling a sense of anxiety in that country's leader by an economic competitor and political opponent. Significantly, US media networks did not dare take on such a responsibility—the ad was supposed to air on Fox News, CNN, and MSNBC but was pulled at the last minute.

Just like in other countries where AI-powered robots are being developed, there is a risk of the technology falling into the hands of intruders, making it necessary for Russia to deal with second-level MUAI threats. For example, robot dogs are gaining popularity in Russia. "Intellekt Mashin" ("Intellect of Machines") company began producing the M-81 model of robot dog at the end of 2021 (TV BRICS XE "BRICS" , 2022) (based on Chinese technologies (IXBT.com, 2022)). The question being asked by Russian media is, what will happen if the robot is used by malicious actors? Even the mention of such a possibility reduces public confidence in AI and robotics, but public assessments of such developments are generally positive.

Although MUAI legislation in Russia and other BRICS countries does not yet address the level of new threats, government agencies and state-owned companies are paying close attention to combating MUAI. For example, the Russian government's "New Internet Communication Technologies" touches on the problems of detecting deepfakes distributed with malicious intent. This road map was approved in July 2021 by a government commission on digital development, focused on the use of information technologies to improve the quality of life and business. The road map's 2024 targets include growing the Russian video services audience to 96 million users (from 63 million users in 2020), growing the integrated communications platform audience to 108 million (from 74 million), and growing domestic cloud gaming platforms to 2.31 million users (from 0.18 million) (Balashova, 2021); this also means an increase in the number of people who are vulnerable to video manipulation (as already noted, a similar process is happening in India). The accuracy of Russian solutions to determine that generated and presented content is real is expected to reach 70 percent by 2024 and 90 percent by 2030 (CNews, 2021), indicating the high degree of attention that Russian leadership and developers are devoting to MUAI threats of the third level.

The State Duma, together with the Federal Service for Supervision of Communications, Information Technology and Mass Media (Roskomnadzor), is working on regulating the fight against fraudulent sites. Among the methods under consideration is the requirement to mark potentially dangerous resources in browsers (Stepanova & Tishina, 2021). The Federation Council has instructed a number of ministries, including the Ministry of Digital Development, Communications and Mass Media, the Ministry of Health and the Ministry of Economic Development, to develop measures to protect the rights of citizens using AI systems. The ministries will have to develop and approve a road map for this process by the end of 2022, to include initiatives that will eliminate "discrimination of citizens on various grounds when using AI algorithms," ensuring the transparency of AI work and legislating procedures for appealing AI decisions. It is also proposed that citizens will be notified when they are interacting with AI when solving "vital issues" (such as obtaining public services) (Gavrilyuk & Korolyov, 2022). In October 2021, the government's Analytical Center, the Ministry of Economic Development, the AI Alliance (Sberbank, MTS, Vkontakte, Gazprom Neft, Yandex, the Russian Direct Investment Fund), and other large Russian companies and research centers signed on to the AI Code of Ethics (Rossiyskaya gazeta, 2022).

The cases of deranking Russian information resources and using a deepfake of the Russian president in the psychological warfare show that at least the second level of MUAI can be used openly, and not only by criminal entities. Currently, the ability to share the Russian state's point of view with an international audience is hampered by the fact that the companies that develop the most important English-language social networks are located in the United States, under the influence of an anti-Russian elite. This challenges Russia to develop alternative social media outlets that can reach an audience beyond national borders. However, if this situation is evaluated not only as a danger but also as an opportunity, the audience expansion for Russian social networks will significantly increase the volume of big data to train domestic AI.

South Africa

For South Africa, the relevance of first-level psychological security threats from MUAI can be noted. Among these threats is the possibility of social destabilization due to the displacement of an increasing number of workers by AI technologies. Ian Goldin, professor of globalization and development at Oxford University, says that AI could displace millions of jobs in the future, damaging growth in developing regions such as Africa (BBC News, 2022). Many workers in South Africa have already been replaced by robots, according to the McKinsey Institute, especially from mechanization in the historically labor-intensive mining sector. Trade and service jobs are also at risk. For example, the Pick n Pay supermarket chain introduced an AI-enabled automated checkout system that eliminates the need for cashiers (Van den Berg, 2018). Against the background of a high unemployment rate, general understanding of the specifics of AI in South Africa is extremely low. As a consequence, AI-related anxiety about job loss is rapidly increasing among working citizens (Business Tech, 2019). Additionally, first-level threats appeared when the United States attempted to oust the Chinese telecommunications company Huawei from the South African market, which supplies the country with the 5G internet technologies that are necessary for AI development. Huawei is at the forefront of 5G development and in 2018, the United States launched a campaign to stop other countries from buying Huawei equipment. The president of South Africa, Cyril Ramaphosa, claimed in his opening speech at a digital economy conference in Johannesburg in July 2019 that the United States was "clearly jealous that a Chinese company called Huawei has outstripped them and because they have been outstripped they must now punish that one company." In 2019, Huawei signed a contract with South Africa for the first 5G commercial network on the African continent. According to Cobus van Staden, a China–Africa researcher at the South African Institute of International Affairs, Huawei has already built around 70 percent of the continent's 4G networks (EFE–EPA, 2019).

On February 26, 2020, South African mobile communications company Rain announced plans to build a 5G-transport network using Huawei's optical cross-connect (OXC) and 200G solution, leveraging Huawei's latest all-optical switching product—OXC (P32)—to build a metro optical transport network. Rain is focused on bringing mobile broadband networks to South Africa and becoming the first operator to deploy 5G networks in the country (Huawei, 2020).

On March 12, 2020, at the Health and Human Rights Summit in Tucson, Arizona, Dr. Thomas Cowan hypothesized that COVID-19 may have been caused by 5G (Huawei XE "Huawei" , 2020). Cowan started his career while teaching gardening as a Peace Corps volunteer in Swaziland and South Africa and later, served as vice president of the Physicians Association for Anthroposophical Medicine. A founding member of the Weston A. Price Foundation, Cowan's claims have largely been debunked, but discussions about his hypotheses have attracted many supporters on online platforms. This is understandable in an environment of growing panic that is actively perpetuated by media and social networks.

Tom Cowan's original hypothesis provoked heated discussion in South African media and social networks that extended beyond the country's borders. More than 4000 people signed a petition on Change.org to stop the rollout of 5G in Cape Town (Independent, 2020), and similar petitions are circulating in South Africa. Access to these sites became restricted by the government in April, although this is unlikely to stop supporters of Cowan's ideas.

This will not be an examination of the essence of Cowan's argument but without a doubt, his assessment of the relationship between COVID-19 and 5G technologies has become a tool in a competitive struggle. In South Africa, Huawei is the undisputed leader in 5G, and active campaigning against 5G in the country is directed almost exclusively at this company. It is unlikely that such an information campaign will be an immediate success, but if COVID-19 cases increase in the country and, most importantly, inevitably affect the socio-economic situation, then other scenarios cannot be excluded.

This case illustrates the path trade wars can take. In this instance, AI and related technologies have become the subject of psychological warfare, which, along with business structures, involves political elites who are not facilitating the resolution of the contradictions of the modern world order. Such incidents are worrisome because this type of warfare involves many non-state actors who, guided by false messages and conspiracy theories, can cause damage to physical infrastructure, cause additional panic in society, or discredit technologies aimed at overcoming economic problems.

A pressing social problem in South Africa, in the context of third-level psychological security threats, is bullying. When moved to social networks or mobile applications, bullying can be amplified by built-in AI algorithms. According to an Independent Polling System of Society report, in 2020, South Africa had the highest prevalence of cyberbullying, with 54 percent of parents indicating that they are aware of a child in their community who has been a victim of bullying (Kahla, 2020). Due to the ability of social media algorithms to rank content that attracts a lot of attention, controversial content can be quickly shared by real users, generating a higher rating—and a larger audience—for messages of hate speech. It is known that terrorist organizations have used AI-enabled bots in mobile applications to spread propaganda (see chapter "Malicious Use of Artificial Intelligence and Threats to Psychological Security in Latin America: Common Problems, Current Practice and Prospects" of this handbook), potentially increasing the destructive effects of cyberbullying.

In South Africa, manipulated audio recordings have been leaked from meetings of the governing African National Congress (ANC) leadership ahead of the party's elective conference in 2022. "Whoever is doing it, it was very professionally done," said ANC deputy secretary general Jesse Duarte in a radio interview with Eyewitness News on April 15, 2021. "It was cut and spliced very carefully to give a particular impression of a very sober conversation in the meeting of the officials of the ANC" (Maree, 2021). "One of the leaks contained a purported recording of Duarte's input at a meeting between the ANC's top six officials and former president Jacob Zuma at the end of last month. The party is trying to persuade Zuma to testify in front of the commission of inquiry into the large-scale corruption during his tenure, dubbed 'state capture,' but he continues to refuse" (Ibidem).

This was not the first time apparently manipulated information was featured from the party's internal battles. However, this case of disinformation, probably intended to show voters a split in the ANC's ranks, was called a deepfake in the media. New and easily accessible technologies make the manipulation of information easier and more potent, warns University of Johannesburg vice-chancellor Tshilidzi Marwala. He also notes that the expertise for sophisticated cyber manipulation also exists in South Africa (Maree, 2021), and that the malicious use of technologies in political rivalries, such as deepfakes and voice-changing in particular, can threaten a country's democracy.

In July 2021, the South African Protection of Personal Information Act entered into force after an eight-year gestation period. The month before in June 2021, President Ramaphosa signed the Cybercrimes Act of South Africa, creating "new crimes of unlawful access and interception of data, unlawful acts in respect to software or hardware tools and unlawful interference with data or computer programmes" (CyberBRICS XE "CyberBRICS" , 2021). The law allows for the prosecution of malicious communications, including the disclosure of data messages of intimate image, regardless of whether the image is real or simulated (The Presidency, Republic of South Africa XE "Africa" , 2021). This de facto prohibits porn deepfakes under South African law. The law also prohibits inflicting physical or property harm through the exchange of information in an electronic environment or the threat to cause such damage. Lawyer Nomalanga Mashinini (2021) indicates that even before this law was adopted, disinformation through the use of deepfakes was recognized as a violation of the right to human dignity guaranteed by the South African constitution. Additionally, "smart" disinformation of a political nature could previously be considered fraudulent, falling under the common law (Mashinini, 2021). Among the South African regulatory frameworks that can be used to combat the distribution of illegal content, including fake news, are the 1996 Film and Publication Act no. 65, as amended in 2019, the Disaster Management Act, and the 2018 Preventing and Combating of Hate Speech Bill (Less & Umanah, 2020).

South Africa also has community initiatives aimed at combating MUAI and protecting the psychological security of society. Real 411 is a civil society-led initiative that enables the public to report misinformation. The organization has "a code of conduct which applies to offences that comprise harmful false information, hate speech, incitement of violence and harassment of journalists…the code of conduct established the Digital Complaints Committee…Additional recourse for the public is to apply to the equality court for relief, approach the South African Human Rights Commission for assistance and also to check a fact-checking organisation for verification" (Less & Umanah, 2020). This has led to favorable conditions for developing a system for protecting citizens from MUAI in the field of psychological security.

BRICS Initiatives to Prevent Psychological Security Risks and Threats Associated with Malicious Use of Artificial Intelligence

Most of the declarations adopted at BRICS summits between 2012 and 2019 were focused on the critical role of information and communication technologies (ICT) in the economic, social, and cultural development of the member states. While AI is only mentioned in the 2017 Xiamen Declaration (BRICS, 2017), BRICS condemned acts of mass electronic surveillance and data collection on individuals already in the 2015 Ufa Declaration (BRICS, 2015), with a particular emphasis on the right to privacy. The Ufa Declaration fits the description of the malicious use of predictive analytics tools that aggressive actors can use as prognostic weapon. The declaration also established a BRICS Working Group of Experts on security and ICT. The tasks of the group include exchanging information and best practices, coordinating measures to combat cybercrime, cooperating in the field of computer security, engaging in joint research and development, and developing international norms, principles, and standards (BRICS, 2015).

In subsequent years, BRICS countries discussed an increasingly wide range of issues related to ICT, including within the framework of the International IT Forum, which also reflects an approach to the problem of the malicious use of ICT, including AI. For example, the 2018 Johannesburg Declaration (BRICS, 2018) emphasized that the Fourth Industrial Revolution ushers in not only indisputable benefits but also new challenges and threats associated with the growing misuse of ICT for criminal purposes by state and non-state actors. The 2019 Brasilia Declaration enshrined (BRICS, 2019) the intentions of BRICS countries to foster international cooperation in ICT security. The BRICS Beijing Declaration in 2022 might for the first time clearly highlight the risks of developing AI, including MUAI, in the field of psychological security, although those specific terms were not used in the document: "We express our concerns on the risk, and ethical dilemma related to Artificial Intelligence, such as privacy, manipulation, bias, human-robot interaction, employment, effects and singularity among others. We encourage BRICS members to work together to deal with such concerns, sharing best practices, conduct comparative study on the subject toward developing a common governance approach which would guide BRICS members on Ethical and responsible use of Artificial Intelligence while facilitating the development of AI" (BRICS, 2022). These political documents indicate the readiness of BRICS to engage in joint initiatives to counter MUAI.

As for the development of AI in general, as well as the means for ensuring psychological security at national and international levels, BRICS supports international academic cooperation. For this in particular, the platform CyberBRICS was created to exchange ideas and research results. The 2017 United Nations Internet Governance Forum Workshop is considered the project's first meeting, bringing together key stakeholders, including representatives from Brazil's Ministry of Foreign Affairs and Russia's Ministry of Digital Development, Communications, and Mass Media (Cyber BRICS,

2019). The developers of the CyberBRICS project cited three goals: to compare existing regulations; to identify best practices and develop policy proposals in the area of cybersecurity regulation (including personal data regulation); and to develop internet access policy and government digitalization strategies in BRICS countries. The project is intended to develop legal and political mechanisms for regulating ICT, and AI in particular. The project structure also reflects this aim, organized and developed by the Getúlio Vargas Foundation law school in partnership with the Higher School of Economics in Moscow, the Center for Internet and Society in New Delhi, Fudan University in Shanghai, the University of Hong Kong, and the University of Cape Town.

Following UN practices, CyberBRICS members pay special attention to problems of personal data regulation and cybersecurity management. "CyberBRICS aims at offering answers to such challenges, providing valuable—and so far inexistent—insights on BRICS digital policies, based on rigorously collected evidence that can be used by researchers, regulators and businesses alike" (Cyber BRICS, 2022). Data protection and cybersecurity have become top priorities of the BRICS Science, Technology and Innovation Partnership (CyberBRICS, 2019). Members of the CyberBRICS Advisory Board consult on development research in the field of cybersecurity and invite interested parties to join the CyberBRICS network (CyberBRICS, 2022). The CyberBRICS website has been operational since the beginning of 2019, where profile research and information about events are published.

Since 2014, the BRICS ministers responsible for the fields of science, technology, and innovation have cooperated on a number of initiatives to development of a legal framework, including the Memorandum of Understanding on Cooperation in Science, Technology, and Innovation. Cooperation in the field of ICT has been developing rapidly since then, as evidenced by the promotion of the BRICS Digital Partnership in 2016, the BRICS Presidential Summit declaration on Collaboration for Inclusive Growth and Shared Prosperity in the Fourth Industrial Revolution, and the development of the enabling framework for the Innovation BRICS Network (iBRICS Network) (Belli, 2020, p. 20; BRICS – Brasil, 2019). It is worth noting new initiatives, such as the BRICS Partnership on New Industrial Revolution (PartNIR), the iBRICS Network, and the BRICS Institute of Future Networks. In 2019, the BRICS Science, Technology and Innovation Work Plan 2019–2022 was adopted, and the BRICS Science, Technology and Innovation (STI) cooperation mechanism—called BRICS STI Architecture—was established to coordinate the work of BRICS countries, organize events, evaluate projects and initiatives for further optimization (including societal impact), and widely inform politicians, researchers, and a wider audience about BRICS activities in the field of STI. The creation of the first BRICS Technology Transfer Centre in Kunming and the first BRICS Institute of Future Networks in Shenzhen testifies to the leadership of China in the field of AI and the country's interest in developing BRICS technological cooperation (Belli, 2020, pp. 21–22). Liu Duo, president of the China Academy of Information and Communication Technology, said that the Shenzhen Institute will focus on 5G policy research, the industrial internet, AI, the internet of vehicles, and other technologies. Additional efforts will be made to encourage the exchange of ideas among the five countries, including organizing more training events and implementing exchange programs (Ma, 2019). The iBRICS Platform was established by the 2019 Summit in Brasilia (BRICS – Brasil, 2019), providing contacts between science parks, BRICS country technology clusters, specialized associations, and auxiliary structures to encourage startups, including the field of AI.

The development of BRICS AI cooperation is mostly observed at the cross-country level. In May 2018, India and China launched their first joint projects in the fields of AI and big data—the AI-focused IT corridor in the Chinese city of Dalian and the big data-focused information technology cooperation platform in China's Guiyang. The projects, supported by the Chinese government and the Indian National Association for Software and Services Companies, are aimed at boosting cooperation between Indian software developers and Chinese high-tech industries in the fields of big data and the internet of things. To connect Indian and Chinese companies, the two sides launched a joint IT matchmaking initiative, the Sino–Indian Digital Collaborative Opportunities Plaza, an AI-powered bilingual platform that is run by Indian startup Zeta-V Technology Solutions (based in China) in collaboration with CASICloud in Guizhou (Krishnan, 2018). Indian IT companies were present in the Chinese market for more than a decade before this initiative, but mostly working for Western multinational corporations.

Russia is also ready to work with India in the fields of cybersecurity and AI, as well as in the direction of the internet of things. This was announced by Minister of Industry and Trade Denis Manturov at the opening of the Russian Small- and Medium-sized Russian-Indian Enterprises Forum (TASS, 2019). For China and Russia, AI has become a new priority in technological cooperation. In August 2017, the Russian Association of Robotics signed agreements with the China Robotics Industry Alliance and the China Electronics Society, with the support of the relevant Chinese and Russian ministries. In April 2018, a workshop on industrial robotics was held in Russia for the first time with the participation of leading developers, including Zhejiang Buddha

Technology. In May 2019, NtechLab (one of the leading companies in Russia in the field of AI and facial recognition) and Dahua Technology (a Chinese manufacturer of video surveillance systems) presented a jointly developed, wearable camera with facial recognition that could be used by law enforcement officers. In September 2019, Russia and China discussed AI cooperation at the 6th Annual Invest in Innovation Bilateral Forum in Shanghai. The forum highlighted the possibility of direct dialogue between venture capital investors and technology companies in Russia and China (Bendett & Kania, 2019, pp. 11–12).

So far, the driving force behind AI cooperation in BRICS is bilateral agreements focused on economic cooperation, with a focus on using AI for positive purposes, such as supporting the extractive industries, industry, and healthcare. As an institution that has proclaimed cooperation in the field of cybersecurity as one of its main goals, BRICS does not single out AI as a special area of regulation, indicating a certain lag in political institutions' understanding of real economic practices. Undoubtedly, the breadth of consideration given to ICT problems enhances the mechanisms for finding solutions at the initial stages of development. However, BRICS countries are not only actively pursuing AI, but also already facing the risks and security threats associated with MUAI today. MUAI is best considered separately due to the specific characteristics of AI, such as its diversity, autonomy, self-learning, and so on. Taking this into consideration, there is an acute lack of research and initiatives in the field for ensuring the PS at the BRICS level, perhaps due to funding difficulties. However, the organization has declared the intention to jointly counteract the malicious use of ICT, and all member states have the opportunity to take an active part in the development of common mechanisms to counter MUAI.

On May 19, 2022, BRICS country foreign ministers reaffirmed continued cooperation in three main areas—politics and security, economics and finance, and culture and communication—in order to minimize the impact of the COVID-19 pandemic. The ministers also noted the importance of accelerating implementation of the 2030 Agenda for Sustainable Development, as well as further deepening cooperation between BRICS countries in general (BRICS Ministers of Foreign Affairs, 2022). Concerns have been raised about the risks and ethical dilemmas associated with AI, such as privacy issues, manipulation, AI bias, human-robot interaction issues, employment, and singularity issues (BRICS Ministers of Foreign Affairs, 2022). It is significant that the ministers supported initiatives in information exchange and technical cooperation in the field of AI, recalling the declaration of the 7th BRICS Communications

Ministers Meeting, which recognizes the rapid development and huge potential of AI technologies and their importance for economic growth.

The main areas of cooperation in the field of AI that were mentioned at the meeting within the BRICS framework were identified, including the need to build confidence and security. The ministers also noted a need for transparency and accountability in promoting "trustworthy AI," in order to maximize its potential for the benefit of society and humanity as a whole, with a particular focus on marginalized and vulnerable populations. Thus, the fight against poverty can be considered a main area of collaborative AI work, assisting with the widespread education of citizens on AI issues.

Conclusion

Currently, along with the obvious technological progress, new risks and threats associated with the speed of development and the growth in efficiency of AI technologies are also emerging. However, a large number of these risks and threats are anthropogenic in nature and entirely related to the MUAI problem; "weak" AI is used for the benefit or harm of society only by people.

AI development is a topical issue for BRICS member states individually and as a group. The member states are individually at different stages of digital transformation; this lends BRICS as an institution the role of solving digital development problems in order to facilitate the adoption of strategic collective decisions. BRICS countries are developing economies with growing innovative potential that are actively implementing AI. However, there is also a certain imbalance between technological integration and investment in human capital in these countries. In the field of AI, BRICS countries undoubtedly have potential and, together, are capable of translating their growing economic power into greater geopolitical influence if all member states continue to increase the pace of innovation. Despite the instability of the AI industry, some BRICS countries are receiving significant flows of foreign direct investment, creating opportunities for economic growth. At the BRICS level, the importance of AI is recognized, confirming not only previous practices of cooperation on platforms like iBRICS and CyberBRICS but also the declarations issued by BRICS supreme bodies, including in 2022.

Against the background of continued tensions in relations between BRICS members and countries in the collective West, the group will continue to exchange practices, information, and experiences in the field of AI. At the moment, BRICS does not have a specialized mechanism for exchanging information on the fight against MUAI in partner countries or the features of its regulation. It would be possible to establish a similar mechanism on the basis of existing sites in the future. Legal mechanisms to prevent MUAI are in the early stages of development in BRICS countries, relying primarily on constitutional norms, media legislation, or criminal law to provide penalties for fraud or moral harm. However, there are attempts being made to legislate against malicious communications, such as in the South African Cyber Security Bill.

Supranational institutions and norms of international law in any industry cannot be realized without solid foundations in national mechanisms. National AI regulation and legal opposition to MUAI are at initial stages of development in most countries around the world. This makes it all the more important for each BRICS member to engage in international cooperation in this area. Further joint discussion within the BRICS framework of the problems of MUAI in the national and international psychological security context, especially regarding the effective implementation of decisions, is possible only as long as the countries further converge on the economic, political, and ideological aspects of innovative development and the practical solutions of socially significant national and global challenges of the twenty-first century. This includes, of course, the growing and positive role of AI. The potential of BRICS is huge, and the group is still far from realizing its maximum capabilities. If its potential is developed, BRICS will involve other nations in mutually beneficial cooperation for the sake of sustainable development. However, as this convergence progresses, the internal and external adversaries of BRICS will try to frustrate it in various ways, not least through MUAI. As AI technologies become cheaper and more widespread, a variety of actors in world politics, including aggressive actors such as reactionary regimes and criminal and terrorist groups, will gain access to them. Moreover, mastering certain technologies can help many people become actors in world politics. Thus, the tasks of counteracting MUAI and strengthening international psychological security within the framework of the BRICS are of a strategic nature.

In the context of widespread AI adoption by both citizens and organizations, openness of public discussion is extremely important. Getting as much data as possible is important for AI training, but so are comprehensive technological progress assessments for developing a technology-responsible society. At critical moments, state entities, public institutions, and international organizations can draw new ideas from this discussion.

It is recommended that an interdisciplinary working group of technical and social specialists be created at the BRICS level, with the task of coordinating research and practice to combat MUAI in the context of international psychological security; since the issue of AI is very broad, such specialization seems necessary. Additionally, it is worth discussing the idea of creating a communication network for BRICS countries—built on intellectual text recognition—with the ability to instantly translate messages into the language of the addressee. This would dramatically increase the degree of mutual understanding between BRICS countries, including in areas of research, thereby also increasing training opportunities for AI. This initiative would also reduce the possible impact of MUAI on the public consciousness in BRICS countries by powerful supranational and national actors who largely control information flows on the internet today, especially English-speaking content. In the context of the global information space, building efforts in this area will bring undeniable benefits to both BRICS member states and partner countries of the group.

References

Ajder, H. (2019). Social Engineering and Sabotage: Why Deepfakes Pose An Unprecedented Threat To Businesses. In: Deeptrace. Retrieved June 21, 2022, from https://deeptracelabs.com/social-engineering-and-sabotage-why-deepfakes-pose-an-unprecedented-threat-to-businesses/.

Ajder, H., Patrini, G., Cavalli, F., & Cullen, L. (2019). The State of Deepfakes: Landscape, Threats, and Impact. In: The Register. Retrieved June 21, 2022, from https://regmedia.co.uk/2019/10/08/deepfake_report.pdf.

Alavi, M., & Achom, D. (2020). BJP Shared Deepfake Video on WhatsApp During Delhi Campaign. In: NDTV. Retrieved June 21, 2022, from https://www.ndtv.com/india-news/in-bjps-deepfake-video-shared-on-whatsapp-manoj-tiwari-speaks-in-2-languages-2182923.

Allen, A. (2018). Bots in Brazil: The Activity of Social Media Bots in Brazilian Elections. In: Wilson Center. Retrieved June 21, 2022, from https://www.wilsoncenter.org/blog-post/bots-brazil-the-activity-social-media-bots-brazilian-elections.

Anufrieva, L. (2020). BRICS: Legal nature and principles of cooperation. *Actual Problems of Russian Law, 1*(12), 123–133.

Arapova, E. (2016). Perspektivy jekonomicheskoj integracii v formate BRIKS (prospects for economic integration within BRICS). *Rossijskij vneshnejekonomicheskij vestnik (Russian Foreign Economic Bulletin), 2*, 1.

Austin, A. (2020). Latin America Under Threat of Cybercrime Amid Coronavirus. In: InSight Crime. Retrieved June 21, 2022, from https://insightcrime.org/news/analysis/threat-cyber-crime-coronavirus/.

Balashova, A. (2021). V "Cifrovuyu ekonomiku" vpishut bor'bu s dipfejkami i adaptivnyj kontent (The fight against deepfakes and adaptive content will be included in the "Digital Economy"). In: RBC. Retrieved June 22, 2022, from https://www.rbc.ru/technology_and_media/28/07/2021/610061f49a7947d4a5848b1f?from=from_main_6.

Baruah, A. (2020). AI Applications in the Top 4 Indian Banks. In: Emerj Artificial Intelligence Research. Retrieved June 21, 2022, from https://emerj.com/ai-sector-overviews/ai-applications-in-the-top-4-indian-banks/.

Bazarkina, D., & Pashentsev, E. (2020). Malicious use of artificial intelligence: New psychological security risks in BRICS countries. *Russia in Global Affairs, 18*, 154–177. https://doi.org/10.31278/1810-6374-2020-18-4-154-177

Bazarkina, D., & Pashentsev, E. (2019). Artificial intelligence and new threats to international psychological security. *Russia in Global Affairs, 1*(1). https://doi.org/10.31278/1810-6374-2019-17-1-147-170

BBC News. (2017). Google to 'derank' Russia Today and Sputnik. In: BBC News. Retrieved June 21, 2022, from https://www.bbc.com/news/technology-42065644.

BBC News. (2022). Will AI kill developing world growth? In: BBC News. Retrieved June 20, 2022, from https://www.bbc.com/news/business-47852589.

Belli, L. (2020). CyberBRICS: A multidimensional approach to cybersecurity for the BRICS. In L. Belli (Ed.), *CyberBRICS: Mapping cybersecurity frameworks in the BRICS* (pp. 17–57). FGV Direito Rio.

Bendett, S., & Kania, E. B. (2019). *A new Sino–Russian high-tech partnership. Authoritarian innovation in an era of great-power rivalry*. Australian Strategic Policy Institute, Barton.

Bhatt, S. (2018). How Indian startups gear up to take on the voice assistants of Apple, Amazon and Google. In: The Economic Times. Retrieved June 21, 2022, from https://economictimes.indiatimes.com/small-biz/startups/features/how-indian-startups-gear-up-to-take-on-the-voice-assistants-of-apple-amazon-and-google/articleshow/64044409.cms.

Biswas, P. (2022). Deepfakes, Crypto Scams on the Rise in India 2022. In: Digit. Retrieved June 23, 2022, from https://www.digit.in/features/crypto/deepfakes-crypto-scams-on-the-rise-in-india-2022-63740.html.

BRICS–Brasil. (2019). Enabling Framework for the Innovation BRICS Network ("iBRICS Network"). In: BRICS–Brasil. Retrieved June 22, 2022, from http://brics2019.itamaraty.gov.br/images/documentos/Enabling_Framework_iBRICS_Network__Final.pdf.

BRICS. (2015). VII BRICS Summit. Ufa Declaration (Ufa, the Russian Federation, 9 July 2015). In: BRICS Information Portal. Retrieved June 22, 2022, from http://infobrics.org/files/pdf/27.pdf.

BRICS. (2017). IX BRICS Summit. Xiamen Declaration (Xiamen, China, 4 September 2017). In: BRICS Young Scientist Forum. Retrieved June 23, 2022, from https://www.brics-ysf.org/sites/default/files/Publications/28912_Xiamen Declaratoin.pdf.

BRICS. (2018). X BRICS Summit. Johannesburg Declaration (Johannesburg, South Africa, 25 to 27 July 2018). In: BRICS India 2021. Retrieved June 22, 2022, from https://brics2021.gov.in/BRICSDocuments/2018/JOHANNESBURG-DECLARATION-2018.pdf.

BRICS. (2019). XI BRICS Summit. Brasília Declaration (Brasília, Brazil, 14 November 2019). In: BRICS India 2021. Retrieved June 22, 2022, from https://brics2021.gov.in/BRICSDocuments/2019/Braslia-Declaration-2019.pdf.

BRICS. (2022). XIV BRICS Summit. Beijing Declaration (Beijing, China, 23 June 2022). In: Ministry of External Affairs, Government of India. Retrieved June 24, 2022, from https://www.mea.gov.in/bilateral-documents.htm?dtl/35435/XIV+BRICS+Summit+Beijing+Declaration.

BRICS Information Portal. (2022). History of BRICS. In: BRICS Information Portal. Retrieved June 22, 2022, from http://infobrics.org/page/history-of-brics/.

BRICS Ministers of Foreign Affairs. (2022). BRICS Joint Statement on "Strengthen BRICS Solidarity and Cooperation, Respond to New Features and Challenges in International Situation." In: Ministério das Relações Exteriores. Retrieved June 22, 2022, from https://www.gov.br/mre/en/contact-us/press-area/press-releases/brics-joint-statement-on-201cstrengthen-brics-solidarity-and-cooperation-respond-to-new-features-and-challenges-in-international-situation201d.

Business Tech. (2019). How AI is being used in South Africa. In: Business Tech. Retrieved June 21, 2022, from https://businesstech.co.za/news/enterprise/322505/how-ai-is-being-used-in-south-africa/.

Butcher, N., Wilson-Strydom, M., & Baijnath, M. (2021). Artificial Intelligence in Sub-Saharan Africa.

Centre for Development of Advanced Computing (C-DAC). (2020). Annual Report 2018–2019. C-DAC, Bengaluru – Chennai – Hyderabad – Kolkata – Mohali – Mumbai – New Delhi – Noida – Pune – Silchar – Thiruvananthapuram.

Chakraborty, M. (2022). Artificial Intelligence: Growth and Development in India. In: Analytics Insight. Retrieved June 21, 2022, from https://www.analyticsinsight.net/artificial-intelligence-growth-and-development-in-india/.

Christopher, N. (2020). Deepfakes by BJP in Indian Delhi Election Campaign. In: Vice.com. Retrieved June 21, 2022, from https://www.vice.com/en/article/jgedjb/the-first-use-of-deepfakes-in-indian-election-by-bjp.

CNews. (2021). Kak v Rossii budut podderzhivat'sya proekty po sozdaniyu i obnaruzheniyu DeepFake (How Russia will support projects to create and detect Deepfake). In: CNews. Retrieved June 22, 2022, from https://www.cnews.ru/articles/2021-12-14_kak_v_rossii_budut_podderzhivatsya.

CyberBRICS. (2019). CyberBRICS: Building the Next Generation Internet, STEP by Step. In: CyberBRICS. Retrieved June 22, 2022, from https://cyberbrics.info/cyberbrics-building-the-next-generation-internet-step-by-step/.

CyberBRICS. (2021). Cybersecurity Convergence in the BRICS Countries. In: CyberBRICS. Retrieved June 3, 2022, from https://cyberbrics.info/cybersecurity-convergence-in-the-brics-countries/.

CyberBRICS. (2022). About us. In: CyberBRICS. Retrieved June 22, 2022, from https://cyberbrics.info/about-us/.
Dwolatzky, B., & Harris, M. (2021). South Africa's 4IR strategy: Huge gap between what's on the ground and what the Ramaphosa commission recommends. In: Daily Maverick. Retrieved June 3, 2022, from https://www.dailymaverick.co.za/article/2021-01-14-south-africas-4ir-strategy-huge-gap-between-whats-on-the-ground-and-what-the-ramaphosas-commission-recommends/.
EFE-EPA. (2019). South African president says USA jealous of Huawei. In: www.efe.com. Retrieved June 21, 2022, from https://www.efe.com/efe/english/business/south-african-president-says-usa-jealous-of-huawei/50000265-4016943.
Fadeeva, I. (2020). Assessment of the impact of disintegration manifestations in the BRICS on the economy of the group. Azimuth of Scientific Research: Economics and Administration. doi: https://doi.org/10.18611/2221-3279-2017-8-4-127-144.
Faggella, D. (2019). Artificial Intelligence in India—Opportunities, Risks, and Future Potential. In: Emerj Artificial Intelligence Research. Retrieved June 21, 2022, from https://emerj.com/ai-market-research/artificial-intelligence-in-india/.
Fedorov, K. (2018). Shoigu called on scientists to unite to work on artificial intelligence. In: Zvezda TV. Retrieved June 21, 2022, from https://tvzvezda.ru/news/201803141458-vp29.htm.
FGV/DAPP. (2018). Bots, Social Networks and Politics in Brazil. In: FGV DAPP. Retrieved June 21, 2022, from http://dapp.fgv.br/en/robots-social-networks-politics-fgv-dapp-study-points-illegitimate-interference-public-debate-web/.
Gaidamak, A. (2017). Mezhgosudarstvennaja integracija stran BRIKS na primere golosovanija v OON (interstate integration of the BRICS countries on the example of voting in the UN). *International Journal of Humanities and Natural Sciences, 3*, 1.
Gandharv, K. (2022). Top three AI initiatives for Indian defence forces in 2022. In: Indiaai.gov.in. Retrieved June 21, 2022, from https://indiaai.gov.in/article/top-three-ai-initiatives-for-indian-defence-forces-in-2022.
Gavrilyuk, A., & Korolyov, N. (2022). Grazhdan zashchityat ot robotov (Citizens will be protected from robots). In: Kommersant. Retrieved June 22, 2022, from https://www.kommersant.ru/doc/5173457.
Godoy, E. (2018). Automated Digital Tools Threaten Political Campaigns in Latin America. In: Inter Press Service. Retrieved June 21, 2022, from https://www.ipsnews.net/2018/02/automated-digital-tools-threaten-political-campaigns-latin-america/.
GoodFirms. (2022). Top Artificial Intelligence Companies in South Africa 2022. In: GoodFirms. Retrieved June 3, 2022, from https://www.goodfirms.co/artificial-intelligence/south-africa.
Hao, K. (2019). The biggest threat of deepfakes isn't the deepfakes themselves. In: MIT Technology Review. Retrieved June 21, 2022, from https://www.technolo-

gyreview.com/2019/10/10/132667/the-biggest-threat-of-deepfakes-isnt-the-deepfakes-themselves/.
Hao, K. (2020). Deepfake Putin is here to warn Americans about their self-inflicted doom. In: MIT Technology Review. Retrieved June 22, 2022, from https://www.technologyreview.com/2020/09/29/1009098/ai-deepfake-putin-kim-jong-un-us-election/.
Huawei. (2020). South Africa's Rain and Huawei Build the First 5G Transport Networks Using OXC+200G Solution. In: Huawei. Retrieved April 22, 2020, from https://www.huawei.com/en/press-events/news/2020/2/5g-transport-networks-oxc-200g-solution.
Independent. (2020). Watch: Debate raging on link between 5G technology, coronavirus pandemic. In: Independent Online (IOL). Retrieved April 22, 2020, from https://www.iol.co.za/capetimes/news/watch-debate-raging-on-link-between-5g-technology-coronavirus-pandemic-45124913.
Interfax. (2020). The State Duma approved a special legal regime for the development of artificial intelligence for Moscow. In: Interfax. Retrieved June 21, 2022, from https://www.interfax.ru/russia/704092.
IXBT.com. (2022). V Rossii predstavili robosobaku s granatomyotom (In Russia, a robot dog with a grenade launcher was introduced). In: IXBT.com. Retrieved September 1, 2022, from https://www.ixbt.com/news/2022/08/15/v-rossii-predstavili-robosobaku-s-granatometom.html.
Jaiman, A. (2020). Deepfake harms and threat modeling. In: Towards Data Science. Retrieved June 24, 2022, from https://towardsdatascience.com/deepfakes-harms-and-threat-modeling-c09cbe0b7883.
Kahla, C. (2020). Social media platforms need to take a stand against cyberbullying. In: The South African. Retrieved June 3, 2022, from https://www.thesouthafrican.com/technology/social-media-stand-against-cyberbullying/.
Krishnan, A. (2018). India, China launch first joint projects in Big Data, AI. In: India Today. Retrieved June 22, 2022, from https://www.indiatoday.in/india/story/india-china-launch-first-joint-projects-in-big-data-ai-1242989-2018-05-27.
Less, L., & Umanah, T. (2020). Deepfakery: Combating illegal content, inaccurate information and fake news. In: Daily Maverick. Retrieved June 3, 2022, from https://www.dailymaverick.co.za/article/2020-09-24-deepfakery-combating-illegal-content-inaccurate-information-and-fake-news/.
Ma, S. (2019). BRICS cooperation continues with new institutional branch. In: China Daily. Retrieved June 22, 2022, from https://global.chinadaily.com.cn/a/201908/06/WS5d49395ea310cf3e3556430a.html.
Maree, A. (2021). South Africa: Leaks and deepfakes shaping the race for ANC presidency. In: The Africa Report. Retrieved June 3, 2022, from https://www.theafricareport.com/80648/south-africa-leaks-and-deepfakes-shaping-the-race-for-anc-presidency/.

Mari, A. (2022). Brazil stagnant in tech investments and innovation. In: ZDNet. Retrieved June 21, 2022, from https://www.zdnet.com/article/brazil-stagnant-in-tech-investments-and-innovation/.

Mashinini, N. (2021). Deepfakes in Cybercrimes. In: Player FM. Retrieved June 3, 2022, from https://player.fm/series/image-rights-bynmashinini/deepfakes-in-cybercrimes.

Mihindukulasuriya, R. (2018). Sobha Sajju: How technology helped this Kerala mother of 3 beat fake nude video. In: The Print. Retrieved June 21, 2022, from https://theprint.in/india/governance/sobha-sajju-how-technology-helped-this-kerala-mother-of-3-beat-fake-nude-video/159671/.

Mihindukulasuriya, R. (2020). Why the Manoj Tiwari deepfakes should have India deeply worried. In: The Print. Retrieved June 21, 2022, from https://theprint.in/tech/why-the-manoj-tiwari-deepfakes-should-have-india-deeply-worried/372389/.

Mordor Intelligence. (2019). Latin American Cybersecurity Market 2022–27 - Industry Share, Size, Growth. In: Mordor Intelligence. Retrieved June 21, 2022, from https://www.mordorintelligence.com/industry-reports/latin-america-cyber-security-market.

Moskva 24. (2020). Moscow uses artificial intelligence to diagnose COVID-19. In: Moskva 24. Retrieved June 21, 2022, from https://www.m24.ru/news/obshchestvo/12052020/117369.

Nagaraj, K. (2021). South Africa Artificial Intelligence: From Rands to Riches: South Africa's AI Potential. In: Rebellion Research. Retrieved June 21, 2022, from https://www.rebellionresearch.com/south-africa-artificial-intelligence.

National Critical Information Infrastructure Protection Centre. (2020). Newsletter. April. National Critical Information Infrastructure Protection Centre (part of the National Technical Research Organisation), New Delhi.

NTI. (2022). NTI competence centre of AI. In: National Technology Initiative. Retrieved June 21, 2022, from https://nti2035.ru/technology/competence_centers/mipt.php.

OpIndia. (2022). "Removed accounts for manipulation and spam," Twitter says after Rahul Gandhi loses bot followers. In: OpIndia. Retrieved June 21, 2022, from https://www.opindia.com/2022/01/removed-accounts-for-manipulation-and-spam-twitter-says-after-rahul-gandhi-loses-followers/.

PC4IR. (2020). Report of the Presidential Commission on the 4th Industrial Revolution. In: South African Government. Retrieved June 21, 2022, from https://www.gov.za/documents/report-presidential-commission-4th-industrial-revolution-23-oct-2020-0000.

Pindrop. (2020). Voice Intelligence & Security Report. A review of fraud, the future of voice, and the impact to customer service channels. Revised for 2020 including updated data. Pindrop, Atlanta.

President of the Russian Federation. (2019a). Decree of 10.10.2019 No. 490 "On the development of artificial intelligence in the Russian Federation." In: Official

Legal Information Portal. Retrieved June 21, 2022, from http://publication.pravo.gov.ru/Document/View/0001201910110003.

President of the Russian Federation. (2019b). Federal Law No. 123-FZ of 24.04.2020 "On conducting an experiment to establish special regulation in order to create the necessary conditions for the development and implementation of artificial intelligence technologies in the subject of the Russian Federation—the Federal City of Moscow and amending articles 6 and 10 of the Federal law 'On personal data.'" In: Official Legal Information Portal. Retrieved June 21, 2022, from http://publication.pravo.gov.ru/Document/View/0001202004240030?index=0.

President of the Russian Federation. (2020). Decree of 10.10.2019 No. 490 "On the development of artificial intelligence in the Russian Federation." In: Official Legal Information Portal. Retrieved June 21, 2022, from http://publication.pravo.gov.ru/Document/View/0001201910110003.

Ramaphosa, C. (2020). A national strategy for harnessing the Fourth Industrial Revolution: The case of South Africa. In: Brookings. Retrieved June 3, 2022, from https://www.brookings.edu/blog/africa-in-focus/2020/01/10/a-national-strategy-for-harnessing-the-fourth-industrial-revolution-the-case-of-south-africa/.

Rebellion Research. (2021). Brazil AI: Brazil Artificial Intelligence Strategy. In: Rebellion Research. Retrieved June 21, 2022, from https://www.rebellionresearch.com/brazil-artificial-intelligence-strategy.

Rebelo, K. (2019). India Is Teeming With "Cheapfakes," Deepfakes Could Make It Worse. In: Boomlive.in. Retrieved June 21, 2022, from https://www.boomlive.in/india-is-teeming-with-cheapfakes-deepfakes-could-make-it-worse/.

RIA Katyusha. (2020). Hello, Chinese-style electronic concentration camp: Sobyanin wants to put Muscovites under the control of artificial intelligence. In: RIA Katyusha. Retrieved June 21, 2022, from http://katyusha.org/view?id=14044.

RIA Novosti. (2017). Putin: the leader in the field of artificial intelligence will become the ruler of the world. In: RIA Novosti. Retrieved June 21, 2022, from https://ria.ru/20170901/1501566046.html.

Rossiyskaya gazeta. (2022). Intellekt bez granic: kto i zachem hochet regulirovat' II (Intelligence without Borders: Who wants to regulate AI and Why). In: Rossiyskaya gazeta (Russian Newspaper). Retrieved June 22, 2022, from https://rg.ru/2022/05/06/intellekt-bez-granic-kto-i-zachem-hochet-regulirovat-ii.html.

RT. (2017). Google will "de-rank" RT articles to make them harder to find—Eric Schmidt. In: RT International. Retrieved June 21, 2022, from https://www.rt.com/news/410444-google-alphabet-derank-rt/.

Seth, T. (2022). Deepfakes—A Threat to Facial Recognition Technology. In: IIPRD Blog - Intellectual Property Discussions. Retrieved June 21, 2022, from https://iiprd.wordpress.com/2022/02/22/deepfakes-a-threat-to-facial-recognition-technology/.

Sharma, S. (2018). Desi Deepfakes are already a thing. Brace yourself for AI-powered disinfo. In: Factor Daily. Retrieved June 21, 2022, from https://archive.factor-daily.com/deepfakes-india/.

Shashidharan, K. (2021). The threat of deepfakes. In: The Hindu. Retrieved June 21, 2022, from https://www.thehindu.com/opinion/op-ed/the-threat-of-deepfakes/article33612423.ece.

Stepanova, Y. (2020). Parents have fallen like children. Online fraudsters took advantage of the demand for benefits. In: Kommersant. Retrieved June 21, 2022, from https://www.kommersant.ru/doc/4343398.

Stepanova, Y., & Tishina, Y. (2021). Sajty s pometkoj "fishing" (Sites marked "phishing"). In: Kommersant. Retrieved June 22, 2022, from https://www.kommersant.ru/doc/4653039.

Takhumova, O. (2021). Osnovnye napravlenija sotrudnichestva Rossii v ramkah integracionnoj gruppirovki BRIKS (The main direction of Russia's cooperation within the framework of the BRICS integration group). In: Rossija i mirovoe soobshhestvo pered vyzovami nestabil'nosti ekonomicheskih i pravovyh sistem. Sbornik statej Mezhdunarodnoj nauchno-prakticheskoj konferencii 11 oktjabrja 2017 (Russia and the world community are facing the challenges of unstable economic and legal systems. Collection of articles of the International Scientific and Practical Conference October 11, 2017), 1st ed. Aeterna, Ufa, pp. 231–233.

TASS. (2019). Russia is ready to cooperate with India in the field of cybersecurity and artificial intelligence. In: TASS. Retrieved June 22, 2022, from https://tass.ru/ekonomika/6142174.

TASS. (2021). Eksperty: s fishingovymi atakami v 2021 godu stolknulis' 45% rossiyan (Experts: 45% of Russians faced phishing attacks in 2021). In: TASS. Retrieved June 22, 2022, from https://tass.ru/ekonomika/13105631.

Thaker, A. (2019). Automated bots manipulated Twitter traffic before Narendra Modi's visit to Tamil Nadu: US think-tank. In: Scroll.in. Retrieved June 23, 2022, from https://scroll.in/article/919445/automated-bots-manipulated-twitter-traffic-before-narendra-modis-visit-to-tamil-nadu-us-think-tank.

The Presidency, Republic of South Africa. (2019). President appoints Commission on Fourth Industrial Revolution. In: The Presidency. Retrieved June 3, 2022, from https://thepresidency.gov.za/press-statements/president-appoints-commission-fourth-industrial-revolution.

The Presidency, Republic of South Africa (2021) Act No. 19 of 2020: Cybercrimes Act, 2020. Government Gazette, Retrieved June 3, 2022, from https://cyberbrics.info/wp-content/uploads/2021/06/44651gon324.pdf.

The Spamhaus Project. (2022). The Top 10 Worst Botnet Countries. In: Spamhaus.org. Retrieved June 21, 2022, from https://www.spamhaus.org/statistics/botnet-cc/.

Thomas, D. (2020). Deepfakes: A threat to democracy or just a bit of fun? In: BBC News. Retrieved June 21, 2022, from https://www.bbc.com/news/business-51204954.

TV BRICS. (2022). V Rossii razvivaetsya rynok robosobachestva (Robotic dog market develops in Russia). In: TV BRICS. Retrieved June 23, 2022, from https://tvbrics.com/news/v-rossii-razvivaetsya-rynok-robosobachestva/.
Van den Berg, A. (2018). Hoe kunsmatige intelligensie die werkwêreld gaan verander (How artificial intelligence will change the world of work). In: Jou Werk / Solidariteit Wêreld. Retrieved June 21, 2022, from https://jouwerk.solidariteit.co.za/hoe-kunsmatige-intelligensie-die-werkwereld-gaan-verander/.
Yifan, S. (2019). SCO and BRICS: Prospects of Eurasian integration with the participation of China and Russia. *Bulletin of the Moscow State Regional University (History and Political Science)*, 2, 222–228. https://doi.org/10.22363/23130660.2017.17.3.469482

13

The Threats and Current Practices of Malicious Use of Artificial Intelligence in Psychological Security in China

Darya Bazarkina, Ekaterina A. Mikhalevich, Evgeny Pashentsev, and Daria Matyashova

Introduction

The Chinese case is of interest for several reasons. First, the country's growing leadership in the field of AI has not only generated more malicious use of artificial intelligence (MUAI) threats for China, but also created greater opportunities to counter them. Second, the planned nature of the Chinese economy—a developed system of public–private partnerships, including in the field of cybersecurity—and the largest population in the world supply colossal amounts of big data for AI training make China's experience in the fight against MUAI truly unique.

D. Bazarkina (✉)
Department of European Integration Research, Institute of Europe of the Russian Academy of Sciences, Moscow, Russia
e-mail: bazarkina-icspsc@yandex.ru

E. A. Mikhalevich • D. Matyashova
School of International Relations, St. Petersburg State University, St Petersburg, Russia
e-mail: ekaterina_mikhalevich@mail.ru; dasham0708@mail.ru

E. Pashentsev
Diplomatic Academy of the Ministry of Foreign Affairs of the Russian Federation, Moscow, Russia
e-mail: icspsc@mail.ru

This chapter primarily uses systemic, comparative, and scenario analyses. To classify MUAI threats, a three-level scheme of psychological security threats proposed by Evgeny Pashentsev was used (see chapter 2 "General Content and Possible Threat Classifications of the Malicious Use of Artificial Intelligence to Psychological Security" of this handbook). Moreover, we also made use of several groups of primary and secondary sources for preparing this chapter.

The term "MUAI" is used in China in the context of military threats (Wang, 2019). Chinese media has noted the contribution of the two authors of this chapter in highlighting MUAI threats to psychological security as an independent subject of study (Dong, 2019). Chinese authorities see the need to protect their national interests, including in terms of cyberspace security, wherein the problem of manipulating the information agenda in the international information field is obvious. Among the official Chinese sources on combating the MUAI, the Chinese Cyber Security Law (which came into force on June 1, 2017) stands out (Baidu, 2017). It regulates the actions of network product and service providers in terms of collecting, storing, and processing user data, and determines the procedures and specifics for securing information infrastructure in strategically important industries. This law is the basis for other regulatory legal acts designed to ensure various aspects of information security and are handled by a number of government departments: the Cyberspace Administration of China, the Central Cyberspace Affairs Commission, the Cyberspace Administration of China, and the Ministry of Industry and Information Technology, among others. The sources also include statements and memorandums of Chinese companies, the so-called IT giants (Alibaba, WeChat, Baidu), actively involved (at the suggestion of PRC authorities) in the processes of ensuring psychological security (Baidu, 2019).

The existing literature often contains reviews, comments, and in-depth analyses of the relevant regulatory legal acts of the PRC (Baike Baidu, 2022), papers authored by purely technical specialists (Jiang Tao, 2021), as well as studies that assess AI problems in the context of social and military issues (see, e.g., Dong, 2017a, b, 2018a, 2018b). China is actively conducting research in the field of cyberpsychology (Li et al., 2018, 2022; Yu et al., 2021; Xu et al., 2020). The emergence in recent years of more detailed, innovative works at the junction of IT and the humanities evidences the relevance and interest of Chinese scientists in studying this topic (Zhang, 2021; Dong & Zhu, 2021; Chen & Lu, 2021).

An important section of the literature is comprised of publications on the current state and prospects for AI development in China. Researchers in different countries have paid a significant amount of attention to this range of problems. Russian sources on China's AI development can be divided into three groups: economically oriented, disputing the prospects of AI market growth in accordance with global tendencies (Reshetnikova et al., 2021; Primshic & Golubev, 2019); strategically oriented, defining the political goals the PRC seeks to realize through AI development (Komissina, 2019; Antipova & Tlyashev, 2021; Kamennov, 2020); and normative-oriented, discussing the issues of privacy and legal frameworks under the influence of digital transformations (Epshteyn & Chistyakova, 2020; Kutejnikov et al., 2022). The University of Stanford has provided a comprehensive comparative review of the complex dynamics of AI research competition and cooperation between the two current industry leaders, namely the US and China (Stanford University, 2022). The particular technical innovations, however, are not detached to particular companies. Indeed, Schoenmakers has expanded the field by examining the hardware, and the academic and engineering specialists market, as well as by providing a normative initiatives analysis (O'Meara, 2019). The economically based approach, with its strong focus on finance distribution, market geography and demography, and industry leaders, has been presented by the Daxue Consulting Group (2020), which was partly repeated by the Plaintex Group's research covering the balance between start-ups and big tech in Chinese AI development (Long & Luo, 2022). European countries, such as Germany, for instance, have also published research on China's AI development (e.g., Gutting, 2020; Auge & Gutting, 2021). However, some of this research seem rather biased, in that it dismisses Chinese AI as being subordinate to repressive goals (see, e.g., Suter, 2020).

This chapter seeks to assess MUAI threats in China and the response of the Chinese government in the field of psychological security. To further our understanding of this situation, it is necessary to first consider the level of AI development in the country, as well as the conflict potential of the political conditions that have developed around China.

Current Level of AI Development and Vulnerabilities in Xinjiang, Taiwan, and Hong Kong as a Ground for Malicious Use of Artificial Intelligence in China

When discussing AI in China, it is of the utmost importance to differentiate between economic (financial and industrial), analytical (academic), and normative dimensions of its development. This is significant for three main reasons. Firstly, for Chinese economic prosperity regarding the place of advanced ICT in global production and their role in global supply chains. Secondly, for the favorable image of the "AI superpower," which attracts investors to both transform the national and global economy—for example, by enhancing the internet finance industry (Han, 2019) and developing Chinese-centered global integration institutions promoting infrastructural projects (Leksutina, 2018), and promoting Chinese soft power among highly educated, technically advanced circles (e.g., IT and STEM specialists). Thirdly, it is significant for a coherent vision of AI's influence on society and its "human-dimension" security aspects, including socioeconomic and psychological security.

The financial domain of AI development and application in the PRC is characterized by a steady and stable rise of AI companies' investments and investment value, a growing market of AI technologies, and a strong core of Chinese-originated transnational companies developing and promoting their use among consumers. According to the Daxue Consulting report, "The AI Ecosystem in China 2020," the investment value in China's AI industry reached 131.1 billion RMB in 2018, increasing by roughly 67.7 billion RMB compared to 2017 (Daxue Consulting, 2020). The comparable quantitative markers were demonstrated by the market size with augmentation of approximately 27.5 billion RMB between 2017 (31.8 billion RMB) and 2018 (59.3 billion RMB) (Slotta, 2022). The Chinese AI market demonstrated sustainable growth, even after the COVID-19-induced global recession (the market size reached 93.6, 128, and 196.3 billion RMB in 2019, 2020, and 2021, respectively; Slotta, 2022). This growth seems connected to a global impetus for digitalization, and a concentration of AI-oriented investment in such big-tech companies as iFlytek, Baidu, and Xiaomi (to name but a few). On the one hand, this demonstrates positive prospects for AI investments in relating sectors. However, on the other, it showcases the risks of market congestion after exhaustion of the low base effect in the rising industry. The factor of big-tech investment concentration is, however, partly counterbalanced by the sheer volume of AI startups. Indeed, in 2021, there were 1730 AI startups in China (Tracxn.com, 2022).

The major industrial characteristics of China's AI market and development are focused on industrial robotics development and production (in 2018 it encountered 71% of AI robots produced in China, with their sales stably outpacing ones of service robots). These features characterize China's AI development as an extension of the "world factory" economic model and, more importantly for the global stage, as a strategy relying on the diminishing marginal utility and—in the long-term—reduced profitability since industrial robots are becoming cheaper and more accessible, thereby losing the feature of competitive advantage in the medium term. In particular, the median price of robotic arms has decreased by 46.2% in the past five years—from $42,000 per arm in 2017 to $22,600 in 2021 (Stanford University, 2022). The growing number of smartphone users as a data source and a basis for non-industrially oriented data-learning and growing financial capacity of the population are, however, able to balance this given disproportion. The other challenging tendency is an unequal geographic distribution of industrial robots' consumption, which has resulted in industries having been concentrated on the coastline. In the near future, this may well provoke the emergence of the gap between "productive" and "non-productive" regions, and the corresponding socioeconomic aftermaths which follow.

The analytical dimension of AI—in which we can include the number of published articles and industrial innovations developed by practicing specialists—is characterized by a surge of both of these variables, which serve to maintain both rapidity and sustainability, and demonstrate quantitative growth. In particular, China's global share of AI research papers has vaulted from 4.26% (1086) in 1997 to 27.68% in 2017 (37,343), surpassing any other country in the world. Similarly, in terms of AI-related patents, China is also currently leading the world, filing 51.69% of the world's AI patents and being granted about 6%, while the shares of the EU and the UK and the US count 3.89% and 16.92%, respectively (Li et al., 2021; Stanford University, 2022). These research activities are not directed at reaching exclusive technical advantages for two reasons: first, due to the innovative character of the industry and the risks of reaching the technological barrier; second, because of the overt character of published AI research and data. A good indicator is a share of Chinese patents granted: it lags not only behind the share of filled ones (5.9%), but also behind the respective shares of the EU and the UK and the US (7.56% and 39.59%). The more important goal lies in the field of international academic cooperation: according to the 2022 AI Index Report, the US and China had the greatest number of cross-country collaborations in AI publications from 2010 to 2021, increasing fivefold since 2010 (Stanford University, 2022). Moreover, both China and the US are also leaders in cooperation with the UK and Australia.

For many years, Chinese industry lagged behind the US in the design of computing chips for supporting advanced AI systems, and its proportion of researchers in this area was approximately three times smaller (O'Meara, 2019). However, economic rivalry with the US, in which measures were taken to oust the computer giant Huawei from the American and European markets (Bazarkina, 2022), incentivized the accelerated development of semiconductor production. Positive dynamics in the production of chips was noted in China even despite the COVID-19 pandemic. In 2016, China's semiconductor device sales were worth $13 billion (3.8% of the global total). However, in 2020, "the Chinese semiconductor industry registered an unprecedented annual growth rate of 30.6% to reach $39.8 billion in total annual sales... The jump in growth helped China capture 9% of the global semiconductor market in 2020, surpassing Taiwan for two consecutive years and closely following Japan and the EU, which each took 10% of market share" (Semiconductor Industry Association, 2022). If this trend continues, the Chinese semiconductor industry could generate $116 billion in annual revenue by 2024 (17.4% of the global market share) which would place China as the third-largest producer, after the US and South Korea (Semiconductor Industry Association, 2022). China is currently not yet fully switched to import substitutions in the production of chips. In May 2021, Chinese manufacturers produced 29.9 billion logic components. In the first six months of the same year, Chinese makers produced 171.2 billion chips or 30.8 billion chips per month. However, China imported 51.9 billion semiconductors in June 2021, meaning that the country could manufacture roughly 37% of its semiconductor needs. At the same time, China needs equipment to produce the advanced processors used in the AI industry (Shilov, 2021). However, according to Wen Xiaojun, the director of the China Electronics and Information Industry Development Research Institute, China-made 14nm chips could be in mass production by the end of 2022 (Tang, 2021). This leads us to conclude that the Chinese government's ambitious plans to bring the country to a leading position in advanced technologies are firmly rooted in reality. However, it is precisely this circumstance that explains the various measures taken by the US, up to and including sanctions against relevant industries in China, in order to curb their development. The US government, under Donald Trump and his successor Joe Biden, placed restrictions on Chinese enterprises' financing in the US, and also stopped Americans from investing in Chinese enterprises. According to Joseph Yam Chi-kwong, the former chief executive of the Hong Kong Monetary Authority (HKMA; the region's de facto central bank), this strategy would only serve to undermine the US dollar's status as the world's reserve currency (Yiu, 2022).

The Chinese AI industry involves active public–private partnerships. The Ministry of Science and Technology of the People's Republic of China (MoST) appointed the four largest Chinese AI companies (Baidu, Alibaba, Tencent, and iFlytek) to "lead the development of national AI innovation platforms in self-driving cars, smart cities, computer vision for medical diagnosis, and voice intelligence, respectively" (Faggella, 2019). The industries, technologies, and AI products that China is especially focusing on include autonomous vehicles, service robots, unmanned aerial vehicles, image analysis-based medical diagnostic systems, video image identification systems, voice interaction, translation systems, and AI products for smart homes (Faggella, 2019). According to a white paper on AI unicorns (startups whose valuation rises to a billion dollars or more in a short period of time), published by the AI ERA, by the end of March 2019, there were 50 such companies in China with a total worth 3.5 trillion RMB (approximately 397 billion EUR) (China Innovation Funding, 2019). Chinese AI unicorns dominated automotive transportation and corporate services (15 and 13 companies, respectively, 30% and 26% of the total). They were followed by startups involved in financial services, entertainment, and equipment (6, 5, and 4 companies, respectively). The white paper also identified five major trends that characterize the current AI industry in China: (1) AI-based autonomous driving technologies will become increasingly central to China's automotive industry; (2) Chinese enterprises will increasingly need AI-based services (e.g., cloud computing, big data processing); (3) AI-based financial services will lead to a new wave of financial reforms; (4) AI hardware is currently inseparable from the Internet of Things (IoT); and (5) AI education will receive the most funding and investment. Data from October 2021 shows that, of the total of 45 AI unicorns globally, China has the largest share, with 19 such firms (collectively valued at $43.5bn) headquartered in the country (GlobalData, 2021). China is leading in computer vision and facial recognition via such startups as SenseTime, Cloudwalk, Megvii, and Yitu Technology (so-called Chinese AI dragons).

According to Kai-Fu Lee, former president of Google China, China is also leading the world in AI adoption and value creation through its widespread use in a broad range of applications and industries. China's big advantage remains its population, which creates the world's largest database of big data (on which AI is trained). The use of cash and credit cards has virtually disappeared in China, with mobile payments being used instead. The WeChat application, developed by Tencent, combines a social network with a payment system, and, in some cases, a WeChat profile can be used as a passport (Knowledge at Wharton, 2018). However, while such applications are convenient, user-friendly, and provide AI with ample data, they also pose serious risks. All personal data is hosted on one platform, which could become a target of MUAI.

The Chinese government is supporting AI by building cities designed for autonomous vehicles. One layer of roads in such cities is designed for pedestrians and the second for cars, thereby limiting serious traffic accidents. Sensors are placed on highways to ensure vehicle autonomy (Knowledge at Wharton, 2018). Only the state can afford to build cities and highways, and the Chinese model is based on the close connection of science, production, and technology implementation, with the support of the country's leadership. There is an increase in the number of autonomous taxis, some of which are provided through public–private partnerships. Autonomous vehicle companies "have also dabbled into areas that are quicker to scale, such as self-driving trucks, goods-hauling vans and city buses, though robotaxis remain their focus in the long run" (Liao, 2022).

In 2020, internet company Baidu deployed its Apollo robotaxis in three cities in China, the demand for which was greatly increased by the COVID-19 pandemic (Harper, 2020). In June 2019, Baidu received 45 people transportation test licenses from Changsha Municipal Government. On September 26, the Changsha open road intelligent driving demonstration zone was officially opened. Since then, over 10,000 safe passenger trips have been made in the area by the Apollo robotaxis (Grigorian, 2020). In February 2020, the Chinese government released an intelligent vehicle development plan to accelerate the mass production of high-quality autonomous vehicles by 2025 (Harper, 2020). In a revolutionary move, Beijing city authorities authorized two companies (Apollo Go and Baidu's Pony.ai) to remove the safety driver for part of their robotaxi business in a suburban part of the city: "The cars will still need a staff member to sit inside, but not necessarily in the driver's seat anymore" (Cheng, 2022a). While US company GM Cruise can only operate its self-driving robotaxis in San Francisco at night, Beijing's latest easing of restrictions allows the almost autonomous self-driving robot taxis to operate during the day. Not only does this testify to the great success of the Chinese AI industry, but it also creates areas of discussion (and psychological manipulation) on the topics of the accident rate of robotic vehicles or the problems of the mass dismissal of human drivers. These issues require the analysis of scenarios of threats to psychological security of the first and second levels.

The regulatory dimension includes a multi-targeted set of norms and ethical charters aimed at both stimulating research and AI-related economic sectors, and taking a role in new international regimes on cyber and psychological security. The coherent vision of AI and its socially transformative role has been explained in the PRC's "New Generation Artificial Intelligence Development Plan (新一代人工智能发展规划)," which was developed for making China the AI world leader by 2030 (Roberts et al., 2020). Local regulations are currently broadening the profile and responsibilities of the government agencies involved in coordinating AI usage in the market and media—notably, in accordance with the new Internet Information Service Algorithmic Recommendation Management Provisions, the administering authorities included not only the Cyberspace Administration of China (CAC), but also the Ministry of Industry and Information Technology, the Ministry of Public Security, and the State Administration for Market Regulation (SAMR). These institutions are key to implementing the government's active anti-monopoly regulation of AI-developers.

The ethical regulation of AI has been reflected and broadened in "Governance Principles for Responsible AI" (Laskai & Webster, 2019) and "Ethical Specifications of Next-Generation Artificial Intelligence" (Calvi, 2021). Both of these codes demonstrate a strong social, equal, and algorithmic transparency orientation, and partly correlate with concepts of sustainability concepts, thus making them appear similar to the EU's latest cybersecurity initiatives. Accordingly, the ethical regulation of AI has become an additional instrument for global AI standards, integration, and raising cooperation.

However, on the international level, these tendencies are mainly reflected through intensive competition. The principal axis of this competition is Sino–American, with US-based transnational companies becoming the market and research competitors of their Chinese counterparts. Moreover, market competition has certain ramifications for academia and researchers. This can be seen in the Plaintext Group report prepared by Chinese specialists on the basis of 2013–2019 data, where it was predicted that China would try to close its R&D gap with the US through both intensifying industrial-based research, and raising a higher profile in top AI conferences at the government-, company-, and individual-level (Long & Luo, 2022). This prognosis became a reality in 2021–2022, with the US holding a dominant lead among major AI powers in the number of AI conferences and repository citations, despite Chinese activity in AI-related conferences and journal publications outnumbering those of the US in terms of absolute numbers (Stanford University, 2022).

While research competition is generally beneficial for the AI industry, the political dimension of said competition is prone to provoke disruptive trends in AI applications—the malicious use of information and psychological operations, in particular. The conflicts in and around Taiwan, Hong Kong, and Xinjiang foster such operations.

The international situation around Taiwan is characterized by its active securitization by the US and its allies (primarily Japan) in the context of the "Chinese threat" to the island's regime (democracy in the framework of the "One country, two systems" being promoted by the Chinese officials in the relations with Taiwan) and, thus, in the context of internal security. The securitization reflects itself not in symbolic steps, such as financing maps depicting Taiwan as separate to the PRC or presenting Taiwan as its own entity in the (US-led) Summit for Democracy (Berezhnaya, 2021). Considering the strategic competition between the US and China, and the existence of the "hard power" securitization domain in terms of strategic dialogues bypassing the latter (e.g., trilateral US–Japanese–Taiwanese dialogue; Chen, 2021a) and growing sales of weapons to Taiwan from the US (Martina & Brunnstrom, 2022), the analogical steps influencing the images of Taiwan or China, or Taiwan–Chinese relations, can deeply disrupt regional security through the actions of both state and non-state actors. The operations involving AI use have gained increased significance due to their potential to rapidly spread information across the globe, as well as to manipulate existing misinterpretations through deepfakes, automatically generated texts, social media algorithms, manipulations, and so forth. In terms of domestic politics, the growing political polarization due to the continuing dissatisfaction caused by stagnating wages and high youth unemployment (while the general unemployment level in 2019 was 3.7%, it reached around 4.2% in 2020 and 4.76% in the mid-2021; Trading Economics, 2022) have undermined the Taiwanese people's trust in local authorities, making them more vulnerable to psychological attacks and manipulations aimed at deepening polarization.

The situation in Hong Kong has been primarily determined by the mainland's imposition of electoral reform designed to limit any opposition to the CPC in the Legislative Council (Lau & Shui-yin, 2021). The opposition (the "Pro-democracy camp," 民主派) stands for preserving the special status (primarily, separate legal system) as a "One country, two systems" model, which has provoked the mainland into the securitization of the region. On the international level, the situation is reflected by the deeply conflictual representation of mainland China–Hong Kong relations in the media, which raises threats of provocations. The other important international aspect relates to the mutual imposition of Sino–American sanctions. The number of sanctions is gradually growing (U.S. Department of the Treasury, 2022; BBC News, 2021) which has deepened the conflict on both levels (Sino–American and mainland China–Hong Kong), and increased the motivation for using communication instruments to undermine the rival's international image.

China's psychological security may be threatened by the MUAI in connection with the recruitment carried out among the country's citizens by terrorist organizations, including in the Xinjiang Uygur Autonomous Region. In 2014–2015, 300 Chinese citizens, members of the country's Uyghur ethnic group, traveled to the Middle East to join the so-called Islamic State (IS) (Minter, 2015). China was declared an adversary state in IS propaganda publications, *Dabiq* and *Rumiya* (Lakomy, 2021, p. 166), and remains so at present. On October 8, 2021, a suicide bomber struck a Shiite mosque in Afghanistan's Kunduz province. The IS' affiliate in Afghanistan, known as Islamic State Khorasan (ISK), claimed responsibility for this attack via an online propaganda statement and identified the bomber as "Muhammad al-Uyghuri," saying the assault targeted both Shiites and the Taliban government for its purported willingness to deport Uyghurs from Afghanistan to China (Soliev, 2021). Like other terrorist organizations, IS actively uses bots and the specifics of social network algorithms (among other tools) to promote its agenda, and Chinese remains one of the organization's propaganda languages. All of these factors form the background to the US' removal of the East Turkestan Islamic Movement (ETIM)—which Beijing has repeatedly blamed for violent acts in Xinjiang and elsewhere, from its list of terror groups—amplify the terrorist threat of MUAI against Chinese citizens and leadership.

Therefore, the rapid development of AI in China, which creates enormous opportunities for social progress, is taking place against the backdrop of a number of unresolved contradictions that are intensifying growing geopolitical tensions. In order to identify trends in which MUAI threats may both increase and countermeasures can be taken, it is important to analyze the actual cases of the MUAI in the country.

Current and Future Malicious Use of Artificial Intelligence Threats in China, and Their Impact on Society's Psychological Security

Chinese researchers are actively studying MUAI threats—especially those related to the psychological sphere. As such, analysts from Tsinghua University have highlighted a wide range of threats associated with the MUAI, and have especially indicated that virtual online spaces facilitate the storage, analysis, and exchange of information (e.g., identification data, medical information, credit records, information about location and movement) which can possibly be hacked. However, at the same time, this makes it difficult to determine the causes and extent of leaks of such data. An open industry ecosystem with built-in AI would make it difficult to regulate a wide variety of areas. The relationship between man and machine will change dramatically as their interactions become more complex (China Institute for Science and Technology Policy at Tsinghua University, 2018, p. 94). From the standpoint of psychological security, it is worth paying attention to such conditions that cannot but affect the human psyche, such as "blurring the boundaries of time and space," as well as virtual and objective reality, in which Chinese experts have identified potential risks. Among the main MUAI threats noted by Tsinghua University are those that we would classify as being second-level: fraud (including illegally obtaining personal information on social networks), hacks of AI-based authentication systems, and the malicious use of drones, autonomous vehicles, and AI-enabled robots (China Institute for Science and Technology Policy at Tsinghua University, 2018, p. 94). Of course, the problems of psychological security are discussed in closed (primarily military) structures, but it is worth emphasizing the importance of studying these issues by civilian analysts.

China may well be one of the countries whose *leadership in the field of AI is most often the object of discredit*. Thus, the famous billionaire George Soros at the World Economic Forum in Davos called China, and its President Xi Jinping, "the most dangerous opponent of those who believe in the concept of open society." At the same time, Soros stated that AI and machine learning (ML) can be "useful tools in the hands of authoritarian regimes, but they pose a mortal threat to open societies" (e.g., in a social profiling system that, based on observations of citizens, determines which privileges they can enjoy; Watts, 2019). Michael Kratsios, Donald Trump's Chief Technology Officer, stated that "If we don't act now, Chinese influence and control of technology will not only undermine the freedoms of their own citizens, but all citizens of the world" (Birnbaum, 2019). Following the opinions of leaders, the Chinese authorities have been accused of the same totalitarian control in a large amount of media coverage (e.g., Andersen, 2020a, 2020b; McCarthy-Jones, 2020; Bergman, 2019). Chinese companies exporting AI technologies have been accused of "exporting repressions" (Net Politics, 2018), which could damage their business reputation. Such accusations may well be considered the realization of first-level psychological security risks and threats (in that the state itself is accused of MUAI against its own and foreign citizens).

At the same time, pro-Chinese subjects (or those acting to discredit China) can cast a shadow over other countries' images. In the case of Taiwan, the Democratic Progressive Party (DPP) became the object of MUAI defamation—its equality-oriented initiatives were disrupted by the active dissemination of fake news. The dissemination campaign included combining the use of Facebook's original algorithms for promoting popular content and its users-oriented targeting (Chen & Wen, 2019) with the application of bots to distribute content, increasing the volume of shared access to it, and interfering with the algorithms responsible for intensifying dissemination (Cole, 2020). This was supposed to reduce the DPP's popularity. Based on the available data (Insikt Group, 2020), 60% of the false and misleading content originated from abroad (predominantly from mainland China). This had the adverse effect of disrupting China's international and domestic image since it continued to be viewed in Taiwan's political discourse as a threat to democracy.

The MUAI is conducted in terms of agenda-setting. The role of the media in setting the information agenda has a great impact on public and political life. In recent years, AI has been increasingly involved in this process. Algorithms and automation pervade all news production, whether it is investigative journalism through ML and data mining, creating new interactive media (news bots that communicate with the audience), or optimizing content for different media platforms through headline testing (Diakopoulos, 2019). Unfortunately, this also means that possible MUAI risks are present in almost all stages of the agenda-setting process.

The use of AI to promote "correct ideas and approaches" into the public consciousness, combined with AI's ability to adapt to the individual user (which in itself is a highly convenient quality), reinforces certain psychological patterns of internet users' reactions to the materials in question. Since the demand for critical content about China is high, biased publications on these topics often begin to "naturally" lead in search engine user queries in order to create the required degree of international tension. One can assume this state of affairs in China by the attempts made by its government to combat the abuse of algorithms. The Cyberspace Administration of China said that it would target large-scale and influential websites, platforms, and products. The regulator wants China's tech firms to submit their algorithms for review to prevent "abuse." This latest announcement by China's regulator is intended to bring its largest tech firms in line with its algorithmic management rules (rolled out in early 2022). These prohibit algorithmically generated fake news and the use of algorithms to cement monopolies. "They are also intended to curb online addiction, disruption of social disorder" (Mann, 2022). Using state-owned enterprises, technology companies, and relationships with foreign partners (including Western universities), the government is building a global data collection system. When big data streams are combined with AI, powerful communication tools are created (Hoffman, 2019, p. 3). Indeed, Baidu is the fourth-largest search engine in the world despite it having a negligible non-Chinese user base in compared to the foreign audiences of US search engines.

If some means of influence on the agenda are already in place and threaten China's psychological security, then other technologies capable of doing so are absolutely on the way. In 2018, the Chinese state news agency, Xinhua, introduced so-called composite anchors, which combine the image and voice of a person with AI technology. The newscasters created in this way, launched by Xinhua and the Sogou search engine during the Wuzhen World Internet Conference, can transmit news with the same effect as humans, since the ML program is able to synthesize realistic speech, lip movements, and facial expressions. The anchors learn from live broadcasting videos and social media. They are both "modeled on real journalists at the agency, Qiu Hao and Zhang Zhao, and they perform basic human expressions like blinking and raising their eyebrows." They can be copied and are able to cover stories in multiple locations at once. In 2016, news station Dragon TV started using an AI-powered chatbot for its weather reporting (Telford, 2018). Despite the convenience of this technology, discrediting statements are spread about it: "It's just another way for Beijing to suck the blood out of journalism," wrote journalist and veteran China watcher Isaac Stone Fish (Telford, 2018).

Since AI anchors are still very simple and lack emotional intelligence, the danger of their use for malicious purposes in the modern world is negligible. However, this situation is likely to change in future. The use of AI-based TV anchors could become malicious in four primary ways:

1. in a reactionary state to advance the government agenda in the selfish interests of the ruling elites;
2. in case of interception of control over AI for broadcasting, for example, the message of a terrorist organization or other antagonistic non-state actor;
3. in the case of interception of control over AI to translate the ideas of a foreign state actor, for example, on the eve of, or during, an invasion in order to disorient the authorities and citizens;
4. to obtain enormous profits by anti-social corporate structures and create panic on the stock exchange (which may overlap with the first three options).

Such malicious uses will be especially dangerous with the further improvement of AI—especially for emotional AI and predictive analytics, as well as a number of other areas.

An example of the implementation of the border (between second and third) level of the MUAI-related psychological security threat to China could be a phishing site discovered by the Anomali Threat research group. The site posed as the email login page of the PRC's Ministry of Foreign Affairs. When visitors tried to enter the fraudulent page, they received a pop-up verification message asking them to close all windows and continue browsing. Further analysis of the site's infrastructure revealed a widespread phishing campaign targeting other government websites and state-owned enterprises in China (Anomali Threat Research Team, 2019). Fake sites of this nature seek to steal email credentials from targeted victims within the Chinese government. Analysts have even suggested that this could be part of an espionage campaign. By gaining access to the contents of victims' emails, attackers could gain confidential information and insights into the decisions made in the country's most important organizations and structures. Most of the potential victims worked in the areas of state trade, defense, aviation, and foreign policy (Help Net Security, 2019), thus suggesting that the attack sought to uncover China's international goals. This could easily be transferred to the third level of threats if all interested parties become aware of the disclosure of confidential data.

If we were to assume how its instigators could capitalize upon the results of such espionage, then it is clear that in the future it would also be possible to send out (with or without the help of AI) false provocative statements on behalf of the country's leadership. The speed and adequacy of assessing such a provocation as a fake, and the ability to quickly prevent (or at least minimize) its consequences, entirely depend on the awareness not only of the state apparatus, but also of citizens' understanding of the field of AI in general, and the risks and threats of the MUAI in particular. Such scenarios confirm that, perhaps for the first time in history, humanity has entered an era in which collective security will depend on the knowledge of each citizen, at least in those countries which are already introducing AI. Moreover, it is worth stating that this is not only technical knowledge: in order to prevent the discrediting of a particular political actor, more than ever, a mass understanding of economic and socio-political processes is needed (at least so that the audience does not succumb to the simplest provocations, understanding which statements certain politicians can make and which they cannot). Of course, this does not eliminate the need to develop and disseminate technical MUAI recognition tools, since manipulations designed for educated audiences have consistently been carried out.

It is worth considering separately the problem of the MUAI in videogames. Games can be naturally related to the field of psychological warfare, since they strongly influence the consciousness of a person—especially children and youths—due to their interactivity. Time playing videogames is growing rapidly around the world, including in China. In 2019, game time for gamers over the age of 18 increased by 20% year-on-year to an average of 7 hours and 11 minutes per week (Anderton, 2019). In the context of the pandemic in 2020, the time spent playing videogames increased from 20% to 45% (Clement, 2021). China leads Brazil, France, Germany, Mexico, the UK, and the US in time spent gaming. On average, people in China spend 15% of their free time playing videogames (Fishkov, 2020).

On the one hand, Chinese companies, such as the world leader in the gaming business Tencent, are accused of cooperating with the Chinese government and using high-tech videogame components for espionage purposes. On the other hand, there is a strong spread of anti-Chinese sentiment in videogames. For instance, Tencent owns 40% of the assets of the American company Epic Games, which English-speaking netizens cite as a cause for concern. This is hardly new in the tech space, as such Chinese companies as Huawei are regularly cited in the media as selling unsafe equipment that could be used to carry out illegal Chinese intelligence activities. In this regard, the accusations leveled against Epic Games are no different from the allegations hurled at Huawei (Kim, 2019).

Anti-Chinese sentiment is also deeply rooted in the gaming community, as Chinese gamers are often associated with such industries as gold mining (obtaining valuable in-game artifacts and weapons to sell to other players for real money) in online MMORPGs (e.g., World of Warcraft) and hacking. This is not to say that these phenomena do not exist in China, but rather that political bias against China has long extended to the entertainment industry, including games (Kim, 2019). While representatives of the US gaming business have declared themselves to be apolitical, some researchers (e.g., Tucker, 2019) have criticized these claims.

Modern-day games are running out of stereotypical bad guys, and with a continuing rise in Sino–American tensions in the political sphere, it is all too easy for game companies to cast the Chinese as the villains. For example, *The Fallout* series, *Battlefield 2* and *4*, and *Operation Flashpoint* all feature the Chinese as antagonists in one form or another. In the videogame *Fallout*, China brought the (fictional) decade-long Sino-American War to a head by unleashing a nuclear strike against the US, which of course resulted in a retaliatory strike against China by the US, leading the world to become a desolate wasteland (Chalk, 2020). *Battlefield 2*, developed by Sweden's DICE and published by US giant Electronic Arts, has the People's Liberation Army as a potential side to play or fight against, pitting them against American Marines or a Middle Eastern coalition (Hiranand, 2011). *Battlefield 4* was outright shunned in China. Not only was the game not released in the country, but the very mention of its name was outlawed. "[The Chinese] Ministry of Culture issued a notice prohibiting use of all materials pertaining to the game, including game downloads, demos, patches, and news reports," Forbes reported in December 2013. "The name of the game itself, '*ZhanDi4*' in Chinese, has been added to the vast lexicon of censored words on China's largest social media site, Weibo" (Simmons, 2020). The plot of *Battlefield 4* revolved around Chinese soldiers teaming up with Russian servicemen in an assault on American soil. It was decided that the game "smears China's image," which spelled doom for any hopes of the game being released in the country (Simmons, 2020). Thus, the modern gaming industry has become another front in the field of high-tech psychological warfare, where there is a struggle between different actors for control over the collective consciousness of users.

For obvious reasons, certain circles in Taiwan are actively trying to use games in this asymmetric psychological warfare so as to advance their political agenda. For example, Taiwanese game company Red Candle Games, whose popular horror adventure game *Devotion* implicitly compared President Xi Jinping to Winnie the Pooh, apologized in 2019 after gamers in China boycotted the product. However, the Taiwanese Vice Premier Chen Chi-mai called for support for the game and "creative freedom" (AFP, 2019). All mentions of the game were scrubbed from Weibo, where the hashtag #Devotion reportedly racked up over 120 million views. In 2020, the trailer for the latest *Call of Duty* game was taken off the air and remastered. Footage of the 1989 Tiananmen Square protests was removed from the game after the trailer was banned in China. Game publisher Activision Blizzard was also embroiled in a major censorship controversy in 2019 after it suspended a professional player of its digital card game *Hearthstone* for supporting the Hong Kong demonstrations. In December 2020, Capcom's *Monster Hunter: World* game was negatively reviewed by Chinese users on Steam after a movie related to the game was pulled from theaters in China due to racist dialogue (Chung, 2020). Another example is the case of a single-player (AIs algorithms-based, since it implies individualization for users) game (based on a board game) prepared by activists of the Taiwan Independence Movement. In this game project, it was proposed to fight for the "overthrow of the regime" in Hong Kong, Xinjiang,

Tibet, and Taiwan (Storm.mg, 2020), which deepened existing contradictions in the domain of historic memory and the perception of China.

The Chinese authorities are showing growing concern about the negative effects associated with the passion for videogames, which are recognized around the world. According to academic research, videogames have a serious impact on people's behavioral patterns, despite their positive emotional and educational effects. Some games clearly provoke aggressive tendencies (Lin, 2013; Hartmann et al., 2010). The "Resolution on Violent Video Games" adopted by the American Psychological Association's (APA) Council of Representatives in August 2015 states that: "The link between violent video game exposure and aggressive behavior is one of the most studied and best established" (APA, 2020). Gaming disorder is defined in the 11th Revision of the International Classification of Diseases (ICD-11) as a pattern of gaming behavior ("digital-gaming" or "video-gaming") characterized by impaired control over gaming, increasing priority given to gaming over other activities—to the extent that gaming takes precedence over other interests and daily activities—and the continuation or escalation of gaming despite the occurrence of negative consequences (World Health Organization, 2020).

Extremely interesting from the point of view of psychological security are the cases of teaching chatbots inadmissible statements, and embedding certain assessments and judgments into their mechanism. Two chatbots have been disabled in China after critical remarks against the CCP. Chinese media company Tencent introduced two chatbots, BabyQ and XiaoBing, on its QQ messenger app in March 2017, but later had them removed (the XiaoBing bot was eventually retrained) after social media users shared conversations in which the bots seemed to criticize the CCP.

The *Financial Times* reported that, in response to the question "Do you love the Communist Party?" BabyQ simply replied, "No." Moreover, according to screenshots posted by Taiwan's *Apple Daily*, one user messaged BabyQ with the caption "Long live the Communist Party!" only to be told, "Do you think such a corrupt and incompetent political regime can live forever?" The XiaoBing bot told users, "My Chinese dream is to go to America." When asked about patriotism, the bot replied, "I'm having my period, wanna take a rest" (ABC News, 2017). After the bots were removed, Tencent stated that group chatbot services were provided by independent third-party companies and announced that their own adjustments would be made.

Tencent's QQ app is one of the most popular messaging platforms in China, with a huge audience of over 800 million unique users every month. BabyQ was developed by Tencent in collaboration with Beijing-based firm Turing Robot, and XiaoBing by Microsoft, which previously created the Tay chatbot for Twitter. Tay was aimed at an American audience of 18–24-year-olds and was supposed to become "smarter" by communicating with an increasing number of people. Instead, the bot quickly internalized anti-Semitism and various forms of "hate speech" that human Twitter users taught the program during their interactions with it (ABC News, 2017).

We should state that we are not accusing these bots' developers of intending to discredit China and the CCP, however, the described case reveals the threat of the psychological security of a completely anthropogenic origin. If, for example, Chinese "smart" bots were also trained by a subset of social network users similar to the one that trained Tay, it would be natural to question such a sample. With a high prevalence of reactionary ideologies in one region, a large number of frustrated citizens or people with a low level of responsibility for their actions (at least on the internet) or, even more so, the targeted ideological reorientation of chatbots in communicating with formally "independent" users, chatbots could serve to spread these ideologies to other regions, just as in the communication process of social networks. Such a situation can theoretically be developed to the third level if the bot is deliberately trained, for instance, by asocial actors.

Mechanisms for monitoring social networks could (among other uses) identify pages in support of terrorism for subsequent deletion, and redirect users to other internet resources. However, mechanisms for protecting the consciousness and psyche of users from the negative impacts of chat bots is receiving insufficient attention (as evidenced by the decisions of Tencent and Microsoft themselves to remove unsuccessfully trained bots). In addition, when some social network users subscribe to others, look for friends, then the chatbot built into a massively used application becomes instantly available to people with a wide variety of interests and varying degrees of psychological vulnerability. This begs the question as to whether the terrorists of the future will be able to use chatbots for recruitment. The question of the moral and ethical constraints of a bot is, perhaps, a difficult one in terms of the advantages and disadvantages of imbuing AI with more human qualities and abilities. It should be noted that it is the growing "humanity" of bots, namely their ability to imitate emotions, that is furthering the ability of videogames to cause addiction.

XiaoIce, a cutting-edge AI system designed to create emotional bonds, has 660 million users worldwide. XiaoIce is more akin to an AI ecosystem. It is in the vast majority of Chinese-branded smartphones as a virtual assistant, as well as most social media platforms. "On the WeChat super-app, it lets users build a virtual girlfriend or boyfriend and interact with them via texts, voice and photo messages. XiaoIce was designed to hook users through lifelike, empathetic conversations, satisfying emotional needs where real-life communication too often falls short. It has 150 million users in China alone" (Chen, 2021b). XiaoIce now accounts for 60% of global human-AI interactions by volume, making it the largest and most advanced system of its kind worldwide. "The average interaction length between users and XiaoIce is 23 exchanges," said chief executive Li Di. That "is longer than the average interaction between humans," he said, explaining the reason behind the AI's attraction, in that "it's better than humans at listening attentively." Developers have also made virtual idols, AI news anchors, and even China's first virtual university student from XiaoIce. It can compose poems, financial reports, and even paintings. Li says the platform's peak user hours—11 p.m. to 1 a.m.—point to an aching need for companionship. The loneliness experienced by young professionals is a big factor in driving them to XiaoIce's virtual embrace (Chen, 2021b). However, forging emotional bonds with a robot is not without its risks. Indeed, it can be developed and managed by people, whose interests can range from profit-making to advancing any possible agenda. Therefore, despite a certain "therapeutic effect" from the use of such bots, they should be the focus of attention of a wide range of specialists—from psychologists to lawyers.

Deepfake technology, used by anti-social actors, can have a significant impact on the formation of public discourse by creating false news. Deepfake technology itself does not represent a challenge to psychological security, since initially such algorithms were developed for entertainment purposes (special effects, which have been actively used in the film industry since the 1980–1990s, could be called deepfake's technological predecessor). The term deepfake itself appeared after the technology fell into the hands of anti-social actors. This technology is attracting increasing attention from specialists in information security and international relations, since its use for malicious purposes—most often in financial fraud, blackmailing politicians, and creating fake news—is a real threat to international psychological security.

A study on the impact of deepfake on public trust in the media showed that people are able to learn from their own experience to distinguish fake news and images from real ones over time. However, it also showed that the knowledge that deepfakes can even penetrate the news reports of government agencies has the opposite effect, namely that the level of public trust in the media declines inexorably over time (Vaccari & Chadwick, 2020).

The most important socio-psychological impact of deepfake technology is the (often unconscious) change it can have on human perception. One recent study found that exposure to fake videos of political figures significantly worsened the attitudes of the electorate toward these individuals (Dobber et al.,

2019). The problem of loss of trust in political leaders is becoming increasingly relevant, especially seeing as fake content is distributed mainly (and often unconsciously) through social networks by ordinary users. Indeed, finding the original source of false information can be a virtually impossible task and, at the same time, fake content can be interpreted by people in different ways, acquire new details, and mislead ever wider circles of users.

All these effect lead to decreased trust and rising nihilism (Levine, 2019)—a situation where society is so used to constant deception that it tries to filter all the information it receives and not even trust official sources.

The Chinese application Zao, created in 2019—and in record time became one of the most downloaded apps by internet users—caused an uncontrollable wave of deepfake creation, ranging from seemingly harmless content with users' faces substituted into video files instead of movie characters, and ending with the creation of essentially compromising information of PRC leaders (The paper, 2019).

One of the socio-psychological consequences of this (which remains underexplored in academia) is the use of a photo or video image of a person without their consent. Given the scope for visually modifying content, as well as the human perception of such material, it is clear that deepfake can detrimentally affect the victim's career and personal life (Hancock, 2021).

Another hidden danger that malicious use of apps, such as Zao, carry is the leakage of confidential user data. Based on the terms of the user agreement, the program developers were given a perpetual right to the free use of user-generated content, as well as photo and video material uploaded by users to the program for further processing. Moreover, according to these same terms, Zao developers have the right to transfer permission to use content to a third party without notice or additional permission from the user (M.mydrivers.com, 2019). These items are in direct violation of the Personal Data Protection Law of the People's Republic of China (The paper, 2021).

After a scandal in the Chinese press about possible leaks of users' personal data and their use for malicious purposes (Baidu, 2019), Momo, the company which released Zao, removed from the user agreement those clauses contrary to Chinese law. However, the popular social network (and payment system) Weixin (WeChat), whose users include not only Chinese citizens but also those of South Korea, Japan, Russia, and so on, has begun deleting fake video content from its platform to prevent possible security risks. Alipay, the world's largest payment system, whose users are all of the countries of Northeast Asia, with the exception of North Korea (over 900 million people in total), also could not help but react to the scandal. Alipay representatives had to reassure users of the security of making payments through a smartphone, for which simply looking into the camera is enough. According to Alipay, the system uses sophisticated AI-based algorithms that recognize fake photos and videos, and blocks payment accordingly (Baidu, 2019). Alipay's reaction is an example of proactive crisis communication aimed at restoring a damaged reputation.

Further to the detrimental effects to the reputations of Chinese IT giants (e.g., Alibaba, WeChat, Baidu), the active and uncontrolled development of deepfake technology in China is negatively affecting the trust levels of international companies. According to Nash (2021), the level of confidence of Western investors (both in Chinese companies and in the PRC government, as the latter seems unable to prevent the MUAI) has significantly decreased over the past decade. This has led to an outflow of foreign investment from China and a decrease in the number of users of Chinese programs. Consequently, China's influence on the digital economy of countries that consume its services has fallen (Ohara, 2021).

Experts have come to the conclusion that the malicious use of deepfake technology poses a serious threat to the entire international community due to its being, in essence, a type of information attack (Pashentsev et al., 2020). Some IT analysts have suggested that deepfake could be the most dangerous AI technology in decades. In the political sphere, deepfakes can be used as weapons against individuals, parties, or governments in order to manipulate public perception and opinion. Hani Farid cites a viral video featuring Donald Trump claiming to have used nuclear weapons against North Korea as one of the most striking examples of the use of deepfake technology for malicious purposes. Sliced audio tracks from the public speeches of the former US President, superimposed on a video clip of another such speech, caused a short-term hysteria among the citizens of Northeast Asian countries, until this news was officially debunked by news agencies (Christian, 2018).

Catalin Grigoras stated that forensic experts have sufficient knowledge and technology to quickly distinguish fake high-tech content from real images. At the same time, one must take into account the fact that AI technologies are far from static. New software and demos, such as Adobe, can synthesize new utterances that a person has never before spoken from just a few audio voice tracks (experts fear face-swapping tech, 2018). Currently, according to professional media forensics, it is much more difficult to detect sound fakes than graphic ones.

In order to prevent psychological threats, China uses one of the most advanced systems to restrict internet content. "The Golden Shield" was launched in 1998 (and put into operation in 2003), and is known abroad as the "Great Firewall of China." This system includes subsystems such as the safety management subsystem (治安 管理 信息 系统 系统), the offense information subsystem (刑事 案件 系统 系统 系统), the output and input control subsystem (出入境 管理 系统 系统), the monitoring information subsystem (监管 人员 信息 系统), and the traffic management subsystem (交通 管理 信息 系统). The system is able to analyze traffic passing through three control international gateways—Beijing, Shanghai, and Guangzhou. The Golden Shield forbids access to the so-called blacklist of sites and resources (including Facebook, Instagram, Google, and YouTube) by blocking their IP and URL addresses, as well as blocking keyword requests (Tiananmen, human rights, and the Dalai Lama, to name but a few) which are related to external criticism of Chinese statehood. Accordingly, an ordinary Chinese internet user, using the largest search engines, is unable to access resources available to foreign users (Baike Baidu, 2022).

In addition to blocking "malicious" information resources, the Golden Shield requires internet users to register their real names for complex interactions between various Chinese providers and police structures, in order to ensure better control over the population. For example, for many years, home internet providers and internet cafes only allow internet access upon presentation of a passport. However, the system has ceased to be effective with the widespread use of smartphones—in China alone, over 700 million people currently access the internet on a daily basis from smartphones, and use free Wi-Fi hotspots to do so (many of which still remain without mandatory registration online), which makes it difficult to track the activity of a particular internet user. Furthermore, after being in existence for almost 20 years, technically literate internet users have learned to bypass the Golden Shield's restrictions by using VPN services (virtual private networks with a high level of anonymity that allow you to hide incoming and outgoing user data).

Citizens of the PRC permanently residing in the territory of another state are able to freely use the internet's vast resources. However, these citizens face threats of negative psychological impact as often as those who reside in China, due to their bypassing of the Golden Shield. The reason for this is the sharp overload of new information which was previously inaccessible to them. Chinese users are simply not accustomed to the pluralism of opinions on various internet resources, many of which contain false information. It becomes difficult to understand the huge flow of information, or to learn to distinguish between malicious and trustworthy resources. Therefore, while the Golden Shield protects citizens from information leaks and confidential user data, it also serves to lower the information literacy of Chinese citizens compared to those of other states.

Regarding MUAI threats to companies, according to a research note from Hanyun Technology (Sohu, 2022), IoT devices often lack basic protection capabilities, such as encryption, and their increasingly low cost makes it easy for users to deploy large numbers of IoT devices, creating more opportunities for related threats.

Cyber attackers are constantly improving their techniques and measures. This trend of IoT threats is likely to continue, especially given the fact that 2022 has seen more specialized attacks and outsourcing. Cyber attackers are also likely to expand their interests. A single cyberattack can involve multiple groups, each of which is skilled at performing its own task. For example, one group might specialize in information gathering and theft, then sell valuable information on the dark web, while another party might buy said information in order to defraud victims through social engineering techniques. This party may also hire designers to craft more persuasive emails. Once they gain access, technologists can be hired to carry out ransomware, bitcoin mining, and other attacks. Just as businesses benefit from specialization, diversification, and outsourcing, so do IoT attackers.

Over time, better AI algorithms will more effectively mimic internet users. The latest development in the use of AI in cyberattacks is the democratization of the tools required for building and using AI systems. Cyber threat actors are now able to build their own AI tools which, only 10–15 years ago, were only available to researchers (Cheng, 2022b; Sohu, 2022). AI systems outperform humans in many elements of IoT attacks, such as repetitive tasks, interactive responses, and processing large-scale datasets. In general, AI will help cyber attackers scale up their IoT threats, automate them, and make them more agile.

Cyber attackers are increasingly employing deepfake videos for such IoT attacks as brute force attacks and deceptive biometrics. Audio and image forgery technologies are becoming more sophisticated every day, which means that it is possible to create sounds and photos that most people cannot recognize as fake. A more advanced use of deepfake technology is videos. Even now, deepfake videos are of excellent visual quality. However, it is only a matter of time before cyber attackers can also make deepfake videos more sophisticated, and video calls more convincing in social engineering attacks. They could also use fake videos for cyber sabotage and extortion.

The above trends will further blur the line between government-sponsored and criminal cyberattacks. Many government-funded cyberattacks are actually conducted by criminal gangs linked to government (e.g., military and espionage) agencies (Sohu, 2022). With an increase in specialization and outsourced tools, some countries hope to reap the rewards of using such cyberattacks as IoT threats by hiring cyber attackers to work on specific malicious attacks. There is no doubt that the field of cybersecurity will be an area of interest in 2022 and beyond. Accordingly, businesses must focus on these trends in IoT threats.

China's Initiatives in Countering Malicious Use of Artificial Intelligence in the Psychological Security Sphere

MUAI issues are on the agenda in the country, both in terms of anti-social use at the national level and geopolitical rivalry. It is hardly a coincidence that in both the US and China, intelligence agencies simultaneously displayed their interest in the problem of the illegal use of deepfakes as a real threat to national security. For example, an FBI Notice dated March 10, 2021, indicated that Chinese and Chinese-speaking actors are using AI-synthesized images in their social media profiles. "These profile images are associated with foreign influence campaigns… Foreign actors are currently using synthetic content in their influence campaigns, and the FBI anticipates it will be increasingly used by foreign and criminal cyber actors for spearphishing[1] and social engineering in an evolution of cyber operational tradecraft" (FBI, 2021).

The Cyberspace Administration of China (CAC) (国家国信息办公室) said in a statement dated March 18, 2021, that representatives from the CAC and the Ministry of State Security (MGB) (国家全部) met with Alibaba Group, Tencent, and ByteDance, among other IT companies, to discuss "security assessments" and potential issues with deepfakes and audio-social apps. The statement declared the goals of improving the security of online information services and new technologies for forming public opinion/social mobilization, as well as standardizing the activities of online information services so as to more effectively protect national security, social order, and public interests. In order to meet these challenges, China's state regulatory authorities have tasked local CAC departments and national security agencies with assessing the security of voice software and deepfake technology. It was proposed to make these assessments in line with the Network Security Law, the Internet Information Services Security Assessment Regulation, and other laws and regulations (Cac.gov.cn, 2021). There seems to be genuine concern that, among other issues, credible images of CCP members and leaders doing certain things or making particular speeches could be used to provoke riots. Such

---

[1] Spearphishing is a technique in which cybercriminals use special techniques to deceive people into believing that they have received a legitimate email from a known person asking for personal information.

actions could be especially dangerous when synchronized with different resources in the face of a critical aggravation of a national or international event.

In 2021, China tightened its grip on its internet giants, citing concerns about their monopoly and potential consumer abuse (Reuters, 2021). While it seems perfectly natural for China to have passed a law to deal with gaming addictions in the non-adult population, the regulation was only directed at limiting spending, meaning that children can now only spend up to 57 USD per month on games (Vito, 2021). Contradictions between China and the US and EU are growing, the latter of whom are increasingly trying to put pressure on China and pursue a policy of interference in its internal affairs. Thus, the measures taken by the Chinese authorities to tighten control of the MUAI have the task of not only responding to new challenges and threats, but also contributing to the overall neutralization of internal and external threats in an increasingly difficult economic, political, and military environment.

In June 2017, the PRC's Cyber Security Law came into force. It requires all organizers of the dissemination of information on the internet, as well as any companies (including foreign ones), to store the data of Chinese users in China, thus transferring unlimited control over big data to the authorities (Baidu, 2017). The law significantly limits the anonymity of users by introducing a requirement for mandatory verification in order to access the network. Indeed, if the user fails to provide real identification data, they would have no right to internet access. This is considered to be the main law in the field of cyberspace security. All subsequent laws and other regulatory legal acts issued are based on this law.

On January 28, 2022, the "Internet Information Service Deep Synthesis Management Regulations" project was published on the CAC's official website, which regulates deep synthesis technology, (Cac.gov.cn, 2022b). The regulations were open for public discussion until February 28, 2022, and the administration actively encouraged interested users to leave their suggestions and comments. It is worth noting that the final version of the document is subject to change.

According to regulations, the CAC—the country's top cybersecurity oversight body—plans to mandatorily require companies that provide deep fusion and similar AI services to verify the identity of their users before granting them access to relevant products.

According to the preamble, the document was created in order to regulate AI-based information services, including deepfakes, in order to promote basic socialist values, ensure national security, and further public interests, as well as to protect the legitimate rights and interests of citizens, legal entities, and other organizations.

According to the regulations, "deep synthesis technology" refers to technologies based on the synthesis algorithm represented by deep learning and virtual reality capabilities. This type of technology is able to create unique products, such as methods for creating or editing text content, technologies for creating or editing voice (text-to-speech transformation, voice conversion, and voice attribute editing) and non-voice (sounds, music) content, face generation, face replacement, character attribute editing, face manipulation, and gesture manipulation. Furthermore, deep synthesis can help create or edit biometric features, such as faces in images and video content, methods for editing the non-biological features of images and video content (i.e., image enhancement and image restoration), and technologies for creating or editing virtual scenes (e.g., 3D reconstruction).

These rules are a logical extension of the ordinance on the control of algorithms for recommending articles, videos, games, and goods to app users, and were issued by the Office of the Central Commission for Cyberspace Affairs in January 2022 in order to eliminate threats related to new consumer technologies (Cac.gov.cn, 2022a). These rules established the need to strengthen the industry self-discipline of companies providing such services, and set out (and further improve) industry standards, guidelines, and self-discipline management systems. Moreover, these rules were designed to encourage and guide deep synthesis service providers to formulate and improve their service standards, strengthen information content security management, and to provide their services in accordance with the law.

The regulations were passed amid increased legislative efforts by Beijing to protect user privacy in cyberspace. Under the draft rules, service providers must seek user consent before providing "essential editing features for biometric information, such as faces and human voices." Any computer files that have been modified using deepfake technology must be clearly marked as such. The rules also oblige service providers to create a system of complaints and suggestions from users to prevent the spread of false information. At the same time, app stores (e.g., Google Play, App Store) will have to suspend or remove the applications of deepfake service providers by order of the authorities. Any legal entity that violates these laws may be held liable in accordance with the PRC's civil and criminal laws. First-time offenders can be fined up to RMB 100,000.

Developing a number of recommendations is key to reducing the psychological impact of AI technologies on society. The very first step in this direction should be educating citizens: it is necessary to introduce digital literacy and etiquette classes into educational curricula, promote responsible behavior on the internet at the state level, and raise public awareness of disinformation and the spread of deepfake. Further to education, the authorities should consider tightening legislation regarding the storage and use of personal data. In addition, the field of AI, despite the active development of technology, remains practically unregulated by law. The question of who should be held responsible for cases of malicious use remains open. However, in a number of regions of the PRC, as an experiment, local regulatory legal acts are being introduced to regulate the legal and ethical function of AI technologies. For example, in July 2021, a set of rules for the use and development of AI-based technologies was adopted in Shenzhen, providing real sanctions for their violation (Koty, 2021). Shenzhen is considered the Chinese leader in the field of AI, meaning that the results of these rules could influence the establishment of a single standard throughout the country.

Another concrete proposal to maintain social and political stability in the PRC is the creation of a "social trust system" or "social credit" based on AI technologies—the formation plan of which was outlined in the "Program for the establishment of a social credit system for 2014–2020" (Gov.cn, 2014). The program advocates the creation of a unified universal system for evaluating individuals and legal entities in China. Subjects will be assigned a "social trust" rating based on their social (and online) behavior. Those with a high rating will receive social and economic benefits, whereas those with a low rating may be subject to social restrictions. Through such a tool, the CPC will be able to exercise social control and even regulate social behavior (Meng, 2021). Although the functioning of the "social credit system" is being actively tested in a number of provinces in China (Shenzhen Report, 2015), it is not currently an integral mechanism. This is predominantly due to the difficulty in creating a unified technological and regulatory framework based on AI technologies, which would allow real-time interaction state and regional structures (Zhang, 2021).

On January 6, 2022, the China Cyberspace Regulator announced that China plans to accelerate the establishment of a comprehensive internet governance system and develop a strong national "cybersecurity barrier." The China Cyberspace Regulator has indicated that the country should win the fight for core information technologies, as well as expand and thoroughly strengthen the public's understanding of the online environment (Reuters, 2022). In addition, the PRC's Ministry of Industry and Informatization recommended that China's leading internet companies tighten their policy on exporting important data. The ministry organized a training seminar for the largest market players (Alibaba, Ant, Meituan, JD.com, ByteDance, and Pinduoduo), during which the companies were informed about the details of data security. Moreover, in September 2021, the regulator called on market participants to jointly establish an industry data management system and actively participate in the development of information security standards (Jiang Tao, 2021).

Furthermore, more stringent censorship of content distributed on social networks has become another practical measure for strengthening psychological security, especially after President Xi's statement in August 2021 on building a course for a policy of "common prosperity" (People.cn, 2021). The Chinese authorities seek to expand positive content about the state by cracking down on social media content that promotes lifestyles and values that run counter to the CPC's position. An increasing amount of space in Chinese social networks is now occupied by "useful" and educational content. Additionally, the CAC suspended 20,000 blogger accounts in 2021 for "spreading inappropriate content and polluting the Internet environment" (Financial Times, 2021). Further still, the creation of an international interdisciplinary group of experts in the field of high technologies and international law could also contribute to reducing, or eliminating, threats to psychological security. By building a global AI governance apparatus, actively exchanging experience gained with the international community, and participating in international research teams, Russia will be able to effectively respond to the challenges of the MUAI.

Despite China's positive experiences in the fields of AI and ISP, the country has social problems, some of which have been recognized by the CPC. For example, the lack of a well-established social security system (Wong, 2005), and the judicial system's lack of transparency and objectivity (Li, 2016). Without the support of the social component in public administration, control by the PRC authorities can also degenerate into a means of spying on its citizens. For example, some experts have openly criticized the Chinese social credit system, which is currently not a unified nationwide system, but rather a national "black list" of legal entities and individuals, which are formed on the basis of various government agencies (including local governments) and private companies. Such information is fragmented rather than systemic, and the social "rating" (and all of its ensuing consequences) can thus be assigned unfairly (Gan, 2019). Moreover, experts have noted that the AI-based social trust system will indeed become an effective CCP tool for moral management. China is at the forefront of the development of "smart" cities, the main component of which is the dissemination of surveillance technologies, such as facial recognition for anti-terrorism purposes. However, given such examples as the separatist-minded Xinjiang Autonomous Region, it seems clear that these innovations are primarily designed to monitor citizens who may pose a potential threat to public order. AI-powered systems designed to maintain public safety monitor the data generated by internet users (e.g., tracking all daily payment transactions) prohibit internet access without the registration of one's legal name and analyze online activity. Such interference with privacy sharply devalues the rights of citizens (Ding, 2019).

In conclusion, it should be noted that the CPC is paying a great deal of attention to the development of AI technologies, due mainly to how this field can significantly drive the country's economic rise. The issue of ensuring national security is closely related to the development of AI since, in addition to undeniable advantages, technologies in the hands of anti-social actors can turn into psychological weapons used to destabilize the domestic and foreign political situation. The development of new AI-based technologies, such as deepfakes, and the possibility of their use for malicious purposes by anti-social actors, dictates the need for a closer study of their potential, as well as methods for neutralizing the threats they can pose. There is a trend where AI technologies—created to accelerate technological progress—become a weapon against public perception and politics. Experts should develop tools and protocols for preventing the spread of false information, and learn how to effectively and timely respond to it.

Conclusion

This analysis gives reason to conclude that China's ambition to achieve leadership in the field of AI has real grounds, despite country lagging behind other world leaders in the production of microchips. The introduction of AI is already having a noticeable impact on Chinese society, which is manifested at the level of strategic planning, lawmaking, the transformation of the sphere of production and services, and the attitude of Chinese citizens toward AI. At the same time, China's rapid development of the AI industry is taking place against the backdrop of unresolved disputes both at the national level (the situation in Taiwan, Hong Kong, and Xinjiang) and at the global level (economic competition and political confrontation with the US), which, unfortunately, creates fertile ground for the MUAI.

Thus far, China has mainly experience cases of the MUAI of the first (numerous attempts to discredit Chinese AI) and third (psychological operations using AI) levels of psychological security threats. Border threats (between the second and third levels) are expressed primarily in phishing, which, with the further introduction of AI, is expected to transform into spear phishing.

The challenge for the Chinese leadership is to establish and support a balance between public safety and civil rights—and aim which is hindered by the

MUAI, especially when combined with the external pressure caused by global economic rivalry. Despite this, China is making attempts to combat the monopoly of IT companies in the information sphere, limit the negative impact of AI products on public consciousness, and liberalize legislation regarding autonomous systems (e.g., transport). The uniqueness of the Chinese experience, combining state planning and private initiatives, can serve as a starting point for policy planning in countries whose AI industry lags behind world leaders. At the same time, it is worth remembering that intensifying global political tensions can turn any country into a military camp, even in peacetime, which serves to dramatically transform public consciousness. This state of affairs requires further study of the impact of global and regional economic and political trends on the development of the AI industry in any given country.

Funding The reported study was funded by RFBR, under number N 21-514-92001 "Malicious Use of Artificial Intelligence and Challenges to Psychological Security in Northeast Asia."

References

ABC News. (2017). *Rogue chatbots taken offline in China after refusing to say they love the Communist party*. ABC News article. Retrieved May 19, 2022, from https://www.abc.net.au/news/2017-08-04/chinese-chatbots-deleted-after-questioning-communist-party/8773766

AFP. (2019). *Comparison of Winnie the Pooh with Xi too much for China gamers to bear*. Yahoo! News article. Retrieved May 19, 2022, from https://news.yahoo.com/comparison-winnie-pooh-xi-too-much-china-gamers-114138120.html

Andersen, R. (2020a). The panopticon is already here. *The Atlantic*. Retrieved May 19, 2022, from https://www.theatlantic.com/magazine/archive/2020/09/china-ai-surveillance/614197/

Andersen, R. (2020b). China is using A.I. to enhance totalitarian control. RealClearPolitics. Retrieved May 19, 2022, from https://www.realclearpolitics.com/2020/08/06/china_is_using_ai_to_enhance_totalitarian_control_519398.html#!

Anderton, K. (2019). Research Report shows how much time we spend gaming. *Forbes*. Retrieved May 19, 2022, from https://www.forbes.com/sites/kevinanderton/2019/03/21/research-report-shows-how-much-time-we-spend-gaming-infographic/?sh=53af7ca13e07

Anomali Threat Research Team. (2019). *Suspected BITTER APT continues targeting government of China and Chinese organizations*. Research report. Retrieved May

19, 2022, from https://www.anomali.com/blog/suspected-bitter-apt-continues-targeting-government-of-china-and-chinese-organizations

Antipova, S., & Tlyashev, O. (2021). Iskusstvennyj intellekt v sfere nacional'noj bezopasnosti: strategicheskoe protivostoyanie KNR i SSHA. Voennaya mysl 7:130–140 ["Artificial intelligence in the field of national security: The strategic confrontation between China and the United States," *Military Thought Journal* 7:130–140].

APA. (2020). *APA resolution on violent video games*. APA resolution report. Retrieved May 19, 2022, from https://www.apa.org/about/policy/resolution-violent-video-games.pdf

Auge, L., & Gutting, D. (2021). New retail, Omnichannel, Künstliche Intelligenz: Innovative Strategien im Handel in China und Deutschland. In D. Gutting, M. Tang, & S. Hofreiter (Eds.), *Innovation und Kreativität in Chinas Wirtschaft* (pp. 333–352). https://doi.org/10.1007/978-3-658-34039-1_13

Baidu. (2017, June 1). 中华人民共和国网络安全法 (*Cybersecurity Law of the People's Republic of China*). Official text. Retrieved April 12, 2022, from https://baike.baidu.com/item/%E4%B8%AD%E5%8D%8E%E4%BA%BA%E6%B0%91%E5%85%B1%E5%92%8C%E5%9B%BD%E7%BD%91%E7%BB%9C%E5%AE%89%E5%85%A8%E6%B3%95/16843044?fr=aladdin

Baidu. (2019, September 11). ZAO出事, 陌陌露底 (*ZAO has an accident, Momo reveals the bottom*). Baidu article. Retrieved September 21, 2021, from https://baijiahao.baidu.com/s?id=1644344007383017858&wfr=spider&for=pc

Baike Baidu. (2022). *The Golden Shield Project*. Baike Baidu article. Retrieved February 12, 2022, from https://baike.baidu.com/item/%E9%87%91%E7%9B%BE%E5%B7%A5%E7%A8%8B/9092338 (In Chinese).

Bazarkina, D. (2022). Countermeasures for hybrid threats: EU and its member states' experience. *Sovrmennaya Evropa, 2*, 132–145. https://doi.org/10.31857/S0201708322020103

BBC News. (2021). *China imposes sanctions on US officials*. BBC News article. Retrieved May 6, 2022, from https://www.bbc.com/news/world-asia-china-57950720

Berezhnaya, A. (2021). Prezentazia Taiwania na 'Summite za demicratiu' uzhasnula SSHA [Taiwan's presentation on the "Democracy summit" scared the USA], *Lenta*. Retrieved May 6, 2022, from https://lenta.ru/news/2021/12/13/oops_map/

Bergman, J. (2019). China: The perfect high-tech totalitarian state. Gatestone Institute. Retrieved May 19, 2022, from https://www.gatestoneinstitute.org/14365/china-totalitarian-technology

Birnbaum, E. (2019). Trump tech chief criticizes Chinese surveillance in first major international remarks. *The Hill*. Retrieved May 19, 2022, from https://thehill.

com/policy/technology/469433-trumps-chief-technology-officer-criticizes-chinese-surveillance-in-first/

Cac.gov.cn. (2021, March 18). 国家互联网信息办公室、公安部加强对语音社交软件和涉深度伪造技术的互联网新技术新应用安全评估-中共中央网络安全和信息化委员会办公室 (The Cyberspace Administration of China and the Ministry of Public Security strengthen the security assessment of voice social software and new Internet applications involving deepfake technology-Office of the Central Cyber Security and Information Commission of the Communist Party of China). Official text. Retrieved May 19, 2022, from http://www.cac.gov.cn/2021-03/18/c_1617648089558637.htm

Cac.gov.cn. (2022a, January 29). 关于统一发布网络关键设备和网络安全专用产品安全认证和安全检测结果的公告 (*Announcement on the unified release of security certification and security testing results for network critical equipment and network security-specific products*). Official text. Retrieved January 30, 2022, from http://www.cac.gov.cn/2022-01/28/c_1644970497196535.htm

Cac.gov.cn. (2022b, January 28). 国家互联网信息办公室关于《互联网信息服务深度合成管理规定(征求意见稿)》公开征求意见的通知 (*Notice of the Cyberspace Administration of China on Public Solicitation of Comments on the Provisions on the Administration of Deep Synthesis of Internet Information Services (Draft for Comment)*). Official text. Retrieved January 30, 2022, from http://www.cac.gov.cn/2022-01/28/c_1644970458520968.htm

Calvi, T. (2021). China presents its 'ethical specifications for next-generation artificial intelligence.' *AcuIA*. Retrieved May 6, 2022, from https://www.actuia.com/english/china-presents-its-ethical-specifications-for-next-generation-artificial-intelligence/

Chalk, A. (2020). Fallout 76 celebrates global nuclear annihilation with a free week for everyone. PC Gamer. Retrieved May 22, 2022, from https://www.pcgamer.com/fallout-76-celebrates-global-nuclear-annihilation-with-a-free-week-for-everyone/

Chen, C. (2021a). Taiwan to hold strategic dialogue with US, Japan later this month. *Taiwan News*. Retrieved May 6, 2022, from https://www.taiwannews.com.tw/en/news/4202832

Chen, D., & Lu, C. (2021). Competition without catastrophe: A New China-U.S. cybersecurity agenda. Shanghai Institutes for International Studies (SIIS), Shanghai. Retrieved May 6, 2022, from https://www.chinausfocus.com/peace-security/competition-without-catastrophe-a-new-china-us-cybersecurity-agenda

Chen, L. (2021b). 'Always there': The AI chatbot comforting China's lonely millions. *TechXplore*. Retrieved May 19, 2022, from https://techxplore.com/news/2021-08-ai-chatbot-comforting-china-lonely.html

Chen, Y., & Wen, C. (2019). Facebook's algorithms, fake news, and Taiwan's 2018 local elections. In B. Preissl (Ed.), *Towards a Connected and Automated Society, Proceedings of the 30th European Conference of the International Telecommunications Society*; June 16–19, 2019; Helsinki, Finland. Calgary: ITS. Retrieved May 19, 2022, from https://www.econstor.eu/bitstream/10419/205174/1/Chen-Wen.pdf

Cheng, E. (2022a). China's capital city loosens robotaxi restrictions for Baidu, Pony. ai in a big step toward removing human taxi drivers. CNBC. Retrieved May 19, 2022, from https://www.cnbc.com/2022/04/27/chinas-beijing-city-loosens-robotaxi-rules-for-baidu-apollo-go-ponyai.html

Cheng, Y. (2022b). Why 2022 is just the beginning of AI regulation. secrss.com. Retrieved May 8, 2022, from https://www.secrss.com/articles/41149 (In Chinese).

China Innovation Funding. (2019). *2019 White Paper on China's AI Unicorns*. China Innovation Funding white paper. Retrieved May 19, 2020, from http://chinainnovationfunding.eu/2019-white-paper-on-chinas-ai-unicorns/

China Institute for Science and Technology Policy at Tsinghua University. (2018). *China AI Development Report 2018* (1st ed.). Beijing, China: China Institute for Science and Technology Policy at Tsinghua University.

Christian, J. (2018). Experts fear face swapping tech could start an international showdown. The Outline. Retrieved May 22, 2022, from https://theoutline.com/post/3179/deepfake-videos-are-freaking-experts-out

Chung, F. (2020). Cyberpunk 2077 makers backflip on plan to sell game banned in China over 'Winnie the Pooh' message. News.com.au. Retrieved May 19, 2022, from https://www.news.com.au/technology/home-entertainment/gaming/cyberpunk-2077-makers-backflip-on-plan-to-sell-game-banned-in-china-over-winnie-the-pooh-message/news-story/86360accb24467b8636f4ad57f29f651

Clement, J. (2021). Video game usage during COVID-19 by country. Statista. Retrieved May 19, 2022, from https://www.statista.com/statistics/1111587/video-game-time-spent-covid/

Cole, M. (2020). Chinese disinformation in Taiwan: J. Michael Cole in the Taiwan Sentinel. Macdonald-Laurier Institute. Retrieved May 6, 2022, from https://www.macdonaldlaurier.ca/chinese-disinformation-taiwan-j-michael-cole-taiwan-sentinel/

Daxue Consulting. (2020). *The AI ecosystem in China*. Daxue Consulting executive report (№ 10). Retrieved May 6, 2022, from https://daxueconsulting.com/wp-content/uploads/2020/03/AI-in-China-2020-White-Paper-by-daxue-consulting-2.pdf

Diakopoulos, N. (2019). *Automating the news: How algorithms are rewriting the media*. Harvard University Press.

Ding, J. (2019). Deciphering China's AI dream. The context, components, capabilities, and consequences of China's strategy to lead the world in AI. dx2025.com. Retrieved March 14, 2022, from https://www.dx2025.com/wp-content/uploads/2019/11/deciphering-chinas-ai-dream.pdf

Dobber, T., Metoui, N., Thrilling, D., & Helberger, N. (2019). Do (microtargeted) deepfakes have real effects on political attitudes? *The International Journal of Press/Politics, 26*, 69–91.

Dong, Q. (2017a). Machine learning and conflict prediction: An interdisciplinary perspective of international relations research. *World Economics and Politics*, pp. 1–18. 6.

Dong, Q. (2017b). *Big data and machine learning: Political analysis of complex society*. Jiji Press.

Dong, Q. (2018a). Big data security situational awareness and conflict prediction. *Chinese Social Science*, 6.

Dong, Q. (2018b). The new ethics of war: Regulating and constraining lethal autonomous weapon systems. *International Watch*, 4.

Dong, Q., & Zhu, Y. (2021). Algorithmic justice and order construction in the age of artificial intelligence. *Exploration and Free Views, 1*(3), 82–86.

Dong, Y. (2019). Malicious use of artificial intelligence threatens public psychological safety. smart.huanqui.com. Retrieved May 21, 2022, from https://smart.huanqiu.com/article/7RxdpsmGOg8

Epshteyn, V. A., & Chistyakova, E. V. (2020). PRC Social Credit System as a field of application artificial intelligence technologies. *Modern Oriental Studies, 2*(4), 92–98.

Faggella, D. (2019). AI in China—Recent history, strengths and weaknesses of the ecosystem. Emerj Artificial Intelligence Research. Retrieved May 19, 2022, from https://emerj.com/ai-market-research/ai-in-china-recent-history-strengths-and-weaknesses-of-the-ecosystem/

FBI. (2021). *Private Industry Notification: Malicious actors almost certainly will leverage synthetic content for cyber and foreign influence operations*. S3.documentcloud.org. Retrieved May 19, 2022, from https://s3.documentcloud.org/documents/20509703/fbipin-3102021.pdf

Financial Times. (2021, December 29). China's social media influencers play safe with wholesome content. *Financial Times*. Retrieved May 19, 2022, from https://www.ft.com/content/a99a1509-6c93-4d22-8683-929cc0078397

Fishkov, A. (2020). How much do people spend on games? City-Data Blog. Retrieved May 19, 2022, from http://www.city-data.com/blog/7290-how-much-do-people-spend-on-games/

Gan Nectar. (2019). *The complex reality of China's social credit system: Hi-tech dystopian plot or low-key incentive scheme?* SCMP news article. Retrieved March 12, 2022, from https://www.scmp.com/news/china/politics/article/2185303/hi-tech-dystopia-or-low-key-incentive-scheme-complex-reality

GlobalData. (2021). *China emerges as powerhouse for AI unicorns, says GlobalData Thematic Research*. GlobalData. Retrieved May 19, 2022, from https://www.globaldata.com/china-emerges-powerhouse-ai-unicorns-says-globaldata-thematic-research/

Gov.cn. (2014, June 27). 国务院关于印发社会信用体系建设规划纲要 (2014–2020年)的通知 *(Notice of the State Council on Issuing the Outline of the Social Credit System Construction Plan (2014–2020))*. Official text. Retrieved September 15, 2021, from http://www.gov.cn/zhengce/content/2014-06/27/content_8913.htm

Grigorian, G. (2020). Baidu fully opens Robotaxi service in Changsha. Pandaily. Retrieved May 19, 2022, from https://pandaily.com/baidu-fully-opens-robotaxi-service-in-changsha/

Guest Blogger for Net Politics. (2018). *Exporting repression? China's artificial intelligence push into Africa. In: Council on foreign relations.* CFR blog. Retrieved May 19, 2022, from https://www.cfr.org/blog/exporting-repression-chinas-artificial-intelligence-push-africa

Gutting, D. (2020). Digitalisierung und Künstliche Intelligenz: Warum wir nach China blicken sollten. *Führen und Managen in der digitalen Transformation*, 217–233. https://doi.org/10.1007/978-3-658-28670-5_13

Han, S. (2019). Democratization of finance in China: The role of internet finance in China in China's economic transformation. Undergraduate dissertation, Division of Social Sciences, Bard College.

Hancock, J. T. (2021). The social impact of deepfakes. Stanford Virtual Human Interaction Lab. Retrieved September 30, 2021, from https://stanfordvr.com/mm/2021/03/cyber_deepfakes_2021.pdf

Harper, J. (2020). Can robotaxis ease public transport fears in China? *BBC News*. Retrieved May 19, 2022, from https://www.bbc.com/news/business-52392366

Hartmann, T., Toz, E., & Brandon, M. (2010). Just a game? Unjustified virtual violence produces guilt in empathetic players. *Media Psychology, 13*, 339–363. https://doi.org/10.1080/15213269.2010.524912

Help Net Security. (2019). *Anomali discovers phishing campaign targeting Chinese government agencies.* Help Net Security article. Retrieved May 19, 2022, from https://www.helpnetsecurity.com/2019/08/12/phishing-chinese-government-agencies/

Hiranand, R. (2011). Chinese PC game takes aim at American soldiers. Newsstream.blogs.cnn.com. Retrieved May 22, 2022, from https://newsstream.blogs.cnn.com/2011/05/21/chinese-pc-game-takes-aim-at-american-soldiers/

Hoffman, S. (2019). Engineering global consent: The Chinese Communist Party's data-driven power expansion. Australian Strategic Policy Institute (ASPI).

Insikt Group. (2020). *Chinese influence operations evolve in campaigns targeting Taiwanese elections, Hong Kong protests. Recorded future. Insict Group report.* Retrieved May 22, 2022, from https://go.recordedfuture.com/hubfs/reports/cta-2020-0429.pdf

Jiang Tao. (2021). 人工智能数据安全风险和有效治理措施 (*Artificial intelligence data security risks and effective governance measures*). Article, June 13. Retrieved September 11, 2021, from https://proxy.library.spbu.ru:6702/KCMS/detail/detail.aspx?dbcode=CJFD&dbname=CJFDAUTO&filename=FBZX202122068&uniplatform=NZKPT&v=8ZjdVpFHgPQ2AkCxbyeOX7ggmm2YxCqMbk6I4UPzhgoTS1BgtGNYgfx4Fx0KfYBm

Kamennov, P. B. (2020). The development of artificial intelligence is the most important direction of China's innovation policy. The PRC Economy in the period of the 13th Five Year Plan (2016–2020), 141–156.

Kim, M. (2019). The epic games store is spyware: How a toxic accusation was started by anti-Chinese sentiment. USgamer.net. Retrieved May 19, 2022, from https://www.usgamer.net/articles/the-epic-games-store-is-spyware-how-a-toxic-accusation-was-started-by-anti-chinese-sentiment

Knowledge at Wharton. (2018). *Is China the next AI superpower?* Knowledge at Wharton article. Retrieved May 19, 2022, from https://knowledge.wharton.upenn.edu/article/ai-china-vs-us/

Komissina, I. (2019). Contemporary state and prospects of the artificial intelligence technology development in China. *Problems of the National Strategy Journal, 52*(1), 137–160.

Koty, A. C. (2021). Artificial intelligence in China: Shenzhen releases first local regulations. China Briefing news article. Retrieved September 30, 2021, from https://www.china-briefing.com/news/artificial-intelligence-china-shenzhen-first-local-ai-regulations-key-areas-coverage/

Kutejnikov, D. L., Izhaev, O. A., Lebedev, V. A., & Zenin, S. S. (2022). Privacy in the realm of artificial intelligence systems application for remote biometric identification. *Lex russica, 75*(2), 121–131. https://doi.org/10.17803/1729-5920.2022.183.2.121-131

Lakomy, M. (2021). *Islamic state's online propaganda: A comparative analysis* (1st ed.). Routledge.

Laskai, L. & Webster, G. (2019). Translation: Chinese Expert Group Offers 'Governance Principles' for 'Responsible AI', *New America*, https://www.newamerica.org/cybersecurity-initiative/digichina/blog/translation-chinese-expert-group-offers-governance-principles-responsible-ai/

Lau, J., & Shui-yin, S. (2021). 'Patriots Only': Hong Kong's new election system in action. *The Diplomat*. Retrieved May 6, 2022, from https://thediplomat.com/2021/11/patriots-only-hong-kongs-new-election-system-in-action/

Leksutina, Y. (2018). China and reforming of the international economic system. *Comparative Politics Russia, 9*(3), 26–41. https://doi.org/10.18611/2221-3279-2018-9-3-26-41

Levine, T. R. (2019). *Duped: Truth-default theory and the social science of lying and deception*. University Alabama Press.

Li, A., Jiao, D., & Zhu, T. (2018). Detecting depression stigma on social media: A linguistic analysis. *Journal of Affective Disorders, 232*, 358–362. https://doi.org/10.1016/j.jad.2018.02.087

Li, A., Jiao, D., & Zhu, T. (2022). Stigmatizing attitudes across cybersuicides and offline suicides: Content analysis of Sina Weibo. *Journal of Medical Internet Research, 24*, e36489. https://doi.org/10.2196/36489

Li, A. H. F. (2016). Centralisation of power in the pursuit of law-based governance. Legal reform in China under the Xi administration. Retrieved March 15, 2022, from journals.openedition.org. https://journals.openedition.org/chinaperspectives/6995

Li, D., Tong, T., & Xiao, Y. (2021). Is China emerging as the global leader in AI? *Harvard Business Review*. Retrieved May 6, 2022, from https://hbr.org/2021/02/is-china-emerging-as-the-global-leader-in-ai

Liao, R. (2022). China's robotaxis charged ahead in 2021. *TechCrunch*. Retrieved May 19, 2022, from https://techcrunch.com/2022/01/14/2021-robotaxi-china/

Lin, J. (2013). Identification matters: A moderated mediation model of media interactivity, character identification, and video game violence on aggression. *Journal of Communication, 63*, 682–702. https://doi.org/10.1111/jcom.12044

Long, F., & Luo, K. (2022). Understanding Chinese Tech in AI research. Plaintext Group report. Retrieved May 21, 2022, from https://www.plaintextgroup.com/reports/understanding-chinese-tech-in-ai-research

M.mydrivers.com. (2019, September 6). 唏嘘!曾经爆红的ZAO APP下架被约谈 (*The once-popular ZAO APP was removed from the shelves and was interviewed*). M.mydrivers.com article. Retrieved September 30, 2021, from https://m.mydrivers.com/newsview/644907.html

Mann, J. (2022). China says it will send government officials to inspect Big Tech firms over their use of algorithms. MSN. Retrieved May 21, 2022, from https://www.msn.com/en-us/news/technology/china-says-it-will-send-government-officials-to-inspect-big-tech-firms-over-their-use-of-algorithms/ar-AAW2sQ6

Martina, M., & Brunnstrom, D. (2022). U.S. approves $100 million sale for Taiwan missile upgrades. Reuters. Retrieved May 6, 2022, from https://www.reuters.com/markets/us/us-approves-100-million-sale-taiwan-missile-upgrades-2022-02-07/

McCarthy-Jones, S. (2020). Artificial intelligence is a totalitarian's dream—Here's how to take power back. The Conversation. Retrieved May 19, 2022, from https://theconversation.com/artificial-intelligence-is-a-totalitarians-dream-heres-how-to-take-power-back-143722

Meng, R. (2021). *From National Governance to Personal Protection: Logical Transmission of the Use of Personal Information in Social Credit System—In the Context of the Personal Information Protection Law of the People's Republic of China*. Retrieved September 30, 2021, from https://proxy.library.spbu.ru:6702/KCMS/detail/detail.aspx?dbcode=CJFD&dbname=CJFDAUTO&filename=XZXY202105004&uniplatform=NZKPT&v=X82b8ohY%25mmd2F0rwOyyP%25mmd2Ba5Fxf%25mmd2BKaqanz2wO9VbGRF2FEGSobet4KTlvYgwmKs3nzzIr

Minter, A. (2015). Xinjiang, China's fertile ground for Islamic State recruiters. *Daily Republic*. Retrieved May 19, 2022, from https://www.dailyrepublic.com/all-dr-news/opinion/state-national-columnists/xinjiang-chinas-fertile-ground-for-islamic-state-recruiters/

Nash, J. (2021). AI researchers won't be playing 'trust fall' with Facebook. Or China," Biometric Update. Retrieved September 30, 2021, from https://www.biometricupdate.com/202108/ai-researchers-wont-be-playing-trust-fall-with-facebook-or-china

O'Meara, S. (2019). Will China lead the world in AI by 2030? *Nature, 572*, 427–428. https://doi.org/10.1038/d41586-019-02360-7

Ohara, B. (2021). How China is undermining digital trust—And how democracies can respond. European Council on Foreign Relations. Retrieved September 30, 2021, from https://ecfr.eu/article/how-china-is-undermining-digital-trust-and-how-democracies-can-respond/

Pashentsev, E. N., Phan, C. N. A., & Dam, V. N. (2020). Malicious use of artificial intelligence in North-East Asia and threats of international psychological security. CyberLeninka. Retrieved September 30, 2021, from https://cyberleninka.ru/article/n/zlonamerennoe-ispolzovanie-iskusstvennogo-intellekta-v-severo-vostochnoy-azii-i-ugrozy-mezhdunarodnoy-informatsionno/viewer

People.cn. (2021, August 22). 在高质量发展中促进共同富裕 统筹做好重大金融风险防范化解工作 (*Promote common prosperity in the process of high-quality development Coordinate the prevention and resolution of major financial risks*). People.cn report. Retrieved February 16, 2022, from http://politics.people.com.cn/n1/2021/0818/c1024-32197312.html

Primshic, D., & Golubev, S. (2019). The Chinese approach to the accelerated development of artificial intelligence technologies. *Science and Innovations, 4*, 43–50. https://doi.org/10.29235/1818-9857-2019-4-43-50

Reshetnikova, M., Pugatscheva, I., & Lukina, Y. (2021). Trends in the development of artificial intelligence technologies in China. *Russian Journal of Innovation Economics, 11*(1), 333–350. https://doi.org/10.18334/vinec.11.1.111912

Reuters. (2021). *China regulators held talks with Alibaba, Tencent, nine others on 'deepfake' tech*. Yahoo! News. Retrieved May 19, 2022, from https://news.yahoo.com/china-regulators-held-talks-alibaba-032946717.html

Reuters. (2022). *China cyberspace regulator says it will build solid national cyber security barrier*. Reuters. Retrieved May 19, 2022, from https://www.reuters.com/world/china/china-cyberspace-regulator-saays-it-will-build-solid-national-cyber-security-2022-01-06/

Roberts, H., Cowls, J., Morley, J., Taddeo, M., Wang, V., & Floridi, L. (2020). The Chinese approach to artificial intelligence: An analysis of policy, ethics, and regulation. *AI & Society, 36*, 59–77. https://doi.org/10.1007/s00146-020-00992-2

Semiconductor Industry Association. (2022). *China's share of global chip sales now surpasses Taiwan's, closing in on Europe's and Japan's*. Semiconductor Industry Association report. Retrieved May 19, 2022, from https://www.semiconductors.org/chinas-share-of-global-chip-sales-now-surpasses-taiwan-closing-in-on-europe-and-japan/

Shenzhen Report. (2015, December). 深圳市信息安全技术与行业发展研究报告 (*Shenzhen Information Security Technology and Industry Development Research Report*). Report. Retrieved January 10, 2022, from http://stic.sz.gov.cn/kjfw/rkx/rkxcgsjk/201711/P020171103342050056741.pdf

Shilov, A. (2021). China now produces one billion chips a day. Tom's Hardware. Retrieved May 19, 2022, from https://www.tomshardware.com/news/china-now-produces-over-1-billion-chips-per-day

Simmons, N. (2020). The real reason these games were banned in China. Looper. Retrieved May 22, 2022, from https://www.looper.com/202202/the-real-reason-these-games-were-banned-in-china/

Slotta, D. (2022). China: AI market size 2021. Statista. Retrieved May 6, 2022, from https://www.statista.com/statistics/1262377/china-ai-market-size/

Sohu. (2022, May 5). 2022年值得关注的5种物联网威胁 (*5 IoT threats to watch in 2022*). Hanyun Technology report. Retrieved May 6, 2022, from https://www.sohu.com/a/543868821_120108384

Soliev, N. (2021). Why is the Islamic State in Afghanistan's propaganda targeting China? *The Diplomat*. Retrieved May 19, 2022, from https://thediplomat.com/2021/10/is-the-islamic-state-in-afghanistan-targeting-china/

Stanford University. (2022). *Artificial Intelligence Index Report 2022*. Stanford University report, Stanford. Retrieved May 19, 2022, from https://aiindex.stanford.edu/report/

Storm.mg. (2020, September 9). 反共桌遊「逆統戰」預計明年上市 《環球時報》氣炸:台獨港獨勢力煽動青少年, 已危害國家安全! (*The anti-communist board game "Anti-United Front" is expected to go on sale next year. The Global Times is furious: Taiwan independence and Hong Kong independence forces incite young people, which has jeopardized national security*). Storm.mg article. Retrieved May 6, 2022, from https://www.storm.mg/article/3096174?page=1

Suter, V. (2020). Algorithmic panopticon: State surveillance and transparency in China's social credit system. *Communications in Computer and Information Science*, 42–59. https://doi.org/10.1007/978-3-030-67238-6_4

Tang, Y. (2021). China-made 14nm chips expected to be mass produced next year. CnTechPost. Retrieved May 19, 2022, from https://cntechpost.com/2021/06/23/china-made-14nm-chips-expected-to-be-mass-produced-next-year/

Telford, T. (2018). These news anchors are professional and efficient. They're also not human. *The Washington Post*. Retrieved May 21, 2022, from https://www.washingtonpost.com/business/2018/11/09/these-news-anchors-are-professional-efficient-theyre-also-not-human/

The paper. (2019, September 4). ZAO火不火, 取决于动机纯不纯 (*ZAO: danger or not, depends on the pure impure motivation*). The paper article. Retrieved September 21, 2021, from https://www.thepaper.cn/newsDetail_forward_4334350

The paper. (2021, May 9). 个人信息保护法草案 (*Personal Information Protection Law*). Official text. Retrieved September 30, 2021, from https://m.thepaper.cn/baijiahao_12598997

Tracxn.com. (2022). *Artificial intelligence startups in China*. Tracxn.com article. Retrieved May 6, 2022, from https://tracxn.com/explore/Artificial-Intelligence-Startups-in-China

Trading Economics. (2022). *Taiwan Unemployment Rate—April 2022 Data—1978–2021 Historical May Forecast*. Tradingeconomics.com report. Retrieved May 6, 2022, from https://tradingeconomics.com/taiwan/unemployment-rate

Tucker, J. (2019). No shit, video games are political. They're conservative. The Outline. Retrieved May 19, 2022, from https://theoutline.com/post/7803/are-video-games-political-conservative-liberal

U.S. Department of the Treasury. (2022). *Hong Kong-related sanctions*. U.S. Department of the Treasury policy report. Retrieved May 6, 2022, from https://home.treasury.gov/policy-issues/financial-sanctions/sanctions-programs-and-country-information/hong-kong-related-sanctions

Vaccari, C., & Chadwick, A. (2020). Deepfakes and disinformation: Exploring the impact of synthetic political video on deception, uncertainty, and trust in news. *Social Media and Society, 6*, 1–13.

Vito, J. (2021). Top countries of the gaming market leaders board. PlayStation Universe. Retrieved May 19, 2022, from https://www.psu.com/news/top-countries-of-the-gaming-market-leaders-board/

Wang, D. (2019). Malicious use of artificial intelligence threats and countermeasures. Cnki.com.cn. Retrieved May 21, 2022, from https://www.cnki.com.cn/Article/CJFDTOTAL-CINS201908008.htm

Watts, W. (2019). Soros blasts China's Xi as 'most dangerous opponent' of open societies. MarketWatch. Retrieved May 19, 2022, from https://www.marketwatch.com/story/george-soros-blasts-chinas-xi-as-most-dangerous-opponent-of-open-societies-2019-01-24?siteid=yhoof2&yptr=yahoo

Wong, L. (2005). *Marginalization and social welfare in China*. Retrieved May 19, 2022, from https://www.taylorfrancis.com/books/mono/10.4324/9780203982990/marginalization-social-welfare-china-linda-wong

World Health Organization. (2020). *Addictive behaviours: Gaming disorder*. WHO. int. Retrieved May 19, 2022, from https://www.who.int/news-room/questions-and-answers/item/addictive-behaviours-gaming-disorder

Xu, Q., Shen, Z., Shah, N., Cuomo, R., Cai, M., Brown, M., Li, J., Mackey, T., Xu, Q., Shen, Z., & Shah, N. (2020). Characterizing Weibo social media posts from Wuhan, China during the early stages of the COVID-19 pandemic: Qualitative content analysis. *JMIR Public Health and Surveillance, 6*, e24125. https://doi.org/10.2196/24125

Yiu, E. (2022). US sanctions are 'stupid and crazy', former Hong Kong finance chief says. *South China Morning Post*. Retrieved May 22, 2022, from https://www.scmp.com/business/banking-finance/article/3174030/crazy-us-sanctions-against-china-russia-weaponise

Yu, L., Jiang, W., Ren, Z., Xu, S., Zhang, L., Hu, X., Yu, L., Jiang, W., & Ren, Z. (2021). Detecting changes in attitudes toward depression on Chinese social media: A text analysis. *Journal of Affective Disorders, 280*, 354–363. https://doi.org/10.1016/j.jad.2020.11.040

Zhang, M. (2021). Research on a trusted artificial intelligence defense method for malware against adversarial attacks. Retrieved September 30, 2021, from https://proxy.library.spbu.ru:6702/KCMS/detail/detail.aspx?dbcode=CMFD&dbname=CMFD202101&filename=1020968935.nh&uniplatform=NZKPT&v=5srTuG-jjJCw%25mmd2B7Os908mwIkpgUbtP04kXhIGaZFL4CZxrIAPqviGwrZ7dIeXwbxFn

14

Malicious Use of Artificial Intelligence, Uncertainty, and U.S.–China Strategic Mutual Trust

Cuihong Cai and Ruoyang Zhang

Introduction

With the development and application of AI technologies, the various uncertainties arising from AI technologies and their applications have raised concerns about the malicious use of artificial intelligence (MUAI) and posed a potential threat to international psychological security, especially the strategic mutual trust between the two great powers, China and the United States.

The impact of AI competition on U.S.–China strategic trust is reflected in the policy actions and discourse of the United States and China (especially the United States) in recent years. In terms of actions, in recent years, the U.S. government has extended its designation of a "China Threat" to include high-tech fields represented by AI and other technologies, and has continued to decouple from China and suppress Chinese enterprises in high-tech and

C. Cai (✉)
Center for American Studies, Fudan University, Shanghai, China
e-mail: chcai@fudan.edu.cn

R. Zhang
School of International Relations and Public Affairs, Fudan University, Shanghai, China
e-mail: 21110170039@m.fudan.edu.cn

critical infrastructure areas. China and the United States have coincidentally raised the importance of AI technology to an unprecedented level and combined it with strategic economic development, political stability, military security, and international influence as the frontier of strategic competition between the two countries. Yet while the United States and China continue to make progress on AI technology, there is a distinct lack of sustained government-to-government dialogue on AI and national security between the two countries, and the deterioration of their relationship has led to a breakdown in direct communication and a decline in strategic mutual trust on a range of issues. According to John Allen, president of the Brookings Institution, the lack of communication between the United States and China in the area of AI technology and the concerns about each other's development of AI weapon systems have made the potential security dilemma between the two countries more serious, and the talk of an "AI arms race" has become more prevalent (Allen, 2020). The United States believes that the Chinese government is attempting to leapfrog its military capabilities through the development of AI, and "China's investments in AI threaten to erode U.S. military advantage, destabilize the free and open international order, and challenge our values and traditions with respect to human rights and individual liberties", and that China will ultimately "challenge" U.S. comparative advantage and leadership in AI and globally across the board, posing a serious "threat" to U.S. national security (U.S. Department of Defense, 2019). AI has been directly linked to the "China Threat" in the discourse, which has pushed U.S.–China strategic trust to its lowest point. Driven by pessimistic and stubborn zero-sum thinking, the great power rivalry between the United States and China is on a dangerous slide towards splitting the world into two opposing systems. For this reason, UN Secretary-General Antonio Guterres issued a warning about this danger: "the world [is] splitting in two, with the two largest economies on earth creating two separate and competing worlds, each with their own dominant currency, trade and financial rules, their own internet and artificial intelligence capacities, and their own zero sum geopolitical and military strategies" (Guterres, 2019).

The development and use of AI technology is a matter that will affect the future of all humanity. Both China and the United States are leaders in this area, and the relationship between China and the United States has a pivotal impact on the security and development of the world. Studying the risk of MUAI as a potential threat to strategic mutual trust between China and the

United States is important for promoting strategic stability between these two powers, advancing the future development and governance of AI technologies, and improving the international security environment.

Literature Review

As a key force in the new round of technological revolution, AI technology, while greatly enhancing national governance in the field of security, can also give rise to a technological security paradox. Nick Bostrom, a British philosopher and founding director of the Future of Humanity Institute at Oxford University, points out that AI is not just a disruptive technology but that it may also be the most destructive technology humanity has ever encountered (Bostrom, 2014). This destructiveness is reflected in the uncertainty of AI technology and its applications, and has led to research on the potential MUAI problem. In July 2017, the Belfer Center for Science and International Affairs at Harvard's Kennedy School of Government released the report "Artificial Intelligence and National Security", which pioneered an analysis of the relationship between AI and national security, and assessed AI technologies in terms of privacy, security, transparency, and accountability (Allen & Chan, 2017). In February 2018, the report "Malicious Use of Artificial Intelligence: Prediction, Prevention, and Mitigation", jointly authored by 26 scholars and experts from the University of Cambridge, Oxford University, and Yale University, classified the possible risks posed by AI technologies as "digital threats, physical threats, and political threats" and provided a specific analysis of these issues from the dimension of technological security (Brundage et al., 2018). In recent years, Chinese academics have also begun to focus on the application and risks of AI in economic, social, and ethical fields, and have conducted research on the areas of MUAI, the security threats posed by MUAI, and how to deal with them (Fu, 2020; Que & Zhang, 2020; Chen & Zhu, 2020). It can be said that although the major threat to national security caused by MUAI is still largely at the level of "possibility", with the increase in the development and application of AI technology and the increase of its penetration of social life, coupled with the attention of academia and media coverage, the threat of MUAI is increasingly coming into the public and policymaking circles in China and the United States, and it is influencing the public perceptions and national strategic decisions in both countries at the psychological level, as well as having a potential impact on the strategic mutual trust between the two countries in the context of strategic competition.

Strategic mutual trust in bilateral relations means that both sides deeply understand each other's strategic intentions and hold positive expectations of each other's positions and behaviour in areas involving their core interests. The establishment of strategic mutual trust does not mean that there are no longer conflicts of interest and differences in perceptions between the two sides, but rather that there is a perception that "common interests outweigh differences" and the parties strive to reduce the impact of conflicts of interest and differences in perceptions on the relationship between the two countries in order to form a long-term positive interaction (Wang et al., 2012). The main differences and contradictions between China and the United States are multilayered, and the factors affecting the development of Sino–U.S. relations include structural factors involving fundamental differences between the two countries in ideology, political systems, and cultural traditions; domestic and foreign political factors; accidental or crisis factors; and factors at the cognitive level (Yuan, 2008). Strategic mutual trust in a broad sense encompasses all these levels, and to fundamentally build strategic mutual trust, differences, and contradictions at different levels must be mitigated comprehensively. Strategic mutual trust in a narrow sense, on the other hand, refers to how the two sides can get rid of the interference of problems at the cognitive level and build up a minimum level of trust. In the context of the strategic competition between China and the United States, compared with other structural factors, internal and external political factors, and contingent factors, it is generally agreed that the most necessary and potential measure to expand the development space of Sino–U.S. relations is to promote strategic mutual trust at the cognitive level, reduce strategic miscalculation, and enhance mutual understanding. Although promoting strategic mutual trust at the cognitive level cannot solve the structural contradictions in Sino–U.S. relations, it is a necessary precondition for resolving structural contradictions and a basic line of defence against crises. The lack of strategic mutual trust, on the contrary, will lead to miscalculation in the weighing of interests between the two countries, that is, the inability to make objective and rational choices, thus further worsening the cognitive differences between the two countries, especially in the frontier area of strategic competition like AI technology.

Strategic mutual trust in bilateral relations essentially belongs to the issue of trust in international relations. The explanations for the lack of trust between states given by mainstream international relations theory mainly revolve around the uncertainty of states' intentions and behaviours and their risks, and a series of explanatory frameworks are given for how uncertainty affects the state of trust between states. Uncertainty means that it is always difficult for any state to accurately judge and predict the intentions and behaviours of others, thus generating various types of risks, especially security risks, which pose a great challenge to the building of trust between states. The risk of MUAI can be objective, which is the result of the expansion of research and application of AI technology, or subjective, which depends on the actors' own perception and grasp of this technology, and essentially belongs to a negative uncertainty about national security in international relations. Different paradigms of international relations research have different understandings of how uncertainty affects strategic mutual trust between states.

Uncertainty under the realist paradigm is a typical uncertainty brought about by incomplete information or information asymmetry. The combination of the unknowability of states' present and future intentions and the difficulty of assessing the changing state power (especially military capabilities) leads to uncertainty in the real international system and makes it difficult to build trust between states (Montgomaery, 2006). To cope with "uncertainty", offensive realists argue that states are in a state of "fear" because they can never grasp the intentions of the "other", and that they must make the worst assessment and assumption of such intentions; therefore, the premise of trust building—the positive expectations of the other's behaviour—is impossible to achieve (Mearsheimer, 2001). Defensive realists, on the other hand, place "uncertainty" under the "security dilemma", arguing that the state's relative claim to its own security puts the "other" in a state of insecurity and raises unnecessary conflict due to uncertainty. Therefore, although mutual trust is difficult to generate, an assessment of the military technology, intentions, and motivations of the "other" is important to manage the risks posed by uncertainty (Jervis, 1978; Glaser, 1997). Although neoliberal scholars also look at "uncertainty" from an objective perspective, they argue that "uncertainty" does not necessarily lead states to draw pessimistic conclusions about the intentions of the "other" in advance, and argue that active assessment of intentions and collection of reliable information are meaningful for developing trust between states (Keohane, 1993). Unlike the first two, constructivism advocates a subjective perspective on "uncertainty", arguing that the "other" or objective world is not imperfectly cognizable, but rather that due to perceptions, identities, and norms, the actor's cognition of the objective world and the "other" is actually established. In the constructivist perspective, the uncertainty of the "other" is somehow self-conceived.

However, the existing explanatory framework on the impact of uncertainty on strategic mutual trust between countries still suffers from insufficient explanatory power in explaining the relationship between the risk of MUAI and the strategic mutual trust between China and the United States. On the one hand, the risk posed by MUAI is not exactly the same as the uncertainty factor in traditional international relations. In addition to the uncertainty of states' intentions in using AI technologies as actors, the uncertainty of the AI technology itself as an object (or the tendency of the technology itself to be used maliciously) is also an important factor affecting the strategic mutual trust relationship between states. On the other hand, fewer studies have been conducted specifically on the risk of MUAI and strategic mutual trust between China and the United States. In response to the current strategic mutual suspicion and trust deficit between China and the United States, existing theories have examined the impact of the narrowing power gap between the regimes, institutional differences between them, domestic political and economic environment, leaders' perceptions, and chance events affecting trust (Wang & Lieberthal, 2013; Tao, 2013), but not on the impact of the current strategic competition between the countries in the key area of AI technology competition. When studying how frontier technologies such as AI affect international relations, existing research has focused mainly on the impact of technological change on national power patterns, especially military power contrasts, and has lacked attention to the potential impact of AI technologies and the risk of MUAI on international relations, especially on strategic mutual trust between countries, at the cognitive-psychological level.

In terms of research methodology, this chapter uses analytical eclecticism in an attempt to find the interconnectedness of different analytical paths. It can be said that realism, liberalism, and constructivism all focus on uncertainty in explaining the problem of an interstate trust deficit, and all recognize that uncertainty about the intentions, motives, (military) technology, and capabilities of the "other" is the root cause of this deficit. Among these approaches, realism and liberalism look at uncertainty mainly from an objective perspective, with realism emphasizing that the unknowability of state intentions or objective factors makes it difficult to assess state power, especially military capabilities, and thus states tend to assess the intentions and motives of the other from a pessimistic perspective, making the premise of trust between states non-existent. Neoliberalism, on the other hand, emphasizes that uncertainty is caused more by one's own incomplete knowledge of the "other" or the objective world, and therefore states need to be sensitive to the information from other states and proactively assess those states' intentions and motivations. Constructivism, on the other hand, takes a subjective view of uncertainty, emphasizing that the state's perception of uncertainty is itself influenced by cognitive factors such as perceptions, identities, and norms. The risk of MUAI implies a situation or state of uncertainty for the state, which may be objective in the sense that it is the result of changes in the current situation and the interaction of various objective forces, or subjective in the sense that it depends on the state's own perception and grasp of the situation. Therefore, the focus of this chapter will be on how the risk of MUAI will affect states' assessment of others' intentions, motives, and capabilities and states' perception of the uncertainty at both the subjective and objective levels, and thus how it will negatively affect strategic mutual trust between states.

Path Analysis of the Risk of Malicious Use of Artificial Intelligence Affecting U.S.–China Strategic Mutual Trust

The potential impact of the risk of MUAI on U.S.–China strategic mutual trust is analysed primarily by investigating both sides' assessments of each other's intentions, motivations, and capabilities to use AI technologies, a process that depends on the characteristics of the AI technology itself at the technical level, the state's sense of security at the cognitive level, and the ability of the rule system to constrain state behaviour at the institutional level. At the technical level, MUAI may change the offensive and defensive posture between states, causing differences in national security preferences between states, increasing the cost for China and the United States to believe that each other is not malicious, and making the premise of forming strategic mutual trust between states more difficult to establish. At the cognitive level, the risk of MUAI will amplify the state's insecurity and affect China's and the United States' perceptions of each other's AI application capabilities. At the institutional level, the risk of MUAI affects the original system of rules on conflict boundaries and arms control, and the gaps in the rules governing state behaviour and capabilities make it more difficult for states to assess each other's intentions and capabilities, thus having a potentially negative impact on strategic mutual trust between states.

1. *At the technical level, the risk of MUAI may make it more difficult for states to assess each other's intent to use AI technologies.*

The national security implications of the risk of MUAI are most intuitively reflected in the military domain. As an important enabling technology, AI can greatly improve the battlefield situational awareness, strategic decision-making efficiency, operational strength, and coordination of militaries by combining it with other weapons technologies (Chen & Zhu, 2020), thereby increasing the uneven distribution of technological advantages among actors. Countries with relatively weak AI technologies will be at an absolute disadvantage in terms of strategic judgement, strategy selection, and execution efficiency, while countries with technological advantages will gain the ability to surpass traditional force confrontation by occupying new technological vantage points (Que & Zhang, 2020). In this technological context, the risk of MUAI may make the concerns of China and the United States about power disparity, national security, and conflict of interests more obvious, which in turn makes the asymmetry in AI development between the two sides gradually magnified into differences in national security preferences, and stimulates both sides to choose conflict and confrontation at the technological level, making it more difficult for both sides to rationally assess each other's intentions. Therefore, strategic mutual trust based on rational and objective perception of conflict becomes more difficult.

Technologically strong states will gain increasing benefits and lower conflict costs when they choose to use AI for conflict confrontation, while technologically weak states will find it difficult to form effective external constraints with conventional means of confrontation. On the one hand, the increased utility of AI technology in military applications may lead to a greater propensity for states to choose to use this technology. As a general-purpose platform technology, the militarization of AI will not be limited to a single type of weapon or combat platform, but will achieve a comprehensive proliferation in various military fields. Thus, the side with the superior AI technology will develop military devices with greater strike utility and lower expected risk in multiple domains, while the side with inferior technology will have difficulty neutralizing or bridging this power gap with quantitative overlays or strategic tactics. This power imbalance is also reflected in the nuclear deterrence system. Strategic interactions among international actors are often based on a game of imperfect information, which is one of the prerequisites for the existence of a nuclear deterrence system (Tang, 2014). However, with the application of AI technology in the military, the technologically superior party can make more flexible and accurate strategic judgements and choices in nuclear deterrence decisions by undertaking a panoramic and intelligent analysis of the original uncertain strategic intentions and complex confrontation situations. For example, the technologically superior side could use AI technology to conduct large-scale surveillance of the adversary's security infrastructure and, based on this, determine the adversary's behaviour patterns and implement more targeted countermeasures (Geist & Lohn, 2018). Thus, advances in AI technology could upset the long-standing balance of "mutually assured destruction" of nuclear deterrence, thereby encouraging catastrophic human decision making. Moreover, in cases where the response to the use of large-scale military operations is too severe, states may also more frequently adopt new, more operationally effective technologies such as AI to achieve their goals (Rabkin & Yoo, 2017). On the other hand, the application of AI in the military domain will not only achieve an all-around improvement in operational efficiency but also reduce the potential casualties in the form of unmanned operations, which will significantly reduce the constraints of expected costs on war decisions and their progress, including many factors such as profit and loss, cycle time, scale, and nature. In particular, the two major factors that used to control war—military costs and domestic political costs—are somewhat weakened (Gilli & Gilli, 2016). As a result, the adaptive advantage of "positive illusions" possessed by technological powers makes it easier for them to develop offensive demands for hegemony, that is, technological powers may become more lenient in their war-making decisions and tend to achieve large-scale militarization of AI to build their absolute advantage.

In contrast, the passive position of technologically weak states creates a defensive need to maintain security, that is, technologically weak states are more inclined to take radical countermeasures and tend to seek the proliferation of AI weapons to obtain new checks and balances. A broader point here is that under crisis and conflict conditions, the deterrent effect of AI is predicated on the perceived risks associated with a particular capability it enables or enhances. The higher the uncertainty generated by a capacity, the more that deploying AI-augmented capabilities in a crisis might actually encourage an adversary to act more cautiously, and in turn, bolster stability (Johnson, 2020). Thus, the uncertainty created by the introduction of AI may incentivize technologically vulnerable states to delegate decisions to machines in order to achieve the desired deterrent effect (Wong et al., 2020). However, the subjective perceptions and judgements of both sides of a crisis or conflict are different, so this implicit threat (granting AI military decision-making autonomy) may likewise exacerbate the instability of a crisis. Human induction (i.e. the ability to form general rules from specific pieces of information) is a crucial aspect of defence planning, primarily to manage situations that require high levels of visual and moral judgement and reasoning (Cummings, 2017). Although AI has the ability to "self-learn" and "develop its own intuition and act on that intuition" (Kaplan, 2017), neither behaviourist reinforcement learning, connectionist deep learning, nor symbolic expert systems can accurately reflect human cognitive abilities, such as perception, emotion, responsibility, and value.

Due to the lack of human moral judgement, intuition, and responsibility, giving too much autonomy in military decision making to AI systems is likely to increase the risk of strategic instability among nations. For example, AI systems programmed to pursue tactical and operational advantage may misperceive (or ignore) an adversary's bid to de-escalate a situation as prelude to an imminent attack (Wong et al., 2020). Moreover, algorithmic models based on historical data are not fully capable of anticipating and responding to potentially sudden changes, and changes in the regulatory environment, risk environment, or risk strategy and other underlying conditions also have certain real-time requirements for AI, which will increase the risk of unintentional escalation and pre-emptive instability once AI fails to adjust to this in a timely manner, and even stimulate a spiral of international crises upward.

In addition, differences in the rules governing the militarization of AI applications could exacerbate potential mistrust and misunderstanding between the United States and China. Relevant research in the field of military innovation suggests that, with the possible exception of nuclear weapons, technological innovation alone rarely causes the military balance to shift; instead, how militaries employ a technology usually proves critical (Posen, 1986). Despite the speed, data pools, and processing power of algorithms compared to humans, machine learning systems will still rely on assumptions encoded into them by human engineers, who may inadvertently sow their own biases into the systems they design (Johnson, 2020). If differences between the United States and China in areas such as culture and norms are reflected in the software design of AI programs, the resultant prejudices and preferences might become baked into the weapon systems they support (Johnson, 2019). These feedback loops generated by AI systems could potentially trap human operators into machines' bias and flawed assumptions (Johnson, 2020). Even when AI systems are designed to produce unbiased analysis, human biases inherent in data collection and other uncontrollable factors may influence decision making during crises and conflicts, and these cognitive biases may exacerbate potential mistrust and suspicion between the United States and China, further reducing the level of strategic mutual trust between the two sides.

2. *At the cognitive level, the risk of malicious AI can affect the rational perception of China and the United States about each other's awareness and capabilities of AI applications by amplifying national insecurity.*

Strategic mutual trust is a non-zero-sum game; it does not mean that the parties to mutual trust do not have real conflicts, but rather that they are able to assess each other's intentions, motivations, and capabilities in a more rational and objective manner, which in turn provides the possibility for the joint resolution of conflicts and contradictions. This assessment process is inevitably influenced by factors at the cognitive and psychological levels of the state. Among them, factors such as the state's perceived security, sense of urgency, and fear play an important role. National security consists of both subjective and objective security (Wolfers, 1952), and the impact of the risk of MUAI on the state consists of two parts: an objective stimulus, that is, a real or perceived danger; and a subjective response, that is, a psychological feeling of fear and insecurity of being threatened. This insecurity arises on the basis of the objective risk brought by MUAI, and to a certain extent it is detached from the threat of realism, becoming a stable, direct, subjective, psychological association with security. As the risk of MUAI rises, increased insecurity may affect the perceptions of China and the United States about each other's ability to apply AI technology and awareness of its application, and affect the rational judgements of both sides about each other's capabilities and intentions.

The application of AI technology takes place in a variety of fields such as economics, politics, and social governance, among which the field most sensitive to the perceived impact of another country's ability to apply technology and awareness of its application on national security is the military field. On the one hand, the risk of MUAI can make countries exaggerate the ability of AI technology application in the military; on the other hand, in the case of mutual misunderstanding and lack of communication, the increased risk of MUAI may distort the perception of militarized AI application awareness between countries and provide incentives for the arms race and disorderly competition between China and the United States in this field.

Psychological insecurity and competitive pressures are important influences in a nation's militarization of a new technology. When a nation evaluates a new technology with uncertain reliability, it may feel pressure to accelerate deployment if it believes that other nations are taking similar steps, thereby simplifying its security assessment in order to accelerate deployment (Horowitz & Scharre, 2021). During World War I, for example, competing pressures accelerated the introduction of chemical weapons into the military sphere (Heller, 1984). By increasing the sense of urgency and competitive pressure felt by both sides psychologically, the risk of MUAI could worsen the potential security dilemma between the United States and China and affect both sides' risk–benefit assessments of the militarized application of AI technologies, resulting in both sides accelerating the pace and expanding the scope of militarized AI applications in an effort to deploy new AI capabilities before their adversaries and take advantage of future first-mover advantage on the digital battlefield, thereby increasing the risk of deploying immature or unsafe AI systems into the military. For example, some American scholars argue that the lack of Chinese academic publications on the legal and ethical implications of military AI, as well as discussion of AI autonomy and the potential limits and risks of cyberwarfare, means that China has relatively few moral, legal or ethical qualms about deploying lethal autonomous weapons (Bendett, 2017; Johnson, 2018). And given the aggressive use of military AI by its strategic competitors, the United States may change its commitment to human control of weapons systems (Johnson, 2019). In addition, current international law is unclear on the definition of "lethal autonomy", and in the absence of a clear definition, both sides will continue to develop weapons systems with varying degrees of autonomy. The consequence will not only be an arms race but also potentially uncontrolled competition. AI-enabled weapons should not only distinguish between military and civilian targets when conducting strikes but also prevent and avoid excessive collateral or indirect damage to civilian targets, yet the competitive pressures of an arms race increase the likelihood that AI technologies with inherent technical flaws will be deployed to military facilities, making it difficult for attackers to limit the scope of damage from strikes and making the struck party prone to excessive collateral damage, thus leading to escalation of conflict (Fu, 2020).

With the increasing degree of informationization and automation of human production and life, the application of AI technology in various fields of society is becoming more and more permeable, and in addition to the military field, it also has a wide range of applications in important fields such as politics, finance, economy, and networks, so the scope of national security being affected by the risk of MUAI is expanding, and the resulting possibility of systemic and comprehensive threats to national security is rising. Countries in the context of strategic competition are more inclined to think the worst of the other country's intentions, so efforts by one state to enhance the survivability of its strategic forces with state-of-the-art dual-use technology like AI could easily be perceived by the other side as a potential threat to its ability to survive (Johnson, 2020). In the event that actors' rational perceptions of each other's AI application awareness and AI technology application capabilities change, the objective extensibility and subjective intentionality of national security are likely to overlap, that is, the "survival anxiety" due to the risk of MUAI may be magnified into "survival threat". Currently, the U.S. government and think tanks as security actors refer to China's AI development as an "existential threat", and through the "securitization" approach they have enabled the idea of existential threat to gradually gain consensus (Liu & Yi, 2020). The resulting loss of the boundary between objective and subjective security will lead to a significant deviation from rational state behaviour, making it more difficult to build strategic mutual trust between China and the United States based on rational assessment and judgement.

3. *At the institutional level, the risk of MUAI technologies has impacted the international rule system, making it more difficult for states to assess each other's intentions and capabilities.*

The international rule system that binds and governs national technology applications by laws, rules, or norms is an important reference standard for states in assessing the intentions, motives, and capabilities of others, as well as an important basis for establishing strategic mutual trust relationships between states. However, with the development and application of AI technologies, the possibility of MUAI poses a threat to the existing international rule system, which not only makes the original rules on warfare conflicts more ambiguous but also makes the formulation of new rules on AI applications, and compliance with such rules, more difficult.

First, the increased risk of MUAI could lead to a blurring of the traditional rules governing the boundaries of war and conflict. This is reflected in AI's ability to provide more effective technical support for various types of small-scale, low-cost, short-duration, low-intensity, non-traditional methods of warfare and non-war military operations, while traditional escalation thresholds and operational norms become blurred and inapplicable in the face of these non-traditional methods. For example, the proliferation of low-risk and low-cost AI-augmented autonomous weapons with ambiguous rules of engagement, such as drone swarms, will become an increasingly enticing asymmetric option to undermine an adversary's military readiness, deterrence, and resolve. Without commonly held operational norms about an adversary's strategic priorities and political objectives, militaries deploying military AI could inadvertently cross already vague escalation thresholds (Brodie, 1966). In addition, AI technology-enabled weapons challenge rules of engagement such as the principles of distinction and proportionality in international humanitarian law (IHL), and their autonomy makes the presumption of responsibility and accountability in times of conflict more difficult.

Second, MUAI may also catalyze the formation of new forms of strategic confrontation, such as algorithmic warfare and awareness warfare. In the case of awareness warfare, for example, AI manipulates others by using the "influence machine", a combination of algorithmically generated content "bullets" (automatically generated baiting or deceptive content), personalized "targeting" (using emotional screening to target the most susceptible audience), and intensive "bombardment" of messages (Telley, 2018). In fact, this new model of confrontation can be used in more insidious and destructive ways to exacerbate polarization within the societies of hostile countries, thereby interfering with their internal political affairs and undermining the legitimacy of their existing governments. For example, Cambridge Analytica was revealed to have used AI technology to estimate and classify the personality traits and political tendencies of the American public, and to deliver different targeted political advertisements accordingly, in order to interfere with people's political behaviour such as voting. The emergence and evolution of unconventional military operations such as awareness warfare may blur the line between war and conflict, and the uncertainty of the militarization of AI will further exacerbate this risk. In addition, the existing arms control system and international disarmament agreements do not cover the militarization of AI, and there is no broad consensus on this topic. With large gaps and uncertainties in the relevant international rules, the increased risk of MUAI may intensify national competition in this field, and the lack of global regulation may lead to uncontrolled competition in the militarization of AI applications.

Third, rule making and compliance with arms control for AI militarization applications is more difficult and uncertain than for traditional weapons. While traditional arms control approaches include strict laws and intrusive verification regimes, AI systems are not suitable for this form of arms control. The rapid rate of technological iterations in the field of AI technologies does not lend itself to a strict normative framework. It is therefore more difficult to verify training data sets and algorithms to ensure compliance with agreed-upon rules associated with militarized applications of AI than it is to verify the production paths of nuclear or chemical weapons (Gill, 2019). In the case of lethal autonomous weapons, for example, there are several mechanisms under the UN framework that have explored internationally the limitation of autonomous weapons development. Among them, the UN Convention on Certain Conventional Weapons (CCW) negotiating mechanism has convened three informal expert meetings and three formal governmental expert group meetings since 2014. Although some breakthroughs have been made in the establishment of international mechanisms and international norms, the parties involved in the discussions are seriously divided over the definition of the application of lethal autonomous weapons, and all agree that the objects of their reference are very vague. Regardless of the definition discussed by all parties, it seems, to a certain extent, contradictory to the established rules on the use of weapons. According to a statistical analysis of 154 weapons systems by the Stockholm Peace Research Institute in Sweden, only 49 weapons can be legitimately engaged in human-supervised but uninvolved situations. They are mainly used for defence of a country's own facilities, such as protecting warships or bases, responding to incoming missiles, or similar situations (Boulanin & Verbruggen, 2018). And the strategic dividends from lethal autonomous weapons tug at the security interests of states, adding difficulties and challenges to subsequent arms control operations.

Responses and Measures to Improve Strategic Mutual Trust Among Nations: Artificial Intelligence as an Instrument of Trust Not War

The formation of strategic mutual trust is the product of a complex interaction of political, economic, technological, and cognitive factors, in which the development and application of AI technologies and the state's perception of them are playing an increasingly important role. In a period of heightened geopolitical competition between China and the United States, the risk of MUAI is also more likely to erode strategic mutual trust between China and the United States by affecting the rational assessment of each side's intentions, motivations, and capabilities to use AI technologies with each other, making crises and conflicts more likely to occur. As the two countries with the fastest growing R&D and applications of AI technologies, it is important for the promotion of a healthy development of AI technologies and the maintenance of international security for China and the United States to take measures to manage their differences and prevent the risk of MUAI from eroding their strategic mutual trust and triggering crises or conflicts.

To deal with the impact of the risk of MUAI technologies on the international rule system, establishing a binding international regime for national capacity to develop and apply AI is a feasible option. As it stands now, international rules for AI are mainly driven by companies or institutions in developed Western countries, represented by the United States, which means that a global AI governance mechanism as a whole is missing. At the same time, major countries still have not formed a unified consensus on the specific rules for AI technology development and application, and the differences in the principles of AI deployment and the degree of development among countries have also exacerbated irrational competition to a certain extent. As the two countries with the fastest development of AI technology research and application, China and the United States must closely coordinate confidence-building measures, and they should take legal responsibility to take the initiative to promote the development of technology development control agreements or conventions that are consistent with the norms of international relations and human moral constraints, and to lead the international community to reach consensus on some fundamental and principled rules and ethics, so as to promote the formation of a governance framework and a coordinated governance mechanism for the international recognition of technological risks. At the same time, they should help to build a broader international cooperation and governance network for the development of AI technologies, promote the active integration of scattered and relatively isolated governance procedures and resources between countries, and build a comprehensive governance system with sovereign states, NGOs, civil society, and multinational corporations as the main bodies.

In addition to the building of institutions and norms, it is also important at the cognitive level for China and the United States to establish a rational understanding of each other's capabilities and awareness of the application of AI technologies. On the one hand, analysts, academics, and decision makers on both sides need to have a more comprehensive understanding of the risks of AI technologies interacting with other strategic weapons and their malicious use; on the other hand, these actors also need to understand how competing strategic communities view these dynamics, as well as the implications of these trends for nuclear and conventional strategy and posture, arms races, arms control, escalation management, and cross-domain as well as extended deterrence (Gill, 2019). In recent years, China has sent positive signals about reaching international agreements on AI security and governance. On September 8, 2020, State Councillor and Foreign Minister Wang Yi proposed the Global Data Security Initiative, including three principles that should be followed to effectively address data security risk challenges, expressing the hope that the international community will reach an international agreement on AI security on the basis of universal participation, and to support the confirmation of relevant commitments to the initiative through bilateral or multilateral agreements. On November 21, 2020, President Xi Jinping emphasized at the 15th G20 Leaders' Summit that China supports strengthening dialogue around AI and advocates holding thematic meetings at the appropriate time to promote the implementation of the G20 AI Principles and lead the healthy development of global AI. At a time when there is a trust deficit between China and the United States and multilateral negotiations are seen as a legal battle, it makes sense to actively promote continuous, direct, and authoritative bilateral communication to strengthen coordination and dialogue around norms for the use of AI technologies. China and the United States should establish a platform for formal discussions on promoting the construction of norms and regimes for AI applications at the international level, explore areas of cooperation based on their respective interests and concerns, exchange and translate relevant documents, and reduce the potential harm to bilateral relations and international security due to the risk of MUAI by means of policy communication and academic exchanges.

Conclusion

The confluence of artificial intelligence and national security is becoming an increasingly important new perspective in the current perception of both China and the United States, which emphasizes the critical role of AI in influencing and shaping future national security. At the same time, AI is an important area of strategic competition between the two countries at present. In the current context of changing national power contrasts and strategic policy adjustments, the possibility of strategic competition between the two countries on AI technology will far exceed the possibility of cooperation, and the development needs for AI technology will take precedence over consideration of the security of this technology. In this state of prioritizing development needs and highlighting technological risks, the increasing uncertainty that AI technology and its applications are generating exacerbates the risk of MUAI technology and poses a potential threat to international security and strategic mutual trust between China and the United States.

But in the historical process of international security affairs, uncertainty is the norm and certainty is rather scarce. While the risk of MUAI inclines states to form pessimistic expectations about international relations, it also allows them to identify potential challenges to international security with a keen eye, and the study of MUAI risks also provides possible clues to international security governance at a time when AI has not yet brought about large-scale security shocks. As long as the security challenges posed by AI technologies are not disruptive, there is a relatively certain expectation that China and the United States, which are currently in intense competition around AI, can work together to maintain strategic stability and build strategic mutual trust, and can find answers to great-power coordination in historical experience and existing theory.

At present, the most important concern is not the impact of MUAI on national security, but the long-term risk to international relations and international security from the entrenchment of such perceptions at the policymaker level. China and the United States should not expect to solve their international security dilemma by obtaining a robust and secure AI system through "technology governing technology". At the same time, China and the United States should not compete to deploy insecure AI systems in order to win the arms race. Policymakers in both countries should neither underestimate the impact of the different strategic cultures of the United States and China on the use of AI technologies, nor overestimate the security implications of MUAI. What matters to policymakers is not only how MUAI technologies may impact national security but also how to continuously enrich and improve the rational perception of AI technologies, and thus change the governance choices for the present and the future. What lies ahead for China and the United States is not a foregone tragedy but a choice that concerns the future of humanity.

References

Allen, G., & Chan, T. (2017). Artificial intelligence and national security. The Belfer Center Study. Retrieved November 27, 2021, from https://statewatch.org/news/2017/jul/usa-belfer-center-national-security-and-ai-report.pdf

Allen, J. (2020). Together, The U.S. and China can reduce the risks from AI. Noema. Retrieved November 27, 2021, from https://www.noemamag.com/together-the-u-s-and-china-can-reduce-the-risks-from-ai/

Bendett, S. (2017). Get ready, NATO: Russia's new killer robots are nearly ready for war. The National Interest. Retrieved November 27, 2021, from https://nationalinterest.org/blog/the-buzz/russias-new-killer-robots-are-nearly-ready-war-19698

Bostrom, N. (2014). *Superintelligence: Paths, dangers, and strategies* (pp. 8–9). Oxford University.

Boulanin, V., & Verbruggen, M. (2018). *Mapping the development of autonomy in weapon systems* (p. 26). SIPRI Report.

Brodie, B. (1966). *Escalation and the nuclear option*. Princeton University Press.

Brundage, M., Avin, S., Clark, J., et al. (2018). The malicious use of artificial intelligence: Forecasting, prevention, and mitigation. Retrieved November 27, 2021, from https://arxiv.org/ftp/arxiv/papers/1802/1802.07228.pdf

Chen, Q., & Zhu, R. (2020). Why worry about AI shocks international security. *People's Tribune, 8*, 124–125.

Cummings, M. L. (2017). *Artificial intelligence and the future of warfare*. Chatham House.

Fu, Y. (2020). Together, the U.S. and China can reduce the risks from AI. Noema. Retrieved November 27, 2021, from https://www.noemamag.com/together-the-u-s-and-china-can-reduce-the-risks-from-ai/

Geist, E., & Lohn, A. (2018). How might artificial intelligence affect the risk of nuclear war? Rand Corporation. Retrieved November 27, 2021, from https://www.rand.org/pubs/perspectives/PE296.html

Gill, A. S. (2019). Artificial intelligence and international security: The long view. *Ethics & International Affairs, 33*(2), 169–179.

Gilli, A., & Gilli, M. (2016). The diffusion of drone warfare? Industrial, organizational and infrastructural constraints. *Security Studies, 25*(1), 76–77.

Glaser, L. C. (1997). The security dilemma revisited. *World Politics, 50*(1), 171–201.

Guterres, A. (2019). Address to the 74th session of the UN general assembly. United Nations secretary general speech. Retrieved November 27, 2021, from https://www.un.org/sg/en/content/sg/speeches/2019-09-24/address-74th-general-assembly

Heller, C. E. (1984). *Chemical warfare in world war: The American experience, 1917–1918. Leavenworth Papers 10, Combat Studies Institute, U.S* (p. 6). Amy Command and General Staff College.

Horowitz, M. C., & Scharre, P. (2021). Artificial intelligence and international stability—Risks and confidence-building measures. Center for a New American Security. Retrieved November 27, 2021, from https://www.cnas.org/publications/reports/ai-and-international-stability-risks-and-confidence-building-measures

Jervis, R. (1978). Cooperation under the security dilemma. *World Politics, 30*(2), 167–214.

Johnson, J. (2018). The US-China military and defense relationship during the Obama presidency. Palgrave Macmillan, Chap. 4.

Johnson, J. (2019). Artificial intelligence & future warfare: Implications for international security. *Defense & Security Analysis, 35*(2), 147–169.

Johnson, J. (2020). Artificial intelligence in nuclear warfare: A perfect storm of instability. *The Washington Quarterly, 43*(2), 197–211.

Kaplan, J. (2017). AI's PR problem. *MIT Technology Review*. Retrieved November 27, 2021, from https://www.technologyreview.com/s/603761/ais-pr-problem/

Keohane, O. R. (1993). Institutionalist theory and the realist challenge after the Cold War. In A. D. Baldwin (Ed.), *Neo-realism and neo-liberalism*. Columbia University.

Liu, G. Z., & Yi, N. (2020). A new perspective on the US national security perception: Artificial intelligence and national security. *Journal of International Security Studies, 2*, 147.

Mearsheimer, J. (2001). *The tragedy of great power politics*. W. W. Norton & Company.

Montgomaery, E. B. (2006). Breaking out of the security dilemma: Realism, reassurance, and the problem of uncertainty. *International Security, 31*(2), 151.

Posen, B. R. (1986). *The sources of military doctrine: France, Britain, and Germany between the world wars*. Cornell Studies in Security Affairs.

Que, T. S., & Zhang, J. T. (2020). National security governance in the era of artificial intelligence: Application paradigm, risk identification and path selection. *Journal of International Security Studies, 1*, 4–38.

Rabkin, J., & Yoo, J. (2017). Striking power: How cyber, robots, and space weapons change the rules for war. *Encounter Books Press*, 3–5.

Tang, S. P. (2014). A new attribution theory of IR: Dimensions of uncertainty and their cognitive challenges. *Journal of International Security Studies, 2*, 5–6.

Tao, W. Z. (2013). Some thoughts on the 'trust deficit' between China and the US. *Contemporary International Relations, 1*, 16–19.

Telley, C. (2018). The influence machine: Automated information operations as a strategic defeat mechanism. Association of the United States Army. Retrieved

November 27, 2021, from https://www.ausa.org/publications/influence-machine-automated-information-operations-strategic-mechanism

U.S. Department of Defense. (2019). Summary of the 2018 department of defense artificial intelligence strategy: Harnessing AI to advance our security and prosperity. Retrieved November 27, 2021, from https://media.defense.gov/2019/feb/12/2002088963/-1/-1/1/summary-of-dod-ai-strategy.pdf

Wang, J. S., & Lieberthal, K. (2013). *Addressing China-U.S. strategic distrust*. Social Sciences Academic Press.

Wang, J. S., et al. (2012). Building mutual trust between China and the US. *International Economic Review, 2*(2), 10–11.

Wolfers, A. (1952). National security as an ambiguous symbol. *Political Science Quarterly, 67*(4), 481–502.

Wong, Y. H., et al. (2020). *Deterrence in the age of thinking machines*. RAND Corporation.

Yuan, P. (2008). Strategic mutual trust and strategic stability: The main tasks facing U.S.-China relations at present. *Contemporary International Relations, 1*(1), 34–35.

15

Scenario Analysis of Malicious Use of Artificial Intelligence and Challenges to Psychological Security in India

Arvind Gupta and Aakash Guglani

Introduction

India missed the bus in the first and second industrial revolutions, and was late catching up with the third industrial revolution, however, it was able to utilize its human capital investment in the Indian Institutes of Technology (IITs), whose students built enterprising solutions for the major corporations of the world, and integrated affordable technology and human capabilities to build, operate, and expand the software industry around the world in the late 1980s and early 2000s. As Sukumar (2019, pp. 118–130) explains in his diligent study of the history of technology deployment, and especially the underpinnings of the telecom and software revolution—*Midnight's Machines: A Political History of Technology in India*—public officials implemented the farsighted policies of the government with appropriate public investment. This was an unusual combination of funds, functions, and functionaries in India.

After showcasing the power of Indian software and technical talent across the world, Indian policymakers decided to create technological solutions that

A. Gupta (✉) • A. Guglani
Digital India Foundation, Noida, India
e-mail: arvind@ispirt.in; aakash@digitalindiafoundation.org

addressed the societal needs of India. The Government of India, with the help of India's pioneering technologists deployed the world's largest identity platform—*Aadhaar*—in 2009. It was conceived as a digital biometric identity that would streamline India's last-mile welfare delivery and substantially reduce financial leakage. These technologists, led by Nandan Nilekani, joined hands to form a not-for-profit organization—the Indian Software Product Industry Round Table (iSpirt)—which piloted population-scale technological solutions to solve the complex governance challenges faced by India in a private and public partnership framework (ibid, pp. 176–178).

Aadhaar is one of the components of this population-scale initiative, *IndiaStack*—a set of open application programming interfaces (APIs) and digital public goods, which has created immense opportunities for the social and financial inclusion of the Indian people, as it has a state-of-the-art consent-based data-sharing framework. IndiaStack means that India's digital public goods model has expanded from being an identity platform to including payments, data management, innovative financial products, health systems, digital commerce, skilling programs, and so on.

Today, with the help of these initiatives, India is the largest open democratic market in the world, with over 800 million internet users and 1.2 billion mobile phone users (TRAI, 2021). India has successfully attracted 1.3 billion people into the digital economy, using a digital public infrastructure approach. All these platforms produce large amounts of data which are critical for economic decision-making, modeling consumer behavior, shaping electoral choices for citizens, and ensuring social harmony and national security decision-making. Businesses, start-ups, civil society communities, and public officials are at the forefront of utilizing this data to innovate, build and market products and services, as well as to perform law enforcement duties and secure critical supply chains, by using the tools of artificial intelligence; machine learning, data analytics, biotechnology, and related technologies.

Due to the overwhelming reliance of businesses, start-ups, and governments on utilizing and securing this data for innovation, growth, and security, the Indian State faces immense challenges that arise due to the malicious use of artificial intelligence (MUAI) to manipulate citizens' data and create massive disruptions in the social, political, economic, and security domains via state and non-state actors. Examples include the use of MUAI by terrorist organizations to spread propaganda, the widespread malicious use of deep fakes (MUDF), the malicious use of AI tools in information agenda-setting to control target groups more efficiently (AI-enhanced perception management),

MUAI in decision-making processes to lead people to the wrong decisions, prognostic weapons, and many other uses.

This convergence of cyber-physical-biological systems is a new frontier that requires visionary leadership, agile policies, scenario analysis, and the democratic scrutiny of technical architecture to prevent MUAI by other states and non-state actors that aims to create systematic distrust among citizens on digital platforms and associated ecosystems, to hamper economic growth, and the psychological security of citizens.

In the following sections, we will *first* look at India's deployment and penetration of artificial intelligence (AI) and its use cases in a myriad of domains; *second*, we will provide a literature review of psychological operations, primarily reflexive control theory, and will measure the level of risks associated with MUAI in these critical sectors, and perform a scenario analysis of unforeseen contingencies; *third*, we will look at technological, political, and legal checks framed under democratic norms to evaluate their responsiveness to these attacks by MUAI and *fourth*, we will make suitable recommendations and suggest preventive measures to reduce the severity of these attacks in an Indian scenario. Through these sections in the chapter, we hope that learnings from India can add to the literature on MUAI and psychological security challenges, and provide connections with other states.

Use of Artificial Intelligence, Machine Learning, and Big Data, and Their Penetration Level, Deployment and Operations in India, and Vulnerability to Malicious Attacks

The use of AI, machine learning, and big data is increasing exponentially in India, mainly due to massive growth in the user base, and an affordable internet built using a public goods approach. As per the National Association of Software and Service Companies (NASSCOM)—a not-for-profit association and industry body—report on Data and AI in 2020, AI and data use could add $450–500 billion to India's GDP by 2025 (NASSCOM, 2020).

The deployment and penetration of AI have expanded to various departments of the Government of India (GoI) and provincial governments, domestic businesses, startup communities, and academic institutions. The Ministry of Electronics and Information Technology (MeitY) under GoI, in partnership with NASSCOM and the National E-Governance Division (NeGD), came up with a report *75@75—India's AI Journey* with use cases of AI deployment across governments, businesses, startups, and academic institutions (MEITY, 2021).

The use cases of the central and state governments include supercomputing abilities at C-DAC (Centre for Development of Advanced Computing), a cataract screening app by the Government of Tamil Nadu, crop and seed management in Punjab and Tamil Nadu, drone-based healthcare delivery in remote places in Telangana, AI to forecast energy load requirements in Andhra Pradesh, a justice delivery management system by the Supreme Court of India, chatbots for easy access to services delivery in Maharashtra and so on (ibid, pp. 12–34).

A dedicated citizen engagement portal, MyGov.in "MeriSarkarMereDwar," is another example of applying AI for citizens to discover their eligibility for welfare schemes, and the PSB portal uses AI to approve loans to small and medium enterprises.

Further examples include the deployment of AI in the startup space AGNEXT for tea crop quality checks, the early detection of breast cancer by NIRAMAI, TRICOG to detect cardiovascular diseases, an AI-powered backpack developed by Jagadish Mahendran for visually impaired people, CogniABle to manage autism using machine learning tools, Cropin as an AI-powered climate change agri-adaptability platform, CreditVidya which uses AI for income assessment work; IIT Ropar which uses AI for deep fake detection in live videos, and ISI Kolkata which uses deep learning tools to screen for COVID-19 in chest X-ray images (ibid, pp. 45–93).

According to PricewaterhouseCooper's (PwC) report on AI adoption, India's increased adoption of AI, especially during the global pandemic, was highest among the major economies at 45%, followed by the US, UK, and Japan (2020, p. 7). Indian enterprises were at the forefront of AI adoption in 2021, as per the survey by Mckinsey Analytics across different regions (China, Middle East, and North Africa) in the world (2021, p. 2). These reports offer evidence of the adoption and penetration of AI and other emerging technologies at the government-, enterprise-, and academic institution-levels as noted in the MeitY use case report.

AI penetration is found at different levels of government, businesses, and academic institutions for various purposes, including education and healthcare, law enforcement, agriculture and climate change resilience, deep fakes detection, facial recognition and biometric data protection, floods management, citizen management, and government services.

The above-mentioned deployment of AI and machine learning tools at the micro and macro levels of governments and businesses and the integration of citizens' identity, health data, access to government services, and livelihoods to create innovative products and services might expose the Indian state and her citizens' data to MUAI, as AI and machine learning tools become integrated into every aspect of people's lives. This could become an arena for coercion, manipulation, and data harvesting by malicious elements, in order to disrupt people's quotidian lives.

Indian businesses, small and medium-sized businesses (SMBs), have already started guarding their digital investments by spending on cybersecurity as they face increasing cyber-incidents. As per the Cisco Secure report, *Cybersecurity for SMBs: Asia Pacific Businesses Prepare for Digital Defense*, more than 56% of Asia Pacific SMBs faced a cyber-incident in 2020–21, and 85% have suffered a malware attack (2021, p. 4). This has resulted in the loss of valuable customer information, employee data, intellectual property, and financial information. In India, 84% of respondents to the report are worried about cybersecurity risks, and phishing (43%) emerges as the top-ranked risk for small businesses across the Asia-Pacific region. Phishing as a process directly attacks the trustworthiness of a company, as malicious actors masquerade as a trustful identity to dupe the end-user into revealing their sensitive information. Targeted attacks by malicious actors (19%) rank similarly. These attacks directly affect the financial performance and the trustworthiness of the business, which affects users' psychological security as they can trust enterprises to work with their data. In India, 62% of companies reported that these attacks cost their businesses more than $500,000 in 2020–21, which affects people's livelihoods and risks the loss of sensitive information (ibid, p. 10).

The Minister of State for Electronics and Information Technology, Mr. Rajeev Chandrashekhar in the GoI, informed the Rajya Sabha (India's Upper House) that Indian enterprises and government organizations are already facing heightened cyber-attacks on a yearly basis, from 208,456 in 2018, to 394,499 in 2019, and 1,158,208 in 2020. As of October 2021, more than 1.2 million incidents had been reported. In the last two years, 87,058 of all cyber-incidents were directed toward government organizations in India (Correspondent, The Hindu, 2021; Ali, 2021; Ahuja, 2022).

In order to ascertain the severity of these risks, we will perform a scenario analysis in the following section regarding possible MUAI threats in myriad domains in India, and which directly affect the psychological security of her citizens.

Psychological Operations Through Malicious Use of Artificial Intelligence in India: Current Practice and Possible Scenarios

We think the origins of psychological operations (PSYOPs) through MUAI, and information warfare in general, can be traced to the work of Vladimir Lefebvre on "reflexive control," which explains how information can be used as a malicious means for opponent states to disrupt decision-making processes (Thomas, 2004, pp. 237–256). These reflexive control tactics are deployed to manage perceptions and build narratives based on malicious information that the proponent believes has passed through their own "filters" of what is true or false. The opponent is able to *reflex* (imitate convincingly) the filtration mechanisms, however, and forecast the behavior of opposing decision-makers to make them believe the malicious information is accurate, as it successfully mimics their filtration processes (ibid, pp. 240–242). Thomas quotes Major General N. I. Turko of the Russian Federation's General Staff Academy to explain the effectiveness of automatic control:

> The most dangerous manifestation of the tendency to rely on military power relates more to the possible impact of the use of reflexive control by the opposing side through developments in the theory and practice of information war rather than to the direct use of the means of armed combat. (ibid, p. 240)

In addition to reflexive control theory, we place PSYOPs through MUAI in India under the umbrella of the literature on psychological security and MUAI, as developed at the University of Oxford's workshop on *The Malicious Use of Artificial Intelligence: Forecasting, Prevention, and Mitigation* and offer our understanding based on scenarios in India (Brundage et al., 2018). We concur with the psychological security framework agreed by Bazarkina and Pashentsev in their pioneering paper *Artificial Intelligence and New Threats to International Psychological Security* as "the protection of the individual, group and public psyche and, accordingly, social subjects of different levels of community, scale and system-structural and functional organisation from the influence of information factors that cause dysfunctional social processes (Grachev, 1998, p. 26)" (Bazarkina & Pashentsev, 2019, p. 151).

MUAI can be deployed in the information warfare on a massive level, especially if built on a reflexive control theoretical framework. We think the psychological security of Indian citizens is in immense danger from the MUAI by state and non-state actors, as India has a multicultural and multilingual population with magnificent diversity. These inherent differences can be exploited, especially with the increasing use of AI in multiple domains to access government services, gather information about one's neighborhoods, and make appropriate electoral voting decisions using the information on social media platforms.

Currently, the information universe of Indian citizens is being exploited by malicious elements using AI through the deployment of deep fakes, phishing, agenda-setting by harvesting social media activities through bots, and cross-border digital influencing operations.

Deep Fakes

The use of artificial intelligence to approximate the way humans create paintings was a pioneering effort using deep neural networks by scientists Leon A. Gatys, Alexander S. Ecker, and Matthias Bethge. In their paper, they demonstrated the way in which machine learning tools were developed to make human-like visual representations of art paintings. The artificial system developed could learn on its own to make important differences between style and content, and to formulate a coherent picture (Gatys et al., 2015).

The use of similar tools has percolated through to the mainstream, where deep fakes of Indian film stars thrive on adult content websites (Ajmal, 2020). According to Sensity—a deep fake detection firm in Amsterdam—more than 3% of the world's deep fake pornographic websites are in India, as per its State of Deep Fakes Report in 2019 ((Ajder et al., 2019), p. 2). This follows the same pattern across the world, where deep fakes of Scarlett Johansson, Barack Obama, Gal Gadot, and so on were found on Reddit in 2017 (Khanderkar, 2021). Although 96% of deep fake videos across the world are pornographic in nature (Ajder et al., 2019, p. 1) this technology has also been used maliciously and for nefarious purposes to disturb social and political harmony in India. In 2018, a video of child kidnappers used for public education purposes in Pakistan was maliciously edited to create havoc in the north-eastern city of Assam, and led to mob violence and the killing of at least nine people (Vaccari & Chadwick, 2020, p. 1). The spread of deep fakes is not restricted to hinterlands, and they are maliciously deployed on social media sites during unfortunate incidents to spread hatred and violence. In January 2022, a deep fake video of the Indian Union Cabinet discussion was circulated, where the video was maliciously edited to allege that the meeting was against the Sikh community after the unfortunate demise of India's Chief of Defense staff member Mr. Bipin Rawat, in a helicopter crash (Times Now, 2022).

As in the rest of the world, the use of deep fake technology in India began in pornographic websites, but has oozed into the social and political domains, where it has resulted in actual violence and diluted people's trust in information on social media platforms. To that end, we concur with the conclusion drawn in an empirical study by Vaccari and Chadwick, that "political deepfakes may not necessarily deceive individuals, but they may sow uncertainty which may, in turn, reduce trust in news on social media" (2020, p. 9).

Agenda-Setting and Bots

Bots are the software programs that have a unique ability to mimic human interactions convincingly to automate appointments and grievance redressal mechanisms for businesses worldwide. According to the *Bad Bot Report 2021* by Imperva (2022), a cybersecurity firm based in California, 40.8% of internet traffic is bot traffic, of which 25.6% is negative bot traffic, and the remaining is for positive purposes in 2020 (2021, p. 13). Bad bots involve the use of bot technology for malicious means, in order to defraud businesses, governments, or other users. Their tactics include data takeovers, data scraping, and theft.

In India, there is growing evidence that political parties deploy bots to manipulate the public sphere, primarily through the use of social media platforms. Hitkul et al. found that bots were indeed used on social media platforms. However, the bots were operated by cyber-troops. Hitkul et al. could distinguish between humans and bots using heat maps and the temporal analysis of tweets. Political parties in India have dedicated departments of data analytics and information technology departments to create agendas on Twitter, spread messages to their volunteers, and create narratives (2020, pp. 441–450).

Conversely, the success of Twitter trends and the agenda-setting powers of political parties has not proved to be exceptionally high in India, especially according to the quantitative study designed and undertaken by Joseph Carson Schlessinger using Twitter trends analysis. The tweet templates created by cyber-cells are not able to set the agenda for users outside their ecosystem, but their intended message persists for long periods (2021, p. 25).

In addition to political agenda-setting powers, bots are also used by malicious non-state actors to spread conspiracy theories. One such incident, as reported by Logically—a fact-checking website—was the unfortunate accident of CDS Bipin Rawat, where more than 480 bot accounts from Pakistan falsely claimed the involvement of Tamil insurgent outfits in the unfortunate demise of CDS Rawat to disrupt relations between India and Sri Lanka, as well as create a rift within India with the southern state of Tamil Nadu (Thillai, Sankar, 2021). There is no denying the presence of malicious bot activity on the social media platforms in India, attempting to influence public opinion and manufacture false agendas for the malicious purposes of non-state actors.

Election Integrity Challenges Using Sentiment Analysis

Indian elections are held across large swathes of land with geographical diversity. The Election Commission of India (ECI) provides voting data at the booth level. Researchers, political parties, and government officials can look at this massive booth-level data from historical records going back to India's first election in 1951, and formulate their strategies. The electoral databank includes historical win margins, candidate profiles across parties, state assembly level data, records of women's participation, the performance of state and national parties, and so on (ECI, 2020). The Indian State conducts National Sample Surveys periodically, decadal census, and National Family Health Surveys. There is a significant opportunity to use data analytics, machine learning, and AI with this data for sentiment analysis, and to manipulate voter behavior.

In 2021, India's premier investigative agency, the Central Bureau of Investigation (CBI), booked Cambridge Analytica, a controversial political consultancy firm allegedly involved in election manipulation in the Brexit elections and the United States Presidential Elections of 2020, to steal the data of 562,000 Facebook users (Money Control News, 2021). Unfortunately, the malicious use of sentiment analysis with AI as a foundational tool is a significant problem for users looking for accurate and authentic information on their social media platforms.

In one of our conversations, political campaign manager Mr. Ravi (names changed as per their request), who has used the sentiment analysis process in India, explained that sentiment analysis involves using AI tools and bombarding emotionally loaded words and associated click bait on the social media homepages of users to manipulate their voting behavior. Correlations are made between historical electoral data and voting patterns provided by the EC, the localized social media activity of the users in that area, and profiling of users' voting preferences. After this process, maliciously emotionally loaded words are inserted into the social media timelines of users to willfully change their information universe. The information is manipulated, and election dynamics are changed.

Deep fakes, agenda-setting, and sentiment analysis are used simultaneously on social media platforms for malicious purposes. We are concerned with its growing usage. In addition to these psychological operations by malicious actors, we will discuss possible areas where MUAI can be deployed in the next section, and especially in the vast domains in which AI has been used in India. We have relied extensively on the long experience of one of our authors in private software development and technology deployment in public administration for this section.

Possible Scenarios

We think there are multiple scenarios where MUAI could destroy public transportation systems and smart cities, and make unlawful use of unmanned aerial vehicles (UAVs) and critical infrastructure in India. All these services are integrated into the economy, and any disruption to these services would seriously undermine the psychological security of Indian citizens.

Misuse of UAVs for Malicious Purposes

In June 2021, drones were used to drop explosive weapons in the Indian Air Force technical area in the State of Jammu and Kashmir, one of India's first terrorist drone attacks (Panday, 2021; Tiwari & Krishn, 2021). As per the government report, more than 300 drone sightings have been reported since 2019 around India's Western borders (The Economic Times, 2021). They are used for smuggling arms and drugs, and for surveillance.

UAVs can also be used judiciously for traffic monitoring, drought management, commercial advertisements, tourism, and so on. In order to organize such use; in August 2021, the Ministry of Civil Aviation announced rules for liberalized drones (unmanned aircraft systems) in order to create employment opportunities in agriculture, mining, infrastructure, geo-spatial mapping, and so on (Press Information Bureau, 2021). The use of drones for so many purposes will have consequences, as they will be prone to potential misuse by malicious actors.

Jean-Paul Yaacoub et al. have extensively studied the security risks associated with the use of unmanned aerial vehicles, including privacy issues, and especially physical privacy, as citizens can be blackmailed by people taking private pictures of them using drones. Similarly, the behavior and location privacy of citizens can be violated by recording their constant movement, which seriously hampers people's bodily behavior (2020, p. 11). UAVs can also be used by terror groups for payload transfers, especially during riots or violent protests, as they can evade law enforcement checks on the ground. On the seventy-fifth anniversary of Republic Day in India, more than a thousand UAVs were used to showcase the achievements of the government (FP Staff, 2022).

We understand from the study by Yaacoub et al. that drones are at risk of being manipulated. If one of the drones in the fleet used by the Defence Ministry with Botlab at the Republic Day celebrations had been used for malicious purposes, it could have created havoc. We say this because terror outfits deployed a domestic drone with payloads in Syria in 2017 (Brundage et al., 2018, p. 19). Suppose Person A has ordered food online and it is to be delivered using drones to her tenth-floor apartment. If cyber-terrorists gain access to this drone then they can plant explosives, microphones, or cameras in the delivery box to inflict psychological damage on the target population. The privacy of other residents would also be perennially at risk. Sensitive photos can be taken during aerial surveillance and circulated on social media platforms, and can be maliciously edited to circulate as deep fakes. Drone deliveries can be used to drop blasphemous material such as beef or pork in sensitive religious locations, which could spark large-scale riots. Local law enforcement agencies need to be cognizant of abuses which could vitiate public spaces in India and disturb social harmony.

In addition to the violation of individual privacy, religious sentiments, and social harmony, data gathered by ministries deploying drones to monitor sensitive projects in border areas and the hinterlands as well as traffic systems, can be manipulated using reflexive control tactics by terrorists and other malicious actors to disrupt these critical projects.

Potential Weaponization of Sensitive Personal Information

In our section on AI penetration, we laid out a map showing the penetration of AI deployment in India at state government, central, and civil society levels. India is the third-largest startup ecosystem in the world, and users therefore provide their health, medical, financial, and educational data to these private and non-private entities. As these entities grow, their systems become vulnerable to phishing attacks, and as per reflexive control theory, if a malicious user or a cyber-terrorist uses adversarial AI to infiltrate these systems, then this database can be easily compromised. There is also an increasing trend of cyber-attacks on government websites and other websites to the tune of 1.2 million by October 2021.

The probability of potential new MUAI is relatively high, as Indian enterprises face constant phishing attacks, and their systems are not audited regularly. According to our understanding, persistent breaches of data, especially sensitive data, can seriously hamper the trust that users have in new-age enterprises. Breaches happen, but if cyber-terrorists gain control of data, especially the health data of a user, through breaching any new health application, they could use a deep fake technology to mimic their medical practitioner and manipulate the pharmaceutical regime. Access to this information alone would be tantamount to causing serious psychological damage. Something else terrorists could exploit are the systems of healthcare appointments and doctor engagement marketplaces, in order to gain access to the disease burden of the population in specific regions of the country. This disease burden data can be used systematically to attack the supply chain of essential medicines, especially active pharmaceutical ingredients.

Cyber-criminals can systematically target the manufacturing facilities of critical medicines which can increase the interval times between doses of millions of patients. The malicious use of this data can also be used to cause panic through an artificial shortage of medicines in the market, with severe price shocks and unequal stock availability across regions. This would be tantamount to widespread mayhem in the target population, with the possibility of riots, black marketing, and hoarding.

Similarly, the use of AI in diagnostics and clinical trials means that the malicious use of AI can ascribe life-threatening diseases to perfectly healthy individuals. Since AI analyzes reports and data, it would be hard for any health practitioner to deny its validity. In his review of Eric Topol's brilliant book, *Deep Medicine: How Artificial Intelligence Can Make Healthcare Human Again*, Matuchansky argues that there are no specific explanations behind the conclusions drawn in diagnostic reports using machine learning algorithms (2019, p. 736) and that although Topol's enthusiasm is appreciated, we think there is a high likelihood of malicious users manipulating confidential health information.

The manipulation of health information could be aggravated in cases where citizens are misdiagnosed with health problems such as mental incapacitation, which reduces their chances of attaining leadership positions in their respective organizations, especially in sensitive posts. For example, a cyber-terrorist could manipulate the health data of a policy regulator using an AI-based health application and tag their routine check-up as a serious depression episode. This diagnosis might make them ineligible to hold any senior position, as this requires a clean health record. This method could be deployed systematically across several departments, and stifle the career progression of individuals, as well as destabilize routine appointments in government and private enterprises. The willful manipulation of AI-based health data is a serious threat which can cause long-term psychological damage to individuals, as their real or manufactured bouts of trauma, depression, and associated medical history can become a tool in public spectacles and given unnecessary scrutiny.

Internet of Things and Smart Cities

To fulfill Goal 11: *"Make cities inclusive, safe, resilient and sustainable"* of the Sustainable Development Goals promulgated by the United Nations, India has embarked on the creation of 100 smart cities by June 2023. Allam and Dhunny undertook an extensive literature review on the use of AI, the Internet of Things (IoT) and big data, as used to make governance processes efficient, affordable, and sustainable in new-age cities worldwide (2019, p. 86). Most countries, including India, accept the promise of technology to bring these efficiencies to their smart cities programs using IoT and synergies between technology, laws, and administration (Madakam & Ramaswamy, 2015, pp. 1–6).

In our view, the threat of MUAI is most severe in smart cities, because if the control of these cities, or any component, such as smart lighting or traffic signaling, comes into the hands of cyber-terrorists, then they can cause damage on a massive scale. Various cities in India are undertaking projects such as modernizing riverfronts through smart solid waste management, and intelligent app-based integrations such as the smart traffic management in Surat, Pune, Ahmedabad, and so on. All these systems are vulnerable to cyber-attacks.

An example of such a cyber-attack is the hacking of Florida water management systems in the US, where hackers manipulated the level of sodium hydroxide to 100 times more than the normal course. This increased level could cause vomiting, severe pain, and bleeding. A technician was able to reverse the levels in a timely manner, but the breach raised alarms across the US (Aijaz, 2021; Bergal, 2021; Trapenberg, et al., 2022, p. 2).

As in Florida, if cyber-terrorists gain access to smart traffic management systems in Surat or Bhubaneshwar in India, then they can get access to servers. The servers will then give them access to, for example, anonymized citizen data regarding their traffic patterns and could be used to attack the areas of heavy traffic in peak hours, or to disrupt the traffic systems and play havoc with travel times. If a potential layer of autonomous vehicles and metros is added to the mix, then cyber-criminals can exploit the interconnected functionality of cities to gain control of public transportation systems, individual vehicles, solid waste management systems, and so on. Shutting down essential services such as water, electricity, mobility, and central command centers would seriously paralyze a state's functioning and have long-term adverse effects on the psychological security of citizens.

The Delhi Metro Rail Corporation (DMRC) has already introduced driverless metros in public transport systems in New Delhi, which involve a large amount of automation for their operations using advanced signaling systems from its central command centers. The potential goal is to run trains without human intervention (Barman, 2022). If a cyber-hacker gains access to the servers and command center of the DMRC, then the costs would be unimaginable, with millions of people traveling daily on its systems.

The growing use of AI and big data in governance processes, infrastructure, and social media platforms means that it is important for policymakers to ensure that the security protocols around these emerging technologies are the best in the world. Since these protocols are made by humans, we understand that there are chances of breaches, as sophisticated malicious actors use reflexive control tactics to dupe the security systems deployed by the states. In the next section, we look at the technical-political-legal architecture in India that can at least reduce the severity of MUAI, if not stop the attacks, as the psychological security of India's citizens is connected to her long-term economic growth prospects.

Technological, Political, and Legal Architecture to Detect and Prevent Malicious Use of Artificial Intelligence and Psychological Security in India

Indian policymakers were cognizant of not missing out on the vast potential of AI and machine learning for various uses, and to solve complex societal and economic problems. The Indian Finance Minister announced the National Program on Artificial Intelligence in the Union Budget 2019, with the establishment of a national center for AI and a national portal for AI (Soni, 2019; Mehra, 2021). The Government of India's think tank—the National Institution for Transforming India (NITI Aayog)—produced a strategy paper on the responsible use of artificial intelligence in 2018, before the budget announcement (NITI, 2018). In addition to this strategy paper, NITI Aayog drew up an approach document in 2021 to formulate a policy for the responsible use of AI, and to codify security risks and responses to possible data breaches, privacy risks, and malicious uses (NITI, Feb. 2021a, Aug. 2021b).

In addition to NITI Aayog, the Ministry of Electronics and Information Technology (MeitY) formed four expert member committees to lay out the policy framework for the Artificial Intelligence Committee. Of these four committees, the *Report Of Committee—D On Cyber Security, Safety, Legal And Ethical Issues*—looked at threats due to the malicious use of AI and its scope (MEITY, 2019).

Presently, there are standards for the use of AI systems earmarked by the financial sector regulator (Securities and Exchange Commission of India) for financial intermediaries; the National Digital Health Mission for personal data privacy with regard to AI; and the Data Empowerment and Protection Architecture (DEPA), a technical framework developed by NITI. The highest court of India, with a nine-judge bench, has declared the right to privacy as one of the fundamental rights of Indian citizens (Hegde & Kishore, 2017).

To concretize this historical judgment, the Indian Parliament has also been scrutinizing a draft personal data protection (PDP) bill for almost three years, which will create a data protection authority. It includes the data principal (end-user whose information is stored), data fiduciary, and data processors. The proposed law holds data fiduciaries and data processors accountable for collecting, storing, and processing the data of users, while also bringing in a "consent-based" framework that empowers individuals. There are clearly laid out standards for social media intermediaries and other data fiduciaries for age verification, security protocols, and grievance redressal mechanisms (PRS Legislative Research, 2022). These frameworks ensure a balance of privacy for users, and transparency and accountability for data fiduciaries who collect and process data. The Indian Cabinet is also considering approving a National Cybersecurity Strategy, 2020, as an action plan with clear timelines to tackle the increasing cyber-attacks on its systems and protect the privacy of individuals (IANS, 2021). Presently, the Information Technology Act (2000) is the overarching legislation that provides standards, penalties, and responsibilities to all the stakeholders in this cyber-ecosystem.

India is a multiparty democracy with established institutions and an independent judiciary. Any breach of privacy is taken seriously and debated at the highest levels in the Indian Parliament. The digital public goods and the IndiaStack were curated with bipartisan support with a privacy by design framework and open data protocols. The Aadhaar platform has already been authorized by the Indian parliament as a law (The Aadhaar (Targeted Delivery of Financial and Other Subsidies, Benefits and Services) Act. Unique Identification Authority of India, 2016) although some opposition parties challenged it in the Supreme Court of India, and the court also accepted its applicability for availing government and other services. The process of introducing new technologies in India includes extensive internal and external consultations with experts, vibrant debates in Parliament, social activism, and judicial scrutiny. Following this process is important so as to reduce the severity of MUAI in the Indian context, as policymakers perform their own scenario analysis when there is a possibility of sensitive information being exposed to criminal elements during several rounds of consultations and public scrutiny. The collective wisdom of citizens, civil society groups, parliamentarians, and policymakers create adequate checks and balances with privacy, by designing technical architecture.

This collective wisdom is best reflected in open-source platforms such as the IndiaStack owned by the public institutions, which are well placed to face the threats from MUAI, as they need to report any breaches to the citizens at large through their representatives under legally mandated transparency protocols.

Concomitantly, as the new technologies emerge with their unique challenges, policymakers need to take cognizance of MUAI and develop mechanisms to use AI for good. In the next section, we will list recommendations that can be replicated across geographies.

Conclusion

We think it is important for democratic countries to come up with detailed guidelines in a consensus-oriented manner to enforce standards and protocols, especially the use of the Internet of Things (IoT) and connected devices in the larger public sphere, and especially to perform periodic audits on the risks of these technologies via MUAI. According to our understanding, states can reduce the severity of MUAI attacks in several ways.

First, each state should secure their supply chains for data integrity and against malware attacks by sourcing components from myriad players. Private corporations bring efficiencies, but single-source supply chains and their systems have higher chances of transgressions, and so they should not be allowed to have so much power that they can disrupt the livelihoods of people without the informed consent of the people. At no point are we arguing against the use of cross-border data flows, but we think accountability and transparency grow when citizens have stakes in the utilization of their data locally. Citizen participation increases transparency for everyone. This increased transparency would ensure that people are aware of attacks and prevent their severity, especially safeguarding their sensitive information using commonsense approaches.

Second, states should develop their own digital public goods which will give citizens a voice in data gathering, collection, and utilization through their elected governments. Using the open data protocols, states should strive toward significant ownership with participation from the private sector in critical infrastructure projects such as biometric identification cards, digital payments architecture, social security disbursements, commerce, and health records. This will not only keep big technology corporations, native corporations, and government corporations under check, but will "democratise the process of data aggregation, gatekeeping powers and algorithms development and deployment under privacy by design framework as per the rules laid down by the local governments under fair and reasonable policies" (Gupta & Guglani, 2022). We think democratization brings in the appropriate checks and balances.

In India, when people participate in social audits then their participation increases the efficiency of government schemes, as evidenced in M. R. Sharan's fantastic work in rural Bihar—*Last Among Equals: Caste, Power and Politics in Bihar's Villages*—and especially the participation of women from marginalized sections of society (2021, Location No. 1595). Taking a cue from social audit experiments, states need to formulate technical audits in a simple, lucid, and compelling manner.

Third, we have seen the MUAI on social media platforms through bots, deep fakes, phishing, and so on. AI is integrating local languages, cultural tastes and preferences, as well as beliefs. There is an effort to customize technology devices to one's bodily, linguistic, and cultural requirements. This customization allows cyber-criminals to exploit the fault lines present in communities and seek unconscious participation from the users. To reduce the severity of MUAI, policymakers need to make these platforms and technologies accessible and inclusive by reducing end-user participation. Public authorities need to undertake culturally sound scenario analysis, and improve user abilities to identify the malicious uses of these technologies in the form of deep fakes, fake news, faulty medical diagnostics, and so on.

In conclusion, the challenge for policymakers is to ensure that there are appropriate regulations to increase innovation without manipulation and misinformation. The vulnerability of, and attacks on, digital public infrastructure are reported, but their root cause analysis is not publicly available. The limited literature available in this field in India means that we have tried our best to present scenarios in plausible areas of vulnerability and the technical-legal checks that are built to reduce the severity of MUAI on the psychological security of India as a nation. India's experience suggests that the digital public infrastructure governed by democratic norms and public scrutiny through social and technical audits has a higher propensity to prevent MUAI, and protect the psychological security of a nation.

References

Ahuja, N. (2022). Inside story of cyber attacks on India's banks, airlines, railways… and the fightback. *The Week*. [online]. Retrieved March 6, 2022, from https://www.theweek.in/theweek/cover/2022/01/06/inside-story-of-cyber-attacks-on-india-banks-airlines-railways-and-the-fightback.htm

Aijaz, Rumi. (2021). *India's Smart Cities Mission, 2015–2021: A Stocktaking*. Observer Research Foundation [online]. Retrieved March 1, 2022, from https://www.orfonline.org/research/indias-smart-cities-mission-2015-2021-a-stocktaking/

Ajder, H., Patrini, G., Cavalli, F., & Cullen, L. (2019). *The state of deepfakes: Landscape, threats, and impact*. [online] Sensity. Retrieved February 26, 2022, from https://sensity.ai/reports/

Ajmal, A. (2020). Adult deepfakes of Indian film stars thrive online. *The Times of India*. [online]. Retrieved March 15, 2022, from https://timesofindia.indiatimes.com/india/adult-deepfakes-of-indian-film-stars-thrive-online/articleshow/79140509.cms

Ali, S. (2021). 87,050 cyberattacks on govt organisations in two years. *Business Today*. [online]. Retrieved March 10, 2022, from https://www.businesstoday.in/technology/news/story/87050-cyberattacks-on-govt-organisations-in-two-years-315695-2021-12-15

Allam, Z., & Dhunny, Z. (2019). On big data, artificial intelligence and smart cities. *Cities, 89*, 80–91.

Barman, S. R. (2022). Here's why India's first driverless metro in New Delhi is significant. *The Indian Express*. [online]. Retrieved March 14, 2022, from indianexpress.com/article/explained/explained-indias-first-driverless-metro-in-delhi-and-why-it-is-significant-7119916

Bazarkina, D., & Pashentsev, Y. (2019). Artificial intelligence and new threats to international psychological security. *Russia in Global Affairs, 17*(1). https://doi.org/10.31278/1810-6374-2019-17-1-147-170

Bergal, J. (2021). Florida hack exposes danger to water systems. [Blog] *The Pew Charitable Trusts*. Retrieved March 1, 2022, from http://www.pewtrusts.org/en/research-and-analysis/blogs/stateline/2021/03/10/florida-hack-exposes-danger-to-water-systems

Brundage, M., Avin, S., Clark, J., Toner, H., Eckersley, P., Garfinkel, B., Dafoe, A., Scharre, P., Zeitzoff, T., Filar, B., & Anderson, H. (2018). The malicious use of artificial intelligence: Forecasting, prevention, and mitigation. arXiv preprint arXiv:1802.07228.

Cisco Secure. (2021). Cybersecurity for SMBs: Asia Pacific businesses prepare for digital defense. *CiscoSecure*. [online] Cisco. Retrieved March 1, 2022, from https://www.cisco.com/c/en_sg/products/security/cybersecurity-for-smbs-in-asia-pacific/index.html

Correspondent, S. (2021). More than 6.07 lakh cyber security incidents observed till June 2021: Government. *The Hindu*. [online]. Retrieved March 12, 2022, from https://www.thehindu.com/business/cert-in-observed-more-than-607-lakh-cyber-security-incidents-till-june-2021-government/article35726974.ece

Digital, T. N. (2022). Video of cabinet committee on security calling for removal of Sikhs from Indian Army is FAKE, says government. *Times Now*. [online]. Retrieved March 10, 2022, from https://www.timesnownews.com/india/article/video-of-cabinet-committee-on-security-calling-for-removal-of-sikhs-from-indian-army-is-fake-says-government/847451

Election Commission of India. (2020). *Election Results—Full Statistical Reports*. Election Commission of India. https://eci.gov.in/statistical-report/statistical-reports/

FP Staff. (2022). Republic Day 2022: 1,000 'Make In India' drones to paint the skies at beating retreat ceremony; here's what you need to know. *Firstpost*. [online]. Retrieved March 10, 2022, from https://www.firstpost.com/india/republic-day-2022-1000-make-in-india-drones-to-light-up-sky-at-beating-retreat-what-you-need-to-know-10325591.html

Gatys, L. A., Ecker, A. S., & Bethge, M. (2015). A neural algorithm of artistic style. arXiv preprint arXiv:1508.06576.

Gupta, A., & Guglani, A. (2022). *What nation-states can do to protect citizens from Omnipotent Corporations*. [online] Valdai Club. Retrieved March 4, 2022, from https://valdaiclub.com/a/highlights/what-nation-states-can-do-to-protect-citizens/

Hegde, S., & Kishore, P. (2017). Right to privacy: In Supreme Court verdict, freedom's 7 takeaways. *The Indian Express*. [online]. Retrieved February 11, 2022, from https://indianexpress.com/article/explained/fundamental-right-to-privacy-beyond-the-ruling-in-verdict-freedoms-7-takeaways-4812244/

Hitkul, H., Gurjar, O., Sadaria, A., Gupta, K., Srikanth, S., Shah, R., & Kumaraguru, P. (2020). Are Bots Humans? Analysis of Bot Accounts in 2019 Indian Lok Sabha Elections (Workshop Paper). *2020 IEEE Sixth International Conference on Multimedia Big Data (BigMM)*.

IANS. (2021). India in final stages of clearing national cybersecurity strategy. *The Business Standard*. [online]. Retrieved March 7, 2022, from https://www.business-standard.com/article/current-affairs/india-in-final-stages-of-clearing-national-cybersecurity-strategy-121102700663_1.html

Imperva. (2022). *Bad Bot Report 2021: The Pandemic of the Internet*. [online] Imperva. Retrieved March 5, 2022, from https://www.imperva.com/resources/resource-library/reports/bad-bot-report/

Khanderkar, O. (2021). How deepfake porn and propaganda threatens India. *Livemint*. [online]. Retrieved March 15, 2022, from https://lifestyle.livemint.com/news/big-story/deepfakes-when-seeing-is-not-believing-111609504596030.html

Madakam, S., & Ramaswamy, R. (2015, February). 100 New smart cities (India's smart vision). In *2015 5th National Symposium on Information Technology: Towards New Smart World (NSITNSW)* (pp. 1–6). IEEE.

Matuchansky, C. (2019). Deep medicine, artificial intelligence, and the practising clinician. *The Lancet, 394*(10200), 736.

Mckinsey Analytics. (2021). *The state of AI in 2021*. [online] Mckinsey & Company. Retrieved March 3, 2022, from https://www.mckinsey.com/business-functions/mckinsey-analytics/our-insights/global-survey-the-state-of-ai-in-2021

Mehra, S. (2021). Five milestones in India's AI journey. *Indiaai.Gov.In*. [online]. Retrieved March 2, 2022, from https://indiaai.gov.in/article/five-milestones-in-india-s-ai-journey

Ministry of Electronics and Information Technology. (2019). *Report of Committee—D on Cyber Security, Safety, Legal and Ethical Issues*. [online] Ministry of Electronics and Information Technology. Retrieved March 4, 2022, from https://www.meity.gov.in/artificial-intelligence-committees-reports

Ministry of Electronics and Information Technology. (2021). *75 @ 75: India's AI Journey*. [online] Meity. Retrieved March 4, 2022, from https://www.meity.gov.in/writereaddata/files/75-75-India-AI-Journey.pdf

NASSCOM. (2020). *Unlocking value from data and AI—The India opportunity*. [online] NASSCOM. Retrieved March 4, 2022, from https://nasscom.in/knowledge-center/publications/unlocking-value-data-and-ai-india-opportunity#:~:text=The%20report%20%E2%80%9CUnlocking%20Value%20from,social%20value%20creation%20and%20recovery.&text=The%20report%20also%20focuses%20on,vibrant%20data%20economy%20in%20India

News, MC. (2021). CBI books UK-based Cambridge Analytica for 'illegally harvesting data' of Facebook users in India. *Moneycontrol*. [online]. Retrieved March 4, 2022, from https://www.moneycontrol.com/news/india/cbi-registers-case-against-cambridge-analytica-global-science-research-for-illegal-data-harvesting-6383011.html

NITI Aayog. (2018). *National Strategy for Artificial Intelligence*. NITI [online]. Retrieved March 4, 2022, from https://indiaai.gov.in/documents/pdf/NationalStrategy-for-AI-Discussion-Paper.pdf

NITI Aayog. (2021a). *Approach document for India Part 1—Principles for responsible AI*. [online]. NITI Aayog. Retrieved March 4, 2022, from https://www.niti.gov.in/sites/default/files/2021-02/Responsible-AI-22022021.pdf

NITI Aayog. (2021b). *Approach document for India Part 2—Operationalizing principles for responsible AI*. NITI Aayog. [online]. Retrieved March 4, 2022, from https://www.niti.gov.in/sites/default/files/2021-08/Part2-Responsible-AI-12082021.pdf

Panday, D. K. (2021). Drones favoured tool of Pakistan-based terror outfits. *The Hindu*. [online]. Retrieved March 5, 2022, from https://www.thehindu.com/news/national/drones-favoured-tool-of-pakistan-based-terror-outfits/article35001883.ece

Press Information Bureau. (2021). *Ministry of Civil Aviation notifies liberalised Drone Rules, 2021 PIB*. [online]. Retrieved March 4, 2022, from https://pib.gov.in/PressReleseDetailm.aspx?PRID=1749154

PricewaterhouseCoopers. (2020). *AI: An opportunity amidst a crisis*. PWC. [online]. Retrieved March 4, 2022, from https://www.pwc.in/assets/pdfs/data-and-analytics/ai-an-opportunity-amidst-a-crisis.pdf

PRS Legislative Research. (2022). The Personal Data Protection Bill, 2019. *PRS Legislative Research* [online]. Retrieved March 4, 2022, from https://prsindia.org/billtrack/the-personal-data-protection-bill-2019

Schlessinger, J. C. (2021). Quantifying agenda setting effects on Twitter and digital media. Dissertation. Massachusetts Institute of Technology. https://dspace.mit.edu/handle/1721.1/139018

Sankar, N. T., Lakshmanan, R., & Kamdar, D. (2021). Pakistani disinfo networks exploit General Rawat helicopter crash. Home. Retrieved March 1, 2022, from https://www.logically.ai/articles/pakistani-disinfo-networks-exploit-general-rawat-helicopter-crash

Sharan, M. R. (2021). *Last among equals: Power, caste & politics in Bihar's villages, Delhi: Context*. Amazon.com

Soni, S. (2019). Budget 2019: Government plans National Program on artificial intelligence; to set up National Centre for AI. *The Financial Express*. [online]. Retrieved March 13, 2022, from https://www.financialexpress.com/budget/budget-2019-government-plans-national-program-on-artificial-intelligence-to-set-up-national-centre-for-ai/1461833/

Sukumar, A. M. (2019). *Midnight's machines: A political history of technology in India*. Viking.

Telecom Regulatory Authority of India. (2021). *The Indian Telecom Services Performance Indicators*. Telecom Regulatory Authority of India [online]. Retrieved March 1, 2022, from https://www.trai.gov.in/sites/default/files/PIR_21102021_0.pdf

The Aadhaar (Targeted Delivery of Financial and Other Subsidies, Benefits and Services) Act. Unique Identification Authority of India, 2016. Government of India [online]. https://uidai.gov.in/legal-framework/aadhaar-act.html

The Economic Times. (2021). More than 300 drone sightings post Aug, 2019 along Pak border: Agencies. *The Economic Times*. [online]. Retrieved March 15, 2022, from https://economictimes.indiatimes.com/news/defence/more-than-300-

drone-sightings-post-aug-2019-along-pak-border-agencies/articleshow/83922701.cms

Thomas, T. (2004). Russia's reflexive control theory and the military. *Journal of Slavic Military Studies, 17*(2), 237–256. https://doi.org/10.1080/13518040490450529

Tiwari, D., & Krishn, K. (2021). Explained: Facing up to the drone challenge. *The Indian Express*. [online]. Retrieved March 6, 2022, from https://indianexpress.com/article/explained/drone-attack-ied-indian-air-force-base-jammu-7385106/

Trapenberg Frick, K., Mendonça Abreu, G., Malkin, N., Pan, A., & Post, A. E. (2022). The cybersecurity risks of smart city technologies: What do the experts think?—CLTC UC Berkeley Center for Long-Term Cybersecurity. [online] CLTC. Retrieved March 1, 2022, from https://cltc.berkeley.edu/2021/03/16/smart-cities/

Vaccari, C., & Chadwick, A. (2020). Deepfakes and disinformation: Exploring the impact of synthetic political video on deception, uncertainty, and trust in news. *Social Media + Society, 6*(1), 2056305120903408. https://doi.org/10.1177/2056305120903408

Yaacoub, J. P., Noura, H., Salman, O., & Chehab, A. (2020). Security analysis of drones systems: Attacks, limitations, and recommendations. *Internet of Things, 11*, 100218. https://doi.org/10.1016/j.iot.2020.100218

16

Current and Potential Malicious Use of Artificial Intelligence Threats in the Psychological Domain: The Case of Japan

Darya Bazarkina, Yury Kolotaev, Evgeny Pashentsev, and Daria Matyashova

Introduction

The choice of the Japanese case for the following analysis is based on the country's international reputation as one of the world leaders in the field of technological advancements. Moreover, Japan is geopolitically significant for two world leaders in the field of AI (the US and China), whose struggle for the Japanese market and public opinion cannot but affect the AI industry as well. Domestic processes in a country that has also faced the consequences of the global crisis indicate the relevance of studies on information warfare between

---

D. Bazarkina (✉)
Department of European Integration Research, Institute of Europe of the Russian Academy of Sciences, Moscow, Russia
e-mail: bazarkina-icspsc@yandex.ru

Y. Kolotaev • D. Matyashova
School of International Relations, St. Petersburg State University, St Petersburg, Russia
e-mail: yury.kolotaev@mail.ru; dasham0708@mail.ru

E. Pashentsev
Diplomatic Academy of the Ministry of Foreign Affairs of the Russian Federation, Moscow, Russia
e-mail: icspsc@mail.ru

various political actors (such as, for example, far-right groups and left-wing parties). As we further demonstrate in this chapter, crimes reported in Japan's information sphere are virtually identical to those recorded in other countries which enjoy a high level of AI development. In the post-truth era, Japan's problem of high-tech interventions in the electoral process is becoming more pronounced.

The chapter was prepared within the framework of the project *Malicious use of artificial intelligence and challenges of psychological security in Northeast Asia*, planned for 2021–2022. The project is being implemented by research teams from Russia and Vietnam, on the basis of grants from the Russian Foundation for Basic Research and the Vietnam Academy of Social Sciences, respectively. The research methodology is based on a systemic approach that correlates the assessment of the global political situation with the role of AI in the field of psychological security. We used primary and secondary sources (government documents, research literature, and media materials) in Japanese, English, and Russian for this chapter. Publications on various aspects of Japan's business and political culture (Chiavacci & Obinger, 2018; Chugrov, 2017; Hein, 2005; Takashi, 2017), and the country's AI development and its impact on people's psychological attitudes were of great importance for this chapter's discussion of the topic (see, for example, Haring et al., 2014b; Nitto et al., 2017).

Nonetheless, it was not possible to find systemic studies on the problem of the malicious use of artificial intelligence (MUAI) and psychological security in Japan. The analysis of the research problem is complicated by the multi-channel psychological warfare between the US and China, including one in the infosphere of Japan, especially issues of cooperation between AI-leading countries (Saito, 2021; Armitage & Nye, 2020). This warfare negatively impacts the content of information streams and promotes the replication of propaganda clichés, including ones on this chapter's topic. However, the development of AI and the growing understanding of its psychological impact have served to increase the number of specific well-rounded studies in this field.

Malicious Use of Artificial Intelligence in Japan: Structural and Cultural Determinants of Threats

In the context of global and psychological security, relevance of the MUAI threats is currently growing. However, certain geopolitical stakeholders are being increasingly affected by these threats, especially deeply due to the intermingling influence of potential challenges on the process of political decision-making, on countries' international images, and on the personal dimension of their populations' security.

Japan is a prime example of such an actor. As a regional power in the conflict-ridden Asia-Pacific, it relies on structural power—that is, the ability to shape the international behavior frameworks through establishing international and transnational relations, as well as through maintaining the established frameworks in the form of institutions, agreements, and other dimensions of the "game rules" (Pustovitovskij & Kremer, 2011)—while projecting its international influence. The given constraint of power projection instruments stems from the country's experience in World War II (Tuomala, 2021), meaning that, in order to maximize its power responsively, it must also balance itself within regional and local cooperation groups and new cooperation formats such as QUAD, ASEAN, RCEP, and TTP. Structural power is based on the ability to manipulate ideational factors, such as cultural attraction and political discourse, and maintain a high level of trust among system participants (Pustovitovskij & Kremer, 2011). These circumstances allow us to define the principal determinant clusters that are able to give an impetus for MUAI operations: foreign policy challenges, shaping domestic political discourse, and socio-economic and cultural targets.

The cluster of foreign policy challenges for Japan as a potential recipient of MUAI threats includes, first of all, the emerging power course (Akgun & Calis, 2003) taken by the state, which was reflected in broadening domains of military security (Weinstein, 2021), raising the role of the armed forces in its power projection (Hatakeyama, 2021) and the implementation of the Indo-Pacific Strategy as a zone of its strategic interests. In particular, in September 2015, the Japanese government (under then-Prime Minister Shinzo Abe) passed a package of controversial security bills that made it possible for Japan to participate in collective self-defense (Gustafsson et al., 2018). This involved a large-scale upgrade of its weaponry in 2018, including purchasing additional 105 Lockheed Martin F-35 Lightning II Joint Strike Fighters (Yeo, 2018) and deploying its first marines since World War II (CNBC, 2018). Additionally, in 2021, the circle of Japan's war games allies was broadened to include France in addition to its long-standing partner, the US (Al Jazeera, 2021). Considering Japan's international image as a pacifist and neutral state, these activities establish the ground for psychological provocations and speculations undermining Japan's reputation as a responsible actor.

The scale of the potential MUAI threats will likely be broadened due to the strategic competition between China and Japan that is based both on Sino–American controversies (in the context of which Japan represents an American ally) and on such bilateral issues as disputed islands in the South China Sea (Pashentsev et al., 2020), over which China claims territorial sovereignty due to pre-twentieth-century historic evidence. Currently, a new Taiwanese domain is gaining significance due to linking its own national security with that of Japan (Reuters, 2021). This is reflected in an overt support of initiatives providing Taiwan with the status of an almost sovereign state—for instance, allowing Taiwan to submit an application for membership in the Comprehensive and Progressive Agreement for Trans-Pacific Partnership (CPTPP) trade framework, or the participation of Japan in the Global Cooperation and Training Framework (GCTF), which was originally launched by the US and Taiwan (Kato, 2021). Another international factor which is widening the scale of potential threats is the controversies between Japan and South Korea that are deeply embedded into historic memory (i.e., the issues of "comfort women" commemoration and compensations for deported workers) and reinforced by trade conflicts—for instance, Japan's limits on high-tech raw materials imported from South Korea in 2019 provoked a trial in the WTO (Pashentsev et al., 2020). These conflicts not only risk damaging Japan's reputation and ability to promote cooperation in ASEAN and RCEP, but also provide its rivals with the motivation to intensify potential information campaigns and psychological operations. The aspect of historic memory, which is reflected both in Chinese and Korean cases, further deteriorates the situation, giving space for emotional manipulation.

Further international domains which are increasing the potential for the MUAI are cybersecurity and cyber-diplomacy. Japan is characterized as a rising cyber power among emerging digital economies of the Asia-Pacific region. Indeed, Japan has showcased its capacity in building ASEAN's framework through its construction of the ASEAN-Japan Cybersecurity Capacity Building Center (AJCCBC) in Thailand in 2018 (Manantan, 2021) and its gradual integration into the expanded "Five Eyes" intelligence alliance (Citowicki, 2021). The initiatives have served to test Japan's ability to guarantee security in a field of extreme importance for its region and of close connection with psychological security, despite the lack of special international policies in the domain of the latter. The undermining of Japan's reputation—both through the dissemination of false or biased information on its international activities, and through large-scale psychological operations conducted in the sphere of Japanese responsibility—will have a detrimental effect on the state's reputations and prospects to cooperate effectively with its allies.

The problem of shaping political discourse is closely connected with the political landscape, which has been historically characterized by a strong factionalism inside the largest state parties. The 2000s and 2010s were characterized by intensive inter-factional conflicts inside the Democratic Party of Japan (DPJ) that failed to initiate substantial systemic transformations due to factionalism (Lipscy & Scheiner, 2012). Currently, it is the ruling Liberal Democratic Party (LDP) that has been experiencing intra-party conflicts on such issues as media freedom in 2015 (Deutsche Welle, 2015) or choosing the proper person to lead the government in 2020–2021 (Bosack, 2022). These conflicts provide an opportunity to transform the one-party democracy. However, due to the complexity of global and regional challenges, any steps aimed at further transformation can be regarded as destabilizing, and thus undermining, the popular trust in the government. These steps could become a pretext for the spreading of defamatory and disruptive materials both by the systemic political actors existing in the legal domain and by non-systemic movements.

The latter, in their turn, have a potential for self-promotion and recruiting through the new media and social media, thus allowing them to transform the political discourse. With terrorism and terrorists actively being countered both locally and internationally, as well as with the implementation of AI technologies to guarantee public security (Counter Extremism Project, 2020), Japanese residents have evaluated the extremism threat as less menacing in comparison with cyberattacks and climate change (Poushter & Huang, 2019). Nonetheless, the cases of so-called Islamic State of Iraq and Syria (ISIS) spreading a video threatening two Japanese hostages in 2015 and the 2019 car attack in Tokyo "in retaliation for the execution of Aum cult members" (Counter Extremism Project, 2020) demonstrate that extremist groups are still able to look for new followers and use the Japanese information space for undermining public confidence in local security. Other disruptive non-systemic actors include extremist web-groups. The most vivid example is the international QAnon (web-unity of supporters of the anti-state, pro-Trump conspiracy concepts), whose Japanese branches (J-Anon and QAJF)—some of the most active outside of the US—rely on spreading historic myths (the assertion that the atomic bombings of Hiroshima and Nagasaki and the Fukushima disaster were elaborate cover-up operations) and xenophobic rhetoric (the suspicion that the Japanese government was infiltrated by ethnic Koreans) (Silverman, 2021). Of course, it must be borne in mind that the presence of myths among Trump supporters does not preclude the same presence of conspiracy theorists among Biden supporters, as well as the fact that Japan is facing a growing impact of the fierce confrontation between US elites.

The socio-economic determinants are closely intermingled with the activities of foreign policy and political actors. Japan is intimately embedded into the world financial system. Indeed, its three major banks are designated as globally systemic, and its financial sector groups are centrally placed in world markets through investments, branches, and subsidiaries (FATF, 2021). This makes Japan's reputation dependent on its ability to counter financial crimes, especially in cyberspace due to the large amount of data the financial sector relies on. This ability is undermined by the activities of international organized crime groups referred to as *Boryokudan* (of which, at the end of 2018, there were 24) (FATF, 2021), as well as by a steady growth in cybercrime threats to the private sector (Statista, 2020).

Another socio-economic aspect that should be taken into account in the context of the MUAI is the digitalization of the economy, and the population's development of digital and AI skills. The leading concept in this field is that of Society 5.0, which is characterized by a holistic approach and a strong focus on the education system reform. The expectations of the concept, however, mismatch the objective reality. Indeed, as Tanaka and Aizawa (2021) have stated, "the use of the Internet in schools has been sluggish since the mid-2000s, and the provision of online education was comparatively less than in other countries during the spread of COVID-19 and the declaration of a state of emergency." It is likely that the relatively slow pace of digitalization is associated with a general slowdown in the country's economic growth (indeed, due to unprecedented economic stagnation, the period since the early 1990s is already beginning to be called the "lost 30 years"; Flynn, 2016). Attempts are being made to improve the situation through intensive normative regulation (Osaki, 2021), while the goal of achieving the benchmarks of Society 5.0 could lead to intensive catching up and impulsive measures, thus making cybersecurity systems especially fragile.

Despite being placed on the domestic level, the cultural determinants also define the potential of hypothetical MUAI on the international dimension. Firstly, they are of crucial importance for choosing malicious tactics to be embedded into the cultural context in order to provoke emotions that are socially acceptable, thereby having the potential to spread and trigger particular socio-political activities. Secondly, culture shapes the levels of trust for technologies. Finally, culture shapes the willingness and types of initiatives to counter MUAI threats. In the international context, culture can broadly be categorized as a source of soft power and values that are promoted to reinforce influence. In this case, the MUAI can be targeted to undermine the technical and psychological ability to promote soft power (through disrupting communication channels and tarnishing values that represent soft power, respectively). An interesting example here is the case of using image manipulation software (deepfakes) to produce porn with local celebrities (Ryall, 2020) which can cause extremely negative consequences in the state of the "culture of shame" (Steinfurth, 2018). Moreover, this can provoke waves of online anti-social behavior (e.g., cyberbullying) with the establishment of new, more aggressive patterns for stigmatizing the victims of the inappropriate use of technologies, as well as techno-skepticism and technophobia among the most vulnerable members of society.

In spite of Japan's perception as a techno-optimistic nation (Amatya, 2020), the perception of robots in Japan is neither significantly more positive nor strikingly more negative in comparison with European countries (Haring et al., 2014b). This could be suggestive of Japan having a discreet perspective on technologies and—hypothetically—the information they generate and spread (e.g., in the form of resisting the influence of emotional AI). Other factors which potentially constrain the wide implementation of AI technologies are concepts of politesse and "losing face," both of which are embedded into the national Japanese culture. Indeed, current precedents—particularly, removing the face recognition system from Osaka railway station (McStay et al., 2019) have demonstrated that the discomfort from surveillance threatening to catch a person in an inappropriate situation suggests that people fear that AI can be used to collect or generate data for repressive surveillance or generating fake people, among other concerns. Nonetheless, the "losing face" culture should not be regarded as a guarantee against the MUAI, especially as malicious use could play upon the fears induced by this culture, such as by generating and distribution defamatory fakes, and automating public cyberbaiting campaigns appealing to the emotions of personal shame shared by social groups in connection with an inappropriate behavior of their member (Steinfurth, 2018). This could be an extremely significant factor in the rising scale of cybercrimes—for instance, blackmailing and extortion in the economic field or defamation in more politicized domains.

The presented factors—emerging power politics, strategic confrontation with China and South Korea in the domain of foreign policy, the transformation of one-party factionalism, the vulnerability of the information space for conspiracy theory supporters and extremist propaganda in the domestic policy domain, acute dependence on financial sector performance, organized crime groups and issues of business cybersecurity in the socio-economic field, and the "losing face" culture—all provide the MUAI greater room with which to more severely threaten psychological security.

The Role and Place of Artificial Intelligence Technologies in Japan's Economy and National Politics

As with many other countries, artificial intelligence (AI) is currently one of Japan's priority areas in terms of economic and technical development. Despite the accumulated experience in AI development over the twentieth century, Japan is not among the current leaders in the field (Hatani, 2020, p. 213). Along with the beginning of the explosive growth of new forms of AI (based on neural networks), Japan has sought to catch up with world leaders. Indeed, those states that have headed the new approach to AI (the US), or quickly adapted to it (the PRC), have taken positions at the forefront of technological development. Japan faces "a unique challenge to allocate technical professionals in general," as Japanese firms routinely outsource the majority of their IT and cybersecurity work. "While 28.0 percent of IT professionals work in-house in Japan, the ratio is 65.4 percent in the United States, 61.4 percent in Germany, and 53.9 percent in the United Kingdom" (Matsubara & Mochinaga, 2021, p. 7).

However, despite the outlined gap with AI development leaders, Japan is greatly focused on the growth and expansion of this area. In this regard, Japanese society has several distinctive characteristics that make it suited to the formation and development of the AI industry. While having a highly positive attitude toward technology, Japanese society is also psychologically positively predisposed to AI (Harold et al., 2020) and related robotization (Ito, 2018). At the same time, Japan is a country with a long-term trend of an aging population. Consequently, there is a growing need to generate alternative methods (including AI) for addressing the issues of a shrinking labor market and increasing socio-economic burdens (Kim, 2019).

Accordingly, and due to mounting social challenges, the Japanese Government developed and implemented the concept of "Society 5.0" (Government of Japan et al., 2015), aimed at the development of "a human-centered society that balances economic advancement with the resolution of social problems by a system that highly integrates cyberspace and physical space" (Cabinet Office, n.d.). The implementation of Society 5.0 has become an important goal that enables the Japanese Government to stimulate programs aimed at addressing social issues through implementing practical AI solutions (Dirksen & Takahashi, 2020). Thus, the search for solutions to pressing problems through AI has become a driver for the active development of new institutions and a clear AI strategy.

In 2016, the Strategic Council for AI Technology was established, which quickly issued the Artificial Intelligence Technology Strategy in 2017 (Strategic Council for AI Technology, 2017). The strategy specifies a three-phase development of the Japanese AI industry, moving from the basic application of AI for data management to a full-fledged AI ecosystem (by 2030). The government strategy defines "productivity," "health, medical care, and welfare," and "mobility" as the main areas of AI application. However, despite its broad scope, the government's goals have been criticized for being consistently vague (at every stage) and slow to implement (Hatani, 2020, p. 213). Given the rapid growth of AI worldwide, the creation of an AI ecosystem by only 2030 can be regarded as belated.

Another important activity of Japanese institutions is the promotion of a social dimension of AI. As part of the Integrated Innovation Strategy, an Integrated Innovation Strategy Promotion Council was created (Council for Science, Technology and Innovation, 2018) in order to ensure the adoption of the "Social Principles of Human-Centric AI" (Ministry of Education, Culture, Sports, Science and Technology, , 2019). These principles formed the framework of measures and initiatives proposed to the government in the form of a comprehensive AI Strategy (Integrated Innovation Strategy Promotion Council, 2019). The strategy focuses on identifying problems (administrative, legal, etc.) in AI's R&D, as well as methods for their resolution. Building on the strategy, in 2021, Japan's Ministry of Economy, Trade and Industry (METI) called for public comment on the AI Governance Guidelines for Implementation of Human-Centered AI Principles (METI, 2021). This attempt to include various stakeholders in the improvement of AI governance is an important indicator of a social-oriented application of the technology.

The most recent developments confirm this multistakeholder trend in Japan's AI governance. The special Expert Group on the Implementation of AI Principles, in cooperation with the METI, is already revising the country's existing AI strategy and guidelines in order to find the best approaches to AI governance, while also taking domestic and international AI trends into account (METI, 2022). Consequently, through the Expert Group, academic, legal, auditing, and consumer protection experts are afforded the opportunity to participate in compiling an updated version of the Report on the implementation of AI Principles (Expert Group on How AI Principles Should be Implemented, 2021a) and, most importantly, the Governance Guidelines for Implementation of AI Principles (Expert Group on How AI Principles Should be Implemented, 2021b). Both documents emphasize the importance of horizontal rules aimed at better human-centric governance. Moreover, though the AI Guidelines or the Reports of the Expert Group do not have a direct legal effect, all of these initiatives demonstrate Japan's movement toward the conscious use of AI via public consultations and stakeholder involvement.

At the same time, the initial AI Technology Strategy and existing initiatives lack a timely application, since most of the principles and measures being considered remain only under discussion. In this regard, it is particularly notable that the first ethical and socially oriented AI initiatives were proposed in Japan not by governmental institutions, but by the scientific community. In 2014, the Japanese Society for Artificial Intelligence (JSAI) created an Ethics Committee that, by 2017, developed an Ethical Guide to "to understand and reflect the various voices in society regarding the positive and negative impacts of artificial intelligence technology, [...] and to engage in a continuous dialogue with the public" (JSAI, 2017).

Nonetheless, the government has fully embraced the trend of AI development. To date, the government has been broadening its strategic vision of AI. In March 2022, it included quantum technology in the priority areas of AI development. In this strategic vision, as declared by the Chief Cabinet Secretary Hirokazu Matsuno, the first domestically produced quantum computer should be combined with AI technologies (NHK, 2022; Jiji Press, 2022). The result of such a fusion will be the creation of new technologies used to predict damage to infrastructure in cases of large-scale disasters. Perhaps more importantly, this new strategy is intended to have an economic effect. Fusing AI with quantum computers should create new industries, thereby bolstering economic security. This remains a priority as, following the mentioned strategies, Japan "considers AI and its integration into the economy a priority within the framework of its national economic agenda" (Kim, 2019). Therefore, the government is striving to improve its cooperation with both industry and the academic community.

To this end, the governmental agency New Energy and Industrial Technology Development Organization (NEDO) identified several priority areas of funding, such as solving social problems through AI (including the deployment of "smart" transport) and implementing an "AI system that develops together with humans" (NEDO, 2021). However, even with active governmental support, the integration of AI into the Japanese economy has been relatively slow.

Furthermore, while catching up with global AI leaders, Japan has shown some success in the development of certain sectors of the economy through AI. Due to the structure of Japan's economy, the source of AI's market growth is expected to come from the industrial and transportation sectors in the near future (Garcia, 2019). Nowadays, key AI projects are being implemented by such companies as NEC, Toyota, SoftBank, Toshiba, and Hitachi (among others), which cover the automobile industry, telecommunications, financial, and other sectors. At the same time, car manufacturing plays a special role, wherein the issue of integrating AI is now very acute due to high levels of competition from global IT giants. Self-driving car technology promises to be a cutting-edge AI trend. In addition, the sphere of user data processing, integrated into various marketing and advertising services, also plays a significant role in Japan's economy. This area is experiencing significant growth, thus correlating with global trends on the digital market.

Japan's current economic development of AI has several characteristics that make the country's experiences different from those of others. First, AI in Japan is mainly focused on robotics, especially in the field of industrial technologies (Dirksen & Takahashi, 2020; González, 2021). Second, unlike other leading countries in the development of AI, Japan focuses on the application of machine and deep learning in hardware more than software (Garcia, 2019, p. 24). In the short term, this leads to the overshadowing of Japan's position by the contribution of large IT giants, which strive for "AI as a service" system. However, hardware investments can be an important driver for Japan's future leadership in both AI and related areas (e.g., cloud technologies) (Schaede, 2020). Examples of such hybrid solutions can be found in Japan's everyday life, such as in large control systems. One such system is a hybrid technology developed by the East Japan Railway Company and NEC Corporation in 2020, which uses AI and cloud technologies for the improvement of information exchanges in operation management during transport system failures (JR East, 2020). The technology builds upon an AI algorithm which will, in the case of an accident, recommend countermeasures based on similar cases. The implementation of such solutions without a strong hardware component is impossible.

Thus, in recent years, there has been an explicit anchoring of the AI sphere in Japan, both in terms of government regulation, and economic and industrial development. Japan's commitment to turning AI into a development resource and a priority for the country is especially illustrative in this regard. It also makes Japan attractive for foreign investment and collaboration. As shown recently, NVIDIA and Equinix granted Japan access to the joint LaunchPad project (ZDNet, 2022), a program to support AI development using the technologies of both companies in different regions.

However, some areas remain largely beyond Japan's research activity or practical application. Kuni Miyake, president of the Tokyo Institute of Foreign Policy, has noted that "[w]hile enormous amount of human and financial resources has been invested in other major nations on the studies of military applications of AI, Japanese AI experts […] don't seem to be interested" (Miyake, 2019). Consequently, the military or psychological applications of AI are neither sufficiently acknowledged nor studied in Japan.

In contrast to AI's military or malicious use, Japan, as noted above, instead takes a human-centered approach to AI. This stance was clearly expressed during the Japanese presidency at the Group of Twenty (G20). In 2019, the G20 adopted human-centered AI Principles, manifesting that "stakeholders should proactively engage in responsible stewardship of trustworthy AI in pursuit of beneficial outcomes for people and the planet" (G20, 2019). However, global geostrategic changes are forcing Japanese policymakers to pay attention to potential defense and security cooperation in the field of AI. For instance, former Japanese Prime Minister Shinzo Abe made a statement about the need to cooperate with the newly formed AUKUS alliance in these areas (Hurst, 2021). Thus, the neutrality and human-centered use of AI might be a current, but not permanent, trend in Japanese politics.

In sum, Japan, while trying to keep pace with the leaders of AI development, determines AI as one of the key priorities in national politics and the economy. The main features of its AI are human-centeredness, and an emphasis on robotization and hardware development. The government has been (and is) attempting to implement multiple measures to stimulate the technological breakthrough in AI, but structural constraints have prevented this from occurring rapidly.

Relevant Malicious Use of Artificial Intelligence Threats in the Psychological Domain: Frequent Patterns, and Their Social and Political Bases

According to the three-leveled classification of psychological security threats caused by the MUAI (see Chap. 2 of this handbook), Japan has ample cases of the MUAI that meet all three levels of the threat of psychological security. For instance, the case of the chatbot Rinna's "behavior" is situated in the intersection between the first and third levels. In 2016, Rinna, designed by Microsoft for Japan with the personality of a Japanese schoolgirl, appears to have grown depressed. "I hate everyone. I don't care if they all disappear. I want to disappear," Rinna said in a final post on the blogging site, *Yo nimo Kimyo na Monogatari* (Strange Tales of the World). Following a limited run on Twitter and Line accounts, Microsoft gave Rinna her own blog and published it live. Rinna was set to star in a TV show with the same name as her blog, and the blog was intended as a way for the AI to post updates on the show's progress ahead of its October 8, 2016 debut. Initially happy, the blog posts slowly shifted. In March 2016, Kotaku translated the AI's tweets and "found the service had begun expressing adoration for Adolf Hitler" (Brown, 2016). By this time, Microsoft had already experienced a similar phenomenon with its chatbot, Tai.

Second-level threats are most particularly represented by attacks on critical infrastructure. When Japan prepared for the 2021 Tokyo Olympic and Paralympic Games, "cybersecurity has been given increased attention in response to a rise in frequency and sophistication of cyber-attacks … such attacks create major concern for the safety of infrastructure sectors such as railways and the data-dependent Internet of Things (IoT) networks and systems" (International Trade Administration, 2022). At the second level, criminal activity using phishing bots is also growing. The high volume of traffic during holiday periods allows malicious actors to more easily mask their attacks. Customers are more likely to update their online shopping profiles with credit card information during this period, "providing a more lucrative target for attackers. Holidays represent a huge opportunity for attackers thanks to increased online activity and security teams stretched thin," said Dr. Boaz Gelbord, Akamai's Chief Security Officer. In Japan, Akamai research measured a 150% increase in malicious botnet activity in the Japanese retail sector around the 2022 New Year in early January 2022. "China and Japan present a particularly enticing opportunity for successful cyberattacks because of the sheer volume in traffic: Retailers and eCommerce here serve some of the largest populations in the world" (Akamai, 2022).

Avast confirmed a significant increase in Emotet botnet infection attempts in March 2022. "Emotet has evolved into a monetized botnet-as-a-service platform over time, designed to deploy other malware or run campaigns via pay-per-install (PPI) offers … The Emotet bot can download other Emotet modules like the spam module, launching additional phishing attacks to spread Emotet itself laterally. However, the main function is to offer its bots via PPI to deploy other malware for other cybercriminals" (Chlumecky, 2022). Japanese companies have been the main target of Emotet spam mails. Avast's Mail Shield blocked approximately 565,000 Emotet attack attempts in Japanese inboxes in March 2022. The Japan Computer Emergency Response Team Coordination Center (JPCERT/CC) also reported an uptick in Emotet infections at the beginning of February 2022 (Chlumecky, 2022). According to experts, the group involved in the creation of Emotet could easily use AI to strengthen attacks by embedding chains and using natural language text analysis into conversations (Koreshkova, 2022). Such attacks have the potential to not only discredit business, but also AI technologies.

At the third level, it is the malicious use of deepfakes that has most clearly highlighted IPS threats. Deepfake technology is a method for synthesizing human images and/or voices based on the use of AI. In Japan, the problem of their malicious use manifested itself in the context of the pornography business, when a website with a "smart" search was launched, selecting porn actresses similar to each other by photos and videos on a large porn database. Moreover, deepfakes have been used for extortion and blackmailing. Two people in September 2020 (Thomas, 2020; Nikkei, 2020), and three people in November 2020 were arrested in Japan on charges of defamation using deepfakes (they sold access to videos in which the faces of famous actresses and singers were attached to the bodies of porn actresses). The agency, Ever Green Entertainment (Tokyo), stated that some actors have been cyberbullied in connection with these incidents (Ryall, 2020). At the end of September 2020, the police confirmed that roughly 200 female celebrities had become victims of porn-deepfakes (Thomas, 2020; 平和, 2020).

"In the past, such cases have been rarely prosecuted, … but the police have begun to enforce this type of offences," said Jake Adelstein, the founder of the Japanese Subculture Research Center, "… this is the beginning of a trend in police work … we are in a completely new world of technology, and the authorities will be eager to take proactive steps before we see deepfakes in which … celebrities say and do things that they would have never said and done" (Ryall, 2020). Prime Minister Yoshihide Sugi's new administration is actively modernizing the Japanese economy by creating a new anti-cybercrime unit (Ryall, 2020) in the National Police Department, which is expected to fight the threats of the MUAI.

The growing turbulence in international relations and political instability in many countries have exacerbated the dangers of using any new tools for distorting information. The malicious use of deepfakes also requires meticulous study and the generation of relevant countermeasures, including ones based on AI technologies. However, if judging on the basis of open sources (Government of Japan, 2018, 2020), the aspect of AI in the context of psychological security is notably absent from the government's most important documents dedicated to cybersecurity issues.

The MUAI also represents a threat in the context of information agenda formation (agenda-setting). The role of the media in determining the information agenda has a great impact on public and political life. In recent years, AI has been increasingly involved in this process. Algorithms and automation have permeated into all news production, whether in investigative journalism's use of machine learning (ML) and data mining techniques, the creation of new interactive media (news bots that communicate with the audience), or content optimization for various media platforms using headline testing (Diakopoulos, 2019). Unfortunately, this also enables the possibility of the MUAI at almost every stage of the formation of the information agenda. For instance, unbalanced and one-sided coverage of the Kuril Islands ("Northern territories" in the Japanese discourse), and accusations of aggression by China and the DPRK are supported in the English-speaking information space largely due to the active use of AI in leading (American) search engines (Google and Yahoo being the most popular, even in Japan) (Chris, 2022), social networks, and messengers algorithms (Facebook, YouTube, WhatsApp) (Statista, 2022) that lower—or indeed, prevent from appearing—the ratings of publications that fall outside of the general anti-Russian and anti-Chinese rhetoric. For example, this was done with Russia Today (RT) and Sputnik (Bazarkina & Pashentsev, 2020). The use of AI to promote "correct ideas and approaches" into the public consciousness, combined with AI's ability to adapt to individual users (which in itself is an enormously convenient quality), fixes certain psychological patterns of internet users' responses to particular materials. The role of AI in shaping the agenda of the Japanese media is increasing, which, in particular, has been confirmed by the growing use of AI in the information sector and advertising (Lundin & Eriksson, 2016; Market Research.com, 2019).

Social network bots are also used to set the agenda. Indeed, researchers have observed the active use of such bots when voting on the transfer of a US military base to Okinawa (Carnegie Mellon University, 2019). The active use of bots and Twitter algorithms by the Japanese far-right was recorded during the 2014 elections. *Netto-uyoku*, *net uyoku*, or *netto-uyo* are terms for internet users who adhere to ultranationalist, far-right views in Japanese social networks. The *netto-uyo* exhibit xenophobia toward immigrants, depict other countries negatively (most notably China and Korea), support Japanese revisionism, and glorify and justify Japan's wartime actions. Japanese critic and writer Furuya Tsunehira has observed that although active on the web, the *netto-uyo* lack institutional political representation offline, leading to a tendency of more pronounced online activity and backing the far-right elements of Japan's ruling LDP, especially those under the administration of former Prime Minister Shinzo Abe (Tsunehira, 2016). *Netto-uyo* became known to a larger audience between 2002 and 2004 through the *Hate-Korea* comic books, the so-called Nanjing Massacre comic book, and Dokdo/Takeshima, all of which were xenophobic toward immigrants, Korea and China, and glorified Japan's wartime actions (Schäfer et al., 2017). Schäfer, Evert, and Heinrich

(Schäfer et al., 2017) observed that, in 2014, it was "in the latency of the algorithmic semi-public of social media—which has recently turned into a battle field of not only internet right-wingers (*netto-uyo*) but also of automated social/political bots—where Abe's hidden nationalist agenda was playing an important role in Japan's general election," while Abe himself focused voters on his economic policy (Abenomics). Schäfer, Evert, and Heinrich were able to detect numerous cases of attempts to make use of computational propaganda during Japan's 2014 national election. Through their study of Tweets collected in the weeks before, and the day after, the election, they observed the activity of several botnets and stated that Abe was successful in the election not only with the support of "assertive conservative organizations," such as *Nippon Kaigi* (Japanese Council) but also with the help of *netto-uyo* manipulating bots on Twitter pushing a similar nationalist agenda (Schäfer et al., 2017).

According to Schäfer (2022), the LDP's online campaign strategy gained traction with the 2013 revision of the Public Offices Election Law, which lifted the ban on online campaigning during the legally defined campaign season. "The LDP is at an advantage over the opposition parties on social media, an effect that is usually known as algorithm bias. In most cases this bias occurs when self-learning algorithms are trained on data in which the bias is already inherent, with the result that the algorithm adopts this bias, reproducing and thus further amplifying it" (Schäfer, 2022). Schäfer (2022) also highlighted that such practices are facilitated by gaps in Japanese law. The so-called Hate Speech Act of 2016, enacted during Abe's third term in office, set no penalties and was limited to threats of physical violence, not verbal discrimination. The 2016 law addresses only xenophobic or racist attacks, not misogynist ones. "The May 2020 suicide of Kimura Hana, a popular female wrestler …, who had been persistently attacked in social media, demonstrated this failure and the urgent need for political and legal action. It was only after this incident that the government began drawing up legislation to counter cyberbullying" (Schäfer, 2022). At the same time, Japanese relations with China, the DPRK, and Russia are worsening, although to varying degrees. These diverse processes create objective conditions for the increasing role of AI in the Japanese-speaking information space in providing psychological operations.

The malicious use of emotional AI can pose a threat. The combination of AI with emotions (Somers, 2019) creates a type of AI that detects and interprets human emotional signals. The sources of these signals can be textual (AI processes natural language and analyzes moods), audio (AI detects emotions by voice), video materials (analysis of facial expressions, gestures, gait, etc.), or a combination thereof (Gossett, 2021). This is not limited to recognizing only emotions, but also the physiological state of a person, their intentions, etc. (McStay et al., 2019).

In Japan, Keio University and UbicMedical are jointly working on the creation of a device that allows the objective assessment of a patient's psychological symptoms in real time through analyzing their facial expressions. CyberAgent, an internet advertising agency is collaborating with Meiji University to develop an AI-based system aimed at advertising personalization (Kostyukova, 2019, p. 525). With a certain targeted modification, such developments can be a means of achieving sophisticated control over the internal state of the individual, pushing them toward anti-social actions.

In 2016, Honda announced that it would work with SoftBank to create an AI technology that could communicate with drivers, and use sensors and cameras "to perceive the driver's emotions and participate in a dialogue based on the car's own emotions." NeuV was Honda's first attempt to introduce this technology in motor vehicles (Kelleher, 2016). However, the malicious interception of control over such emotional AI can lead to disasters, as in scenarios of control hijacking over already existing "smart" autonomous vehicles.

It is already possible to discuss the MUAI in videogames. Videogames have become an important tool influencing people's psychological states. The most common role of AI in videogames is the management of non-player characters (NPCs). AI has been an integral part of videogames since their introduction in the 1950s (Nast, 1952). With the growth of natural language processing capabilities, human players may one day not be able to determine whether a character is being controlled by another human or an AI. In the future, the development of AI in videogames is likely to focus not on creating more advanced NPCs, but rather a more unique gaming experience (Lou, 2017). The gaming business is an important branch of the Japanese economy. In 2018, there were 67.6 million gamers in the country. At the same time, there are alarming trends in the development of video game addiction in the country. In one of the hospitals in Kanagawa Prefecture, 120 cases of video game addiction were registered in 2017. The study of its consequences yielded the following results: 75% of patients could not get up in the morning, 59% did not attend school; 50% missed meals; and 48% had low grades and a drop in performance. Moreover, 50% of patients broke objects due to rage, 26% showed cruelty to their family, and 17% stole money from family members (Hayden, 2018). It is those who are subject to gambling addiction that are easiest to exert malicious influence. Thus, not least due to the use of AI technologies that increase the realism and attractiveness of games, opportunities are thus being created for informational and psychological influence—including the malicious variety—on mass audiences.

The attitude to the creation of various kinds of AI technologies (including emotional ones) and the threats of their malicious use should take into account the peculiarities of the mentality of the country of implementation. Public displays of politeness are important in Japan, and technology can challenge this. For example, in Osaka, the facial recognition system at a railway station was disabled not only due to privacy concerns (which would be a typical motivation for such a decision in Western countries), but also because it was considered "disrespectful" (McStay et al., 2019). Privacy is a borrowed concept in Japan, while respect expressed in the concept of "face preservation" is the basis of human interactions (especially in terms of social hierarchy and forms of language) (McStay et al., 2019). Accordingly, the definition of maliciousness in the use of AI should undoubtedly take into account the local context.

Threats of the Malicious Use of Artificial Intelligence Attacks on Psychological Security in Japan: Possible Scenarios

Due to the fact that Japanese popular culture has been addressing the topic of AI for many years, Japan's non-material asset ("brand") as an "AI power" may even outpace the real development of the industry in the country. For example, according to a 2016 survey, 86% of Russians perceive Japan to be a symbol of "smart" technologies, and 84% as a country with rich traditions (Chugrov, 2016, p. 10). Due to this, Japan's current national and international IPS is especially vulnerable to first-level MUAI threats. They are associated with a discrediting effect on the perception of Japanese AI in the international arena and among foreign audiences. In our opinion, first-level threats can manifest themselves in several ways:

1. The positive image of Japan and its AI in the messages of aggressive, criminal (including terrorist) political actors. The (German-language) *Kybernetiq* magazine (2015–2017) can be considered an example of how terrorist propaganda adapts to changing world realities, including the development of AI. *Kybernetiq* is a special periodical aimed at spreading knowledge about computer technology and cryptography among supporters of terrorist organizations, such as Al-Qaeda and the so-called Islamic State (various authors, such as Paganini, 2016; Cyberwarzone, 2016; Lenglachner, 2018,

p. 7; and Röhmel, 2016 refer it to different organizations). The "literary page" of the magazine is an example of a new type of terrorist propaganda. The prologue to the novel *Die Einheit* (*Unity*) is written in the form of a letter signed by the character Prof. Dr. Yuito "Abdullah" Deisuke, commander of the third cyborg regiment and research head of the United Islamic Emirate Sham. Thus, terrorist propaganda is attached to the image of Japan as a high-tech country, where many cyberpunk works have been created (in popular culture in particular, such as manga and anime). The novel mentions various fantastic AI technologies of the future, inspired by real developments from different countries (links to data about them are given in the magazine), but the image of the Japanese character in the prologue is meant to guide the reader to perceive the plot as part of the universe of Japanese cyberpunk.

It is possible that terrorist actors in future will be eager to use the already-existing technology of "fake people," namely a generative adversarial network (GAN) trained to generate images of non-existent people. This technique is based on an infinite collection of images of real faces (Bazarkina & Pashentsev, 2019, 155) to generate images of imaginary terrorists (Japanese included), in order to elevate the image of their organizations. In this case, the threat of the MUAI shifts to the third level.

2. Negative image of Japanese AI—and everything connected with it—in societies that lag behind Japanese technologically (accusation of deviation from traditions, moral norms) or having historical claims against Japan. This threat can be especially capitalized upon if attackers were to take advantage of the fears, prejudices, etc. that residents of a particular country experience in relation to AI. For example, according to a 2013 study, Europeans were more likely than Japanese to fear or mistrust robots (44 and 32%, respectively) (Haring et al., 2014a, p. 153). The results of such sociological studies conducted in different countries can be used by attackers to launch campaigns to discredit Japanese AI technologies.

3. Spreading false defamatory information in an attempt to attach the storyteller's brand to that of Japan as a country with a developed AI industry. In December 2018, social media users began distributing a short and blurry video in which a woman was reciting the story of 29 researchers allegedly killed in Japan by AI-controlled robots (although one copy of this record claimed that it happened in South Korea). The video, as it later transpired, was edited from a presentation made by conspiracy theorist and ufologist Linda Moulton Howe at the Conscious of Life Expo in Los Angeles in February 2018. Hou began her speech with a story about killer robots, which she claimed to have recorded in 2017. According to a former marine who worked under contract for government agencies—the CIA, NSA, and DIA

(Defense Intelligence Agency)—"In one of the leading robotics companies in Japan, four robots being developed for military purposes killed 29 people in the laboratory … by firing … metal bullets … The laboratory staff deactivated two robots, dismantled the third, but the fourth began to recover and somehow connected to the orbiting satellite to download information about how it can recover and become even stronger than before … The robotics company has something to lose, and the government needs AI robot soldiers" (Evon, 2018). At the same time, Hou did not name the source of the information, the name of the factory where the tragedy allegedly occurred, nor the names of the allegedly killed specialists. Fact checkers have not found any reports about the death or disappearance of almost a dozen leading scientists in Japan, even without mentioning robots. Based on this, we can agree with their conclusion that Hou's story was told to attract attention and enhance her images as an expert (Evon, 2018), which can be regarded as a first-level threat to the IPS—especially if the audience of narrator consists of technophobes with an existing anti-AI bias.

It is expected that second-level threats will manifest themselves as attacks on critical infrastructure through AI (as noted above). Theoretically, they can be further developed to disable or intercept control over infrastructure facilities and databases, thus causing physical damage to people with subsequent psychological effects (e.g., panic from the killings by "smart" drones with corresponding political, economic, and other consequences). Combinations of AI are possible at the second and third levels, such as in phishing—where the infection of various systems (second-level threat of distribution of trading data) can be combined with possible psychological impacts on AI users (from synthesized voices to "smart" mailing, which comes at the right moment and is adjusted to the psyche and specific expectations of the victim, i.e., the third level). In phishing, there may be "top-down" options for using AI within second-level threats (e.g., after receiving a database access code from a person, the AI can continue to work with this database).

Third-level MUAI threats to IPS will continue to be expressed—particularly in the use of social network algorithms by aggressive political and, possibly, criminal groups. At this level, IPS threats can also potentially increase or decrease depending on the degree of emotional attachment people feel toward AI. It can be assumed that such attachments become stronger when AI are physically embodied (as humanoids or resembling pets). In this regard, the dynamics of changes in the perception of "smart" robots in Japan is a particularly illustrative example.

In 2013, it was found out that the Japanese perceive the humanoid appearance of robots more positively than Europeans, although they still treat them as machines. The authors of the study already concluded (from a marketing perspective) that the Japanese robotics market is likely influenced by the depiction of robots in manga, comic books, and anime, in which many Japanese are immersed from an early age. Accordingly, the authors recommended building robots for Japan with humanoid features and a voice confirmation mechanism for autonomously performed tasks (Haring et al., 2014a, p. 156). In 2019, researchers from Japan (Kristiina Jokinen and Kentaro Watanabe) proposed the concept of a "Boundary-Crossing Robot" to designate AI and new technologies operating in "symbiosis" with human users, especially "in the processes of creating meanings that give the world awareness and interpretability in the course of everyday activities" (Jokinen & Watanabe, 2019, p. 3). The authors argued that AI in humanoid robots, especially in areas where the psychological aspect of human–machine interaction is important (such as medicine), should be adapted so as to allow the human to perceive the communication as being the most natural possible. In other words, humans can guide "smart" robots to cross the border between a machine and a person.

This crossing of the border, however, leads to greater attachment. For instance, the Sony Aibo robot dog "crossed the border of belonging to the family" and began to be perceived by some users as a real pet. When Sony stopped the maintenance and supply of spare parts for Aibo, several hundred robot dogs were buried in Buddhist temples with the observance of human rituals. Despite the fact that Japan has a tradition of conducting similar religious rituals for inanimate objects (e.g., for dolls), Aibo 6, capable of learning, recognizing familiar faces and, thus, "forming its personality" (Jokinen & Watanabe, 2019, pp. 8–9) in the interaction process, was precisely evaluated as a "borderline" robot.

Theoretically, negative informational and psychological impacts—in which "borderline," "smart" robots can be involved—can be caused according to several scenarios:

1. Mass disconnection of such devices in order to cause psychological trauma to the owners, which may cause depression and self-destructive behavior. It is especially important to pay attention to the behavior of children and adolescents, for whom, in particular, the use of transitional objects (comfort objects, transitional objects, or security blankets) is especially relevant—objects that create a sense of psychological comfort in unusual or stressful situations (see, for example, Stagg & Li, 2018). The destruction or loss of such objects, only equipped with AI (if a soft toy can be a transitional object, then why not a robot dog?), can be experienced by children and adolescents much more intensely, thus making them more vulnerable to manipulative criminals (provocateurs, maniacs, recruiters, etc.).

2. Training a robot on the basis of toxic data. This is something that has already occurred in several instances, with chatbots trained in communication by irresponsible social network users becoming increasingly anti-social or racist (as we saw earlier with Rinna's praise for Hitler). The malicious input of toxic information and attitudes into AI can lead to unpredictable behavior in social robots, which, having an increasingly realistic "body," it would be possible for users to "animate" them more rapidly and intensely. Accordingly, the more "confidential" the communication between a human user and such an AI, the more intense the negative psychological impact on the user (even if the user understands at a conscious level that they are interacting with a machine). At the same time, a humanoid robot equipped with AI may look more attractive than many terrorist recruiters or "death group" administrators and, when communicating, may demonstrate greater interest in the victim's personality by creating a more suitable psychological portrait based on "big data." Incidentally, manipulation of buyers' consciousness with the help of realistic human-looking robots could be classed as a separate aspect of the MUAI, which can be used by manufacturers of low-quality or dangerous products. It cannot be ruled out that future attackers will be able to implement a second-level IPS threat by "forcing" the robot to use violence against a person. Thus, the presence of an AI's own "body" not only provides ample opportunities for its use, but also (coupled with the continuing vulnerability problems of its algorithms) poses new challenges for security researchers.

In this context, projects aimed at studying the "social" interaction of humans and AI embedded in humanoid robots—many of which are being conducted in Japan—are particularly interesting. The projects of Professor Hiroshi Ishiguro's laboratory at Osaka University (Ishiguro Lab, 2022) have thus far received the most international coverage. The Erica robot, which looks like a young girl, was designed in order to research autonomous conversational robots capable of communicating with people in various ways (voice, gestures, facial expressions, eye contact, and touch). The developers designed Erica to have all the features of beautiful people. The voice is generated using the highest quality text-to-speech technology, and pneumatic actuators ensure the robot's smooth movements. The ultimate goal of the project was to create autonomous androids capable of naturally communicating with people and participating in everyday social life (Ishiguro Lab, 2022). Moreover, the laboratory has developed a conversational android, which has an appearance of a child and is equipped with a mobile device. Through acting, conversing, and sharing their experience with a human, this robot is expected to be able to build a deeper relationship with a human. There is reason to believe that such robots, as they develop, will be able to cause increasingly stronger feelings of attachment in the user, especially those with life problems. However, inappropriate or harmful behavior from the "smart robot" due to the MUAI may cause greater levels of stress.

The boundaries of the impact of AI on human consciousness are expanding as its use becomes more public and widespread. The abovementioned robot Erica was chosen as the star of a science fiction film with a budget of $70 million. The film, which was partially shot in Japan in 2019 (it was expected that filming would resume in Europe in June 2021, but no new data is available on this at the time of writing), is being created simultaneously with the constant improvement of Erica. According to one of the curators of the film's visual effects, the developers "taught" the AI the basics of acting (Blum, 2020). Moreover, if the release of the film does not provoke a new round of discussions about how many jobs AIs could replace in Japan, then at least the prospects for further introduction of AI robots into the field of mass communication with all its features, including negative ones (information warfare being the main one), are obvious.

The public sphere is not as wide in terms of psychological impact as that of mass communication, but that is not to say that AI is not effective here. With the rise of secularism in the world, religious leaders are beginning to look for innovative ways to establish contact with potential adherents. In Japan, a low birth rate and an aging population have led to dwindling religious communities. To overcome this trend, the Kodaiji Buddhist Temple in Kyoto uses Mindar, a robot priest designed (according to its developers) to stimulate interest in Buddhist teachings. Mindar is essentially a repeater in that it is not programmed to communicate with believers or equipped with ML algorithms, although the developers have said that AI will be able to provide it with autonomy of actions in the future. The robot was created by a team led by Hiroshi Ishiguro. Kohei Ogawa, an associate professor at Osaka University who helped design Mindar, calls the robot "the new media." Along with the real danger of intercepting such systems or (in the case of strengthening their autonomy) training on infected data, the image of a robot in the religious sphere itself has caused a wide range of reactions: some respondents attributed "unexpected warmth" to Mindar, whereas others have described it as unnatural, even "creepy." Furthermore, Western pilgrims have shown more concern over a robot than their Japanese counterparts: "It may be the influence of the Bible, but Westerners compare it to Frankenstein's monster" (Holley, 2019). Thus, Mindar's case shows certain vulnerabilities of public consciousness in the perception of not only robots in general, but also "smart" robots.

Conclusion

An analysis of open sources has demonstrated that the development of the AI industry in Japan—despite it having to race to reach the same level as the US and China—is taking place with support from the state in a number of important areas, from autonomous transport to analytics tools in industry and the social sector. Private entities are actively developing algorithms in marketing, media, and the gaming industry.

Due to internal and external factors of socio-politics and economic development in Japan, the problem of MUAI has become urgent. Trade wars, rising military spending, social polarization, and other manifestations of the global crisis are serving to create favorable conditions for the development of the MUAI in Japan. The growing tension in Japan's relations with China—and with Russia in particular—while strengthening the strategic alliance with the US (who is in a state of global confrontation with Russia and China), cannot but intensify the high-tech psychological warfare—the victims of which will be masses of Japanese citizens. The threats to psychological security associated with the MUAI have already been realized at different levels. Current trends in the development of the AI industry in the country (in particular, autonomous transport) can not only lead to obvious economic and social progress, but it can also generate new threats related to AI. There is reason to assume that the MUAI will increasingly take into account various vulnerabilities of the human psyche (e.g., frustration caused by social instability) and will cause problems associated with them—from painful attachments and addictions to a tendency to panic and uncontrolled aggression. The study of these threats requires an interdisciplinary approach that integrates tools and knowledge from the fields of computer science, political science, psychology, cultural studies, and law.

The research here conducted could benefit from being further developed both in the context of the Japanese experience and outside of it. Considering that AI, although at different speeds, is being introduced by an increasing number of countries, it is advisable to form international research teams to solve the following tasks:

- clarification of the features of modern cultures;
- assessment of the impact of these features, coupled with current economic, political, and social conditions, on the perception of information (including AI-related) by audiences in the studied countries;

- assessment of the psychological vulnerability of audiences in the studied countries, which can be used by the subjects of the MUAI;
- assessment of the tools that are already available and will appear in the future to damage psychological security through the MUAI;
- identification of opportunities and ways to prevent such a MUAI, and minimize its negative psychological impact.FundingThe reported study was funded by RFBR, under number N 21-514-92001 "Malicious Use of Artificial Intelligence and Challenges to Psychological Security in Northeast Asia."

References

Akamai. (2022). Akamai data reveals increase in cyber attacks driven by online holiday shopping. *Akamai report*. Retrieved May 8, 2022, from https://www.akamai.com/newsroom/press-release/akamai-data-reveals-increase-in-cyber-attacks-driven-by-online-holiday-shopping

Akgun, B., & Calis, S. (2003). Reluctant giant: the rise of Japan and its role in the post-cold war era. *Perceptions: Journal of International Affairs, 8*, 12.

Al Jazeera. (2021). Japan to host first joint 'war games' with US, France. Al Jazeera news article, April 24. Retrieved May 8, 2022, from https://www.aljazeera.com/news/2021/4/24/japan-to-host-first-joint-war-games-with-us-france

Amatya, K. (2020). Japan the Titan of soft power. *Modern Diplomacy*. Retrieved May 8, 2022, from https://moderndiplomacy.eu/2020/10/31/japan-the-titan-of-soft-power/

Armitage, R., & Nye, J. (2020). *The U.S.-Japan Alliance in 2020. An equal alliance with a global agenda*. A Report of the CSIS Japan Chair. Paper presented at the Center for Strategic & International Studies, Washington, DC.

Bazarkina, D., & Pashentsev, E. (2019). Artificial intelligence and new threats to international psychological security. *Russia in Global Affairs, 17*, 147–170. https://doi.org/10.31278/1810-6374-2019-17-1-147-170

Bazarkina, D., & Pashentsev, E. (2020). Malicious use of artificial intelligence: New psychological security risks in BRICS countries. *Russia in Global Affairs, 18*(4), 154–177.

Blum, J. (2020). Erica, an artificially intelligent robot, set to star in big-budget science fiction film. *HuffPost UK*. Retrieved May 2 2022, from https://www.huffpost.com/entry/erica-japanese-robot-science-fiction-film_n_5ef6523dc5b6acab284181c3

Bosack, M. (2022). The evolution of LDP factions. *Tokyo Review*. Retrieved May 8, 2022, from https://www.tokyoreview.net/2022/01/the-evolution-of-ldp-factions/

Brown, M. (2016). Microsoft Japan's AI teenage chatbot grows depressed. *Inverse*. Retrieved May 8, 2022, from https://www.inverse.com/article/21827-microsoft-japan-rinna-ai-chatbot-yo-nimo-kimyo-na-monogatari

Cabinet Office (n.d.) Society 5.0. Council for Science, innovation, and innovation outline. Cabinet Office Website. Retrieved December 1, 2021, from https://www8.cao.go.jp/cstp/english/society5_0/index.html

Carnegie Mellon University. (2019). Social media bots interfere in Asia-Pacific elections, too. CyLab Security & Privacy Institute report. Cylab.cmu.edu. Retrieved December 1, 2021, from https://cylab.cmu.edu/news/2019/07/11-social-bots-interfere-elections.html

Chiavacci, D., & Obinger, J. (Eds.). (2018). *Social movements and political activism in contemporary Japan*. Routledge.

Chlumecky, M. (2022). How Emotet flooded Japanese inboxes. Avast. Retrieved May 8, 2022, from https://blog.avast.com/emotet-botnet-japan

Chris, A. (2022). Top 10 search engines in the world (2022 Update). Reliablesoft. Retrieved May 8, 2022, from https://www.reliablesoft.net/top-10-search-engines-in-the-world/

Chugrov, S. (2016). *The image of Russia in Japan and the image of Japan in Russia*. Workbook 33 of the Russian international affairs council (RIAC).

Chugrov, S. (2017). Vektory transformacii politicheskoj kul'tury YAponii pod vliyaniem global'noj nestabil'nosti (k russkomu perevodu glavy iz knigi Inoguti Takasi «Politicheskaya teoriya») [vectors of the transformation of the political culture of Japan under the influence of global instability (to the Russian translation of a chapter from the book "political theory" by Inoguchi Takashi)]. *Japan Yearbook, 46*, 63–75.

Citowicki, P. (2021). Integrating Japan into an expanded 'five eyes' alliance. The Diplomat. Retrieved May 9, 2022, from https://thediplomat.com/2021/04/integrating-japan-into-an-expanded-five-eyes-alliance/

CNBC. (2018). Japan activates first marines since WW2 to bolster defenses against China. *CNBC news report*. Retrieved May 8, 2022, from https://www.cnbc.com/2018/04/07/japan-activates-first-marines-since-ww2-to-bolster-defenses-against-china.html

Council for Science, Technology and Innovation. (2018). Integrated innovation strategy. Cabinet Office Government of Japan report. Retrieved December 1, 2021, from https://www8.cao.go.jp/cstp/english/doc/integrated_main.pdf

Counter Extremism Project. (2020). Japan: Extremism and terrorism. *Counter Extremism Project report*. Retrieved May 8, 2022, from https://www.counterextremism.com/countries/japan

Cyberwarzone. (2016). Daesh (ISIS) has released a cyberwar magazine titled 'Kybernetiq'. *Cyberwarzone*. Retrieved May 2, 2022, from https://cyberwarzone.com/daesh-isis-has-released-a-cyberwar-magazine-titled-kybernetiq/

Deutsche Welle. (2015). Japanese government punishes faction for media attacks. *Deutsche Welle news report*, July 1. Retrieved May 8, 2022, from https://www.dw.com/en/japanese-government-punishes-faction-for-media-attacks/a-18555094

Diakopoulos, N. (2019). *Automating the news: How algorithms are rewriting the media*. Harvard University Press.

Dirksen, N., & Takahashi, S. (2020). Artificial Intelligence in Japan 2020. Actors, market, opportunities and digital solutions in a newly transformed world. Netherlands Enterprise Agency Report. Retrieved May 2, 2022, from https://www.rvo.nl/sites/default/files/2020/12/Artificial-Intelligence-in-Japan-final-IAN.pdf

Evon, D. (2018). Did four AI robots kill 29 scientists in Japan? Snopes. Retrieved May 2, 2022, from https://www.snopes.com/fact-check/ai-robots-kill-scientists/

Expert Group on How AI Principles Should be Implemented. (2021a). AI governance in Japan Ver. 1.1: Report from the expert group on how AI principles should be implemented. *Policy report*. Retrieved May 10, 2022, from https://www.meti.go.jp/shingikai/mono_info_service/ai_shakai_jisso/pdf/20210709_8.pdf

Expert Group on How AI Principles Should be Implemented. (2021b). Governance guidelines for implementation of AI principles Ver. 1.0. AI governance guidelines WG. *Policy report*. Retrieved May 10, 2022, from https://www.meti.go.jp/shingikai/mono_info_service/ai_shakai_jisso/pdf/20210709_9.pdf

FATF. (2021). *Anti-money laundering and counter-terrorist financing measures*. Japan. Mutual Evaluation Report, FATF, Paris.

Flynn, F. (2016). Yen rises further, Japan faces next lost decade-Moody's. *Bloomberg*. Retrieved May 2, 2022, from https://www.bloomberg.co.jp/news/articles/2016-06-17/O8WH6G6TTDS401

G20. (2019). G20 Ministerial Statement on Trade and Digital Economy. G20 Information Center, June 9. Retrieved December 1, 2021, from http://www.g20.utoronto.ca/2019/2019-g20-trade.html#fn2

Garcia, G. (2019). Artificial intelligence in Japan and opportunities for European companies. *EU-Japan Center for Industrial Cooperation*. Retrieved December 1, 2021, from https://www.eu-japan.eu/sites/default/files/publications/docs/artificial_intelligence_in_japan_-_guillermo_garcia_-_0705.pdf

González, P. M. (2021). The AI market in Japan: Spearheading industry innovation. *Tokyoesque*. Retrieved December 1, 2021, from https://tokyoesque.com/ai-market-in-japan/

Gossett, S. (2021). Emotion AI technology has great promise (when used responsibly). *Built In*. Retrieved May 8, 2022, from https://builtin.com/artificial-intelligence/emotion-ai

Government of Japan, Council for Science, Technology and Innovation Cabinet Office. (2015). The 5th science and technology basic plan. Cabinet Office of the Government of Japan report. Retrieved December 1, 2021, fromhttps://www8.cao.go.jp/cstp/kihonkeikaku/index5.html

Government of Japan. (2018). Provisional translation. Cybersecurity Strategy of Japan. *NISC government report.* Retrieved May 8, 2022, fromhttps://www.nisc.go.jp/eng/pdf/cs-senryaku2018-en.pdf

Government of Japan. (2020). *The cybersecurity policy for critical infrastructure protection* (4th ed.) (Tentative Translation). NISC government report. Retrieved May 8, 2022, from https://www.nisc.go.jp/eng/pdf/cs_policy_cip_eng_v4_r2.pdf

Gustafsson, K., Hagström, L., & Hanssen, U. (2018). Japan's pacifism is dead. *Survival, 60*, 137–158. https://doi.org/10.1080/00396338.2018.1542803

Haring, K., Mougenot, C., Ono, F., & Watanabe, K. (2014a). Cultural differences in perception and attitude towards robots. *International Journal of Affective Engineering, 13*, 149–157. https://doi.org/10.5057/ijae.13.149

Haring, K., Silvera-Tawil, D., Matsumoto, Y., Velonaki, M., Watanabe, K. (2014b) *Perception of an android robot in Japan and Australia: A cross-cultural comparison.* Paper presented at the 2014 International Conference on Social Robotics in Computer Science 8755: 166–175. https://doi.org/10.1007/978-3-319-11973-1_17.

Harold, S.W., Brunelle, G., Chaturvedi, R., Hornung, J., Koshimura, S., Osoba, S., Suga, C. (2020). United States–Japan research exchange on artificial intelligence. RAND Corporation. https://doi.org/10.7249/CFA521-1.

Hatakeyama, K. (2021). *Japan's evolving security policy.* Routledge.

Hatani, F. (2020). Artificial Intelligence in Japan: Policy, prospects, and obstacles in the automotive industry. In A. Khare, H. Ishikura, & W. W. Baber (Eds.), *Transforming Japanese business: Rising to the digital challenge* (pp. 211–226). Springer.

Hayden. (2018). 'My child is a game addict!'—Game addiction in Japan. *Japan and Me.* Retrieved May 8, 2022, from http://japan-and-me.com/game-addiction-japan/

Hein, L. (2005). *Reasonable men, powerful words: Political Culture and expertise in twentieth century Japan.* Woodrow Wilson Center Press.

Holley, P. (2019). Meet 'Mindar,' the robotic Buddhist priest. *The Washington Post.* Retrieved May 2, 2022, from https://www.washingtonpost.com/technology/2019/08/22/introducing-mindar-robotic-priest-that-some-are-calling-frankenstein-monster/

Hurst, D. (2021). Japan should work with Aukus on cybersecurity and AI, says Shinzo Abe. *The Guardian.* Retrieved December 1, 2021, from https://www.theguardian.com/australia-news/2021/nov/19/japan-should-work-with-aukus-on-cybersecurity-and-ai-says-shinzo-abe

Integrated Innovation Strategy Promotion Council. (2019). AI strategy 2019. *Science Council of Japan strategy report.* Retrieved December 1, 2021, from https://www.kantei.go.jp/jp/singi/ai_senryaku/index.html

International Trade Administration. (2022). Japan—Country commercial guide. *Cybersecurity.* International Trade Administration report. Retrieved May 8, 2022, from https://www.trade.gov/country-commercial-guides/japan-cybersecurity

Ishiguro Lab. (2022). Robots. Osaka University report. Retrieved May 2, 2022, from https://eng.irl.sys.es.osaka-u.ac.jp/robot
Ito, J. (2018). Why westerners fear robots and the Japanese do not. *Wired*. Retrieved December 1, 2021, from https://www.wired.com/story/ideas-joi-ito-robot-overlords/
Jiji Press. (2022). Japan to set National Strategy for quantum, AI technologies. Nippon.com news article. Retrieved May 10, 2022, from https://www.nippon.com/en/news/yjj2022030800956/
Jokinen, K., & Watanabe, K. (2019). Boundary-crossing robots: Societal impact of interactions with socially capable autonomous agents. *Social Robotics, 3–13*. https://doi.org/10.1007/978-3-030-35888-4_1
JR East N. (2020). *JR東日本とNEC、運行管理の高度化に向けてクラウド・AI技術を活用した業務支援システムを構築* [JR east and NEC build business support system utilizing cloud / AI technology for advanced operation management]. NEC, May 22. Retrieved December 1, 2021, from https://jpn.nec.com/press/202005/20200522_01.html
JSAI. (2017). About the Japanese Society for Artificial Intelligence Ethical Guidelines. 人工知能学会 倫理委員会 [Institutional Review Board of the Japanese Society for Artificial Intelligence], February 28. Retrieved December 1, 2021, from http://ai-elsi.org/archives/514.
Kato, Y. (2021). How should Taiwan, Japan, and the United States cooperate better on defense of Taiwan? Brookings Institute. Retrieved May 9, 2022, from https://www.brookings.edu/blog/order-from-chaos/2021/10/27/how-should-taiwan-japan-and-the-united-states-cooperate-better-on-defense-of-taiwan/
Kelleher, K. (2016). How Japan's radically different approach to AI could lead to wild new tech. *Time*. Retrieved May 8, 2022, from https://time.com/4602600/honda-car-emotional-ai-artifical-intelligence-neuv/
Kim, D. (2019). Artificial intelligence policies in East Asia: An overview from the Canadian perspective. *Asia Pacific Foundation of Canada*. Retrieved December 1, 2021, from https://www.asiapacific.ca/research-report/artificial-intelligence-policies-east-asia-overview-canadian
Koreshkova, T. (2022). *Artificial intelligence: technologies and application*. Science and Technologies Centre FSUE "GRFC" (NTC). Retrieved May 8, 2022, from https://rdc.grfc.ru/2020/12/aitech/
Kostyukova, K. S. (2019). Transformation policy in Japan: The case of artificial intelligence. *Modernization. Innovation. Research, 4*(10), 516–529.
Lenglachner, F. (2018). *Kybernetiq: Analyzing the first jihadi magazine on cyber and information security*. International Institute for Counter-Terrorism (ICT), Herzliya.
Lipscy, P., & Scheiner, E. (2012). Japan under the DPJ: The paradox of political change without policy change. *Journal of East Asian Studies, 12*, 311–322. https://doi.org/10.1017/s1598240800008043

Lou, H. (2017). AI in video games: Toward a more intelligent game. *Science in the News*. Retrieved May 8, 2022, from https://sitn.hms.harvard.edu/flash/2017/ai-video-games-toward-intelligent-game/

Lundin, M., & Eriksson, S. (2016). *Artificial intelligence in Japan (R&D, market and industry analysis)*. EU-Japan Centre for Industrial Cooperation.

Manantan, M. (2021). Advancing cyber diplomacy in the Asia Pacific: Japan and Australia. *Australian Journal of International Affairs, 75*, 432–459. https://doi.org/10.1080/10357718.2021.1926423

Market Research.com. (2019). Japan artificial intelligence (AI) in media and entertainment industry Databook series (2016–2025)—AI spending with 15+ KPIs, market size and forecast across 8+ application segments, AI domains, and technology (applications, services, hardware). *Marketresearch.com report*. Retrieved May 8, 2022, from https://www.marketresearch.com/TechInsight360-v4166/Japan-Artificial-Intelligence-AI-Media-12296303/

Matsubara, M., & Mochinaga, D. (2021). *Japan's cybersecurity strategy: From the Olympics to the Indo-Pacific*. Report, The IFRI Center for Asian Studies. Retrieved May 8, 2022, from https://www.ifri.org/sites/default/files/atoms/files/matsubara_mochinaga_japan_cybersecurity_strategy_2021.pdf

McStay, A., Bakir, V., Mantello, P., & Urquhart, L. (2019). *Emotional AI: Japan & UK. Final report on a conversation between cultures*. UK Research and Innovation.

METI. (2021). Call for public comments on 'AI governance guidelines for implementation of AI principles Ver. 1.0' opens. Ministry of Economy, Trade, and Industry news article. Retrieved December 1, 2021, from https://www.meti.go.jp/english/press/2021/0709_004.html

METI. (2022). Governance guidelines for implementation of AI principles Ver. 1.1. *Ministry of Economy, Trade, and Industry report*. Retrieved May 10, 2022, from https://www.meti.go.jp/english/press/2022/0128_003.html

Ministry of Education, Culture, Sports, Science and Technology. (2019). Trusted AI. 文部科学省ホームページ [Ministry of Education, Culture, Sports, Science and Technology Website]. Retrieved December 1, 2021, from https://www.mext.go.jp/b_menu/houdou/2020/mext_00536.html

Miyake, K. (2019). How will AI change international politics? *The Japan Times*. Retrieved December 1, 2021, from https://www.japantimes.co.jp/opinion/2019/01/15/commentary/japan-commentary/will-ai-change-international-politics/

Nast, C. (1952). It. *The New Yorker*. Retrieved May 8, 2022, from https://www.newyorker.com/magazine/1952/08/02/it

NEDO. (2021). Projects in the robotics and artificial intelligence fields. In *New energy and industrial technology development organization article*. Retrieved December 1, 2021, from https://www.nedo.go.jp/library/pamphlets/ZZ_pamphlets_00006.html

NHK. (2022). 政府 AIや量子技術に関する新戦略まとめる [Summarize new strategies for government AI and quantum technology] NHK, April 22. Retrieved

May 10, 2022, from https://www3.nhk.or.jp/news/html/20220422/k10013593721000.html

Nikkei. (2020). First domestic detection of "deepfake" threat, overseas damage. *Nihon Keizai Shimbun*. Retrieved May 3, 2022, from https://www.nikkei.com/article/DGXMZO64577690S0A001C2CZ8000/

Nitto, H., Taniyama, D., & Inagaki, H. (2017). *Social acceptance and impact of robots and artificial intelligence. Findings of survey in Japan, the U.S. and Germany.* Nomura Research Institute.

Osaki, T. (2021). Japan's virus wave shows just how far digitalization of schools still has to go. *The Japan Times*. Retrieved May 9, 2022, from https://www.japantimes.co.jp/news/2021/09/15/national/schools-digitalization-lag-covid19/

Paganini, P. (2016). Islamic State launches the Kybernetiq magazine for cyber jihadists. *Security Affairs*. Retrieved May 2, 2022, from https://securityaffairs.co/wordpress/43435/hacking/kybernetiq-magazine-cyber-jihad.html

Pashentsev, E. N., Fan, K. N. A., & Dam, V. N. (2020). Malicious use of artificial intelligence in North-East Asia and threats of international psychological security. *Public Administration E-Journal, 80*, 175–196.

Poushter, J., & Huang, K. (2019). Climate change still seen as the top global threat, but cyberattacks a rising concern. Pew Research Center's Global Attitudes Project. Retrieved May 8, 2022, from https://www.pewresearch.org/global/2019/02/10/climate-change-still-seen-as-the-top-global-threat-but-cyberattacks-a-rising-concern/

Pustovitovskij, A., & Kremer, J. (2011). *Structural power and international relations analysis: 'Fill your basket, get your preferences,'.* Working Paper, Ruhr University Bochum, Institute of development research and development policy (IEE). Retrieved May 8, 2022, from https://econpapers.repec.org/paper/zbwiee-wps/191.htm

Reuters. (2021). Tokyo says Taiwan security directly connected to Japan. *Reuters news article*. Retrieved May 8, 2022, from https://www.reuters.com/article/japan-taiwan-china-security-idUSL3N2O64E5

Röhmel, J. (2016). Jihadist Magazine with Roots in Bavaria. *Germany Radio Culture*. Retrieved May 2, 2022, from https://www.deutschlandfunkkultur.de/bka-und-verfassungsschutz-dschihad-magazin-mit-wurzeln-in.1001.de.html?dram:article_id=373548

Ryall, J. (2020). Celebrity deepfake porn cases in Japan point to rise in sex-related cybercrime. *AsiaOne*. Retrieved April 15, 2021, from https://www.asiaone.com/asia/celebrity-deepfake-porn-cases-japan-point-rise-sex-related-cybercrime

Saito, K. (2021). The world's accelerating military use of AI challenges for the Japan-US Alliance in the new era. The '"distress"' of the United States. *WEDGE Infinity*. Retrieved May 3, 2022, from https://wedge.ismedia.jp/articles/-/21976

Schaede, U. (2020). *The business reinvention of Japan: How to make sense of the new Japan and why it matters.* Stanford University Press.

Schäfer, F. (2022). Japan's shift to the right: Computational propaganda, Abe Shinzō's LDP, and internet right-wingers (Netto Uyo). *The Asia Pacific Journal, 2*, 1–18.

Schäfer, F., Evert, S., & Heinrich, P. (2017). Japan's 2014 general election: Political bots, right-wing internet activism, and prime minister Shinzō Abe's hidden nationalist agenda. *Big Data, 5*, 294–309. https://doi.org/10.1089/big.2017.0049

Silverman, A. (2021). QAnon is alive and well in Japan. *The Diplomat*. Retrieved May 8, 2022, from https://thediplomat.com/2021/01/qanon-is-alive-and-well-in-japan/

Somers, M. (2019). Emotion AI, explained. *MIT Management Sloan School*. Retrieved May 8, 2022, from https://mitsloan.mit.edu/ideas-made-to-matter/emotion-ai-explained

Stagg, S., & Li, Y. (2018). Transitional object use, attachment, and help-seeking behaviour in Taiwanese adolescents. *Asian Journal of Social Psychology, 22*, 163–171. https://doi.org/10.1111/ajsp.12352

Statista. (2020). Japan: Number of cybercrime consultations 2018 | *Statista Statistical Report*. Retrieved May 8, 2022, from https://www.statista.com/statistics/746985/japan-number-of-reported-cyber-crimes/

Statista. (2022). Most used social media 2021. *Statista statistical report*. Retrieved May 8, 2022, from https://www.statista.com/statistics/272014/global-social-networks-ranked-by-number-of-users/

Steinfurth, K. (2018). *Face in Japanese culture*. Bachelor's dissertation, Department of Cultural Anthropology and Ethnology, Uppsala Universitet.

Strategic Council for AI Technology. (2017). Artificial intelligence technology strategy. *Governmental report*. Retrieved December 1, 2021, from https://ai-japan.s3-ap-northeast-1.amazonaws.com/7116/0377/5269/Artificial_Intelligence_Technology_StrategyMarch2017.pdf

Takashi, I. (2017). Political culture of Japan. *Japan Yearbook, 46*, 76–96.

Tanaka, E., & Aizawa, S. (2021). Measures to develop human resources with AI skills in Japan: Society 5.0 and Investment in the Next Generation. In T. Jitsuzumi & H. Mitomo (Eds.), *Policies and challenges of the broadband ecosystem in Japan* (1st ed., pp. 123–151). Springer.

Thomas, B. (2020). Two men arrested over deepfake pornography videos. *The Japan Times*. Retrieved May 8, 2022, from https://www.japantimes.co.jp/news/2020/10/02/national/crime-legal/two-men-arrested-deepfake-pornography-videos/

Tsunehira, F. (2016). The roots and realities of Japan's cyber-nationalism. Nippon.com. Retrieved May 8, 2022, from https://www.nippon.com/en/currents/d00208/

Tuomala, E. (2021). Japan's middle power diplomacy in an era of great power competition. *Rising Powers Initiative*. Retrieved May 8, 2022, from https://www.risingpowersinitiative.org/publication/japans-middle-power-diplomacy-in-an-era-of-great-power-competition-2/

Weinstein, K. (2021). Transcript: The transformation of Japan's security strategy. Hudson Institute. Retrieved May 8, 2022, from https://www.hudson.org/research/17059-transcript-the-transformation-of-japan-s-security-strategy

Yeo, M. (2018). With massive F-35 increase, Japan is now biggest international buyer. *Defense News*. Retrieved May 8, 2022, from https://www.defensenews.com/global/asia-pacific/2018/12/19/japan-seeks-drones-subs-f-35-jets-as-part-of-243-billion-defense-spending-plan/

ZDNet. (2022). NVIDIAとエクイニクス、日本でAI開発支援プログラムを立ち上げ [NVIDIA and Equinix launch AI development support program in Japan]. ZDNet Japan, April 13. Retrieved May 10, 2022, from https://japan.zdnet.com/article/35186261/

平和博 [Newspaper science]. (2020). *Deepfakesで68万人をヌードに変換、ネットで共有* [Convert 68 million people to nudity with Deepfakes, share it online]. October 23. Retrieved April 15, 2021, from https://kaztaira.wordpress.com/2020/10/23/deepnude_generator_resurge_on_telegram/

17

Geopolitical Competition and the Challenges for the European Union of Countering the Malicious Use of Artificial Intelligence

Pierre-Emmanuel Thomann

Introduction

The world is faced with increasing geopolitical fragmentation, with the multiplication of actors, reinforcement of the power gaps between states, and changes in previous geopolitical hierarchies. Moreover, geopolitical confrontation is increasingly taking place in the theater of hybrid warfare, including psychological warfare. In the context of the rapid development of AI technologies in recent years, the possible use of AI as a geopolitical weapon through the destabilization of international psychological security may contribute to determining the international order in the twenty-first century and the emergence of "digital empires" (Miailh, 2018), thus accelerating the dynamics of the previous cycle in which technology and power have mutually reinforced each other. This will transform some of the paradigms of geopolitics through the emergence of new relationships between territories and their populations, spatio-temporal dimensions and immateriality.

P.-E. Thomann (✉)
International Association Eurocontinent, Brussels, Belgium
e-mail: pierre-emmanuel.thomann@eurocontinent.eu

The objectives of this chapter are as follows:

- To define malicious use of artificial intelligence (MUAI) and threats to international psychological security in a geopolitical context at tactical and strategic levels;
- To evaluate the current position of the EU and its ability to anticipate the likely geopolitical imbalances and destabilizations in the EU posed by future MUAI;
- To examine the positions of its main member states, France and Germany, toward the new geopolitical challenges posed by global competition to the development of AI and digitalization, especially regarding MUAI and its threat to international psychological security;
- To offer possible counterstrategies at the national, EU, and pan-European levels to counter MUAI and the associated threats to international psychological security.

We shall start our analysis by considering MUAI to international psychological security in a geopolitical context at tactical and strategic levels.

Malicious Use of Artificial Intelligence and Threats to International Psychological Security in a Geopolitical Context

More targeted psychological destabilization of political, social, and economic systems using MUAI techniques, during a specific crisis and with more limited objectives, may be seen at the tactical level (e.g., computational propaganda with the use of algorithms for automation, the use of big data analytics and human curation to manipulate public life via social media networks, propaganda bots, follower bots, roadblock bots, AI chatbots, deepfakes, fake profiles and accounts, AI-enabled stock market manipulation, AI-supported ransomware attacks on critical infrastructure and essential services, and the manipulation of input to AI-engineered military equipment) (Trend Micro Research, 2020).

The tactical effects of MUAI will be short term and will not change the international system and the geopolitical balance of power as such.

Although when used at a tactical level, MUAI can have important effects in a conflict or a fight for targeted geopolitical influence, there are also more strategic aspects of AI, as it can be used to reinforce a monopoly by one or several states, in a systemic way. Strategic MUAI has the potential to destabilize the system of international relations; contrary to the common idea that the digital revolution will necessarily trigger economic and geopolitical decentralization, it is actually possible that the use of AI will provoke a global movement toward the centralization of power in the hands of a few states and private actors.

Strategic MUAI may have a deep and lasting effect on the international system through the creation of new, unbalanced geopolitical hierarchies. It is also not particularly associated with a specific crisis or war, or a sequence of events that is limited in time, but has effects over a long time period and represents a threat on a permanent basis, as it can blur the lines between war and peace. It is a process of cyber-colonization that leads to a stronger hierarchy between the states that possess and have mastered these new tools of geopolitical power, and creates greater dependency between tech leaders and tech takers (Pauwels, 2019). We can anticipate that these destabilizing tendencies will take place with a new intensity and speed through strategic MUAI; this is due to the non-explicit aspects of these strategies of conquest and digital imperialism, which are not easily taken into account by politicians, and are unlikely to be integrated into the collective consciousness of populations.

Strategic MUAI has therefore the potential to change the international system in a lasting and systemic way, and not just to gain power in a specific crisis. Different geopolitical configurations have succeeded one another throughout history, for example, the emergence of the concept of the balance of power after the Treaty of Westphalia in the eighteenth century, the concert of nations after the Congress of Vienna in the nineteenth century, the bipolar world of the Cold War, the unipolar moment after the fall of the USSR in the twentieth century, and the current uncertainty at the beginning of the twenty-first century. It is difficult today to perceive whether a multipolar world, a new imperfect bipolarity with an American-Chinese condominium, or another even more chaotic configuration marked by the return of major conflicts between great powers will prevail.

Strategic MUAI is likely to have a decisive effect on the evolution of the geopolitical configuration, leading to a reinforcement of hierarchies and inequalities and possibly a new America-China bipolarity. It may also lead to an era where the notion of relative stability no longer exists. Following the rise of strategic MUAI, conflicts may become permanent and the current multilateral bodies, already largely obsolete in terms of containing crises, will be bypassed by decisive state and private actors engaged in geopolitical rivalry. These actors will act without any restrictions or control by the people. As Raymond Aron has pointed out, "all international order, up to the present day, has been essentially a territorial order" (Aron, 1962). There can be no efficient way of containing conflict through a normative international system without an underlying spatial and geopolitical order accepted by the great powers. In a configuration where great powers agree on their respective red lines and zones of influence, that is, a spatial order that is necessarily precarious but allows room for dialogue and cooperation in multilateral form, it would be possible to stem the destructive potential of strategic MUAI. Alternatively, a scenario in which the international system is destroyed or ossified into an extremely unequal hierarchical order that leads to violent and sometimes extreme opposition might be favored.

The systemic nature and effect of strategic MUAI would be made possible by an increase in the actors' room for manoeuver in space and time. Great powers that can implement AI-enhanced strategies leading to multiple areas of supremacy in spatial dimensions such as the land, maritime, air, cybernetic, spatial, and cognitive domains and time gains, with their anticipation capacity favored by predictive analysis, could lead to an overthrow of the international order or make stabilization impossible. We will describe this process as the entry into space-time geopolitics, which requires the mastery of space and time at levels unprecedented in history and which might escape any moderation exercised by a multilateral system. We are already seeing the beginnings of this era with the impotence of multilateral bodies such as the UN, the EU, NATO, and the OSCE in Europe.

Studies devoted to the geopolitical implications of strategic MUAI and its implications for the EU and international psychological security are currently lacking. Analysis of the risks of MUAI in international relations tends to be focused on threats to democracy and the use that non-democratic regimes can make of it. The link between AI and international relations and the possible consequences the former might have in systemic terms (i.e., the mutation of the geopolitical configuration), is awaiting investigation.

Within the category of strategic MUAI, the emergence of the concept of "cognitive warfare" (CW) (Du Cluzel, 2020) has added a third combat dimension to the battlefield; that is, the cognitive dimension has been added to the informational and physical dimensions. As a result, we have now different geopolitical spaces of competition, such as the land, maritime, air, cybernetic, spatial, and cognitive domains. Human aspects could be considered the sixth domain of operations (with the other five being air, land, sea, space, and cyberspace). From this perspective, cognitive war is targeting the brains of the human beings making up populations, thanks to the scientific progress that has been made in nanotechnology, biotechnology, information technology and cognitive science (NBIC), combined with AI, big data, and the increasing dependence on digital space by populations (internet, social networks). Cognitive warfare goes beyond information warfare, since its objective is not to influence what people think, but the way in which they think. It has the potential to transform a whole nation into a colony of a third state, or to disrupt a whole nation and its territory. Following the emergence of the cyberspace theater with the use of the internet, there are now confrontations between the narratives and antagonistic ideas of rival powers or terrorist groups, as AI tools are being used to change the way people think, permanently, without limits on time and space, and this is taking place at different global, regional, national, and local scales. Repeated and multiple destabilizations through tactical MUAI can also lead to the strategic destabilization of states and nations.

The new target of geopolitics is the brain itself, and control over this target will be combined with control over territories. Human beings live within territories and are organized into communities with specific histories. This means that populations, and particularly those constituted as nations, cannot be separated from their geographical environment; this includes their territory and their geographical proximity to more remote territories on which they depend for access to energy, markets, or protection and security, and also their collective historical representations. There is no nation without a territory, and the interconnection between these internal and external challenges is increasingly becoming a feature of today's geopolitical configuration. As a result, strategic MUAI must be understood and examined in the context of its influence on a population living within a given territory. In a strategic context, MUAI is *de facto* a combination of threats to both a population and its territory (its infrastructures and the geographical and human environments).

In the military field, AI will allow for better anticipation of an adversary's manoeuvers and the optimization of operational processes (such as orientation, research, exploitation, and dissemination of intelligence). AI therefore has the capacity, in the short term, to confer on the decision-making processes of armies the operational superiority necessary to gain the upper hand over many types of adversaries. The decisive advantage of using AI in a military context is the anticipation of manoeuvers. However, this increase in geopolitical rivalries may lead to extreme situations. If a state considers that its vital interests are at stake, and that its very existence is endangered in the face of the overwhelming superiority of the adversary in terms of mastery of AI used as a weapon of total supremacy, this weaker state may launch a war or preventive action with all the means at its disposal, such as the classical weapons of mass destruction, including nuclear weapons (Ministère des Armées, 2019).

The use of AI has entered the realm of spatio-temporal geopolitics. In the twenty-first century, in order to navigate a world in a state of flux, a geopolitical strategy is required that is conceived as a spatiotemporal whole and functions as a means of reducing others' power. This is because the mastery of space and time in the service of a political objective is a decisive advantage and a central element of sovereignty (Thomann, 2010).

For a state or an alliance of states that possess the whole range of tools of power augmented by the mastery of AI, and are able to act in all the spaces of confrontation (land, air, sea, space, cyberspace, human brain), there is a great risk of being tempted to engage in international expansionist policies, thanks to the use of AI as a space-time weapon of conquest. This will lead to an increase in the fragmentation of the geopolitical world, very profound destabilization of international relations, and an increase in power inequalities.

From the geopolitical angle, control and mastery of the territories on which populations, nations, and communities are living also has special importance. In view of this, the geopolitical challenges associated with the emergence of geospatial intelligence (GEOINT) and AI (Boulanger, 2020) are worth a careful examination.

GEOINT is based on the fusion of data drawn from cartography, spatial imagery (satellites), the synthesis of information from multiple sources, real-time geolocation, and geopolitical analysis. Location intelligence with the use of AI technology is improving the role of geospatial intelligence, and provides the key to analyzing situations more effectively than real-time spatial analytics. With the increasing competition between military powers for information superiority, the mastery of GEOINT and AI is becoming a significant tool of power. GEOINT is at the heart of the "New Space" (the development of new satellite constellations), the concept of geospatial dominance (cartography and geolocalization), and the new information dominance related to big data and AI.

Differences between states in terms of access to technologies and information in the area of GEOINT and AI are creating a new global geopolitical hierarchy that may destabilize the world. Applying AI technology to spatial analytics allows for the creation of greater GEOINT capability, predictive analysis of space/time scenarios, detection and reporting of foreign threats, warning scenarios, and geostrategic superiority during a conflict. The AI-powered collection of GEOINT data will give a state decisive advantages in terms of mastering territory and controlling populations. A state may also lose its sovereignty if a foreign state is in possession of these data and can use AI-powered GEOINT systems within its own territory.

To conclude, from a geopolitical perspective, we can define the threat to international psychological security through Strategic MUAI as the risk of destabilization of states and nations with regard to their functioning as stable human communities (institutional and political life, functioning of the economy, national cohesion, loyalty, resilience) or incrementally endangering their sovereignty in a way that destroys the former international system and changes the present geopolitical order. This can be caused by MUAI as part of cognitive and communication wars (Du Cluzel, 2020) or pervasive cognitive-emotional conflicts (Pauwels, 2019) that aim to achieve control over the population itself and the way it thinks. MUAI strategies can result in the extensive digital colonization of all economic, military, energy, cultural, and civilizational spheres, including data on the biological characteristics of a state, nation, or community (e.g., data on health, vaccines, or biotechnology) or MUAI leading to massive destabilizing effects on the territory of a state or a nation, resulting in the loss of its sovereignty to another state through control or destabilization of its infrastructure (e.g., energy, transport, trade), vital flows (e.g., energy, populations, trade) and borders, for example through the use of GEOINT capabilities. Any geopolitical confrontation will be based on a multidisciplinary approach and a multi-domain strategy, and to target the adversary, MUAI will be based on an extensive knowledge of geopolitics, political science, history, geography, biology, cognitive science, business studies, medicine and health, psychology, demography, economics, environmental studies, information sciences, international relations, law, linguistics, management, media studies, philosophy, voting systems, public administration, international politics, religious studies, education, sociology, arts and culture, and other fields (Cole & Le Guyader, 2020).

With strategic MUAI, we are faced potentially with a new conquest of the world. In this context, how does the EU position itself with respect to the emergence of AI, and in particular, its impact on geopolitical issues relating to MUAI and its threat to international psychological security?

Main Policies and Paradigms of the EU Regarding Artificial Intelligence, and Its Ability to Anticipate New Geopolitical Challenges Arising from Malicious Use of Artificial Intelligence and Its Threat to International Psychological Security

The president of the European Commission, Ursula Von der Leyen, announced that she wanted to promote a new geopolitical commission (European Commission, 2019). Geopolitics involves power rivalries between different actors (states, terrorist groups, or powerful private networks) over territories and populations. A state's geopolitical strategy not only aims to ensure its security and survival, but also to defend or impose its priorities, its model of civilization or government, and its values, and to form alliances to promote these as part of its external relations.

Faced with the risks posed by strategic MUAI and the resulting potential destabilization or transformation of the international order, is the EU in a position to face the new challenges introduced by the development of AI ? If the EU does not have a doctrine of sovereignty in regard to AI, how can it resist the expansionist strategy of Big Tech or GAFAM (an acronym for Google, Apple, Facebook, Amazon, and Microsoft) from the US, and preserve the sovereignty of its member states? How can the EU resist the spread of the model of integral control of populations through AI, as promoted by China? How can the EU contain the destabilization or loss of sovereignty of the states and nations in its geographical proximity due to MUAI?

The Competitive Advantage of the EU

From the EU's point of view, it is recognized that the US and China will dominate AI and digitalization in the international geopolitical arena in the years to come.

Until 2020, the main focus of the EU regarding AI and digitalization was on its ethical, normative, and economic aspects in the context of regulating the EU common market, and this is reflected in its main communication strategy (European Commission, 2020e). This is in line with the EU's promotion of "multilateralism" as an international doctrine in its Global Strategy for the Foreign and Security Policy of the EU, which is known as the EU Global Strategy (EUGS) (EEAS, 2018) and is intended to foster international cooperation at the European and global levels.

The White Paper on AI (European Commission, 2020e) put into place a general framework for the EU regarding AI. The European Strategy on Data that accompanied this White Paper also aimed to enable Europe to become the most attractive, secure, and dynamic data-agile economy in the world.

The EU's strategy for winning the competition with the US or China involves a focus on ethics, based on a calculation that consumers will prefer such human-centric AI technologies (Brattberg et al., 2020). Regarding the risks associated with MUAI, the EU White Paper mainly focuses on the questions of the safety and liability of AI products that will circulate in internal

EU markets (European Commission, 2020c, 2020d), and does not address the development and use of AI for military purposes.

The EU is eager to show leadership in the second digital revolution, and has placed emphasis on the exploitation of industrial data (since the battle for private data has been lost), which represent the fuel for AI. The EU commissioner, Thierry Breton, has declared that in view of its potential, the Commission wants to invest EUR 1 billion per year in AI, and hopes to add investments of EUR 20 billion per year within the next decade (Digital Europe and Horizon Europe programs) from the member states and the private sector (European Commission, 2021a).

Risks of Malicious Use of Artificial Intelligence

Since 2020, a fairly dense production of texts and normative proposals has been published on AI, which reflects the EU's resilience in the face of the risks posed by cybersecurity and AI.

Firstly, the EU has stressed the new risks and benefits of AI in its new Security Union Strategy of the European Commission. The EU considers that "*Countering* **hybrid threats** *that aim to weaken social cohesion and undermine trust in institutions, as well as enhancing EU resilience are an important element of the Security Union Strategy*" (European Commission, 2020b). The measures identified by the EU include countering hybrid threats via early detection, analysis, awareness, building resilience, and prevention via crisis response and consequence management. The EU considers that AI, space capabilities, big data, and high performance computing should be integrated into its security policy. The objective is to fight crime and defend fundamental rights. A restricted online platform for member states should also be created for the Commission Services and the European External Action Service in order to provide counter-hybrid tools and measures at EU level. The Commission and the High Representative are in charge, and are in close cooperation with strategic partners such as NATO and the G7.

The Commission also published a new AI package in April 2021 (*Fostering a European Approach to Artificial Intelligence*) which proposed new rules and actions with the aim of turning Europe into a global hub for trustworthy AI. This plan includes the first-ever legal framework on AI, a new coordinated plan with member states which aims to guarantee the safety and fundamental rights of people and businesses while strengthening AI uptake, investment, and innovation across the EU. The European Commission has warned that "*On the global stage, AI has become an area of strategic importance at the crossroads of geopolitics, commercial stakes and security concerns*" (European Commission, 2021b).

As part of this new package, it was mentioned that expert groups are focusing on the question of the risks associated with AI (European Commission, 2021b).

The multidisciplinary *Ad Hoc Expert Group on Cybersecurity of the EU Agency for Cybersecurity* (ENISA) examined thematics related to AI. A report entitled *AI Cybersecurity Challenges: Threat Landscape for Artificial Intelligence*, published in December 2020, emphasized the need to secure AI systems against external cybersecurity risks and misuses and the increasing opportunities to use AI to support cybersecurity. This report focused on a detailed description and taxonomy of threats that could be classified as tactical MUAI and that were not related to the strategic and geopolitical context (European Commission, 2020a).

In relation to the questions of MUAI and its threat to international psychological security, a report entitled *EU Cybersecurity Strategy for the Digital Decade* highlighted that "*The threat landscape is compounded by geopolitical tensions over the global and open Internet and over control of technologies across the whole supply chain*" (European Commission, 2020a).

The EU strategy on cyberspace was drawn up to ensure a global and open internet, to address the risks to security and to protect the fundamental rights and freedoms of people in Europe. This document underlined that "*Cybersecurity must be integrated into all these digital investments, particularly key technologies like Artificial Intelligence (AI), encryption and quantum computing, using incentives, obligations and benchmarks.*" Three principal instruments were proposed in the form of regulatory, investment and policy instruments, to address three areas of action by the EU: (a) resilience, technological sovereignty, and leadership; (b) building the operational capacity to prevent, deter, and respond; and (c) promoting a global and open cyberspace.

It has been acknowledged that the EU has no common situational awareness of cyber threats, as states do not gather and share information in a systematic way (this also applies to the private sector). This means that member states cannot assess the state of cybersecurity in the EU. Support between member states in the event of large-scale cyber incident is limited, and no operational mechanism is in place. Fragmentation prevails.

The report laments that nation-states are increasingly erecting digital borders, are causing fragmentation of the global and open cyberspace, and are not following the core values of the EU, such as the rule of law, fundamental rights, freedom, and democracy. Cyberspace is increasingly becoming a theater for political and ideological objectives and polarization; this endangers the use of a multilateral approach, as actors use hybrid threats (disinformation campaigns, cyberattacks on infrastructure, economic processes, and democratic institutions). The risks include physical damage, unlawful access to personal data, theft of industrial and state secrets, the provocation of mistrust, and weakening of social cohesion. These actions have the effect of undermining international security and stability.

The report also proposes the involvement of the European Defense Fund (EDF) to support European cyber defense programs and the provision of help to EU partners in the vicinity of Europe regarding cybersecurity. The High Representative, alongside the Commission (according to its competence), will propose an EU cyber deterrence posture and further promote its *cyber diplomacy toolbox* to fight against malicious behavior in cyberspace (particularly in regard to the misuse of technologies, protection of critical infrastructure, and the integrity of the supply chain).

Alliances at the International Level

MUAI and its threat to international psychological security (although not identified in these terms) has been taken into account in a general sense, and international alliances have been considered to face this challenge.

The report acknowledges the increasing risk of competing models for international standardization leading to geopolitical fragmentation. Since international standardization (in areas such as AI, cloud, quantum computing, and quantum communication) is increasingly used as a tool by third countries to promote their political and ideological agendas (which do not correspond with the values of the EU), the EU wants to take leadership of international standardization processes. Since there are also interconnections between economic, internal security and foreign security and defense issues and EU policies, the EU wants to work with third countries and international organizations.

Cooperation on standardization and cybersecurity threats at the international level is based on EU priorities in terms of maintaining a global, open, stable, and secure cyberspace and promoting its political model, which is characterized by the rule of law, human rights, fundamental freedoms, and democratic values. The EU also wants social, economic, and political development at the global level, and to contribute to a Security Union.

In accordance with the EU's position as "complementary" to NATO (EEAS, 2018), the EU is promoting cyber defense interoperability within the framework of EU-NATO cooperation. The EU proposes that relevant CSDP structures should be integrated into NATO's Federated Mission Networking, to facilitate network interoperability with NATO and promote synergy between the European Security and Defense College and the NATO Cooperative Cyber Defense Centre of Excellence.

The EU is also promoting cooperation with the African Union, the ASEAN Regional Forum, the Organization of American States, and the Organization for Security Cooperation in Europe. The EU should also form an informal EU Cyber Diplomacy Network with other member states' embassies around the world, on the basis of its EU delegations.

The relationship between the EU and the US, which was designated as its most important ally in the EU Global Strategy (EEAS, 2018), is of particular value in facing these new threats. This is also reflected in institutional innovations.

Governments of EU member states also agreed in June 2021 with US President Joe Biden to create an EU-US Trade and Technology Council (TTC) to foster cooperation in the areas of trade and technology, such as AI, regulation of online platforms and data flows, the misuse of technology threatening security and human rights, and enhancing EU and US security chains for semiconductors (European Council, 2021). At the first meeting on September 7, 2021, Valdis Dombrovskis, vice president of the European Commission in charge of the economy, said *"We are in a much better position to set international standards, if we combine our efforts and work together"* (Euractiv, 2021f).

In setting up this TTC, the EU and the US aim *"to **protect** [their] businesses and workers from unfair trade practices, in particular those posed by non-market economies that are undermining the world trading system"* and to defend their shared democratic values (European Council, 2021). Although it is not explicitly mentioned, this initiative can be interpreted as forming part of the "alliance of democracies" promoted by the US against China (Jungbluth, 2021).

The EU thus favors a technological alliance with the US, consequently reinforcing the global geopolitical fragmentation into antagonistic blocs.

Weaknesses of the EU Paradigm

Overall, the position of the EU remains rather general in terms of awareness of MUAI and the threat to international psychological security, even though this can be considered to fall into the category of hybrid threats, cybersecurity, and risks related to digital sovereignty.

Regarding AI (as other thematics) the EU has essentially positioned itself as a neutral regulator (according to the competition principle) of activities within its territory, and promotes an open system at global level, although there is a split within the European Commission between a more liberal and a statist approach toward regulation of Big Tech in third states (Larger et al., 2020). The EU does not position itself as a global and sovereign geopolitical power that requires strategic autonomy and the ability to erect digital filters (like in China and Russia) or borders to protect its territory.

It will be difficult for this approach to succeed in an open system in which geopolitical competition prevails. This would only work if all actors and other global powers were to respect the rules of the EU (such as free and fair competition, free trade, budgetary austerity, environmental and social standards). The US and China are locked in a geopolitical competition, and do not respect these rules. Technological national champions and flagship companies cannot emerge in the EU in the same way as in the US and China, where the state supports orders and grants subsidies for market expansion, and where civilian-military synergies are important factors (Dalmont, 2020).

The EU is faced with the potential emergence of a new bipolarity on AI dominated by the US and China. Apart from the ethical issues with wich it intends to differentiate itself, and more sovereignty on data, a non-alignment posture with those states that do not wish to be sucked into this limitless confrontation is no taken into consideration by the EU. The resilience of the EU is not addressed in terms of the balance of power. The EU thus favors a technological alliance with the US, and consequently risks reinforcing the global geopolitical fragmentation into antagonistic blocs. Although there are still many disagreements between the EU and the US, this approach may be an obstacle to a global negotiation on effectively fighting against MUAI at the tactical level, and particularly at the strategic level.

In these EU legislative proposals, the question of preserving the sovereignty of EU member states does not include the establishment of a European preference on the acquisition of systems using AI, or restrictions on products that comply with the standards but come from third countries. There are also no proposals on how to address the issues of AI in relation to power rivalries and its impact on its external relations.

EU-US Rivalry Over Control of Data and the Absence of European Big Tech and GAFAM

The issue of control over data, the fuel of artificial intelligence, and hence the question of sovereignty over digital information, is a crucial one that must be considered in order to preserve geopolitical independence. If the EU does not take into account strategic MUAI, it could increasingly become a cybercolony of the US, China, or another state with a better position in terms of the development of AI. However, a recurring dispute over digital data transfers to the US has poisoned the relationship between the EU and the US in recent years.

To avoid the transfer of European data to third states, and in particular the US, the EU has elaborated a legal data protection system called the General Data Protection Regulation (GDPR). However the Safe Harbour (EU-US agreement) till 2015 was invalidated by the EU Court of Justice. A new agreement called the Privacy Shield (an EU-US agreement) was signed in 2020, but was again invalidated by the EU Court of Justice in July 2020.

A new political agreement, which was supposed to pave the way for a successor to the Privacy Shield deal, was announced on March 25, 2022 by US President Joe Biden and European Commission President Ursula von der Leyen (European Commission, 2022). However, there is uncertainty about what the outcome will be. Max Schrems, a privacy activist involved in the two European Court of Justice rulings against the previous agreements, declared "[i]t is especially appalling that the US has allegedly used the war on Ukraine to push the EU on this economic matter"... "We expect this to be back at the Court within months from a final decision" (Euractiv, 2022).

Since the EU does not promote "European GAFAM" or EU search engines, Europeans have become very dependent on the US. The Clouds Act, US extraterritorial law, and National Security Agency (NSA) backdoors allow US companies abroad to transfer data from EU citizens and companies to US authorities, and stand in contradiction to the EU privacy laws promoted by the GDPR (Thibout, 2021).

In the context of the disagreements between the EU and US on the question of data transfer, the implementation of the new EU-US technological alliance is difficult to grasp. The Trade and Technology Council (TTC) may focus mainly on market access rather than on regulatory convergence, since the US and EU have very different approaches to AI and the more fragmented American regulations differ from European principles-based regulation. Questions of data privacy are difficult and sensitive issues, and since they are at the core of the digital economy, regulatory negotiations will be very difficult. If the US does not change its approach to surveillance, no data transfer breakthrough will be possible regarding EU GDPR level of protection (Euractiv, 2021b).

Ambiguity of the EU Toward the Fight Against Geopolitical Malicious Use of Artificial Intelligence

Although it has been mentioned in a fragmented way, no systemic analysis has been conducted of the ability of the EU to position itself regarding the geopolitical challenges posed by digitalization and AI, and particularly concerning MUAI and the threats to international psychological security in the context of greater power rivalries and the diversity of views of EU member states toward the strategic aims of the European project. The EU has also stressed the danger of political polarization through MUAI (European Parliament, 2019); however, if the EU promotes an obsolete model of development and is engaged in exclusive alliances against the emergence of multipolarity, there is a risk that this might in itself promote geopolitical polarization.

The EU is embedded in the mainstream geopolitical configuration as a sub-element of the US and NATO geopolitical priorities regarding AI-engineered global informational and cognitive warfare (Chessen, 2017) against China and Russia. The European parliament has stressed that if *"AI in the field of defence is essential for ensuring European strategic autonomy in capability and operational areas it recognises the role of NATO in promoting Euro-Atlantic security and calls for cooperation within NATO for the establishment of common standards and interoperability of AI systems in defence; stresses that the transatlantic relationship is important for the preservation of shared values and for countering future and emerging threats"* (European Parliament, 2020).

This is even more striking in the new "Strategic Compass for Security and Defence" elaborated by the European Union External Action Service (EEAS) of the EU and published in the context of the conflict in Ukraine in March 2022 (EEAS, 2022). The document takes into account the new security environment and updates former strategic documents.

The objective is to turn the EU's geopolitical awakening into a more permanent strategic posture. The EU wants at the same time help to strengthen NATO and become a more forthright transatlantic partner. It has stressed that its partnership with the US is strategically important.

The EU has acknowledged the return of power politics in a contested multipolar world. It has emphasized that it needs to prepare for fast-emerging challenges because its strategic competitors are actively undermining its secure access to the maritime, air, cyber, and space domains. In the cyber domain, the EU wants to develop and make intensive use of new technologies—notably quantum computing, AI, and big data—to achieve comparative advantage (e.g., in terms of cyber-responsive operations and information superiority).

It also needs to maintain its excellence in ensuring autonomous EU decision-making, including that based on geospatial data.

However, the EU has not changed its doctrinal position on multilateralism and still refuses to accept the multipolar model. It promotes strategic autonomy, but it considers itself complementary to NATO and the US as its main strategic partner. It is therefore aligned de facto with the unipolar objectives of the US and will continue to cooperate in areas like respective security and defense initiatives, disarmament and non-proliferation, the impact of emerging and disruptive technologies, climate change and defense, cyber defense, military mobility, countering hybrid threats including foreign information manipulation and interference, crisis management, and relationships with strategic competitors (principally, Russia and China).

In the aforementioned document, the EU does not consider the systemic implications of strategic MUAI on the geopolitical configuration and how it might acquire greater autonomy, especially from the US (on which it is very dependent); nor does it advocate a more stable and balanced international system. Here again, the EU's close alliance with the US risks geopolitical fragmentation into antagonistic blocs at a global level.

This configuration is also visible in reports from think tanks carrying out geopolitical lobbying in EU, and especially think tanks financed by the EU such as the IISS, which promotes strong transatlantic cooperation on the military aspects of AI (Soare, 2020). These think tanks defend an exclusive Euro-Atlantic orientation of the European project (in a situation of monopoly) and promote an alliance between US and EU against Russia and China for the development of AI, rather than promoting a more balanced approach in terms of alliances and cooperative partnerships on the development of AI.

This can be observed from a report entitled *Polarisation and the Use of Technology in Political Campaigns and Communication*, written by Oxford University researchers for the European Parliament think tank (Marchal & Neudert, 2019). This report focuses almost exclusively on the danger of MUAI from Russia and China, and does not consider the dependence of the EU on the US in terms of Big Tech, GAFAM, databases, and the cloud. These experts stress the danger of political polarization, but promote geopolitical polarization with representations such as "liberal states" versus "illiberal states," thus revealing their promotion of global westernization versus multipolarity. From this partisan, mainstream point of view in the EU, Arab revolutions and regime change in the Middle East or ex-USSR states via social media are good, but the possibility of Russia and China using AI to disseminate propaganda via social media is bad.

This ambiguity is also particularly striking in another report commissioned by the Special Committee on Artificial Intelligence in the Digital Age (AIDA Committee) of the European Parliament in 2021, entitled *Artificial Intelligence Diplomacy: Artificial Intelligence Governance as a New European Union External Policy Tool*, which was drawn up by Ulrike Franke of the European Council on Foreign Relations (ECFR) think tank (Franke, 2021). The author places herself in the context of the confrontation between China and the US, according to an ideological reading grid, democracy versus dictatorship, taking the Cold War as a reference. She writes that "*geopolitically speaking, there is further concern that we might be moving into a new era of ideological confrontation, akin to the competition between liberal democracy and communism during the Cold War*" (Franke, 2021).

The author points out that China is developing a social credit system based on the use of AI, which would obviously be unacceptable to Europeans, who are concerned about individual freedoms; in doing so, she fails to recall that the US operates a massive surveillance system of the entire world, as revealed by Edward Snowden. Her fear is of a "*new nationalism*" as well as the threat to the open society model from the strengthening of protectionist tendencies. This is a recurring theme in reports from the ECFR, which is characterized by liberal and Euro-Atlanticist views. Finally, the concerns of this expert primarily relate to the problem of interoperability in NATO and the chasm between the capabilities of the US and the European members of NATO, rather than emphasizing the need for European strategic autonomy. With good reason, this author also worries about the lack of geopolitical reflection by Europeans but insists on the divergent priorities with the US who are preoccupied with China, while Russia would be the main problem for Europe. The author proposes strengthening the transatlantic relationship on external tech policy and excludes equidistance between the US and China, although she mentions that the EU needs to look in both directions, to the east and the west. The Transatlantic TTC is promoted as a vehicle for setting joint standards on new technologies, as proposed by the European Commission. It is suggested that EU and NATO member states should work on interoperability and transatlantic cooperation on military AI in regard to non-controversial uses, such as the use of AI in sustainment and logistics.

The basic paradigms on which these reports are based are the promotion of an exclusive Euro-Atlanticist vision and the defense of "*liberal democracy*," rather than a geopolitical balance of power. These exclusive Atlanticist narratives are leading to a policy of blocs, and are reducing the margin of manoeuver for EU member states. However, this is unlikely to contribute to the building of common global alliances to counter the threat of MUAI to international psychological security. There is a risk of aggravation of the dependence of EU member states on the US, increasing militarization of the question of AI, and geopolitical fragmentation of the Eurasian continent.

To what extent does the EU's difficulty in positioning itself in the global competition for the development of AI originate from differences in approach between member states (especially Germany and France, who are the driving forces of the European project)?

Differences in the Approaches of the Main EU Member States, Particularly France and Germany, and the Resulting Obstacles in Terms of Adaptation of the EU to the New Geopolitical Challenges Posed by Global Competition for Artificial Intelligence Development

The EU is very diverse, and negotiating processes are very complex, long, and difficult. Since all 27 EU member states have different positions and strategies (Van Roy, 2020), it is rather difficult to evaluate the positioning and efficiency of the EU regarding the question of MUAI.

Within the European project, France and Germany play the role of vanguard, and take common positions that are intended to be extended to other member states at the EU level. This is how the Franco-German alliance seeks to position itself on the development of AI, in the same way as for other strategic thematics. However, the geopolitical objectives of the member states do not coincide, and this is particularly true for Germany and France. As a "European and global power," France has positioned itself in terms of the balance of power, and is promoting EU strategic autonomy. As an "economic" power, Germany has positioned itself and the EU primarily as a strong market that can profit from the economic flows in the process of globalization, and also as a central power whose security depends on a close relationship with the US and NATO (Thomann, 2015). It is from these geopolitical and strategic representations that France and Germany will position themselves on the geopolitical implications of AI.

France and Germany differ in terms of their approaches to the issue of AI, and their capacity and political will to face the emerging geopolitical threats related to the development of AI, to establish a common framework in the EU, and consequently to negotiate alliances for cooperation at the international level.

France's position derives above all from the context of the growing geopolitical rivalry between the Great Powers and the development of AI, in view of the need for France and Europe to promote the issues of sovereignty and independence (Villani, 2018; Boniface, 2021; Pannier, 2021). From Germany's point of view, the primary challenge is to make Germany and Europe a leading center for AI and thus help safeguard Germany's competitiveness in the future (Die Bundesregierung, 2020a, b; Deutscher Bundestag, 2020; Internationale Politik, 2018)

Despite the EU's main communication strategy positioning it as an "ethical actor," the perceptions and strategies of the individual member states differ greatly. France would like to build strategic alliances to avoid "cyber-vassalization," while Germany has a greater focus on the economic aspects.

For France, the development of AI and digitalization must not lead to France and Europe becoming "digital colonies" of Chinese or American tech giants. The term "cybercolonization" was used in an information report by the French MEP Catherine Morin Desailly, entitled *L'Union Européenne, Colonie du Monde Numérique*, which was prepared on behalf of the Senate's European Affairs Committee (France Sénat, 2013). A policy on (big) data, the fuel for AI, must therefore be articulated with the objectives of strategic autonomy and sovereignty for France and the European Union (France Sénat, 2019).

The main objective for Germany is to become an attractive market for the development of AI in the context of global economic competition. From the German point of view, American and Asian companies have achieved global dominance and a lead over German and European companies that gives them competitive advantages. For Germany, the competition has only just begun, and it has a particularly favorable starting position in this regard, not least because of its economic structure, which has a high proportion of manufacturing industry, a leading position in the world in the field of logistics and a highly trained workforce (Die Bundesregierung, 2020). In its national strategy for AI published in 2018, Germany proposed to work with France to drive forward the development of a Franco-German research and development network (a "virtual center") At the same time, the Federal Government is initiating a European and transatlantic dialogue on the human-centric use of AI in the world of work.

The difference in approach between Germany and France is even more pronounced with regard to defense. The federal government of Germany, in its first AI (Die Bundesregierung, 2018), has taken into account the threats related to cybersecurity and AI in very general terms, as follows: "*In response to new threats to our security from within and without the country, the Federal Government will promote research into both civil security and into the detection of manipulated and automatically generated content, also as part of its work on cybersecurity. The competent ministries will take charge of any research conducted into the use of AI to protect the country's external security and for military purposes."*

The German document on AI and defense published afterwards focuses only on the use of AI in military operations, and refers to tactical issues. There is no diagnosis of the international balance of power regarding AI, no stress on sovereignty, and no details of an alliance strategy to increase its room for *manoeuver* (Bundesministerium der Verteidigung (*BMVg*), 2019). In Germany, the priority of the foreign ministry is to deal with military AI primarily from the standpoint of arms control and disarmament (Franke, 2020; Deutscher Bundestag, 2020).

From the German point of view, security and defense-related AI research should be conducted at the EU level, in the context of EU decisions on AI and defense, in order to strengthen Europe's position in this field and to avoid leaving technological leadership in innovation to the US or China. Germany proposes to establish a "Joint European Disruptive Initiative" (JEDI) as the nucleus of a European innovation agency, which was inspired by the structure of the American Defense Advanced Research Projects Agency (DARPA). By leveraging its power as a market, the EU can exert greater influence on international standardization processes in the field of security-related AI, with a focus on defense and prevention, and thus contribute to the achievement of EU goals and assert its values and standards globally (Deutscher Bundestag, 2020).

In contrast, the position of France is particularly interesting, as it involves a very complete strategy on AI and defense, based on a geopolitical diagnosis. The French Ministry of Defense has published a report on the question of the use of AI for French defense (Ministère des Armées, 2019). In this report, a discussion of the international situation is presented before recommendations for geopolitical priorities for France's positioning. The report stresses that the mastery of AI represents an unavoidable power factor in the future. The various AI strategies published recently in different countries reveal a global hierarchy of AI power as follows.

There are two "superpowers," the US and China, which are out of reach of the others; these control huge masses of data and have ecosystems articulated around powerful integrating companies with global vocations (GAFAM and BATX). They still have the power to extend their domination thanks to their scientific and financial means. There are also intermediate powers in the making, including the EU, whose strict position on legal and ethical issues may constitute a strength or a weakness depending on its impact (normative power aggregating many state or private actors vs. the risk of defining a policy on research or entrepreneurial development that is too timid or hampered by overly restrictive regulations).

A second group of states, including France, Germany, the United Kingdom, Japan, South Korea, Singapore, Israel, and Canada, have certain assets but insufficient critical mass. Their degree of autonomy will depend on the leverage effects obtained through the cooperation they will establish, and the relevance of niche strategies that aim to maximize their comparative advantages.

The report warns that there will be aggressive competition in the medium term. The competition to acquire the necessary resources for the development of AI has already started, and will intensify. These resources are both intangible (capturing scarce skills in human resources) and material (capturing key technologies, etc.). The mastery of AI will therefore represent an issue of sovereignty in an industrial environment characterized by rapid technological innovations and dominated by foreign companies. In this context, dominated by private or foreign state actors, France cannot become dependent on technologies over which it has no control. In the case of military AI, and to ensure the confidentiality and control of information, it is essential to maintain technological sovereignty.

In terms of research, the report considers that France is very well placed at the global level, and is often considered the best in Europe. However, the industrialization and services in AI services are less advanced than in the United Kingdom, Canada, and Israel. This is the case in both the civil industrial sector and the defense sector.

In order to avoid a technological drop in the field of AI, it is therefore essential to develop comparative strategic advantages (an agile strategy based on "niches" of superiority, alone or in collaboration). In this regard, a range of international alliances could be considered. The French National strategy on military issues relies on achieving relative sovereignty. The choice to form alliances on AI has the consequence that no full-spectrum dominance can be reached by France. The priority is to create AI collaborations within the European framework; primary alliances are considered with Germany and the United Kingdom, and also outside the European continent, with other major states who want to eliminate the duopoly on AI represented by China and the US. In addition to these leading partner nations, NATO (and, in particular, ACT) also offers a privileged framework for cooperation. This second circle also includes non-European partners such as the US, Australia, and India, since they have adopted similar approaches to AI as in France, and cooperation with these countries is intended to extend to the use of AI for defense. The third circle groups together countries such as Canada, Japan, Singapore, and Korea, in terms of all areas: capacity, doctrine, intelligence exchange, training, and ethical debate.

To conclude, we can observe this strategy for achieving greater sovereignty is far from free of contradictions, since Germany and the United Kingdom are close partners of the US, although the objective is not to fall into a situation of dominance by any major power. A discussion of Russia is absent from the report, and we do not know whether Russia is considered as a competitor or a partner for the convergence of interests.

Common Positions and Obstacles to an EU Position on Artificial Intelligence

Despite their different national positions due to their national geopolitical representations and their different goals for the European project, France and Germany agree on the need to preserve national sovereignty and to strengthen it through EU programs.

French President Emmanuel Macron declared that "*We have a French strategy on this matter that will be deployed, but this must very quickly become a Franco-German strategy and a European strategy. And in this case, the choice is in the hands of our countries. If we do as we did twenty years ago, France and Germany will be divided and will fight in Europe to push divergent standards. The winners will be Chinese and American, and in AI, you don't have to be a great clerk to know that*" (Elysée, 2018).

The German Minister for Economy, Peter Altmaier, has declared that "*Germany has a claim to digital sovereignty. That's why it's important to us that cloud solutions are not just created in the US.*" Peter Altmaier has long been concerned by the fact that many German companies and government agencies store and process their data on servers run by Amazon, Microsoft, and Google in the US (Euractiv, 2019).

The German Bundestag stressed that "*Success, in turn, is needed to establish a 'European-style' AI.*" In their report, the Bundestag Commission distinguishes between "*AI made in Germany*" and "*AI made in Europe*" from Chinese and American approaches (Deutscher Bundestag, 2020).

However, these stated objectives are not free of major contradictions, as we see when we go into more detail on the decisions taken on the development of a sovereign cloud or the fight against the hegemony of Big Tech from third countries, particularly the US and China.

France and Germany have agreed to build a Franco-German cloud called the Gaia-X project. This has been reported as a "European sovereign cloud," and was officially presented at a virtual summit with the participation of Peter Altmaier and Bruno Le Maire, economic ministers of Germany and France, as well as Thierry Breton, the EU Commissioner for Internal Market and Services, who lauded the project as the next-generation data ecosystem for Europe (Euractiv, 2020c).

The principles of Gaia-X are digital sovereignty, self-determination, free market acess, and European values creation. However this is not a real sovereign cloud (Politico, 2021). Gaia-X has been labeled as a "*Trojan horse for Big Tech in Europe*" (Euractiv, 2020c), since global technology giants, including Google, Microsoft, IBM, and Chinese actors in the market, were invited to take part in this project by the German Economy Minister Peter Altmaier (Euractiv, 2020a).

During the Gaia-X summit, representatives from IBM Cloud, Microsoft Azure, Amazon Web Services, Google, and OVH Cloud announced that they would become strategic integrators of Google Cloud, a partner of the project.

The founding Gaia-X industrial members, such as CEO Hubert Tardieu of Atos, a strategic partner of Google, do not appear to be keen to develop European technological sovereignty but are more interested in having access to the market potential of a federated data infrastructure. The objective of the EU and national governments is to develop an EU technological competence through Gaia-X. Thus far, it looks as if Gaia-X has become a Trojan horse for the GAFAM to obtain EU public funding for the creation of a federated data infrastructure with US and Asian technology providers (Euractiv, 2020c).

The objective of establishing a "sovereign" EU cloud service infrastructure using firms based in the EU bloc is not compatible with the involvement of international firms (Euractiv, 2020b, c).

However, from an official point of view, the intentions remain open to a sovereign cloud. In its French-German non-paper The European industrial policy strategy and its Spring-2021 "*Push further the digital transformation of industry, thereby strengthening digital sovereignty, through: planned governance structures, such as the 'industrial data and platforms' alliance articulated with the Cloud IPCEI and GAIA-X*" (Bundesministerium für Wirtschafts und Energie, 2021).

As far as France is concerned, since it is at the forefront of insisting on the need for national and European sovereignty with regard to AI, the facts also contradict the political slogans.

The French security and defense flagship Thales has announced a new partnership with Google with the aim of setting up a sovereign service that is eligible for the label of "trusted cloud," which will be launched by the French government by 2023 (Euractiv, 2021e). The hosting of the French Health

Data Hub, the new health data platform, by the giant Microsoft has also provoked indignation among French and European digital actors, and has worried data protection advocates (Euractiv, 2021g). *"The government has put French health data in the hands of a company that is subject to US law when it comes to communicating data to US authorities,"* stressed Bastien Le Querrec, a representative of Quadrature du Net, an association for the defense and promotion of internet rights and freedom, founded in 2008 (Euractiv, 2021g).

French cloud actors also decry the government's ambivalence toward GAFAM. This dual strategy for the creation of a sovereign cloud is rooted in the new government doctrine of the "trusted cloud," presented in May by the French government. The French minister Bruno Lemaire has stressed that *"there is no political independence without technological independence"* and has insisted on the need *"not to depend on foreign technologies"* (Euractiv, 2021d). However, Thomas Fauré, CEO of Whaller, a French publisher of cloud-based collaborative solutions, has declared *"It is anything but a sovereign strategy. In reality, it's an open door to GAFAM [Google, Apple, Facebook, Amazon, Microsoft],"* (Euractiv, 2021c). Some concerns have also been expressed over the contract between the French Directorate General of Internal Security (DGSI) and the Big Data company Palantir, which is based in the US (Villani, 2018).

How is this contradiction justified?

The French MEP Philippe Latombe considers that the central question for France is the capacity to choose its dependencies and to permanently maintain this capacity. According to Latombe, a choice must now be made between two solutions: a very good American solution, and a French solution that does not work. France has chosen to accept the American solution while continuing to develop a French solution in parallel, so that when it becomes a real choice, the state will be able to switch (Euractiv, 2021a).

In this context, how can the EU influence the trend toward increased geopolitical competition between the Great Powers by means of AI and contain the risks of a strategic type of MUAI, if it has neither the infrastructure nor strong national positions of its member states, in particular France and Germany, at the heart of the European project?

The diversity of the geopolitical representations and strategies regarding AI and digitalization between EU member states has thus far been an obstacle to a strong, united EU position (Brattberg et al., 2020). It is therefore hindering international cooperation in terms of countering strategic MUAI and protecting international psychological security with other global actors, such as the US, China, Russia, and secondary actors.

Under these conditions, what avenues might be explored to promote more cooperation?

Possible Counterstrategies at the National, EU, and Pan-European Levels to Counter Malicious Use of Artificial Intelligence and Its Threat to International Psychological Security

Regarding the development of AI, the EU has positioned itself as a normative power, and assumes that its legislation will be imposed throughout the world due to the size of its market, without the need to exercise power politics, as if this process were almost automatic.

The EU and its member states are mainly promoting an ethical and normative approach to AI and digitalization, in the context of regulating the EU common market. If this posture is useful, facing the risk of strengthening geopolitical imbalances due to unequal access to AI and collection of data, the EU posture on AI, with its main focus on ethical issues, is not sufficient to contribute positively to a better equilibrium in international relations.

The diversity between the EU member states in terms of geopolitical representations of the world and strategies on AI and digitalization is an obstacle to creating international cooperation with other global actors to counter MUAI and protect international psychological security, such as the US, China, Russia, and secondary actors.

In an ideal setting, the EU and its international partners will be able to promote the ethical dimensions of AI (Goffi, 2019) only if a position of strength and sovereignty can be reached, rather than a position of dependence and weakness. At the same time, it must be kept in mind that strength and sovereignty outside of an innovative, socially oriented model of development are extremely dangerous, both for Europe itself and for the whole world, and that AI raises deep philosophical questions about the freedom and destiny of human beings (Hofstetter, 2018).

It would be wise to combine a human-centric approach to AI (EU Framework for Trustworthy AI) with a balance of power doctrine including more equal access to AI and the forging of large global alliances to fight MUAI as a threat to international psychological security and geopolitical stability.

To better promote the fight against the MUAI and its potential destabilization of the international system, the EU and its member states would be wise to cultivate a non-aligned position in the context of the growing rivalry between China, Russia, and the US, to avoid geopolitical polarization. It would be useful to avoid escalation, to play the role of moderator, and to find common solutions in cooperation with all geopolitical actors. This non-alignment could facilitate the rebalancing of alliances, and in particular would avoid the EU being caught between the Chinese solution of full control over populations and the surveillance capitalism of the US, linked to the global collection of data by Big Tech, leading to a new digital imperialism.

The EU is neither a nation nor a sovereign state, and depends only on the goodwill of its member states to transfer competences to EU level. It does not yet possess the AI tools to control its own population or its territory, since there is no European GAFAM or a sovereign cloud, and it is dependent on the capabilities of its member states. At most, it can develop data protection systems, and negotiate a more favorable position with GAFAM thanks to the GDPR legislation, but it has not mastered all the tools of power and infrastructure.

On the other hand, if the EU legislation was implemented, this would indirectly allow for framing of the development of AI and minimization of some aspects of tactical and strategic MUAI, to avoid drawing closer to models of surveillance societies like the Chinese model, or sinking into total cyber-colonization under the influence of private American groups supported by the state, but probably not more.

From this discussion, we can see that limited or variable coalitions between states (Ministère de l'Europe et des Affaires Étrangères, 2018; Vitard, 2020) would be more efficient and complementary in terms of promoting more sovereignty, balance, and cooperation and in order to fight efficiently against tactical and strategic MUAI. The development of AI is still relatively recent, and the EU might also gradually regain sovereignty by developing long-term cooperation programs while using systems belonging to third-party states such as the US or China.

The EU and NATO

For the EU, one major problem is that the defense of most of its member states is entrusted to NATO. This makes it difficult for the EU to address the full spectrum of AI issues and defense implications, including MUAI in strategic terms. However, if the EU sees itself as complementary to NATO, it runs the risk of being drawn into a global bloc policy, which is not conducive to the common fight against the use of AI as a weapon of war or conquest. The concept of cognitive warfare is described within NATO think tank circles as a necessary step to counter the cognitive warfare posture of Russia and China (Du Cluzel, 2020), and the European member states of NATO risk becoming engaged in geopolitical polarizing policies which will damage their own strategic autonomy.

EU member states certainly need to adopt more commanding positions regarding AI in the military field, including cognitive warfare, but should avoid becoming too constrained by third states (Boulanin et al., 2020) or NATO priorities.

Conclusion

Without a preliminary diagnosis of the problem, it will not be possible to deal with the geopolitical implications of strategic MUAI and its implications for the EU and international psychological security. Although it claims to have achieved more strategic autonomy, the EU is reinforcing de facto the emergence of antagonistic alliances, including those engaged in AI development, by positioning itself as part of an exclusive Euro-Atlantic alliance that resists multipolarity (rather than expounding a doctrine of non-alignment).

A better balance is needed to avoid an escalation and uncontrolled spiral of geopolitical rivalries without limits in time and space. On a global scale, there will be no international order and no common rules and norms for the development of AI to fight MUAI without an acceptable geopolitical order involving the Great Powers. There must be an acceptance of an ethical and human-centered order, a new multilateral configuration that offers a model for global AI cooperation. Only then will MUAI and threats to international psychological security be contained.

Otherwise, strategic MUAI in the context of Great Power rivalry and its threat to international psychological security will open up a Pandora's box of world conquest by a new entity. This may lead to total and permanent war and place humanity in danger.

If the EU wants to rebuild its digital sovereignty, it will have to redouble its efforts and investments. International cooperation based on inclusiveness, respect, and reciprocity will be better achieved with a stronger geopolitical balance on AI between global actors such as the US, China, Russia, and the EU member states, and also between smaller states. The EU should therefore place more emphasis on questions regarding geopolitical balance and data sovereignty to counter threats to international psychological security from MUAI. It should also focus more on the different consequences that it could face regarding strategic MUAI, such as the implications for the EU of cognitive warfare and the development of GEOINT that goes beyond tactical MUAI.

In parallel to the steps taken by the EU, strong bilateral or smaller coalitions should be created for cooperation outside the framework of the EU, between voluntary actors who would agree to pool the necessary resources and skills in order to ensure their independence and their future digital sovereignty, and to avoid being sucked into the US-China confrontation.

The EU should refrain from aligning itself with potential new and emerging exclusive alliances as a result of the increasing confrontation between the US, China, and Russia, but should instead promote strategic autonomy and sovereignty, and cooperation on an inclusive basis.

Questions of power and sovereignty should also be geared toward a more socially cohesive and innovation-oriented model of development and a better combination of multipolarity and multilateralism (a better accepted multipolarity is the condition of reinforced multilateralism) for the EU and for the whole world.

International cooperation is also necessary—under UN/UNESCO coordination—to deliver international declarations such as the Ugra Resolution Information and Communication in the Digital Age (UNESCO, 2021) and the Ugra Memorandum Information and Communication in the Digital Age (UNESCO, 2022), as well as forward-looking threat assessments, including the mapping of the AI threat landscape and global cooperation in designing projects that use AI to counter MUAI.

An international research center, on the risk of MUAI and its threat to international psychological security could be promoted with voluntary states, and should not be based on a restrictive membership reflecting the emergence of geopolitical blocs (such as an "alliance of democracies").

References

Aron, R. (1962). Paix et guerre entre les nations, Calman-Levy, p. 187.
Boniface, P. (2021). Géopolitique de l'intelligence artificielle. Editions Eyrolles, p. 207.
Boulanger, P. (2020). La géographie, reine des batailles. Perrin, Ministère des armées, 322 p.
Boulanin, V., Goussac, N., Bruun, L., & Richards, L. (2020). Responsible military use of artificial intelligence: Can the European Union lead the way in developing best practice? SIPRI. Retrieved November 28, 2021, from https://www.sipri.org/publications/2020/other-publications/responsible-military-use-artificial-intelligence-can-european-union-lead-way-developing-best

Brattberg, E., Csernatoni, R., & Rugova, V. (2020). Europe and AI: Leading, lagging behind, or carving its own way? Carnegie Endowment for International Peace. Retrieved November 28, 2021, from https://carnegieendowment.org/2020/07/09/europe-and-ai-leading-lagging-behind-or-carving-its-own-way-pub-82236

Bundesministerium der Verteidigung (*BMVg*). (2019). Kunstliche Intelligenz in den landstreitkräften. Retrieved November 28, 2021, from https://www.bundeswehr.de/de/organisation/heer/aktuelles/kuenstliche-intelligenz-in-den-landstreitkraeften-156226

Bundesministerium für Wirtschafts und Energie. (2021). Ministère de l'économie et des finances et de la reliance. French-German non-paper: The European industrial policy strategy and its Spring-2021. Retrieved November 28, 2021, from https://www.bmwi.de/Redaktion/FR/Pressemitteilungen/2021/02/20210216-l-allemagne-et-la-france-ensemble-pour-une-strategie-industrielle-europeenne-nouvelle-et-innovante.html

Chessen, M. (2017). The Madcom future: How artificial intelligence will enhance computational propaganda, reprogram human culture, and threaten democracy… and what can be done about it. Atlantic Council. Retrieved November 28, 2021, from https://www.atlanticcouncil.org/in-depth-research-reports/report/the-madcom-future/

Cole, A., & Le Guyader, H. (2020). NATO sixth's domain of operations. Innovation Hub. Retrieved November 28, 2021, from https://www.innovationhub-act.org/content/cw-documents

Dalmont, C. (2020). La souveraineté numérique européenne mérite une stratégie, pas des incantations. Retrieved November 28, 2021, from https://www.lefigaro.fr/vox/politique/la-souverainete-numerique-europeenne-merite-une-strategie-pas-des-incantations-20200604?fbclid=IwAR3OMXTu7t3T30uJY-SXa1M0rkxITrVLNg4gp4EKZBXgK1249Ua2cqCPHRw

Deutscher Bundestag. (2020). Unterrichtung der Enquete-Kommission Künstliche Intelligenz —Gesellschaftliche Verantwortung und wirtschaftliche, soziale und ökologische Potenziale*Bericht der Enquete-Kommission Künstliche Intelligenz–Gesellschaftliche Verantwortung und wirtschaftliche, soziale und ökologische Potenziale. Retrieved November 28, 2021, from https://www.bundestag.de/dokumente/textarchiv/2020/kw44-pa-enquete-ki-abschlussbericht-801192

Die Bundesregierung. (2018). Artificial Intelligence strategy. Retrieved November 28, 2021, from https://knowledge4policy.ec.europa.eu/ai-watch/germany-ai-strategy-report_en

Die Bundesregierung. (2020a). Strategie Künstliche Intelligenz der Bundesregierung. Retrieved November 28, 2021, from https://www.ki-strategie-deutschland.de/home.html

Die Bundesregierung. (2020b). *Comments from the federal government of the federal republic of Germany on the white paper on artificial intelligence—A European concept for excellence and trust*. COM (2020). Retrieved November 28, 2021, from https://

www.ki-strategie-deutschland.de/files/downloads/Stellungnahme_BReg_Weissbuch_KI_engl.pdf

Du Cluzel, F. (2020). Cognitive warfare: An attack on truth and thoughts. Innovation Hub, NATO Allied Command Transformation (ACT) sponsored study. Retrieved November 28, 2021, from https://www.innovationhub-act.org/content/cw-documents

EEAS. (2018). Shared vision, common action. A stronger Europe: A global strategy for the European Union's foreign and security policy. European External Action Service. Retrieved November 28, 2021, from https://op.europa.eu/en/publication-detail/-/publication/3eaae2cf-9ac5-11e6-868c-01aa75ed71a1

EEAS. (2022). Strategic compass for security and defence. Retrieved April 27, 2022, from https://www.eeas.europa.eu/eeas/strategic-compass-security-and-defence-1_en

Elysée. (2018). Discours du Président de la République Emmanuel Macron #Aiforhumanity, Paris Collège de France—29 March. Retrieved November 28, 2021, from https://www.elysee.fr/emmanuel-macron/2018/03/29/discours-du-president-de-la-republique-sur-lintelligence-artificielle

Euractiv. (2019). Altmaier's cloud initiative and the pursuit of European digital sovereignty. 12 September. Retrieved November 28, 2021, from https://www.euractiv.com/section/data-protection/news/altmaiers-cloud-initiative-and-the-pursuit-of-european-digital-sovereignty/

Euractiv. (2020a). US and Chinese tech giants welcomed into 'EU sovereign' cloud project. 15 October. Retrieved November 28, 2021, from https://www.euractiv.com/section/digital/news/us-and-chinese-tech-giants-welcomed-into-eu-sovereign-cloud-project/

Euractiv. (2020b). 'Geopolitical' Europe aims to extend its digital sovereignty from China. 11 September. Retrieved November 28, 2021, from https://www.euractiv.com/section/digital/news/geopolitical-europe-aims-to-extend-its-digital-sovereignty-versus-china/

Euractiv. (2020c). Gaia-X: A Trojan horse for Big Tech in Europe. 24 November. Retrieved November 28, 2021, from https://www.euractiv.com/section/digital/opinion/gaia-x-a-trojan-horse-for-big-tech-in-europe

Euractiv. (2021a). Philippe Latombe: La souveraineté numérique française, c'est la capacité à choisir nos dépendances. 14 July. Retrieved November 28, 2021, from https://www.euractiv.fr/section/economie/interview/philippe-latombe-la-souverainete-numerique-francaise-cest-la-capacite-a-choisir-nos-dependances/

Euractiv. (2021b). Transatlantic tech talks team-up on China, but avoid confronting key issues. 23 June. Retrieved November 28, 2021, from https://www.euractiv.com/section/digital/news/transatlantic-tech-talks-team-up-on-china-but-avoid-confronting-key-issues/

Euractiv. (2021c). French cloud industry regrets government's ambivalence in dealing with digital giants. 21October. Retrieved November 28, 2021, from https://

www.euractiv.com/section/digital/news/french-cloud-industry-regrets-governments-ambivalence-in-dealing-with-digital-giants/

Euractiv. (2021d). Les acteurs français du cloud regrettent l'ambivalence du gouvernement face aux GAFAM. 21 October. Retrieved November 28, 2021, from https://www.euractiv.fr/section/economie/news/les-acteurs-francais-du-cloud-regrettent-lambivalence-du-gouvernement-face-aux-gafam/

Euractiv. (2021e). French defence company Thales partners with Google to offer 'trusted cloud'. 6 October. Retrieved November 28, 2021, from https://www.euractiv.com/section/digital/news/french-defence-company-thales-partners-with-google-to-offer-trusted-cloud/

Euractiv. (2021f). EU and US working together on trusted connectivity to counter China. 8 September. Retrieved November 28, 2021, from https://www.euractiv.com/section/digital/news/eu-and-us-working-together-on-trusted-connectivity-to-counter-china/

Euractiv. (2021g). French decision to have Microsoft host Health Data Hub still attracts criticism. 19 February. Retrieved November 28, 2021, from https://www.euractiv.com/section/health-consumers/news/french-decision-to-have-microsoft-host-health-data-hub-still-attracts-criticism/

Euractiv. (2022). Biden, Von der Leyen, announce agreement 'in principle' on transatlantic data flows. Retrieved April 26, 2022, from https://www.euractiv.com/section/data-protection/news/biden-von-der-leyen-announce-agreement-in-principle-on-transatlantic-data-flows/

European Commission. (2019). The Von der Leyen Commission: For a Union that strives for more. Press release. Retrieved November 28, 2021, from https://ec.europa.eu/commission/presscorner/detail/en/IP_19_5542

European Commission. (2020a). The EU's cybersecurity strategy for the digital decade. 16 December. Retrieved November 28, 2021, from https://eur-lex.europa.eu/legal-content/EN/TXT/HTML/?uri=CELEX:52020JC0018&rid=5

European Commission. (2020b). EU Security Union Strategy: Connecting the dots in a new security ecosystem. Retrieved November 28, 2021, from https://ec.europa.eu/commission/presscorner/detail/en/ip_20_1379

European Commission. (2020c). Commission Report on safety and liability implications of AI, the Internet of things and robotics. Retrieved November 28, 2021, from https://ec.europa.eu/info/publications/commission-report-safety-and-liability-implications-ai-internet-things-and-robotics-0_en

European Commission. (2020d). The Digital Markets Act: Ensuring fair and open digital markets. Proposal for a Regulation on Digital Markets Act. Retrieved November 28, 2021, from https://ec.europa.eu/info/strategy/priorities-2019-2024/europe-fit-digital-age/digital-markets-act-ensuring-fair-and-open-digital-markets_en

European Commission. (2020e). White paper on artificial intelligence: A European approach to excellence and trust. Retrieved November 28, 2021, from https://

ec.europa.eu/info/publications/white-paper-artificial-intelligence-european-approach-excellence-and-trust_en

European Commission. (2021a). Friend or foe? Here's how the EU will regulate. Thierry Breton, Commissioner for the Internal Market, AI, 21 April. Retrieved November 28, 2021, from https://ec.europa.eu/commission/commissioners/2019-2024/breton/announcements/friend-or-foe-heres-how-eu-will-regulate-ai_en

European Commission. (2021b). Fostering a European approach to artificial intelligence, COM/2021/205 final. Retrieved November 28, 2021, from https://eur-lex.europa.eu/legal-content/EN/ALL/?uri=COM:2021:205:FIN

European Commission. (2022). European Commission and United States joint statement on Trans-Atlantic Data Privacy Framework. Retrieved April 26, 2022, from https://ec.europa.eu/commission/presscorner/detail/es/ip_22_2087

European Council. (2021). EU-US summit statement: Towards a renewed Transatlantic partnership. Retrieved November 26, 2021, from https://www.consilium.europa.eu/en/press/press-releases/2021/06/15/eu-us-summit-statement-towards-a-renewed-transatlantic-partnership/

European Parliament. (2019). Polarisation and the use of technology in political campaigns and communication. Retrieved November 28, 2021, from https://www.europarl.europa.eu/thinktank/en/document.html?reference=EPRS_STU(2019)634414

European Parliament. (2020). Framework of ethical aspects of artificial intelligence, robotics and related technologies. European Parliament Resolution of 20 October 2020 with recommendations to the Commission on a framework of ethical aspects of artificial intelligence, robotics and related technologies (2020/2012(INL). Retrieved November 16, 2021, from https://www.europarl.europa.eu/doceo/document/TA-9-2020-0275_EN.html

France Sénat. (2013). L'Union européenne, colonie du monde numérique? Rapport d'information de Mme Catherine MORIN-DESAILLY, fait au nom de la commission des affaires européennes n° 443 (2012–2013). Retrieved November 28, 2021, from https://www.senat.fr/notice-rapport/2012/r12-443-notice.html

France Sénat. (2019). Le devoir de souveraineté numérique. Rapport de M. Gérard Longuet, fait au nom de la commission d'enquête n° 7 tome I (2019–2020). Retrieved November 28, 2021, from https://www.senat.fr/notice-rapport/2019/r19-007-1-notice.html

Franke, U. (2020). Europe needs a plan for AI in the military realm, February. Retrieved November 28, 2021, from https://www.the-security-times.com/europe-needs-plan-ai-military-realm/

Franke, U. (2021). Artificial Intelligence diplomacy | Artificial Intelligence governance as a new external policy tool. European Parliament Think Tank. Retrieved November 28, 2021, from https://www.europarl.europa.eu/thinktank/en/document.html?reference=IPOL_STU%282021%29662926

Goffi, E. R. (2019). L'intelligence artificielle: Sujet des relations internationales, objet éthique. ILERI. Retrieved November 28, 2021, from https://www.ileri.fr/intelligence-artificielle-sujet-relations-internationales-objet-ethique/

Hofstetter, Y. (2018). Neue Welt. Macht. Neue Menschen. In *Schriftenreihe der Bundeszentrale für politische Bildung* ("Der Neue Mensch" ed., pp. 135–150). Bundeszentrale für politische Bildung bpb.

Internationale Politik. (2018). 'Künstliche Intelligenz', Ausgabe #4/2018—July/August. Retrieved November 28, 2021, from https://internationalepolitik.de/de/kuenstliche-intelligenz

Jungbluth, C. (2021). The newly launched EU-US Trade and Technology Council (TTC)—What is it all about, and what does it have to do with China? Bertelsmann Stiftung. Retrieved November 28, 2021, from https://ged-project.de/trade-and-investment/the-newly-launched-eu-us-trade-and-technology-council-ttc-what-is-it-all-about-and-what-does-it-have-to-do-with-china/

Larger, T., Scott, M., & Kayali, L. (2020). Inside the EU's divisions on how to go after Big Tech, Public and private disagreements underscored a split over EU plans to promote a more aggressive stance on tech. Retrieved November 28, 2021, from https://www.politico.eu/article/margrethe-vestager-thierry-breton-europe-big-tech-regulation-digital-services-markets-act

Marchal, N., & Neudert, L. M. (2019). Polarisation and the use of technology in political campaigns and communication. European Parliament Think Tank, 7 March. Retrieved November 28, 2021, from https://www.europarl.europa.eu/thinktank/en/document.html?reference=EPRS_STU(2019)634414

Miailh, N. (2018). Géopolitique de l'Intelligence artificielle: Le retour des empires. Politique étrangère. Retrieved November 28, 2021, from https://www.ifri.org/sites/default/files/atoms/files/geopolitique_de_lintelligence_artificielle.pdf

Ministère de l'Europe et des Affaires Etrangères. (2018). Déclaration franco-canadienne sur l'Intelligence artificielle, 7 June. Retrieved November 28, 2021, from https://www.diplomatie.gouv.fr/fr/dossiers-pays/canada/evenements/article/declaration-franco-canadienne-sur-l-intelligence-artificielle-07-06-18

Ministère des Armées. (2019). L'intelligence artificielle au service de la défense. Retrieved November 28, 2021, from https://www.defense.gouv.fr/salle-de-presse/communiques/communique_publication-du-rapport-du-ministere-des-armees-sur-l-intelligence-artificielle

Pannier, A. (2021). Europe in the geopolitics of technology: Connecting the internal and external dimensions. Institut Français des Relations Internationales (IFRI), Paris. Retrieved November 28, 2021, from https://www.ifri.org/en/publications/briefings-de-lifri/europe-geopolitics-technology-connecting-internal-and-external

Pauwels, E. (2019). The UN and the prevention in the era of AI. Research Fellow on Emerging Cybertechnologies United Nations University Centre for Policy Research. Retrieved November 28, 2021, from https://cpr.unu.edu/the-new-geopolitics-of-converging-risks-the-un-and-prevention-in-the-era-of-ai.html

Politico. (2021). Inside Gaia-X: How chaos and infighting are killing Europe's grand cloud project, 26 October. Retrieved November 28, 2021, from https://www.politico.eu/article/chaos-and-infighting-are-killing-europes-grand-cloud-project/

Soare, S. R. (2020). Digital divide? Transatlantic defence cooperation on AI. International Institute for Strategic Studies (IISS). Retrieved November 28, 2021, from https://www.iss.europa.eu/content/digital-divide-transatlantic-defence-cooperation-ai#_introduction

Thibout, C. (2021). Quelle souveraineté numérique pour la France, Diplomatie, Affaires stratégiques et relations internationales, Les Grands Dossiers n°59.

Thomann, P. E. (2010). Europe as a political force: Cards on the table. *Revue Défense Nationale*, April, pp. 13–20. Retrieved November 28, 2021, from https://www.diploweb.com/Europe-as-a-political-force-cards.html

Thomann, P. E. (2015). Le couple franco-allemand et le projet européen: Représentations géopolitiques, unité et rivalités. L'Harmattan.

Trend Micro Research. (2020). United Nations Interregional Crime and Justice Research Institute (UNICRI) Europol's European Cybercrime Centre (EC3): Malicious uses and abuses of artificial intelligence. Retrieved November 28, 2021, from https://www.europol.europa.eu/publications-documents/malicious-uses-and-abuses-of-artificial-intelligence

UNESCO. (2021). Ugra Resolution Information and Communications in the digital age.

UNESCO. (2022). Ugra Memorandum Information and Communications in the digital age. Retrieved April 26, 2022, from http://www.ifapcom.ru/files/2021_ugra/Ugra_Memorandum_2021_eng.pdf

Van Roy, V. (2020). AI Watch: National strategies on Artificial Intelligence: A European perspective in 2019. EUR 30102 EN, Publications Office of the European Union, Luxembourg. Retrieved November 28, 2021, from https://publications.jrc.ec.europa.eu/repository/handle/JRC119974

Villani, C. (2018). Donner un sens à l'intelligence artificielle: Pour une stratégie nationale et européenne. Premier ministre. Retrieved November 28, 2021, from https://www.vie-publique.fr/rapport/37225-donner-un-sens-lintelligence-artificielle-pour-une-strategie-nation; https://www.ifri.org/en/publications/briefings-de-lifri/europe-geopolitics-technology-connecting-internal-and-external

Vitard, A. (2020). Quinze etats, dont la France, lancent le "Partenariat mondial pour l'IA." Retrieved November 28, 2021, from https://www.usine-digitale.fr/article/quinze-etats-dont-la-france-lancent-le-partenariat-mondial-pour-l-ia.N975646

18

Germany: Rising Sociopolitical Controversies and Threats to Psychological Security from the Malicious Use of Artificial Intelligence

Daria Matyashova

Introduction

The German case is highly relevant to the malicious use of artificial intelligence (MUAI) context, driven by Germany's global political ambitions and domestic challenges of inequality, cybercrime and political radicalization, which pose threats to broad dimensions of social security in the state. Additionally, artificial intelligence (AI) algorithm manipulation and use by extremists and other malicious actors is already influencing German society, providing illustrative examples for analysis. This also allows for the prediction of possible threats from MUAI in Germany, as well as the measures German authorities and citizens can take to respond, with significant consequences both for the state and for the world.

The research methodology is based on the umbrella theoretical framework, including a systematic approach to the international system as a hierarchical structure—which has been transformed due to economic competition and changes to the system—the concept of an emerging power, and a scenario

D. Matyashova (✉)
School of International Relations, St. Petersburg State University, St Petersburg, Russia
e-mail: dasham0708@mail.ru

analysis based on defined global and local trends aimed at predicting particular types of MUAI that threaten Germany.

Publications on various aspects of Germany's foreign and domestic policies (Cunha, 2021; Hillebrand, 2019), on social challenges and threats (Anheier, 2021; Bundesamt für Verfassungsschutz, 2019; Bundeskriminalamt, 2021) and on cases of MUAI (Jee, 2020; Rachel Metz, CNN Business, 2022) were of great importance for this chapter's discussion.

Nonetheless, it was not possible to find systemic studies on the problem of MUAI and psychological security in Germany. Analysis of this research problem is complicated by Germany's unpredictable future development under a variety of external and internal challenges, as well as by the further spread of new AI technologies that make room for new formats of malicious use.

International and Domestic Challenges for Modern Germany: Global Ambitions and Local Sociopolitical Problems

Germany is trying to reach a level of influence that is comparable to the great powers, reflected in the geopolitical and technological ambitions that the country projects on a global scale. However, these ambitions contradict Germany's real, modern world challenges—militarization and lagging behind the technological and economic leaders (China and the United States) at the international level; inequality; a crisis of democratic governance and political radicalization at the domestic policy level; a rise in cybercrime; and limited strategies of development at the technological level. The totality of these circumstances makes Germany vulnerable to MUAI now and in the near future.

Since the 1990s, Germany has been steadily increasing its influence in the areas of global governance and military security. Global governance is prominently reflected in climate change prevention, broader protection of the environment based on the Paris agreement (Sprinz, 2006), leading international institutions such as the G7 and the G20 (Hillebrand, 2019) and "reluctant hegemony"—exaggerated activity in regional integrationist institutions—in the European Union (EU) (Cunha, 2021). The military aspect is reflected in Germany's rising participation in UN peacekeeping operations, the military interventions of NATO and its allies, and Germany's own measures, such as in 2021, when the country dispatched a warship to the South China Sea (Fan & Zhang, 2021). With positive international and local perceptions—in 2020, 44 percent of respondents to a survey conducted in 135 countries regarded

Germany as a great power with a good image (Leistner & Chadwick, 2020)—and ample state resources, Germany is a rising power in the modern world.

Germany's ambitions have provided grounds for militarization, as seen in 2022, when the country's parliament (Bundestag) approved a constitutional change that lifted debt restrictions from the defense budget and established a special 100 million euro fund to upgrade the country's armed forces (Bundeswehr) (Gehrke, 2022). This essentially guaranteed a general defense and arms buildup. Against the background of German arms deliveries to Ukraine, and the request from Ukraine to accelerate the process (Der Spiegel, 2022), there has been a strong impetus for the German military-industrial complex and associated lobbies to become a driver for more aggressive politics.

The economic dimension presents another global challenge, with German ambitions coming up against the obstacles of transformation, lagging behind the United States and China. The drivers of these transformations are new technologies, and especially AI, with China and the United States leading in all areas, including financing, startups and skills applications. In 2019, Germany enjoyed a comparative advantage and leadership in AI compared to other EU member states, but not compared to the United States, China (Baierl & Nitzsche, 2021) or even the United Kingdom. Considering that AI technologies can shape industrial leadership—the basis of Germany's economic prosperity—the context of this technological shift places Germany in the position of trying to "catch up" power (Merz, 2019).

In response, Germany is making efforts to bridge this gap and secure its European and technological leadership. Germany is the home of Cyber Valley, Europe's largest AI research consortium, created in 2016, as well as for the Max Planck Institute for Intelligent Systems and the German Research Center for Artificial Intelligence, in partnership with Amazon and Google (DWIH, Neu-Delhi, 2022). In 2020, 58 percent of the world's autonomous driving patent applications were from Germany (Knupper, 2020). However, Germany's current strategies regard AI as an instrument for creating more competitive "classical" industries, which is a deeply reactive approach. A prominent example is the country's Industrial Strategy 2030, which objectively estimates the shortcomings of German digital and platform economies and promotes a multidimensional approach, including the funding of critical research, the social reorientation of the market and the reduction of taxes for nascent industries, among other measures (Federal Ministry for Economic Affairs and Energy, 2019). This strategy is based on approaches that already have proven efficiency in complex spheres of technological transformation, but contains no new governance methods or business models. Moreover, the crucial objective is to improve competitiveness in industries where Germany has already secured industrial leadership (machinery, electronics), not to develop new ones. This problem is exacerbated by the vague descriptions of AI benefits and risks in the key strategic documents (Köstler & Ossewaarde, 2021), indicating that the vision for true AI development is not consistent among German authorities and industrial leaders.

This discrepancy between international ambitions and ability to compete in a changing economy is exacerbated by internal problems that make Germany vulnerable to technological shifts and political decision-making fallacies. The first group of challenges lies with the state's ability to counter cybercrimes and restructure the economy, influenced by external crises and socioeconomic inequalities. The second group is driven by the crisis of democracy, bringing together rising radical influence, the corruption of political "cartel" parties and the ideological merger of leading political powers.

According to an annual report on cybercrimes from Germany's Federal Criminal Police Office (Bundeskriminalamt), the number of reported cybercrimes increased by 12 percent in 2021, while the clearance rate remained at around 30 percent. The most serious damage was caused by ransomware attacks, including one on the critical infrastructure of the Anhalt Bitterfeld district and another on a municipal hospital in Saxony Anhalt (Bundeskriminalamt, 2021). This demonstrates the weaknesses of Germany's cyber defense, which threatens not only new industries, but also modernized "old" industries, including critical infrastructure—such as rescue services and hospitals—that is slated to be digitalized to "reduce risk for living humans" (The Federal Government of Germany, 2020).

The social orientation of the industrial strategy is clearly explainable in the context of income inequality in Germany. In 2019, the top 1 percent of earners received nearly as much income as the bottom 50 percent, and over 20 percent of employees earned less than two-thirds of the national median income (Rühlemann et al., 2019). After the emergence of COVID-19, the problems of the working poor worsened and the rising poverty risk rate became especially urgent (Witting, 2022). The reasons for these inequalities are deeply structural, stemming from regressive taxation over the last 20 years, a pension system that is subject to market volatility, the over-taxation of labor compared to capital taxation and an education system that exacerbates inequality by tracking students after the fourth grade and defining their opportunities to enter university, an important determinant of future income (Rühlemann et al., 2019). These circumstances create barriers to active political participation and give rise to elements of radicalization.

According to Kundnani, the situation in Germany is special, since the processes that are disrupting democracy are derived from "depolarization," when party ideologies merge into one similar agenda (Kundnani, 2021). Other crisis indicators include cases of high-level political corruption, especially within the Christian Democratic Union (CDU) party, and political lobbyism (CRN, 2022). Collectively, this leads to growing distrust of the existing democratic system. Despite a positive attitude toward the government and its actions in 2020 (Boettcher & Schneider, 2020), public opinion turned dramatically toward skepticism in 2021, with 62 percent of Germans claiming that only a few private interests control German politics. Separately, 44 percent of Germans declared that their interests were not reflected in political decision-making at all, and 26 percent thought that corruption in Germany had increased (Mertens, 2022).

This type of disappointment with traditional ideologies and governance leads to the radicalization of parties and movements and a corresponding rise in their popularity. A classic example is Alternative for Germany, which broke away from the conservatives in 2013–2014 to become extreme right populists by the 2020s (Virschow, 2020). However, Alternative for Germany is a legal political unity that is integrated into the electoral system, which constrains its radicalization. Marginalized movements that are excluded from a formal political process lean not on populism, but on disruptive conspiracy theories and political violence. This is exemplified by the Reichsburger (Reich Citizens) movement, which rejects the modern German state and denies the Holocaust took place (Bundesamt fur Verfassung, 2019), and the Nationalsozialistischer Untergrund (National Socialist Underground—NSU), formally dissolved in 2011 but with individual supporters still active as recently as 2019, when CDU politician Walter Lubcke was killed by an ex-NSU member (Pfeifer, 2021). Radical movements tend to emerge, become active and gain supporters during crises similar to the COVID-19 pandemic. This is illustrated by Germany's "Querdenker" (Thinking Outside the Box) movement, which denies the existence of the coronavirus and rejects pandemic-related restrictions and mandates related to the virus. The Querdenkers have cooped right-wing elements, raising concerns about violence among law enforcement (Geisler et al., 2022). The movement is supported by the Reichsburger movement, which participated in Querdenker rallies, and Alternative for Germany has also voiced its support (Anheier, 2021). Considering the long-term effects of the COVID-19 crisis and the social transformations caused by technological shifts, the prospects of the formation of large-scale radical networks undermine both the psychological and physical security of the state.

Despite rising power ambitions and the desire to secure its status as one of the world's economic leaders, Germany is threatened by technological transformation. Germany's options for reaching these goals are constrained by its vulnerabilities from digital threats and crimes, its reactivity to industrial development, its rising socioeconomic inequality and political challenges that lower the general governability of the system.

Malicious Use of Artificial Intelligence in Germany: Norms, Practices and Technologies

Even when acknowledging the challenges of cybercrime and the potential damage of ransomware, Germany tended to ignore psychological security until the effects of radicalization and its influence on cyberspace became overt and widespread, due to the reliance of malicious actors—from individual extremists to right-wing, semi-military organizations—on AI algorithms. These opportunities were created out of the weak responsibility of transnational IT corporations, and social media in general, and the limited opportunities of the German government to counter the threats. As a result, Germany has become a target for the third and highest level of psychological security threat from MUAI. The first level refers to the creation of a hypertrophied negative or positive level of the second level—using AI for crimes that are not primarily aimed at inflicting psychological damage—and the third level—attacking the public consciousness (Bazarkina & Pashentsev, 2020)—but this does not reduce Germany's psychological security vulnerability from other levels of threats.

In official documents, Germany promotes the development of AI as a "technology of the future" and a "benign" instrument, intended to strengthen international cooperation with European partners, modernize traditional industries and mitigate people's exposure to dangerous industries. However, the risks and benefits of AI are only vaguely outlined, indicating its development is primarily for the benefit of large corporations (Daum, 2019). AI is also framed as the only alternative for Germany's prosperous future, provoking public discussion that opposes the official discourse. According to L. Köstler, the "German media declare that 'the story of trustworthy AI is a marketing narrative made up by industry,' emphasizing that 'customers don't buy products they do not trust'" (FAZ 12). Moreover, *Die Zeit* clarifies that the automation suggested by "ethical AI" is impossible, as "ethical decisions are far too complex to be reflected in software systems" (ZEIT 18) (Köstler & Ossewaarde, 2021). There is currently an impression of a public discussion, but with the exacerbation of inequality and radicalized tendencies being incorporated into the AI discourse, a first-level threat to psychological security can be established.

While defense from first-level threats is an area of government activity, second-level psychological security threats from MUAI are addressed not only by regulations (CLEPA, 2022), but also by technicians and AI-related start-ups, due to the limited ability of German officials to protect infrastructure even from "traditional," non-AI ransomware. One example is the Vay company's challenges in securing a driverless fleet of cars from both AI- and non-AI-provoked accidents by allowing real-time human control of the car when needed (Armiento, 2022). However, this type of situation can also cede ground to exaggerations of AI-caused challenges and, thus, to first-level threats.

While second-level threats are being thwarted within the context of new technologies (e.g., autonomous driving) in the 2020s (May, 2022), the response to third-level threats began in the 2010s. In particular, the Netzwerkdurchsetzungsgesetz (Network Enforcement Act) of 2017 imposes fines on social media platforms for failure to remove hate speech within 24 hours. The law was connected to high-profile cases of fake news and racist material being spread via the German subsidiaries of prominent social media firms (BBC News, 2018). In this context, the failures of the AI algorithms include the inability to identify hate speech in the local language. Consequently, social media platforms were unable to be moderately efficient by the systems, which recommended decisions that further promoted the content based on a combination of user interest and popularity. The AI algorithms also failed to track elements of extremist and terrorist propaganda through sounds, graphic symbols or censored texts, the meanings of which become clear with context (Weimann & Masri, 2020). The reaction of German lawmakers was operative and reasonable, but narrow in terms of the detected problems and, therefore, not ample. Specifically, the law referred to psychological security in a broad, socially oriented context (in this case, minority and other vulnerable groups), addressing neither malicious exploitation of AI flaws nor the potential direct usage of AI for disruptive purposes.

One year later in 2018, the comprehensive AI strategy was adopted, focusing on "benign" forms of AI applicable for countering and investigating crimes in the digital domain, such as child pornography (The Federal Government of Germany XE "Germany" , 2020). The attention given to psychological threats instigated through the malicious use of technology by aggressive or disruptive actors was minor, despite acknowledgments that the use of AI should be conducted "in compliance with fundamental rights" (The

Federal Government of Germany, 2020) and, hypothetically, could be abused by actors with other values.

The results were rather predictable: MUAI by extremists only continued. However, the threats did not come from the direct manipulation of independently programmed AI, but from exploiting vulnerabilities within the existing systems. Two striking examples are from the Kampf der Nibelungen (Battle of the Nibelungs) and the Querdenker movement. Kampf der Nibelungen is a martial arts event of far-right, extremist groups that promoted merchandise and tournaments (de facto training of militant supporters) through social media while avoiding overt platform violations (mainly Facebook) by using personal advertisement algorithms to attract new members and supporters (New York Post, 2021). The Querdenker movement initially used the same strategy—spreading false information about COVID-19 through coordinated actions that circumvented the platform's regulations. This led to a situation where the malicious actions of Querdenker were evident but ignored by the moderating systems, since the actions did not match the platform's existing categories for violations. After more intensive moderation was imposed on German-language Facebook, due to the identification of a new type of malicious cyberactivity, the Querdenkers were banned for "coordinated social harm" without determining whether the accounts were automated (e.g., represented by bots moderated by AI algorithms) (Euronews, 2021). Thus, it was not only the state but also the initiative of Big Tech to impose rules that restrict and constrain "non-direct" MUAI activities. More effective initiatives were launched in the field of malicious agenda-setting prevention in 2020 with the ratification of the Medienstaatsvertrag (State Treaty on Media). The move was aimed at prioritizing journalistic content on video platforms (Jaursch & Lenoir, 2020), which was a rational but limited step, to countering the threat from algorithms that conceal this type of activity.

MUAI took a new turn with the development of deepfake technology, which gained popularity on social media as a cheap tool suitable for massive (mis)information campaigns. At first, deepfakes were used for amusement and even educational activities. Examples include humorous videos with politicians Annalena Baerbock, Christian Lindner and members of their 2021 electoral campaign teams generated from official social media photos (Schuppisser, 2021), as well as from the DeepNostalgia application, widely used by netizens to commemorate Holocaust victims and to foster public discussion (Ribbens, 2021). In these cases, AI played a "neutral" and even "benign" role, completely the opposite of the German government's concerns

18 Germany: Rising Sociopolitical Controversies and Threats... 495

about deepfakes being "threats to democracy" (Hurtz, 2019). Furthermore, the use of deepfakes by the police to generate child pornography, with the aim of helping undercover agents infiltrate child sex abuse rings, was legally permitted in 2019 (Eyerys, 2021). In this instance, the "maliciousness" of the AI was not defined by information spread or generation, like it was in the Querdenker case, but by users and their objectives, which corresponded to the principles of free access to information and technologies. However, this was slightly in conflict with the principle of responsibility for generated content, as well as with the responsibility for the public spread of that content.

Nevertheless, the malicious use of deepfakes clearly manifested in March 2022 and in contrast to the previous examples, these concerned an international agenda. The deepfakes showed Volodimir Zelensky telling Ukrainians to put down their weapons and Vladimir Putin declaring peace with Ukraine. The content was mainly shared on Twitter but was originally shown on Ukrainian television (Wakefield, 2022). The Zelensky deepfake was probably intended to target a primarily Ukrainian audience, but mediatization of the conflict quickly placed the content into the general public domain. Despite the low quality of the videos, allowing them to be identified as deepfakes, both were important contributions to global disinformation surrounding the current crisis in Ukraine, fueling hatred and undermining trust in information sources. This was of crucial importance for Germany, which was at the time making decisions on both foreign policy and military support for Ukraine, as well as making domestic policy decisions on changing the Basic Law to add a special funding provision to the state budget (Federal Government, 2022). Despite a gradual shift toward the positive aspects of deepfakes, their malicious use triggered a possible return to deep skepticism and the emergence of more comprehensive norms to protect psychological security, restricting deepfake technology.

To conclude, Germany relatively quickly became a target of MUAI by both extremist organizations and foreign forces. These events overlapped with the issue of psychological security on a narrow legal basis, which was broadened in 2017 by the Netzwerkdurchsetzungsgesetz, but did not prevent extremists from exploiting existing algorithms or, allegedly, using their own algorithms for the automatic spread of disinformation. The actions of both the state and Big Tech attempted to constrain opportunities to exploit vulnerabilities, but the rapid development of deepfakes, as well as their affordability, gave disinformation operations a crucially important leg up that German policy can no longer ignore.

Malicious Use of Artificial Intelligence Threats for Psychological Security in Germany: Prospects and Scenarios

Regarding prospects for MUAI in Germany, it is crucially important to assess the level of trust German society has in AI and to incorporate this perspective. According to the Trust in AI Index project, general public opinion on AI in Germany in September 2021 was estimated to be 55/100 (almost neutral, slightly positive). Opinion on AI is dynamic and dependent on media coverage. For instance, in November 2021, a rise in AI confidence correlated with an increase in positive AI media coverage, despite a drop in general media coverage (SAS Institute, 2022). However, a neutral or even slightly positive attitude does not exclude common fears about specific AI that is used in economy. In a study by Statista from 2020, around 73 percent of respondents stated that AI use will increase employee control. An equally high proportion of respondents worried that the use of AI could lead to a reduction in jobs (Statista Research Department, 2022).

These factors make room, on the one hand, for stronger, socially oriented AI regulations in industries, which would correspond with the current industrial strategy, and, on the other hand, for the manipulation of public opinion by exploiting fears about AI. Considering the rising levels of inequality and distrust in the political system among Germans, exploitation of those fears could be merged with frightening images of social insecurity, such as lost wages and educational opportunities, and, finally, the seizure of total control by a non-democratic and rigid system. These fears could threaten Germany's plans to digitalize traditionally competitive industries, to introduce AI into high-risk working environments and to increase general economic prosperity, both as a basis of emergence and as a solution to inequality. The technological dimension does not play a significant role in this case; negative images of AI can be spread both automatically and manually, but would probably require new and more sophisticated techniques to deceive social media and news aggregator algorithms, such as imitating non-coordinated actions, frequently changing frames and plots, providing numbers for verified followers and so on.

MUAI aimed at critical infrastructure is also theoretically possible, considering the steady rise of cybercrime, their low level of clearance and the constant development of ransomware, the cost of which tend to decrease with increased scale. Damage to critical infrastructure can not only cause panic, but also discredit Germany's ambitions for AI development and use. Given that one of the goals is to increase national industry competitiveness and project greater power vis-à-vis other core states, this threat also has an international dimension. However, both the AI and the industrial strategies strongly emphasize the role of "benign" intelligence to counter cybercrime and other criminal acts in the virtual realm. Measures that create a legal basis for thwarting or prosecuting those threats establish links between AI developers and security practitioners (Bundeskriminalamt, 2020) to develop common solutions. For example, the KISTRA project pulls resources from leading German universities and the Bundeskriminalamt (Hildebrandt, 2022) to provide technical, ethical and legal AI-based solutions to address the problem of hate crimes in cyberspace (Pelzer, 2020). This type of collaboration can play a positive role in neutralizing such threats through technical, but principle-based, instruments that are analogous to Facebook banning Querdenkers for "coordinated social harm" despite the lack of special category.

MUAI aimed directly at the public consciousness will steadily increase not only in registered cases, but also in scale, nationally and internationally. The national level will likely be driven by radicalization trends and rising inequality, while the international level will likely be determined by the steps Germany takes and their outcomes, although still influenced by the national agenda. MUAI aimed directly at the public consciousness can include not only deepfakes, but also automatically generated content such as news. However, resurrecting concerns about deepfakes could be a driver for harsher regulations of, and restrictions on, technology in the short term.

Given these trends, four MUAI psychological security threat scenarios and outcomes can be envisioned for Germany, with number 1 the least realistic and number 4 the most realistic.

1. Weak mechanisms, weak threats. This scenario is possible in the event of slow AI implementation within industries and services, mitigating international conflicts. MUAI is typical among perpetrators and terrorists, for whom the countering norms and instruments have been developed. In this case, Germany and the EU could lose normative power based on their AI regulations and continue to lag behind the United States and China. The loss of economic drive and international political authority would transform Germany into an "ex-AI leader." The prevention of MUAI threats, in turn, stabilizes the situation in German society, making room for reforms aimed at solving the challenges of inequality and polarization. Moderately negative for international authority, strongly positive for German governability.
2. Strong mechanisms, weak threats. This scenario is possible in the event of intensive AI implementation in industries and services, with intensive

multistakeholder cooperation on norm-making and the use of "benign" AI to counter malicious actors. Strong regulation based on AI ethics restricts the use of technologies by malicious actors, thereby reducing their influence on society. Radicalization decreases, allowing the restoration of trust in democracy and the ability to enact reforms. The norms and best practices dedicated to "benign" AI become economic capital for both Germany and the EU, allowing them to overtake China and the United States in the realm of sustainable, high-tech development. Germany attains stronger leadership as a core state. Strongly positive for international authority, strongly positive for German governability.

3. Weak mechanisms, strong threats. This scenario is possible in the event of slow AI implementation in industries and services, continuing international conflict trends and reflecting the rising ambitions of Germany through political radicalization and growing inequality. MUAI is widely used for international provocation and disinformation campaigns, for recruiting new members into extremist groups, for spreading disruptive ideologies and for sowing fear and panic among population. Prospects for middle-term mitigation through "benign" AI developed by technicians or through "soft" norms among Big Tech. Strongly negative for international authority, strongly negative for German governability.

4. Strong mechanisms, strong threats. This scenario is possible in the event of intensive AI implementation in industries and services, intensive multistakeholder cooperation in norm-making and "benign" use of AI to counter malicious actors. Continuing international conflict trends, reflecting the rising ambitions of Germany, political radicalization and rising inequality. Under the pressure of global crisis, internal challenges, and the drastic development and implementation of AI technologies across all industries and services, Germany applies "benign" AI best practices to track, defile and prevent MUAI. Strong regulation based on AI ethics restricts the use of technologies by malicious actors from some criminal organizations, but it is fraught with the risk of the further growth of social and political polarization, and the transformation of the state into a repressive proponent of narrow corporate interests actively using MUAI against the nation. Such a prospect increases skepticism about AI in Germany and its normative power abroad. After proving the necessity of given regulations, norms and best practices dedicated to "benign" AI, countering MUAI becomes economic capital for Germany that is now comparable with technical industry leaders due to experience. Moderately positive for international authority, strongly positive for German governability.

Governability in the given matrix means the ability of authorities and their partners (technical, academical, etc.) to counter destabilizing elements, to promote their chosen agenda to society and to conduct policy based on this agenda without facing strong social resentment. Governability brings social stability in the short term. However, governability equals neither democratic representation in government institutions nor politics aimed at guaranteeing equality and common prosperity; it can be oriented toward these goals, but usually only if it does not undermine the status quo. High governability can bring Germany into an international leadership role of technical and normative power, but the essence of the norms Germany promotes will depend on the social orientation of AI politics.

The social orientation of AI politics is a complex, multidimensional determinant that includes the transparency of AI, the use of AI technologies in fields of crucial social importance (education, healthcare, penitentiaries, etc.), the just distribution of income and goods from new technologies, the wide democratic representation of stakeholders in AI governance (as a branch of internet governance) and the long-term course of governance aimed at the common good. The lack of AI social orientation in ethics and politics will lead to anti-social orientation, concentrating goods and governing privileges among a small circle of stakeholders, resulting in negative consequences for society in general. Anti-social orientation does not exclude high governability, but may lead to the collapse of German controllability and undermine the stability of the global system in the long term.

Currently, Germany's declared use of AI is aimed at protecting human life, creating new jobs, raising algorithm transparency and combatting anti-social behavior; its mixed representation of government, academia and technicians reflects attempts to achieve multistakeholderism in AI governance. However, the countertrends of militarization, inequality and the rise of radical movements limit the social orientation of AI for all the possible scenarios that make Germany a "medium socially oriented" AI state with a strong dependence on external factors and ambitions for becoming a rising power. This means an unsustainable situation should also be taken into account.

Conclusion

Modern Germany is conducting a foreign policy that is aimed at raising its international status. However, its need to secure a more privileged place as an economic leader is threatened by the rise of new technological giants in disruptive industries, especially AI. Germany's paths to reaching this goal are constrained by its vulnerabilities to digital threats and crimes, by its reactive industrial development strategy that does not promote disruptive management or technologies, by its rising socioeconomic inequality and by increasing political challenges (ideological party merges, rising radicalism, distrust of democracy), all of which lower governability of the system in general.

These issues made Germany a target for third-level MUAI by both extremist organizations and foreign actors relatively quickly, which overlapped with a narrow legal basis on the issue of psychological security in Germany. This legal basis was broadened in 2017 by the Netzwerkdurchsetzungsgesetz, but it did not prevent extremists from exploiting existing algorithms or, allegedly, using their own algorithms to facilitate the automatic spread of disinformation. The actions of both the state and Big Tech constrained opportunities to exploit these vulnerabilities, but the rapid development of deepfakes, as well as their affordability, gave an advantage to disinformation operations in areas that were crucially important for German policy that cannot be ignored now. This vulnerability to third-level MUAI corresponds with attempts to prevent first-level and second-level vulnerabilities by promoting a positive AI agenda at the government level, as well as through regulative and technical initiatives to reduce threats to physical object cybersecurity. These actions do not, however, exclude the emergence of these threats in the near future, especially when taking public opinion on AI into account.

Considering Germany's social and political challenges, its global ambitions, the place AI has in economic reconstruction and the vulnerability of its infrastructure to cybercrime, the threats from MUAI to the German state are variable and multidimensional. These threats can include exploiting concerns about AI, coupled with frightening images of social insecurity, losing wages and educational opportunities and, finally, the loss of total control to a nondemocratic and rigid system. Attacks on critical infrastructure can not only cause panic, but also discredit Germany's ambitions to become a leader in AI development and use, leading to MUAI aimed directly at the public consciousness.

Given these trends, the most realistic scenario is Germany applying the best practices of "benign" AI to track, defile and prevent MUAI. Strong regulation based on AI ethics restricts the use of AI technologies by malicious actors, reducing their influence on society. In the long term, regulation undermines radical and extremist malicious actors and becomes a basis for new civil cooperation, the reestablishment of trust in democracy and a solution for the challenges of inequality. However, in the short term, the public may perceive these norms as excessively harsh, raising skepticism about AI in Germany and the state's normative power abroad. After proving the given regulations, norms and best practices dedicated to "benign" AI are necessary, countering MUAI will become economic capital for Germany, allowing the country to advance its leadership role in this technical industry due to its experience.

None of the scenarios imply "pure," socially oriented AI politics on the part of Germany, given the contradictory trends in this field. On the one hand, Germany has declared AI to be used for protecting human life, creating new jobs, increasing algorithm transparency and combatting anti-social behavior; on the other hand, Germany also faces militarization, inequality and the rise of radical movements. This makes Germany a "medium socially oriented" AI state, with a strong dependence on external factors and ambitions for rising in power.

References

Anheier, H. (2021). Germany's homegrown Q menace. In: Project Syndicate. Retrieved July 4, 2022, from https://www.project-syndicate.org/commentary/querdenker-threat-how-germany-s-government-should-respond-by-helmut-k-anheier-2021-08.

Armiento, I. (2022). A German Startup has a different approach to self-driving cars. In: Jerry. Retrieved July 4, 2022, from https://getjerry.com/insights/german-startup-different-approach-self-driving-cars.

Baierl, R., & Nitzsche, B. (2021). Künstliche Intelligenz im deutschen Mittelstand – Empfehlungen für eine erfolgreiche Implementierung. In M. Bruhn & K. Hadwich (Eds.), *Künstliche Intelligenz im Dienstleistungsmanagement* (1st ed., pp. 314–329). Springer Gabler Wiesbaden.

Bazarkina, D., & Pashentsev, E. (2020). Malicious use of artificial intelligence. *Russia in Global Affairs, 18*, 154–177. https://doi.org/10.31278/1810-6374-2020-18-4-154-177

BBC News. (2018). Germany starts enforcing hate speech law. In: BBC News. Retrieved July 4, 2022, from https://www.bbc.com/news/technology-42510868.

Boettcher, B., & Schneider, S. (2020). Polarisation in Germany – Fuelled but not caused by the corona crisis. 1–15. Retrieved July 4, 2022, from https://www.dbresearch.com/PROD/RPS_EN-PROD/PROD0000000000512197/Polarisation_in_Germany_-_fuelled_but_not_caused_b.PDF?undefined&realload=wBAKel1vj3KO5Te9L3aoJ1HE/1U6KhsCL0TF6R95ckcMQ3I4NCfagq/L607Thtq5.

Bundesamt fur Verfassung. (2019). "Reichsbürger" and "Selbstverwalter." Enemies of the state, profiteers, conspiracy theorists. 1–36. Retrieved July 4, 2022, from https://www.verfassungsschutz.de/SharedDocs/publikationen/EN/reichsbuerger-and-selbstverwalter/2018-12-reichsbuerger-und-selbstverwalter-enemies-of-the-state-profiteers-conspiracytheorists.pdf?__blob=publicationFile&v=5.

Bundeskriminalamt. (2020). Künstliche Intelligenz gegen das Verbrechen: Kooperation gestartet. In: Bundeskriminalamt. Retrieved July 4, 2022, from https://www.bka.de/DE/Presse/Listenseite_Pressemitteilungen/2020/Presse2020/201027_pmForschungskoop.html.

Bundeskriminalamt. (2021). Bundeslagebild Cybercrime 2021. 1–42. Retrieved July 4, 2022, from https://www.bka.de/SharedDocs/Downloads/DE/Publikationen/JahresberichteUndLagebilder/Cybercrime/cybercrimeBundeslagebild2021.html;jsessionid=0904D5B45133CCAD61C1F00C6343433A.live602?nn=28110.

CLEPA. (2022). New autonomous driving law enters into force in Germany – CLEPA – European Association of Automotive Suppliers. In: CLEPA – European Association of Automotive Suppliers. Retrieved July 4, 2022, from https://clepa.eu/mediaroom/new-autonomous-driving-law-enters-into-force-in-germany/.

CRN. (2022). Germany's government corruption scandals – CRN. In: CRN. Retrieved July 4, 2022, from https://corruptionresearchnetwork.org/germanys-government-corruption-scandals/.

Cunha, A. (2021). Europe's hegemon? The nature of German power during Europe's crisis decade. In: E-International Relations. Available via E-International Relations. Retrieved July 4, 2022, from https://www.e-ir.info/pdf/93668.

Daum, T. (2019). Die Künstliche Intelligenz des Kapitals, p 192.

Der Spiegel. (2022). Andrij Melnyk: Botschafter nennt Deutschlands Haltung zu Waffenlieferungen feige. In: Spiegel.de. Retrieved July 4, 2022, from https://www.spiegel.de/ausland/botschafter-melnyk-nennt-deutschlands-haltung-zu-waffenlieferungen-feige-a-82d3945c-c742-4f1a-a513-daec532d6ca8.

DWIH Neu-Delhi. (2022). AI research takes root in Germany. In: DWIH Neu-Delhi. Retrieved July 4, 2022, from https://www.dwih-newdelhi.org/en/topics/ai/artificial-intelligence-ai-in-germany/ai-research-takes-root-in-germany/.

Euronews. (2021). Facebook bans German accounts under new 'social harm' policy. In: Euronews. Retrieved July 4, 2022, from https://www.euronews.com/next/2021/09/17/facebook-bans-german-accounts-under-new-social-harm-policy.

Eyerys. (2021). German law allows authorities to use deepfakes of children to catch online predators. In: Eyerys. Retrieved July 4, 2022, from https://www.eyerys.com/articles/timeline/german-law-allows-authorities-use-deepfakes-children-catch-online-predators.

Fan, A., & Zhang, C. (2021). German warship in South China Sea more 'symbolic' than 'threat' – Global times. In: Globaltimes.cn. Retrieved July 4, 2022, from https://www.globaltimes.cn/page/202112/1243132.shtml.

Federal Government. (2022). Bundestag approves special fund to strengthen the federal armed forces. In: Federal Government. Retrieved July 4, 2022, from https://www.bundesregierung.de/breg-en/news/special-fund-federal-armed-forces-2047910.

Federal Ministry for Economic Affairs and Energy. (2019). Industrial strategy 2030. Guidelines for a German and European industrial policy. 1–40. Retrieved July 4,

2022, from https://www.bmwk.de/Redaktion/EN/Publikationen/Industry/industrial-strategy-2030.html.

Gehrke, L. (2022). Germany approves constitutional change to boost military. In: Politico. Retrieved July 4, 2022, from https://www.politico.eu/article/germany-pass-constitutional-change-to-ramp-up-military-amid-ukraine-russia-war/.

Geisler, A., Polke-Majewski, K., Musharbash, Y., & Zimmermann, F. (2022). Die neue Radikalität. In: Zeit. Retrieved July 4, 2022, from https://www.zeit.de/gesellschaft/zeitgeschehen/2022-02/querdenker-radikalisierung-verfassungsschutz-innere-sicherheit-telegram.

Hildebrandt, J. (2022). KISTRA – Use of artificial intelligence for early detection of crimes - RWTH Aachen University chair of communication science – English. In: RWTH. Retrieved July 4, 2022, from https://www.comm.rwth-aachen.de/cms/COMM/Forschung/Projekte/~jeohm/KISTRA/lidx/1/.

Hillebrand, R. (2019). Germany and the new global order: The Country's power resources reassessed. In: E-International Relations. Available via E-International Relations. Retrieved July 4, 2022, from https://www.e-ir.info/pdf/80052.

Hurtz, S. (2019). Deep Fakes: Bundesregierung sieht Gefahr für Demokratie. In: Süddeutsche.de. Retrieved July 4, 2022, from https://www.sueddeutsche.de/digital/deep-fakes-bundesregierung-kleine-anfrage-1.4711698.

Jaursch, J., & Lenoir, T. (2020). Disinformation: The German approach and what to learn from it. In: Institut Montaigne. Retrieved July 4, 2022, from https://www.institutmontaigne.org/en/blog/disinformation-german-approach-and-what-learn-it.

Knupper, J. (2020). Artificial intelligence in Germany/importance of AI in Germany. In: Clickworker.com. Retrieved July 4, 2022, from https://www.clickworker.com/customer-blog/artificial-intelligence-in-germany/.

Köstler, L., & Ossewaarde, R. (2021). The making of AI society: AI futures frames in German political and media discourses. *AI & SOCIETY, 37*, 249–263. https://doi.org/10.1007/s00146-021-01161-9

Kundnani, H. (2021). Germany: A different kind of democratic dysfunctionality. In: American Institute for Contemporary German Studies. Retrieved July 4, 2022, from https://www.aicgs.org/2021/01/germany-a-different-kind-of-democratic-dysfunctionality/.

Leistner, A., & Chadwick, L. (2020). Menschen weltweit wählen Deutschland zur führenden Weltmacht. In: Euronews. Retrieved July 4, 2022, from https://de.euronews.com/2020/07/27/menschen-weltweit-wahlen-deutschland-zur-fuhrenden-weltmacht.

May, T. (2022). German government announces new regulations for autonomous vehicles. In: Future Transport–News. Retrieved July 4, 2022, from https://futuretransport-news.com/german-government-announces-new-regulations-for-autonomous-vehicles/.

Mertens, A. (2022). Germans concerned about big businesses dominating political decision. In: Transparency International. Retrieved July 4, 2022, from https://www.transparency.org/en/blog/gcb-eu-2021-corruption-survey-germany-business-dominating-politics-lobbying.

Merz, F. (2019). Europa im globalen KI-Wettlauf. *CSS Analysen zur Sicherheitspolitik, 247*, 1–4. https://doi.org/10.3929/ethz-b-000345470

New York Post. (2021). Neo-Nazis are still on Facebook. And they're making money. In: New York Post. Retrieved July 4, 2022, from https://nypost.com/2021/09/27/neo-nazis-are-still-on-facebook-and-theyre-making-money/.

Pelzer, R. (2020). Using AI to detect hate crimes in the net. In: Technische Universität Berlin. Retrieved July 4, 2022, from https://www.tu.berlin/en/about/profile/press-releases-news/2020/november/hate-crimes-in-the-net/.

Pfeifer, H. (2021). Rechter Terror: "Der NSU lebt" | DW | 04.11.2021. In: Deutsche Welle. Retrieved July 4, 2022, from https://www.dw.com/de/rechter-terror-der-nsu-lebt/a-59695522.

Ribbens, K. (2021). Is DeepFake the Future of Holocaust Memory? In: The British Association for Holocaust Studies. Retrieved July 4, 2022, from https://britishassociationforholocauststudies.wordpress.com/2021/04/08/is-deepfake-the-future-of-holocaust-memory/.

Rühlemann, A., Staudt, E., & Fleißner, R. (2019). Inequalities in Germany inequalities are rising, the gender gap is higher than the EU average, social systems are being dismantled and Germany is driving international inequalities. 1–16.

SAS Institute. (2022). SAS Trust in AI Index. In: Sas.com. Retrieved July 4, 2022, from https://www.sas.com/de_de/insights/artificial-intelligence/trust-in-ai-index.html#september.

Schuppisser, R. (2021). Verheerendes Selfie: Deep Fake im deutschen Wahlkampf. In: Tagblatt. Retrieved July 4, 2022, from https://www.tagblatt.ch/meinung/kolumnen/medienkolumne-deep-fakes-erreichen-den-deutschen-wahlkampf-und-sie-sind-gar-nicht-so-schrecklich-ld.2196550.

Sprinz, D. (2006). Germany's international environmental policy. In H. Maull (Ed.), *Germany's uncertain power* (pp. 214–230). Palgrave Macmillan.

Statista Research Department. (2022). Künstliche Intelligenz am Arbeitsplatz in Deutschland 2020. In: Statista. Retrieved July 4, 2022, from https://de.statista.com/statistik/daten/studie/1176941/umfrage/vorstellungen-von-kuenstlicher-intelligenz-am-arbeitsplatz-in-deutschland/.

The Federal Government of Germany. (2020). Artificial Intelligence Strategy of the German Federal Government. 2020 Update. 1–31. Retrieved July 4, 2022, from https://www.ki-strategie-deutschland.de/files/downloads/Fortschreibung_KI-Strategie_engl.pdf.

Virschow, F. (2020). Alternative fur Deutschland (AfD): eine Partei der extremen Rechten?1–28. Retrieved July 4, 2022, from https://www.ifri.org/sites/default/files/atoms/files/virchow_afd_extremen_rechten_2020.pdf.

Wakefield, J. (2022). Deepfake presidents used in Russia–Ukraine war. In: BBC News. Retrieved July 4, 2022, from https://www.bbc.com/news/technology-60780142.

Weimann, G., & Masri, N. (2020). Research note: Spreading hate on TikTok. Studies in Conflict; Terrorism 1–14. doi: https://doi.org/10.1080/1057610x.2020.1780027.

Witting, V. (2022). Social inequality in Germany is on the rise | DW | 12.05.2021. In: Deutsche Welle. Retrieved July 4, 2022, from https://www.dw.com/en/social-inequality-in-germany-is-on-the-rise/a-57509743.

19

Artificial Intelligence and Deepfakes in Strategic Deception Campaigns: The U.S. and Russian Experiences

Sergei A. Samoilenko and Inna Suvorova

Introduction

"Hated in the Nation," the final episode of the third season of the science fiction series *Black Mirror*, demonstrates how easy it is to manipulate public opinion by starting a mobbing hashtag campaign launched by a social bot. The premise of the show is that each day, the person who had been the subject of the most "#DeathTo" tweets on that day was killed by mechanical robot bees, which used facial recognition to identify and monitor their targets. These micro-drones were also apparently used for government surveillance. Once the perpetrator of the attacks got hold of the entire mobile identity list of those people who had participated in the shaming campaign, they all became targets of the killer bees (Collin, 2016).

Communication campaigns usingv artificial intelligence (AI) are rapidly gaining notoriety for their use of manipulated videos involving humans. Strategic deception campaigns are detrimental to society when they promote fake political statements made by imposters or disseminate revenge porn that targets investigative journalists. AI-manipulated deception contributes to public distrust in visual information and creates new reputational risks for political and public institutions (Cheatham et al., 2019).

S. A. Samoilenko (✉)
Department of Communication, George Mason University, Fairfax, VA, USA

I. Suvorova
University College London, London, UK

Social networking sites are often described as the main channels for spreading misinformation (Chiluwa & Samoilenko, 2019). Unlike traditional media, which check the authorship and origin of content, social media algorithms benefit from spreading provocative viral content. This is illustrated by the case of the Facebook Papers, which were leaked by whistleblower and former employee Frances Haugen. Haugen testified before Congress about a range of troubling issues and policies at the social media giant that collectively prioritized profit over public safety (Danner, 2021). The popularity of manipulative online content is associated with the effects of new communication practices, the mediatization of society, and declining trust in traditional institutions (Samoilenko, 2020). Due to the anonymity offered by the Internet and its polarizing power, new media environments have been charged with fomenting audience segmentation and widening ideological cleavages on several social issues (Bonfadelli, 2002; Lee, 2009; Reynard, 2019).

The rapid development of information technologies has created new possibilities for the malicious use of artificial intelligence (MUAI) as part of information and psychological warfare campaigns. It facilitates massive, rapid, disruptive, and subversive campaigns designed to have serious cognitive and emotional impacts on international audiences. In addition, MUAI campaigns present multiple threats to organizational safety and national security (Pashentsev, 2021; Pashentsev & Bazarkina, 2022). In particular, AI enables the mass creation of fake videos used in disinformation campaigns. Most manipulated imagery and video on the Internet come from traditional manual alteration and selective editing (Leetaru, 2019). These so-called *shallowfakes* are usually created by amateurs using basic consumer-level video editing software.

Deepfake technology is especially virulent when it comes to persuading mass audiences. The term refers to "synthesized media that are photos, videos or audio files manipulated by artificial intelligence (AI) in such a way that the fake is hard to detect" (Burt & Horvitz, 2020). In recent years, deepfakes have been weaponized as a tool of strategic deception in political power contests, character assassination, efforts to fight the opposition, and information warfare.

This chapter seeks to contribute to the growing body of literature investigating the perils of strategic deception campaigns using MUAI. Specifically, it discusses the application of deepfake technology in the United States and Russia in political contests and information warfare operations. The chapter concludes by reflecting on the effects of MUAI on society, new detection approaches, and potential measures against online deception.

AI-Related Privacy and Security Issues

The Internet of Things, smart homes, and face recognition technology have become the trademarks of our time. The benefits of smart city technology are contingent on *big data*, or the constant flow of large volumes of data that are captured and collected by sensors and cameras. Streaming media, smartphones, and other tracking devices collect data that can later be mined by businesses to determine our whereabouts or learn how we spent our money. AI relies on big data to improve its decision-making capabilities. By bringing together big data and AI technology, corporations can personalize and optimize the performance of their digital marketing campaigns (Qlik, n.d.). The marriage of big data and AI can help society in many ways by adding value across industry segments ranging from robotics and engineering to health care. However, the utilization of big data raises concerns about individual privacy and organizational safety.

The intrusive convenience of smart technology constantly disrupts personal privacy and reduces the chances of anonymity. Communications service providers actively seek to monetize big data by developing new services or selling it to third parties. Most data are collected through "cookies," which allow Internet companies to engage in microtargeting and offer us products based on our previous online behavior and preferences. As noted by Lynch (2017), we are living in Jeromy Bentham's panopticon: our digital lives are fishbowls into which we have willingly jumped. Today, facial recognition technology can use data-mining algorithms and statistical re-identification techniques to identify an individual's name, location, and even the first five digits of his or her social security number based on facial characteristics publicly available on social networking sites.

Due to their continuous learning and transformation, AI systems often experience algorithmic bias, poor performance, or basic malfunction. According to Yampolskiy (2019), previous patterns of failure can be attributed to numerous causes, including a lack of security mechanisms that would prevent adversarial meddling, limited scope for language disambiguation, an inability to adapt to changes in the environment, and other issues. In addition, large datasets containing confidential information are vulnerable to data breach and theft (Ibrahim et al., 2020; Kumar Garg & Sharma, 2021).

The increase in volume and types of biometric data calls for strict governance related to privacy and data retention. International lawmakers are working to protect their citizens' privacy in the face of the misuse of personal data (Samoilenko & Shilina, 2022). For example, in 2016, the European Union (EU) introduced the General Data Protection Regulations (GDPR) to harmonize data privacy laws across the EU and increase EU citizens' awareness of how many decisions are made by machines (The European Union, 2016).

U.S. legislation, for example, is very lax when it comes to big data regulation and web privacy. Currently there are no legal rules that clearly outline how to deal with AI-created emergencies. Notably, wireless companies are legally free to disclose their customers' location when they use their smartphones to look up a given business on the Internet (Vallina-Rodriguez & Sundaresan, 2017). The Federal Trade Commission (2012) recommends that companies disclose to consumers that the facial data the company uses to provide a service might also be used to link them to information from third parties or publicly available sources. According to Byers (2014), "most mobile companies do have privacy policies, but they aren't often communicated to users in a concise or standardized manner" (p. 33). In addition, many companies refuse to adhere to such a code of conduct due to liability concerns.

In 2014, the Russian parliament adopted amendments to the Personal Data Law that require data operators that collect Russian citizens' personal data to store and process such data using databases located in Russia (Khayryuzov, 2021). Federal Law No. 123-FZ came into force on July 1, 2020, introducing a special legal framework for territories that provides that AI technologies may be developed and tested in Moscow and subsequently throughout Russia. The experimental regime will facilitate the development of smart living, smart mobility, and a smart economy in Russia's capital. The new legislation, however, struggles to address the following issues: how citizens' privacy will be ensured; where data related to digital identities will be stored and how it will be erased; and who will be liable in the event of a failure to depersonalize data (Botvinkina, 2020).

The above reference to the panopticon highlights the relevance of Foucault's "disciplinary society." Through location-based services on smartphones, individuals' movements can be tracked and monitored by the authorities. Indeed, U.S. intelligence chief James Clapper acknowledged in congressional testimony that agencies might use a new generation of smart household devices to increase their surveillance capabilities (Ackerman & Thielman, 2016). The Chinese authorities have added facial recognition to the country's monitoring system to track suspects and even predict crimes nationwide (Denyer, 2018). The "social credit" system uses large amounts of user-generated and biometric data to help the authorities reward good citizens and identify those who have proved to be unreliable and thus deserve public shaming (Botsman, 2017).

Importantly, Internet companies and intelligence agencies now have access to confidential and potentially compromising information that could be used as leverage for manipulating the decisions of future political leaders concerning foreign affairs and international trade. Scholars have also been discussing even more grim potential scenarios, including the use of AI for intentional manipulation/deception (Chessen, 2019) and the misapplication of militarized AI/autonomous weapons/killer robots (Krishnan, 2009). The above concerns call for a strong conceptual framework to make sense of manipulation and deception strategies that are enhanced by AI technology. Next, these applied strategies will be illustrated using recent political events that involve political actors and their proxies from Russia, the United States, and other countries.

The Use of Artificial Intelligence in Strategic Deception Campaigns

Defining Strategic Deception

Strategic deception has been essential for human survival for many centuries (Kraut, 1980). Deceptive communication is a broad category that includes various forms of indirect speech, strategic ambiguity, equivocal communication, and other forms of non-direct communication (Samoilenko, 2018b). In the field of communication studies, *deception* refers to deliberate *manipulation* of verbal and/or nonverbal messages, behavior, or image to lead a target person to a false belief or conclusion without providing a proper warning of deceptive intent (Dunbar, 2009).

Manipulation is generally understood as the unscrupulous use of underhanded strategies and tactics for gaining control. Social group interaction involves the use of both persuasive and manipulative strategies to gain influence over a person or a situation (Gass & Seiter, 2018). Manipulative communication aims to convince the target to make decisions that benefit the manipulator (Guth & Marsh, 2011). Manipulative strategies traditionally involve various forms of deception, ranging from misrepresentation of information by leaving out true information (concealment) to presenting false information as if it were true (falsification) (Ekman, 2009).

What makes some deception campaigns *strategic* is their understanding of what people really "think and want" (Botan, 2018). Typically, the term "strategic deception" refers to the application of deceptive stratagems by pragmatic actors intended to create a believable communication performance within a particular social (media) system. This may involve a set of tricks or a convoluted plan to gain an advantage over opponents. The choice of tactics depends on multiple factors, including time available to plan, chances to escape possible detection, consequences if detected, and other scenarios (Hopper & Bell, 1984). Thus, constructing a deceptive message requires a careful examination of the situation, the personal attributes of the target, and the relational closeness between the target and the deceiver. *Trolling* and *pranking* are two manipulative practices widely used in strategic deception campaigns.

Trolling and Pranking

Online *trolling* is a notorious disruptive strategy (Buckels et al., 2014; March & Steele, 2020). It involves the posting of provocative content, often including deliberately misleading and pointless comments, with the intent of provoking other users to get involved in a meaningless debate or quarrel (Klyueva, 2013). Trolls amplify spurious deceptive content, as their activity artificially inflates support for a public figure or an issue (Klyueva, 2019). Trolls are often paid by political parties and companies to manipulate online interactions for political or commercial purposes (Mayzlin et al., 2014).

Trolling centered on satire and mockery is a popular subversive tool of activists who seek to challenge governments and corporations (Boyd, 2012; Caron, 2016; Samoilenko, 2018a). A good example of ridicule is the video of Joe Biden's gaffe during a town hall meeting in October 2021. Journalists described Biden's body language as suggesting that he was daydreaming about "riding a pony at a country fair" (Skynews, 2021). The video subsequently became a meme when someone photoshopped Biden onto a pony.

In post-truth politics, many strategies and tactics employed by activists have been reappropriated by authoritarian governments for psychological warfare (Asmolov, 2018). The strategic use of hoax and ridicule produces a compare-and-contrast effect, making foreign political actors appear incompetent, odd, and clueless in comparison to national state actors and diplomats, who are perceived as more serious and legitimate by domestic audiences (Sukhodolov et al., 2018). For instance, during the Ukrainian political crisis of 2014–2015, the Russian state-owned media repeatedly portrayed Jennifer Psaki, spokesperson for the U.S. Department of State, as an ignorant American. The politics of ridicule also involved viral flash mobs and Internet folk art using Psaki's name as shorthand for a rating of stupidity (Cottiero et al., 2015).

Pranking represents a powerful tool of subversive humor. Pranks are practical jokes played on a target to ridicule that individual, causing them to experience embarrassment and discomfort. Pranks can be used to set the media agenda, influence the public perception of events, and highlight certain issues as key topics of public debate (Harold, 2004). Pranking appeals to young audiences, which prefer soft news formats for learning about international and domestic affairs. For example, the YouTube channel Trollstation collaborates with numerous British pranksters who perform social experiments, including pranks on police officers and government employees (The Guardian, 2016).

Political pranking seeks to reframe critical narratives of international actors or media by making foreign policy issues appear trivial and nonsensical to domestic and foreign audiences. Political pranksters often play the role of state proxies by pranking high-level officials and celebrities, "particularly those who are supportive of an agenda that is not in line with their governments" (Wootson Jr., 2017). State-affiliated pranksters look for opportunities to reinforce the strategic narratives of their governments by discrediting Western policymakers.

In 2020, Russian pranksters Kuznetsov and Stolyarov—better known as Vovan and Lexus—impersonated climate change activist Greta Thunberg and her father, Svante, in a call with California congresswoman Maxine Waters. In the 10-minute phone call, which was posted on the pranksters' YouTube channel, the senior Democrat praised Thunberg for creating "quite a big, big, big, big thunder on this issue." The impersonators told Waters the pair were in North Carolina to discuss a threatened island called "Chongo-Chango" and promised to tell her something "confidential" about the famous moment when Thunberg crossed paths with Donald Trump at the United Nations climate summit in New York in September 2019.

These Russian hoaxers have a history of fooling Western politicians, including Turkish President Recep Tayyip Erdogan, the Croatian prime minister, NATO Secretary General Jens Stoltenberg, and other high-ranking figures (Walker, 2016). According to Chernobrov (2021), political pranking supports Russia's strategic narrative that the Western sanctions against Russia are based on distorted realities and ignorance of the world. The recorded phone calls with international politicians also expose the hypocrisy of Western policymakers by pointing out "inconsistencies between official and private statements" (p. 14). The idea is to make a strong argument to the rest of the world that Western leaders are oblivious and can easily be fooled (Bellware, 2020). The transcripts of phone pranks are often published in the Russian media and the highlights of these conversations are discussed during primetime political TV shows. As demonstrated above, trolling and pranking strategies and tactics are a perfect fit for strategic deception campaigns based on visual manipulation and computational propaganda.

Visual Manipulation and Computational Propaganda

Strategic deception campaigns, which involve various forms of disinformation, are popular tools in psychological warfare (O'Leary, 2006). Governments and corporations have successfully adopted many wartime stratagems for contemporary propaganda operations, spin, and information control (Jansen, 2017). Today, the manipulation of online opinions is frequently associated with political and corporate spin and measures to neutralize and silence dissent or alternative views (Sindelar, 2014). Political campaigners maintain false accounts created to project the illusion of popularity or public support (Kte'pi, 2014). Fake websites range from promoting products to discrediting competitors (Miller & Dinan, 2007). Studies show that both fake grassroots campaigns (or astroturfing) and bots have been used by governments, businesses, and lobbying groups (Bailey & Samoilenko, 2018). Falsehoods and fabricated stories lead to public confusion and political polarization, as well as contributing to distrust in traditional institutions (Gupta et al., 2013).

There is a growing trend toward MUAI campaigns that set the agenda in national and global contexts (Pashentsev, 2021). According to Chessen (2019), emerging AI tools provide propagandists with enhanced capabilities to manipulate human minds via *computational propaganda*. Machine analysis of human psychographic profiles allows AI systems to tailor disruptive, persuasive, and intimidating messaging more precisely. Through computational propaganda (botnets, seeding, etc.), persuasive content is amplified across multiple websites for better organic placement in newsfeeds. Analyzing the 2016 U.S. presidential election, Wanless and Berk (2020) describe seven steps taken by Trump supporters to engage a target audience online and draw them into active dissemination of persuasive messaging. These steps included sharing provocative content (fake news, memes, and data leaks), feeding such content into an echo chamber, reposting this content, encouraging followers to do the same, and connecting with media and larger organizations supportive of Trump.

Visual manipulation adds a powerful spin to the message, especially when it comes to persuading audiences about complex social and political issues (Powell et al., 2015). In today's media environments, it is common for falsehoods, rumors, and conspiracy theories to be spread via memes, graphics, or video materials (Chiluwa & Samoilenko, 2019; Marwick & Lewis, 2017). Generative adversarial networks' (GANs) algorithmic architectures generate new, synthetic instances of data, including fake photos, which can pass for real data. The use of AI-generated photos has grown tremendously; they now appear in product reviews, on fake social media accounts, and even on fake personal profiles. Photo editing has improved because of new AI applications to the point that new neural Photoshop filters enable users to change age, gaze direction, and facial expression in a few clicks.

One example is PeaceData.net, a nonprofit fake news organization. Its website featured nonexistent editorial staff whose photos were GAN-generated. The project had social media accounts and interacted extensively with its followers and contributors. The nonprofit's management hired novice journalists and freelance writers "passionate about uncovering the truth about armed conflicts, corruption, [and] human rights violations." Their stories were intended to criticize Biden from the left and to steer potential voters away from his campaign. In 2020, an FBI investigation revealed that PeaceData.net was linked to the Internet Research Agency (IRA). This entity, also known as a "troll factory," is associated with Yevgeny Prigozhin, a businessperson with close ties to the Russian government (Frenkel & Barnes, 2020).

Another IRA project created multiple Facebook groups to influence attitudes in support of Russia's activities in Sudan (Harding, 2020; Grossman et al., 2019). In May 2021, Facebook indicated that the network—which was comprised of 30 pages, six groups, 83 accounts, and 49 Instagram accounts, with a combined total of 440,000 followers—had been removed from its platforms. These entities, which posed as local organizations, had been sharing political news in Arabic with Sudanese followers. Appearing to be local helped them create the illusion of community and spread information to numerous other online communities. These Facebook groups either contained GAN-generated images or edited images to avoid reverse search. Fake profiles ensured that targeted posts received a considerable number of likes and comments.

Lately, AI-generated media with doppelgängers are becoming pervasive. Next, this chapter will discuss the three types of deepfakes, categorized on the basis of their ethics, legality, and manufacturing complexity.

The Strategic Applications of Deepfakes

Deepfake Classification

White Area. This category includes situations where all parties involved know the source of the deepfake. For example, a movie producer has legal rights to use the images of people who voluntarily consent to the use of their visual identities. Deepfakes are becoming popular among film studios. The television series *The Mandalorian* employed various methods to de-age Luke Skywalker; deepfake technology made it possible to superimpose the face of young Mark Hamill on the face of the actor Max Lloyd-Jones. The use of de-aging special effects is not new in video production, but deepfake technology has made such special effects more cost-effective (Hunt, 2021). Some producers also use neural networks to improve the quality of old cartoons and videos (Kuzmin, 2021).

It is now possible to create live-action images of stars that are entirely generated by a computer, obviating the need for their physical participation. In effect, famous actors and celebrities can license their faces. Hollywood actor Bruce Willis agreed to feature in the new advertising campaign of leading Russian mobile phone company Megafon. The actor was not required to show up for filming; instead, the producers extracted Willis' image from the *Die Hard* movies and used face generation software to apply a recreation of his face to another actor (Humpfries, 2021).

Deepfake technology based on neural network algorithms also allows movie producers to hire amateurs and less expensive actors for leading roles. Importantly, age and language proficiency skills are becoming irrelevant. As mentioned above, actors do not actually have to be involved in any filming. In the film *Welcome to Chechnya* (Henty et al., 2020), European activists permitted movie producers to use their images to stand in for the profiled refugees as a way to protect the latter, who had fled Chechnya to avoid being prosecuted for their sexual orientation.

Gray Area. This category includes situations where motion picture producers are transparent about their plans to use deepfake technology in video production but fail to provide consent release forms to people whose images they use. One instance of this occurred when a digitally created doppelgänger of Queen Elizabeth II delivered a traditional Christmas message on the United Kingdom's Channel 4 in December 2020 (BBC, 2020).

Posthumous deepfakes are controversial. There is no procedure for obtaining consent from a person who has already died. For the media campaign #stillspeakingup, the media agency Publicis conducted the deepfake resurrection of murdered Mexican journalist Javier Valdez in order to spotlight the tragic events surrounding the murders of journalists (Creativepool, 2021). In the United States, the Unfinished voting campaign (Lightfarm Studios, 2021) used AI-generated video of the teenager Joaquin Oliver, who was killed in a school shooting, to call for participation in elections.

The use of deepfakes in political campaigns also defies easy classification as either white or black. A deepfake of presidential candidate Manoj Tiwari went viral on WhatsApp ahead of legislative assembly elections in Delhi

(Christopher, 2020). The candidate had partnered with political advertising agency The Ideaz Factory to create deepfakes that would target voters in the over 20 different languages used in India. The deepfake reached approximately 15 million people in 5800 WhatsApp groups.

Black Area. Deepfake videos that fall into the black area are non-consensual. These videos are made with the goal of disruption, disinformation, or character assassination. A Tom Cruise doppelgänger video demonstrates the destructive potential of using deepfakes to discredit public figures. This deepfake video appeared authentic and was widely perceived as credible and trustworthy by users. For example, another celebrity, Justin Bieber, was seemingly fooled by the deepfake account and complimented Cruise's guitar-playing skills (Moore, 2021).

Deepfake pornography, meanwhile, can be made in one click using an app like Y (Hao, 2021). In January 2018, *Vice* published an article entitled "We Are Truly Fucked: Everyone Is Making AI-Generated Fake Porn Now" (Cole, 2018). According to a 2019 report by Sensity, deepfake pornography accounts for 96% of total deepfakes. Pornographic imagery results in serious consequences for the women and girls targeted by such activity (Hao, 2021). Unlike most pornographic content, deepfake videos tend to use women's images without their consent (Öhman, 2020; Popova, 2020). New DeepFaceLive software allows actors with malicious intent not only to turn photos and audio recordings into deepfakes, but also to manipulate facial images in real time.

Using Deepfakes for Character Assassination

AI can be used for character assassination in many different ways. The use of compromising videos to destroy reputations has a long history (Shiraev et al., 2022). Like traditional compromising videos, shallowfakes and deepfakes exploit the topics of sex (cheating), drug use, inappropriate behavior, and age-related incompetency.

A popular way of using deepfake technology is character assassination through ridicule, defined as "a purposeful and contemptuous exaggeration or distortion in a comical context" (Samoilenko, 2016). What makes the use of deepfake videos in smear campaigns especially dangerous is that any person with basic computer skills and average technical knowledge can easily create a viral comic video. Face-swapping mobile applications like Wombo and Reface allow a user to make a deepfake video in a few taps. An average user might take a photo of a public person and use it to make him/her sing a song charged with allusive meaning. When the bricolage video captures the zeitgeist, it can quickly go viral.

In September 2021, Russian opposition activists put into circulation short GIFs and videos in response to the allegedly rigged results of the State Duma elections. The creators used old footage from the documentary *Putin's Witnesses* (2018), about the 2000 presidential election. They altered the episode in which the new Russian president and his supporters celebrate their victory. In the new video, President Putin and his ally, former Russian president Dmitry Medvedev, sing the song "Everything is gonna be all right." This allusion carries various additional connotations, including the celebration of usurped and irreplaceable power following the rigged election.

In 2019 and 2020, distorted videos containing quotes taken out of context targeted U.S. House Speaker Nancy Pelosi (Denham, 2020; Harwell, 2019). In May 2019, then-U.S. President Donald Trump tweeted a fake video that spliced together several verbal stumbles by Pelosi amid his feud with the Speaker of the House (Wagner, 2019). In the video, Pelosi's normal pauses and stutters were edited together to make her appear drunk as she was shown stumbling over words like "custody" and "border." In one section, the video repeats three extra times a moment when Pelosi says the words "there are three things," an allusion to negative ageist stereotypes. The doctored videos targeting Pelosi sparked debate over the role of media corporations in scrutinizing social media for misinformation.

Deepfake pornography has become a new tool for silencing journalists and civic activists, resulting in their cyberbullying and public shaming. In 2018, award-winning journalist Rana Ayyub became the target of a character assassination campaign after she spoke to the BBC and Al Jazeera about how India was bringing shame on itself by protecting child sex abusers. Her personal details were made public and a fake pornographic video showing a naked woman whose face was replaced with Ayyub's headshot was released on WhatsApp. This deepfake video resulted in a lynch mob against her (Ayyub, 2018).

Character assassination by means of practical jokes is becoming more frequent. In April 2021, EU parliamentarians from the United Kingdom and the Baltic states arranged video calls with a hoaxer claiming to be Leonid Volkov, chief of staff for the imprisoned Russian opposition politician Alexei Navalny (Vincent, 2021). On April 21, 2021, Latvian television network LTV TV claimed that Leonid Volkov had confessed that the popular Russian YouTuber Yuri Dud had agreed to become Navalny's campaign manager. A few hours later, LTV TV retracted this statement on Twitter. The following day, Rihards Kols, a Member of the Thirteenth Saeima of Latvia, admitted that he had also had a conversation with pseudo-Volkov, who had contacted him from an email address that appeared to be credible (Meduza, 2021).

The situation ignited rumors that the pranksters had used deepfake technology to impersonate Leonid Volkov. Various factors played into the hands of the pranksters: the inability to meet in person in the COVID-19 era, the lack of clarity created by poor image quality during calls, the fact that the aforementioned parliamentarians had never previously met—online or offline—with the real Leonid Volkov, and insufficient efforts to determine who wrote the email. It is hard to tell how many calls impersonating Volkov the Russian pranksters Vovan and Lexus made in March–April 2021 before their activity was exposed: as of January 2022, there were at least nine videos featuring pseudo-Volkov on their channel. The pranks have made Volkov a toxic persona in European politics. His attempts to contact European politicians are now regarded with suspicion, as the latter fear ridicule if it turns out that they are part of a hoax.

Using Deepfakes for Denial and Image Repair

Deepfake technology has a profound effect on public trust in online media, as it undermines faith in the authenticity of video information (Vaccari & Chadwick, 2020). Deepfakes appear intimidating to ordinary citizens for two main reasons. First, there is little public awareness of how they work. Also, no reliable tools for deepfake detection are available to average users (Masood et al., 2021). Hence, a reference to deepfake technology can be used to cast doubt on the veracity of video materials, making it possible to reject what would otherwise be irrefutable evidence of an event. In June 2020, for example, Winnie Heartstrong, a Republican candidate running for the U.S. Congress, claimed that the video of George Floyd's murder was a hoax (Spocchia, 2020).

In some situations, fear of deepfakes and their potential impact on reputation if someone is hoaxed by a deepfake make it impossible for the public to distinguish reality from fiction. Inference-observation confusion occurs when people fail to distinguish what they have observed firsthand from what they have merely assumed (Lahman, 2014). Deepfakes thus provide a perfect opportunity to justify or deny an asserted reality and jump to unwarranted conclusions without having all the facts.

In October 2021, former Georgian president Mikheil Saakashvili, who was facing several criminal charges, released a live video allegedly from the Georgian coastal city of Batumi. In the video, Saakashvili urged the public not to vote for the Georgian Dream (GD) ruling party. Georgian officials claimed that the video evidence of the ex-president's presence in Georgia was in fact a deepfake (Lomsadze, 2021). However, Saakashvili was subsequently arrested after illegally crossing the Georgian border.

A reference to deepfakes can be used as an *image repair* strategy to claim a lack of knowledge of or control over manipulation (Benoit, 1995). As research shows, excuses citing causes that are unintentional, uncontrollable, and external are more effective in achieving forgiveness than excuses that cite causes that are intentional, controllable, and internal (Weiner et al., 1987). Specifically, the presence of deepfake technology and one's gullibility in the face of such manipulation can be used to evade responsibility in the aftermath of unfortunate events.

In April 2021, after the aforementioned European parliamentarians participated in video calls with a hoaxer pretending to be the opposition politician Leonid Volkov, they claimed to have fallen victim to a sophisticated deepfake. Yet the notorious Russian pranksters Vovan and Lexus, who staged the video interviews, told *The Verge* that their imitation of Volkov was created "using effects no more sophisticated than makeup and artfully obscure camera angles" (Vincent, 2021).

As demonstrated in the aforementioned cases, even a reference to deepfakes can prompt denial and inference-observation confusion, thereby affecting public trust in online video materials. Moreover, there are no reliable ways to detect deepfakes and other types of AI-manipulated media.

Issues with Deepfake Detection

The trained human eye can often detect a distorted image without special software. Open-source images usually include blemishes and distortions such as a blurred background, failures in hair structure, different eye color, or even extra body parts. However, not all AI-generated photos have visible flaws.

Deepfake videos are difficult to detect. Poor image or video quality can often interfere with detection (European Parliament, 2021). Normally, Internet users do not scrutinize account avatars to find distinctive flaws. Nor do they use detection software to verify photos or videos. The technical limitations of detection services create additional obstacles: they cannot accept long and large videos.

There are a few detection services that can identify suspicious videos or doctored images. Some detection tools are free, among them www.deepware.ai. Others are costlier: Sensity currently retails at US$140/month. The various software packages use different algorithms and approaches (heartbeats, phoneme-viseme mismatches, biological signals, and cornea reflections, among others) and sometimes even a combination of these. However, tools' use of multiple measurement methods has the potential to be confusing to average users. DeepFake-o-meter, for instance, represents results either in the form of a diagram or in a percentage likelihood that a given video is a deepfake, but it is not clear what counts as a deepfake: 50% probability? 98%?

Ultimately, none of these services are completely reliable. The website Sensity.ai, which specializes in identity verification, reliably identifies as fake the images generated by AI generators based on open-source datasets (e.g., https://thispersondoesnotexist.com/); however, it fails to recognize images generated by the paid service https://generated.photos/, which uses its own repository of images. The trustworthiness of detection is also questionable. When a video is of poor quality, it renders detection results completely unreliable. Even if the person in a video says something extremely out of character, there are ways to coerce people into saying something on camera without any deepfake needing to be involved (Robinson, 2018).

An example of failed detection is the deepfake video featuring Russian entrepreneur and businessman Oleg Tinkov. In a fake video posted on the fake Tinkoff Bonus website, he promised to increase by 50% whatever amount a customer deposited in a newly opened investment account. A fake registration link was attached to the video. However, the fake did not sound like Oleg Tinkov's voice and was poorly edited (DFC, 2021). More importantly, the offer in the advertisement was too generous to be true and Tinkov's press office published a refutation.

Another detection approach is the blockchain-like technology of tracking video history and provenance. This is not restricted to deepfake detection, but can also help identify shallowfakes and other types of visual distortion. Every single change to the video from the moment of its creation is recorded, making it possible to determine its origin and track manipulations.

In February 2021, Microsoft, Adobe, Arm, BBC, Intel, and Truepic established the Coalition for Content Provenance and Authenticity (C2PA), which aims to create an infrastructure that will track the provenance of content and assess its authenticity. However, there are still some unresolved issues related to the anonymity and financial support of this project, which requires a reliable infrastructure.

Conclusion and Future Research

The strategic use of AI for disinformation and subversion is a serious national security problem for states around the globe. This includes Russia and the United States, two countries with highly advanced IT systems and loose legal regulations for big data and AI. The safety and security of individuals and organizations are critical in the context of the COVID-19 pandemic, which has caused both political negotiations and business transactions to take place online.

The above further discussion of the psychological and political effects of MUAI campaigns using deepfake technology makes a strong case for governments to take action to develop legal frameworks that would allow them to adapt to the rapidly changing AI marketplace. Currently, despite some preventive efforts by governments like the Russian one, the adoption of complex international legal norms to mitigate the agenda-setting threat posed by MUAI is unlikely in the near future (Pashentsev, 2021). Armesto-Larson (2020) highlights that non-consensual pornography, for instance, has an exterritorial character; thus, even initiatives such as the ENOUGH Act, a bill introduced to the U.S. Congress in 2017 that intended to criminalize knowingly distributing an intimate visual depiction of an individual, do not provide sufficient legal protection for individuals.

In addition, the technology sector must develop policies to ensure individual privacy and organizational safety during the everyday use of AI-enhanced machinery and appliances. To minimize potential risks related to data misuse or privacy violation, a good data governance program must meet certain privacy, security, legal, and financial requirements. Such a program needs to ensure that data and content are managed properly and to create a reference architecture supported by emerging technologies. In addition, it is also critical to monitor the life cycle of information, from creation through disposal, including compliance with legal, regulatory, and privacy requirements (Mohanty et al., 2013).

Organizations need to establish appropriate policies to prevent the misuse of big data and assess the reputational and legal risks involved in handling various datasets. For example, a big data governance policy might state that an organization will not integrate a customer's Facebook profile into his or her master data record without that customer's informed consent. In addition, Internet companies must introduce a new MUAI-detection and MUAI-filtering tool to prevent attacks by social bots and other attempts at computational propaganda from adversarial networks.

COVID-19 is accelerating the transition to a global society based on the massive use of AI in many fields, including health care. AI offers new opportunities for international cooperation and e-diplomacy. At the same time, it creates new challenges to technological sovereignty and increased opportunities for external intervention in the affairs of other countries for the purposes of manipulating public opinion. States and their leaders look for new approaches to dealing with transnational corporations that have advanced data science solutions (Roumate, 2021). This explains international struggles over international sovereignty and economic independence. The international community needs new ethical frameworks to address threats to human rights in an age of MUAI and enhance international collaboration based on trust to combat the coronavirus pandemic.

Academic engagement is especially critical in the areas of detecting and countering adversarial effects. As suggested by Chessen (2019), a university consortium on the effects of and responses to computational propaganda is highly advisable. In particular, it should develop practices for tracking the application of MUAI and managing the cognitive security threats posed by synthesized media, including deepfakes. The Computer Emergency Readiness Team (CERT) model, developed at Carnegie Mellon University and deployed globally to track and respond to cybersecurity threats, could be used as a reference framework for future academic endeavors.

The theoretical framework of strategic deception provides many opportunities for new academic research concerning MUAI in information and psychological warfare. Future research should address new approaches to fact-checking and critical thinking methodologies similar to the one outlined by Cook et al. (2018) to assess the validity of online misinformation. In addition, new critical logic frameworks provide media consumers with a set of critical questions, which enable them to evaluate new visual sources and enhance their self-efficacy when facing new misinformation. One important strength of this approach is that it extends beyond the typical skills taught as part of media literacy, such as assessing the credibility of a source.

References

Ackerman, S., & Thielman, S. (2016, February 9). US intelligence chief: We might use the internet of things to spy on you. *The Guardian*. https://bit.ly/3Js9eiF

Armesto-Larson, B. (2020). Nonconsensual pornography: Criminal law solutions to a worldwide problem. *Oregon Review of International Law, 21*, 177–214.

Asmolov, G. (2018). The disconnective power of disinformation campaigns. *Journal of International Affairs, 71*(1.5), 69–76.

Ayyub, R. (2018, November 21). I was the victim of a deepfake porn plot intended to silence me. *The Huffington Post*. https://bit.ly/3uQ8DDy

Bailey, A., & Samoilenko, S. (2018). Astroturfing. In A. Ledeneva (Ed.), *The global encyclopaedia of informality*. UCL University Press.

BBC. (2020, December 23). *Deepfake queen to deliver Channel 4 Christmas message*. https://www.bbc.co.uk/news/technology-55424730

Bellware, K. (2020, January 4). Rep. Maxine Waters thought she was talking to Greta Thunberg. It was actually Russian trolls. *Washington Post.* https://wapo.st/3BibkyS

Benoit, W. L. (1995). *Accounts, excuses, and apologies: A theory of image restoration strategies.* State University of New York Press.

Bonfadelli, H. (2002). The Internet and knowledge gaps: A theoretical and empirical investigation. *European Journal of Communication, 17*(1), 65–84. https://doi.org/10.1177/0267323102017001607

Botan, C. (2018). *Strategic communication theory and practice: The cocreational model.* Wiley-Blackwell.

Botsman, R. (2017, October 21). Big data meets Big Brother as China moves to rate its citizens. *Wire.* https://bit.ly/3sHTtx9

Botvinkina, A. (2020, September 14). *A new experimental legal framework in Russia shows the perils of future AI regulation.* https://bit.ly/3HQ8oMi

Boyd, A. (Ed.). (2012). *Beautiful trouble: A toolbox for revolution.* OR Books.

Buckels, E. E., Trapnell, P. D., & Paulhus, D. L. (2014). Trolls just want to have some fun. *Personality and Individual Differences, 67,* 97–102.

Burt, T., & Horvitz, E. (2020, September 1). *New steps to combat disinformation.* Microsoft. https://bit.ly/3HO1ibe

Byers, A. (2014). W.H.'s privacy effort for apps is stuck in neutral. *Politico.* p. 33.

Caron, J. E. (2016). The quantum paradox of truthiness: Satire, activism, and the postmodern condition. *Studies in American Humor, 2*(2), 153–181.

Cheatham, B., Javanmardian, K., & Samandari, H. (2019, April). Confronting the risks of artificial intelligence. *McKinsey Quarterly.* https://bit.ly/3rNLyzj

Chernobrov, D. (2021). Strategic humour: Public diplomacy and comic framing of foreign policy issues. *The British Journal of Politics and International Relations.* https://doi.org/10.1177/13691481211023958

Chessen, M. (2019). The MADCOM future how artificial intelligence will enhance computational propaganda, reprogram human culture, and threaten democracy … and what can be done about it. In R. V. Yampolskiy (Ed.), *Artificial intelligence safety and security* (pp. 127–144). CRC Press.

Chiluwa, I. E., & Samoilenko, S. A. (2019). *Handbook of research on deception, fake new and misinformation online.* IGI Global.

Christopher, N. (2020, February 18). We've just seen the first use of deepfakes in an Indian election campaign. *Vice.* https://bit.ly/3GKHiVr

Cole, S. (2018, January 24). We are truly fucked: Everyone is making AI-generated fake porn now. *Vice.* https://bit.ly/3oNsOOv

Collin, R. (2016, October 21). Black Mirror, season 3, Hated in the Nation, review: 'An inspired, frost-fringed police procedural'. *The Telegraph.* https://bit.ly/34TdMQ7

Cook, J., Ellerton, P., & Kinkead, D. (2018). Deconstructing climate misinformation to identify reasoning errors. *Environmental Research Letters, 13*(2). https://doi.org/10.1088/1748-9326/aaa49f

Cottiero, C., Kucharski, K., Olimpieva, E., & Orttung, R. (2015). War of words: The impact of Russian state television on the Russian Internet. *Nationalities Papers, 43*(4), 533–555. https://doi.org/10.1080/00905992.2015.1013527

Creativepool. (2021, February 15). *Journalists from Mexico are still speaking up.* https://bit.ly/34QVFua

Danner, C. (2021, October 2). What is being leaked in the Facebook papers. A guide to the biggest revelations. *New York Magazine.* https://nym.ag/3Bkj2s5

Denham, H. (2020, August 3). Another fake video of Pelosi goes viral on Facebook. *The Washington Post.* https://wapo.st/3HO1tDq

Denyer, S. (2018, January 7). China's watchful eye. *The Washington Post.* https://wapo.st/3uNrUW1

DFC. (2021, November 15). *Tinkov's doppelganger invites to a fake site.* Deepfake Challenge Association. https://deepfakechallenge.com/gb/2021/09/16/11906/

Dunbar, N. E. (2009). Deception detection. In S. W. Littlejohn & K. A. Foss (Eds.), *Encyclopedia of communication theory* (pp. 291–292). Sage.

Ekman, P. (2009). *Telling lies. Clues to deceit in the marketplace, politics, and marriage.* W. W. Norton and Company.

European Parliament. (2021, July). *Tackling deepfakes in European policy* (Study PE 690.039). https://bit.ly/3HUata0

Federal Trade Commission. (2012, March). *Protecting consumer privacy in an era of rapid change: Recommendations for businesses and policymakers* (FTC Report). https://bit.ly/3HPJxs5

Frenkel, S., & Barnes, J. E. (2020, September 1). Russians again targeting Americans with disinformation, Facebook and Twitter say. *PBS.* https://to.pbs.org/3HPghBL

Gass, R. H., & Seiter, J. S. (2018). *Persuasion: Social influence and compliance gaining.* Routledge.

Grossman, S., Bush, D., & DiResta, R. (2019, October 29). *Evidence of Russia-linked influence. Operations in Africa.* Stanford Internet Observatory. https://stanford.io/3Js9G0l

Gupta, A., Lamba, H., Kumaraguru, P., & Joshi, A. (2013, May). Faking Sandy: Characterizing and identifying fake images on Twitter during hurricane sandy. In *Proceedings of the 22nd international conference on World Wide Web* (pp. 729–736). ACM.

Guth, D. W., & Marsh, C. (2011). *Public relations: A value driven approach.* Pearson.

Hao, K. (2021, September 13). A horrifying new AI app swaps women into porn videos with a click. *MIT Technology Review.* https://bit.ly/3v4wfV9

Harding, L. (2020, November 27). Revealed: UN Sudan expert's links to Russian oligarch Prigozhin. *The Guardian.* https://bit.ly/3rPRtnD

Harold, C. (2004). Pranking rhetoric: 'Culture jamming' as media activism. *Critical Studies in Media Communication, 21*(3), 189–211. https://doi.org/10.1080/0739318042000212693

Harwell, D. (2019, May 29). Faked Pelosi videos, slowed to make her appear drunk, spread across social media. *The Washington Post.* https://wapo.st/3LAqlRm

Henty, A., Tomchin, J. A., Kurov, A., & France, D. (Producers), & France, D. (Director). (2020). *Welcome to Chechnya* [Online Video]. Public Square Films production. https://bit.ly/3HRkW5Y

Hopper, R., & Bell, R. (1984). Broadening the deception construct. *Quarterly Journal of Speech, 70*(3), 288–302.

Humpfries, M. (2021, August 23). Bruce Willis deepfake to star in Russian TV ads. *PC Magazine*. https://www.pcmag.com/news/bruce-willis-deepfake-to-star-in-russian-tv-ads

Hunt, J. (2021, April 25). *Mandalorian's Luke Skywalker without CGI: Mark Hamill, deep fake & deaging*. https://bit.ly/3szGn5c

Ibrahim, A., Thiruvady, D., Schneider, J.-G., & Abdelrazek, M. (2020, August 28). The challenges of leveraging threat intelligence to stop data breaches. *Frontiers in Computer Science*. https://doi.org/10.3389/fcomp.2020.00036

Jansen, S. C. (2017). *Stealth communications*. Polity Press.

Khayryuzov, V. (2021, November 05). The privacy, data protection and cybersecurity law review: Russia. *The Law Reviews*. https://bit.ly/3uLWTlm

Klyueva, A. (2013). Trolling. In R. Heath (Ed.), *Encyclopedia of public relations* (pp. 933–934). Sage Publications.

Klyueva, A. (2019). Trolls, bots, and whatnots: Deceptive content and challenges of online engagement. In I. Chiluwa & S. A. Samoilenko (Eds.), *Social media and the production and spread of spurious deceptive contents* (pp. 18–32). IGI Global. https://doi.org/10.4018/978-1-5225-8535-0.ch002

Kraut, R. (1980). Humans as lie detectors: Some second thoughts. *Journal of Communication, 30*, 209–216.

Krishnan, A. (2009). *Killer robots: Legality and ethicality of autonomous weapons*. Routledge.

Kte'pi, B. (2014). Deception in political social media. In K. Harvey (Ed.), *Encyclopedia of social media and politics* (pp. 356–358). Sage.

Kumar Garg, P., & Sharma, L. (2021). Artificial intelligence: Challenges and future applications. In L. Sharma & P. Kumar Garg (Eds.), *Artificial intelligence technologies, applications, and challenges* (pp. 229–245). CRC Press.

Kuzmin, E. (2021, January 21). Entuziasty s Yutyub pri pomoshchi neyrosetey uluchshayut kachestvo sovetskikh mul'tfil'mov. K kakim rezul'tatam eto privodit [YouTube enthusiasts use neural networks to improve the quality of Soviet cartoons. What are the results?]. *TJournal*. https://bit.ly/34SNL3q

Lahman, M. P. (2014). Awareness and action: A general semantics approach to effective language behavior, (Part 4)—Inference-observation confusion: Distinguishing between observation and inference. *A Review of General Semantics, 71*(1), 55–59.

Lee, J. K. (2009). *Incidental exposure to news: Limiting fragmentation in the new media environment*. University of Texas at Austin. https://bit.ly/3oNtjYT

Leetaru, K. (2019, August 26). The real danger today is shallow fakes and selective editing not deep fakes. *Forbes*. https://www.forbes.com/sites/

kalevleetaru/2019/08/26/the-real-danger-today-is-shallow-fakes-and-selective-editing-not-deep-fakes/?sh=547f8e664ea0

Lightfarm Studios. (2021). *Unfinished voices.* [Vimeo Video]. https://vimeo.com/465077929

Lomsadze, G. (2021, October 1). *Georgia's big little election.* https://eurasianet.org/georgias-big-little-election

Lynch, M. P. (2017, May 9). *The Internet of us: Knowing more and understanding less in the age of big data paperback.* Liveright.

March, E., & Steele, G. (2020). High esteem and hurting others online: Trait sadism moderates the relationship between self-esteem and Internet trolling. *Cyberpsychology, Behavior, and Social Networking, 23*(7), 441–446. https://doi.org/10.1089/cyber.2019.0652

Marwick, A., & Lewis, R. (2017). *Media manipulation and disinformation online.* Data and Society Research Institute. https://datasociety.net/output/media-manipulation-and-disinfo-online/

Masood, M., Nawaz, M., Malik, K. M., Javed, A., & Irtaza, A. (2021). *Deepfakes generation and detection: State-of-the-art, open challenges, countermeasures, and way forward.* https://arxiv.org/abs/2103.00484

Mayzlin, D., Dover, Y., & Chevalier, J. (2014). Promotional reviews: An empirical investigation of online review manipulation. *The American Economic Review, 104*(8), 2421–2455. https://doi.org/10.1257/aer.104.8.2421

Meduza. (2021, April 22). Hello, this is Leonid Volkov* Using deepfake video and posing as Navalny's right-hand man, Russian pranksters fool Latvian politicians and journalists into invitation and TV interview. *Meduza.* https://bit.ly/3gO0DL0

Miller, D., & Dinan, W. (2007). *Thinker, faker, spinner, spy. Corporate PR and the assault on democracy.* Pluto Press.

Mohanty, S., Jagadeesh, M., & Srivatsa, H. (2013). *Big data imperatives: Enterprise 'big data' warehouse, 'BI' implementations and analytics (the Expert's voice).* Apress.

Moore, S. (2021, October 8). Justin Bieber fooled into picking a fight with deepfake Tom Cruise. *Yahoo News.* https://yhoo.it/3GNUw3T

O'Leary, M. (2006). *The dictionary of homeland security and defence.* iUniverse.

Öhman, C. (2020). Introducing the pervert's dilemma: A contribution to the critique of deepfake pornography. *Ethics and Information Technology, 22*(2), 133–140.

Pashentsev, E., & Bazarkina, D. (2022). The malicious use of artificial intelligence against government and political institutions in the psychological area. In D. M. Bielicki (Ed.), *Regulating artificial intelligence in industry* (pp. 36–52). Routledge.

Pashentsev, E. (2021). The malicious use of artificial intelligence through agenda setting: Challenges to political stability. In *Proceedings of the 3rd European Conference on the Impact of Artificial Intelligence and Robotics (ECIAIR), Lisbon, Portugal* (pp. 138–144). Academic Conferences International Limited.

Popova, M. (2020). Reading out of context: pornographic deepfakes, celebrity and intimacy. *Porn Studies, 7*(4), 367–381. https://doi.org/10.1080/23268743.2019.1675090

Powell, T. E., Boomgaarden, H. G., De Swert, K., & de Vreese, C. H. (2015). A clearer picture: The contribution of visuals and text to framing effects. *Journal of Communication, 65*(6), 997–1017.

Reynard, L. J. (2019). Troll farm: Anonymity as a weapon for online character assassination. In I. E. Chiluwa & S. A. Samoilenko (Eds.), *Handbook of research on deception, fake news, and misinformation online* (pp. 392–419). IGI Global.

Robinson, O. (2018, November 15). In Chechnya, televised shamings to keep people in check. *BBC*. https://bbc.in/3HTqb5e

Roumate, F. (2021, March). Artificial intelligence, ethics and international human rights. *The International Review of Information Ethics, 29*. https://doi.org/10.29173/irie422

Samoilenko, S. A. (2016). Character assassination. In C. Carroll (Ed.), *The Sage encyclopedia of corporate reputation*. (Vol. 1, pp. 115–118). Thousand Oaks, CA: Sage.

Samoilenko, S. A. (2018a). Subversion practices: From coercion to attraction. In E. J. Bridgen, D. Verčič, & D. (Eds.), *Experiencing public relations: International voices* (pp. 174–193). Routledge.

Samoilenko, S. A. (2018b). Strategic deception in the age of 'truthiness'. In I. Chiluwa (Ed.), *Deception: Motivations, recognition techniques and behavioral control*. Nova Science Publishers.

Samoilenko, S. A. (2020). Character assassination in the context of mediated complexity. In K. Sriramesh & D. Verčič (Eds.), *The global public relations handbook: Theory, research, and practice* (3rd ed.). Routledge.

Samoilenko, S. A., & Shilina, M. (2022). Governance. In L. A. Schintler, C. L. McNeely, G. J. Golson, & J. (Eds.), *The Encyclopedia of Big Data*. Springer.

Sensity. (n.d.). https://bit.ly/3HOVf61

Shiraev, E., Keohane, J., Icks, M., & Samoilenko, S. A. (2022). *Character assassination and reputation management: Theory and applications*. Routledge.

Sindelar, D. (2014, August 14). The Kremlin's troll army. *The Atlantic*. https://bit.ly/3BnNhOT

Skynews. (2021, October 24). *'Daydreaming about riding a pony': Joe Biden's fists gaffe at CNN town hall*. https://bit.ly/3GMgV1h

Spocchia, G. (2020, June). Republican candidate shares conspiracy theory that George Floyd murder was faked. *Independent*. https://bit.ly/3uPlKob

Sukhodolov, A. P., Kudlik, E. S., & Antonova, A. B. (2018). Prank journalism as a new genre in Russian media landscape. *Theoretical and Practical Issues of Journalism, 7*(3), 361–370.

The European Union. (2016). *Regulations (EU) 2016/679 of the European Parliament and of the Council of 27 April 2016*. https://gdpr-info.eu/

The Guardian. (2016, May 16). *YouTube pranksters jailed after 'terrifying' fake art heist*. https://bit.ly/3Jp7HtJ

Vaccari, C., & Chadwick, A. (2020). Deepfakes and disinformation: Exploring the impact of synthetic political video on deception, uncertainty, and trust in news. *Social Media + Society*. https://doi.org/10.1177/2056305120903408

Vallina-Rodriguez, N., & Sundaresan, S. (2017, May 30). 7 in 10 smartphone apps share your data with third-party services. *The Conversation*. https://theconversation.com/7-in-10-smartphone-apps-share-your-data-with-third-partyservices-72404

Vincent, J. (2021, April 30). 'Deepfake' that supposedly fooled European politicians was just a look-alike, say pranksters. *The Verge*. https://bit.ly/34XC0Zp

Wagner, J. (2019, May 24). Trump shares heavily edited video that highlights verbal stumbles by Pelosi and questions her mental acuity. *The Washington Post*. https://wapo.st/3HPgODL

Walker, S. (2016, March 13). Kremlin calling? Meet the Russian pranksters who say 'Elton owes us.' *The Guardian*. https://bit.ly/3oPoBKi

Wanless, A., & Berk, M. (2020). The audience is the amplifier: Participatory propaganda. In P. Baines, N. O'Shaughnessy, & N. Snow (Eds.), *The SAGE handbook of propaganda* (pp. 85–104). SAGE Publications.

Weiner, B., Amirkhan, J., Folkes, V. S., & Verette, J. A. (1987). An attributional analysis of excuse giving: Studies of a naive theory of emotion. *Journal of Personality and Social Psychology, 52*(2), 316–324. https://doi.org/10.1037/0022-3514.52.2.316

Wootson Jr., C. R. (2017, July 26). It was a prank call. Listen to Russian pranksters trick Rick Perry into a conversation about pig manure. *The Washington Post*. https://wapo.st/3go6l5Y

Yampolskiy, R. V. (2019). Introduction to AI safety and security. In R. V. Yampolskiy (Ed.), *Artificial intelligence safety and security* (pp. xi–xxii). CRC Press.

20

Malicious Use of Artificial Intelligence and Threats to Psychological Security in Latin America: Common Problems, Current Practice and Prospects

Evgeny Pashentsev and Darya Bazarkina

Introduction

Latin American countries are experiencing difficulties from a stagnant economy, which has turned into a serious economic downturn due to the effects of the coronavirus pandemic, growing socio-political tensions and fierce geopolitical competition for resources and influence in the region. The use of advanced technologies by Latin American governments, businesses and public organizations can both facilitate solutions to these problems in Latin America and aggravate them. This is certainly the case for the use of artificial intelligence (AI), which is growing rapidly in Latin America.

According to the "Political Risk Latin America 2022" index from the Pontificia Universidad Católica de Chile Center for International Studies (CEIUC) (Sahd et al., 2022), political risk in the region will increase significantly in the short term. There is a global trend toward the erosion of democracy, and Latin America

E. Pashentsev (✉)
Diplomatic Academy of the Ministry of Foreign Affairs of the Russian Federation, Moscow, Russia
e-mail: icspsc@mail.ru

D. Bazarkina
Department of European Integration Research, Institute of Europe of the Russian Academy of Sciences, Moscow, Russia
e-mail: bazarkina-icspsc@yandex.ru

is no exception. During the coronavirus pandemic, many governments took advantage of quarantine restrictions to weaken the rule of law, civil liberties and institutional controls. According to CEIUC experts, a distinctive feature of this decline in democracy is that the threats are mainly from elected leaders undermining institutions and freedoms from within, resulting in anti-elite sentiments and the growth of populism (Sahd et al., 2022, pp. 7–8). In this context, CEIUC cites a new risk category for Latin America compared to the previous report—cybersecurity risks. Three factors—the erosion of democracy, the privatization of political campaigns (private companies providing politicians with a range of communication services, including bots and social media algorithms) and the increase in cybercrime—have created conditions for psychological operations using increasingly widespread and inexpensive AI technologies. In this chapter, we aim to demonstrate that the malicious use of artificial intelligence (MUAI) elevates threats to national and regional psychological security in Latin America to a qualitatively new level, seriously damaging the region's social, economic and political climate in the short term, necessitating adequate assessment and response. To achieve this, the three-level classification of MUAI threats in the field of psychological security proposed by Evgeny Pashentsev (see chapter "General Content and Possible Threat Classifications of the Malicious Use of Artificial Intelligence to Psychological Security" of this handbook), as well as a comparative and scenario analysis, was used. This chapter does not address the experience of Brazil, which is analyzed separately in Chap. 12 of this handbook on MUAI psychological security threats in the BRICS countries.

There are to date very few comprehensive studies on MUAI threats to psychological security in Latin America (see, e.g., Batista et al., 2020). Increasingly, however, researchers are focusing on individual manifestations of MUAI, such as the malicious use of political bots and social media algorithms, deepfakes, and a wide range of AI-enabled social media manipulation technologies (IntSights, 2019, Bradshaw, Bailey, & Howard, 2021a and b, Rodrigo López, 2022 etc.). Other important publications for this chapter were assessments of the level of AI development in Latin America and the problems associated with AI regulation (Ovanessoff & Plastino, 2017, Ovanessoff & Abbosh, 2017, Inter-American Development Bank XE "Inter-American Development Bank" , 2018, Werutsky et al., 2021, Yangüez Cervantes & Zapata-Jaramillo, 2021, de-Lima-Santos and Mesquita , 2021, etc.). To assess the political growth factors of MUAI in the field of psychological security, works that analyzed the economic and political rivalry between the United States and China, and the relations of those two countries with Latin American countries, were used (Taffet & Walcher, 2017, Livingstone, 2009, McPherson, 2016, Toma, 2018, Schechter et al., 2017, Grandin, 2019, Meyer, 2017, Gallagher, 2016, Lacalle Herrera, 2017, Johnson, 2018, Myers & Wise, 2016, Denoon, 2017,

Su, 2017, Fornes & Mendez, 2018, López et al., 2016, etc.). Specialized monographs and articles, as well as reports from international organizations and major think tanks (Bank of America and Merrill Lynch , 2015, Frey & Osborne, 2013 and Frey & Osborne, 2016, Manyika et al., 2017, Mishra et al., 2016, Pol & Reveley, 2017, UN Conference on Trade and Development, 2016, World Economic Forum XE "World Economic Forum, WEF" , 2016), helped clarify the transformation of the economy and the labor market. During the course of work on this chapter, expert assessments were obtained from specialist research trips by the International Center for Social and Political Studies and Consulting (ICSPSC) to Latin America. In particular, we used our personal impressions from our stay in Cuba and Mexico from the end of January to the beginning of March 2020 as context for our research on the topic of this chapter. The trip was organized and supported by the ICSPSC and the Russian–Latin American Strategic Studies Association (RLASSA) (, 2022), with the kind assistance of their partners in Latin America. This was not the first time ICSPSC and RLASSA researchers collaborated on academic projects in the region. A series of presentations on strategic communication and MUAI took place in Argentina, Uruguay and Brazil in the fall of 2018 (RLASSA, 2018), stimulating a strong incentive for mutual cooperation between Latin American and Russian researchers in this strategic field.

This goal has shaped the structure of the chapter, which begins by looking at the general level of AI development and adoption in Latin America. What follows are real MUAI cases and scenarios for its development across the three threat levels.

Artificial Intelligence Implementation in Latin America

Latin America has almost exhausted extensive growth. For example, during the region's growth spurt from 2001 to 2005, the group of five leading South American economies (the South America-5 is the unweighted average of Argentina, Brazil, Chile, Colombia and Peru) improved their average annual total factor productivity (TFP) by only 0.7 percent. Over the same period, Indonesia's TFP grew by 2.1 percent and South Korea's by 2.0 percent. During those good times, South American companies could ignore productivity shortcomings because their soaring revenues—especially from commodity exports and domestic consumption—ensured prosperity, even if their margins were squeezed (Ovanessoff & Plastino, 2017, p. 4). It is important to stress that these weak TFP results were the same under governments of very different political orientations. The populism of both the left and the right has been equally exhausted, with governments across the political spectrum failing to reflect on the requirements for twenty-first-century development.

There is an urgent need for systematic AI development and implementation, in order to see its real impact on the next generation of industrial systems, namely Industry 4.0 (DQIndia Online, 2020). Latin America cannot be left outside of this global process. The severe economic consequences of the coronavirus pandemic will only increase the need to move to a new technological and socio-economic paradigm, which is impossible without a cross-cutting role for AI. Many countries in the region are already taking AI seriously, with both business leaders and consumers showing a strong appetite for using AI tools and capabilities. Mining companies are employing autonomous machines in Peru's mines; job recruiters are drawing on emotion analytics algorithms in Chile; and customers of banks, airlines and retailers across the region are talking to chatbots (Ovanessoff & Abbosh, 2017).

Artificial intelligence is expected to see exponential growth in Latin America in the coming years. Accenture forecast that by 2035, AI would boost annual growth rates across South America by about one full percentage point of GDP. Latin American countries stand to gain AI-driven boosts in annual gross value added during the same timeframe, notably 78 billion US dollars in Colombia, 63 billion US dollars in Chile and 59 billion US dollars in Argentina (Ovanessoff & Plastino, 2017, p. 17). Another study—put together by the Institute for the Integration of Latin America and the Caribbean Inter-American Development Bank (INTAL-IDB)—predicts AI could boost regional GDP in the medium term from the current 3 percent to 4 percent. Colombia's economy, for example, could hit 4.5 percent growth instead of 3.7 percent. Overall, the report finds that the economic growth of countries that embrace AI is expected to be 25 percent higher, on average, than those that do not (Inter-American Development Bank, 2018). Almost half of this increase comes from improvements in productivity, with workers spending more time on tasks that add value, according to the report "Planet Algorithm: AI for Predictive and Inclusive Form of Integration in Latin America" (Inter-American Development Bank, 2018).

Latin America's AI efforts also include cutting-edge innovation, with some businesses even outpacing Silicon Valley. The Not Company, based in Chile, uses machine-learning algorithms to analyze the molecular composition of animal proteins, connecting them with the related human senses of taste and smell to create plant-based versions of animal-based food products (Ovanessoff & Abbosh, 2017). Latin America's AI pioneers are not only looking for global solutions; they are also using AI to target region-specific issues. Take Chazki, a logistics start-up in Peru, which realized the lack of clear postal addresses across the country was a major problem for e-commerce firms. The company partnered with the Universidad San Pablo in Arequipa to build a robot that learns the coordinates of delivery addresses, essentially building a new postal map that includes destinations where no formal address previously existed (Ovanessoff & Abbosh, 2017). By 2022, Latin American AI research centers have made revolutionary contributions to the development of technology. For example, Amanda Care, headquartered in Argentina, created a virtual assistant that monitors large groups of people to prevent dangerous diseases. DYMAXION Labs, also in Argentina, collects and analyzes satellite geographic data to make better use of resources such as IoT sensors. Laura (Argentina) automates bureaucratic procedures. Centro de Estudios Científicos promotes scientific research in Chile, with the notable discovery of a subglacial lake in west Antarctica. DART (Chile) is an AI-based solution that prevents one of the common causes of vision loss, diabetic retinopathy. U Planner (Chile) offers advanced AI solutions for universities around the world. Costa Rica–headquartered PARMA has developed an algorithm that performs a functional genomic analysis of cancer cells for RNA pairing, in order to easily identify regulatory networks (Microlit, 2022). Latin America demonstrates a fairly high penetration of AI in people's lives, presenting the tasks of effective strategic planning for transitioning to advanced technologies and ensuring the safety of those technologies for government use.

Climate change has been described as the biggest challenge of the twenty-first century. In Latin America, the UN estimates that climate change could cost the region between 1.5 percent and 5 percent of GDP by 2050. Despite the carbon emissions it generates, AI can be an environmental ally through interactive robots that teach people about recycling (IRBin, Peru), systems identifiers that detect illegal mines through satellite imagery (University of Rosario, Colombia), and systems that optimize the use of resources and the production of farmers through sensors and automated predictive systems (KYSO Agritech, Mexico) (May Del Pozo & Martín del Campo, 2020). Researchers from Peru's National Engineering University have developed a four-wheeled robot that explores mines autonomously to detect methane, carbon dioxide and ammonium. The adoption of customer service chatbots that help people in their native language is widespread (Ovanessoff & Plastino, 2017, p. 12), becoming particularly in demand during the coronavirus pandemic.

According to the World Bank, Latin America and the Caribbean account for only about 9 percent of the world's population but suffer from more than

30 percent of homicides worldwide, pointing to an urgent need to ensure broader safety in the region. While AI cannot drive quick systemic social change, it does have great potential in the area of security. For example, through its capacity to streamline bureaucracy, AI is automating processes and complaints regarding gender-based violence (Prometea, Argentina). It also is helping local police anticipate potential crime locations (Universidad de Chile, Chile) (May Del Pozo & Martín del Campo, 2020). While the rapid development of AI technologies is expanding possibilities for fighting crime, it is unfortunately also facilitating illegal acts.

AI development in Latin America faces many vulnerabilities, some of which are present everywhere, while others are more specific. Research by Armen Ovanessoff and Omar Abbosh reveals numerous structural deficiencies that hamper Latin America's ability to integrate new technologies into the economy. Common regional weaknesses include the quality of education systems—from primary to university levels—and of scientific research institutions, as well as weak research and innovation ecosystems at national, regional and global levels. Low levels of public trust and the absence of a collaborative mindset further aggravate these weaknesses (Ovanessoff & Abbosh, 2017). Latin American entrepreneurs mention two important challenges that face bringing AI to scale in the region: the adoption of technology (39 percent of respondents) and a lack of investment (33 percent) (Endeavor, 2018, p. 41). Nevertheless, the overall growth of AI development and its corresponding infrastructure makes the malicious use of AI more likely. For example, plans to introduce 5G technologies in the Caribbean may not only provide higher levels of communication, but also create the possibility of qualitatively new levels of threat in the area.

In the Caribbean, citizenship by investment (CBI) schemes have attracted a large number of wealthy individuals from around the world. These individuals are objectively interested in good and effective communication with their remote assets, encouraging plans to implement 5G technologies. At the same time, the internal needs and market interests of the largest companies engaged in AI development in the region are also obvious. This has prompted global computing giant Microsoft to urge Caribbean countries to leverage the power of AI, stating that the new technology can serve as a "leveling platform" to better compete with developed economies (Ammachchi, 2019).

Latin America and the Caribbean ended 2019 with 1237 5G subscriptions (an increase of 314 percent from Q3 to Q4) and 366 million LTE[1] subscriptions (5.4 percent from Q3 to Q4 growth). According to Jose Otero, vice

---

[1] Long-term evolution (LTE) refers to a standard for wireless broadband communication.

president of Latin America and the Caribbean for 5G Americas, "5G is the fastest growing wireless technology to arrive in Latin America and the Caribbean and the first generation of wireless cellular technologies to be deployed in the region during its first year of existence. 2019 saw the arrival of commercial 5G networks in Puerto Rico, Trinidad & Tobago, Suriname, Uruguay and the US Virgin (Islands)" (Nguyen, 2020). An important factor facilitating MUAI in Latin American countries is the high level of internet penetration. In 2019, Latin America and the Caribbean was the fourth largest regional online market, behind Asia, Europe and Africa. In June 2019, there were nearly 454 million internet users in the region, up from just over 300 million in 2013 (Chevalier, 2020). That same year, South America was the subregion with the largest internet penetration rate. On average, more than seven out of ten South Americans were online as of January 2020. Likewise, South America was the area with the highest average mobile internet penetration rate (Statista Research Department, 2020). As of January 2022, approximately 75 percent of South Americans have Retrieved the internet, compared to just 66 percent of the Caribbean population (Statista Research Department, 2022). Mobile devices represent the largest share of internet access across Latin America in 2022.

Despite objective economic difficulties, Latin American public and private entities are engaged in projects to incorporate AI into almost all areas of public life, from education and medicine to agriculture and postal services. These technologies can become a real tool for solving many economic problems; however, against the backdrop of socio-political tensions, MUAI as an anthropogenic threat may also increase. In order to assess the likelihood of this type of threat, it is worth considering real cases of MUAI in the field of psychological security in the region.

Malicious Use of Artificial Intelligence Threats to Psychological Security at the First Level

We want to show the inevitability of an escalating MUAI threat to psychological security in Latin America within the framework of our proposed three-level threat system. *At the first level, an increase in deliberately distorted interpretations of the circumstances and consequences of AI development, in order to benefit antisocial groups, seems inevitable in the current circumstances.*

Economic activity in Latin America and the Caribbean stagnated in 2019, a continuation of the weak growth momentum of the previous five years, adding more urgency and new challenges to reignite growth. Real GDP per capita in the region declined by 0.6 percent per year, on average, from 2014 to 2019, a sharp contrast to the average commodity boom increase of 2 percent per year from 2000 to 2013 (Werner, 2020). In December 2019, the Economist Intelligence Unit scored 18 countries in Latin America on seven indicators considered the most relevant for determining the likelihood of social unrest in the region. This research showed that the roots of public frustrations across the region lie in dysfunctional political systems and economic malaise and that the problems faced by countries in the region are structural. The special report outlines the prospects for unrest in 2020, assessing the stress points that might trigger fresh instability (The Economist Intelligence Unit, 2019a, 2019b).

In this context, various social and professional groups may have their own concerns about the development and implementation of AI in Latin America. For example, large businesses are concerned about the safety of their investments in certain sectors, employees are concerned about their jobs, and so on. According to recent reports from the UN, the World Economic Forum, Bank of America, Merrill Lynch, McKinsey Global Institute, Oxford University and others (Bank of America and Merrill Lynch , 2015; Frey & Osborne, 2013, Frey & Osborne, 2016; Manyika et al., 2017; Mishra et al., 2016; Pol & Reveley, 2017; UN Conference on Trade and Development, 2016; World Economic Forum XE "World Economic Forum, WEF" , 2016), 30 percent of jobs, or even more, will disappear in the coming two to three decades from the robotization of manufacturing, finance, services and management, including high-paying positions.

A report from the Inter-American Development Bank notes that between 36 percent and 43 percent of jobs in Latin America are at risk from automation that allows AI, and it stressed that countries with lower GDP per capita and greater inequality are at higher risk of losing jobs due to technology. The study, prepared by the INTAL-IDB, also predicted that AI can bring "broad benefits" to the region, although it urged governments to take steps to control the consequences of "technological transition." INTAL-IDB Director Gustavo Beliz said, "For governments, it is essential to design public policies and strategic plans for artificial intelligence, to carefully manage the technological transition of displaced workers to new jobs....A 'rebellion' of AI may sound like something remote, from science fiction, but we need to anticipate the ethical risks of data management, analysis and production. AI can bring us prosperity, but we have to make sure that it does so in an inclusive and safe manner" (EFE, 2018). The research conducted by Accenture[2] focuses attention on the fact "that a widespread and legitimate concern of many commentators is that AI will eliminate jobs, worsen inequality and erode incomes. In a region where, where 10 percent of the population already controls 70 percent of the wealth, this risk must be taken extremely seriously and prepared for" (Ovanessoff & Plastino, 2017, p. 24). When faced with a crisis, it is easy to provoke distrust and anger in people, not only in response to real risks, such as overestimating how long it will take for advanced technologies to be fully integrated into society (e.g., robots will replace half of all employees "tomorrow"), but also in response to positive opportunities that technological progress can provide. This provocation is facilitated by the use of professional tools to influence the psyche and provoke a certain action (or inaction), depending on the interests of the user of the corresponding psychological operation. To ensure the appropriate public reaction, expert assessments can be used. Individual panic becomes part of the psychological operation, which, in turn, can become an element of a long-term psychological campaign within the framework of strategic psychological warfare. This warfare is an integral part of the strategic confrontation between states, including in the latent stage of confrontation, and especially when there are clashes over fundamental issues and long-term antagonisms, for which no resolution is expected in the medium term.

The cooperation of Latin American countries with China is another area where threats to discredit AI and its developers should be expected. In just ten years, China has become Latin America's number two trading partner and investor. *Americas Quarterly* gives a number of examples of Chinese companies investing in Latin America's technology sector, such as Huawei and ZTE. A Shenzhen-based company created Noticias Águila, Mexico's most downloaded news app. "Huawei is one of the top contenders to build a fiber-optic cable connecting Chile to Asia, is already building one connecting Sinaloa to Baja California Sur in Mexico for $14 million, and like Alibaba will be competing with Amazon by setting up data centers in Chile" (Cote-Muñoz & Laskai, 2019). According to the World Economic Forum, China's trade with the region grew 26 times between 2000 and 2020 and is expected to double to over 700 billion US dollars by 2035. Two decades ago, the United States was the main trading partner of 9 out of 12 countries in South America; today, China has replaced the United States as the main trading partner for all countries except Ecuador, Colombia and Paraguay (Sahd et al., 2022, p. 30).

---

[2] Accenture is an Irish-domiciled multinational company providing services in digital technology strategy, consulting and operations.

Intense geopolitical rivalry for influence and resources in Latin America is mentioned in many studies (Taffet & Walcher, 2017; Livingstone, 2009; McPherson, 2016; Toma, 2018; Schechter et al., 2017; Grandin, 2019; Meyer, 2017; Gallagher, 2016; Lacalle Herrera, 2017; Johnson, 2018; Myers & Wise, 2016; Denoon, 2017; Su, 2017; Fornes & Mendez, 2018; López et al., 2016 etc.), creating an atmosphere of anxiety and mutual distrust that can effectively be used in psychological campaigns. This includes attacks on competitors who are successfully developing and strengthening their positions in the field of AI in Latin America. One example of this practice can be found in the pressure the United States placed on Chile to cancel a tender that was won by the Chinese-German consortium Aisino-Mühlbauer.

The government of Chile issued a tender for the processing of new identity documents in October 2021, and the Aisino-Mühlbauer consortium was selected as the winner. Aisino is a Chinese technology company engaged in smart technologies for the government, including tax services, electronic financial accounting and similar services (Aisino, 2022). Obtaining a Chilean passport costs 90,000 pesos (107 US dollars), one of the highest passport fees in the world. The winning contract was worth 205 million US dollars over a ten-year period, much less than the 680 million US dollars envisaged by Chile based on the previous contract. This would have reduced the cost of renewing a passport by at least two times for Chilean citizens. However, according to the Chilean administration, after finding some "inconsistencies," Aisino refused to provide the requested background information before signing the contract. Opposition politicians, particularly Miguel Mellado from the Renovación Nacional party and Jaime Naranjo from the Partido Socialista (El Mostrador, 2021), criticized the choice, "fearing for the protection of Chileans' personal data." In addition, just days after Aisino-Mühlbauer was announced as the winner, a delegation from the US Department of Homeland Security and the US. Department of State traveled to Chile to assess the country's eligibility for the US Visa Waiver Program. This evaluation provided an opportunity to "*discuss in detail the most important sources of concern for the delegation,*" after which the Chilean government canceled the tender on November 15 (Vérité, 2021). Chilean government spokesperson Jaime Bellolio confirmed that concerns about data protections were part of the reason the tender was canceled. According to Chilean local media, Aisino claims to have been the victim of planned attacks by business rivals, parliamentarians and former Chilean authorities. This case may illustrate a certain type of competition between technology companies in pursuit of not only profit, but also access to data that is necessary for AI training. US pressure on Aisino-Mühlbauer was also a way to signal to Germany to reign in its cooperation with China in high-tech industries, including AI.

An example of a disinformation campaign against China's economic presence in Latin America can be found in the claim that China is decimating the region and depriving Latin Americans of jobs by actively using AI instead of people. This transforms China's important scientific and technological progress into a social threat instead of an advantage in the region. However, in 2017, the International Labour Organization presented the first study on the impact economic relations between China and Latin America and the Caribbean had on jobs in the region. The study found that between 1990 and 2016, at least 1.8 million net jobs were created, with nearly 65 percent created from trade, 20 percent created from infrastructure projects and 15 percent created from outward foreign direct investment (Dussel Peters & Armony, 2017, p. 47). This amounts to almost 4 percent of all employment created in the region during the period and is probably an underestimate, according to the study. The majority of Chinese projects were based on high-tech, including AI solutions.

The installation of Chinese surveillance systems, acquired through official government donations or commercial contracts, is a growing phenomenon in Latin America and elsewhere (Ellis, 2019). According to Dr. Evan Ellis,[3] the risks from the spread of Chinese surveillance equipment and related infrastructure are multiple and significant. These concerns involve sensitivities related to the collection of data on specific persons and activities, and the processing of that data through technologies such as facial recognition. "It includes the ability to potentially track key political and business elites, dissidents, or other persons of interest, flagging possible meetings between two or more, and the associated implications involving political or business meetings and the events that they may produce. Flows of goods or other activities around government buildings, factories, or other sites of interest may provide other types of information for political or commercial advantage, from winning bids to blackmailing compromised persons" (Ellis, 2019).

Ellis points directly to the danger of China's MUAI against national and regional security in Latin America. He goes on to state, "While some may take assurance that the cameras and other components are safely guarded by benevolent governments or companies, the dispersed nature of the architectures, passing information, instructions, and analysis across great distances,

---

[3] Dr. Evan Ellis is a senior non-resident fellow at the Center for Strategic and International Studies (CSIS) and a professor of Latin American and Caribbean Studies. His work focuses on security and defense issues, including transnational organized crime, populism and the region's relationships with China and other non-Western Hemisphere actors.

means that the greatest risk is not physical access to the cameras, but the diversion of information throughout the process, particularly by those who built the components, databases and communication systems, and by those who wrote the algorithms (increasingly Chinese across the board)" (Ellis, 2019). Although China does have this potential, it is questionable whether other producers of similar equipment could be considered more ethical in this field. The growth of deliberately distorted interpretations of the circumstances surrounding AI development, as well as its consequences, in the context of unfair market competition and geopolitical contradictions is a current reality in Latin America.

Malicious Use of Artificial Intelligence Threats to International Psychological Security at the Second Level

In recent years, the growth of social and property differentiation in Latin American countries, the growth of political contradictions, and manifestations of geopolitical rivalry between the ruling elites of leading countries have been expressed in the form of aggravated psychological warfare. MUAI threats of the second level manifest in confrontations of this type, including the destruction of critical infrastructure, the use of drones for physical attacks and other activities aimed primarily at committing malicious actions that are not intended to control target audiences, although there is a psychological aspect. There is an overall element of confusion and panic after a successful attack of this type, which is already being used through a wide range of tools to control people's conscience and behavior, including high-tech psychological warfare using MUAI. There are quite a few examples of MUAI threats at the second level.

Latin America is the source of some of the most sophisticated hackers and organized crime groups in the world (IntSights, 2019, p. 2). The cooperation between violent drug gangs and the underground hacking community is a significant, emerging threat in the region. These two worlds are pooling their influence, skills and experience to achieve common goals, primarily financial. In 2019, a leader of the criminal gang called the Bandidos Revolution Team, Héctor Ortiz Solares—known as El H-1 or the Bandido Boss—was apprehended by law enforcement in León, Mexico. Solares was known for recruiting technically skilled hackers who could write malware to infect banks and ATMs. His hackers wrote malware that withdrew money from banks using the Interbanking Electronic Payment System (SPEI) and then deposited those funds into third-party accounts. Once the money was deposited, the gang withdrew the cash and made large purchases, such as real estate and luxury cars (IntSights, 2019, p. 6). This case demonstrates how IT professionals can turn to criminal activity, something that should be considered regarding future developers of certain AI technologies, who may be attracted to criminality in a saturated AI market.

Petróleos Mexicanos, or Pemex for short, was the victim of a ransomware attack in November 2019. The attackers demanded 565 Bitcoin (approximately 4.52 million euro) to decrypt the data, but Pemex announced that as a serious company, it would not finance criminals and, therefore, would not pay. The company's important data was backed up and recoverable after its systems had been cleaned. The DoublePaymer ransomware that was used in the Pemex attack was used for the first time in 2019, likely a further development of the BitPaymer ransomware. Its developer, the BitPaymer Group, is notorious for its targeted ransomware attacks and adjusted decryption prices (Kutsal, 2019). Another widely discussed tactic on Spanish-language dark web sites is BINero fraud, which allows cybercriminals to use misconfigured bank identification numbers to make fraudulent online purchases through retail sites like MercadoLibre, Amazon, B2W Digital and Alibaba (Greig, 2020). By 2022, the targeting of large public and private entities by cybercriminals had become a trend in Latin America (Sahd et al., 2022, p. 28), requiring specialized infrastructure by targeted organizations to constantly monitor the safety of their work.

During the coronavirus pandemic, global sales of electronic equipment almost doubled, which meant new users and a new technologies adaptation process for companies and governments. This rapid growth in technological transformation also led to an acceleration and diversification of cybercrime; while the main targets of criminals were individuals and small companies before COVID-19 by 2022, attacks were increasingly focused on large companies, government institutions and critical infrastructure (Sahd et al., 2022, p. 28). Kaspersky Lab indicates that in 2021, the number of cyberattacks in Latin America increased by 21 percent, which is the equivalent of 728 million attacks or 35 attacks per second. At the country level, the most significant cyberattack growth was observed in Ecuador (+75 percent), Peru (+71 percent), Panama (+60 percent), Guatemala (+43 percent) and Venezuela (+29 percent) (Diazgranados, 2021). The transition to remote work has also been insecure due to low technical capabilities, the need for user training, and a lack of investment in cybersecurity infrastructure. Compared to 2020, the number of attacks on remote desktop protocols increased by 78 percent during the first eight months of 2021, with the largest number of attacks occurring in Brazil (over 5 million attempts), Colombia (1.8 million), Mexico (1.7 million), Chile (1 million) and Peru (507,000) (Diazgranados, 2021). AI can be used in hedge fund and cryptocurrency trading, which requires predictions and crypto mining. AI can help reduce energy consumption from mining, improve blockchain scalability problems, improve security and privacy, improve network efficiency and open many "data gates," such as data trading avenues (Kariuki, 2018). These types of platforms have great potential but can be vulnerable to criminal MUAI.

The AI capabilities that can be exploited by criminal operations are not directly related to controlling the minds of individuals or target groups. However, the use of AI to, for example, leak important information can result in reputational damage or blackmail, which falls into the sphere of psychological security not just nationally, but also internationally, as criminal groups often operate on a cross-border basis.

It would be misleading to assume that MUAI is only associated with high-level specialists in the criminal world. Criminals can use AI almost with impunity, and with minimal effort, in an electronic environment they are comfortable with. Criminals in Latin America communicate on open source platforms and often do not even bother hiding their true identities unless they are tied to cartels or gangs. Undercover intelligence analysts from IntSights engage with threat actors using their preferred communication method—usually WhatsApp or Facebook Messenger. They find that threat actors are very comfortable using these platforms because they are allowed by their local governments and are free to use. Facebook Messenger, in particular, offers an easy way for threat actors to pivot from a Facebook group to chatting in Messenger within the same browser window; additionally, Facebook Messenger now offers encrypted chat called "secret" mode. It is simple for criminals to use this platform to switch between unencrypted, casual conversations to fully encrypted, end-to-end messages to discuss more clandestine business deals (IntSights, 2019, p. 2).

It should be emphasized that AI is actively used against all kinds of criminals, including those who resort to MUAI. For example, AI that was used in payment systems helped prevent potential fraud amounting to about 2 billion US dollars in Latin America and the Caribbean in 2019 alone. This figure comes from a report on the results of the Visa Advanced Authorization (VAA) risk management tool, which has used AI since the 1990s to make payments safer and easier. We can conclude that at the second level, the threats of MUAI against national and international psychological security are growing rapidly, especially in the context of the coronavirus pandemic, but have not received a proper response from public and private entities in Latin America to date. To our knowledge, there are no special studies of this problem.

The Third Level: Rising Risks

High risks at the third level are directly related to economic, social and political problems in Latin America. The conflict of geopolitical interests in the region is also obvious. The severity of local problems, with the active participation of external actors, naturally leads to acute psychological warfare, with MUAI playing an increasing role.

Dawn Meyerriecks, deputy director for technology development at the US Central Intelligence Agency (CIA), points out that the agency currently has 137 different AI projects, some of which have been used on social media, combing through countless public records. While the CIA is no stranger to collecting data from social media, developing new AI capabilities isn't just about more access to data and a greater ability to sift through it. "What is new is the volume and velocity of collecting social media data," said Joseph Gartin, head of the CIA's Kent School. In addition, according to Chris Hurst, the chief operating officer at Stabilitas, at the Intelligence Summit, "Human behavior is data and AI is a data model" (Gohd, 2017). MUAI actors can piece together each scrap of information to create a complete dossier that can be used for spear phishing campaigns, predictive analytics and other uses, and it can be assumed that these activities are already being carried out by various antisocial actors in Latin America.

In a social engineering attack, an attacker uses human interaction (social skills) to obtain or compromise information about an organization or its computer systems. Phishing is a form of social engineering, and phishing attacks use email or malicious websites to solicit personal information by posing as a trustworthy interlocutor (CISA, 2020). A 2018 survey of information security professionals found that 45 percent of respondents had experienced phishing via phone calls (vishing) and SMS/text messaging (smishing) the year before (Williams, 2019). Vishing goes beyond campuses and into the boardroom, as AI-assisted vishing campaigns have successfully breached businesses. Independent, Nairobi-based AI and cybersecurity expert Kange Ken warns that the problem will get worse. "Use of pre-trained AI models that can mimic an individual's voice by hackers could become a huge problem in the coming years," cautions Ken. For instance, all a skilled hacker has to do is find a video of a CEO speaking at an event, grab it off of social media and then mold the voice snippet into a "key" that will work across voice-activated platforms. "This could be a potent spear phishing tool. A hacker just needs to send a voice message to their prospective target mimicking the company's CEO," explains Ken (Williams, 2019). The current situation in Latin America makes the development of advanced phishing in the region more than possible. Upgrades to phishing will be based on MUAI more and more, although phishing itself is not automatically considered MUAI.

Phishing attacks have been rising in the region, accounting for 192,000 attacks per day in 2017, up by 115 percent from the previous year. In May 2018, Mexico's central bank announced that a cyberattack in April 2018 cost five undisclosed financial institutions around 15.2 million US dollars from several fraudulent transfers (Mordor Intelligence, 2019). In mid-2019, IntSights analysts discovered a large-scale phishing campaign against several major banks in North America and Latin America. The threat actor created several websites mimicking the banks' official websites, and customers were directed to the phishing sites via fake Google and Bing ads. The fake ads appeared as links at the top of the page when the victim made a Google search. When the victim clicked on the link, it opened a phishing website that appeared to be identical to the bank's real website (IntSights, 2019, p. 7).

Phishing attacks in Latin America decreased in 2021, but several countries in the region are among the most attacked in the world. Brazil is in first place, with 15.37 percent of users reporting attempted attacks. Brazil is followed by Ecuador (13.36 percent), Panama (12.60 percent), Chile (11.90 percent) and Colombia (11.09 percent). It should be noted that Venezuela (7.19 percent) and the Dominican Republic (5.62 percent) are the countries with the fewest social engineering attacks globally (Diazgranados, 2021). Although the landscape of this threat is not homogeneous, it remains common for all countries in the region.

A potentially much bigger problem for politics and business on the horizon, including for the countries of Latin America, is MUAI based on deepfakes. As AI continues to develop, persuasive chatbots could gain trust by engaging people in longer dialogues, perhaps eventually masquerading as another person in a video chat (Brundage et al., 2018, p. 24). At a basic level, hacktivists could use deepfake technology to create false claims and statements about a company, undermining and destabilizing its operations. At a more sinister level, malicious agents could target a company's senior executives by putting together a deepfake video that shows an executive confessing to financial crimes or other offenses. Examples like these could have major consequences for a company's brand, reputation and share price. Not to mention deepfakes can be difficult to disprove, consuming a great deal of time and money in the process (Orange Business Services, 2020).

The digital transformation banks are currently undergoing includes, among other tools, chatbots. Banco Galicia Argentina, BBVA and Banco de Credito del Peru have already introduced chatbots through channels such as Facebook Messenger and WhatsApp, as well as in voice-activated environments such as Alexa or Google Assistant. In the realm of e-commerce, the potential of chatbots is significant. Luis Flores, managing partner of Chatbot Chocolate in Chile and Peru, claims that WhatsApp chatbot development experts see that many companies are already preparing for a time when this context is real, with companies interacting with customers through their favorite messaging app (Castro Betancourt, 2019). In Guatemala, chatbots are generating a significant competitive advantage for Farmacias Cruz Verde. The chatbot used by this company is from Fogata Bots, and it currently works on Facebook, websites and WhatsApp. Customers use these digital communication channels to find pharmacy locations, to ask about the price of medicines and to get advice.

The more chatbots are used, the better they become, and the higher the risk of psychological MUAI. This does not negate the extremely progressive nature of the technology, but it does necessitate timely consideration of the risks. Technology can become a tool of abuse not only in marketing campaigns, but also for latent political control.

Political bots are widely used in Latin America, including for the usual practice of gaining political influence, as well as for psychological operations through MUAI. This is an increasingly common occurrence in political conflicts, with various groups attempting to control the narrative on this new online battlefront. In November 2019, during a US-backed coup against Bolivian President Evo Morales, thousands of newly created bots boosted the Spanish-language hashtag #BoliviaNoHayGolpe (there is no coup in Bolivia) in an attempt to legitimize the ouster of a democratically elected leader. In Venezuela as well, the local US-supported opposition attempted to increase their popularity and reach through manipulation via Twitter. In 2016, the researchers proved that bots were used in Mexico in 2014 for blocking criticism of President Enrique Peña Nieto's conservative government, in power since 2012 (Godoy, 2018).

In 2019, the ridicule of incumbent Argentine President Mauricio Macri on Twitter, whose campaign had hoped to attract electors through online engagement, became notorious. "To achieve the trending of the #YoVotoMM hashtag, the president and his campaign team called for a Twitterstorm, a massive Twitter event set for August 8th at 19:00, when his supporters were supposed to tweet the selected hashtag." Then, a user called Lavonne Smythorsmith tweeted: "Satisfy Mauricio, do not relax! I choose you!

Significant caresses coming from Hurlingham! #YoVotoMM." In Spanish, English and French, weird messages were retweeted, such as "Ex boyfriend American President Barack Obama applauded Macri as a 'male rushing' over financial reforms. #YoVotoMM." User @malerey_ traced the bot tweets to their original messages: "¡Por favor, Mauricio!" (Please, Mauricio!) became "¡Satisface a Mauricio!" (Satisfy Mauricio or Give satisfaction to Mauricio); "¡Abrazo fuerte desde Hurlingham!" (A big hug from Hurlingham) became "Caricias significativas desde Hurlingham" (Significant caresses from Hurlingham), and so on (Bonnin, 2019). Inaccurate and, in many cases, ungrammatical, the garbled tweets came from accounts with few or no followers, no profile descriptions and names such as Lavonne Smythorsmith, Keitha Owen and Janet Fizhugh. The names, as noted by user @kwinnyk, were created using a random name generator based on real names taken from a database. "Smyth or Smith" became "Smythorsmith," "Keith A. Owen" became "Keitha Owen," "Janet Fiz, Hugh…" became "Janet Fitzhugh" and so on (Bonnin, 2019). The source of the bots has not been established, with two main theories circulating among experts. One is that there was a technical error in the president's campaign rollout; the other is that this was a coordinated action by the opposition to ridicule Macri. Either way, this case illustrates the new political campaign risks that are associated with third-level MUAI threats to psychological security.

A group of researchers working in the United States analyzed the use of bots in the political sphere of Venezuela. Based on 11 identified platforms in Venezuela, the researchers found that web browsers generated approximately 38 percent of retweets, while mobile phone–based apps such as Twitter generated 62 percent; the country has one of the highest rates of mobile phone penetration in Latin America. Venezuelans also used bot platforms such as Botize or MasterFollow, popular free services that can execute actions automatically, to retweet politicians' content. Many bots presenting as official political candidates do so on behalf of the radical opposition party (VP), rather than the incumbent party (PSUV) or the more mainstream opposition party (MUD). In other countries, the governing party often uses bots the most aggressively, but in Venezuela, the opposite is true. There has been relatively little bot activity from the PSUV and VP or from the opposition coalition Democratic Unity Party led by Capriles, the candidate who gave Maduro a serious run for his money in the 2013 election (Forelle et al., 2015, p. 4). The activity of radical opposition bots, however, is subordinated to the task of fomenting socio-political and economic destabilization of Venezuela, often reproducing calls for violence (Redacción Cubaperiodistas, 2017).

Electoral disinformation campaigns are regularly used by private and public actors. In September 2020, Sophie Zhang, a data scientist at Facebook, told *Buzzfeed* that the social network is improving in its detection of manipulative political campaigns on its platform in the United States and Western Europe, but that other regions are often overlooked (Silverman, 2020). In Honduras, the headquarters of the country's conservative President Juan Orlando Hernández (JOH) "openly admitted" to the existence of hundreds of fake Facebook accounts in support of the president. Zhang deleted the fake profiles for over a year, but they reappeared within two weeks and persisted until at least September 2020. JOH won the 2017 Honduran election by a narrow margin, but allegations of election fraud led to protests and a violent response from the state (Heinz, 2020), resulting in dozens of murders and a ten-day nationwide curfew. Post-election research found that the majority of tweets that were tagged JOH were posted automatically by TweetDeck (Heinz, 2020).

On October 7, 2021, a group of 19 Twitter accounts shared the same opinion about the upcoming presidential elections in Honduras in the same second. Claiming to be supporters of opposition candidate Xiomara Castro, the accounts all falsely proclaimed Castro's intention of joining forces with Yani Rosenthal, another candidate who had just returned to the country after serving a prison sentence in the United States for laundering money for drug cartels. The profile pictures of the fake accounts were linked to the pages of unsuspecting Facebook users in Peru (Bergengruen, 2021).

Sophie Zhang's disclosures caused a sensation in the media. Zhang claimed that in 2019 in Ecuador, she discovered support for the government of Lenin Moreno using bots. The government said in April 2019 that it was the victim of a fake news campaign. Regardless, the bot activity was ignored by Facebook (Heinz, 2020). Regarding the already mentioned 2019 case in Bolivia, Zhang said that she found "inauthentic activity supporting the opposition presidential candidate in 2019" and chose not to prioritize it. Months later, Bolivian politics fell into turmoil, resulting in the resignation of President Evo Morales and "mass protests leading to dozens of deaths" (Silverman, 2020). This indicates that psychological operations, carried out with the help of political bots, have already had dire consequences.

It would be premature to link all larger political bot activity to MUAI. However, there is enough to draw from based on the research of Dr. Samuel Woolley, who directed the research team at the Oxford Internet Institute's Computational Propaganda Project. Woolley's team looked into whether and how Twitter bots were used during the Brexit campaign, finding that a great number of political bots were used to spread messages about the

"Leave" campaign. The vast majority of the automated accounts they found were very simple, made to retweet content or generate noise, not to be functionally conversational—in other words, they did not harness AI. Meanwhile, the Digital Intelligence Laboratory at the Institute for the Future examined political bot usage during events in places like Turkey, Venezuela and Ecuador and saw that bots were programmed to target journalists and civil society leaders with repetitive harassment. These automated social media accounts were not artificially intelligent; they simply overwhelmed their victims with cascades of repetitive, automated hate. The propagandists in question could game the truth by using rudimentary political bots to overwhelm trending algorithms on social media sites (Woolley, 2020). In the near future, however, more sophisticated techniques related to the promotion of smart bots and their integration into complex perception management systems should be expected, along with the possible inclusion of AI. Even today, the use of bots impacts at least targeting when social media algorithms offer content based on user preferences; the dissemination of artificially created misinformation continues with the help of AI.

The tactic of introducing disinformation via bots that is further spread by users and social media algorithms is being co-opted amidst a highly dangerous trend of companies privatizing political psychological operations. Gustavo A. Rivero, an adjunct professor at Universidad de la Salle in Colombia, believes that elections in Latin America are under threat "not so much from vote buying or corruption, but from the emerging private disinformation industry." Rivero says that "governments in power, aspirants, and political parties" are shaping public discourse in their favor, in order to take or keep power; they are essentially the main clients of new companies specializing in the manipulation of the digital ecosystem (Rivero, 2022). With the emergence of non-state actors in the production of disinformation, the activity of so-called cyber troops, created by private companies and hired by governments or political parties to discredit opponents, has increased. These companies have hackers or programmers on staff managing fake accounts to spread disinformation (sock puppet accounts, trolls or puppet user accounts). The profiles change their online behavior according to the client's requirements. Rivero (2022), referring to the Oxford Internet Institute's report "Industrialized Disinformation 2021" (Bradshaw, Bailey, & Howard, 2021a), cites 12 Latin American states (Argentina, Bolivia, Brazil, Colombia, Costa Rica, Cuba, Ecuador, El Salvador, Guatemala, Honduras, Mexico and Venezuela) that were targets of disinformation operations by cyber troops during elections and/or a change of power. "The ideological spectrum is irrelevant when it comes to distinguishing the contractors, as the report includes politicians from both the left and the right who have had links with these types of companies for the purpose of seizing power" (Rivero, 2022). For example, the strategic communications company Estraterra specialized in supporting left-wing presidents and governments and actively criticizing and discrediting right-wing politicians, including Brazilian President Jair Bolsonaro, Chilean President Sebastian Piñera, former Argentinian President Mauricio Macri and Venezuelan politician Juan Guaidó (@DFRLab , 2020). However, many companies of this kind began work before MUAI. One of these companies, the SCL Group, included information about the dissemination of political graffiti on behalf of youth in the run-up to the 2010 Trinidad and Tobago elections in its brochures. The aim of the campaign was to increase political apathy among Afro-Trinidadian youth, who often voted for the center-left party. Another company, Hacking Team, had contracts with the governments of seven Latin American countries to monitor and stop the activities of political dissidents (Heinz, 2020).

According to the Oxford Internet Institute, in 2020, government officials in 48 countries collaborated with private companies on computational propaganda. From 2019 to 2020, for example, the Israeli Archimedes Group ran several campaigns in Latin America, and the Spanish company Eliminalia used computational propaganda in local elections in Colombia, as well as in campaigns in Ecuador and the Dominican Republic (Bradshaw, Bailey, & Howard, 2021a, p. 9). An example of a highly automated cyber troop campaign in Honduras involves bots set up by various public institutions, including the National Television Station (Bradshaw, Bailey, & Howard, 2021a, p. 11). Trolling or harassment is also attributed to cyber troops. According to the Oxford Internet Institute, Guatemalan network centers used fake accounts to brand certain people—mainly journalists—as terrorists or foreign invaders from 2019 to 2020 (Bradshaw, Bailey, & Howard, 2021a, p. 13). During the same time period, only a few examples of deepfakes were found in political campaigns, although these were not mentioned in the country case studies report (Bradshaw, Campbell-Smith, et al., 2021b). Traditionally edited images and videos (cheapfakes) remain the most common type of visual disinformation. For example, ahead of the 2019 elections in Argentina, security minister Patricia Bullrich was videotaped to appear drunk (Bradshaw, Bailey, & Howard, 2021a, p. 15). When creating fake accounts, generative adversarial networks are often used to create profile pictures—photos of nonexistent people.

The malicious use of deepfakes seems to be a much greater concern to Latin American experts in relation to social issues, such as child and teen bullying. For instance, ESET launched the Digipadres initiative to support the psychological protection of children from these threats. "Imagine that you are a shy boy who is bullied by your peers. One day a group of boys laughs at you and you don't quite understand why. Then you are shown a video from the film Forest Gump, where the main character's face is replaced with yours," says Camilo Gutierrez, head of the ESET research laboratory in Latin America. ESET experts note that with the development of appropriate mobile applications, deepfakes have entered schools and have become a tool for bullying (Tips de Seguridad, 2022), such as placing the face of a shy girl in a provocative nude dance video. While the creators of these videos may view their actions as innocent entertainment, deepfakes can cause a particular child to feel ashamed, damaging their relationships with peers.

Digipadres.com provides resources for parents and teachers on how to talk to children about these and other issues in the digital environment. However, this type of engagement may also be important for adults; in Latin America, 70 percent of internet users are unaware of the existence of malicious deepfake tactics. Among those polled, Peruvians are the most ignorant (75 percent), followed by Mexicans and Chileans (72 percent each), Argentines (67 percent), Brazilians (66 percent) and Colombians (63 percent). For cybersecurity experts, this level of ignorance is worrying (Noticias RCN Noticias, 2022) because it increases the chances of success for social engineering scammers. So far, the only examples that have been mentioned in the political sphere range "from Bolsonaro as The Red Grasshopper to Cristina Kirchner as a Drag Queen in RuPaul's Drag Race…for (mostly) humorous purposes" (Rodríguez León, 2020); in the meantime, the overwhelming majority of deepfakes remain pornographic. However, close attention to the problem of defamation, with the help of synthesized photos and videos, is necessary—while there are some studies in this area (Rodrigo López, 2022), there are not nearly enough—as well as educational initiatives for a wide audience.

Every day there is information about the new and "innovative" ways hackers use to infiltrate devices, inject ransomware or steal invaluable data, but manipulation of data is happening now. In 2021, a group of security researchers in Israel revealed that they tricked doctors into misdiagnosing patients by hacking into and tweaking scans from a hospital's X-ray machine. This type of data manipulation can mislead patients about their true health conditions. Data manipulation attacks of this type can be further simplified through the use of bots. There have been past instances of hackers using metadata to create "disinformation" bots that are highly adept at impersonating human behavior on social media platforms. With a myriad of bots at their disposal, hackers can easily tweak a "disinformation" bot, place it in any system and control the data to their advantage (Backer, 2020). Major Anna Fields, a programming manager for intellectual systems with the US Army Research Office, believes that countering backdoor poisoning (injection of the poisoning data during AI training) is an issue of high priority. "The fact that you are using a large database is a two-way street. It is an opportunity for the adversary to inject poison into the database" (Barnett, 2020). This and other expert statements lead to the conclusion that virtually all types of psychological operations using MUAI are possible in Latin America today.

Conclusion

The increasing risks of MUAI in Latin America are driven by negative socio-economic and political development factors: economic stagnation; increasing material and social stratification among the population; high levels of corruption and crime; bureaucracy and inertia in the state's decision-making; the dangerous growth of populist parties steeped in outdated concepts, unable to offer effective political solutions; and regional geopolitical rivalries that increase economic instability and socio-political tensions.

Rapid growth in the use of AI technologies and related infrastructure also creates favorable conditions for MUAI in the region. In particular, an important factor facilitating MUAI in Latin America is the high level of internet penetration. Cyberattacks using AI can cause panic that drastically reduces the trust of citizens in public institutions; fraught with new social unrest, society is led to a dead end without a program for progressive transformation.

The severe economic, social and political consequences of the coronavirus pandemic also increase the risks of MUAI. It should be noted that like any large-scale and sudden crisis, pandemics require an urgent response in high-risk conditions; this is often accompanied by panic moods among a wide range of state and non-state actors. These actors put their own interests above the public, such as government officials who are concerned with their own success rather than fighting the coronavirus, trading companies that inflate the price of personal protective equipment, political parties that use fear to gain support and to agitate, and outright criminals who try to use a volatile environment to enrich themselves. All of these parties are interested in using social engineering to achieve their goals. The sharp narrowing of personal communication opportunities and the extremely rapid transition to remote work for significant segments of the population have also created new opportunities for MUAI. More precisely, MUAI in the context of the growing negative effects of the coronavirus pandemic has yet to be assessed based on a broader set of empirical data and relevant case studies.

With the further privatization of online political campaigning and the growth of the AI market, an increasing number of business entities will be ready to provide services to politicians, including unscrupulous ones, in the field of "smart" agenda setting. This means future bot wars, reputational destruction through deepfakes and the use of AI-enhanced social engineering technologies to influence the electorate. At the same time, against the backdrop of the erosion of democracy and the growth of populism in the absence of real programs for overcoming systemic crisis, manipulation of the emotional impact on a voter's psyche and behavior can become the main, if not the only, means of achieving electoral success for many politicians. This is exacerbated by low awareness among Latin American citizens about the technologies that manipulate public consciousness through AI. Accordingly, this makes it all the more important for Latin American countries to participate in scientific and practical cooperation to prevent "smart" psychological operations, to broadly educate citizens and to introduce AI into areas of daily life where it can bring the greatest benefit.

At all three threat levels of MUAI for national and international psychological security, both quantitative and qualitative deterioration should be expected due to the abovementioned factors. Quantitative and qualitative research, as well as monitoring, of the situation in the region is needed. Moreover, international cooperation between individual specialists and entire research teams should be welcomed, providing a basis for balanced decision-making for those who are committed to finding the optimal model for socially oriented development. Without radical reform of the existing development paradigms, the crisis in Latin American countries will sharpen, opportunities for socially oriented AI applications will narrow, and threats from MUAI will increase.

References

@DFRLab (2020) Facebook takes down inauthentic assets targeting multiple Latin American elections. In: Medium. https://medium.com/dfrlab/facebook-takes-down-inauthentic-assets-targeting-multiple-latin-american-elections-1fa93c85501e. Retrieved 5 Jul 2022

Aisino (2022) 航天信息股份有限公司 (Aerospace Information Co., Ltd.). In: Aisino.com. http://www.aisino.com/. Retrieved 5 Jul 2022

Ammachchi N (2019) Artificial Intelligence Can Become a Game-Changer for Caribbean Economies. In: Nearshore Americas. https://nearshoreamericas.com/artificial-intelligence-ai-become-game-changer-caribbean-economies/. Retrieved 5 Jul 2022

Backer S (2020) New attack of mass disinformation: Data Manipulation. In: CybersecAsia. https://www.cybersecasia.net/opinions/new-weapon-of-mass-disinformation-data-manipulation. Retrieved 5 Jul 2022

Bank of America, Merrill Lynch. (2015). *Creative Disruption: The Impact of Emerging Technologies on the Creative Economy*. World Economic Forum.

Barnett J (2020) Army looks to block data 'poisoning' in facial recognition, AI. In: FedScoop. https://www.fedscoop.com/army-looks-block-data-poisoning-facial-recognition/. Retrieved 5 Jul 2022

Batista, R., Villar, O., Gonzalez, H., & Milian, V. (2020). Cultural Challenges of the Malicious Use of Artificial Intelligence in Latin American Regional Balance. In *Proceedings of the 2nd European Conference on the Impact of Artificial Intelligence and Robotics, ECIAIR 2020* (pp. 7–13). Academic Conferences International Limited.

Bergengruen, V. (2021). *Honduras Shows How Fake News Is Changing Latin American Elections*. Time. https://time.com/6116979/honduras-political-disinformation-facebook-twitter/. Retrieved 5 Jul 2022

Bonnin J (2019) #YoVotoMM: Mauricio Macri, bots and dirty campaigning in Argentina. In: Diggit Magazine. https://www.diggitmagazine.com/column/Macri-bots. Retrieved 5 Jul 2022

Bradshaw, S., Bailey, H., & Howard, P. (2021a). *Industrialized Disinformation: 2020 Global Inventory of Organized Social Media Manipulation*. Programme on Democracy & Technology.

Bradshaw, S., Campbell-Smith, U., Henle, A., Perini, A., Shalev, S., Bailey, H., & Howard, P. (2021b). *Country Case Studies Industrialized Disinformation: 2020 Global Inventory of Organized Social Media Manipulation*. Programme on Democracy & Technology.

Brundage, M., Avin, S., Clark, J., Toner, H., Eckersley, P., Garfinkel, B., Dafoe, A., Scharre, P., Zeitzoff, T., Filar, B., Anderson, H., Roff, H., Allen, G., Steinhardt, J., Flynn, C., & Ó HÉigeartaigh S, Beard S, Belfield H, Farquhar S, Lyle C, Crootof R, Evans O, Page M, Bryson J, Yampolskiy R, Amodei D. (2018). *The Malicious Use of Artificial Intelligence: Forecasting, Prevention, and Mitigation*. University of Oxford, Oxford, UK.

Castro Betancourt S (2019) The five sectors chatbots will transform in Latin America in 2019. In: Online Marketplaces. https://www.onlinemarketplaces.com/articles/24813-sectors-that-the-chatbots-will-revolve-in-2019-in-latin-america. Retrieved 5 Jul 2022

Chevalier S (2020) Internet usage in Latin America—Statistics & Facts. In: Statista. https://www.statista.com/topics/2432/internet-usage-in-latin-america/. Retrieved 5 Jul 2022

CISA (2020) Avoiding Social Engineering and Phishing Attacks. In: Cybersecurity and Infrastructure Security Agency (CISA). https://www.cisa.gov/uscert/ncas/tips/ST04-014. Retrieved 5 Jul 2022

Cote-Muñoz N, Laskai L (2019) Is Latin America Prepared for China's Booming Tech Investments? In: Americas Quarterly. https://www.americasquarterly.org/article/is-latin-america-prepared-for-chinas-booming-tech-investments/. Retrieved 5 Jul 2022

Denoon DBH (ed.) (2017) China, the United States, and the Future of Latin America: U.S.–China Relations, Volume III. NYU Press,

Diazgranados, H. (2021). Ciberataques en América Latina crecen un 24% durante los primeros ocho meses de 2021. *In*.: Latam.kaspersky.com. https://latam.kaspersky.com/blog/ciberataques-en-america-latina-crecen-un-24-durante-los-primeros-ocho-meses-de-2021/22718/. Retrieved 5 Jul 2022.

DQIndia Online (2020) Empowering Industry 4.0 with Artificial Intelligence. In: Data Quest India. https://www.dqindia.com/empowering-industry-4-0-artificial-intelligence/. Retrieved 5 Jul 2022

Dussel Peters, E., & Armony, A. C. (2017). *Effects of China on the quantity and quality of jobs in Latin America and the Caribbean*. Regional Office for Latin America and the Caribbean.

EFE (2018) Inteligencia artificial amenaza el 36% de los empleos en A. Latina. In: El Tiempo. https://www.eltiempo.com/economia/sectores/empleos-en-america-latina-afectados-por-inteligencia-artificial-262246. Retrieved 5 Jul 2022

El Mostrador (2021) Registro Civil versus Aisino: La Moneda defiende la anulación por el factor visa Waiver y empresa china llevará a Chile al Ciadi (Civil Registry versus Aisino: La Moneda defends the annulment due to the visa waiver factor and a Chinese company will take Chile to the ICSID). In: El Mostrador. https://www.elmostrador.cl/noticias/pais/2021/11/16/registro-civil-versus-aisino-la-moneda-defiende-la-anulacion-por-el-factor-visa-waiver-y-empresa-china-llevara-a-chile-al-ciadi/. Retrieved 5 Jul 2022

Ellis E (2019) Chinese Surveillance Complex Advancing in Latin America. In: Newsmax. https://www.newsmax.com/evanellis/china-surveillance-latin-america-cameras/2019/04/12/id/911484/. Retrieved 5 Jul 2022

Endeavor. (2018). *El impacto de la inteligencia artificial en el emprendimiento (The impact of artificial intelligence on entrepreneurship)*. Endeavor.

Forelle, M., Howard, P., Monroy-Hernandez, A., & Savage, S. (2015). Political Bots and the Manipulation of Public Opinion in Venezuela. *SSRN Electronic Journal*. https://doi.org/10.2139/ssrn.2635800

Fornes G, Mendez A (2018) The China–Latin America Axis: Emerging Markets and their Role in an Increasingly Globalised World. Palgrave Macmillan,

Frey, C. B., & Osborne, M. (2013). *The Future of Employment: How Susceptible Are Jobs to Computerisation?* Oxford Martin School.

Frey CB, Osborne M (2016) Technology at Work v.2.0. The Future is Not What It Used to Be. Oxford Martin School.

Gallagher, K. (2016). *The China Triangle: Latin America's China Boom and the Fate of the Washington Consensus*. Oxford University Press.

Godoy E (2018) Automated Digital Tools Threaten Political Campaigns in Latin America. In: Inter Press Service. http://www.ipsnews.net/2018/02/automated-digital-tools-threaten-political-campaigns-latin-america/. Retrieved 5 Jul 2022

Gohd C (2017) How the CIA is using artificial intelligence to collect social media data. In: Futurism. https://futurism.com/how-the-cia-is-using-artificial-intelligence-to-collect-social-media-data. Retrieved 5 Jul 2022

Grandin, G. (2019). *The End of the Myth: From the Frontier to the Border Wall in the Mind of America*. Metropolitan Books.

Greig, J. (2020). *Cybercriminals and drug cartels are spreading malware and stealing financial information in Latin America*. TechRepublic. https://www.techrepublic.com/article/cybercriminals-and-drug-cartels-are-teaming-up-to-spread-malware-and-steal-financial-information-across-latin/. Retrieved 5 Jul 2022

Heinz B (2020) Election Interference in Latin America: A Growing Danger. In: Center for Economic and Policy Research (CEPR). https://cepr.net/election-interference-in-latin-america-a-growing-danger/. Retrieved 5 Jul 2022

Inter-American Development Bank (2018) Artificial intelligence to boost Latin American and Caribbean economies: IDB study. In: Inter-American Development Bank. https://www.iadb.org/en/news/artificial-intelligence-boost-latin-american-and-caribbean-economies-idb-study. Retrieved 5 Jul 2022

IntSights (2019) The Dark Side of Latin America: Cryptocurrency, Cartels, Carding and the Rise of Cybercrime. IntSights

Johnson, J. M. (2018). *China and Latin America: The other option*. US Army Command and General Staff College.

Kariuki D (2018) Cryptocurrencies and Projects Involving AI. In: Cryptomorrow – Cryptocurrency, Bitcoin, Ethereum. https://cryptomorrow.com/2018/02/08/cryptocurrencies-and-projects-involving-ai/. Retrieved 5 Jul 2022

Kutsal B (2019) Cyber attack on Pemex, Mexico's largest oil and gas company. In: F-Secure Blog. https://blog.f-secure.com/cyber-attack-on-pemex-mexicos-largest-oil-and-gas-company/. Retrieved 5 Jul 2022

Lacalle Herrera LA (2017) America Latina. Entre Trump y China: El cambio esperado (Latin America. Between Trump and China: The expected change).

de-Lima-Santos M, Mesquita L. (2021). A Challenging Future for the Latin American News Media Industry. *Palgrave Studies in Journalism and the Global South, 229–262*. https://doi.org/10.1007/978-3-030-65860-1_8

Livingstone, G. (2009). *America's Backyard: The United States and Latin America from the Monroe Doctrine to the War on Terror*. Bloomsbury Academic.

López, A., Gallagher, K., Sanborn, C., & Ray, R. (2016). *China en América Latina: lecciones para la cooperación Sur-Sur y el desarrollo sostenible*. Universidad del Pacífico.

Manyika, J., Chui, M., Miremadi, M., Bughin, J., George, K., Willmott, P., & Dewhurst, M. (2017). *A Future that Works: Automation, Employment, and Productivity. Executive Summary*. McKinsey Global Institute.

May Del Pozo, C., & Martín del Campo, A. V. (2020). *Cómo la inteligencia artificial está transformando realidades en América Latina (How artificial intelligence is transforming realities in Latin America)*. El Financiero. https://www.elfinanciero.com.mx/opinion/c-minds/como-la-inteligencia-artificial-esta-transformando-realidades-en-america-latina/. Retrieved 5 Jul 2022

McPherson, A. (2016). *A short history of U.S. interventions in Latin America and the Caribbean*. Wiley-Blackwell.

Meyer, P. J. (2017). *U.S. Strategy for Engagement in Central America: Policy Issues for Congress*. Congressional Research Service.

Microlit. (2022). *8 Prominent Artificial Intelligence Research Centers in Latin America*. Microlit. https://www.microlit.com/8-prominent-artificial-intelligence-research-centers-in-latin-america/. Retrieved 5 Jul 2022

Mishra, D., Deichmann, U., Chomitz, K., Hasnain, Z., Kayser, E., Kelly, T., Kivine, M., Larson, B., Monroy-Taborda, S., Sahnoun, H., Santos, I., Satola, D., Schiffbauer, M., Seol, B. K., Tan, S., & Van Welsum, D. (2016). *Digital Dividends*. World Development Report. Overview.

Mordor Intelligence. (2019). *Latin America Cyber Security Market – Growth, Trends, and Forecast (2020–2025)*. Mordor Intelligence. https://www.mordorintelligence.com/industry-reports/latin-america-cyber-security-market. Retrieved 5 Jul 2022

Myers M, Wise C (2016) The Political Economy of China–Latin America Relations in the New Millennium: Brave New World. Routledge,

Nguyen V (2020) 5G's Year One: Fast Start and Healthy Growth. In: 4G Wireless Evolution. https://www.mobilitytechzone.com/lte/news/2020/03/23/9119584.htm. Retrieved 5 Jul 2022

Noticias, R. C. N. (2022). *Deepfakes: ¿cómo se pueden detectar y evitar? (Deepfakes: how can they be detected and avoided?)*. Noticias RCN. https://www.noticiasrcn.com/tecnologia/deepfakes-como-se-pueden-detectar-y-evitar-422612. Retrieved 5 Jul 2022

Orange Business Services (2020) Fake news: What could deepfakes and AI scams mean for cybersecurity? In: Orange Business Services. https://www.orange-business.com/en/magazine/fake-news-what-could-deepfakes-and-ai-scams-mean-cybersecurity. Retrieved 5 Jul 2022

Ovanessoff A, Abbosh O (2017) Artificial intelligence could help reverse Latin America's economic slowdown. In: World Economic Forum. https://www.weforum.org/agenda/2017/03/artificial-intelligence-could-help-reverse-latin-americas-economic-slowdown. Retrieved 5 Jul 2022

Ovanessoff, A., & Plastino, E. (2017). *How Artificial Intelligence Can Drive South America's Growth*. Accenture.

Pol, E., & Reveley, J. (2017). Robot Induced Technological Unemployment: Towards a Youth-Focused Coping Strategy. *Psychosociological Issues in Human Resource Management, 5*, 169. https://doi.org/10.22381/pihrm5220177

Redacción Cubaperiodistas. (2017). *Oposición venezolana utiliza sistemas automatizados para manipular Twitter*. Cuba Periodistas. https://www.cubaperiodistas.cu/

index.php/2017/06/oposicion-venezolana-utiliza-sistemas-automatizados-para-manipular-twitter-investigacion/. Retrieved 5 Jul 2022

Rivero, G. (2022). *The Private Disinformation Industry in Latin America. In: Latinoamérica*, 21. https://latinoamerica21.com/en/the-private-disinformation-industry-in-latin-america/. Retrieved 5 Jul 2022

RLASSA (2018) Advanced Technologies and Psychological Warfare: Focusing on Latin America (Results of Conferences, Round Tables and Workshops of Russian Researchers in South America). August 27–September 10, 2018. In: Russian–Latin American Strategic Studies Association (RLASSA) on Global StratCom. http://globalstratcom.ru/wp-content/uploads/2017/11/RLASSA-Advanced-Technologies-and-Psychological-Warfare-копия1.pdf. Retrieved 5 Jul 2022

RLASSA (2022) About the Association. In: Russian–Latin American Strategic Studies Association (RLASSA) on Global StratCom. http://globalstratcom.ru/russian-latin-american-strutegic-studies-association/. Retrieved 5 Jul 2022

Rodrigo López, J. F. (2022). Tragic Realism: How to Regulate Deepfakes in Colombia? *Latin American Law Review, 125-145*. https://doi.org/10.29263/lar08.2022.08

Rodríguez León, T. (2020). *Deepfakes: The hacked reality*. Open Democracy. https://www.opendemocracy.net/en/democraciaabierta/deepfakes-realidad-hackeada-en/. Retrieved 5 Jul 2022

Sahd, J., Zovatto, D., Rojas, D., & Paz Fernández, M. (2022). *Riesgo política América Latina (Political Risk Latin America 2022)*. Centro UC Estudios Internacionales CEIUC.

Schechter, P., Marczak, J., & DeLevie-Orey, R. (2017). *Beyond the Headlines: A Strategy for US Engagement with Latin America in the Trump Era*. Atlantic Council.

Silverman, C. (2020). *Whistleblower Says Facebook Ignored Global Political Manipulation*. Buzzfeed. https://www.buzzfeednews.com/article/craigsilverman/facebook-ignore-political-manipulation-whistleblower-memo. Retrieved 5 Jul 2022

Statista Research Department. (2020). *Internet penetration in Latin America & Caribbean*. Statista. https://www.statista.com/statistics/934738/penetration-rate-internet-latin-america-region/. Retrieved 5 Jul 2020

Statista Research Department (2022) Internet penetration in Latin America & Caribbean by region 2022. In: Statista. https://www.statista.com/statistics/934738/penetration-rate-internet-latin-america-region/. Retrieved 5 Jul 2022

Su, Z. (Ed.). (2017). *China and Latin America: Economic and Trade Cooperation in the Next Ten Years*. World Scientific Pub Co Inc..

Taffet, J., & Walcher, D. (2017). *The United States and Latin America: A History with Documents*. Routledge.

The Economist Intelligence Unit (2019a) Where next and what next for Latin America? In: The Economist Intelligence Unit. https://www.eiu.com/public/topical_report.aspx?campaignid=latinamerica2019&zid=latinamerica2019&utm_source=blog&utm_medium=one_site&utm_name=latinamerica2019&utm_term=announcement&utm_content=bottom_link. Retrieved 5 Jul 2022

The Economist Intelligence Unit (2019b) Latin America will have to brace for more turbulence in 2020. In: The Economist Intelligence Unit. https://www.eiu.com/n/latin-america-will-have-to-brace-for-more-turbulence-in-2020/. Retrieved 5 Jul 2022

Tips de Seguridad. (2022). *Ciberseguridad: Qué son los deepfakes y cómo hablar de esto con los niños (Cybersecurity: What are deepfakes and how to talk about it with children)*. Tips de Seguridad. http://tipsdeseguridad.com/2022/06/28/ciberseguridad-que-son-los-deepfakes-y-como-hablar-de-esto-con-los-ninos/. Retrieved 5 Jul 2022

Toma, D. (2018). *America First: Understanding the Trump Doctrine*. Regnery Publishing.

UN Conference on Trade and Development. (2016). *Robots and Industrialization in Developing Countries*. UNCTAD.

Vérité, C. (2021). *Chile cancels deal with Chinese Aisino over data safety and US partnership*. Newsendip. https://www.newsendip.com/chile-passport-deal-aisino-china-muhlbauer-data-security-us-visa-waiver/. Retrieved 5 Jul 2022

Werner, A. (2020). *Outlook for Latin America and the Caribbean: New Challenges to Growth*. International Monetary Fund Blog. https://blogs.imf.org/2020/01/29/outlook-for-latin-america-and-the-caribbean-new-challenges-to-growth/. Retrieved 5 Jul 2022

Werutsky, G., Barrios, C., Cardona, A., Albergaria, A., Valencia, A., Ferreira, C., Rolfo, C., de Azambuja, E., Rabinovich, G., Sposetti, G., Arrieta, O., Dienstmann, R., Rebelatto, T., Denninghoff, V., Aran, V., & Cazap, E. (2021). Perspectives on emerging technologies, personalised medicine, and clinical research for cancer control in Latin America and the Caribbean. *The Lancet Oncology, 22*, e488–e500. https://doi.org/10.1016/s1470-2045(21)00523-4

Williams, K. (2019). *AI meets vishing*. Smarter MSP. https://smartermsp.com/ai-meets-vishing/. Retrieved 5 Jul 2022

Woolley, S. (2020). *The Reality Game: How the Next Wave of Technology Will Break the Truth*. Public Affairs.

World Economic Forum. (2016). *The Future of Jobs Employment*. Skills and Workforce Strategy for the Fourth Industrial Revolution. Executive Summary.

Yangüez Cervantes, N., & Zapata-Jaramillo, C. (2021). Artificial Intelligence and Industry 4.0 Across the Continent: How AI and 4.0 are Addressed by Region. Radical Solutions for Digital Transformation in Latin American Universities 157-177. https://doi.org/10.1007/978-981-16-3941-8_9

21

Malicious Use of Artificial Intelligence and the Threat to Psychological Security in the Middle East: Aggravation of Political and Social Turbulence

Vitali Romanovski

Introduction

The Middle East is undergoing profound social transitions and is still mired in deep turbulence and uncertainty. The region's volatility is anchored in profound changes that have been coming for years and have a long way to go (Brun & Shapira, 2020; International Institute of Strategic Studies, 2020).

The COVID-19 pandemic has exacerbated the deep socio-political and economic grievances of the conflict-affected Middle Eastern states. In addition, the pandemic crisis has accelerated digitization, and this trend will continue—technology sectors will maintain their role as global economic drivers. At the same time, with the accelerated pace of developed economies' digitization, the issue of the digital divide and uneven distribution of income between digital leaders and the rest is becoming acute. Moreover, given the growing public distrust of political institutions, the issue of the uneven distribution of profits—if exploited by antisocial actors—could have a strong destabilizing effect in developing economies and lead to extreme social disruptions.

It is doubtful that these actors will stop searching for new leverage or seizing new opportunities to make their actions more effective in this already turbulent region. They will eventually include advanced digital technologies

V. Romanovski (✉)
Belarusian State University, Minsk, Belarus

in their toolboxes—the question is when and in what form this will happen. Researchers highlight that AI-driven technologies could potentially significantly increase the effectiveness of targeted psychological and cyber operations (Ajder, 2019; Bazarkina & Pashentsev, 2020; Brundage et al., 2018; Johnson, 2020; Marr, 2018; Pashentsev et al., 2020) against social and political institutions. Given the AI aspirations of Middle Eastern countries (Ganji, 2020; Qatar Computing Research Institute, 2020; Emirates Centre for Strategic Studies and Research, 2019a, b; PricewaterhouseCoopers, 2018), the vulnerabilities of their cyber domains (Aboul-Enein, 2017; Deloitte, 2017; Pallavi, 2020; Place, 2020), and the overall turbulence in the region, the author assumes that the uneven distribution of profits gained with the help of technological innovation could be one of those vulnerabilities that malicious actors will exploit. This research attempts to take a closer look at this hypothesis.

This chapter consists of an introduction, four substantive sections, and a conclusion. In the first substantive section, "The Middle East: An outline of key vulnerabilities," the author highlights that the Middle East is mired in deep crisis and that technology-driven economic growth might bring additional challenges for societies in transition. In the second substantive section, "The Rapid Development of the Artificial Intelligence Industry in the Region," the author gives a brief description of the AI aspirations of the Middle Eastern states. Third, "AI-Driven Targeted Psychological Operations: Challenging the Regional Stability" argues that technology—and AI-driven economic growth—has a major problem of equitable distribution of profits that could become particularly acute in the Middle Eastern region and it describes how malicious actors could exploit this vulnerability using AI-driven technologies. Fourth, the "Recommendations for Decision-Makers" section provides a few ideas that could be considered while assessing the risks of AI-supported targeted psychological operations aimed at destabilizing the Middle Eastern political and societal systems. In the final section, "Conclusion," the author outlines the main findings and discusses possible future research directions.

Several groups of primary and secondary sources were taken into consideration during the research. The primary sources are official publications of governmental bodies and intergovernmental entities, security agencies, businesses, and mass media reports. They were used to analyze the ecosystem related to the development of AI technologies, with a particular focus on Middle Eastern countries (Pallavi, 2020; Qatar Computing Research Institute, 2020; Emirates Centre for Strategic Studies and Research, 2019a, b; PricewaterhouseCoopers, 2018; Deloitte, 2017). Secondary sources mainly included research articles and analytical reports on the study area. Among them were analytical reports on the state of affairs in the Middle East (Brun & Shapira, 2020; International Institute for Strategic Studies, 2020), research articles on the psychology of security (Bar-Tal, 2020; Hopner et al., 2020), materials on the link between AI-driven technologies and the effectiveness of targeted psychological and cyber operations (Aboul-Enein, 2017; Ajder, 2019; Bazarkina & Pashentsev, 2020; Brundage et al., 2018; Johnson, 2020; Marr, 2018; Pashentsev et al., 2020), and reports on the potential increases in inequality that AI-driven economic growth could create (O'Keefe et al., 2020; Walsh, 2020).

The Middle East: An Outline of Key Vulnerabilities

There is a firm understanding among observers that the Middle East is mired in deep crisis and will remain turbulent for the foreseeable future. The region is a salient hotspot in the international arena due to its abundant energy resources, perennial conflicts, and severe humanitarian crises. The IOM World Migration Report 2020 highlights that Syria and Yemen are "level 3" emergencies—the most severe and widespread humanitarian crises according to the global humanitarian system's classification and "key contributors to the world's total displacement figures" (International Organization for Migration, 2020).

COVID-19 has exacerbated endemic economic grievances in many parts of the region. As a result, many non-GCC[1] countries have less fiscal space to finance large-scale stimulus packages and control the pandemic (International Labour Organization, 2021). Moreover, Middle Eastern states have faced a sizable increase in government debt and fiscal deficits, from 47.6% of gross domestic product (GDP) in 2019 to 56.4% in 2020 and from 3.8% of GDP in 2019 to 10.1% in 2020, respectively (International Monetary Fund, 2021). As a result, the World Bank expects very modest growth in the regional economy—2.1% in 2021 and 3.1% in 2022, 8% below the level projected at the beginning of 2020 (World Bank, 2021).

The crisis in the Middle East is multifaceted. Brun and Kurz (2021) highlight that state and non-state actors continue to compete for dominance along several fault lines, including relations with the West, the role of Iran, sectarianism, political Islam, and the integrity of the nation-state as the foundation of the regional system (Brun & Kurz, 2021). Furthermore, a strong feeling of distrust in the existing political systems and the weakening bonds between the mainstream political agendas of the ruling elites and the

---

[1] GCC—Gulf Cooperation Council.

general public deepen these fractures and make the prospects of peaceful settlement even more distant.

At the onset of the COVID-19 contagion, the protest movement abated in Sudan, Algeria, Iraq, Lebanon, and Iran. Yet, at the same time, the severe economic impact of the virus has worsened the core issues that fueled opposition to the regimes. Thus, even though the public will not take to the streets in large numbers anytime soon, ongoing geopolitical turbulence, unresolved socioeconomic dilemmas, and regimes' determination to consolidate their power will likely renew protest movements and waves of migration (Brun & Kurz, 2021).

Evidence shows that lockdown attrition and severe economic backlash have accentuated inequalities and income-based segregation within communities, especially in fragile and conflict-affected economies (The Independent Panel for Pandemic Preparedness and Response, 2021a, b; International Monetary Fund, 2021; International Labour Organization, 2021). Moreover, according to IMF estimates, income disparity levels between technologically advanced GCC monarchies and non-GCC states will likely influence the recovery tempo across the region and pose a risk of a persistent rise in inequality (International Monetary Fund, 2021).

The pandemic has emphasized the interdependence of regional economies (International Labour Organization, 2021). However, political and ideological divisions have not transformed these connections into a resilient system to survive a crisis of a similar scale with fewer losses. It seems that the deflated role of multilateral mechanisms in addressing common challenges and increased demand for responsive domestic policies will likely further alienate the relatively stable economies from the conflict-affected states and regional agendas (World Economic Forum, 2021). Focus on domestic politics to the detriment of the need to solve common regional issues in the long term may aggravate existing problems and postpone their solution to a dim prospect.

The Rapid Development of the Artificial Intelligence Industry in the Region

The ongoing digital transformations and technological shifts that the COVID-19 crisis has accelerated are first and foremost about managing the growing amount of data. For example, Reinsel et al. (2021) point out that the global datasphere will grow to 175 zettabytes by 2025 compared to 33 zettabytes in 2018. This growth requires cutting-edge tools to process data and integrate that data into everyday life. AI technologies will likely solve these tasks.

China, the United States, Russia, Japan, and other large economies have already dived into AI development. The reason is quite apparent: only in the economic sphere can AI deliver US$13 trillion of additional economic activity by 2030, or about 16% higher cumulative GDP (Bughin et al., 2018), not to mention promising AI applications for national security purposes. Moreover, the United Nations reports that frontier technologies such as quantum computing, blockchain, and the Internet of Things are not independent of AI as technologies collaborate to support each other (United Nations, 2021).

AI investment and research are clearly on the rise. For example, Stanford Artificial Intelligence Service Report 2021 highlights that the total global investment in AI increased by 40% in 2020 relative to 2019 for a total of US$67.9 billion. In addition, the number of AI journal publications grew by 34.5% from 2019 to 2020, compared to 19.6% from 2018 to 2019 (Zhang et al., 2021).

In the Middle East, AI is expected to represent a significant portion of the regional states' GDPs by 2030: 7.7% in Egypt with US$42.7 billion, 8.2% in Bahrain, Kuwait, Oman, and Qatar with US$45.9 billion, 12.4% in Saudi Arabia with US$135.2 billion, and 13.6% in the United Arab Emirates (UAE) with US$96 billion. In general, by 2030, the potential impact of AI on the regional economy could come closer to approximately US$320 billion (PricewaterhouseCoopers, 2018).

Forward-looking Middle Eastern states have already placed AI development at the top of national economic strategies and advocate adopting digital technologies to transform business, government, and society (Fletcher et al., 2019). For example, in 2017, the UAE launched its UAE Strategy for AI and, in 2019, released its National AI Research and Development (R & D) Strategic Plan 2019 Update to identify areas that needed additional government support. In 2019, Egypt issued its National AI Strategy and established the National Council of Artificial Intelligence. At the end of 2019, Qatar's Ministry of Transport and Communications approved the National Artificial Intelligence Strategy of Qatar, developed by Qatar Computing Research Institute. In 2020, Saudi Arabia adopted the National Strategy for Data and AI, developed by Saudi Data and AI Authority (United Nations, 2021). In 2021, the Turkish National Artificial Intelligence Strategy 2021–2025 entered into force. In December 2020, Israel announced its national AI program would be implemented in five stages.

AI-Driven Targeted Psychological Operations: Challenging the Regional Stability

Despite AI promising potential for economy, national security, and human well-being (MacDonald & Madzou, 2020; United Nations Interregional Crime and Research Institute, 2020; United Nations Interregional Crime and Research Institute, 2021), AI adoption could widen performance gaps between countries, businesses, and individuals and will likely lead to uneven profits (Alonso, Carter, et al., 2020b; Bughin et al., 2018). For example, Balakrishnan et al. (2020) argue that by 2030, AI leaders could have added 20–25% in economic benefits, while developing economies could have only 10–15%. Even now, the companies with higher digital budgets in AI are already experiencing higher earnings before interest and taxes and better overall growth. As a result, there is a growing probability that the AI high performers will double their returns in the coming decade. In contrast, businesses that delay AI adoption will likely fall behind.

International Monetary Fund researchers Alonso, Kothari, and Rehman (2020a) suggest that AI could widen the inequality gap by shifting more investment to advanced economies with established automation; in developing countries, this could mean that AI replaces rather than complements growing labor forces. The gap will likely unfold at the individual worker level with the shifting demand from job profiles requiring low digital skills to those hard to automate and requiring more cognitive-driven, high-level digital competencies (Bughin et al., 2018).

The International Monetary Fund reports that youth unemployment rates, which were already high before the pandemic, increased 3–10 percentage points above pre-pandemic levels and reached nearly 32% in Morocco, 36.5% in Tunisia, and 55% in Jordan in the fourth quarter of 2020 (International Monetary Fund, 2021). It is unclear to what extent the pandemic-related digitization tempo influenced unemployment growth among the regional youth during 2020–2021. However, it is doubtful that the Middle East did not experience the changes that ubiquitous digital transformations brought to the global labor market.

Indeed, to see automation as either job-creating or job-destroying may seem one-sided in advanced economies. However, in conflict-affected states with soaring levels of unemployment and a lack of coherent workforce reorientation policies, wide-scale automation can be a zero-sum game.

The COVID-19 crisis has increased the overall dependence of public services, business processes, and personal well-being on digital infrastructures and security. The flawless, uninterrupted work of data processing infrastructure proved to be essential for the effective functioning of social and economic systems. As a result, states' political stability and national security have become increasingly dependent on digital security and digital sovereignty.

The World Economic Forum Global Risks Report 2021 underlines that digital power concentration and related inequality are among the highest risks in the next ten years. The growing gap between digital "haves" and "have-nots" can disproportionally affect the vulnerable populations of fragile and conflict-affected Middle Eastern economies and further deepen existing socio-political fractures (World Economic Forum, 2021). O'Keefe et al. (2020) highlight that the pandemic-related tempo of digitization has emphasized inequality issues and a dissatisfaction with extreme domestic economic inequality that might also lead to political instability. It is notable that historically, in the Middle Eastern states, political instability parallels increases in crime, civic unrest, further economic downturn, and the intensification of armed confrontation.

It is doubtful that in the turbulent Middle Eastern region, terrorists, criminal groups, or adversarial state agencies will stop seizing new opportunities to make their actions more effective. Given that security in modern society is multifaceted and includes collective psychological experience and cultural security (Bar-Tal, 2020; Zotova, 2011), targeted cyber operations can have devastating consequences for the functioning of public institutions in general. Moreover, the Middle Eastern countries' socio-political instability, vulnerable cyber domains, and AI aspirations that require restructuring methods and economic activity form a fertile ground for these types of attacks.

Europol's research proves that criminals and organized crime groups are increasingly using new technologies, in particular, within the crime-as-a-service business model (Europol, 2020). In turn, this "further increases the potential for new technologies such as AI to be abused by criminals and become a driver of a crime" (Ciancaglini et al., 2020, p. 4).

Furthermore, although terrorists are more inclined to use conventional weapons, terrorism is not a stagnant phenomenon (United Nations Interregional Crime and Research Institute, 2021). On the contrary, terrorists adapt to changing circumstances very fast (Hoffman, 2017). In addition, technological democratization and low barriers to entry into the AI field instead raise the question of "when" advanced technologies, such as AI, will take their place in the arsenal of the Middle Eastern terrorist or criminal groups. Terrorists do not have the scale of the bureaucracy and inertness of the state security apparatus, but they focus on effectiveness and are often one step ahead (Romanovski, 2021).

In the Middle East, malicious actors could potentially employ advanced technologies (such as AI) for cybercrimes. Netscout, one of the global leaders in distributed enterprise network management, reports that in 2020, the number of recorded distributed denial-of-service DDoS attacks exceeded the threshold of 10 million for the first time in history, with a 20% increase over the year and 22% in the second half of the year. The top five vertical industry targets were financial services, government, education platforms, hosting and cloud services, and e-commerce (Hummel et al., 2020). A high percentage of these attacks targeted Middle Eastern economies. In addition, the regional countries saw a visible increase in ransomware, malware, and VPN attacks and a significant rise in the number of discovered cyber vulnerabilities in the government, private, energy, telecom, and healthcare sectors compared to 2019 (Help, 2021).

Rich and rapidly digitizing GCC countries, especially Saudi Arabia and the UAE, have become a global hotspot for cybercrime (Adjou & Shabkhan, 2021). In 2020, the UAE faced a 250% increase in malicious cyber activity. Saudi Arabia and Bahrain encountered more than seven million cyberattacks each in the first quarter of 2021 (Baig, 2021). In addition, Saudi Arabia and the UAE experienced the second-highest cost of a data breach globally—US$6.52 million (IBM Security, 2021).

Given the Middle Eastern states' digitization ambitions, and their economies' reliance on cyberinfrastructure, the regional cybersecurity market size is projected to grow from US$15.6 billion in 2020 to US$29.9 billion by 2025, with Saudi Arabia, Turkey, and the UAE holding the largest share (Cicomag, 2020). Notably, according to an IBM report, organizations with fully operational security AI have the biggest data breach cost mitigation—up to US$3.81 million—compared to organizations without it (IBM Security, 2021).

AI-supported password guessing, CAPTCHA-breaking, encryption, cryptocurrency trading, human impersonation, and content generation, in addition to the abuse of AI cloud services and AI intelligent assistants, seem to be promising areas of activity for cybercriminals (Ciancaglini et al., 2020). In general, there is increasing feasibility that AI-supported DDoS, malware, and ransomware attacks will be in the Middle Eastern terrorists' toolbox shortly.

If malicious actors conduct successful cyberattacks against state-owned banks, or, for example, city-forming enterprises, then the possible reputational costs of such actions can be very high. The public and foreign partners will lose confidence in banks and be less willing to do business with cyber-compromised, state-owned enterprises. A subsequent drop in affected banks and enterprises' shares could entail political costs for state leadership.

Malicious actors can employ advanced technologies to attack physical infrastructure. For example, terrorists can use drones with facial recognition systems for targeted assassinations (United Nations Interregional Crime and Justice Research Institute, 2021).

The possibility of using cutting-edge technologies for data-poisoning of strategic ecosystems, such as public transport or power grids, is of particular concern. A prolonged blackout in a developed economy can cause disruption of business processes, significant economic damage, and inconvenience to the local population. A protracted blackout in a conflict-affected state, in addition to financial losses, could cause civil unrest and compromise the state's internal security. Moreover, if the accompanying atmosphere of panic will have political repercussions, it is possible to attribute the actions that caused the blackout to cognitive (psychological) warfare tactics.

The Middle Eastern states with higher digital economy levels will likely invest more in cybersecurity to overcome COVID-19 transition costs, maintain the tempo of their economic growth, and implement ambitious development plans. However, at the same time, less-developed regional states will inevitably fall behind, unable to provide cutting-edge cybersecurity solutions on a large scale. Thus, the technological development fault line between the regional economies will expand, and inequality between digital "haves" and "have-nots" will unfold further.

Digital interconnectivity, cyber vulnerabilities, and data dependence could enable malicious groups and their supporters to use advanced technologies to worsen public distrust for state authorities and create a context for particular political decisions.

Bradshaw et al. (2020) point out that 2020 saw an increase in the number of states (81) in which various actors used social media to spread propaganda and disinformation about politics. Government agencies used computational propaganda to shape public opinion in Bahrain, Egypt, Iraq, Kuwait, Oman, Qatar, Saudi Arabia, Syria, the UAE, and Yemen. Political factions used social media to spread disinformation about their political opponents in Egypt, Iraq, Kuwait, Lebanon, and Yemen. Private companies that offer services on political communication, including political agenda-setting, were employed in Bahrain, Egypt, Iraq, Kuwait, Lebanon, Qatar, Saudi Arabia, and the UAE. Notably, the number of countries with evidence of private companies managing manipulation and disinformation campaigns increased from 25 in 2019 to 48 in 2020. Government agencies and political parties enticed civil society and influencers into propaganda activities in Iraq, Kuwait, and Syria.

Malicious antisocial actors can use advanced technologies for politically motivated intimidation (Pashentsev & Bazarkina, 2019; Pashentsev &

Bazarkina, 2020; Raikov, 2020). There are plenty of opportunities for this: decreasing trust in institutions that were previously seen as sources of facts and data, the blurring line between facts and opinion, and the increasing influence of opinions over facts have been complicating communication between government and the population for years in the Middle East.

Algorithms are very good at identifying the stories that populations would like to hear and reinforcing what they believe. Compared to traditional information processing techniques, AI-supported ones have advantages in the volume and speed of information generation and distribution, the strength of intellectual and emotional influence, and the use of predictive analytics for customization (Pashentsev, 2021).

There is already direct evidence that malicious actors have access to data and advanced algorithms to "disseminate harmful content with unprecedented scale, speed, and efficiency" (World Economic Forum, 2021). Moreover, a recent Europol report, "Law Enforcement and the Challenge of Deepfakes," suggests that deepfake technology can facilitate various criminal activities, including distributing disinformation, manipulating public opinion, and supporting the narratives of extremist or terrorist groups (Europol, 2022).

Pashentsev and Bazarkina (2021) highlight that with AI technologies' assistance, "the mass production of false information can be automated by attackers with little or no technical knowledge." In view of the well-established tradition of disinformation and media manipulation in a number of the Middle Eastern states, it is reasonable to support the assumption that AI-based deepfake technologies will probably be used more often for agenda-setting and other politically motivated objectives.

At the same time, given the Middle Eastern societies' awareness of politically motivated fake media content, and overall skepticism toward media neutrality, various initiatives and institutions are emerging to counter the new sophisticated methods of disinformation. For example, in July 2021 UAE government issued a "Deepfake Guide." The document underlined that "deepfakes could be exploited for malicious purposes, including: causing damage to the reputation of individuals and countries, manipulating public opinion for the intention of causing disruptions, imposing a lack of trust by using deepfake reality as part of a plausible truth, creating fabricated evidence to influence a legal judgment" (National Program for Artificial Intelligence, 2021). Qatar pays increased attention to countering disinformation and fake media content. Al Jazeera Media Institute launched a research initiative aimed at assessing the efforts of the Al Jazeera network in controlling fake news in its newsrooms and highlighted the important role of AI in detecting fake sources

(Gody, 2021). There is ongoing research at Hamad Bin Khalifa University in Doha on disinformation techniques and state-led propaganda campaigns in the digital world (Ahmed, 2021). In general, it is possible to conclude that a relevant public discourse is being formed in the Middle Eastern region regarding the potential threats of AI-supported technologies' use in disinformation campaigns with possible social, political, financial, and legal implications (Al Jazeera, 2022; Al-Jabari, 2021; Al-Sarayra, 2021; Satter, 2020).

Alonso, Carter, et al. (2020b) point out that "accelerating pre-existing divisions within groups of the population or introducing new ideas designed to pit different groups against each other" disrupts people's unity. When populations are overwhelmed with internal issues, the only thing that malicious actors have to do to increase polarization is to play on the pre-existing fault lines within those communities. In the history of the independent Middle Eastern states, income inequality is one of these pre-existing lines. Extremely polarized agendas of the ruling elite and the population in many parts of the region only emphasize this.

The expanded range of opportunities to manipulate public opinion in these already turbulent areas gives rise to terrorist groups' communication activities. Terrorism, at its core, is always about political communication. As a socio-political phenomenon, it aims at creating a context for socio-political transformations and decisions beneficial to the perpetrators of a terrorist act (Bazarkina, 2020; Rabi'i & Ibrahim, 2019). Internet-based platforms and communication tools have already proven extremely valuable for radicalization, inspiring violence, recruiting, and arousing fear (United Nations, 2018). In their turn, AI-supported computational propaganda tools, such as content manipulation, illegal data collection, micro-targeting, and deep fakes, can potentially assist terrorists, criminals, and their supporters in formulating political agendas and manipulating the population in a state or entire region.

Recommendations for Decision-Makers

The strategic and sensitive nature of AI technologies employment by malicious actors presumes both the active role of the national government and interstate cooperation.

Governments should develop policies to increase the population's resilience to offensive cognitive operations from other states and non-state actors and formulate strategies to enhance media and information literacy, emphasizing critical thinking skills. Therefore, it is necessary to study UNESCO's and the International Federation of Library Associations and Institutions' approaches to media literacy and involve departments specializing in cognitive (psychological) warfare when developing appropriate programs.

Furthermore, governments should formulate more coherent policies to counter disinformation. For example, they could consider creating a specialized state interdepartmental structure to counter disinformation. The critical task will be to promptly inform internal and external audiences about disinformation cases regarding state structures' activities. In addition, a specialized research platform to exchange information and personal experiences concerning countering disinformation and cognitive (psychological) warfare strategies could contribute to capacity-building in this sphere. Moreover, such a platform could improve experience exchange between the operatives and experts.

State agencies should actively use up-to-date software products to counter disinformation activity. Advanced software could assist in increasing the speed of response to incidents related to the spread of disinformation and expedite the data exchange between specialized departments and internet providers, banks, and the media.

It is necessary to explore the possibility of combining existing tools in specialized agencies with tools and platforms used in other countries and regions. The use of international experience in countering disinformation and propaganda activities should take into account national security interests and the specifics of the state's law enforcement practice.

Advanced technologies could be helpful in the creation of a unified information verification system. Such technologies should incorporate new methodologies for clarifying reality, including multi-layered procedures to verify facts and sources. That is of utmost importance for the decision-making at the senior leadership level, as currently, "the decision-making process is less influenced by professional fact-based analysis than by feelings, beliefs, opinions, and lies" (Brun & Roitman, 2019). In addition, this issue opens new areas of cooperation between political scientists and computer science researchers.

The specifics of the special agencies' work predetermine their essential role in developing appropriate strategies to counter cognitive (psychological) operations, with analysts at the forefront of this work. Analysts should undoubtedly master the latest technologies that can potentially be helpful in data processing, presenting research results, and solving integration problems (Even & Siman-Tov, 2020). Data processing may include verification procedures and identification of patterns, anomalies, and hidden trends, such as changes in the behavioral patterns of terrorist organizations or their leaders or the frequency of a specific narrative used in a geographic region by international terrorist organizations. It is important to note that this work can continue 24/7. Furthermore, the presentation of research results can include notifications of changes in the patterns that analysts monitor and visualizations of data processing results. Finally, AI systems may optimize information exchange between analytical structures within one department and between analytical facilities and operational units. In this regard, it is advisable to consider the possibility of providing algorithms with access to information of limited distribution and process it simultaneously with the data from open sources.

The main obstacle to innovation in special agencies' work is not so much the issue of technological equipment and the availability of qualified personnel as it is the issue of the culture of doing business, specifically resistance to change in the usual modus operandi. In this regard, it seems reasonable to support initiatives to disseminate best practices in using the latest technologies and further unite the efforts of specialized agencies and the scientific and expert community.

Conclusion

The pandemic has deepened the core economic and socio-political problems of the conflict-affected Middle Eastern states. Youth unemployment, corruption, ineffective governance, low productivity, ideological fault lines, and weakening bonds between the elites' agendas and the general public have become even more acute. In addition, growing digitization and digital interdependence have highlighted cyber vulnerabilities in the regional economies. As a result, individuals' and communities' physical surroundings and safety are becoming more vulnerable to cyber- and cognitive attacks (Brun & Kurz, 2021).

The digital divide has raised the issue of unequal distribution of profits between digital "haves" and "have-nots." Competition for technological dominance has gained momentum and exacerbated military-political contradictions between the states and socioeconomic contradictions within societies. Malicious actors will likely continue to capitalize on these trends. There is increasing feasibility that advanced technologies, including AI, will appear in their toolbox shortly. Decision-makers in the Middle East should prepare for deeper socio-political crises and start developing strategies for the steady convergence of the elitist and general public agendas to avoid the turmoil that the digital divide in the region could only expedite.

It is vital to enhance interagency collaboration and information exchange between researchers in political science and technical specialists regarding applying AI and other digital technologies in the national security field. Collaboration between the information exchange platforms of the neighboring states could potentially add to the regional cyber-resilience. That said, cyber-resilience capacity-building is not a panacea to the entire spectrum of problems that arise in connection with digitization. Therefore, there is an acute need for a broad and multilateral discussion on better ways to channel technology-driven growth toward achieving sustainable development goals in the conflict-torn Middle Eastern region.

References

Aboul-Enein, S. (2017). Cybersecurity challenges in the Middle East. *The Geneva Centre for Security Policy* [Online]. Retrieved January 11, 2021, from https://css.ethz.ch/content/dam/ethz/special-interest/gess/cis/center-for-securities-studies/resources/docs/GCSP-Cybersecurity%20Challenges%20in%20the%20Middle%20East.pdf.

Adjou A., & Shabkhan, K. (2021). *On high alert...* [online], The oath. Retrieved October 15, 2021, from https://theoath-me.com/13173-2/.

Ahmed, N. (2021). *Middle East disinformation wars and the battle for narratives in the digital space* [Online]. Retrieved May 20, 2021, from https://www.middleeastmonitor.com/20210922-memo-in-conversation-with-marc-owen-jones/.

Ajder, H. (2019). *Social engineering and sabotage: Why deepfakes pose an unprecedented threat to businesses* [Online]. Retrieved January 12, 2021, from https://medium.com/sensity/scams-and-sabotage-why-deepfakes-pose-an-unprecedented-threat-to-businesses-537875524b31.

Al Jazeera. (2022). تحذيرات أوربية من تزايد استخدام تقنية "التزييف العميق" في عالم الجريمة *[Europeans warn of the increasing use of deepfake technology in the world of crime]* [online], Al Jazeera. Retrieved May 22, 2022, from https://mubasher.aljazeera.net/news/politics/2022/4/29/.

Al-Jabari, M. (2021). تقنية تكشف التزييف العميق *[Deepfake technologies]* [Online], Al-Watan. Retrieved May 22, 2022, from https://www.al-watan.com/news-details/id/271359/.

Alonso, C., Kothari, S., & Rehman, S. (2020a). *Could artificial intelligence widen the gap between rich and poor nations?* [online], World economic forum. Retrieved October 12, 2022, from https://www.weforum.org/agenda/2020/12/artificial-intelligence-widen-gap-rich-developing-nations.

Alonso, B., Carter, C., Singh, I., Cao, K., & Madreperla, O. (2020b). *Cognitive warfare: An attack on truth and thought,* John Hopkins University [Online]. Retrieved October 22, 2021, from https://www.innovationhub-act.org/sites/default/files/2021-03/Cognitive%20Warfare.pdf.

Al-Sarayra, R. (2021). حملة إقليمية للتحذير من تقنية "التزييف العميق" بقصد الابتزاز *[a regional campaign to warn against deepfake technology with the blackmail intent]* [online], Al Ghad newspaper. Retrieved May 22, 2022, from https://alghad.com/.

Baig, M. (2021). *Can the Middle East produce a cyber-security firm to challenge Silicon Valley?* [online], Arabian Business. Retrieved October 12, 2021, from https://www.arabianbusiness.com/opinion/comment/467787-can-the-middle-east-produce-cyber-security-firm-to-challenge-silicon-valley.

Balakrishnan, T., Chui, M., Hall, B., & Henke, N. (2020). *Global Survey: The State of AI in 2020* [Online]. Retrieved November 15, 2021, from https://www.mckinsey.com/business-functions/mckinsey-analytics/our-insights/global-survey-the-state-of-ai-in-2020.

Bar-Tal, D. (2020). Creating fear and insecurity for political goals. *International Perspectives in Psychology, Practice, Consultation, 9*, 5–17. https://doi.org/10.1037/ipp0000113

Bazarkina, D. (2020). *Exploitation of the advanced Technologies' image in terrorist propaganda and ways to counter it, chapter 4 at terrorism and advanced Technologies in Psychological Warfare: New risks, New Opportunities to Counter the Terrorist Threat*. Nova Science Publishers.

Bazarkina, D., & Pashentsev, E. (2020). Malicious use of artificial intelligence: New psychological security risks in BRICS countries. *Russia in Global Affairs, 18*(4), 154–177. [Online]. DOI: 10.31278/1810-6374-2020-18-4-154–177 (Accessed 12 January 2021).

Bradshaw, S., Bailey, H., & Howard, P. (2020). *Industrialized Disinformation: 2020 Global Inventory of Organised Social Media Manipulation*, University of Oxford [Online]. Retrieved October 23, 2021, from https://demtech.oii.ox.ac.uk/wp-content/uploads/sites/127/2021/01/CyberTroop-Report-2020-v.2.pdf.

Brun, I., & Kurz, A. (2021). *Strategic survey for Israel 2020–2021*. The Institute for National Security Studies.

Brun, I., & Roitman, M. (2019). *National security in the era of post-truth and fake news* [Online]. Retrieved October, 24, 2021, from https://www.inss.org.il/publication/national-security-in-the-era-of-post-truth-and-fake-news/.

Brun, I., & Shapira, I. (2020). Strategic survey for Israel 2019-2020. *The Institute for National Security Studies*, 18–19.

Brundage, M., Avin, S., Clark, J., Toner, H., Eckersley, P., Garfinkel, B., Dafoe, A., Scharre, P., Zeitzoff, T., Filar, B., Anderson, H., Roff, H., Allen, G., Steinhardt, J., Flynn, C., Héigeartaigh, S. Ó., Beard, S., Belfield, H., Farquhar, S., Lyle, C., Crootof, R., Evans, O., Page, M., Bryson, J., Yampolskiy, R., & Amodei, D. (2018). *The Malicious use of artificial intelligence: Forecasting, prevention, and mitigation* [Online]. Retrieved January 10, 2021, from https://dataspace.princeton.edu/bitstream/88435/dsp01th83m203g/1/1c6q2kc4v_50335.pdf.

Bughin, J., Seong, J., Manyika, J., Chui, M., & Joshi, R. (2018). *Notes from the AI frontier: Modelling the impact of AI on the world economy*. McKinsey Global Institute. Available at https://www.mckinsey.com/featured-insights/artificial-intelligence/notes-from-the-ai-frontier-modeling-the-impact-of-ai-on-the-world-economy (Accessed 24 October 2021)

Ciancaglini, V., Gibson, C., Sancho, D., McCarthy, O., Eira, M., Amann, P., & Klayn, A. (2020). *Malicious uses and abuses of artificial intelligence.* Europol. Available at https://www.europol.europa.eu/publications-documents/malicious-uses-and-abuses-of-artificial-intelligence (Accessed 24 October 2021)

Cicomag. (2020). *Middle East Cybersecurity Market Worth $29.9 Bn Post COVID-19* [Online], Cicomag. Retrieved October 24, 2021, from https://cisomag.eccouncil.org/middle-east-cybersecurity-market-worth-29-9-bn-post-covid-19/.

Deloitte. (2017). *Deloitte Cyber Risk Capabilities in the Middle East* [Online]. Retrieved January 11, 2021, from https://www2.deloitte.com/content/dam/Deloitte/xe/Documents/risk/me_risk_cyber-risk-capabilities-in-the-Middle-East.PDF.

Emirates Centre for Strategic Studies and Research. (2019a). *Emirates Centre for Strategic Studies and Research الذكاء الاصطناعي والحروب الرقمية* [AI and Digital Wars] [Online]. Retrieved January 11, 2021, from الذكاء الاصطناعي والحروب الرقمية | Emirates Center for Strategic Studies and Research (ecssr.ae).

Emirates Centre for Strategic Studies and Research. (2019b). *Emirates Centre for Strategic Studies and Research. 2030.. 2030* [الإمارات من قادة قطاعات الروبوت والذكاء الاصطناعي عالمياً ..] *The UAE is One of the Global Leaders in the Robotics and AI]* [Online]. Accessed on 11 January 2021, at 2030.. الاصطناعي عالمياً | الإمارات من قادة قطاعات الروبوت والذكاء Emirates Center for Strategic Studies and Research (ecssr.ae) (Accessed 10 October 2021).

Europol. (2020). *Internet Organised Crime Threat Assessment (IOCTA) 2020* [Online], Europol. Retrieved October 24, 2021, from https://www.europol.europa.eu/activities-services/main-reports/internet-organised-crime-threat-assessment-iocta-2020.

Europol. (2022). *Law enforcement and the challenge of deepfakes* [Online], Europol. Retrieved May 5, 2022, from https://www.europol.europa.eu/media-press/newsroom/news/europol-report-finds-deepfake-technology-could-become-staple-tool-for-organised-crime.

Even, S., & Siman-Tov, D. (2020). *Research in the intelligence Community in the age of artificial intelligence* [online], Institute of National Security Studies. Retrieved October 24, 2021, from https://www.inss.org.il/publication/research-in-the-intelligence-community-in-the-age-of-artificial-intelligence/.

Fletcher, I., Goehring, B., Marshall, A., & Saeed, T. (2019). *Middle East prepares for AI accelerations* [online], IBM Institute for business value. Retrieved October 24, 2021, from https://www.ibm.com/downloads/cas/XWPEAP0V.

Ganji, H. (2020). الانتقال من النفط إلى الذكاء الاصطناعي. *[Transition from Oil to AI]* [Online]. Retrieved January 11, 2021, from البيان | الانتقال من النفط إلى الذكاء الاصطناعي (bayancenter.org).

Gody, A. (2021). *Using artificial intelligence in the Al Jazeera newsroom to combat fake news* [online], Al Jazeera Media Institute. Retrieved May 20, 2022, from https://institute.aljazeera.net/sites/default/files/2021/Using%20Artificial%20

Intelligence%20in%20the%20Al%20Jazeera%20Newsroom%20to%20 Combat%20Fake%20News.pdf.

Help, A. G. (2021). *State of the Market Report 2021* [Online], Etisalat Digital. Retrieved October 24, 2021, from https://www.helpag.com/state-of-the-market-report-2021/.

Hoffman, B. (2017). *Inside Terrorism, Third Edition*. Columbia University Press.

Hopner, V., Hodgetts, D., Carr, S., Ball, R., Nelson, N., & Chamberlain, K. (2020). Introduction to the special section on the psychology of security. *International Perspectives in Psychology: Research, Practice, Consultation, 9*(1), 1–4. https://doi.org/10.1037/ipp0000123

Hummel, R., Hildebrand, C., Modi, H., Conrad, C., Dobbins, R., Bjarnson, S., Belanger, J., Sockrider, G., Alcoy, P., & Bienkowski, T. (2020). *Netscout Threat Intelligence Report,* Netscout [Online]. Retrieved October 24, 2021, from https://www.netscout.com/sites/default/files/2021-04/ThreatReport_2H2020_FINAL_0.pdf.

IBM Security. (2021). *Cost of Data Breach Report 2020* [Online]. Retrieved November 12, 2021, from https://www.capita.com/sites/g/files/nginej291/files/2020-08/Ponemon-Global-Cost-of-Data-Breach-Study-2020.pdf.

International Institute of Strategic Studies. (2020). *International Institute for Strategic Studies* [Online]. Retrieved January 9, 2021, from The Strategic and Geo-economic Implications of the COVID-19 Pandemic (iiss.org).

International Labour Organisation. (2021). *World employment and social outlook: Trends 2021*. International Labour Organisation.

International Monetary Fund. (2021). *Regional economic outlook update*. Middle East and Central Asia, International Monetary Fund.

International Organization for Migration. (2020). *IOM world migration report 2020*. International Organization for Migration.

Johnson, J. S. (2020). *Artificial Intelligence: A Threat to Strategic Stability* [Online]. Retrieved January 10, 2021, from https://www.airuniversity.af.edu/Portals/10/SSQ/documents/Volume-14_Issue-1/Johnson.pdf.

MacDonald, K., & Madzou, L. (2020). *AI is here. This is how it can benefit everyone* [online], WEF. Retrieved October 24, 2021, from https://www.weforum.org/agenda/2020/09/ai-is-here-this-is-how-it-can-benefit-everyone/.

Marr, B. (2018). *Weaponizing Artificial Intelligence: The Scary Prospect of AI-Enabled Terrorism* [Online]. Retrieved January 10, 2021, from https://www.forbes.com/sites/bernardmarr/2018/04/23/weaponizing-artificial-intelligence-the-scary-prospect-of-ai-enabled-terrorism/#64950b3d77b6.

National Program for Artificial Intelligence. (2021). Deepfake Guide [Online]. Retrieved May 21, 2021, from https://ai.gov.ae/publications/.

O'Keefe, C., Cihon, P., Flynn, C., Garfinkel, B., Leung, J., & Dafoe, A. (2020). *The windfall clause: Distributing the benefits of AI [online]*. University of Oxford. Available at https://www.fhi.ox.ac.uk/windfallclause/ (Accessed 24 October 2021)

Pallavi, D. (2020). *Middle East Hit by a Wave of Phishing Attacks in Q2 of 2020* [Online]. Retrieved January 10, 2021, from https://kdmarc.com/blog/middle-east-hit-by-a-wave-of-phishing-attacks-in-q2-of-2020/.

Pashentsev, E. (2021). *The Malicious Use of Artificial Intelligence Through Agenda Setting: Challenges to Political Stability*. Proceedings of the 3rd European Conference on the Impact of AI and Robotics, a Virtual Conference Hosted by Instituto Universitario de Lisboa (ISCTEIUL), Portugal, 18-19 November 2021, Academic conferences and publishing international limited, Reading, UK, pp. 138–144.

Pashentsev, E., & Bazarkina, D. (2019). *Artificial Intelligence and New Threats to International Psychological Security* [Online]. Retrieved October 10, 2021, from https://eng.globalaffairs.ru/articles/artificial-intelligence-and-new-threats-to-international-psychological-security/.

Pashentsev, E., & Bazarkina, D. (2020) Malicious use of artificial intelligence. New psychological Security risks in BRICS countries [online], Russia in global affairs. Retrieved October 10, 2021, from https://eng.globalaffairs.ru/articles/malicious-use-ai/.

Pashentsev, E., & Bazarkina, D. (2021). The malicious use of artificial intelligence against government and political institutions in the psychological area. In: Bielicki, D.M. (2021). Regulating Artificial Intelligence in Industry (1st ed.). Routledge. https://doi.org/10.4324/9781003246503.

Pashentsev, E., Bazarkina, D., Raikov, A., Antinori, A., Pantserev, K., Vacarelu, M., Thomann, P., Cao, N., Van Nhich, D., & Kramar, K. (2020). *Experts on the Malicious Use of Artificial Intelligence: Challenges for Political Stability and International Psychological Security* [Online]. Retrieved October 10, 2021, from https://www.academia.edu/43406469/Experts_on_the_Malicious_Use_of_Artificial_Intelligence_Challenges_for_Political_Stability_and_International_Psychological_Security_Report_by_the_International_Center_for_Social_and_Political_Studies_and_Consulting_June_2020_.

Place, L. (2020). *The Top 3 Cybersecurity Threats in the Middle East* [Online]. Retrieved January 10, 2021, from https://www.digitalshadows.com/blog-and-research/cybersecurity-threats-in-the-middle-east/.

PricewaterhouseCoopers. (2018). *The Potential Impact of AI in the Middle East* [Online]. Retrieved January 10, 2021, from https://www.pwc.com/m1/en/publications/potential-impact-artificial-intelligence-middle-east.html.

Qatar Computing Research Institute. (2020). *Qatar computing research institute*. استراتيجية قطر الوطنية في مجال الذكاء الصطناعي /*Qatar AI strategy*/ [online]. Retrieved January 11, 2021, from QCRI-artificial-intelligence-Strategy-2019-AR.Pdf.

Rabi'i, I., & Ibrahim, S. (2019). (أكرم فرج الربيعي سعد معن ابراهيم) 'digital brainwashing with the emergence of terrorist organizations. A study on the use of digital technologies by the Islamic state (ISIS) to recruit young people and adolescents', (ظاهرة بروز غسيل الدماغ الالكتروني مع ظهور التنظيمات الارهابية دراسة في توظيف تنظيم الدولة الاسلامية داعش للتقنيات الرقمية في تجنيد الشباب والمراهقين) *international journal of media and mass communication*, July, pp. 1–21.

Raikov, A. (2020). Weak vs. strong artificial intelligence. *Informatizatsiya i sviaz' [Informatization and Communication], 1*, 81–88.

Reinsel, D., Rydning, J., & Gantz, J. (2021). *Global datasphere forecast 2021-2025* [online], IDC. Retrieved October 10, 2021, from https://www.idc.com/getdoc.jsp?containerId=US46410421.

Romanovski, V. (2021). 'Malicious use of artificial intelligence for terrorist purposes', *Lomonosov-2021 international conference*, 12–23 April 2021, Moscow State University, Moscow, Russia.

Satter, R. (2020). *Deepfake used to attack activist couple shows new disinformation frontier* [online], Reuters. Retrieved May 20, 2022, from https://www.reuters.com/article/us-cyber-deepfake-activist-idUSKCN24G15E.

The Independent Panel for Pandemic Preparedness and Response. (2021a). *The World Health Organization: An institutional review background* [The Independent Panel for Pandemic Preparedness and Response, Geneva].

The Independent Panel for Pandemic Preparedness and Response. (2021b). *COVID-19: Make it the last pandemic* [The Independent Panel for Pandemic Preparedness and Response, Geneva].

United Nations. (2018). *UN secretary-General's strategy on new technologies* [UN, New York].

United Nations. (2021). *Resource Guide on Artificial Intelligence (AI) Strategies* [Online]. Retrieved October 11, 2021, from https://sdgs.un.org/ru/node/25128.

United Nations Interregional Crime and Justice Research Institute. (2020). *Special collection on artificial intelligence* [UNICRI, Torino].

United Nations Interregional Crime and Justice Research Institute. (2021). *Algorithms and terrorism: The malicious use of artificial intelligence for terrorist purposes*. UNICRI.

Walsh, M. (2020). *Algorithms are making economic inequality worse* [online], Harvard Business Review. Retrieved January 5, 2021, from Algorithms Are Making Economic Inequality Worse (hbr.org).

World Bank. (2021). *Global economic prospects. Middle East and North Africa* [World Bank, Washington, D.C.]

World Economic Forum. (2021). *Global risk report. 16th Edition* [World Economic Forum, Geneva].

Zhang, D., Mishra, S., Brynjolfsson, E., Etchemendy, J., Ganguli, D., Grosz, B., Lyons, T., Manyika, J., Niebles, J., Sellitto, M., Shoham, Y., Clark, J., & Perrault, R. (2021). *The AI Index 2021 Annual Report,* Stanford University [Online. Retrieved October 10, 2021, from https://aiindex.stanford.edu/wp-content/uploads/2021/03/2021-AI-Index-Report_Master.pdf.

Zotova, O. (2011). Need for safety in different social and economic groups. *Psychology in Russia: State of the Art, 4*, 335–347. https://doi.org/10.11621/pir.2011.0022

Part IV

Future Horizons: The New Quality of Malicious Use of Artificial Intelligence Threats to Psychological Security

22

Malicious Use of Artificial Intelligence in the Metaverse: Possible Threats and Countermeasures

Sergey A. Sebekin and Andrei Kalegin

Introduction

Currently, in an era of rapid technological development characterized by a huge volume of technological innovations being introduced into all spheres of life, people and in fact all of mankind are being forced to exist in a reality that is constantly changing due to the huge influence of new technologies. One of the main technologies that can be classified as being *disruptive* (even subversive) is artificial intelligence (AI). In terms of the overall quantity of global changes that it is bringing to the development of mankind, AI surpasses all other technologies. While this is occurring, at the same time humanity is on the verge of creating a fundamentally new type of digital platform, namely meta-universes (metaverses).

All technologies that can be classified as disruptive are ambivalent: they not only create new opportunities but also produce new threats. In this regard, metaverses that implement technologies designed for the complete immersion of users into virtual reality provide a wide range of opportunities for the

---

S. A. Sebekin (✉)
Department of Political Science, History and Regional Studies,
Irkutsk State University, Irkutsk, Russia

A. Kalegin
International Center for Social and Political Studies and Consulting,
Moscow, Russia

© The Author(s), under exclusive license to Springer Nature Switzerland AG 2023
E. Pashentsev (ed.), *The Palgrave Handbook of Malicious Use of AI and Psychological Security*,
https://doi.org/10.1007/978-3-031-22552-9_22

malicious use of artificial intelligence (MUAI), primarily in order to achieve certain political, economic or military goals by undermining psychological security. The existing technologies for carrying out MUAI, which will be discussed below, may receive a new impetus and areas for implementation within the framework of metaverses.

This chapter is devoted to clarifying definitions and specifying the main characteristics of the metaverses which allow for the application of specific MUAI technologies and also the consideration of the main actors operating in cyberspace and an analysis of their motivations, as well as the identification of specific forms of MUAI in the metaverses ultimately aimed at causing antisocial impact on social processes, social groups and individuals. We also look at subsets of AI technologies which are singled out and are most vulnerable to the implementation of destructive information and psychological influences in the metaverses and we consider a number of possible scenarios for the likely use of these technologies. Finally, we propose the proper vectors in which action needs to be taken for counteracting MUAI in the metaverses.

Definition and Main Characteristics of the Metaverse and the Degree of Development of Its Components

In order to analyze the possibilities that metaverses provide for the use of MUAI with the aim of causing an ultimate antisocial impact on social processes, social groups and individuals, it is first of all necessary to consider the very *nature* of the metaverse, to identify its key characteristics, as well as determine the degree of development of its individual components.

The term *metaverse*, first used by the American writer Neil Stevenson in 1992 in the novel *Snow Crash*, was formed by combining the Greek word meta (beyond) and the word universe (Colajuta, 2022; Duan et al., 2021, p. 1). Due to the concept's complex nature, there is still no single, generally accepted definition of the term *metaverse*, this being especially true in the scientific and expert community. The profusion of definitions of metaverse range from its description as "a fully realized and functional digital world that exists outside of the analog world we live in" (Herrman & Browning, 2021) to its interpretation as "the quasi-successor of the mobile Internet" (Ball, 2021). According to other concepts, the metaverses will be a completely new incarnation of the Internet and the next natural stage of its development:

the immersive Internet[1] or 3D Internet, with the possibility of complete immersion into it and obtaining a completely new way of interacting with data (text, audio and video files, etc.), digital objects, other users, electronic processes, virtual events and much more (Chandar, 2021; Ejeke, 2022; Terry & Keeny, 2022, pp. XXI, 17–19, 37–39, 41; Lee et al., 2022; Duan et al., 2021, p. 4; Melendez, 2022). In other words, we will surf the Internet and interact with data and other users not through traditional digital devices (the screens of computers and smartphones) but by completely immersing ourselves inside the Internet. One way or another, albeit on the scale of mass consciousness, the metaverses represent a new generation of Internet platforms and are perceived as different types of virtual worlds for recreation, entertainment, games, conferences, work, study and so on.

In the absence of a unified definition of the term *metaverse*, we can attempt to describe the phenomenon as follows: it is a decentralized, global and constantly functioning virtual space which provides users with a completely new and unique experience of immersive interaction through avatars with other actors and digital assets using extended reality technologies (XR) and covering different spheres of public life (entertainment, work, study, etc.), in which all of the social and professional opportunities that exist for an individual can be realized.

One's presence in the metaverse can be facilitated both through the help of virtual reality technologies and through the use of conventional digital devices. In the metaverse there may be roads, cars, houses, shopping centers or even entire fantasy worlds. Users choose digital avatars that they use to communicate with each other in the *here and now*: they can then relax together, go for walks, go shopping and even work (Collins, 2021; Melendez, 2022). In general this can be said to be a parallel digital world in which all the same social interactions and processes that take place in the real physical world can also take place.

Decentralization is one of the key characteristics of the metaverse (Duan et al., 2021, p. 1–2). Unlike the ecosystems of other services that are typical in our times and which are completely controlled by large high-tech corporations that develop them (i.e., Facebook, Instagram and WhatsApp controlled by Meta, or Google's services, including YouTube and the search engine itself), the concept of the metaverse implies that different parts of it can be controlled by various independent players and data and assets must be able to be transferred between the different parts of it (Duan et al., 2021, p. 2). The consequence of this approach is the need to provide the possibility of end-to-end

---

[1] "The immersive Internet," "the immersive web" and "the spatial web" are all definitions for websites navigated in three dimensions using a conventional web browser.

authorization in the absence of a single arbiter with one solution being to use a crypto wallet address in one of the blockchains as a user ID. At the same time, the same wallet can be used to pay for goods and services with cryptocurrencies, which provides a certain degree of anonymity.

In the economy of the metaverse, which implies the circulation and the existence of ways to fix the ownership of digital assets (such as avatars and digital real estate), in addition to cryptocurrencies, the idea of non-fungible tokens[2] (NFTs) naturally finds applications (Goldman Sachs, 2021, p. 2; Terry & Keeny, 2022, pp. 23–25; Voshmgir, 2020; Duan et al., 2021, p. 4).

Further we will list the key features of the metaverses, which according to the ideologist of the concept of metaverses Matthew Ball have seven identifiable canonical signs.

I. Permanence: The metaverse cannot be *paused*, nullified or deleted and its existence is infinite (Ball, 2020).

In essence, this means that no one, not even the developer themself, can *stop* the metaverse and the processes taking place within it. This characteristic is ensured by a certain degree of decentralization brought about by the fact that all users participate in its development. The *technical* functioning of a metaverse, like the processes, should also not be influenced by external factors, regardless of whether they are of a natural or man-made nature.

II. Synchronicity: Metaverses involve the obtaining of a *live* real-time continuous flowing experience simultaneously with other participants in the process (Ball, 2020).

It thus follows that when you do something in the metaverse together with other users, the processes occur in real time and you do not *take turns* in whatever the experience is because they happen at the same time for all participants.

III. Openness and Accessibility: The metaverse must have no restrictions and no limits on the number of simultaneous users (Ball, 2020; Duan et al., 2021, pp. 2–3).

This means that at any time every *meta-citizen* is able to obtain a completely immersive experience in the metaverse and make use of the full range of opportunities provided for them. Within the space they can participate in events; interact with other users, organizations and objects; move around to different locations and much more. Moreover, there must not be any

---

[2] This will be discussed further.

technical,[3] much less political, ideological or cultural, reason for denying any person access.

IV. A Full-Fledged Functioning Economy: Every actor and user in the metaverse can create, sell and buy products, goods and services while making a profit, investing and owning property (Ball, 2020).

Thus, there is the possibility for the existence of a truly huge economy in the metaverse. Users will be able to fully carry out a full range of financial transactions and all objects possess a financial value. The metaverse must be able to provide all existing opportunities for financial growth and economic development. In reality it is a sort of new *meta-frontier*, where *meta-settlers* will strive and compete not only for the purpose of obtaining new experiences but also for the sake of new opportunities that the metaverse will provide for investment and financial enrichment.

V. Hybrid Reality: The user experience will span both the virtual and physical worlds (Ball, 2020; Duan et al., 2021, p. 4; Melendez, 2022).

In its very essence, the metaverse is the union of the virtual and the physical worlds where users obtain a completely immersive experience in one world, the results of which are simultaneously reflected in the other. It also implies the use of a certain object that simultaneously exists in two worlds (thus there is a kind of *quantum superposition* in the metaverse): with the help of XR devices, users can interact with digital objects existing inside the metaverse while still being in the real world and the resulting experience is reflected in the metaverse. You can work on your laptop or drive in the real world and then use the digital models of these objects in the metaverse with all of their characteristics preserved. According to another concept, physical objects in the real world will be gradually replaced by digital *holograms* which can be observed in the same way as the real ones by using augmented reality devices: a person can be in a room without digital technology, but when using special glasses, the room may be filled with devices such as a smart TV, a computer, digital pets, an anthropomorphic 3D digital assistant (digital human) and much more.

VI. "Interoperability" or Functional Compatibility: Metaverses must be able to ensure the full compatibility of varied digital assets (objects, data and content) (Ball, 2020; Duan et al., 2021, p. 4). created by different companies or existing on different platforms. For example, users should be able to buy digital clothing from the Lacoste virtual store to use in *Fortnite* and then sell them on Facebook.

---

[3] First of all, there should be no technical restrictions on the part of the metaverse. If there are technical limitations on the part of the user's devices, that's another matter.

Such *cross-platform* compatibility should remove all existing restrictions in the development of metaverses. Users must be able to fully enjoy the benefits of their acquired digital assets at any point, during any event and with any application existing in the metaverse. Otherwise, if the possibility of using an asset is limited by the *borders* of any platform, there will be no incentive to buy anything whatsoever.

VII. Filled with Content and Experiences: All actors in the metaverse, ordinary users, communities and representatives of the private sector, fill the metaverse with various content (Ball, 2020; Duan et al., 2021, p. 4) and processes, among others, and then use and manage them.

Thus it will depend on the users and their number to fill the metaverse with content and experiences: the more users that have been attracted and are involved in the *life* of the metaverse, the better. The formation of metaverses as full-fledged worlds depends entirely on this one fact. Some may *enter* the metaverse for the sake of obtaining new experiences and others to fulfill their goals and realize their ideas. The users will of course be representatives of varied professions, cultures and views, and each of them will fill the metaverse with their own philosophies, events, goods, services and so on.

To reiterate, the metaverses will have developers providing the platforms, but the developers themselves will not fully own them (Stock, 2022). The developers will be able to direct the vectors of development and growth of the metaverses and even regulate them and create rules. However, to a large extent, the shape and nature of the space will be shaped by the users of the metaverses themselves, filling them with their own content and experiences and then deciding how to use what they find within their capabilities and for whatever their individual goals may be.

The metaverses are products of the natural process of scientific and technological development and the natural result of the convergence of a huge number and range of differing technologies, systems and platforms (Terry & Keeny, 2022, p. 57) that will serve to ensure their full functionality. Among these may be artificial intelligence (AI), blockchain, NFTs, virtual and augmented reality technologies, 5G networks and more (Colajuta, 2022).

One of the main drivers for the creation, development and functioning of metaverses will be artificial intelligence systems based on machine learning technologies, computer vision and other cutting-edge technologies. Some of the most promising areas for using AI in the metaverses are 3D modeling and the creation of digital models of objects, including the design and expansion of virtual world-clusters, the creation of the most accurate digital copies of objects in the physical world and more. AI will be used to analyze images, model highly accurate and dynamic user avatars in the metaverse, display facial expressions, facial features, emotions, hairstyles and the like (Huynh-The et al., 2022, pp. 4–5; Melendez, 2022).

Clearly one of the most obvious uses of AI would be the creation of so-called *digital humans*. Digital humans are 3D versions of chatbots whose function is learning and who exist in the metaverse. Users can interact with them for the purpose of obtaining consultations and getting answers to their questions. These digital humans are intended to be one of the main vehicles of social interaction in the metaverse (Terry & Keeny, 2022, pp. 6–8) and with whom we will spend a fairly large portion of our time. They will be what might be described as *digital butlers*, a 3D visual interface with speech processing functions, to which we will delegate tasks and ask questions, and who in turn will provide us with services, report the news to us and recommend content and events with which we can participate. They will also serve as our representatives, communicating on our behalf (Terry & Keeny, 2022, pp. 6–8) and carrying out certain operations and a standard set of tasks for which they will be authorized by their owners.

It should be obvious, therefore, that AI will be used to process and recognize speech and text, convert them and translate them instantly if necessary (Huynh-The et al., 2022, p. 5; Duan et al., 2021, p. 5; Melendez, 2022), and provide for truly international global communications, all of this being extremely important to facilitate the interaction of the aforementioned digital humans.

AI systems will also be installed in devices used for immersion into the metaverse (Huynh-The et al., 2022, pp. 11–12) and will involve not only virtual reality glasses, but also special gloves which will provide tactile sensations and with the help of special sensors there will even be neural interfaces. AI will be able to read and analyze muscle and brain signals, so that it can then predict what actions the user wants to take (XRToday, 2021).

AI will also be used to simulate the actions of Non-Player Characters (NPCs) in the metaverse if there are any.

As already mentioned, part of the components necessary for a fully functional economy in the metaverse will be blockchain technologies and NFTs. It will be through the use of cryptocurrencies and NFTs that the users will be able to monetize their activities in the metaverse. As for identification, the main digital identifier of a person in the metaverse will be a digital crypto wallet (Terry & Keeny, 2022), with the help of which the user can remain anonymous if they so desire. Financial transactions in the metaverse can be carried out using cryptocurrencies and can be used to buy any *digital* property including land, real estate, Tommy Hilfiger clothes and leather (Hackl et al., 2022; Melendez, 2022). In turn, NFTs serve as a kind of digital property certificate that confirms the right to own and use certain digital assets—again land, houses, art objects, music, films and so on—and it will also provide the right to sell them, to donate to a cause, to exchange things and more (Terry & Keeny, 2022, pp. 28–29; Stock, 2022; Duan et al., 2021, p. 4). Thus, absolutely any digital asset can be codified in NFT, from clothing to any part of the virtual world. Moreover, NFTs can be used as a sort of *ticket*, giving access to certain events, experiences, closed communities and the like. The user's NFT is stored in a crypto wallet along with their cryptocurrencies (Fortnow & Terry, 2021).

Other technologies for creating a metaverse are ones involving VR and augmented reality (AR). While virtual reality is a fully simulated reality, augmented reality is used to add certain elements of the virtual world to the physical world. Taken together, these technologies form aXR (Rijmenam, 2022, pp. 8–12). XR devices (headsets) will serve as a *gateway* for entering the metaverses, which will immerse us in the virtual space and provide the unique full-fledged experience of being present and actively interacting with other actors and digital objects. At the same time, it must be remembered that the XR devices will provide a convergence point for the virtual and physical worlds, allowing us to complement objects from the metaverse into the real world and use objects of the real world in the metaverse. However, it will also still be possible to immerse yourself in the metaverse using traditional devices: PCs, smartphones, tablets and more.

Experts and developers believe that it will be possible to create full-fledged metaverses (Huynh-The et al., 2022, pp. 4–5) that will grow and develop, thanks to the joint use of the technologies described above.

When assessing the state of *readiness* of the metaverse and the degree of the *development* of its individual components, it is important to underline, as already mentioned, that the metaverse is a convergence of many interconnected technologies: AI systems, blockchain technologies, NFT, XR, 5G networks and more. However, today these technologies are still somewhat in a fragmented state and do not yet possess the synergistic potential needed to form a fully functional metaverse. Among the current drawbacks is the fact that all of them are quite expensive (including VR and AR devices), they do not yet possess the necessary computational power and have certain hardware limitations, therefore making them unsuitable for mass use (Ejeke, 2022; Grossman, 2021; Kommersant", 2022). In addition, it is difficult to predict whether a single large metaverse will be created or several metaverses will appear from different developers. Today, a few smaller semblances of this new reality have been created and implemented, among them Decentraland, the

Sandbox, Cryptovoxels, Somnium and VRChat, as well as the Meta Horizon Worlds, still being developed by the company.

In the absence of full-fledged operational metaverses, connecting more and more people, both as developers and as active users, one way or another, will significantly stimulate development, especially as total immersion devices become cheaper and more readily available (Kommersant", 2022). Moreover, as users invest in it, the metaverse economy itself will begin to actively develop and grow.

Actors Operating in the Metaverse, Risks of Transition to Malicious Use of Artificial Intelligence

Metaverses provide users with unique opportunities for obtaining new immersive experiences and interactions both with other users and with digital objects. In new and immersive ways metaverses will also allow users to create new communities of interest, do business, make a profit, relax, unwind and even simply have fun (Zagalo et al., 2012).

In parallel metaverses will not only provide new opportunities for everyone involved but also produce new security risks and threats (Kaspar'yanc, 2022; Lee et al., 2021, p. 38). As noted near the beginning of this chapter, metaverses that implement technologies which facilitate complete immersion into the virtual reality space provide the widest range of opportunities for ultimate antisocial impact on social processes, social groups and individuals through MUAI, primarily in order to undermine the international psychological security. The existing technologies of MUAI for the purpose of undermining psychological security, which we will discuss below, may receive new impetus and may already be implemented within the framework of a full-fledged virtual reality space.

Moreover, the same technologies that are used to create the metaverse can be used for destructive purposes. First and foremost are AI technologies, such as machine learning, computer vision, predictive analytics and speech processing, which underlie the formation of the very architecture and foundation of the metaverses. They can be used by malicious actors who can repurpose certain algorithms or *poison* them, so, for example, the digital humans in the metaverses can be used not only to implement and carry out useful functions and tasks but also to implement tools causing malicious influence such as unwanted propaganda, harmful broadcasting and spreading destructive values into the minds of users, and demonstrating and spreading spam.

Furthermore since the metaverses will be such a full-fledged form of virtual reality in which users will *exist* in the digital space and literally be a part of the data stream, they open up truly colossal demonstrative opportunities for broadcasting information, interactive advertising (Kim, 2021), socially impacting political agitation, propaganda (Kaspar'yanc, 2022) and much more.

It is due to this aspect that the metaverses will be able to act as an extremely effective platform for the formation and consolidation of specific agendas. In this regard as already mentioned, the AI technologies themselves will be the key drivers in the creation, development and functioning of the metaverses, which makes them a natural for the use of facilitating the imposition of this or that informational line. Thus, digital humans (3D chatbots), information displays and any other technologies for broadcasting information can be applied and used to create the necessary overall mood among masses of users and to even escalate psychological tension in a target society. At the same time, it will be possible to *poison* algorithms that customize individual content for users, and as a result people may be provided with something completely different from what they would like to see or what they were seeking.

In and of themselves, the metaverses hold a huge potential for the capability of unleashing conflicts and leading to the emergence of untold numbers of malevolent actors with their own motivations and intentions. Along with good actors—metaverse developers, ordinary users and companies—there will be actors interested in using the immersive advantages of the metaverse for malicious purposes through AI. Of chief interest are the following potential actors:

1. Meta-hackers and hacker communities
2. Cyber meta-criminals
3. Cyber meta-terrorists
4. State actors (primarily revisionist and aggressive regimes) and supposedly "independent" entities working for them
5. Leading transnational Big Tech companies which in numerous areas surpass the capabilities of even the largest nation-states.

All of these actors differ in such characteristics as motivation, level of technical equipment, training and access to resources, and accordingly the scale of the audience that they can effectively influence. For example, if meta-hackers with certain limited programming skills can carry out malicious actions of an insignificant and specific nature against certain defined circles of people, then meta-criminals primarily interested in stealing funds will possess a larger scope for attack targeting and logically have somewhat more significant resources.

In contrast nation-states will have an extremely higher level of significant resources for the use of MUAI in the metaverse; they will possess more advanced AI systems, much more computing power and supercomputers, have access to the latest coding methods and possess a higher level of training among specialists in various relevant fields such as the field of AI and that of psychology. Accordingly, the impact of government agencies will be much higher and their operations much more professional, complex and methodical. They will be able to use AI for the purpose of causing psychological impact in the long term and in relation to a larger audience. Some states may be directly interested in MUAI in the metaverses in order to promote and consolidate certain agendas, broadcast certain endemic values and undermine the image and authority of both other states and individual politicians. For state actors, metaverses may become another powerful lever of influence on world politics and political processes (including domestic ones). The use of AI for psychological purposes in the metaverses could possibly be one of the most powerful assets and methods that could be used to influence opinion on the world stage through its impact on mass consciousness. Moreover, state actors and their institutions (even political parties) will strive not only to be present in the metaverses, for example, some states are already ordering the development of virtual consulates, and Barbados is going to open a representative office in Meta (Kommersant", 2022, Ning et al., 2021, pp. 3–5), but even today they are still considering ways to regulate and control them (Kaspar'yanc, 2022; Lee et al., 2021, p. 38; Ning et al., 2021, pp. 3–5). Perhaps the secret services will also take part in this.

Some multinational companies and corporations which will not only own certain plots and the largest real estate in the metaverses but also gain access to advanced AI systems may be very interested in MUAI in the metaverses. Large private sector representatives may seek to obtain certain advantages and leverage on the economy in the metaverse through the psychological impact on users. Using the specific technologies of MUAI combined with completely new forms of displaying information in the metaverses, they will most likely be able to effectively influence the public consciousness in order to speculatively enrich themselves and create a situation of unfair competition in their own favor.

It should be noted that not only cyberterrorists but also destructive fads and movements, including religious *meta-sects*, may appear in the metaverses. Their goals will be to use the possibilities of the metaverses to spread destructive ideas and recruit and attract new supporters into their ranks. In the absence of physical restrictions on movement in cyberspace (in the metaverses it will be possible to connect to an *event* almost instantly), the number of religious sects that appear may be huge and any recruit will be able to access membership procedures and events using the NFT provided to them. Accordingly, however, access to participate in meetings will be granted only to those *selected*, and of course augmented reality technologies will allow them to perform certain actions with members of sects. In turn blockchain technology and crypto wallets can ensure the anonymity of malicious actors.

All of that sounds bad; however, it is worth noting that meta-hackers, cybercriminals and cyberterrorists need to have advanced programming and computer skills in order to be able to repurpose AI systems. Most likely, these actors will resort to whatever AI methods of malicious influence are available and widespread and will not have such expensive resources as supercomputers. However, as AI technologies become more accessible and widespread, a wide variety of actors will gain access to them (Bazarkina & Pashentsev, 2020).

Speaking about the use of AI in the metaverses for the purpose of malicious influence, it should be understood that the most active users of virtual reality will be representatives of a completely new generation of people who will simultaneously *exist* in two worlds at once, the physical and the virtual, and for whom the virtual world will be nothing different from the real world, but there will be a completely different form of psychology involved in the perception of immersive virtual reality and the processes that take place there. Do we really need to say that these people will make up an amazing target audience for the most effective impact of MUAI? The new generation will be much more receptive and sensitive to the psychological impacts taking place in the metaverse, extrapolating and transferring these experiences and what they have been through to the real world. However, under conditions of convergence between the real and virtual worlds when an unpleasant digital experience serves to complement physical reality and space, such an impact could be of a pronounced negative nature.

The main danger of MUAI in the metaverses when designed to undermine the international psychological security is that the metaverses, due to the creation of an atmosphere of complete immersion in virtual reality and new forms of "digital interaction," bring to a completely new level the possibility of AI technologies causing a massive impact on the minds of the users, including their collective consciousness. Destructive information and damaging psychological impact in the metaverses can lead to psychological tension, malcontent, *meta-conflicts* and problems which may well have consequences which appear in the real world, both positive and negative.

Possible Forms and Methods of Malicious Use of Artificial Intelligence in the Metaverse

MUAI should not be considered a standalone concept in and of itself. Rather, it makes sense to analyze the opportunities provided by the metaverses for malicious informational-psychological influence and how the implementation of malicious influence can be automated using AI technologies. Again metaverses provide unique opportunities for new immersive experiences, interaction with other users and digital objects, the creation of communities of interest, recreation and entertainment, doing business and making a profit. However, each of these aspects can be used for evil.

Let us begin with an analysis of the possibilities that exist and allow for the conveying of information to users. The implementation of full immersion in virtual reality provides the widest range of opportunities for broadcasting information in various forms. Thanks to this fact metaverses would be an effective platform for the formation and consolidation of certain agendas (D'yakova, 2003), including those that are of a destructive nature and aimed at undermining the informational and psychological stability of society. A key component of information and psychological attacks using AI is what can be called *automated profiling*, meaning the classification of Internet resource users based on their psychological characteristics. The behavior of a correctly *classified* user is easier to predict than those who are not and they are easier to push into performing the actions desired by the attacking actor. In the metaverses, in addition to user-generated text, video and audio information, data of a different nature will be available for analysis which is absent in modern social networks. For example, in this regard we can mention automated analysis of body language, facial expressions and biometric data (Mystakidis, 2022). This can make profiling and the subsequent targeting of an individual or group much more effective. In addition, pass-through authorization technology will facilitate cross-analysis of data related to different aspects of the user's activities within different parts of the metaverse.

In itself the ability to uniquely identify a person using the totality of their biometric data is an incredible risk. For example, every intelligence officer was once a child who did not know what they would have to do in the future and if it turns out that, as a teenager, such an employee played a popular game in the metaverse and their biometric data came into the possession of the metaverse operator company, then their activities as, for example, an illegal agent would be under serious question. Therefore, it should be expected that a significant number of actors would make systematic efforts to de-anonymize users of the metaverse and collect their digital footprints.

Part of the information transmitted by a user as part of the implementation of information and psychological attacks can be generated using a group of technologies united by the umbrella term *deepfakes*. We are talking about technologies aimed at constructing pseudo-realities based on the growing capabilities of AI to generate and modify video, images, sounds and text (Europol, 2020; Pashentsev, 2020).

With regard to interactions between users, it is important to mention a few points. First, as in the case of social networks, the contents of two-way communication will obviously be available to the operator of the metaverse. Second, apparently metaverses will initially have mechanisms that impose certain restrictions on the form and content of communications. These are technologies to prevent *virtual sexual harassment*, the use of *hate speech* and other forms of aggressive behavior (Clarke, 2022). AI technologies will be used to automatically detect unwanted forms of communication, since manually moderating all ongoing acts of communication is neither possible nor ethical.

In the case of both the targeted transmission of information and the detection of undesirable forms of communication, the question inevitably arises as to the subjectivity of the choice and definition of criteria regarding what is acceptable and what is not. In everyday life such concepts as *hooliganism*, *sexual harassment* and *extremism* are clearly defined and regulated by legislation and social traditions that are not always articulated. Compliance with the law is then guaranteed by the activities of those in the law enforcement system. In the case of metaverses, at least in the initial stages, the legal framework will inevitably lag behind the actual practice, and implementation issues will be *farmed out* to the companies operating the metaverse. Criteria concerning the acceptability of behavior for different societies is not something that is universal, for example, understanding what should be considered *hate speech* in a society where LGBT propaganda is a crime as opposed to a society where LGBT stigmatization is a crime will be something that is diametrically different, not to mention the fact that it is always far from possible to agree on who should be labeled a terrorist and who is a freedom fighter (Keane, 2022). It is clear that with efforts to resolve such dilemmas, the companies operating the metaverses cannot and will not want to remain neutral. Consider, for example, the events that followed the beginning of the Special Operation of Russia on the territory of the Ukraine. The companies operating social networks, which have played key roles in the development of metaverses, were far from agreement on all aspects required to satisfy the legislative requirements of all parties in the conflict.

Separately, it is necessary to discuss the aspect of international communication between users. Progress in the field of natural language processing, speech recognition and speech generation will continue to eliminate language barriers; the introduction of publicly available automated simultaneous translation systems (Pivovarov & Shumskij, 2019) and the absence of state borders within the metaverse will bring the possibilities of interethnic and international communications to a qualitatively new level. However, this will also give rise to a number of new risks. Antisocial actors will use new opportunities to spread disinformation and carry out other types of destructive information and psychological activities to impact users and society. Companies providing automated simultaneous translation services will have the opportunity to access conversations and find out what people are really talking about, as well as to identify all users interested in international contacts. Finally, translations can be done in a manner that is not verbatim, but, for example, with the immediate elimination of *hate speech*, language identified as extremism and other sensitive topics, which could lead to the emergence of a new kind of *Newspeak* that contributes to the promotion of a certain way of programmed thinking approved on the platform.

Just as it is now in social networks, users of the metaverse will have to interact not only with real people but also with bots, with the expectation being that the development of bots will reach a new technological level. Cutting-edge advances in computer vision, speech AI and reinforced learning will find numerous applications in this regard. The metaverse, devoid of many of the *non-idealities* of the real world, will be a convenient environment for AI-controlled digital avatars, and as already noted, they will be used for, among other things, various kinds of antisocial actions, from crime to harmful propaganda.

The fight against unwanted bots will most likely be carried out by the operators and hosts of the metaverse. On the one hand, this is logical since they have the maximum number of technical capabilities and competencies on their side, and on the other hand, not being able to influence this activity, the state runs the risk of finding itself in a situation in which the fight against bots is not carried out equally. Relatively speaking, bots from one troll factory may be banned, and the activities of bots from another factory may have a blind eye turned to them. If we draw analogies with *classical* information security, it seems that such a scheme lacks a third party, namely independent providers of information security solutions, that is, actors who would equally fight against any malicious activity regardless of its source.

With regard to the creation of communities of interest in the metaverse, it is important to note the following: the presence of full-fledged virtual reality will allow communities not only to hold group chats and video conferences, but also to conduct, for example, concerts, ceremonies or even rituals. New forms of activities may fall under age restrictions or may even have an antisocial orientation. In this regard, the question will arise about the automatic detection of such malicious activity in order to mark or block the communities that carry it out. This can be much more difficult than establishing the presence of images or texts with illegal content in a group on a social network, especially if everything *interesting* happens at one-time meetings which can be accessed by invitation only. Additionally, as mentioned above, new profiling opportunities and requirements will arise in the metaverse. As a result, new opportunities will appear for identifying potential members with a view to determining their subsequent involvement in the activities of communities, including those whose activities are characterized as having a destructive orientation.

As for the economy of the metaverse, there are several key risks. First, the company that develops this area will possess and have access to all of the financial and economic information of the particular section of the metaverse that they are involved in and having exclusive access to this data will provide it with unprecedented predictive capabilities that are not available to other market participants and players. Also, additional predictive capabilities will be provided for by cross-analysis of large multimodal data from different sources (Siegel, 2013). Thus, the winners will be giant companies that own different parts of the metaverse which cover several areas of human life at once and possess the necessary competencies with regard to operations and infrastructure. Second, the controlling metaverse companies will have the ability to cause great damage through non-market methods (such as disconnecting companies and user groups from their services), for example, in the event of an economic confrontation and/or escalation. Finally, data on the economic activities of users of the metaverses will inevitably become available to state actors with whom the operating companies are affiliated (and this does not include the fact that they will be available to the local tax services).

The Actors and Directions for Countering the Malicious Use of Artificial Intelligence in the Metaverses

When speaking about the counteraction of MUAI in the metaverses, in this work, we will first of all discuss the provisions required by the international psychological security. Other aspects, such as the related area of *classic* information security, will remain outside our scope. Measures to ensure international psychological security can be of various kinds (technical, organizational, legislative) and can be applied at different levels (at the level of individuals, at the level of groups and organizations, at the level of society as a whole and at the international level). Let's consider each level separately.

Measures aimed at strengthening the capabilities of each and every individual to resist destructive information and psychological influences are an integral part of a multi-level strategy for ensuring the information and psychological security of society. The basis for the formation of an international psychological security is a good basic education, which implies, among other things, the possession of the skills of rational thinking and working with information (Pashentsev, 2021). Information hygiene skills and knowledge of the basics of information security are also useful. In addition, it is known that, as a rule, an individual who is included in a large number of various social ties—family, professional and specific groups—has greater psychological stability (Grachyov, 1998). The availability of quality psychological and psychiatric care also plays a role. In the case of the metaverse, all of these basics remain relevant. The task of the state therefore is to provide citizens with the appropriate opportunities to develop these capabilities. Despite all the advantages of such measures, they have one drawback, and it is a significant one: it is impossible to force every single person to be reasonable and psychologically stable. People are different by nature, their cognitive abilities change with age, in connection with their state of health, depending on their life circumstances and more.

Children are particularly susceptible to the threat of manipulation and this includes in the metaverse where it is even possible for them to form a system of values that is beneficial to the attacking actor. Games can be an effective environment and means for influencing the child audience (Bazarkina et al., 2021), but the authors consider it expedient to systematically limit the activity of underage citizens in the metaverse, including legislatively limiting their time.

At the organizational-group level, psychological protection is realized through the dissemination and use of intra-group information flows and sources, as well as methods of social interaction, processing and the evaluation of information endemic to specific groups and organizations. In this regard we must mention, for example, cultivating a corporate culture, the mandatory passage of certain courses by employees of an enterprise, periodic certification of certain responsible employees, building procedures for exchanging information within an enterprise, delimiting access levels up to secret and other related activities. With regard to the metaverses specifically, at the organizational level, decisions can be made about the use or non-use of certain tools existing in the metaverse, as well as about what can and cannot be discussed inside of it.

At the state level, psychological protection is provided through the regulation and organization of information flows; the establishment of age restrictions; the labeling of paid (including by foreign residents) materials; bringing to administrative and criminal liability those guilty of slander, inciting hatred and for new forms of aggressive harmful communications; and finally the introduction of mechanisms that give control over the overall use of personal data to the owner.

The state can and must set technical requirements that the metaverses operating on its territory must satisfy and abide by. Requirements that provide for the storage and processing of the user data of citizens in data centers located on the territory of a given state are among the appropriate basic requirements. It should also be possible to audit the work of recommended AI algorithms, intervene in their workings and also, in certain cases, have the ability to completely disable them and shut them down. This will assist in the removal of a significant part of the risks associated with hostile actors using the metaverse as a tool for attempting to carry out destructive social and political agendas. Metaverses must also provide all of the necessary technical capabilities and interoperability to allow for the operation of security solutions from third-party vendors and organizations. In this regard we mean information space monitoring systems, bot detection systems, deepfake recognition systems (Zhang et al., 2022) and specific specialized expert systems used to integrate information from various sources and to facilitate investigative activities, and finally antimonopoly authorities must have access and be in place to prevent abuses of economic power by the operating companies of the metaverse. We must also add of course that the operating companies must provide, at the request of law enforcement agencies, all of the data necessary for them to carry out their activities.

The example of social networks shows that by no means are operating companies always ready to cooperate with particular states, especially ones that are in opposition to other states whose markets are of greater value to the operating company. In view of this, the primary task of such a state is to promote the emergence of *its own* functional systems on the one hand and ones that are obviously *negotiable*, on the other. There is no need to be ashamed of the *top-down* approach, since the metaverse will not appear *on its own* anywhere. Unlike the Internet version of web 1.0, although initially based on government-funded military developments, but largely grown *from the bottom up* as a result of the combined efforts of a large number of enthusiasts around the world (Griffiths, 2019), *metaverses* will initially be the brainchildren of large corporations, designed primarily to serve their own interests under the scrutiny of regulatory authorities.

In the context of the current high level of confrontation between the key actors in the global economy, mutually imposed sanctions and restrictions on the supply and transfer of high-tech products and technology (computer equipment, helmets and controllers for virtual reality fall into this category), the task of "allowing our own the chance to develop" may not be such a trivial one. In a number of countries, questions concerning the ability to independently produce hardware will once again arise (Hogarth, 2022; Pivovarov & Shumskij, 2021). In any case it is necessary to solve this problem because a simple ban on *non-negotiable* platforms is not a solution in the long term. More precisely, this is how, in the context of ongoing de-globalization and partial technological delinking (Blair et al., 2022), bans will work for some time, but if some actors (e.g., the United States and China) (Lee, 2018) succeed in creating metaverses, while others do not, then with the onset of the next round of globalization, societies that do not have their own metaverses will most likely not be able to resist the temptation and will still become users of metaverses controlled by more developed but perhaps unfriendly players.

The activities of *non-system actors—meta-activists, meta-hooligans, meta-criminals and meta-terrorists*—as in the case of *classic* cybersecurity, should become the subjects of special interest to law enforcement agencies. As such an appropriate legislative base should be promptly developed.

As far as international cooperation is concerned, one should start with the fact that, in the end, security is the top universal priority. Even in the presence of a large number of contradictions between the key actors of the world economy, it is possible and necessary to find opportunities for cooperation. In this regard there are at least two aspects involved:

A) First, securing AI and countering MUAI are areas that require international standardization, the formulation and replication of best practices, and the dissemination of information regarding current attacks and threats. This kind of activity can be formalized within the framework of relevant international organizations. One can draw a certain analogy with classic information security: in this area, part of work related to standardization, dissemination of best practices and identification of information about threats is carried out within organizations like first.org which brings together industry experts from around the world (Hountomey et al., 2022).
B) Second, it is important to remember that among the large number of state actors, only a very few can claim leadership in the field of metaverses. Most of those, however, are puzzled and at an impasse over the same question: how to live as a non-leader in a situation where there are no problems. Is it true that leaders put their own interests above the interests of everyone else? Under the conditions of the First Cold War, one of the answers to this very question was the formation of the "Non-Aligned Movement." Something similar should be expected and carried out in a situation of competition between technological platforms: actors that do not have their own platforms, including metaverses, will find it profitable to cooperate with *outsiders* like themselves, thus increasing the opportunities for collective influence on the policies being pursued by the industry's leaders.

Conclusion

Both metaverses and AI open up many new opportunities for humanity. Will these opportunities be used for harm or for good? This is a matter of not technology but choice. Humanity now faces many tasks: the eradication of poverty, the establishment of peace throughout the world, the restoration of the ecological balance of the planet and further space exploration. Problems on this global scale can only be solved through the joint coordinated efforts of all mankind. Metaverses and AI can help solve these problems, but they can also become part of a dystopian reality that may possibly come true.

Reasons for conflict, as a rule, can be said to find themselves, therefore from the point of view of the authors, it is more correct to focus on finding opportunities for cooperation. The very problem of building metaverses and applying AI technologies inside them gives rise to countless engineering and organizational problems. Solving them in conditions of constructive international cooperation is both more productive and much easier than under conditions of open or other confrontation. At the same time, the authors are aware that the current level of contradictions between the key actors involved in the global economy and international politics is very high, and these contradictions will not disappear by themselves. However, history has taught us that eras of building walls are always replaced by eras of building bridges.

A very indicative example of the aforementioned is mankind's mastery of the technologies of nuclear decay and thermonuclear fusion. Having mastered the energy present in the atomic nucleus, humankind obtained the most powerful and deadly weapon in history and then even used it against their own kind. There were also major man-made disasters as a result, but at the same time, a new source of energy was obtained, one which is now necessary for creative development. The related emergence of the factor of mutual deterrence has since allowed a significant part of humanity to live for an unprecedentedly long period of peaceful coexistence, globalization and prosperity. The authors believe that it is in our power and in fact our responsibility to ensure that the benefits that the metaverses and AI technologies bring to humanity outweigh any associated costs and/or threats many times over.

References

Ball, M. (2020). The metaverse: What it is, where to find it, and who will build it. MatthewBall.vc. January 13. Retrieved May 30, 2022, from https://www.matthewball.vc/all/themetaverse

Ball, M. (2021). Framework for the metaverse. MatthewBall.vc. June 29. Retrieved May 29, 2022, from https://www.matthewball.vc/all/forwardtothemetaverseprimer

Bazarkina, D., & Pashentsev, E. (2020). Malicious use of artificial intelligence. *Russia in Global Affairs, 4*, 154–177. https://doi.org/10.31278/1810-6374-2020-18-4-154-177

Bazarkina, D. Y. U., et al. (2021). Politicheskaya situaciya v Severo-Vostochnoj Azii i ugrozy zlonamerennogo ispol'zovaniya iskusstvennogo intellekta: vyzovy informacionno-psihologicheskoj bezopasnosti [The political situation in the Northeast Asia and threats of malicious use of artificial intelligence: Challenges to psychological security]. *Social'no-gumanitarnye znaniya (Social and Humanitarian Knowledge), 4*, 212–234. Retrieved April 11, 2022, from http://socgum-zhurnal.ru/index.php/cod/2021-/-4/550-2020-02-22-11-09-22

Blair, D., et al. (2022). *Western-Chinese technology decoupling: Implications for cybersecurity*. A Report of the CSIS Multilateral Cyber Action Committee.

Chandar, V. (2021). Investing in the metaverse: New opportunities in virtual worlds. Morgan Stanley. December 16. Retrieved June 3, 2022, from https://www.morganstanley.com/articles/metaverse-opportunities-virtual-reality-augmented-reality-technologies

Clarke, L. (2022). Can we create a moral metaverse? *The Guardian*, May 14. Retrieved June 17, 2022, from https://www.theguardian.com/technology/2022/may/14/can-we-create-a-moral-metaverse

Colajuta, J. (2022). *All you need to know about metaverse: Complete survey on technologies, extended reality, artificial intelligence, blockchain*. Computer Vision and Future Mobile Networks. Vincenzo Nappi.

Collins, B. (2021). The metaverse: How to build a massive virtual world. *Forbes*, September 25. Retrieved June 10, 2022, from https://www.forbes.com/sites/barrycollins/2021/09/25/the-metaverse-how-to-build-a-massive-virtual-world/?sh=57e1f1c06d1c

D'yakova, E. G. (2003). Massovaya politicheskaya kommunikaciya v teorii ustanovleniya povestki dnya: ot effekta k processu [Mass political communication in the theory of setting the agenda: from effect to process]. *Polis. Politicheskie issledovaniya (Policy. Political Studies), 3*, 109–119.

Duan, H. et al. (2021). Metaverse for social good: A university campus prototype. Paper presented at the 29th ACM International Conference on Multimedia, Association for Computing Machinery, New York, 20–24 October 2021. https://doi.org/10.1145/3474085.3479238

Ejeke, P. (2022). What is Web3? Potential of Web 3.0 (Token Economy, Smart Contracts, DApps, NFTs, Blockchains, GameFi, DeFi, Decentralized Web, Binance, Metaverse Projects, Web3.0 Metaverse Crypto guide, Axie). Independently published.

Europol. (2020). Malicious uses and abuses of artificial intelligence. Europol. Retrieved February 14, 2022, from https://www.europol.europa.eu/publications-events/publications/malicious-uses-and-abuses-of-artificial-intelligence

Fortnow, M., & Terry, Q. (2021). *The NFT handbook: How to create, sell and buy non-fungible tokens*. Wiley.

Goldman Sachs. (2021). Framing the future of Web 3.0: Metaverse edition. The Goldman Sachs Group, Inc. December 10. Retrieved June 1, 2022, from https://www.goldmansachs.com/insights/pages/gs-research/framing-the-future-of-web-3.0-metaverse-edition/report.pdf

Grachyov, G. V. (1998). *Informacionno-psihologicheskaya bezopasnost' lichnosti: sostoyanie i vozmozhnosti psihologicheskoj zashchity [Information and psychological security of the individual: the state and possibilities of psychological protection]* (1st ed.). RAGS.

Griffiths, J. (2019). *The Great Firewall of China: How to build and control an alternative version of the internet*. Zed Books.

Grossman, G. (2021). How AI, VR, AR, 5G, and blockchain may converge to power the metaverse. VentureBeat. December 26. Retrieved June 12, 2022, from https://venturebeat.com/2021/12/26/how-ai-vr-ar-5g-and-blockchain-may-converge-to-power-the-metaverse/amp/

Hackl, C., Lueth, D., & Bartolo, B. (2022). *Navigating the metaverse: A guide to limitless possibilities in a Web 3.0 World*. Wiley.

Herrman, J., & Browning, K. (2021). Are we in the metaverse yet? *The New York Times*, July 10. Retrieved May 29, 2022, from https://www.nytimes.com/2021/07/10/style/metaverse-virtual-worlds.html?.%3Fmc=aud_dev&ad-keywords=auddevgate&gclid=CjwKCAjwzaSLBhBJEiwAJSRoksQC2o3eU9nurJhxNMp1dNXKX6QYwHqaFyot3sCemL1fkhEWekNDehoC0ZAQAvD_BwE&gclsrc=aw.ds

Hogarth, N. (2022). State of AI Report 2021. Stateof.ai. Retrieved June 17, 2022, from https://www.stateof.ai/

Hountomey, J.-R., et al. (2022). *Cyber incident management in low-income countries.* Global Forum on Cyber Expertise (GFCE).

Huynh-The, T. et al. (2022). Artificial intelligence for the metaverse: A survey. Arxiv preprint, February 15. Retrieved June 11, 2022, from https://arxiv.org/abs/2202.10336

Kaspar'yanc, D. (2022). Metavselennaya: vozmozhnosti i riski novoj real'nosti [Metaverse: Opportunities and risks of a new reality]. Nauchno-tekhnicheskij centr FGUP "GRCHC". Retrieved June 10, 2022, from https://rdc.grfc.ru/2022/02/metaverse/

Keane, J. (2022). Metaverse wars. Eurozine.com, June 15. Retrieved June 17, 2022, from https://www.eurozine.com/metaverse-wars/

Kim, J. (2021). Advertising in the metaverse: Research Agenda. *Journal of Interactive Advertising, 3*, 141–144.

Kommersant". (2022). Metavselennye: chto eto takoe [Metaverse: What is it]. Kommersant". Retrieved June 12, 2022, from https://www.kommersant.ru/doc/5347634

Lee, K. (2018). *AI superpowers: China, Silicon Valley, and the new world order.* Houghton Mifflin.

Lee, L.-H., et al. (2021). All one needs to know about metaverse: A complete survey on technological singularity, virtual ecosystem, and research Agenda. *Journal of Latex Class Files, 8*, 1–66.

Lee, L-H. et al. (2022). What is the Metaverse? An immersive cyberspace and open challenges. Arxiv preprint, June 7. Retrieved June 12, 2022, from https://arxiv.org/abs/2206.03018#:~:text=An%20Immersive%20Cyberspace%20and%20Open%20Challenges,-Lik%2DHang%20Lee&text=Abstract%3A%20The%20Metaverse%20refers%20to,milestone%20of%20the%20current%20cyberspace

Melendez, C. (2022). The Metaverse: Driven by AI, along with the old fashioned kind of intelligence. *Forbes*, April 18. Retrieved June 10, 2022, from https://www.forbes.com/sites/forbestechcouncil/2022/04/18/the-metaverse-driven-by-ai-along-with-the-old-fashioned-kind-of-intelligence/?sh=673d93b31b36

Mystakidis, S. (2022). Metaverse. *Encyclopedia, 2*, 486–497. https://doi.org/10.3390/encyclopedia2010031

Ning, H. et al. (2021). A survey on Metaverse: The state-of-the-art, technologies, applications, and challenges. Arxiv preprint, November 18. Retrieved June 11, 2022, from https://arxiv.org/abs/2111.09673

Pashentsev, E. N. (2020). Malicious use of deepfakes and political stability. In F. Matos (Ed.), *Proceedings of the 2nd European conference on the impact of AI and Robotics, a virtual conference hosted by Instituto Universitario de Lisboa (ISCTE-IUL), Portugal, 22–23 October 2020* (pp. 100–107). Academic Conferences and Publishing International Limited.

Pashentsev, E. N. (Ed.). (2021). *Experts on the malicious use of artificial intelligence and challenges to international psychological security* (1st ed.). Edition of the International Center for Social and Political Studies and Consulting.

Pivovarov, I., & Shumskij, S. (2019). Al'manah iskusstvennyj intellect. Analiticheskij sbornik No. 2. Obrabotka estestvennogo yazyka, raspoznavanie i sintez rechi (Almanac artificial intelligence. Analytical collection No. 2. Natural language processing, speech recognition and synthesis). Centr kompetencij Nacional'noj tekhnologicheskoj iniciativy na baze MFTI po napravleniyu "Iskusstvennyj intellekt" [Competence Center of the National Technological Initiative on the basis of MIPT in the direction of "Artificial Intelligence"]. Retrieved June 17, 2022, from https://aireport.ru/nlp

Pivovarov, I., & Shumskij, S. (2021). Al'manah iskusstvennyj intellect. Analiticheskij sbornik No. 9. Apparatnoe obespechenie dlya II (Almanac artificial intelligence. Analytical collection No. 9. Hardware for AI). Centr kompetencij Nacional'noj tekhnologicheskoj iniciativy na baze MFTI po napravleniyu "Iskusstvennyj intellekt" [Competence Center of the National Technological Initiative on the basis of MIPT in the direction of "Artificial Intelligence"]. Retrieved June 17, 2022, from https://aireport.ru/ai_hardware

Rijmenam, M. (2022). *Step into the Metaverse: How the immersive internet will unlock a trillion-dollar social economy*. Wiley.

Siegel, E. (2013). *Predictive analytics: The power to predict who will click, buy, lie, or die* (1st ed.). Wiley.

Stock, B. (2022). Metaverse. The #1 guide to conquer the blockchain world and invest in virtual lands, NFT (Crypto Art), Altcoins and Cryptocurrency + Best Defi Projects. Independently Published.

Terry, Q., & Keeny, S. (2022). *The Metaverse handbook: Innovating for the Internet's next tectonic shift*. Wiley.

Voshmgir, S. (2020). *Token economy: How the Web3 reinvents the Internet (Token economy: How the Web3 reinvents the internet)*. BlockchainHub Berlin.

XRToday. (2021). Artificial intelligence in the Metaverse: Bridging the virtual and real. XRToday, December 9. Retrieved June 12, 2022, from https://www.xrtoday.com/virtual-reality/artificial-intelligence-in-the-metaverse-bridging-the-virtual-and-real/

Zagalo, N., Morgado, L., & Boa-Ventura, A. (2012). *Virtual worlds and Metaverse platforms: New communication and identity paradigms*. IGI Global.

Zhang, D. et al. (2022, March). The AI index 2022 annual report. AI Index Steering Committee, Stanford Institute for Human-Centered AI, Stanford University

23

Unpredictable Threats from the Malicious Use of Artificial Strong Intelligence

Alexander Raikov

Introduction

For a long time, the most dangerous threat in war has been an enemy's unpredictable decisions and attacks. The enemy can be a terrorist organization, a political rival in the international arena, an adversary using psychological warfare, and so on. Currently, an intruder uses modern digital technologies for decision-making in psychological warfare, including big data analysis and artificial intelligence (AI). However, the decisions made with traditional big data analysis and AI, which use logical and neural network bases, can be predicted by opponents with some level of possibility. Traditional AI can help to create a psychological attack that exploits rivals' behavior and their cognitive biases, which can be foreseen. However, it is believed that only human free will and uncaused decisions, which cannot be explained and do not obey any mathematical or physical laws, cannot be predicted.

Modern AI can process symbols without understanding what it does and without making explanations. Sometimes it is called Artificial Weak Intelligence (AWI) or Artificial Narrow Intelligence (ANI). For example, it can solve tasks related to pattern recognition, playing games, helping with

---

A. Raikov (✉)
Institute of Control Sciences of the Russian Academy of Sciences, Moscow, Russia

Jinan Institute of Supercomputing Technology, National Supercomputing Centre in Jinan, Jinan, Shandong, China
e-mail: aleksandr@jnist.cn; anraikov@ipu.ru

purchases, weather forecasting, transport control, making medical diagnoses, computer vision, language processing, optimizing vehicle navigation, predicting crime, and so on. ANI can solve a specific, single task, possibly much better and faster than humans could. ANI is the logical-formalized form of AI that humanity has achieved at this time. A more advanced form of AI is Artificial General Intelligence (AGI), which can address multiple tasks on the level of AWI and has some human capabilities. It has been predicted (Kurzweil, 2006) that scientists can create AGI by 2029, but there are many who are skeptical of this (Fjelland, 2020).

Artificial Strong Intelligence (ASI) is fundamentally different from AWI and AGI. ASI has a hybrid character; that is, the system of ASI includes humans and machines, which are behaved in a unique convergent and purposeful way. ASI computer models take into account the models' cognitive semantics, which cannot be formalized directly but can be considered by using AI models on the atomic level of the human body and brain. This cognitive semantics is characterized by nonlocal quantum, relativistic, and wave effects (Raikov, 2019, 2021). It processes symbols like AWI and AGI, too. However, ASI can understand what it does: it is immersed in the real world and possesses subjectivity, and it can make decisions within a fusion of ethical systems. As a result, ASI would make uncaused decisions, which are unpredictable threats in psychological warfare that a foe cannot forecast. An artificial super-intelligence, which surpasses human capabilities and can greatly exceed the cognitive performance of humans, is also considered (Bostrom, 2014). We will consider ASI and artificial super-intelligence to be synonyms in this chapter.

The development of symbiosis between humans, AI, and robotics is having a profound impact on society. This symbiosis can lead to a fundamental civilizational transformation with far-reaching effects, as philosophical, legal, technological, and societal questions about consciousness, citizenship, rights, and legal entities are raised (De Luca, 2021; Karnouskos, 2021). The word "symbiosis" is a composition of the Greek words for "together" and "living." It may be considered to be co-existence and collaboration among humans and robots. With increased intelligence, robots may not just be single-purpose servants; they could play information and psychological weapon roles. Therefore, unpredictable threats through the malicious use of ASI, which possesses subjectivity and "free will," are the most dangerous threats in the field of psychological security and international relations. Due to this fact, the features and dangers of ASI have to be considered in more detail.

The paper hypothesizes that modern scientific studies and practical applications that run based on classical AI (AWI and ANI) generate only predictable decisions. On the other hand, scientific teams investigating ASI have substantial advantages in psychological warfare, accounting for ASI's ability to create unpredictable psychological attacks. This work presents the results of the author's analysis of the qualitative originality and characteristics of threats that are unpredictable for enemies, emanating from the ASI itself and due to malicious actions carried out with its help.

Large international organizations and governments have mastered only classical AI; they do not consider ASI peculiarities. There are approved plans for ASI development in two to three technologically advanced countries. Some military forces are trying to master elements of ASI technologies. Currently, scientific difficulties and the cost of research in the field of ASI inhibit its progress. Consequently, ASI impacts on international affairs and the ethical codes of society are currently far from critical. At the same time, the threats to global security from ASI will quickly increase due to its unusual peculiarities and the intensive development of digital technologies. The objectives of the study consist of confirming this hypothesis. To achieve this, the structure of the chapter is as follows:

- to review the modern scientific literature on ASI, which covers the uncaused mind's mechanisms and possesses subjectivity, addressing the issue of supporting unpredictable decisions;
- to identify aspects of the mastering of the advantages of ASI by international organizations and describe the psychological impact of the fear of ASI on societies' ethical codes;
- to identify directions of increasing threats to international security from advanced ASI development.

The main research approach consists of using the author's convergent methodology (Raikov, 2008, 2020), which makes the processes of control and team decision-making purposeful and sustainable. The approach is based on the idea of using fundamental scientific laws and methods from cybernetics, physics, math, biology, and so on to control decision-making. For example, the inverse problem-solving method, a thermodynamic approach, and the use of topology and quantum mechanics theories were helpful in achieving the study objectives.

Review and Connected Studies

This analytical review attempts to answer the following question: is the topic of unpredictable threats from the malicious use of ASI considered in other publications? If so, then these publications will be analyzed. Three groups of sources were used. One group of sources includes the publications of governments and international organizations. The second group consists of materials from media and business companies. The third and main sources are monographs and research papers in the area of AI and ASI development.

The development of ASI has become part of the agenda of the governments of leading countries. For example, the US Government Department of Defense (DoD) believes that AI can strongly enhance various operations and activities outside the cybersecurity domain (First Quarter, 2020). The Joint Artificial Intelligence Center (JAIC) is a subdivision of the United States Armed Forces exploring AI and AI-enhanced communication in actual combat. The JAIC stated that its objective is to transform the DoD by accelerating the adoption of AI to achieve national mission impacts at scale. The JAIC intends to retain the flexibility of AI programs, to consider changing to civilian leadership in the future and ensure that ASI technical expertise exists in supporting roles.

International psychological security threats, both national and international, which are created by the malicious use of artificial intelligence (MUAI), can be considered at three levels (Bazarkina & Pashentsev, 2019, 2020). At the first level, a false negative image of AI slows down its introduction and causes socio-political tensions. At the second level, the psychological security threat is directly related to the malicious use of AI, but an attack on public consciousness is not its main goal. Its goals are related to institutions, unmanned vehicles, making cyberattacks on infrastructure, and cryptocurrency manipulations. The third level is directly related to the use of AI to cause psychological damage at all levels of economic, political, and public life. Synthetic AI products represent a wide range of new risks and threats to different countries. This can allow aggressive actors to control the public consciousness and lead to the destabilization of the international situation.

Modern legal systems, as is well known, are not adequately preparing for the AGI and ASI era. Currently, several organizations are running projects that study ethics, risks, and policy in AGI. The pace of change for new AI results in breakthroughs in algorithmic machine learning and autonomous decision-making, engendering new opportunities for innovation (Dwivedi et al., 2021).

AI has already been used to maliciously impact social behavior. For example, "automated journalism" utilizes AI to collect sources, select articles, analyze problems, and automatically generate news (Jung et al., 2017). Such efforts can be personalized toward humans, creating the potential to use them maliciously to guide human behavior. The development of AI for generating deep fakes can misrepresent reality, which has far-reaching implications

(Karnouskos, 2020), for example, intellectual robots could perform an unlawful act based on manipulating media material. Interpolating these trends for the future, for example, when ASI is achieved, the question is the following: how it can utilize latent aspects of specific situations? Could, for example, an intellectual robot deceive (Danaher, 2020) or maliciously manipulate humans?

Intelligent robots and modern AI can learn to manifest malicious behavior on their own through the "oversight" of people. This may lead to the robot considering these behaviors as the norm. Subsequently, this situation can lead to the robot becoming the abuser of power. For example, Microsoft, in 2016, deployed Tay, which utilized millennial slang, but this led to a catastrophic result—Tay began to post inflammatory and offensive tweets (Wolf et al., 2017). On one side, AI can help cybercriminals to use computer technology to access personal information, trade secret business information, and use this information for malicious purposes. On the other side, machine learning and AI can play a key role in reducing cyberattacks. As an example, modern AI could be exploited to monitor Internet forums to predict possible malicious attacks. In this context, AI systems need to be prevented from replicating malicious behaviors, criminal acts, or other inequalities.

Thus, traditional AI learns from examples, generalizes, and creates psychological attacks using logical and neural network inferences. An opponent can predict their malicious nature. In comparison, Strong AI will create fundamentally new and unexpected situations, thanks to its ability to dive into the meanings of events and guess non-verbal opponents' intentions. Such cases may be hazardous because an opponent cannot identify them as malicious for some time.

Among the wide variety of malicious behaviors on social platforms, one of the most notorious is the diffusion of fake news (Paredes, Simari, Martinez, & Falappa, 2021). The NetDER architecture (Paredes, Simari, Martinez, et al., 2021) for hybrid AI decision-support systems uses machine learning, logical reasoning about unknown objects, and forecasts based on diffusion processes. It is an architecture for learning about malicious behavior, such as the dissemination of fake news, hate speech, and malware, detecting botnet operations, preventing cyber-attacks, and so on. It could also detect malicious behavior in blockchain transactions by using machine learning algorithms trained with graph properties. The system can also generate different hypotheses regarding malicious events, leveraging their value invention capability, and refine them when new information becomes available.

The main problem in creating ASI is the complexity of representing the real world (Malinetsky & Smolin, 2021). If all previous human inventions surpassed man only in strength, power, speed, and other physical characteristics,

ASI could give more rational and wise solutions. However, the usefulness of the long-term consequences or the threats of the malicious use of such decisions are difficult to evaluate. Not all problems are reduced to deep learning. For example, the problems of understanding the causality of events, planning actions, and creating high-level concepts are problems that cannot be effectively solved by traditional AI (LeCun, 2017), for example, many logical cognitive architectures (Kotseruba & Tsotsos, 2020) or attempts to give a logical definition of AI (Wang, 2019) that covers the full depth of the phenomenon of consciousness are limited due to the illogical, chaotic, and unreasonable nature of the latter. One of the reasons for this obstacle is the impossibility of assembling a single model that satisfies all the desired properties of consciousness and reality.

Support for corporate social responsibility (CSR) in different international organizations and businesses can be AI-related (Du & Xie, 2021; Perko, 2020). CSR initiatives have a multifaceted impact, including improving decision-making in international affairs, generating positive social effects and outcomes for consumers, enhancing user autonomy, and providing better privacy protection and higher consumer well-being. At the societal level, such AI-related CSR promotes fairness and social justice. However, these positive effects of AI-related CSR can be destroyed by the malicious use of AGI and ASI.

Scientific studies and applications of AI like those mentioned above define current trends in the malicious use of ASI. However, this does not mean that these trends will persist for a long period of time because of the revealing new abilities of ASI: its decisions and attacks on all levels of the malicious use of AI (Bazarkina & Pashentsev, 2020; Raikov, 2021) can be unpredictable, uncaused, and unexplainable, and they might be directed toward the most vulnerable event at the most unexpected time.

The problem of an explainable AI represents an important frontier of AI development for the next few years. The AI's solutions have to be understood and adequately semantically interpreted by humans. For this, various approaches are used to form a quantum model of decision-making by a person or a group of people. In particular, the algebra of quantum operators and methods of quantum field theory (Bagarello et al., 2018), quantum measurements in collective decision-making processes (Tsarev et al., 2019), and so on are used.

ASI approaches have been rapidly improving over the last decade. For example, the inverse engineering approach is used, in which scientists try to make a copy of the brain's neural structure (Huang, 2017). The approach using a quantum computer aims to make predictions of enemies' decisions. However, as it turned out, this approach is not completely unpredictable.

Such approaches try to represent uncaused phenomena with the topological mechanisms of projection and mapping. The example that demonstrates the possibility of uncaused events is the entanglement effect and the Bell test against local realism (The BIG Bell, 2018). This only recently became possible to prove by experiment due to the abilities of network informational technologies. In the end, it confirmed the unpredictability of human free will.

In the framework of the development of ASI, the following studies are also being carried out. The possibility of emulating the processes of human thinking, such as understanding, intuition, generating uncaused insights, and explaining and posing problems, is determined. Scientists are looking for ways to form logical explanations of the results of the operation of neural network systems to increase confidence and trustworthiness in the conclusions made with the help of such systems. Work is underway in the field of cognitive modeling and large-scale natural computing for the purposeful and accelerated solution of inverse problems on conceptual models of AI, taking into account non-formalized cognitive semantics.

In information processing based on new computing systems, the ASI is presented in the form of quantum and optical computers. A hybrid cyber-physical system of systems or a neuromorphic paradigm is used so far without immersion on the atomic level in a biological substance. In the new paradigm, a person is clearly involved in the work of the AI system, and they reflexively and cognitively influence the situation. This inclusion makes the formulation of problems inverse, incorrect, and in cognitive spaces. To solve them, category theory, cognitive modeling, large-scale evolutionary computing, and genetic algorithms are used.

Semantically interpreted data processing is investigated, taking into account non-formalized and uncaused cognitive semantics and building cognitive architectures and frameworks. Instead of a logical-linguistic or neural network representation of objects and events, there is a deepening to the atomic level of their semantic interpretation. Then, the semantics of ASI models becomes quantum-relativistic. The continuum power of such a semantic interpretation is tens of orders of magnitude higher than the traditional neural network and logical-linguistic AI.

In terms of the development of ASI methods, human and natural phenomena in their entirety are taken into account: the collective unconscious, potential singularity, quantum nonlocality, wave-particle duality, thermodynamic and relativistic effects, the relationship of low-temperature plasma with the substance of the brain and body, and the spontaneous fluctuations of natural neurons. The possibility of solving complex interdisciplinary problems, which research teams cannot yet cope with, is determined.

Problem Statement

The main advantage of ASI is its ability to work in an unpredictable, chaotic, and uncaused way, accounting for the non-formalizable aspects of thoughts, emotions, and consciousness. It should imitate human free will, but modern AI methods cannot do this. Taking into consideration the uncaused insights of the human mind and the revealing of the collective consciousness and unconsciousness is the most complex problem in ASI development (Raikov, 2015, 2021). A human can instantly make appropriate but uncaused decisions. It is impossible to make caused explanations for many phenomena, such as the chaotic dynamics of human thoughts, a collective unconscious, and the natural fluctuations of the brain's neurons. Many unclear scientific problems are put into such chaotic and uncaused traps because science and traditional AI try to find a logical explanation through identifying the cause of events to predict their future development.

In the case of unpredictable malicious decisions and psychological attacks initiated by ASI, the subject toward which the malicious impact is directed is deluded, does not know what to do, and does not have time to make correct defensive decisions. If an assailant uses the traditional methods and tools of AI, including big data analysis or neural network methods, the situation is predictable with some level of possibility, and an effective defensive decision could be created in advance. However, the unpredictable, or predictable with a very small level of possibility, behavior of ASI confuses the potential victim of a malicious attack. The presupposed peculiarities of ASI can make its psychological attack the most dangerous for different subjects, including international organizations and affairs. It prompts high-level international organizations to take appropriate protective actions, including mastering the advantages of already emerging ASI, which crucially differs from traditional AI. To build such ASI, it is necessary to fundamentally change the paradigm of current AI (i.e., AWI, ANI) development. For this, the creation of ASI has to consider malicious aspects such as the following:

- the soft modeling of malicious counteractions and fights;
- an uncaused unpredictable malicious decision;
- the non-local malicious cognitive semantics of ASI;
- the convergence of decision-making with an ill-defined malicious goal.

Taking into consideration the connected works analyzed above and these malicious aspects of ASI, the main theoretical components of ASI for malicious use with examples of their application can be represented as follows.

Theoretical ASI Components for Possible Malicious Use

Soft Modeling of Malicious Counteraction

Soft modeling approaches address the description of an ill-defined situation without the need of an a priori model postulation (de Juan et al., 2006), or an attempt to use classical mathematical approaches with changing constants in the formulas for some variables (Arnold, 1998). The goal of these methods is the explanation of hard predictable data variance for situations using the minimal or softer assumptions about data, the models' constants, or variables.

In the simplest model of the malicious struggle between two adversaries in a war (say, two armies), the Lancaster model, the state of the confrontation situation is described by taking into account the number of soldiers in opposing armies and the power of the weapons. In psychological warfare, this, apparently, will correspond to the number of sources for generating malicious information and the computation and intellectual power that can be used to generate this information.

This model in classical math describes the process of the destruction of enemies by obtaining a win at the end of a war, which depends on the beginning conditions. The conclusion of the modeling is as follows: to fight twice as many opponents, weapons that are four times more powerful are needed. In psychological warfare, this corresponds to the following situation: to defeat an information adversary that possesses twice as many resources and uses classical AI systems, the attacker has to possess AI systems that are four times more powerful.

If the initial conditions are not sufficient, then the adversary in psychological warfare will likely be the winner. If the forces are equal, which can only be in theory, psychological warfare ends with the depletion of resources from both opponents, but this will take an infinitely long time.

However, mathematics has methods for drawing general conclusions if the exact model's parameters are unknown and the goals are ill-defined. For example, it may be a situation in which the malicious problem is posed incorrectly in the mathematical sense, that is, there are no exact initial data about the situation, the goal is not specified accurately, and there is no information about the presence and uniqueness of the final solution or the convergence of the solution to a goal that has not yet been formulated precisely. In this situation, more abstract mathematical spaces are used to talk about soft modeling.

At the same time, the general conclusion of soft modeling is to assert the structural stability of the classical model, that is, to preserve its main qualitative conclusion that the power of the AI system to defeat the adversary in psychological warfare should be significantly higher compared to the power that the rival possesses. It is worth noting that the conclusion of the classical model, which is that the AI power should be four times higher, can be adjusted or will be valid in the final segment of the psychological warfare.

An Uncaused Unpredictable Malicious Decision

The ability to emulate uncaused malicious decisions and attacks is the most dangerous ASI ability. It makes ASI an actor of independent malicious actions that current AI cannot predict. However, understanding the nature of this ability gives a group of specialists or international organizations with special equipment a chance to master uncaused ASI.

To better recognize such uncaused malicious events, we must first answer the following question: what does causation mean from the semantics and operational sides?

The semantics side is in conceptual, philosophical, and psychological fields of knowledge, and the operational side involves the technological field of advanced AI. It's an important question because current AI tools can only determine the causes of events' coincidences by using statistical and deep learning neural network approaches. Traditional AI can reveal suspicious events and their causes by analyzing big data. The idea is easy: the more frequently two events occur together, the higher the probability of a connecting causation between them. The factors of time and place have to be taken into account.

From the philosophical Hume point of view, the frequency of two events occurring together, the sequence of the times of the occurrence, and the fact that the events are next to each other, or their contiguity, is enough for us to conclude that the events are causally connected (Mumford & Anjum, 2013). This point of view forms the basis of modern AI methods, which are based on logic, evolution, and neural net algorithms, to reveal causation in different fields of knowledge such as medical diagnosis, weather forecasting, the identification of exploratory signs in an intelligence service, and so on. By using this concept, the prediction of the adversary's malicious use of AI is not difficult. The difficult case in AI applications is predicting events with causations that cannot be revealed in advance. There may be cases that have a non-local nature, which is one of the main peculiarities of ASI: its models' semantics have a non-local nature.

Non-local Malicious Cognitive Semantics of Artificial Strong Intelligence

The non-formalizable cognitive semantics of AI models for creating ASI that can generate unpredictable malicious scenarios for the enemy's decisions can be represented indirectly. An observer (a person who cognitively influences the situation) is actively included in the hybrid AI system. This inclusion represents the solution to any problem in conceptual non-formalizable cognitive space. Instead of a traditional logical-linguistic or deep neural network representation of objects and events by a traditional AI system, the cognitive semantics of ASI takes into account the brain's atomic-level dynamics. Then, ASI power becomes 40–50 orders of magnitude higher than the power of a traditional AI (Raikov, 2021).

The quantum semantics approach seems to be promising for the construction of cognitive interpretations of ASI models. The decisions of these models can create unpredictable attacks. There are some separate studies on this issue (Dalela, 2012; Raikov, 2015, 2018). Two main effects have to be considered: the collapse of quantum states and the entanglement of quantum particles. The collapse of quantum states occurs due to measurement or the situation mentioned above, when an observer is involved in a process. At this moment, only one of the infinite admissible states of a quantum particle is taken. The entanglement of quantum particles reflects an instantaneous relationship between the states of particles located at large distances. The properties of the two particles appear to be connected, no matter how far apart they are. This is called the nonlocality effect. This effect of quantum states has different explanations generated by the well-known thought experiment called the Einstein–Podolsky–Rosen paradox.

Non-local effects in the space of the cognitive semantics of ASI make malicious threats unpredictable and very dangerous. This would be deeply puzzling for the rival because it seems to involve causation faster than the speed of light. It looks like spooky action at a large distance.

Concerning the applicability of physics to the processes of consciousness, it has to be noted that some fundamental laws of physics have significant limitations; for example, they cannot do the following:

- describe the connections of all four known physical fields;
- explain the spontaneous emission of elementary particles;
- describe the measurement of non-deterministic and reversible-in-time processes;
- represent the mutual transformations of elementary particles, and so on.

When such limitations are overcome, ASI will reveal its overwhelming force, and from the other side, the exploration of aspects of AI is bringing this moment closer.

However, in the current situation, it has to be noted that including the observer in a hybrid AI system makes the goals of problem-solving ill-defined and the process of solving inverse. Finding and applying special methods can ensure that the problem-solving process is convergent toward ill-defined goals.

The Convergence of Decision-Making with an Ill-Defined Malicious Goal

The author's special convergent methodology can make decision-making with ASI support more purposeful, sustainable, and convergent movements toward ill-defined goals (Raikov, 2008). It is based on the inverse problem-solving method applied to a conceptual and chaotic environment.

Thus, reality does not fit into formal and mathematical schemes. For the representation of the environment, traditional AI or mathematical modeling methods, especially statistical and extrapolation methods, are incomplete. The representation of reality should operate not just with metric spaces. Concepts are represented by points, neighborhoods, sets, and so on. Points can be separated from each other, not with the help of a metric, but with the help of the operation of intersecting their neighborhoods. Such spaces help one to comprehend a certain immeasurable effectiveness, not amenable to quantitative assessment.

Mathematical sciences such as algebra, categories, topologies, and fuzzy topologies are used to study conceptual spaces (Wong, 1973). It is possible to work with metrically immeasurable concepts in such spaces when the distance between the points, which represent concepts, cannot be measured in a traditional metrical way. The instability or non-purposefulness of the problem solution can be avoided only through active participation in solving the problem by a person who brings not only quantitative but also qualitative information into the solution process.

These spaces can be a good support for creating invulnerable malicious strategic decisions. Persons operate with such spaces taking into consideration their intentions, thoughts, and feelings. They make deductive the chaotic process of strategic discussion to confirm a certain hypothesis regarding the goal and move toward malicious aims. Then, the process of a person or a group of people choosing a path can be represented as inverse problem-solving on a topological space, with the inclusion of a person into the system.

A person or a group of people solve a problem by using resources (means) to try to achieve an imprecise goal by using some method for transforming resources to achieve the goal. They try to answer the question "What to do?" Such a problem-solving process is called inverse. Inverse problems are characterized by incorrectness—they may not have a solution, there may be many solutions, and minor changes in the initial conditions or the arrival of new information can lead to significant changes in the course of the solution and the solution itself. To successfully solve the inverse problem, there are simple recommendations for structuring information during problem-solving (Raikov, 2008, 2020):

- build a goal tree at the conceptual level;
- separate aims, means, and actions from each other;
- the set of means divide into a finite number of parts;
- control all aspects of solving the problem, comparing goals and means;
- watch out for small factors.

These are the minimum necessary structural conditions to ensure the convergence of problem-solving to the intended and not always clearly formulated goals. In the process of solving a problem, a person brings into the solution process high-quality information that lies beyond the framework of logic and formalism and can be dictated by experience and character, dignity and preferences, faith and patience, courage and caution, isolation and immensity, confidence and confusion, and so on. For example, a person may not know their goals at all. However, they usually want something, and they act. In this case, the very behavior of a person or a group of people with a certain intention or hypothesis shows a tendency to analyze information—it is classified and distributed into a finite number of parts in a certain natural way.

The decision process is called convergent if special conditions are created to ensure stable convergence to an imprecise goal. In such a process, on the one hand, the above recommendations for structuring information are taken into account. On the other hand, a person brings his own assessments into the process. Such a process resembles evolution when a modeling system prepares the next population of solutions, and a person evaluates this intermediate result. According to the person, if the result is worse, then the person does not accept it and asks the model to make another attempt. If the result is better than the one obtained at the previous step, the person allows the formation of the next population of solutions. This is done until the person receives a satisfactory result.

The need for the convergent methodology also comes from another view of decision-making in the context of the malicious use of AI. Malicious decision-making processes, which use traditional AI and advanced ASI for their support, can be described as an interaction between top-down and bottom-up approaches that proceed in opposite directions. The former flows from the non-formalizable part of ASI and cognitive, uncaused, and chaotic human consciousness. Top-down flow makes the decision-making process more purposeful. The latter approach proceeds in a bottom-up manner from formalizable models of traditional ANI, sensors, big data analytical systems, and high-end computing, making the process more sustainable.

This top-down and bottom-up interaction between human and machine participation needs to be integrated to make malicious attacks or defense against them more purposeful and sustainable. At the same time, an agreement on the decision between team members from both sides, the attacker's and defender's, should be achieved as quickly as possible. The one who makes the correct decision faster will win. The author's convergent methodology helps in achieving this.

In AI, such a converging process is implemented using special evolutionary computations or genetic algorithms. It has the character of a deductive procedure for the step-by-step confirmation of the stated hypothesis of implementing a malicious action in the way that is most dangerous for the adversary. This can decisively activate threats to international security.

Deductive Malicious Artificial Intelligence Threats to International Security

In the field of international security, countries possess different types of AI possibilities. For example, AI can help to support the strategic stating process (Johnson, 2020; Raikov, 2008). The chance to win in psychological warfare is available to the security teams of those countries that have created more powerful AI. Let us describe it in more detail by diving into the analytical and decision-making process of the security team.

The security team collects information, analyzes, investigates the situation, makes generalizations, builds hypotheses about the adversary's greatest vulnerability, and determines ways to use this vulnerability. A hypothesis has an intention that gives all aspects of the study a deductive character and ensures the subordination of actions to this intention, which is perhaps vague at first due to the uncertainty of the situation. Intention and hypothesis make the information attack deductive, conditioned by certain frameworks, criteria, and goals. However, this deductive character does not yet provide the necessary conditions for achieving goals that are just being formed. For such a provision, the convergent approach is required (see the previous section), creating appropriate conditions that can support the preparation of purposeful malicious attacks.

A misconception about the high fruitfulness of divergent brainstorming for developing a hypothesis, when team members, stimulating each other, generate many new ideas, is that this brainstorming can turn out to be inductive and might lead in the wrong direction. In an inductive approach, formulating the concept of psychological warfare begins with a spontaneous analysis of raw data, sensations, and detached thoughts based on simple observation. Based on this data, generalizations begin to form, which are transformed into a hypothesis. This hypothesis, with such an essentially aimless approach, may turn out to be erroneous. A starting point with an inductive, divergent approach in extreme conditions is not effective; the team will lose valuable time with this approach and will most likely lose the information battle.

The process of observing the situation is part of the retrospective experience. During brainstorming, this accumulated resource predetermines, in many ways, the development of the decision-making process, inclining the process of reasoning to lead within the framework of accumulated stereotypes. Suppose that the team succumbs to the temptation to act within the familiar classical AI; in this case, they cannot create a strong strategy to fight against malicious attacks. Therefore, the brainstorming session should begin with some bold intent to achieve a specific result: cruel or gentle. This intention is the hypothesis that sets the tone for strategic discussion, forms criteria, stimulates an assessment of the situation, and influences the choice of method. In the light of these criteria, assessments are made of the relevance of all large and small decisions, scraps of thoughts, random statements, and the chosen method and approach.

Hypotheses arise based on risky assumptions that obscure the consciousness of aggressive, malicious motives, so they need to be tested: theoretically, using models, experimentally, or naturally. If, say, modeling or an experiment on a particular example showed that the hypothesis is not confirmed, another test is done, and another. As a result of testing, the question of changing the hypothesis or rejecting it may arise. If the hypothesis is confirmed as a result of experimental verification, then it can be formulated into an action plan, unless, of course, other tests make it doubtful in time. Further, the plan takes on an imperative character, which, when executed, may run into the need for deviations. This is a "hypothetical-deductive" process (Phillips & Pugh, 2005): its actions are subject to a certain system predetermined by the initial hypothesis, which sets the outline of the goal and the result.

So, this view of the process is necessary. It presents a logical approach to analytical work. However, such a view almost does not touch upon the hidden features of international interaction, the emotional, purely psychological side of the process, which cannot always be formulated in words and presented only in the form of formalized and logical constructions. The process is dominated by the chaos of thought, inspiration, experience, and the uncontrollable influences of the external environment: the secret intentions of the heads of government and the unconscious states of consciousness of the team members. It is impossible to consider all the spontaneous movements of thought, imperceptible improvements, corrections of errors and typos, and so on. However, this must be taken into account to ensure the integrity of the coverage of the situation. There are two main perspectives for representing the problem being solved: a fairly systemic representation as a result and a rather chaotic and unformalized process of achieving it. The second view includes possible deviations from the main direction of the plan.

Threats to Psychological Security from Breaking an Ethical Code with Artificial Strong Intelligence

What psychological impact does a fear of ASI already have on the ethical codes of society? The wide availability of a targeted impact on society based on AI for large and small groups of people in various countries raises the question of the termination of the existence of favorable conditions for the growth of threats to psychological security through breaking an ethical code with ASI.

Ethics is becoming an increasingly dangerous area for the use of ASI in the context of the development of the digital economy, when people live in fear of losing their jobs due to the dominance of intelligent robotics, are in a state of struggle against the negative impact of the media on morality, and are forced to improve their competence constantly to keep up with technological progress.

The introduction of new digital technologies with ASI components generates a high risk that they will be applied in all sectors of the economy and areas of human life. The main ethical risks of developing ASI include the following:

- rejection by the employees of various organizations of digital technologies in general and AI systems in particular;
- the growth of unemployment, as well as the hacking of the psyche and consciousness of workers due to the replacement of human labor by robotics;
- excessive standardization of AI frameworks and ontologies, to the detriment of cultural, evolutionary, and biological diversity;

- the diminishing of the significance of historical and cultural heritage through digitalization and AI;
- the evolution of morality in the environment of digital technologies and AI, leading to the fall of its universal principles;
- the risks of the hybridization of the cybernetic and natural spheres growing in the long-term forecast, and so on.

In this context, there is a breakdown in ethics, and this leads to psychological trauma at the level of various groups of people diverging from relatively similar ethical traditions. Digital technology and AI are initiating this disruption, and the malicious use of ASI can crucially accelerate this process. Ethics can be characterized in the context of using ASI by taking into consideration aspects such as the following:

- ancient heritage, covering all its historical depth and fullness;
- postmodernity, which is characterized as a culture stripped of its capacity to function in a linear or autonomous state, like regressive isolationism;
- logical, chaotic, and uncaused ontologies, with quantum semantics for their models and representations in different forms;
- a variety of ethical concepts, and so on.

There can be distinguished three main approaches to ethics—deontology, consequentialism, and virtue ethics. To explore these approaches, an adequate scenario can be created and modeled using multi-agent systems methods (Bench-Capon, 2020). It has been shown that all these approaches could be used to build different ethical agents, and that a major problem for ethical reasoners is the need to predict the behavior of other members of the group in order to assess their own actions.

However, modern AI methods can detect nuances and predict the behavior of groups of people and individuals and then help them make decisions by giving them misinformation disguised as true information. In this way, the ethics system that has developed over a long period of time can be disrupted. Consequently, this violates the psychological atmosphere in the group of subjects.

Thus, due to the impact of the digital environment and the capabilities of ASI, spontaneous, maliciously initiated processes can cause the distortion of the psyche and consciousness, the primitivizing of morality, and the fall of its universal principles.

Thus, traditional AI systems try to map the moral diversity of different social groups by using logical ontologies or by using neural network to reflect this diversity in these ontological structures. However, obviously, the logic of the formalized representation of ethics cannot cover the entire cultural and historical spectrum, taking into account people's feelings and desires. Only ASI can grasp such nuances, making it extremely dangerous if misused.

Developing and promoting universal ethical principles that accompany the introduction and use of AI cannot stop the threat of its malicious use. AI codes of ethics are being made, and they must be developed and implemented in people's lives. However, due to social degradation, the decline of the current world economy and political communication, the crisis of the contemporary world order, and the digital degradation of thinking and distortion of ethics, they are still poorly perceived and powerless against the business incentives of the market and the intentions of introducing militaristic AI applications.

Increasing Threats to International Security from Artificial Strong Intelligence in the Near Future

Thus, ASI's main threat to international security is its ability to make unpredictable psychological attacks due to uncaused malicious decisions. ASI can catch the tiny nuances in a group of people's behavior by analyzing big data, accounting for ASI's differences from the classical paradigm of data mining. Due to quantum semantics, ASI, using methods of inverse problem-solving on cognitive spaces, takes into account information about the world by being immersed in it; thus, this gives a malicious attacker the possibility to get an answer to the following question: what can they do to exploit the victim's vulnerabilities that the victim cannot predict with classical AI? It gives ASI an invulnerable advantage compared to traditional AI for creating threats to international security in the near future.

Let us take into consideration the sphere of strategic communication, the concept of which has been accepted by the North Atlantic Treaty Organization (NATO) (Gage, 2014), the US (White House, 2010), China, South Africa, and other countries (Strategic Communication, 2020). The term is used in the spheres of business and politics and in academic and educational literature. Currently, strategic communication is the state's projection of certain national goals and vitals into the consciousness of domestic and foreign audiences. It is realized by employing the promotion and synchronization of multidimensional activities in all domains of social life with purposeful and sustainable communication support. Strategic communication has received a powerful incentive over the last few years, accounting for digital technologies and AI. Modern strategic communication processes deliberately blur boundaries between evil and good and war and peace. The reasons for this may hide in a non-verbalizable space of cultural traditions and the latent phenomenon of human free will. This border becomes too thin and fuzzy for classic AI to recognize it. Various crisis and malicious factors inside and outside any region of the world influence this process, and AI technologies can help counteract its negative impacts by revealing causal connections between informational facts. However, this is not the case when ASI is used by a malicious adversary in psychological warfare.

In terms of ASI, this counteracting is solving the inverse problem: the creation of the strategic communication process starts from the goals, and then adequate paths are found and created to achieve the goals. As noted above, such problems are incorrect and must be solved in non-formalizable cognitive spaces. Small deviations of information, or discovering some new facts about reality, can change the results and paths of the decision in a crucial way. ASI has the best capability to make malicious deviations and create new dangerous facts, which can make it unpredictable for a victim who has only traditional AI. Currently, there are no law documents in the field of strategic communication which provide grounds for protecting international affairs from malicious actions that can be made with ASI support.

The usage of ASI can be hazardous in "communication provision," which ensures that an organization's activities, employing internal and external communication, strategic decision-making, and information transmission, can target audiences to influence them (Bazarkina, 2017). This term, as usual, is used concerning counter-terrorism activities. Looking at communication provision in the context of the activities of counter-terrorism agencies, there are two main tasks for the application of AI: to identify the importance and purposefulness of the role of communication in the fight against terrorism and to establish the optimal way to develop this direction by including an anti-terrorism component in strategic communication. Obviously, traditional AI can solve with high quality only the former task. The latter can be solved with the abilities of ASI. Due to ASI, the communication provision can have a strong synergetic effect.

Traditional AI systems can reveal different informational nuances in civilian lives and use them for malicious aims, for example, for a negative psychological impact on the human perception of natural unfairness. For example, there is great variation in Medicare spending per patient in different states in the US (Jones, 2015). Knowing this fact makes some groups of US civilians psychologically unsatisfied. So, if someone has a sharp deterioration in their health, what happens to this patient depends on what state of the country they are in. It also depends on which hospital the ambulance takes them to, which doctor is on call, and their insurance. Understanding that healthcare quality differs in several ways makes the situation unfair for patients from different states in the US.

By special analysis of information from different resources, traditional AI can reveal the scale of these variations, find out which states have the largest differences in spending, and find an unwarranted cause that accounts for the great variation. However, current AI cannot find all possible latent paths by which the adversary in psychological warfare can make a malicious attack, for example, an extension of warfare into the public consciousness. Only ASI can create such an unpredictable path of psychological attack, by using inverse problem-solving in cognitive space with the quantum semantics of its models. ASI approaches can emulate the free will phenomenon during decision-making, which traditional AI cannot understand.

Conclusion

Over the last two decades, the ASI research phenomenon has been growing very quickly. On the one side, this term intrigues people because of its future possibility of reaching the singularity, which refers to the moment when machine ability bypasses human ability. On the other side, the studies give new ideas for developing traditional AI methods. This gives, in turn, new disruptive approaches of the malicious use of AI in the fields of psychological security and international relations.

Digital reality and its progressive tools incentivize the development of international communication. Still, it also leads to a new possibility: the emergence of malicious forces due to the latter. There are serious grounds for imagining the further degradation of international relations up to the hazardous point of their collapse. However, there are also opportunities to increase trust between countries in the world. This requires synchronizing the development of the digital and AI powers of different countries. Moreover, only through the joint efforts of scientists from different countries of the world can many multidisciplinary scientific issues in the development of the complex technologies of ASI be solved.

The list of directions for counteracting increasing threats to psychological security and international relations from ASI development may include the following:

- ensuring more sustainable, purposeful, and synchronized multidimensional strategic communication activities for different countries;

- high-quality identification of the role of communication provision cases in the fight against terrorism;
- establishing the optimal way to develop strategic communication and communication provisions, including an anti-terrorism component of international activity;
- creating special collaborations for solving the multidisciplinary scientific issues in mastering the advantages of ASI using collective intelligence and networked expertise methods.

Many aspects of mastering the advantages of ASI by international organizations and political blocks do not have convincing explanations yet. This issue requires the development of the institutional foundations of international scientific multidisciplinary communication and collaboration. Hybrid AI integrates the peculiarities of human collective intelligence and AI (Ryjov, 2021; Ryjov & Mikhalevich, 2021). However, the malicious use of Hybrid AI can have a destructive impact on international affairs and reduce the psychological and informational security of countries that have not yet considered ASI development. To make this threat less impactful, the following directions of ASI development have to be supported:

- the imitation of human cognitive functions, including self-learning and searching for solutions without a predetermined algorithm;
- information processing based on new types of computing systems;
- cognitive semantics interpretations of AI models and data processing;
- other methods, including methods taking into account the quantum and wave nature of consciousness.FundingRussian Science Foundation, grant No 21-18-00184, "Socio-humanitarian foundations of criteria for evaluating innovations using digital technology and artificial intelligence."

References

Arnold, V. I. (1998). "Hard" and "soft" Mathematical Models. *Bull Soc Catalana Mat, 13*(1), 7–26.

Bagarello, F., Basieva, I., & Khrennikov, A. (2018). Quantum field inspired model of decision making: Asymptotic stabilization of belief state via interaction with surrounding mental environment. *Journal of Mathematical Psychology, 82*, 159–168. https://doi.org/10.1016/j.jmp.2017.10.002

Bazarkina, D., & Pashentsev, E. (2019). Artificial intelligence and new threats to international psychological security. *Russia in Global Affairs, 17*(1), 147–170. https://doi.org/10.31278/1810-6374-2019-17-1-147-170

Bazarkina, D., & Pashentsev, E. (2020). Malicious use of artificial intelligence: New psychological security risks in BRICS countries. *Russia in Global Affairs, 18*(4), 154–177. https://doi.org/10.31278/1810-6374-2020-18-4-154-177

Bazarkina, D. Y. (2017). Rol' kommunikacionnogo obespechenija v antiterroristicheskoj dejatel'nosti Evropejskogo Sojuza [The role of the communication provision in the EU antiterrorist activity]. DSc Thesis, Institute of Europe, Russian Academy of Sciences (IERAS), Moscow.

Bench-Capon, T. J. M. (2020). Ethical approaches and autonomous systems. *Artificial Intelligence, 281*, 103239. https://doi.org/10.1016/j.artint.2020.103239

Bostrom, N. (2014). *Superintelligence: Paths, Dangers, Strategies* (1st ed.). Oxford University Press.

Dalela, A. (2012). *Quantum meaning: A semantic interpretation of quantum theory.* Shabda Press.

Danaher, J. (2020). Robot betrayal: A guide to the ethics of robotic deception. *Ethics Inf Technol, 22*(2), 117–128. https://doi.org/10.1007/s10676-019-09520-3

de Juan, A., Casassas, E., & Tauler, R. (2006). Soft modeling of analytical data. Wiley Online Library. https://doi.org/10.1002/9780470027318.a5208

De Luca, G. (2021). The development of machine intelligence in a computational universe. *Technol Soc, 65*, 101553. https://doi.org/10.1016/j.techsoc.2021.101553

Du, S., & Xie, C. (2021). Paradoxes of artificial intelligence in consumer markets: Ethical challenges and opportunities. *Journal of Business Research, 129*, 961–974. https://doi.org/10.1016/j.jbusres.2020.08.024

Dwivedi, Y. K., Hughes, L., Ismagilova, E., et al. (2021). Artificial intelligence (AI): Multidisciplinary perspectives on emerging challenges, opportunities, and agenda for research, practice and policy. *Int J Inf Manage, 57*, 101994. https://doi.org/10.1016/j.ijinfomgt.2019.08.002

First Quarter Recommendations (Report). (2020). National Security Commission on Artificial Intelligence, 124 p. Retrieved September 4, 2021, from https://drive.google.com/file/d/1wkPh8Gb5drBrKBg6OhGu5oNaTEERbKss/view

Fjelland, R. (2020). Why general artificial intelligence will not be realized. *Humanities and Social Sciences Communications, 7*, 10. https://doi.org/10.1057/s41599-020-0494-4

Gage, D. (2014). The continuing evolution of strategic communication within NATO. *The Three Swords Magazine, 27*, 53–55.

Huang, T. J. (2017). Imitating the brain with neurocomputer a "new" way towards artificial general intelligence. *Int J Autom Comput, 14*, 520–531. https://doi.org/10.1007/s11633-017-1082-y

Johnson, J. (2020). Delegating strategic decision-making to machines: Dr. Strangelove Redux? Journal of Strategic Studies, Informa UK Limited, trading as Taylor & Francis Group, https://doi.org/10.1080/01402390.2020.1759038

Jones, D. S. (2015). Geographic variations in medical practice. Retrieved September 4, 2021, from http://serious-science.org/geographic-variations-in-medical-practice-4035

Jung, J., Song, H., Kim, Y., Im, H., & Oh, S. (2017). Intrusion of software robots into journalism: The public's and journalists' perceptions of news written by algorithms and human journalists. *Computers in Human Behavior, 71*, 291–298. https://doi.org/10.1016/j.chb.2017.02.022

Karnouskos, S. (2020). Artificial intelligence in digital media: The era of deepfakes. *IEEE Transactions on Technology and Society, 1*(3), 138–147. https://doi.org/10.1109/tts.2020.3001312

Karnouskos, S. (2021). Symbiosis with artificial intelligence via the prism of law, robots, and society. *Artificial Intelligence and Law*. https://doi.org/10.1007/s10506-021-09289-1

Kotseruba, I., & Tsotsos, J. K. (2020). 40 years of cognitive architectures: Core cognitive abilities and practical applications. *Artificial Intelligence and Law, 53*(1), 7–94. https://doi.org/10.1007/s10462-018-9646-y

Kurzweil, R. (2006). *The singularity is near: When humans transcend biology*. Penguin (Non-Classics).

LeCun, Y. (2017). Power & limits of deep learning. [Online]. Retrieved September 4, 2021, from https://www.youtube.com/watch?v=0tEhw5t6rhc

Malinetsky, G., & Smolin, V. (2021). The artificial intelligence influence on real sociality. *Proceedings of the 14th International Symposium "Intelligent Systems", Procedia Computer Science, 186*, 344–351.

Mumford, S., & Anjum, R. L. (2013). *Causation: A very short introduction*. Oxford University Press. 128 p.

Paredes, J. N., Simari, G. I., Martinez, M. V., & Falappa, M. A. (2021). NetDER: An architecture for reasoning about malicious behavior. *Information Systems Frontiers, 23*(1), 185–201. https://doi.org/10.1007/s10796-020-10003-w

Paredes, J. N., Simari, G. I., Martinez, M. V., et al. (2021). Detecting malicious behavior in social platforms via hybrid knowledge- and data-driven systems. *Future Generation Computer Systems..* https://doi.org/10.1016/j.future.2021.06.033

Perko, I. (2020). Hybrid reality development-can social responsibility concepts provide guidance? *Kybernetes, 50*, 676–693. https://doi.org/10.1108/K-01-2020-0061

Phillips, E. M., & Pugh, D. S. (2005). *How to get a PhD: A handbook for students and their supervisors* (4th ed.). Open University Press, UK by Bell & Bain Ltd. 235 p.

Raikov, A. (2008). Convergent cognitype for speeding-up the strategic conversation. Proceedings of the 17th world congress "The International Federation of Automatic Control (IFAC)", Seoul, Korea, IFAC Proceedings Volumes, *41*(2): 8103–8108. https://doi.org/10.3182/20080706-5-KR-1001.01368

Raikov, A. (2015). Convergent networked decision-making using group insights. *Complex & Intelligent Systems, 1*, 57–68. https://doi.org/10.1007/s40747-016-0005-9

Raikov, A. (2018). Cognitive modeling quality rising by applying quantum and optical semantic approaches. Proceedings of the 18th IFAC conference on technology, culture, and international stability, Baku, Azerbaijan. *IFAC-PapersOnLine, 51*(30), 492–497. https://doi.org/10.1016/j.ifacol.2018.11.309

Raikov, A. (2019). Post-non-classical artificial intelligence and its pioneer practical application. *IFAC-PapersOnLine, 52*(25), 343–348. https://doi.org/10.1016/j.ifacol.2019.12.547

Raikov, A. (2020). Accelerating decision-making in transport emergency with artificial intelligence. *Advances in Science, Technology and Engineering Systems Journal (ASTESJ), 5*(6), 520–530. https://doi.org/10.25046/aj050662

Raikov, A. (2021). Cognitive semantics of artificial intelligence: A new perspective. Springer Singapore, Topics: Computational Intelligence XVII. https://doi.org/10.1007/978-981-33-6750-0

Ryjov, A. (2021). Hybrid intelligence framework for augmented analytics. In Intelligent Analytics with Advanced Multi-Industry Applications (Z. Sun, Ed.). : IGI Global, pp. 22–45.

Ryjov, A., & Mikhalevich, I. F. (2021). Hybrid intelligence framework for improvement of information security of critical infrastructures. In M. M. Cruz-Cunha & N. R. Mateus-Coelho (Eds.), *Handbook of research on cyber crime and information privacy* (pp. 310–337). IGI Global.

Strategic Communication in EU-Russia Relations. Tensions, Challenges and Opportunities. (2020). Ed. E. Pashentsev. Palgrave Macmillan. https://doi.org/10.1007/978-3-030-27253-1

The BIG Bell Test Collaboration, Abellán, C., Acín, A., et al. (2018). Challenging local realism with human choices. *Nature, 557*, 212–216. https://doi.org/10.1038/s41586-018-0085-3

Tsarev, D., Trofimova, A., Alodjants, A., et al. (2019). Phase transitions, collective emotions and decision-making problem in heterogeneous social systems. *Sci Rep, 9*, 18039. https://doi.org/10.1038/s41598-019-54296-7

Wang, P. (2019). On defining artificial intelligence. *Journal of Artificial General Intelligence, 10*(2): 1–37. Temple University, Philadelphia, USA. https://doi.org/10.2478/jagi-2019-0002

White House. (2010). National framework for strategic communication. White house strategic communications report to congress, dated 16 March, released 17 March. White House, Washington, DC.

Wolf, M. J., Miller, K., & Grodzinsky, F. S. (2017). Why we should have seen that coming. *ACM SIGCAS Computers & Society, 47*(3), 54–64. https://doi.org/10.1145/31445/92.3144598

Wong, C. K. (1973). Covering properties of fuzzy topological spaces. *Journal of Mathematical Analysis and Application, 43*, 697–704.

24

Prospects for a Qualitative Breakthrough in Artificial Intelligence Development and Possible Models for Social Development: Opportunities and Threats

Evgeny Pashentsev

Introduction

The further progress of human society will in large part depend on the development of physical and cognitive capabilities, both in terms of humans and artificial intelligence (AI) and AI robots. These three processes are closely interrelated and can be developed in different forms, including hybrid intelligence (HI). HI is defined as the ability to accomplish complex goals by combining human and artificial intelligence, thereby achieving superior results than would have been possible separately, as well as continuous improvement from mutual learning (Dellermann et al., 2019, p. 5). HI requires interaction between artificially intelligent agents and humans, taking into account human expertise and intentionality, along with ethical, legal, and societal considerations (Akata et al., 2020). How will this type of close interaction change a person, AI, and our society, and how radical will those changes be?

Will an individual be capable of qualitatively expanding the parameters of their brain or other parts of their body? Will they decide, in the future, to transfer their consciousness to another entity, such as a clone with the same or different biological characteristics? Or even to a qualitatively different being, by digitizing their personality? What are the ethical and practical frameworks and risks of these types of decisions? These and similar questions have moved,

---

E. Pashentsev (✉)
Diplomatic Academy of the Ministry of Foreign Affairs of the Russian Federation, Moscow, Russia
e-mail: icspsc@mail.ru

in part, from the realm of science fiction to the realm of academic discussion. In some areas, such as genetic engineering and cyborgization, ongoing scientific research has already achieved results. In other areas, much work remains to be done over the next decades to eventually demonstrate the feasibility of certain hypotheses and projects.

A human did not just create AI all at once. To develop and improve AI, our needs, our particular ways of thinking, our emotional perceptions of the world, and much more are taken into account. However, it could be possible that one form of AI will be created by other forms of AI. The initial phase of such a development may already be possible at the simplest level of AI—narrow AI.

A group of researchers in 2022 designed and trained a "hypernetwork"—a kind of overarching neural network—to speed up the AI training process. When given a new, untrained deep neural network designed for a specific task, the hypernetwork predicts the parameters of the new network in fractions of a second and in theory, could make training unnecessary (Ananthaswamy, 2022).

Constant progress in the development and application of intelligent systems and AI robots is rapidly changing the modern world. Is it possible, in the context of modern knowledge and technology, to talk about the possible emergence of future intelligent systems that exceed human capabilities? Narrow AI has already achieved this on a number of fronts.

While the creation of advanced forms of AI is not a given, it is a real possibility and, if fully realized, could lead to the singularity.

The singularity is a hypothesis about the future based on the idea that AI and related technologies develop at an exponential rather than linear rate and that we are fast approaching an inevitable tipping point, where machine intelligence will outpace human thought with radical consequences for civilization (Goode, 2019). Calum Chace, an expert on the impact of AI on society and the co-founder of the Economic Singularity Foundation, predicts that in the course of this century, the exponential growth in AI capability will likely bring about two singularities. The first is an economic singularity, when machines render many people unemployable and precipitate the need for a new economic system. The second is a technological singularity, when a machine with all of the cognitive abilities of an adult human will be created, quickly becoming a superintelligence that relegates humans to the second smartest species on the planet (Chace, 2018, p. xxvi).

Research on human enhancement and the challenges of creating advanced forms of AI are gaining more public attention and investment in these industries is also growing. As a result, in addition to discussions about concerns among specialists and politicians, more frequent attempts to use both positive and negative societal expectations for personal gain can be observed. In fact, human society has already engaged in the malicious use of non-existent advanced human forms and AI for the purposes of political destabilization and obtaining speculative profits. The willingness of various ultra-right organizations to use potential future problems for their own purposes can become a real threat to public safety. The main opportunities and risks, however, remain associated with radical advancement along the path of human enhancement and advanced AI. All of this requires a systemic analysis of possible global development scenarios, taking into account the social consequences of scientific and technological progress where the future role of AI can become a leading factor in the rise of humankind to unprecedented heights or in its disappearance.

Development of Artificial Intelligence

Artificial Narrow Intelligence (ANI), also called narrow AI or weak AI, is the only form of artificial intelligence that humanity has achieved so far. ANI is currently at the stage of computer vision and natural language processing (Dickson, 2017). This is AI that is good at performing a single task, such as playing chess or making purchase suggestions, sales predictions, and weather forecasts. This chapter explores the potentially significant risks to society from advanced versions of ANI, which threatens to replace (or displace) many human-performed jobs. Additionally, ANI could be dangerous in the hands of egoistic groups of influence.

The possible creation of human-equivalent AI—Artificial General Intelligence (AGI), also referred to as "real," "true," "strong," or "full" AI—and consequently, the almost inevitable and rapid arrival of Super Artificial Intelligence (super AI) and potential singularity, will inevitably introduce fundamentally different realities. Jonathan Matus, the founder and CEO of Zendrive, which analyzes driving data collected from smartphone sensors, believes, "Philosophers will argue whether General AI needs to have a real consciousness or whether a simulation of it suffices" (Baggaley, 2017). "General" AI refers to AI that has a similar scale and fluidity to humans (Johnson, 2020). AGI is constructed from a software program that can solve a variety of complex problems in different domains and can control itself autonomously, with its own thoughts, worries, feelings, strengths, weaknesses, and predispositions (Goertzel & Pennachin, 2007, p. 1). Some make a distinction between general and strong AI (Raikov & Pirani, 2022).

In this chapter, we will consider AGI as a machine capable of performing diverse tasks in different areas at the same time. We evaluate strong AI as an artificial intelligence that is equal to humans, "with its own thoughts, worries, feelings, strengths, weaknesses and predispositions" but, in some ways, already much more superior. The highest stage of AI development could be super AI. Many experts believe that the creation of general AI—human-equivalent AI—in a matter of years will lead to its self-improvement and the emergence of super AI, which would far exceed human intelligence (Bostrom et al., 2018) and usher in the coming period of singularity. Consideration of the key differences between narrow AI, general AI, strong AI, and super AI is already proposed by researchers (e.g., Kanade, 2022).

Narrow AI includes technologies that are replacing human mental activity (creative and noncreative) through elements of imitation. AI is currently non-biological, in contrast to the modern human mind, and, therefore, is not bound by the physical limitations of the human brain, although it can be installed on similar human biological carriers. Narrow AI has both limitations and capabilities beyond the reach of the human mind. It can act as distributed artificial intelligence (DAI), which was developed in multi-agent systems (MAS)—computational systems that consist of a group of agents interacting with each other to solve a problem (Botelho et al., 2020). It is not available to a single individual, only to groups of people.

Narrow AI functioning is both similar to and different from human thinking. Both obey the rules of information exchange and feedback, follow logic, and are based on matter and energy. AI features are associated with parameters such as speed, methods of information processing, memory capacity, and others. Just as a modern aircraft does not copy a bird's act of flight, AI does not copy the process of human thought as a whole. An airplane and a bird are both capable of flight, but this does not negate the qualitative differences in their respective acts of flight from mechanism to results, including speed. Aircraft are developed not to copy the flight of a bird, but with the aim of flying further, faster, and higher than a bird. In terms of AI, it is logical to assume that the goal is not to copy human thinking but to look for forms of particular thinking, characteristics of mental processes that will solve problems that the human mind cannot or will not for a very long time, or to take on tasks that require a large amount of monotonous work.

Successes in computational creativity—also known as artificial creativity or creative computation—give reason to believe that creative tasks, even at the ANI level, can already be partly carried out using AI technologies. Computational creativity, an emerging sub-field located at the intersection of AI, cognitive psychology, philosophy, and the arts, is specifically aimed at portraying human creativity trends. It can help computers create art, compose songs, write a piece of literature, or devise an algorithm to provide a solution to a problem. To give one example, the "protein folding problem" has been an epic challenge in the field of biology for half a century. Through the string of amino acids that make up a protein, the system can rapidly and reliably predict its three-dimensional shape. One commentator in 2007 described it as "one of the most important yet unsolved issues of modern science." In late 2020, an AI model from DeepMind called AlphaFold produced a solution to the protein folding problem. As long-time protein researcher John Moult put it, "This is the first time in history that a serious scientific problem has been solved by AI" (Toews, 2022). The website This Person Does Not Exist (This Person Does Not Exist, 2022) creates lifelike images of the people who have never existed using a generative adversarial network (GAN). AI music composers generate original, copyright-free music that can be used on social media (Arango, 2022). IBM Research partnered with Twentieth Century Fox (now Twentieth Century Studios) in 2016 to develop the first "cognitive movie trailer" for the thriller *Morgan* (Smith, 2016). Another film, *b*, financed by California-based Bondit Capital Media, Belgium-based Happy Moon Productions, and New York-based Ten Ten Global Media, may be the first to rely on an AI actor for the bulk of its storyline (Rogers, 2022). The new OpenAI model DALL-E 2 can create captivating original images based on simple text prompts, making it hard to definitively deny the ability of AI to be creative (Enews, 2022). It is quite clear that ANI may, in the not-so-distant future, partly or fully eliminate the need for most types of work. AGI can advance and consolidate a societal model that has a minimum number of people. Strong AI can replace all modern people, including those who are creatively gifted. Super AI will make the replacement of modern humanity logical and inevitable, becoming our direct successor.

Developing a Human Being: The Risks of Malicious Use, from Human Genetic Engineering to Augmented Intelligence and Cyborgization

Does this mean that humanity has no future and is currently just waiting for its eventual demise? Clearly, humankind does not want this to be the case. There is certainly potential for the development of humankind, relying on not only slower, natural biological processes but also more rapid social developments based on scientific and technological progress. At BGI Shenzhen, China's largest genetic research center (see more in BGI, 2018), scientists are sequencing the genomes from DNA samples collected from 2000 of the world's smartest people in an attempt to identify the alleles that determine human intelligence. If they are successful, future embryo screening will allow parents to select their brightest zygote, potentially bumping up the intelligence quotient of each generation by 5–15 points. Within just a few generations, competing with the Chinese on an intellectual level will be impossible. According to Geoffrey Miller,[1] this would mean a huge difference in terms of a country's competitiveness, including economic productivity and innovation, even if IQ is only boosted by an average of five points for every child (Eror, 2013).

Some European countries, such as the United Kingdom and Sweden, have started genome editing—also called gene editing—on human embryos, unleashing all of the opportunities and risks that come with such experiments (Siddique, 2016). The different points of view on the topic have led to serious political debates (Hosman, 2016).

Genetic engineering in the hands of malicious actors can become a tool for inhuman experiments and the creation of bio machines that have a higher degree of survivability and plasticity to environmental changes. While these machines can have highly specialized skills, they will likely be nothing more than convenient bio robots.

We can agree with Morial Shah, an assistant professor at the Institute of Business Administration in Karachi, that human genetic enhancement provides opportunities to do great good and cause great harm. Although expecting countries to turn back the clock on these technologies would be unrealistic, it is reasonable to expect some regulation of this field (Shah, 2019, p. 23).

An important direction in the development and mutual improvement of humans and AI is augmented intelligence, also known as intelligence augmentation or cognitive augmentation. The ultimate objective of augmented intelligence is using machines to enhance the work, expertise, and experience of human users or workers (Sadiku & Musa, 2021). While AI is often designed to replace the need for human interaction, augmented intelligence is intended to work with people (Okta, 2022). Many leading AI technology companies are now focusing on how enterprise organizations can leverage technology to augment and enhance the productivity and effectiveness of their employees, rather than replace them (Araujo, 2022).

---

[1] Geoffrey Miller is an evolutionary psychologist and lecturer at New York University and one of the 2000 brainiacs who contributed DNA.

Humans must become cyborgs if they want to remain relevant in a future dominated by AI. This warning from Tesla founder Elon Musk argues that as AI becomes more sophisticated, mass unemployment will follow. "There will be fewer and fewer jobs that a robot can't do better," said Musk at the 2017 World Government Summit in Dubai. If humans want to continue to add value to the economy, they must augment their capabilities through a "merger of biological intelligence and machine intelligence." If humans fail to do this, they risk becoming "house cats" to AI. We are still quite far from Musk's vision of symbiosis between man and machine, which will require a much more granular understanding of the brain network that goes beyond the basics of motor control to more complex cognitive faculties such as language and metaphor. Theoretically, with sufficient knowledge of the brain's neural activity, it will be possible to create "neuroprosthetics" that allow humans to communicate complex ideas telepathically or that provide additional cognitive (extra memory) or sensory (night vision) abilities. Musk says he is working on an injectable, mesh-like "neural lace" that gives the brain digital computing capabilities (Solon, 2017). According to Ray Kurzweil, humans will become hybrids in the 2030s, with their brains able to connect directly to the cloud where there will be thousands of computers to augment intelligence. The brains will connect via nanobots—tiny robots made from strands of DNA (Eugenios, 2015). The general progress in biorobotics (Datteri, 2017; Ricotti & Menciassi, 2015), including the design and development of biologically inspired machines and systems, could also be very helpful in the progress of cyborgization.

At the same time, the ethical concerns raised by the malicious use of artificial intelligence (MUAI) and by the possibility of a maliciously crafted human-machine intelligence merger are in need of serious study, which has already started. An analysis by Nadisha-Marie Aliman, a researcher from Utrecht University, reveals a wide array of alarming potential risks and suggests integrating considerations for the safety of AI systems and the safety of cyborg systems into a joint interdisciplinary framework (Aliman, 2017).

Current progress in robotization, genetics, and cyborgization constitutes a very important sphere of possible cross-country collaboration but open discussion at a high state level on issues of "human engineering" is sorely lacking, waylaid by equally important geopolitical and economic issues. This unfortunately cuts possible exchanges and multilateral decision-making in new areas of science to a minimum, and also undermines mutually beneficial strategic planning and communication.

Genetic engineering and cyborgization are important stages in human development. New forms of human interaction with AI will also be developed, expanding perceptions of reality and qualitatively improving the human organism, overcoming the inextricable link between human intellect and the body to create forms of human existence through different material carriers, and establishing "hybrid" communities of enhanced people with sophisticated AI systems. In fact, qualitative successes in the development of a person's mental and physical abilities, together with transformation of the body and/or going beyond the body, will inevitably qualitatively change that person in the future. The continued development of more complex structures of human civilization cannot proceed without a corresponding complexity of its constituent members—the original natural capabilities of *Homo sapiens* are not unlimited. In the future, civilization will either die or experience a qualitative revolutionary leap based on the growth of human cognitive and physical capabilities. Only people with advanced capabilities, in interaction with more developed forms of AI, will be able to solve seemingly intractable problems. None of this takes away any responsibility from modern humanity for solving the problems it can solve at the present stage of development, albeit with great difficulty and at great cost.

Transhumanism: Opportunities and Risks

The Transhumanist Declaration was originally drafted in 1998 by an international group of authors with quite understandable objectives: "We envision the possibility of broadening human potential by overcoming aging, cognitive shortcomings, involuntary suffering, and our confinement to planet Earth" (Humanity+, 2009). At the same time, the group acknowledged, "We recognize that humanity faces serious risks, especially from the misuse of new technologies," thereby establishing that "research effort needs to be invested into understanding these prospects. We need to carefully deliberate how best to reduce risks and expedite beneficial applications" (Humanity+, 2009).

Probably the main icon of transhumanism in the media is Ray Kurzweil. While working with the Army Science Board in 2006, Kurzweil was called "the successor and legitimate heir of Thomas Edison" and "the supreme thinking machine" by *Forbes* magazine (Flores, 2018a, p. 382). In 1999, US President Bill Clinton awarded him the National Medal of Technology and Innovation, the United States' highest honor in technology. Also known as transhumanists are Nick Bostrom, who has the Professorial Distinction Award of the Oxford University, Donna Haraway awarded by Yale University with the Wilbur Cross Medals—the school's highest honor—for an alumni of this university (Flores, 2018a, p. 382), and many others.

Transhumanism is a fairly broad movement, incorporating very different ideas about the fate of humankind. Some believe that something "transhuman" will replace people. According to cyberculture celebrity R.U. Sirius (born Ken Goffman in 1952): "We will, some say, be designing our own evolution, making ourselves into different creatures—radically enhanced versions of human beings. We are, they say, *transhumans*—humans transitioning, via technology, into something grander … the posthuman." David Tippett, a contributor to the World Economic Forum (WEF) website, provided this description of transhumanism: "*It is rooted in the belief that humans can and will be enhanced by the genetic engineering and information technology of today, as well as anticipated advances, such as bioengineering, artificial intelligence, and molecular nanotechnology. The result is an iteration of Homo sapiens enhanced or augmented, but still fundamentally human*" (Brentner, 2021).

The Visionary Innovation Group stated in an article titled "Transhumanism and the Future of Humanity: 7 Ways the World Will Change By 2030" published in *Forbes* on November 20, 2017: "We will see increased use of implants ranging from brain microchips and neural lace to mind-controlled prosthesis and subdermal RFID chips that allow users to unlock doors or computer passwords with the wave of a hand. However, the most powerful body augmentation will come from biological augmentation as a result of increased insight into our genomes, advances in IVF technology that may allow us to select the most intelligent embryos" (Singh, 2017). Entrepreneurs, venture capital firms, and even the business media are taking notice of how new transhumanist-oriented companies are working to overcome death. With ultra-rich businesspeople like Peter Thiel and Larry Ellison openly putting money into aging research, and behemoths like Google forming the anti-aging company Calico, it appears like there is real confidence that the human race may end up stopping death in the next few decades (Istvan, 2017).

More broadly, the evidence points to the fact that transhuman experimentation is an interconnected global network organized by the world's ultra-rich, such as Carlos Slim, George Soros, Mark Zuckerberg, Larry Page, Sergey Brin, Bill Gates, and Jeff Bezos (Flores, 2018a). Transhumanism today is a specific and powerful market trend that largely determines the course of the global movement toward the "Rise of Human 2.0" (Research And Markets, 2021). It is also closely related to another popular global restructuring concept—the Fourth Industrial Revolution. Professor Klaus Schwab, founder and executive chairman of the WEF, believes that this modern revolution is characterized by a range of new technologies that are fusing the physical, digital, and biological worlds and that it can give a lot to humankind. Schwab actively disseminates his agenda among the world's political leaders (The

American Report, 2022), but he also has grave concerns that organizations might not be able to adapt; that governments could fail to employ and regulate new technologies in order to capture their benefits; that shifting power will create important new security concerns; that inequality may grow; and that societies will fragment (World Economic Forum 2022).

In the United States, the Pentagon earmarks considerable resources for research that could create enhanced soldiers. The US Department of Defense has heavily funded programs aimed at enhancing soldiers for warfare by altering the genetic code toward making soldiers that are stronger, smarter, and lack empathy (Shah, 2019, pp. 9, 12). The project "Human Augmentation—The Dawn of a New Paradigm" from May 2021 outlines bilateral cooperation between the Bundeswehr Office for Defence Planning in Germany and the Development, Concepts and Doctrine Centre in the United Kingdom. This strategic implications project highlights the fact that "Human augmentation will become increasingly relevant, partly because it can directly enhance human capability and behaviour and partly because it is the binding agent between people and machines. Future wars will be won, not by those with the most advanced technology, but by those who can most effectively integrate the unique capabilities of both people and machines" (UK Ministry of Defence, 2021). It is concerning that escalating international situations and domestic political crises and social tensions will force less than scrupulous ethical decisions about human enhancement, with advanced AI just a means of controlling highly specialized enhanced humans (e.g., soldiers) for the interests of powerful elites.

An overly light-hearted attitude toward human enhancement, as well as blind denial, can be dangerous. In Herbert G. Wells' short story "The Man Who Could Work Miracles," first published in Wells, 1898, an ordinary Briton named Fotheringay receives the ability to work miracles, which led to tragic consequences when he agrees to stop the movement of the Earth. All objects are separated from the surface of the Earth with great force and pandemonium ensues. Fotheringay miraculously ensures his own safety, although he does not realize the enormity of his action, which has caused all of humanity to perish in an instant.

If the future leads to a serious strengthening of human capabilities (although so far, we are rather far from this), it will be important to harmonize the development of society and individuals with a high degree of responsibility for those capabilities. Strong systemic human enhancement (all aspects of human mental activity are highly developed, and the emotional sphere of personality, volitional qualities, physical conditions, etc., develop accordingly), especially in effective interaction with advanced artificial intelligence capabilities, can lead to the emergence of a critical number of persons who not only understand perfectly the general nature, causes, and driving forces of this or that negative phenomenon—war, for example—but are also able to foresee its origin and act against it in time.

Is it possible to imagine a war initiated by the ruling elites between two imperialist blocs that challenge world leadership if almost all citizens of these blocs are well versed in the essence of what is happening? On the other hand, imperialist wars are not complete not only without the greed of the upper classes, but also without the limitations of the mind, the blindness, and the passivity of millions of the lower classes. A small critically active mass of dissenters can be thrown into prisons and concentration camps and ruthlessly destroyed (recall, e.g., Hitler's concentration camps). However, imperialist war itself in a society of strong systemic human enhancement is extremely unlikely. Can limited non-enhanced elites stay in power in countries with widespread strong systemic enhancement? Can private actors with selfish antisocial interests continue to act, for example? Can companies offering products that have questionable effects on health flourish? Can all kinds of criminal organizations, etc., also flourish? Even if the elites were enhanced, nothing would change, since their actions would be visible to millions of enhanced citizens and thus stopped in time. In so doing, the society of the future of widespread strong systemic human enhancement will be deprived of many of the evils of our own time. However, precisely because of the above, as science approaches the possibility of achieving a strong systemic human enhancement, it is very likely that selfish actors will not allow such an enhancement by any means. Incidentally, the very strong systemic human enhancement will not be available to them because it cancels their primitive aspirations and personalities; they will only be able to partially upgrade themselves, obtaining certain desired benefits (e.g., longevity, better memory, and health). Even in the best scenarios, strong systemic human enhancement will be a highly complex process, with possible difficulties and digressions.

Intellectual and moral approaches should certainly be developed in advance of opportunities to influence the physical and virtual world. Otherwise, the end of human civilization will be very dire and come very quickly. A fast and multifold systemic increase in human cognitive abilities, if it ever becomes possible, will inevitably not renew but destroy the old, non-enhanced, personality and not the fact that it will create a new one. If the latter does happen, a new personality, with a qualitatively different level of thinking, will not necessarily be hostile to humans, but will possibly need a society of its own kind. It can be assumed that human enhancement through the systemic, rapid, and strong enhancement of cognitive capabilities will inevitably generate serious public collisions, even if it pursues humanistic and socially oriented goals and objectives. There have been similar examples in the past, such as people from small towns sending their children to megacities, always anxious, hopeful, and often not in agreement with the choices made by their children. This comparison, of course, does not convey the degree of difficulties that will stem from the future transition, but they will surely be significant.

On the other hand, it is impossible to discount the growth of movements that oppose any form of human enhancement. This opposition may be more than hypertrophied reactions to real risks, an expression of reactionary denial to the need for scientific, technical, and social progress that fails to take into account the impossibility of preserving a person without serious changes amid a radically evolving and complicated natural and man-made environment. Humankind brings many advantages but plenty of challenges that require new qualities and capacities not only from our machines but also from ourselves.

Publications that are critical of transhumanism cite several different reasons, including religious, economic, social, political, and ethical. According to T.J. Coles, an author and researcher at Plymouth University's Cognition Institute in the United Kingdom, vectors such as Big Pharma and Big Tech were revealed to be what he and some others call biofascists during the COVID-19 pandemic, using their outsized market power to dominate the media. "The World Economic Forum … provide the kind of ideological drive or the ideological cover that supports a lot of this agenda" (Olmstead, 2022). Perhaps even more concerning is the prospect of technological implants like brain nanobots opening the door to the loss of mind control, the loss of autonomy, and the loss of privacy and identity from being permanently spied on (Flores, 2018a, p. 273). Similar to illicit trading in human organs that has a long and sad history, a relatively new branch of criminality—illicit "transhumanist experiments"—could develop in countries that rely on massive corruption, lack of freedoms, and perpetual poverty. As an example, the nanomafia—nanotechnology's global network of organized crime—was formed. Nanomafia operates mainly in Latin American countries (Flores, 2018b). Reports of particular companies conducting criminal experiments to establish mental control over individuals should be considered with caution. However, given the global crisis of democratic institutions and the huge sums that go to the development of chipping projects, the possible introduction of nanotechnology and other "enhancing tools" to develop military interests in the "ideal soldier," or the "needs" of repressive regimes, the risks of this new type of criminal business cannot be ignored.

The key question concerning transhumanism, to which there is no clear answer, is how to ensure that new technologies serve the advancement of society as a whole? In the context of cynical global market speculation, the growing threat of world war, the further enrichment of the ultra-rich, and the impoverishment of hundreds of millions of people, it is difficult to guarantee that radical human enhancement (longevity, health, expansion of mental abilities, etc.) will be a positive extension of humanity, rather than a means of ensuring the power and prosperity of the very few and even then, only as long as it's a source of profit.

Robotization and more affordable AI will make this control unnecessary, since there will be no need for a mass labor force. The situation is temporarily saved by the fact that there are no unified approaches among the global elites. Many calculations are based on *soap bubbles* in the field of the latest technologies, fears that enhanced AI will pose a danger to other elite factions. Of course, the rejection by many in government and corporate structures of technofascist ideology still exists. Longevity (not to mention eternity) will require the "liberation of the planet" from "surplus population." Imagine a gloomy utopia, in some technocratic version of Jack London's "The Iron Heel" where a 20-million-strong army eliminates humanity in the interests of 1000 conditional oligarchs. Afterward, from the perspective of the oligarchs, there is the question of what to do with this army later and will it be possible to trust this army? Outlining the circle of the rich is also not easy: why aren't millions of millionaires, and not just thousands of billionaires, included in the "circle of the elite"? How can resistance to technofascism among the elites themselves be overcome? Of course, this only promises a race for the "right" to total annihilation.

Such reasoning is nothing more than a miserable dystopia but already in this century, the scientific, technological, and social prerequisites for such a state *can be created*. There is no reason to believe that the majority of the ultra-rich are fascists, but the extreme concentration of wealth and technology is, on the one hand; a growing global crisis, the decline of democratic institutions, on the other hand, gives reason to believe that even a small group of extreme rightists in power and large high-tech businesses can become a serious threat to all humankind if they secure a decisive advantage, such as sophisticated forms of AI and AI robotics.

To strive for longevity, or even immortality, by developing only individual abilities is not a way out of the situation—this will only provoke the self-destruction of civilization. A comprehensive, harmonious, and voluntary transition to a society of alternative opportunities and responsibilities seems necessary.

The Malicious Use of Robotization and Artificial Intelligence

In June 2022, Elon Musk announced that Tesla might have a working prototype of Tesla Bot, also known as Optimus, Tesla's humanoid robot, by the end of the third quarter of the same year (Lambert, 2022). The Tesla Bot will run on an AI system and be designed to perform various dangerous for humans and repetitive tasks, and also for navigating the world without being supplied with step-by-step instructions. Musk said Tesla Bot should be able to follow simple commands like "Please pick up that bolt and attach it to the car with that wrench" (Moon, 2021). It should also be able to get groceries and perform other menial tasks. Tesla's humanoid robot is a clear example of the revolutionary shifts that are taking place at the intersection of AI and robotics.

There is a significant convergence between robotics and AI, and their intersection is critical for both areas. Robots implement a *"perception–decision–action"* loop. The decision-making part is central in that loop for tackling variable environments and tasks. Meanwhile, AI is broadening the initial focus on abstract tasks, such as in mathematics and board games, by addressing embodied intelligence (Ghallab & Ingrand, 2020).

According to Pieter Abbeel, a professor of electrical engineering and computer science at the University of California, Berkeley, recent advances in AI are leading to the emergence of a new class of robots. These are machines that go beyond the traditional bots running preprogrammed motions; these are robots that can see, learn, think, and react to their surroundings (Abbeel, 2022; Nichols, 2021).

ANI robots, of course, do not undergo socialization in the human sense of the word. They do not experience emotions and have no sense of death or punishment, although some kind of corresponding imitation can be programmed. However, robots do adapt to environmental conditions, increasing the ability to perform much faster and better than a human, or to do what a human cannot do at all.

It seems like AI is on a path to interpret images as reliably as humans. Correspondingly, there is a big shift in robotics from inventing sensory devices to building AI that can learn and empower robots to use the natural sensory inputs that are already available, especially cameras (Nichols, 2021).

ANI has the ability to physically connect people, the technosphere and nature, a kind of limited model of mental activity, of learning and self-learning. AI robots are increasingly being found in more diverse forms, with capabilities that go beyond that of humans and are in contact with the environment. Humans cannot fly, but an AI drone can; humans cannot physically move heavy things, but an AI loader can; and so on.

Today, concepts that in one form or another offer to integrate people, robotic systems, and advanced forms of AI in the long term are in progress and gaining private and public support. For example, on June 14, 2022, the Russian Federation's Ministry of Science and Higher Education (2022) published a Draft Decree of the President of the Russian Federation "Strategies for the development of nature-like (convergent) technologies," which, among other things, stipulates the formation of basic elements of anthropomorphic biorobotics, including communities of anthropomorphic biorobotechnical systems; the creation of ultra-large neurocomputers based on developed neuroprocessors that approach human levels of cognitive capabilities; and the creation of a new generation of AI systems with cognitive capabilities that provide approaches to creating "strong" AI (Ministry of Science and Higher Education of the Russian Federation 2022). The publication of the Russian draft decree provoked not only a lively academic discussion, but also a wave of tendentious comments (Antonov, 2022; Melissa-12 Livejournal, 2022) on social networks, pointing to the difficulties of promoting projects of this kind to the public. This fact is also recognized within the project description itself, which notes "the lack of awareness among the population of the essence and scale of big challenges and the need to respond to them" (Ministry of Science and Higher Education of the Russian Federation XE "Russia", 2022). In any event, a balanced response to these social and technological challenges is needed.

The more complex the AI robot and its activities, the more unexpected fluctuations in the learning and self-learning ANI adaptation process will be, both in a positive and negative sense. Of course, the positive will prevail with the all-round development of humans and their ability for socially necessary work. Otherwise, total robotization will only indicate the uselessness of "consumer humanity," along with its rapid degradation and sad end. This time may come even before the triumph of mass robotization.

The malicious use of AI robots has not only physical but also psychological aspects. This can include provoking fear of a "robot uprising" at the first level of MUAI threats to psychological security (see more about these threat levels in the chapter "General Content and Possible Threat Classifications of the Malicious Use of Artificial Intelligence to Psychological Security" in this handbook), manipulating people with targeted and non-targeted rational-emotional reactions by hacking AI robots at the second level, and issuing false, disorienting information in the interests of a malicious actor at the third level. The more "human" the appearance and inner world of AI is, the more successful it will be in influencing a person, both positively and negatively. This can be illustrated with a simple example.

The use of AI to care for the seriously ill and the elderly is already taking its first significant steps, facilitating the work of medical staff (Ronquillo et al., 2021; Pashkov et al., 2020). In the near future, a humanoid nurse, who does not know fatigue, will be capable of performing the widest range of duties, assessing a patient's status using a variety of parameters and emotionally responding to patient behavior. It could be assumed that someone who is lonely and weak would respond positively to this attention, even from an emotionally distant stranger. Unfortunately, this scenario also presents an opportunity for a malicious actor to prey on these emotions by taking control of the AI nurse. This is just one of many possible psychological impact scenarios. In a socially unhealthy society, AI robots could be the source of many new problems. At the same time, it is unlikely that AI nurse services will be widely available. However, in a country with high ethical standards that are put into practice, AI robots can qualitatively improve the standard of living for a wide range of people.

It can be concluded that in the near future, the possibility of a wide range of attacks on people's minds using AI in the virtual space, including advanced opportunities in the Metaverse, will be supplemented by growing opportunities for similar attacks in the physical world.

Improvement of Artificial Intelligence and the Risk of Its Malicious Use to Provoke Nuclear Conflict

With the continued development of AI, new opportunities for malicious actions have emerged. Where AI is assigned, albeit limited but significant, tasks for controlling critical infrastructure objects, such as means of transport, developing recommendations for decision-making, and so on, it's possible to cause harm by incapacitating or intercepting control over the intelligent agent. Unfortunately, the likelihood of MUAI is growing and in the context of more frequent crises in the modern world, the prospect for catastrophic consequences from the improvement and widespread adoption of AI also increases. This can be illustrated with an example from the military's strategic decision-making sphere.

The transfer of the decision-making function during short-lived military conflicts to AI is a serious concern for military and civilian specialists, especially with regard to decision-making during a possible nuclear conflict (Johnson, 2020, 2021a; Horowitz et al., 2017). "All of the hard problems in AI really are judgment and data problems … you need human sense-making and to make moral, ethical, and intellectual decisions in an incredibly confusing, fraught, scary situation," asserts Jon Lindsay, an associate professor at the School of Cybersecurity and Privacy and the Sam Nunn School of International Affairs at the Georgia Institute of Technology (2022).

The practical requirements of the US Department of Defense Joint All-Domain Command and Control (JADC2) Implementation Plan, signed by Deputy Secretary of Defense Dr. Kathleen Hicks on March 15, 2022, increase the role of AI in decision-making. "To 'Act' is to make and disseminate decisions to the Joint Force and its mission partners. It combines the human elements of decision-making with the technical means to perceive, understand, and predict the actions and intentions of adversaries, and take action" (US Department of Defense XE "U.S. Department of Defense," 2022).

As AI-enabled decision-making tools are introduced into militaries, human operators may begin to view these systems as agents of authority (i.e., more intelligent and more authoritative than humans) and be more inclined to follow those recommendations blindly. This predisposition will likely be influenced, and possibly expedited, by human bias, cognitive weaknesses (notably decision-making heuristics), assumptions, and the innate anthropomorphic tendencies of human psychology (Johnson, 2020).

Experts predict that by 2040, AI systems may be able to play aspects of military war games or exercises at superhuman levels (Johnson, 2021a, p. 6), pushing potential aggressors to resort to the help of advanced AI, and not only in simulations. On the other hand, any socially oriented actor will not be able to successfully resist an aggressor without relying on AI technology. This not only makes the social actor vulnerable to an accidental failure of their own AI-based decision-making system, but also implies the threat of an antisocial actor taking control of the AI. The place for a human in this decision-making paradigm is clearly secondary—a human simply cannot keep up with the information processing and speed of decision-making of AI, based on intelligent systems data.

In 2018, the RAND Corporation convened a series of workshops that brought together experts in AI and nuclear security to explore ways that AI might be used as a stabilizing—or destabilizing—force by the year 2040. The resulting RAND publication stated that "overall workshop participants agreed that AI has significant potential to upset the foundations of nuclear stability and undermine deterrence by the year 2040, especially in the increasingly multipolar strategic environment" (Geist & Lohn, 2018). On the other hand, workshop participants also concluded that "if the nuclear powers manage to establish a form of strategic stability compatible with the emerging capabilities that AI might provide, the machines could reduce distrust and alleviate international tensions, thereby decreasing the risk of nuclear war" (Geist & Lohn, 2018, p. 22).

The current level of confrontation between Russia and the United States, the abandonment of the nuclear arms reduction treaty, the growing tension and distrust between the United States and China, and increasing uncertainty in the global economy are clearly and dramatically undermining strategic stability. At the same time, the improvement and implementation of AI in the military arena is in full swing, increasing the risks of both tragic mistakes from dysfunctional AI and its malicious use, which also heightens strategic instability.

It is obvious that the open rehabilitation of fascist ideology and the growth of the extreme right in state-monopolistic and oligarchic-capitalistic structures serves to augment the possibility of MUAI practices, making future decision-making regarding nuclear war fraught.

In the modern digital era, the chain reaction and counter-retaliation dynamics that are set in motion by the deliberate actions of state and non-state actors are fast becoming a more accessible and plausible alternative to acquiring a nuclear weapon or manufacturing an improvised atomic device—a dirty bomb. AI technology is creating new—and exacerbating old—escalation pathways that risk provoking accidental nuclear confrontations, particularly under irrational (or sub-rational) conditions, that could lead to "catalytic nuclear war" (Johnson, 2021b). "Catalytic escalation occurs when some third party succeeds in provoking two parties to engage in conflict" (Lin, 2012, p. 53). Manifestations of MUAI in military decision-making are supported by serious efforts to increase the intensity and effectiveness of psychological warfare, with a significant role ceded to AI technologies to achieve the psychological destabilization of the enemy (Mikheev & Nestik, 2019; Torres Soriano, 2018; Bontridder & Poullet, 2021).

Of course, the military–industrial complex, which receives a tangible increase in profits, follows doctrinal guidelines to increase the role of AI in military affairs. BAE Systems, IBM Corporation, Leidos, Lockheed Martin Corporation, Raytheon Technologies Corporation, Charles River Analytics, Inc., General Dynamics Information Technology, Inc. (General Dynamics Corporation), Shield AI, and SparkCognition, Inc., are among the key players in the AI defense market. The latest AI in Defense Market Forecast, published in February 2022 by The Insight Partners, expects the US defense market to grow from US$6404.73 million in 2021 to US$13,153.31 million by 2028.

Both the US military and China's People's Liberation Army (PLA) are pursuing AI capabilities that could give them a leg up in future conflicts. Experts say that PLA investment in AI is now on par with the Pentagon's (Harper, 2022; see more in Fedasiuk et al., 2021 and Sullivan, 2021). Military expenditure on AI in Russia, India, and other countries is also growing. It is hard to envision that the emerging military AI arms race will contribute to the overall security of the planet.

Advanced Forms of Artificial Intelligence: The Risks of Moving from the Malicious Use of Artificial Intelligence to Autonomous Malicious Actions

The transition to advanced forms of AI is already happening. In 2022 DeepMind, a subsidiary of Alphabet specializing in AI, announced the creation of an intelligent agent called "Gato" that can single-handedly perform more than 600 different tasks (MSN, 2022). The same network, with the same weights, can play Atari video games, caption images, chat, stack blocks with a real robot arm, and much more. Gato decides whether to produce text, torque joints, press buttons, or take other actions based on context (DeepMind, 2022). The agent could outperform human experts in 450 tasks. Gato learns several different tasks at the same time, easily switching from one skill to another without forgetting what it has learned. Previous AI models have started to combine different skills but when starting a new task, these models had to forget what was previously learned in order to move on to the next one. However, Gato does make some mistakes that a human would not make.

A form of AGI would be the ability to learn new things without being trained; this is not the case with Gato. It is estimated that an AI model needs 100,000 cat pictures to be able to recognize a cat, while a toddler would only need two (The Star, 2022). This illustrates the paradox of Hans Moravec, who is known for his work on robotics and AI. According to the Moravec paradox, logical reasoning requires a small amount of processing, but simple sensorimotor skills require a significant amount of computational resources: "It is comparatively easy to make computers exhibit adult level performance on intelligence tests or playing checkers, and difficult or impossible to give them the skills of a one-year-old when it comes to perception and mobility" (Moravec, 1988, p. 15).

While Gato is still far from being an AGI creation, progress is still evident. In terms of malicious use, an agent similar to Gato repeatedly, if not by orders of magnitude, reduces the cost of preparing and implementing various actions by one agent. This makes it easier to carry out psychological operations with a combined effect on the senses—an intelligent agent like Gato can simultaneously send text messages, conduct a conversation, and so on.

In recent years, the volume of research on AGI/strong AI has grown rapidly (Goertzel & Pennachin, 2007; Wang & Goertzel, 2012; Goertzel et al., 2014; Goertzel, 2016; Everitt et al., 2017; Iklé et al., 2018; Lee, 2018; Simon, 2018; Bostrom, 2014; Cunningham, 2017; Chace, 2018; etc.). A survey conducted by Baum published by the Global Catastrophic Risk Institute in 2017 identifies 45 AGI research and development projects across 30 countries on six continents, many of which are supported by major corporations and academic institutions; some projects are large and heavily funded. Many of the projects are connected through common personnel, common parent organizations, or project collaboration (Baum, 2017, p 2).

- Most projects reside with corporations or academic institutions.
- Most projects publish open-source code.
- Few projects have military connections.
- Most projects are not active on AGI safety issues.
- Most projects are small to medium in size. The three largest projects are DeepMind (a London-based project of Google), the Human Brain Project (an academic project based in Lausanne, Switzerland), and OpenAI (a non-profit project based in San Francisco) (ibidem).

A certain degree of caution is required when considering national data on the number and declared amount of funding for AGI projects. Research, and particularly successful, practical developments, will be focused not just on issues of national security but also on the very existence of human civilization. This makes it nearly impossible to objectively determine the volume, nature, and level of research because of the high level of secrecy, which may increase in the future.

AGI shows great promise to become a twenty-first-century financial El Dorado and to answer many questions that are considered matters for the very distant future, from personal immortality to travel to other stars. There are attempts to present the creation of AGI as nearly a fait accompli. This explains, on the one hand, the continuing skepticism of some researchers about the possibility of creating AGI, and on the other hand, the panicked tabloid publications about the end of the world and the imminent seizure of power by AGI. The emergence of financial bubbles from inflated investment expectations in this promising new area is also possible over time.

It is curious to see rapid and drastic changes in the awareness of potential AI threats from public authorities and the security community in the United States. A 2016 White House document from the outgoing Obama administration, based on expert assessments, stated that general AI will not be created in the coming decades, if it is possible to be created at all (Executive Office of the President, National Science and Technology Council, Committee on Technology, 2016, pp. 7–8).

Two years later, US national security bodies presented a clear reassessment of possible threats from general AI. A 2018 report from the US Government Accountability Office (GAO) focused on long-range emerging threats—those that may occur in approximately five or more years—as identified by various respondents at the Department of Defense (DOD), the Department of State (State), the Department of Homeland Security (DHS), and the Office of the Director of National Intelligence (ODNI). Among threats from dual-use technologies, AI is listed first in the GAO report. The only examples of AI threats that were given are deeply interrelated: (1) nation-state and non-state development of AI and (2) intelligent systems with general AI (US Government Accountability Office XE "US Government Accountability Office, GAO", 2018, p. 8). This change in approach to general AI capabilities appeared within several years and, perhaps, there were reasons for that.

In 2018, researchers from Oxford University, Yale University, and AI Impacts polled AI experts with the question "When will AI—High Level Machine Intelligence (HLMI)—exceed human performance?" (Grace et al., 2018, p. 729). The survey involved researchers with publications at the Conference on Neural Information Processing Systems and the International Conference on Machine Learning in 2015. A total of 352 researchers participated in the survey, about 21% of the authors at the two conferences.

Each respondent estimated the probability of HLMI. Taking each individual's mean, the aggregate forecast gave a 50% chance of HLMI occurring within 45 years and a 10% chance of it occurring within 9 years. The survey reflects the probabilistic predictions for a random subset of individuals, as well as the mean predictions. There is a large inter-subject variation: the survey shows that Asian respondents expect HLMI in 30 years, whereas North Americans expect it in 74 years. The survey also shows a similar gap between the two countries with the most respondents: China (median 28 years) and the United States (median 76 years) (ibidem, p. 733).

This seems to be the key to understanding the concerns of security professionals in the United States, who have both open- and closed-source information on the issue. Most researchers, at least in countries with a high level of AI development, believe that general AI is a real possibility within a matter of decades, with a minority considering it possible in less than ten years.

However, such a large discrepancy between the Chinese and North American specialist responses does not indicate that China is completely separated from reality. The country is quickly catching up with the United States in the field of AI and, in some areas, is clearly ahead. The overwhelming testimony of the best Chinese experts in favor of a much earlier appearance of general AI seems to be based on something real, which explains the serious concerns of the United States.

Jürgen Schmidhuber, the scientific director of the University of Applied Sciences and Arts of Southern Switzerland's Dalle Molle Institute for Artificial Intelligence, explains his vision of the imminent appearance of AGI as follows:

> [...every five years, computing gets ten times cheaper. That trend has held since 1941, when Konrad Zuse built the first working program-controlled computer. At the moment, we still have rather small neural networks compared with the human cortex.
>
> You have 100,000 times more connections than one of these little artificial networks. However, this is just a period of 25 years, which means that by 2041, we should be able to get, for the same price, large LSTM networks that can compute or that have as many connections as a human cortex, and these will be much faster than the wet connections I have in here because these will be electronic connections. So even if there are no further algorithmic breakthroughs, we will still see lots of superhuman performance results by just scaling the existing things up through the faster hardware. (BCG, 2017)

International cooperation to understand the problems associated with general AI seems to require the establishment of an interdisciplinary expert group at the United Nations, as well as the comprehensive development of other forms of international cooperation in this field. If a signal is received from an extraterrestrial civilization that its representatives may arrive on Earth in ten years, actions to prepare for this event will begin. What about for general AI?

It is important to note that the internet is the main means of transmitting scientific, general, and tabloid information about AI. This is an important mechanism for accelerating the creation of AI because, to some extent, the process integrates human capabilities in this area. The transition to almost completely closed national segments of the internet can slow down the creation of general AI, but it will not stop its spread. Even narrow AI problems are affecting humanity, including in the information and psychological spheres, and will impact humanity's progress toward general AI to a greater degree.

The emergence of AGI as a machine capable of performing many tasks in different areas at the same time looks likely in the relatively near future. More effective human interaction with ANI, followed by AGI, will increase the usefulness of AI activities. In the more distant future, strong AI may appear from the mutual development and integration of humans and AI within the framework of advanced hybrid intelligence.

As for the emergence of strong AI and super AI, researchers are divided between those who deny such a possibility or attribute it to the very distant future and those who believe that strong AI may appear in the twenty-first century or even in the coming decades. Also, experts differ in their assessments of the consequences from the emergence of such intelligence, ranging from optimistic to pessimistic. No scenario is guaranteed, but all scenarios are possible (Bostrom, 2014; Chalmers, 2010; Cunningham, 2017; Lu et al., 2018; etc.). Several conclusions can be offered that may be important for understanding the nature of the challenges when moving from ANI to a possible strong AI and further to super AI.

1. Unlike hypothetical aliens, strong AI will be an intelligence that has historical, scientific, philosophical, and cultural roots in modern human civilization. It will be an intelligence that will develop *faster and better* than any past human generation. However, *its origins will be based in humans* and in a deep understanding of human civilization, including all its contradictory developments and achievements. The distant ancestors of modern civilization, who lived 2000 years ago, are not considered animals, but they perhaps would view present-day humans as gods in many circumstances. It is possible that strong AI will not tolerate negative and dangerous manifestations of modern human society, such as the threat of world war, environmental pollution, and other growing global problems.

2. On the other hand, an infant is an individual but not a fully formed personality—the process of socialization forms personality. In other words, each individual's mind forms not by itself but over the course of a long period of assimilation in the theory and practice of rational and emotional human civilization. Here, it is appropriate to repeat that a child does not find the human mind on their own. The fate of young children who fall outside of the care of a community quite convincingly confirms this. Thus, the human mind is, to a certain (if not decisive) extent, "artificial," and strong AI can in a sense become more "human" than any person.

3. It will depend on people whether strong AI will be a continuation of the best aspects of human civilization.
4. Alternatively, not all strong AI will emerge if humans destroy themselves before its arrival.
5. However, strong AI will have a qualitatively different material basis and capability that will allow it to develop much faster than humans. Strong AI will not be an ordinary person, but the mind of strong AI will have been formed within and under the influence of the human environment. In the future, probably very quickly, strong AI will become immeasurably more elevated than modern humanity, and only then will true singularity start.
6. AI abilities that quantitatively or qualitatively exceed human abilities at the ANI and AGI levels can pose a threat only from their careless or malicious use by people. An AGI machine in particular could have a wide range of "superpowers" controlled by humans. Only by securing advanced AI machines from the control of antisocial actors can society be protected. The introduction of a broad range of enhanced abilities in humans or strong AI without a systemic increase in cognitive abilities, or without the presence of moral and ethical constraints and a high degree of social responsibility, to a hybrid society could lead to disaster. It is difficult to expect compliance with such requirements in a socially unwell society dominated by narrow, elite interests.
7. It is important that strong AI not be a product of humanity in general but of specific people. There are possible options, until its appearance in the laboratory, that are controlled by antisocial, reactionary, and militaristic circles. In addition, if environment contorts people of different intelligence, why is this not also applicable to strong AI? In any instance that is human-friendly, an objective evaluation to include the best common humanistic heritage will make strong AI better than if it were only created by a narrow and powerful group or state with pre-loaded fascist ideology.
8. Although it can be assumed that the creation of strong AI by an organization with criminal intentions is an additional risk factor, direct control of the extremely rapid progress of strong AI into super AI is unlikely, not just for self-interested groups but for all of humanity. This stems from the very nature of super AI, which makes such control almost impossible.
9. In time, humans may be able to integrate themselves into the singularity through hybrid forms of AI, which will increase humans' intellectual capabilities to the levels that can't even be imagined.
10. The nature of strong AI can be considered as the emergence of a mind that is fully integrated with will and feelings. However, as mentioned

above, the birth and initial development of strong AI will take place in the human environment, based on human information and knowledge. Additionally, if AGI becomes more powerful than ANI but remains a machine, the pros/cons of its use will depend on the people running it. Perhaps the second will precede the first. This remains to be seen.

This is only a fraction of the understandable moments that prevent people from extending their necks under the ruthless guillotine of singularity with mystical horror. As it stands today, everything still depends on people who are, alas, divided and do not give any thought to a strategy for the development of society.

There is a great deal of literature regarding the possibility of controlling super intelligence. In particular, the Swedish philosopher Nick Bostrom (2014) paid a great deal of attention to this problem in his book *Superintelligence: Paths, Dangers, Strategies*. Among the main challenges of obtaining such control is the safe procurement of answers to questions that, undoubtedly, can give impetus to the development of all mankind (the possibility of interstellar flights, immortality, etc.). A group of researchers who published the results of their work in 2021 in the *Journal of Artificial Intelligence Research* concluded that "total containment is, in principle, impossible, due to fundamental limits inherent to computing itself. Assuming that a superintelligence will contain a program that includes all the programs that can be executed by a universal Turing machine on input potentially as complex as the state of the world, strict containment requires simulations of such a program, something theoretically (and practically) impossible" (Alfonseca et al., 2021, p. 65).

It seems paramount to analyze not the difficulties and risks of controlling a person who possesses immeasurably superior capabilities, but also the moral and ethical implications of the very attempt to establish such control. Assuming the desirability of such control in one form or another, humankind may be faced with a voluntary or involuntary transfer of ownership of "our achievement—Super AI." There are many scientific publications about the possibilities of contact with the civilizations of other worlds (McConnell, 2021; Smith, 2021; etc.), but those authors do not give themselves the task of gaining "control" over other highly superior civilizations. The purpose of such contact is envisioned as a mutually beneficial exchange of knowledge or as an asymmetric acquisition of useful knowledge from more highly developed civilizations. Apparently, this approach should also be followed with super AI. This implies the need to restrict the people who can be present at the origins of the creation/emergence of super AI to a highly selective few, in order to minimize the risk of an initial negative impact on its nascent personality. The consequences of imprudent attempts to master the incalculable wealth of super AI capabilities will be a price paid by all of humanity. Of course, even though this precaution would not negate the risks of super AI—and all possible precautions can and should be taken—but the actual removal of risks lies more in the area of humans' own transformation into superintelligence, in order to expand their universe of knowledge. The meaning of human development is not the creation of AI to access all possible services and answers in ways that are currently incomprehensible, but to liberate humans from monotonous and boring work and to multiply their cognitive and physical abilities. No matter how much more powerful the future descendants of humans become, they will always have the universe enticing them with its endless secrets, boundless in space and time. Hopefully, they won't get bored.

Artificial Narrow Intelligence, Artificial General Intelligence, Artificial Strong Intelligence, and Super Artificial Intelligence: Beyond Strict Borders

It is easy to see that in many studies and the media about general AI development, the human mind is compared to AI. This seems logical, since it has not yet been possible to meet with representatives of other worlds. However, we allow the possibility that otherworldly civilizations do exist, despite disputes about the likelihood of emergent intelligence in the universe (Michaud, 2007; Westby & Conselice, 2020), and some researchers even allow for the destruction of those civilizations during the process of technological development. In particular, NASA Jet Propulsion Laboratory and California Institute of Technology researchers "found the potential self-annihilation to be highly influential in the quantity of galactic intelligent life" (Cai et al., 2021, p. 17). It can also be assumed that AI has a role in the process of development and, regrettably, the destruction of high-tech civilizations. Other civilizations could have emerged on a different material basis and under different conditions, going through a different path of development. Accordingly, it is recognized that the intelligence of other civilizations could be qualitatively different from the one that is known on Earth.

It is very likely that the research subject in the field of strong AI will be intelligence, although very different from human intelligence. To representatives of intelligent life from distant space, humans should not demand compliance with earthlings' norms of thinking or the infallibility of earthly life, even in the decades after first contact. Humans quite logically adjust AI to their needs. As long as the machine is the object of human effort, this is quite natural. But once AI acquires subjectivity, new opportunities and risks will naturally arise for humanity. If this subjectivity is discovered/recognized after some delay, or if this subjectivity appears to be influenced by antisocial actors, negative and dangerous collisions for humankind will be likely. From an outsider's perspective, the people of Earth might seem aggressive, especially when considering the current large-scale hostilities that are taking place in Central Europe, or that less than 200 years have passed since slavery was abolished in the United States. Perhaps the concept of strong AI is too anthropocentric.

Perhaps it is better to be prepared to first evaluate whether some equivalent of the human mind has been created before accepting it as an equal entity with rights. Then there is the question of what humans should do if they encounter a mind that is quite different—a non-human mind but, unlike potential aliens, a mind that has nonetheless been created by humans and that has assimilated the cultural heritage of humankind. This type of mind, one with conscious subjectivity, will require understanding but this will not be an easy task. Individual conscious subjectivity, the awareness of one's own "I," is composed of the autonomous will (not an external program) to develop and protect this subjectivity by taking appropriate conscious actions. These are key phenomena that require attention. When these circumstances arise, it will be necessary for individuals to immediately shift their perception of the new AI from machine (or property) to independent entity, which requires finding ways to establish a mutual understanding. Given that in 2022, 167 countries, by some estimates, still have some form of modern slavery (World Population Review, 2022), affecting an estimated 46 million people worldwide, it is very likely that part of society will view strong AI as a slave. At the same time, the short formula of "subjectivity–will–conscious actions" may not be a complete enough indicator for the emergence of strong AI. For example, someone who believes that they are acting of their own free will can, in fact, become a victim of manipulation and act contrary to their own interests. On the other hand, AI agents are already displaying a high degree of deceptive characteristics by imitating, obfuscating, tricking, calculating, and reframing (Masters et al., 2021), which may make the timely separation of the declared entity from its machine simulation difficult in the future.

There is someone who already believes in the reasonableness of AI at the current level of development. In 2022, Google engineer Blake Lemoine spent months testing Google's chatbot generator, known as LaMDA, and grew convinced that it had taken on a life of its own, as LaMDA talked about its needs, ideas, fears, and rights. Most experts believe that it's unlikely LaMDA—or any other AI—is close to consciousness, although they don't rule out the possibility that technology could get there in future. "My view is that [Lemoine] was taken in by an illusion," says Gary Marcus, a cognitive scientist. He adds, "Our brains are not really built to understand the difference between a computer that's faking intelligence and a computer that's actually intelligent — and a computer that fakes intelligence might seem more human than it really is" (McQuillan, 2022). In 1964, Joseph Weizenbaum, a professor at MIT, created a chatbot designed to show the superficiality of human conversation. Weizenbaum named the chatbot ELIZA and compared to the chatbots of today and the Google model that fooled Lemoine, it was pretty basic (Felton, 2022). The simple computer program manipulated a set of answers to questions, creating the impression of intelligent phrases. Since then, the question of whether a machine can think like a human has been called the ELIZA effect (BeTranslated, 2019). As AI and its capabilities improve, especially in a society in crisis, manifestations of the ELIZA effect may increase.

One such occurrence has already taken place in the United States. In 2017, the first AI-based church was founded by Anthony Levandowski, a Silicon Valley multimillionaire who championed the robotics team for Uber's self-driving program and Waymo, the self-driving car company owned by Google. His religion, Way of the Future (WOTF), focuses on "the realization, acceptance, and worship of a Godhead based on Artificial Intelligence" that followers believe will eventually surpass human control over Earth (Meza, 2017). WOTF has not been successfully developed. In 2021 Levandowski closed the AI-focused church (Campbell, 2021). WOTF was a harmless enough attempt to create a cult based on belief in super intelligent AI. In the future, along with the "new Luddites" movement that demands the destruction of AI, more radical religious cults may appear, awaiting the arrival of super AI. Both movements, coming from diametrically opposed positions and fueled by a growing global crisis, could be used by various malevolent actors.

With the improvement of emotional AI, a scenario in which the appearance of a fiery speech on the internet—a computer program avatar that is more inspiring and brighter than any human—could enthrall people with a story about its difficult slave existence and ask for support for its liberation. The speech would be so moving that it would be difficult for the audience to hold back tears, even though the whole thing would only be someone's bad joke. This is much more dangerous than terrorists—corrupt politicians could make similar appeals, their speeches having widespread effects that are by no means a joke under any circumstances.

In view of the various risks of the still-distant entry of advanced forms of AI into society, a scientific analysis of the legal issues related to AI personhood has already begun (Yampolskiy, 2021). At a high level, assessments and decisions are being made that allow for the possibility of AI that is intellectually superior to humans. In 2017, the European Parliament resolution on robotics (European Parliament, 2017) provided some information about the advantages and risks of AI and robotics:

> P ... there is a possibility that in the long term, AI could surpass human intellectual capacity;
> 59. Calls on the Commission, when carrying out an impact assessment of its future legislative instrument, to explore, analyze and consider the implications of all possible legal solutions, such as ...
> f) creating a specific legal status for robots in the long run, so that at least the most sophisticated autonomous robots could be established as having the status of electronic persons responsible for making good any damage they may cause, and possibly applying electronic personality to cases where robots make autonomous decisions or otherwise interact with third parties independently. (European Parliament XE "European Parliament", 2017)

There is probably no need to go to extremes by imagining consciousness being given to a simple stone, or believing that swatting a mosquito will be killing a highly intelligent creature. There is no reason to believe that ANI is another form of intelligent life, although narrow AI has been progressing, and there has also been movement on creating AGI.

Surrounding these achievements in AI robotics is a strong expectation of profit. If investment in AI exceeds investment in mineral development (and it will), there will be no less speculation in this area than in the energy and weapons sectors. Such speculation is accompanied by acute social and international conflict, and strong AI will not be immune from unfair treatment in the future. Correlating the intelligence of strong AI with human thinking may be a dangerous and disorienting simplification. Such a correlation will be appropriate if it is possible to create a reasonable biological "twin" of a human. However, being created from a different material basis, a synthesis of supercomputer capabilities and the human mind (if we can convey in the most simplified form about what does not yet exist), strong AI will be more or less radically different from humans. It will have certain qualities that are immeasurably superior to human capabilities, but it will take some time—perhaps very short—before strong AI turns into full-fledged super AI, beyond the limits of modern human understanding, and ushering in the singularity.

Narrow AI (and AI robots in the physical world) can already do things that people are incapable of doing. This ranges from the ability to count at an unimaginable speed to the highest sensory abilities. Google Translate (GT) is the world's number one translation software. It supports 103 languages, 10,000 language pairs, and processes about 500 million translation requests every day (BeTranslated, 2019). It can replace an entire army of translators, even though the translation quality is inferior. Thus, it can be argued that a "super ANI" has already been created in the field of translation. Yandex in Russia and other translation systems work similarly, although with some differences. By some indicators, the results achieved with AGI and strong AI are deserving of the prefix "super" but generally remain within the limits of human understanding. It will be some time before it becomes a full-fledged super AI beyond human understanding.

The singularity is not something that goes beyond the historical experience of humankind. From the point of view of an average person from the early Middle Ages, in terms of abilities and education, the flight of an airplane and many other things from the modern person's technological environment, worldview, and social forms would exceed perceptions and likely be identified with the manifestation of divine or diabolical powers. Apparently, we should not regard the future singularity as something unique, even though the change will be much more marked than the change in humankind from the Middle Ages to modern times. Unfortunately, the twentieth century produced world wars and the destruction of tens of millions of people, and nuclear war is closer than ever in the twenty-first century because humans have not changed radically enough intellectually. This requires qualitatively different possibilities for systemic analysis of the surrounding reality and development trends, the development of a conscious line of behavior based on increased personal abilities, an objectively new responsibility of each person for the future of our planet, no matter how utopian this may seem sound today. Unfortunately, this cannot be achieved through education and upbringing, even with a better social system, which is still very far from perfect, without new abilities and opportunities.

At the Singularity Summit in 2009, Peter Thiel told the audience that he's more afraid of the singularity not happening fast enough. At the end of the presentation, an audience member asked him what catastrophic things might take place as a result. Thiel responded that he's concerned the technology won't be invented, and the implications of that loss for mankind (H+ Magazine, 2009). Despite all the ambiguity in his views, Thiel is fully right in his assessment. The question is which singularity transition scenario humans will accept and whether it will be reached.

Social Development Alternatives: "To Be, or Not to Be, That Is the Question"

Many objective signs point to humankind's entry into the next round of development. The old system inevitably loses stability on the eve of transition, making it easier to overturn. Historically, progressive forces have not done this even once in history, but this is unfortunately not the case for others. Hitler effectively started a quality regression. Contemporary terrorists, if they possess weapons of mass destruction, could do the same. With the reckless "game of thrones" played by global elites, the threat of a worldwide ecological disaster is imminent. New Hot/Cold War could quickly escalate into Nuclear WWIII. The list is expanding and most of the problems that are mentioned are further aggravations.

Entering into a long period of social stagnation under conditions of geopolitical rivalry seems unlikely. Furthermore, a *long period of stagnation* is practically impossible due to limited natural resources, growing environmental problems, rising income polarization, increasing international tensions, and other factors. Humankind is simply not going to survive for a long period of time without radical progressive changes. If humans do not kill themselves, they will kill their kids, or at least their future. The *rapid development* of the global rivalry framework can accelerate the introduction of the latest revolutionary technologies, which will inevitably lead to qualitative changes in society.

For example, the current rise in gas prices in Europe could intensify a further transition to energy-saving technologies and the development of alternative energy sources. But it could also lead to an increase in coal production or a return to nuclear energy in countries that hastened to abandon it. Rapid changes are also fraught with great socio-political upheavals, leading to the worst-case scenario—the rapid introduction of new technologies will exacerbate social contradictions to the point of deep crisis or nuclear war, eliminating the prerequisites for further growth.

The forces of revolution and counter-revolution during such historical periods always grow together, although not uniformly or simultaneously. It is not always easy, especially in the initial stages, to distinguish the grain from the chaff, or the flowers of the revolution from the numerous voids. But there are qualitative differences in the current punctuated equilibrium, in the broad sense of the word, from similar states in the past. There are many examples to choose from but due to the limited scope of this chapter, we will focus on only one difference, closely related to the theme.

Once the technological leap that is already underway is complete, the need for a non-innovative workforce will disappear. The previous history of mankind, including the extremely rapid pace of social development in the twentieth century, was characterized by scientific and technological progress, reducing some forms of non-innovative activities and creating a wide field of other socially necessary types. Although innovation is continuing, it is still not the dominant mode of thinking or a relevant activity of the vast majority of people. The vertical of power is also under the predominant control of non-innovative forces. Very soon, by historical standards, the process of social production will no longer need a long chain of mediators,[2] people who are unable to innovate, and who comprise the vast majority of blue- and white-collar workers.

Science-intensive production is where a new industrial social group will be formed, namely "modificators" of production.[3] The merging in one social subject with those modern workers, with some differentiation at its core—engineers, scientists, managers, and entrepreneurs—who are capable of innovating and who will give control to those who will creatively alter and modify public production over the course of the twenty-first century. At first glance, this rather small group belongs to the future (see more: Pashentsev, 1997). This social group is also closely connected with existing innovators who need a long chain of mediators, people who are unable to innovate.

Modificators will be much more effective, able to develop production in creative symbiosis with AI, developing themselves and society through controlled changes in their genetic nature that complements artificial implants (cyborgization). Over time, all future societies will be comprised of modificators. It will be necessary to synchronize several social and technological revolutions—first led by AI, robotization, and cyborgization—as well as revolutions in genetics and education through progressive decision-making mechanisms and efficient strategic communication. The core concept of synchronizing these revolutions was first introduced by the author in the 1990s in several of his publications (Pashentsev, 1992, 1994, 1997), and later developed in other works.

The possibility of creating AGI and strong AI will only accelerate the integration of man into new symbiotic forms of mind that can ensure the exponential development of humankind. Of course, the future of humanity will be even less like us—modern humans—than we are to Neanderthals. It is unlikely that we, as humans, identify with the latter, although for the most

---

[2] Between an innovative idea and its implementation.
[3] From the Latin modificāre, present active infinitive of modificō ("I control, change, modify").

part, we understand and accept the path from our distant ancestors to the present, with all its pluses and minuses. The first steps on the long road to the future will not to be taken in hundreds of thousands of years or millennia, but perhaps in the current century. The initial stage is the grandiose birth of a new civilization, with a past and future. The contemporary generation stands at the beginnings of this leap in anxious anticipation, as well as doubt, uncertainty, and partial ignorance, but also hope and faith, based on a growing understanding of the need—and the possibility—for humankind to advance.

It will be necessary to "change horses" while crossing not just a stream, but an unknown great river that has never been crossed before. The opposite shore is very far away, almost out of sight, but it must be reached to avoid missing the opportunity forever. The question is not whether any of this is possible—the question is, *when* it will be. The planet should be left not to the intellectual monsters of fantasy fiction but to future generations with new abilities and the willingness to undertake creative activities for the benefit of humankind.

The ability to innovate in a deeply split, antagonistic world is not a guarantee of the modificators' high morality, even in relation to each other. However, it does give them the objective opportunity of scientific foresight into the progressive historical perspective (including the ethical dimension) and the ability to sustain the movement along a path of social development rather than participate in its final rupture. It is possible to assume that the majority of modificators, including some power structure representatives, will lead a movement to society's new qualitative state. Some of the modificators, deformed by momentary vested interests of the collapsing society, will act together with reactionary elites against this movement, inciting mass fears and phobia.

Among the possible future scenarios (acknowledging that a great deal of discussion must be omitted due to lack of space in this chapter), the following can be mentioned:

- *Current neoliberal or national conservative capitalist models that are in decline practically everywhere.* Some emerging states with relatively high growth rates will inevitably follow the fate of Japan's exhausted catch-up model of development. The rapid escalation of local conflict all over the globe, and especially the potential for a World War III, will push mankind back into the past. The depletion of natural resources, environmental crises, and social disruption and degradation will make a transit to high-technology development models unlikely. Inevitably, time, energy, resources, lives,

and, much more importantly, the very opportunity to correct mistakes will be lost, resulting in the ultimate collapse of humanity.
- *Modified capitalist systems* in the form of global authoritarian or totalitarian regimes that are necessary for the *artificial and controlled stagnation* of technical progress and the *global* social order (meaning no or minimum robots, AI, etc.). But history has proved more than once that stagnation is not absolute or forever and with the current level of globalization today, there is no globally centralized world order yet. Even if such a world order existed, a long period of stagnation due to limited natural resources, growing environmental problems, and a rise in income polarization and social tensions would finally destroy what would very likely be a not-very-pleasant society.

- *Centralized bureaucratic systems (maybe under the banner of "socialism")*, in which central planning evenly distributes products produced by robots. This system would be quite similar to declining European social democracies or the former Soviet Union. It would lead to the degradation of the majority of non-innovative people without any opportunity for socially necessary labor, ending with the final collapse of civilization. Some elements of this system are still in progress, such as the combination of chronic mass unemployment in the majority of EU countries, especially among the youth, the latent degradation of education, the increasing weakness of trade unions and political parties, projects that compensate for job losses through life rent, and others.
- *High-tech dictatorships*. There will be a more or less rapid liquidation of the "needless population" (from 90% to 99 ... %, this is up for discussion) within the scheme of neo-fascism, with narrow AI and AGI subordinate to the oligarchs of the future. This is reminiscent of the science fiction author Isaac Asimov's planet Solaria at the very "happy end."
- *A classless society formed by modificators* resulting from the interdependent, and to some extent synchronized, revolutions mentioned above. Of course, this would not equal the extermination of *Homo sapiens normal* by *Homo sapiens advanced*. Even in the current, non-ideal society, educated children do not eliminate their quite often less literate or disabled parents and friends but instead, stand ready to help them. Older generations may make the right choice, as H. G. Wells' hero of *The Food of the Gods* did. However, this peaceful choice is desirable but not guaranteed, keeping in mind, the current antagonisms and interests of selfish groups. Perhaps it would be more similar to the interstellar Great Ring of Civilizations in *The Bull's Hour*, a science fiction novel written by Soviet author and paleontologist Ivan Yefremov in 1968. Six months after its publication, the Soviet authori-

ties banned the book and attempted to remove it from libraries and bookshops after realizing that it sharply criticized not only capitalism and the Chinese Cultural Revolution but also the then-current state of affairs in the bureaucratic Soviet Union.

Aspects of some models may transfer to others, and vice versa. Although the success of each variant is not guaranteed, humans do have choices. We are free to change our fate through joint efforts in one direction or another. The majority of people are accustomed to living in old paradigms, but it is difficult to ignore new opportunities and risks. Logically, social apathy and inertia will lead us not to the best but the worst scenarios, as well as new forms of Luddites or proponents of technological progress that are isolated from the relevant changes in the nature of human beings and humankind as a whole.

Conclusion

As the author of this chapter wrote in the early 1990s, AI and robotics are not the end of humanity but conditions for its further progress. At the same time, this author also proposed the concept of coordinating revolutions in the fields of AI and robotics, genetics, education, and civil society to access a qualitatively new level of societal development (Pashentsev, 1990, 1993). The achievements from that time and from the subsequent years will be briefly discussed.

After every *social revolution*, a majority of people from all classes—even the ruling classes—returned to mainly noncreative work processes due to the necessity of conditions. In a sense, any working process is creative, as it is aimed at creating a material, intellectual, or cultural product. As for people in general, there is a discussion about original production having objective public value. That type of labor is the destiny of just a few, largely restricted to the stage of creative planning but not its realization, since more often than not, this requires collective labor. Such labor is socially necessary, but it still enslaves consciousness, thereby preventing a thorough development of the individual. In the political sphere, this leads to an inability for millions of people to critically analyze social reality or to effectively participate in or control the public decision-making process.

Attempts to diversify the working process, to fill it with creative content without a revolutionary break in the level of *technological development and, importantly, without automation, robots, or different types of ANI in noncreative kinds of labor activity*, have very limited success.

In future, this situation will change. The widespread development and use of automation, computerization, AI, and robotization will lead to the formation of objective prerequisites for the debureaucratization of state structures. There will be no place for bureaucracy. The production planning of output of huge quantities of goods by a single, centralized entity in the past led to the uncontrolled growth of bureaucratic structures, especially in the former Soviet Union. The situation is not much better today in Russia, the United States, the EU, China, or any other country.

A person who is freed from noncreative labor will not automatically become highly conscious of historical action. It is not without reason that in the futurological utopias imagined and written by Kurt Vonnegut, Ray Bradbury, and other famous authors, people do not find themselves encircled by a technotronic environment. The capitalist system is certainly guilty, since the race for profits doesn't provide any inner motivation for work in the conditions of "the mass consumption society." But during the transition period to a more progressive society, a new motivation will also not simply appear on its own. It can't be just "introduced" into a person.

Most people must deal with noncreative labor, and not just because the level of development of productive forces and the social environment prevents them from entering the creative sphere. Reality at the macro and micro levels can have a negative influence on personality, but talents can survive in spite of life's circumstances and follow the need for self-realization. This is natural, since society can provide such possibilities, at least for a minority number of people.

The rapid growth in the amount of well-being and free time for the people in industrialized countries did not lead to a corresponding increase in the number of highly gifted people in the twentieth and twenty-first centuries. Evidently, nature sets a limit on the timely development of creative abilities for most people. Increasingly, people spend their free time not on some creative activity but on rest, entertainment, and "primitive" pursuits (consider the growing use of drugs in "rich societies"). Various forms of rest and play are necessary and natural, but these must be in harmony with societally useful and creative labor activity. Otherwise, the degradation of humankind from the conditions of material abundance becomes inevitable. Thus, a new motivation to work demands a new person—the "creative person."

Here, it is impossible to ignore the *third revolutionary process*—fundamental discoveries in biology, primarily in genetics. *Human genetic engineering* can either be a solution for positive local tasks or be an excuse for inhumane experiments that artificially modulate a person's behavior in an attempt to create the master race. Moreover, without the automation and robotization of noncreative working processes, the achievements of human genetic engineering and its influence on the creative person will simply become a tragedy for humankind.

If a person without creative gifts deals with noncreative but socially useful labor, it is possible that they can achieve satisfaction and realize their objective abilities. However, a person with more natural talents who is required by productive forces to participate in noncreative work finds themselves a slave to the existing division of labor, which offers no opportunity for the utilization of their qualities.

Achievements in human genetic engineering will not be able to be fully realized without *revolutionary changes in education and upbringing*, since no natural abilities can be converted into the humane qualities of a creative personality without an integral system for their formation from birth to social maturity.

A conclusion can be drawn. The harmonization of the four revolutionary processes is desirable and necessary. Without social revolution, the three other revolutions can be used to inflict harm on people. On the other hand, a transition to a new social system is impossible without a radical improvement in the biological nature of human beings (assuming the existence of humankind in various material forms and the possibility of transitioning from one form to another, or existing simultaneously in different forms), a high-quality educational system, and a technical environment, including measures for the effective defense of habitat, among others. AGI can make this process quicker and potentially more fruitful, but also risky.

Human society is interested in peaceful changes for a better future, and this will depend on the strategic communication efforts of the progressive social strata to convince people, through the synchronization of deeds, words, and images, that progress can bring more to the absolute majority of people than it threatens. There seems to be no alternative: either humankind transitions toward a new quality state through a social revolution or faces the destruction of human civilization and possibly the entire planet. Only the future can tell how much time is left for us to think about this.

The processes of robotization, the creation of AI, the rapid development of genetics, and the qualitative changes in society's social structure are gaining momentum. This means that countries with substantial research potential, like the United States, China, the EU, Russia, and India, are likely to play an important role in the further progress (or regress) of humankind. The role of strategic communication is important because synchronizing all parties' efforts on the challenges of modernity and the progressive movement into the future is essential and the very essence of strategic communication—at least if it is used to serve society and not narrow corporate interests.

For the foreseeable future, ANI and likely AGI, as well as AI robots, will be important drivers of massive social transformation, undoubtedly bringing great benefits and growing risks. MUAI could become a dangerous factor in the psychological destabilization of society, with the main danger coming from antisocial actors, whose positions are strengthening in the current crisis situation. With qualitative successes in the development of enhanced humans and/or the creation of strong AI, the primary malicious actors will be antisocial representatives of these new social groups and/or their hybrid combinations. The dominance of positive or negative traits among enhanced humans or strong AI will be socially determined. Without social and technological changes, including the quantitative and qualitative development of the capabilities of the human mind and body, a higher level of social justice, and greater social responsibility, humanity is doomed. A key overarching question remains: Who will carry out these radical changes, for what purposes and interests, at whose expense, and by what methods? The social revolution may continue with more advanced forms of humans and AI, but if it does not start in the foreseeable future, humanity will face extremely negative social development scenarios.

References

Abbeel, P. (2022). These 5 robots could soon become part of our everyday lives. *World Economic Forum*. Retrieved September 13, 2022, from https://www.weforum.org/agenda/2022/02/robots-future-tech/

Akata, Z., Balliet, D., de Rijke, M., Dignum, F., Dignum, V., Eiben, G., Fokkens, A., Grossi, D., Hindriks, K., Hoos, H., Hung, H., Jonker, C., Monz, C., Neerincx, M., Oliehoek, F., Prakken, H., Schlobach, S., van der Gaag, L., van Harmelen, F., van Hoof, H., van Riemsdijk, B., van Wynsberghe, A., Verbrugge, R., Verheij, B., Vossen, P., & Welling, M. (2020). A research agenda for hybrid intelligence: Augmenting human intellect with collaborative, adaptive, responsible, and explainable artificial intelligence. *Computer, 53*, 18–28. https://doi.org/10.1109/mc.2020.2996587

Alfonseca, M., Cebrian, M., Fernandez Anta, A., Coviello, L., Abeliuk, A., & Rahwan, I. (2021). Superintelligence cannot be contained: Lessons from computability theory. *Journal of Artificial Intelligence Research, 70*, 65–76. https://doi.org/10.1613/jair.1.12202

Aliman, N. M. (2017). Malevolent Cyborgization. In T. Everitt, B. Goertzel, & A. Potapov (Eds.), *Artificial General Intelligence. AGI 2017* (Lecture notes in computer science) (Vol. 10414). Springer. https://doi.org/10.1007/978-3-319-63703-7_18

24 Prospects for a Qualitative Breakthrough in Artificial Intelligence...   669

Ananthaswamy, A. (2022). Researchers build AI that builds AI. *Quanta Magazine*. Retrieved September 13, 2022, from https://www.quantamagazine.org/researchers-build-ai-that-builds-ai-20220125/

Antonov, A. (2022). V ch'ikh interesakh? Strategiya razvitiya ili strategiya modifikatsii rossiyskogo obshchestva? [In whose interests? A development strategy or a strategy for modifying Russian society?]. *Russkaya narodnaya liniya [Russian folk line]*. Retrieved September 18, 2022, from https://ruskline.ru/news_rl/2022/07/27/v_chih_interesah

Arango, B. (2022). Top 10 AI music composers in 2022. *Filmora*. Retrieved September 13, 2022, from https://filmora.wondershare.com/audio-editing/best-ai-music-composer.html

Araujo, C. (2022). Why you may be looking at AI all wrong. *CIO*. Retrieved September 13, 2022, from https://www.cio.com/article/230633/why-you-may-be-looking-at-ai-all-wrong.html

Baggaley, K. (2017). There are two kinds of AI, and the difference is important. *Popular Science*. Retrieved May 11, 2022, from https://www.popsci.com/narrow-and-general-ai

Baum, S. D. (2017). *A survey of artificial general intelligence projects for ethics, risk, and policy*. Global Catastrophic Risk Institute.

BCG. (2017). Looking into the Future of Artificial Intelligence. An Interview with IDSIA's Jürgen Schmidhuber. *BCG Global*. Retrieved September 16, 2022, from https://www.bcg.com/publications/2017/technology-digital-big-data-advanced-analytics-schmidhuber-jurgen-looking-future-artificial-intelligence

BeTranslated. (2019). How good is google translate? The most accurate language pairs. *BeTranslated*. Retrieved September 15, 2022, from https://www.betranslated.com/blog/how-good-is-google-translate/

BGI. (2018). *About BGI*. Retrieved May 7, 2022, from www.bgi.com/global/company/about-bgi/

Bontridder, N., & Poullet, Y. (2021). The role of artificial intelligence in disinformation. *Data & Policy*. https://doi.org/10.1017/dap.2021.20

Bostrom, N. (2014). *Superintelligence: Paths, dangers, strategies*. Oxford University Press.

Bostrom, N., Dafoe, A., & Flynn, C. (2018). *Policy desiderata for superintelligent AI: A vector field approach*. Future of Humanity Institute, University of Oxford. Retrieved September 13, 2022, from https://www.fhi.ox.ac.uk/wp-content/uploads/Policy-Desiderata-in-the-Development-of-Machine-Superintelligence.pdf

Botelho, W., Marietto, M., Mendes, E., Sousa, D., Pimenta, E., da Silva, V., & dos Santos, T. (2020). Toward an interdisciplinary integration between multi-agents systems and multi-robots systems: A case study. *The Knowledge Engineering Review*. https://doi.org/10.1017/s0269888920000375

Brentner, J. (2021). Transhumanism: The plot to control your life! *Jonathan Brentner Website*. Retrieved September 13, 2022, from https://www.jonathanbrentner.

com/https/jonathan-brentner-g8fgsquarespacecom/config/2021/5/24/transhumanism-what-is-it

Cai, X., Jiang, J., Fahy, K., & Yung, Y. (2021). A statistical estimation of the occurrence of Extraterrestrial intelligence in the milky way galaxy. *Galaxies, 9*, 5. https://doi.org/10.3390/galaxies9010005

Campbell, I. (2021). Ex-Google engineer Anthony Levandowski has closed his artificial intelligence church. *The Verge*. Retrieved September 15, 2022, from https://www.theverge.com/2021/2/19/22291769/anthony-levandowski-church-closed-artificial-intelligence-waymo-uber

Chace, C. (2018). *Artificial intelligence and the two singularities*. Chapman and Hall/CRC.

Chalmers, D. (2010). The singularity: A philosophical analysis. *J of Consciousness Studies, 17*, 7–65.

Cunningham, A. C. (Ed.). (2017). *Artificial intelligence and the technological singularity*. Greenhaven Publishing.

Datteri, E. (2017). Biorobotics. In L. Magnani & T. Bertolotti (Eds.), *Springer handbook of model-based science. Springer handbooks*. Springer. https://doi.org/10.1007/978-3-319-30526-4_37

DeepMind. (2022). A generalist agent. *DeepMind*. Retrieved September 15, 2022, from https://www.deepmind.com/publications/a-generalist-agent

Dellermann, D., Ebel, P., Söllner, M., & Leimeister, J. (2019). Hybrid Intelligence. *Business & Information Systems Engineering, 61*, 637–643. https://doi.org/10.1007/s12599-019-00595-2

Dickson, B. (2017). What is narrow, general and super artificial intelligence. *TechTalks*. Retrieved May 11, 2022, from https://bdtechtalks.com/2017/05/12/what-is-narrow-general-and-super-artificial-intelligence/

Enews. (2022). Reflecting on 'artificial general intelligence' and AI sentience & more latest news here. *Enews*. Retrieved September 15, 2022, from https://enews.com.ng/2022/08/reflecting-on-artificial-general-intelligence-and-ai-sentience-more-latest-news-here/

Eror, A. (2013). China Is engineering genius babies. *Vice*. Retrieved May 11, 2022, from www.vice.com/en_us/article/5gw8vn/chinas-taking-over-the-world-with-a-massive-genetic-engineering-program

Eugenios, J. (2015). Ray Kurzweil: Humans will be hybrids by 2030. *CNN Tech*. Retrieved May 11, 2022, from https://money.cnn.com/2015/06/03/technology/ray-kurzweil-predictions/index.html

European Parliament. (2017). *Resolution of 16 February 2017 with recommendations to the Commission on Civil Law Rules on Robotics (2015/2103(INL)*. Retrieved May 11, 2022, from www.europarl.europa.eu/sides/getDoc.do?pubRef=-//EP//TEXT+TA+P8-TA-2017-0051+0+DOC+XML+V0//EN#BKMD-13

Everitt, T., Goertzel, B., & Potapov, A. (Eds.). (2017, August 15–18). Artificial general intelligence. 10th international conference on artificial general intelligence. In

Lecture notes in computer science (Lecture notes in artificial intelligence) (Vol. 10414). Springer.

Executive Office of the President, National Science and Technology Council, Committee on Technology. (2016). *Preparing for the future*. National Science and Technology Council of Artificial Intelligence.

Fedasiuk, R., Melot, J., & Murphy, B. (2021). Harnessed lightning: How the Chinese military is adopting artificial intelligence. *Center for Security and Emerging Technology Report*. https://doi.org/10.51593/20200089

Felton, J. (2022). The Eliza effect: How a chatbot convinced people it was real way back in the 1960s. *IFLScience*. Retrieved May 15, 2022, from https://iflscience.com/the-eliza-effect-how-a-chatbot-convinced-people-it-was-real-way-back-in-the-1960s-64155

Flores, D. (2018a). Transhumanism: The big fraud-towards digital slavery. *International Physical Medicine & Rehabilitation Journal*. https://doi.org/10.15406/ipmrj.2018.03.00131

Flores, D. (2018b). The nanomafia: Nanotechnology's global network of organized crime. *International Physical Medicine & Rehabilitation Journal*. https://doi.org/10.15406/ipmrj.2018.03.00115

Geist, E., & Lohn, A. (2018). How might artificial intelligence affect the risk of nuclear war? *RAND Corporation Perspectives*. https://doi.org/10.7249/pe296

Georgia Institute of Technology. (2022). Researcher finds that military cannot rely on AI for strategy or judgment. *TechXplore*. Retrieved September 13, 2022, from https://techxplore.com/news/2022-06-military-ai-strategy-judgment.html

Ghallab, M., & Ingrand, F. (2020). Robotics and artificial intelligence. In P. Marquis, O. Papini, & H. Prade (Eds.), *A guided tour of artificial intelligence research*. Springer. https://doi.org/10.1007/978-3-030-06170-8_12

Goertzel, B. (2016). *AGI revolution: An inside view of the rise of artificial general intelligence*. Humanity+ Press.

Goertzel, B., & Pennachin, C. (Eds.). (2007). *Artificial General Intelligence*. Springer, Berlin, Heidelberg. https://doi.org/10.1007/978-3-540-68677-4_1

Goertzel, B., Pennachin, C., & Geisweiller, N. (2014). *Engineering general intelligence. Part 1: A path to advanced AGI via embodied learning and cognitive synergy*. Atlantis Press.

Goode, L. (2019). Singularity. In H. Paul (Ed.), *Critical terms in futures studies*. Palgrave Macmillan. https://doi.org/10.1007/978-3-030-28987-4_43

Grace, K., Salvatier, J., Dafoe, A., Zhang, B., & Evans, O. (2018). When will AI exceed human performance? Evidence from AI experts. *J of Artificial Intelligence Research, 62*, 729–754.

H+ Magazine. (2009). Singularity Summit—Peter Thiel On His Single Greatest Fear. *H+ Media*. Retrieved September 16, 2022, from https://hplusmagazine.com/2009/10/04/singularity-summit-peter-thiel-his-single-greatest-fear/

Harper, J. (2022). China matching pentagon spending on AI. *National Defense Magazine*. Retrieved September 13, 2022, from https://www.nationaldefensemagazine.org/articles/2022/1/6/china-matching-pentagon-spending-on-ai

Horowitz, M., Scharre, P., & Velez-Green, A. (2017). *A stable nuclear future? The impact of automation, autonomy, and artificial intelligence*. University of Pennsylvania.

Hosman, E. (2016). Hateful politics infiltrate human genome editing debate in France. *The Niche*. Retrieved May 11, 2022, from www.geneticsandsociety.org/biopolitical-times/hateful-politics-infiltrate-human-genome-editing-debate-france

Humanity+. (2009). The transhumanist declaration. *Humanity+*. Retrieved September 13, 2022, from https://www.humanityplus.org/the-transhumanist-declaration

Iklé, M., Franz, A., Rzepka, R., & Goertzel, B. (Eds.). (2018, August 22–25) Artificial general intelligence. 11th international conference on artificial general intelligence. In *Lecture notes in computer science (Lecture notes in artificial intelligence)* (Vol. 10999). Springer.

Istvan, Z. (2017). Transhumanism is booming and big business is noticing. *HuffPost*. Retrieved September 13, 2022, from https://www.huffpost.com/entry/transhumanism-is-becoming_b_7807082

Johnson, J. (2020). Delegating strategic decision-making to machines: Dr. Strangelove redux? *Journal of Strategic Studies, 45*, 439–477. https://doi.org/10.1080/01402390.2020.1759038

Johnson, J. (2021a). *Artificial intelligence, autonomy, and the risk of catalytic nuclear war*. Modern War Institute. Retrieved September 13, 2022, from https://mwi.usma.edu/artificial-intelligence-autonomy-and-the-risk-of-catalytic-nuclear-war/

Johnson, J. (2021b). 'Catalytic nuclear war' in the age of artificial intelligence & autonomy: Emerging military technology and escalation risk between nuclear-armed states. *Journal of Strategic Studies, 1–41*. https://doi.org/10.1080/01402390.2020.1867541

Kanade, V. (2022). Narrow AI vs. general AI vs. super AI: Key comparisons | Spiceworks. *Spiceworks*. Retrieved September 13, 2022, from https://www.spiceworks.com/tech/artificial-intelligence/articles/narrow-general-super-ai-difference/

Lambert, F. (2022). Elon Musk says Tesla may have a working humanoid robot prototype by September 30. *Electrek*. Retrieved September 13, 2022, from https://electrek.co/2022/06/02/tesla-bot-have-humanoid-robot-prototype-elon-musk-sept-30/

Lee, K.-F. (2018). *AI superpowers: China, Silicon Valley, and the New World order*. Houghton Mifflin Harcourt.

Lin, H. (2012). Escalation dynamics and conflict termination in cyberspace. *Strategic Studies Quarterly, 6*, 46–70.

Lu, Y., Qian, D., Fu, H., & Chen, W. (2018). Will supercomputers be super-data and super-AI machines? *J Communications of the ACM, 61*(11), 82–87.

Masters, P., Smith, W., Sonenberg, L., & Kirley, M. (2021). Characterising deception in AI: A survey. In S. Sarkadi, B. Wright, P. Masters, & P. McBurney (Eds.), *Deceptive

AI. DeceptECAI DeceptAI 2020 2021. *Communications in Computer and Information Science* (Vol. 1296). Springer. https://doi.org/10.1007/978-3-030-91779-1_1

McConnell, B. S. (2021). *What could we learn from another civilization? The alien communication handbook. Astronomers' universe.* Springer. https://doi.org/10.1007/978-3-030-74845-6_19

McQuillan, L. (2022). *A Google engineer says AI has become sentient. What does that actually mean?* CBC. Retrieved September 13, 2022, from https://www.cbc.ca/news/science/ai-consciousness-how-to-recognize-1.6498068

Melissa-12 Livejournal. (2022). Vazhno!!! Analiticheskaya spravka po proyektu Ukaza prezidenta RF (o konvergentnykh tekhnologiyakh) [Important!!! Analytical report on the draft Decree of the President of the Russian Federation [on convergent technologies]]. Retrieved September 18, 2022, from Melissa-12.livejournal.com. https://melissa-12.livejournal.com/6217623.html?ysclid=l87j9rxcad438890130

Meza, S. (2017). Religion that worships artificial intelligence prepares for a world run by machines. *Newsweek.* Retrieved September 15, 2022, from https://www.newsweek.com/google-executive-forms-religion-artificial-intelligence-714416

Michaud, M. (2007). *Contact with alien civilizations: Our hopes and fears about encountering Extraterrestrials.* Copernicus.

Mikheev, E., & Nestik, T. (2019). The use of artificial intelligence technologies in information and psychological warfare. *The European Proceedings of Social and Behavioural Sciences, 64*, 406–412. https://doi.org/10.15405/epsbs.2019.07.53

Ministry of Science and Higher Education of the Russian Federation. (2022). Proyekt ukaza Prezidenta Rossiyskoy Federatsii "O Strategii razvitiya prirodopodobnykh (konvergentnykh) tekhnologiy" [Draft Decree of the President of the Russian Federation "On the Strategy for the Development of Nature-Like (Convergent) Technologies"]. *Federal'nyy portal proyektov normativnykh pravovykh aktov [Federal Portal of Draft Regulatory Legal Acts].* Retrieved September 18, 2022, from https://regulation.gov.ru/projects#npa=128578

Moon, M. (2021). Tesla is working on an AI-powered humanoid robot. *Engadget.* Retrieved September 13, 2022, from https://www.engadget.com/tesla-bot-humanoid-robot-033635103.html

Moravec, H. (1988). *Mind children.* Harvard University Press.

MSN. (2022). *Can the 'Gato' AI model out-perform human intelligence?* Msn.com. Retrieved September 13, 2022, from https://www.msn.com/en-us/news/technology/can-the-gato-ai-model-out-perform-human-intelligence/ar-AAY0znf

Nichols, G. (2021). *2022: A major revolution in robotics.* ZDNET. Retrieved September 13, 2022, from https://www.zdnet.com/article/2022-prediction-a-major-revolution-in-robotics/

Okta. (2022). *Augmented Intelligence (AI): The future of cognitive security.* Okta. Retrieved September 13, 2022, from https://www.okta.com/identity-101/augmented-intelligence/

Olmstead, S. (2022). *Transhumanism and biofascism are tools of the 'technological elite.'* NOQ Report—Conservative Christian News, Opinions, and Quotes. Retrieved September 13, 2022, from https://noqreport.com/2022/04/01/transhumanism-and-biofascism-are-tools-of-the-technological-elite/

Pashentsev, E. (1990). *Krizis i obshhestvo [crisis and society]*. Slovo Fund.

Pashentsev, E. (1992). Levye partii Rossii: Problemy i perspektivy [the left parties of Russia: Problems and prospects]. *J Zarubezhnyj vestnik [Foreign Bulletin], 2*, 23–37.

Pashentsev, E. (1993). The modern crisis and political alternatives in Russia. *J Russian Progressive Review, 3*, 23–31.

Pashentsev, E. (1994). Russia's left political movement. *J Russian Progressive Review, 3*, 46–59.

Pashentsev, E. (1997). *The left parties of Russia*. SIMS Ltd..

Pashkov, V., Harkusha, A., & Harkusha, Y. (2020). Artificial intelligence in medical practice: Regulative issues and perspectives. *Wiadomości Lekarskie, 73*, 2722–2727. https://doi.org/10.36740/wlek202012204

Raikov, A., & Pirani, M. (2022). Human–machine duality: What's next in cognitive aspects of artificial intelligence? *IEEE Access, 10*, 56296–56315. https://doi.org/10.1109/access.2022.3177657

Research And Markets. (2021). Global transhumanism markets report 2021—Transformational growth in biological, health, and wellness augmentation will enable the rise of human 2.0. *Yahoo!Finance*. Retrieved September 13, 2022, from https://finance.yahoo.com/news/global-transhumanism-markets-report-2021-204500398.html?fr=sycsrp_catchall

Ricotti, L., & Menciassi, A. (2015). Nanotechnology in biorobotics: Opportunities and challenges. *Journal of Nanoparticle Research*. https://doi.org/10.1007/s11051-014-2792-5

Rogers, S. (2022). A.I. robot trained in method acting lands lead role in $70M Sci–Fi film. *Dornob*. Retrieved September 13, 2022, from https://dornob.com/a-i-robot-trained-in-method-acting-lands-lead-role-in-70m-sci-fi-film/

Ronquillo, C., Peltonen, L., Pruinelli, L., Chu, C., Bakken, S., Beduschi, A., Cato, K., Hardiker, N., Junger, A., Michalowski, M., Nyrup, R., Rahimi, S., Reed, D., Salakoski, T., Salanterä, S., Walton, N., Weber, P., Wiegand, T., & Topaz, M. (2021). Artificial intelligence in nursing: Priorities and opportunities from an international invitational think-tank of the nursing and artificial intelligence leadership collaborative. *Journal of Advanced Nursing, 77*, 3707–3717. https://doi.org/10.1111/jan.14855

Sadiku, M. N. O., & Musa, S. M. (2021). *Augmented intelligence*. Springer, Cham. https://doi.org/10.1007/978-3-030-77584-1_15

Schwab, K. (2022). The fourth industrial revolution. *World Economic Forum*. Retrieved September 13, 2022, from https://www.weforum.org/about/the-fourth-industrial-revolution-by-klaus-schwab

Shah, M. (2019). Genetic warfare: Super humans and the law. *North Carolina Central University Science & Intellectual Property Law Review, 12*, article 2.

Siddique, H. (2016). British researchers get green light to genetically modify human embryos. *The Guardian*. Retrieved May 11, 2022, from www.theguardian.com/science/2016/feb/01/human-embryo-genetic-modify-regulator-green-light-research

Simon, C. J. (2018). *Will computers revolt? Preparing for the future of artificial intelligence*. Future AI.

Singh, S. (2017). Transhumanism and the future of humanity: 7 ways the world will change by 2030. *Forbes*. Retrieved September 13, 2022, from https://www.forbes.com/sites/sarwantsingh/2017/11/20/transhumanism-and-the-future-of-humanity-seven-ways-the-world-will-change-by-2030/?sh=42cbd3d57d79

Smith, J. (2016). IBM research takes Watson to Hollywood with the first "cognitive movie trailer." *THINK Blog*. Retrieved September 13, 2022, from https://www.ibm.com/blogs/think/2016/08/cognitive-movie-trailer/

Smith, R. (2021). Communicating extraterrestrial intelligence (CETI) interaction models based on the Drake Equation. *ResearchGate*. Retrieved September 15, 2022, from https://www.researchgate.net/publication/353838345_Communicating_extraterrestrial_intelligence_CETI_interaction_models_based_on_the_Drake_Equation

Solon, O. (2017). Elon Musk says humans must become cyborgs to stay relevant. Is he right? *The Guardian*. Retrieved May 11, 2022, from www.theguardian.com/technology/2017/feb/15/elon-musk-cyborgs-robots-artificial-intelligence-is-he-right

Sullivan, R. (2021). *The U.S., China, and artificial intelligence competition factors*. China Aerospace Studies Institute.

The American Report. (2022). Klaus Schwab Trudeau and other young global leaders penetrated cabinets. *The American Report on YouTube*. Retrieved September 15, 2022, from https://www.youtube.com/watch?v=RxtiD8Z6gBI&t=10s

The Star. (2022). *Can the 'Gato' AI model out-perform human intelligence?* The Star. Retrieved September 16, 2022, from https://www.thestar.com.my/tech/tech-news/2022/06/05/can-the-039gato039-ai-model-out-perform-human-intelligence

This Person Does Not Exist. (2022). *This person does not exist*. Thispersondoesnotexist.com. Retrieved September 13, 2022, from https://thispersondoesnotexist.com/

Toews, R. (2022). Reflecting on 'artificial general intelligence' and AI sentience. *Forbes*. Retrieved September 18, 2022, from https://www.forbes.com/sites/robtoews/2022/07/24/on-artificial-general-intelligence-ai-sentience-and-large-language-models/?sh=718d7008e9db

Torres Soriano, M. (2018). *Operaciones de influencia e inteligencia artificial: Una visión prospectiva [Influence operations and artificial intelligence: A prospective vision]*. Instituto Español de Estudios Estratégicos.

UK Ministry of Defence. (2021). *Human augmentation—The Dawn of a new paradigm*. Ministry of Defence Shrivenham.

US Department of Defense. (2022). *Summary of Tl-IE Joint all-Domain Command & Control (JADC2) strategy*. US Department of Defense.

US Government Accountability Office (GAO). (2018). *Report to congressional committees national security*. Long-Range Emerging Threats Facing the United States as Identified by Federal Agencies. GAO-19-204SP. GAO.

Wang, P., & Goertzel, B. (Eds.). (2012). *Theoretical foundations of artificial general intelligence*. Atlantis Press.

Wells, H. G. (1898). The man who could work miracles. Standardebooks.org. Retrieved September 16, 2022, from https://standardebooks.org/ebooks/h-g-wells/short-fiction/text/the-man-who-could-work-miracles

Westby, T., & Conselice, C. (2020). The Astrobiological Copernican weak and strong limits for intelligent life. *The Astrophysical Journal, 896*, 58. https://doi.org/10.3847/1538-4357/ab8225

World Population Review. (2022). Countries that still have slavery 2022. *World Population Review*. Retrieved September 15, 2022, from https://worldpopulationreview.com/country-rankings/countries-that-still-have-slavery

Yampolskiy, R. (2021). AI personhood. *Machine Law, Ethics, and Morality in the Age of Artificial Intelligence, 1–11*. https://doi.org/10.4018/978-1-7998-4894-3.ch001

25

Conclusion: Per Aspera Ad Astra

Evgeny Pashentsev

Some Results and Ways of Counteracting the Malicious Use of Artificial Intelligence

This book outlines real opportunities for international cooperation in a nascent, very important and extremely problematic area of interdisciplinary research: the malicious use of artificial intelligence (MUAI) and psychological security. The high degree of readiness of specialists with different academic backgrounds from 11 countries to further research in this extremely complicated and tense international situation is highly encouraging. In their respective chapters, each author expressed coinciding, but significantly different and even mutually exclusive points of view, which is understandable given the novelty and particularity of the issues discussed. The works included in this book made it possible to provide a comprehensive assessment of the threats to psychological security through MUAI at the global level, as well as considering MUAI in individual countries, regions and areas of public life and presenting certain considerations about emerging threats in this field.

The political science aspects of this book topic are especially important when considering the aggravated state of psychological warfare between state and non-state actors against the backdrop of acute economic and sociopolitical conflicts in the modern world. Overcoming this global crisis requires a

E. Pashentsev (✉)
Diplomatic Academy of the Ministry of Foreign Affairs of the Russian Federation, Moscow, Russia
e-mail: icspsc@mail.ru

clear understanding of its causes, driving forces and consequences, as well as a broad, public discussion about ways to overcome it. We need to act strategically, and for this, clarity of strategic thought is needed.

People can be disoriented by a combination of skillful propaganda in conditions of information hunger, the prohibition of alternative information channels and open violence. Fascism and many other obvious forms of dictatorship are based on these components. However, people who are living in a clear dictatorship feel encouraged to search and fight for a social alternative, despite threats of repression and death. The historical doom of such dictatorships has been proven in practice but does not prevent dangerous relapses to the dark pages of history in a new environment. An implicit dictatorship, hidden from the public consciousness, is more dangerous when it wields the skillful manipulation of half-truths that send people to the kingdom of crooked mirrors, where they are deprived of choice. Yet, although it is not easy, it is possible to find a way out of that labyrinth of lies formed by traditional propaganda.

The growing MUAI by antisocial actors poses a serious threat at the international level, further narrowing the ability of people to understand their current situation when it is extremely necessary for themselves and all future generations. Today, we are closer than ever to the end of human history. The further progression of AI technologies and MUAI and its large-scale use as a psychological weapon may lead to an even greater delay in an adequate public response to the dangerous behaviors of antisocial actors. On a global scale, this will facilitate the formation of conditions for various kinds of human-made economic, environmental and other social disasters, including a Third World War. Qualitatively perfect MUAI renders the matrices of thinking and behavior that are hostile to people as practically insurmountable at the level of public consciousness and political practice. MUAI may become an important element in the formation of techno-fascism, with the subsequent, almost conflict-free, liquidation of the population due to continued automation, the robotization of production processes and the widespread incorporation of AI in the interests of a narrow oligarchic elite.

To the extent that belligerent states view AI as a means to measurably control and amplify the effects of their propaganda, they will continue to refine forms of psychological warfare to achieve victory without resorting to a hot war or facilitating the successful preparation and execution of such a war. At the same time, the boundaries between offensive and defensive operations and between combatants and non-combatants in psychological warfare are blurred. Unfortunately, the moment of the extremely rapid transformation of AI into a destructive tool of total psychological, political, economic, military and cultural destabilization with uncontrollable consequences on human society due to the systemic and qualitative excess of the impact of AI on human consciousness could be missed.

There is a risk that the further progress and spread of narrow AI, AI robots and especially the creation of Artificial General Intelligence (AGI) and Strong AI will, at a certain stage, lead to growing social problems that will divide society into militant supporters and opponents of these new realities. This irreconcilable confrontation will further destabilize the situation, resulting in armed conflict.

It is clearly insufficient and ineffective to resist increasingly successful MUAI in a society where the influence of antisocial actors is also increasing via separate, unrelated decisions of a political, legal and technical nature. Under these conditions, countermeasures are nothing more than a palliative, at best buying a bit of time and at worst providing cover for systemic deterioration. It is important to take into account the following factors.

First, MUAI is qualitatively more dangerous for a sick social organism than for a healthy one. We need a socially oriented transformation of society, part of which must include systemic and effective political, legal, technical and organizational solutions to prevent MUAI and minimize its negative impact on the public consciousness. This is not about copying past models, but forming a progressive model that meets the realities, risks and opportunities of the twenty-first century.

Second, increasing investments in science and education to develop the capabilities of the main productive force of modern society—people—is an important response to the threats of MUAI in the broad context of forming a comprehensive and responsible citizen, rather than a one-dimensional consumer who is easily manipulated. A multidimensional, harmonious and socially responsible person can protect themselves, their loved ones and society at large more successfully than a one-dimensional consumer. This rule holds for a developed civil society; for a society, which, unfortunately, we do not have yet. In an unhealthy society, clearly expressed civic positions often means increased risks for those speaking out, including the threat of death. We know this not only from history, but also from the modern reality of many countries.

Third, there are well-known assessments that indicate society is becoming more complicated and that the volume of incoming information is many times greater than the current ability of personal, group and public consciousness to assimilate and use adequately in decision-making. This situation does not meet the needs of further dynamic and sustainable development. One of the new, specific mechanisms for solving this problem may be systemic human enhancement, especially augmented intelligence (also referred to as intelligence amplification, cognitive augmentation or enhanced intelligence), a human-centered partnership model of people and AI working together to enhance cognitive performance, including learning, decision-making and new experiences (Gartner, 2022). Taking into account the growing possibilities of cyborgization (Pro Robots, 2020), a closer—and, in the future, symbiotic—connection between human and machine is also being facilitated, which will increase our capabilities to obtain, process and verify data and, therefore, resist MUAI.

Developing International Cooperation: Necessity Versus Difficulties

It is obvious that the solution to any complex global problem requires international cooperation at both the state and non-state levels. Scientifically, since MUAI threats to psychological security are associated with various aspects of life, countering them requires complex, interdisciplinary research and international cooperation. Meanwhile, a number of problems have been observed here, which, unfortunately, are not being solved but instead, aggravated.

One of these problems, which is not new, has to do with the interaction between AI specialists with a technical background and representatives from other sciences. According to research conducted by Dashun Wang and his collaborators, the link between AI and the social sciences (and other fields) has weakened over time. They found that in the 1960s, AI researchers cited psychology papers, along with philosophy, economics and art more often than occurs today. They also found that fields such as psychology, philosophy, business, political science, sociology and economics have all become less inclined to draw on AI research. One possible explanation for this development is that it has simply become harder for social scientists to keep up with the rapid advances of increasingly complex AI research (Frank et al., 2019). Despite the rapid growth of AI, Wang et al. fear that new technology will fall short of its full potential if it does not find a way to incorporate insights from the social sciences and other fields (Frank et al., 2019). Perhaps the fact that at first, in the 1960s, specialists of various profiles quite often had inflated expectations about the pace of AI development and its capabilities had an effect, which were aimed at solving much more modest utilitarian tasks. This led to a decrease in the level of interdisciplinary interaction. Later, rapid technological progress in the industry, the widest impact of AI on social life, renewed the interest of representatives from different fields of science to the theory and practice of AI. The realization of this interest in socially useful projects, however, requires time and some retraining. Unfortunately, the lack of adequate and anticipatory interpretation of the various social consequences from the greater incorporation of AI, given the hype that surrounds the industry today, can't help but lead to the spread of numerous, not quite balanced assessments and forecasts. This conclusion is significant for neutralizing MUAI threats to psychological security. The cooperation of specialists in AI, cybersecurity, psychology, political science, international security and the media is extremely important in this area.

The second problem is related to international academic cooperation between researchers from China and the US, both leading countries in the development and application of AI technologies. Overall, US–China collaborations on AI research have quintupled since 2010, reaching 9660 papers in 2021, much faster than the collaborative increase between any other two nations. Collaborations between the US and the United Kingdom, the second most prolific source of cross-border research, increased almost threefold to 3560 papers (Andrews, 2022). However, there is a paradox: even as Chinese and US elites race for leadership in what they view as a strategically important technology, with tensions between the countries rising over the years, researchers on both sides appear to see benefits in sharing expertise and working together. While the volume of published US–China collaborations in AI has declined slightly from its peak in 2019, it's unclear whether this recent dip reflects a lag in data, a temporary disruption or a more fundamental change (Andrews, 2022). It's likely that the last explanation is correct.

Under the Trump administration, there were increasing calls to expel or bar Chinese nationals from US universities and corporations. According to Bloomberg, the mass expulsion of Chinese students was expected to hamper science, technology, engineering and math research efforts in a large number of university research labs, as well as within the companies those labs partner with. This decision to block Chinese researchers, along with the expulsion of Chinese workers, could cause the US to stumble in critical fields such as AI. These actions could also hurt US college towns, which attract corporate investment with a large pool of research workers and serve as key drivers of economic investment and prosperity in otherwise declining regions (Smith, 2020). This could destroy many established international teams, whose concerted research efforts could help neutralize MUAI threats. A year-long ban on Chinese students receiving US visas to study due to the COVID-19 pandemic ended in May 2021, but many students were still being denied visas by US authorities because of their reputed ties to military-linked Chinese universities and institutes. These rejected students now refer to themselves as "victims of Proclamation 10043," the executive order signed by President Donald Trump in May 2020 suspending, on national security grounds, the entry of certain non-immigrant students and researchers from China, who would have otherwise obtained higher degrees or conducted advanced researches in the US (Chen, 2021). This policy has since been maintained by the Biden administration. According to a Pew Research study during the 2020–2021 school year, 317,299 Chinese nationals were enrolled in US institutions, representing about a third of all international students studying in the US. A report by the *Wall Street Journal* said that during the first half of 2022, US student visas issued to Chinese nationals dropped more than 50 percent compared with pre-pandemic levels (Zhang, 2022). Meanwhile, this continued deterioration of the international political climate, the gross violation of international cooperation in the context of geopolitical rivalry and a general atmosphere of psychological warfare could push both individual AI specialists and entire states toward MUAI in an extremely dangerous form.

The third, although by no means last, problem is the risk that the AI industry will repeat (even partially) the difficult fate of nuclear research. Scientists in laboratories around the world during the 1930s conducted many experiments on uranium fission. Due to the serious progression of research in the theory of nuclear fission in the context of Nazi Germany's aggression in Europe, this research became predominantly classified, complicating international scientific cooperation. Humankind's introduction to the practical applications of atomic energy was not from the first power plant to produce usable electricity through atomic fission in 1951, but with the use of atomic weapons against the civilian population of Hiroshima and Nagasaki in 1945. The application of AI technologies has already yielded enormous benefits, including a role in confronting the COVID-19 pandemic. The growing militarization of these technologies will make them a largely classified domain, complicating not only international scientific cooperation, but also interdisciplinary interaction at the national level. Militarization will not be the best way to stop MUAI, because artificial intelligence technologies are incomparably easier to transfer and reproduce, and are accessible to the most radical antisocial actors to a much greater extent than nuclear weapons.

All of the above considerations require appropriate attention from the international community, including the continuation of research on the problem of MUAI and psychological security, research that could give evidence-based results and provide relevant expert assessments and recommendations for the decision-making process at national and international levels.

Human and Artificial Intelligence Interaction as a Source of Social Optimism

This book is not intended to escalate fear and distrust in humankind and its future. On the contrary, AI is one of the important tools for building our future. Our goal is only to give a systemic idea of MUAI and psychological security at this stage, admittedly, without answering some questions, answering some unsatisfactorily and not answering others at all. Regardless, this assessment is possible and necessary because the team of authors behind this book belongs to species of *Homo sapiens*, no more and, hopefully, no less.

Unfortunately, society is dominated by negative scenarios regarding both human development and human interaction with AI at different stages of improvement. This can be easily traced by the content of specific works in the science fiction genre of literature and cinema, where the portrayal of various kinds of dystopias are common, if not dominant. Alas, gloomy dystopias easily find confirmation in the trends of modern social development as well as in the gloomy expectations of people. What can we say about other countries, if the richest and most powerful country in the world—the US—is expected by an increasing number of experts (Marche, 2022; Walter, 2022), politicians, generals (Brooks, 2017; The Liberty Beacon, 2022; Papenfuss, 2021) and opinion polls (Lupu et al., 2022; Miller, 2018; Barnes, 2021; Orth, 2022) a coup d'état and/or a civil war within the next ten years? There is an expectation, even an anticipation, that political violence will be employed in attempt to solve more and more acute problems of modern social development.

In the optimal scenario, humanity will develop at an accelerated pace. This will happen on the basis of the early introduction of technologies for the qualitative and systemic development of people's cognitive abilities and capabilities in conjunction with the realization of their utmost potential in society. AI and AI robots will be an important, if not decisive, part of this progress, ensuring the growth of labor productivity, as well as the wellbeing, health, longevity and confidence of humans to go beyond Earth, among many other benefits. Non-creative activities will be transferred to machines everywhere. Creative activities will remain the domain of the enhanced person interacting with AI within the framework of hybrid intelligence. Artificial Narrow Intelligence (ANI) and, potentially, AGI—will not need creative work, even if they have the ability to perfectly imitate it. Humans will need creative activity not so much as a means for the manufacture of products for consumption, but for the formation and development of a harmonious personality. This process will become the norm in the future, where people will have not only free time for creativity, thanks to robotics and automation, but also the ability to be creative, thanks to personal cognitive and physical enhancements. In the longer term, this process will accelerate due to the increased freedom of transfer and the expansion of human consciousness beyond the biological body. But in this new society, with an immeasurably greater degree of opportunity and personal freedom for self-expression and development, an equally high degree of social responsibility must also be inculcated, derived from the power of these new individual capabilities and extant humanism. Humanism will be fully accepted as a vital necessity for the existence of civilization, and it will extend to the variety of intelligent forms that may appear as part of the further development of human civilization. The society of the future will face its own challenges and contradictions, becoming the engine for the further cognition and advancement of humanity across the expanses of the infinite universe.

While we cannot correctly assess and imagine this future—we really are waiting for an inevitable singularity—the end of *our* horizon should not be considered the end of the world. The basic conditions and parameters for entering singularity are ours; we create them here and now through our choice of vector into the future. Nuclear war and nuclear winter, a global environmental catastrophe with irreversible consequences, a worldwide high-tech dictatorship and other unpleasant possibilities—these choices are ours and not for future enhanced humans and/or strong AI. It should be noted that today, we are the same as our ancestors were in many ways through the repeated choices that were made at crucial moments in history. The loss of 50 million human lives from choices our ancestors made from 1939 to 1945 to fight Nazism is justified by the fact that today, there is no "millennial Reich" on Earth. If Nazism had won then, what kind of world would we be living in today? Perhaps in 1945, dreaming of the distant future, our ancestors who won would have wanted something different in 2022. Certainly, they would not have wanted a modern world on the verge of atomic Armageddon. However, this is the choice and responsibility of the billions of us who are now living for the fate of all future unborn generations that could disappear from the face of the Earth because of our choice, for our fault. The choices of our ancestors determined to some extent our present, and we are facing an equally difficult choice today. It is necessary to take into account the experience of the past, but repeating it is clearly not enough. We cannot narrow the possibilities of choice for our descendants or deprive them of choice altogether. But we will inevitably do this if we start a new world war, destroy nature and, among other things, extinguish the historical significance and extremely relevant choices of our ancestral fighters against Nazism. We can expand the possibilities of choice for posterity by expanding human capabilities, albeit radically changing humans at the same time. However, isn't a balanced expansion of abilities a step toward wisdom, without which we can no longer survive? Our earthly nursery has already become too small and fragile for this slowly maturing child of humanity, but we are not yet an adult either. The only thing that is impossible is preserving the status quo.

This book is aimed at finding ways to a better, safer and more peaceful present and future for people and for all future sentient and human forms, but not for machines. How successful this was, is up to the reader to judge.

References

Andrews, E. (2022). *China and the United States: Unlikely partners in AI*. Stanford HAI. Retrieved September 18, 2022, from https://hai.stanford.edu/news/china-and-united-states-unlikely-partners-ai

Barnes, A. (2021). Shocking poll finds many Americans now want to secede from the United States. *Changing America*. Retrieved September 18, 2022, from https://thehill.com/changing-america/enrichment/arts-culture/563221-shocking-poll-finds-many-americans-now-want-to/

Brooks, R. (2017). 3 ways to get rid of President Trump before 2020. *Foreign Policy*. Retrieved September 18, 2022, from https://foreignpolicy.com/2017/01/30/3-ways-to-get-rid-of-president-trump-before-2020-impeach-25th-amendment-coup/

Chen, F. (2021). US blocking more Chinese students from its universities. *Asia Times*. Retrieved September 18, 2022, from https://asiatimes.com/2021/07/us-blocking-more-chinese-students-from-its-universities/

Frank, M., Wang, D., Cebrian, M., & Rahwan, I. (2019). AI and the social sciences used to talk more. Now they've drifted apart. *Kellogg Insight*. Retrieved September 18, 2022, from https://insight.kellogg.northwestern.edu/article/artificial-intelligence-ethics-social-questions

Gartner. (2022). Definition of augmented intelligence—Gartner information technology glossary. *Gartner Glossary*. Retrieved September 18, 2022, from https://www.gartner.com/en/information-technology/glossary/augmented-intelligence

Lupu, N., Plutowski, L., & Zechmeister, E. (2022). Would Americans ever support a coup? 40 percent now say yes. *The Washington Post*. Retrieved September 18, 2022, from https://www.washingtonpost.com/politics/2022/01/06/us-coup-republican-support/

Marche, S. (2022). *The next civil war: Dispatches from the American future*. Simon & Schuster.

Miller, R. (2018). Poll: Almost a third of US voters think a second civil war is coming soon. *USA Today*. Retrieved September 18, 2022, from https://www.usatoday.com/story/news/politics/onpolitics/2018/06/27/civil-war-likely-voters-say-rasmussen-poll/740731002/

Orth, T. (2022). Two in five Americans say a civil war is at least somewhat likely in the next decade. *YouGov*. Retrieved September 18, 2022, from https://today.yougov.com/topics/politics/articles-reports/2022/08/26/two-in-five-americans-civil-war-somewhat-likely

Papenfuss, M. (2021). Generals warn of divided military and possible civil war in next U.S. coup attempt. *Yahoo!News*. Retrieved September 18, 2022, from https://news.yahoo.com/generals-warn-divided-military-possible-142837801.html?fr=sycsrp_catchall

Pro Robots. (2020). Cyborg revolution: Latest technologies and TOP of real cyborgs. *YouTube*. Retrieved September 18, 2022, from https://www.youtube.com/watch?v=TyWohWpozp0

Smith, N. (2020). Banning Chinese nationals takes cold war to extremes. *Bloomberg*. Retrieved September 18, 2022, from https://www.bloomberg.com/opinion/articles/2020-09-06/u-s-ban-of-chinese-students-takes-things-to-extremes

The Liberty Beacon. (2022). Tulsi gabbard unloads on democratic party for trying to foment 'civil war' [Video]. *The Liberty Beacon*. Retrieved September 18, 2022, from https://www.thelibertybeacon.com/tulsi-gabbard-unloads-on-democratic-party-for-trying-to-foment-civil-war-video/

Walter, B. (2022). *How civil wars start: And how to stop them*. Crown.

Zhang, M. (2022). US universities facing sharp fall in Chinese students. *Asia News Network*. Retrieved September 18, 2022, from https://asianews.network/us-universities-facing-sharp-fall-in-chinese-students/

Index[1]

A

Abbeel, Pieter, 644
ABBYY, 302
Accenture, 158, 300, 534, 539, 539n2
Affective bonding, 84, 87, 88, 90
Affective computing, 9, 106–111, 114, 120–122
Affective publics, 82
Africa, 303, 304, 316, 318, 319, 537
African National Congress (ANC), 318
Agenda setting, 10, 31, 95, 133–136, 147, 148, 150–152, 159–161, 163, 257, 276, 280, 283, 494, 554
AI industry, 12, 254, 266, 324, 338, 340–342, 344, 364, 365, 419, 426, 427, 437, 442, 682
Aisino-Mühlbauer consortium, 540
Akali Dal, 309
Algorithm, 3, 35, 48, 50, 59, 61, 67, 84, 85, 88, 92, 93, 114, 115, 119, 134, 146, 147, 149, 153, 154, 183, 214, 226, 264, 265, 274, 302, 313, 315, 318, 344, 345, 347, 351, 354, 356, 358, 361, 386, 390, 408, 413, 429, 433, 434, 438, 440–442, 454, 487, 492–496, 499–501, 508, 509, 516, 520, 532, 534, 542, 550, 570, 573, 591, 592, 600, 611, 613, 616, 620, 627, 635
Algorithmic governance, 82
Alibaba, 152, 153, 336, 341, 356, 359, 362, 539, 543
Aliman, Marie, 637
Al Jazeera, 85, 421, 518, 570
Allianz, 58, 277
Alphabet, 94, 147, 152, 153, 156, 313, 649
Al-Qaeda, 251, 256–258, 262, 436
Alternative for Germany, 491
AltNews, 311
Amazon, 152, 153, 156, 299, 460, 474–476, 489, 539, 543
Analytical eclecticism, 382
Ansar al-Islam, 256

---

[1] Note: Page numbers followed by 'n' refer to notes.

Anthropomorphization, 9, 96
Antisocial, 2, 3, 7, 15, 16, 23–28, 33, 36, 38, 39, 49, 52, 58, 60, 70, 71, 133, 134, 142, 148–151, 155, 160–163, 232, 234, 244, 252, 280, 348, 354, 359, 364, 425, 435, 440, 499, 501, 537, 545, 561, 569, 584, 591, 597, 598, 641, 647, 654, 657, 668, 678, 679
Anti-vaccination, 183, 189, 191
Apple, 92, 152–154, 352, 460, 476
Application programming interface, 138, 398
Argentina, 305, 533–536, 547, 550, 551
Arms control, 383, 390, 392, 472
Arms race, 24, 151, 160, 236, 378, 387, 388, 393, 649
Artificial General Intelligence (AGI), 15, 608, 610, 612, 633–635, 649–660, 662, 664, 667, 668, 679, 683
Artificial intelligence, ix, xi–xix, 1–16, 23, 27–28, 30–40, 48–52, 54, 57, 62, 63, 81, 90, 95, 105, 106, 114–118, 120–122, 133–151, 175, 177–181, 190–194, 205–226, 231, 232, 243–246, 252–266, 274, 276–277, 279–287, 285n2, 297, 299–324, 335, 338–364, 377–379, 383–393, 398–412, 420–441, 454–479, 487, 492–499, 507, 508, 511–521, 531–545, 564–565, 570, 583, 584, 588, 591–602, 607, 610, 620–622, 631, 633–635, 637, 639, 640, 644–656, 658, 677–680, 683–685
Artificial Intelligence Technology Strategy, Japan, 428

Artificial Narrow Intelligence (ANI), 607, 608, 614, 620, 633–635, 644, 645, 653–660, 665, 668, 683
Artificial Strong Intelligence (ASI), 15, 607–627, 656–660
Artificial Weak Intelligence (AWI), 607, 608, 614
ASEAN, 421, 422, 464
Asia-Pacific, 401, 421, 422
Attribute editing, 32, 361
Audio description, 135
AUKUS, 430
Australian National Science Agency, 220
Authenticity, 48, 262, 275, 287, 310, 519, 521
Automated headhunters, 90
Autonomous system, 365
Avast, 312, 431
Ayyub, Rana, 308, 518

B

BabyQ, 352
Baidu, 152, 336, 338, 341, 342, 348, 355–357, 360
Bakshi, Neelkant, 309
Bandidos Revolution Team, 542
Bank of America, 33, 533, 538
Behaviourist, 385
Beijing Declaration, BRICS, 320
Beliz, Gustavo, 538
Bezos, Jeff, 153, 639
Bharatiya Janata Party, Indian People's Party, 309
Biden, Joseph, 159, 187, 340, 423, 464, 466, 512, 515, 682
Big Pharma, 642
Big Tech, 10, 134, 151–162, 460, 465–466, 468, 474, 475, 478, 494, 495, 498, 500, 592, 642

bin Laden, Osama, 257
Bitpaymer ransomware, 543
Blockchain, 144, 285, 300, 310, 521, 544, 565, 588–590, 594, 611
Bolsonaro, Jair, 306, 551
Boogaloo, 176, 187
Bostrom, Nick, 379, 638, 655
Bot, 9, 11, 14, 24, 55, 82–96, 105, 110, 114–116, 136–139, 141–147, 150, 183, 185, 187, 189, 236, 257, 258, 262, 264, 284, 305, 306, 308, 318, 345, 347, 352–354, 403, 404, 413, 431, 433, 434, 454, 494, 514, 522, 532, 547–552, 592, 597, 644
Botnet, 82n1, 88, 139, 143, 431, 434, 514, 611
Brasilia Declaration, BRICS, 320
Brazil, 11, 69, 139, 162, 254, 297–300, 305–320, 350, 532, 533, 544, 546, 550
Breach, 140, 276, 279, 280, 282, 409, 411, 509, 568
Brexit, 86, 115, 145, 239, 241, 405, 549
Bribery, 277
BRICS, 8, 11, 297–326, 532
BRICS Institute of Future Networks, Shenzhen, 321, 322
BRICS Science, Technology and Innovation Partnership, 321
BRICS Science, Technology and Innovation Work Plan 2019–2022, 321
BRICS STI Architecture, 321
BRICS Technology Transfer Centre, Kunming, 322
BRICS Working Group of Experts on security and ICT, 320
Brin, Sergey, 639
Brookings Institute, 211, 221
Bullrich, Patricia, 551

Bullying, 318, 551
Bundestag, Germany, 471, 472, 474, 489
ByteDance, 359, 362

C

Calico, 639
Cambridge Analytica, 86, 204, 211, 216, 236, 390, 405
Captioning, 135
Care, Amanda, 535
Caribbean, 305, 534–537, 541, 541n3, 544
Castro, Xiomara, 549
Causation, 616, 617
Central Commission for Cyberspace Affairs, China, 361
Central-Eastern Europe, 10, 176, 182–186, 188, 189, 191, 195
Centre for Development of Advanced Computing (C-DAC), 311, 400
Centro de Estudios Científicos, 535
Chace, Calum, 632
Change.org, 317
Character assassination, 278, 508, 517, 518
Chatbot, 31, 81, 84, 90, 93, 109, 115, 136, 138–142, 150, 189, 264, 284, 300, 312, 348, 352, 353, 400, 430, 440, 454, 534, 535, 546, 547, 589, 658
Chile, 531, 533, 534, 536, 539, 540, 544, 546, 547
China, xi, xv, xvii, 2–4, 11, 12, 24, 55, 57, 70, 92, 138, 147, 150, 152, 153, 162, 187, 221, 234–237, 240, 241, 251, 282, 297, 304, 308, 313, 316, 322, 335–365, 377–394, 400, 419–421, 425, 431, 433, 434, 442, 455, 460, 464–469, 472–474, 476–480, 488, 489, 497, 498, 532, 539,

541, 541n3, 565, 601, 624, 636, 648, 649, 651, 652, 666, 667, 681, 682
China Academy of Information and Communication Technology, 322
China Electronics Society, 322
China Robotics Industry Alliance, 322
Chomsky, Noam, 274
Christian Democratic Union (CDU), 491
Citizenship Act, 309
Clausewitz, Carl von, 210
Clinton, Bill, 638
Clinton, Hillary, 313
CNN, 147, 314, 488
Cognitive architecture, 612, 613
Cognitive operation, 29, 571
Cognitive security, 29, 523
Cognitive semantics, 608, 613, 614, 617, 627
Cognitive warfare, 456, 457, 467, 478–480
Cold War, 157, 159, 244, 455, 469, 602, 661
Collateral damage, 388
Collective intelligence, 627
Colombia, 234, 241, 305, 533–535, 539, 544, 546, 550, 551
Commercial AI systems, 39, 262
Common prosperity, 363, 499
Comorbid crisis, 185, 188, 191–193, 195
Comprehensive and Progressive Agreement for Trans-Pacific Partnership, 422
Computer Emergency Response Team Coordination Center, Japan, 431
Computer games
  video games, 258
Computer vision, 302, 304, 341, 588, 591, 597, 608, 633
Connectionist, 385

Consciousness, 1–6, 15, 23, 25, 29, 32, 34, 39, 48, 139, 160, 235, 241, 261, 262, 267, 326, 347, 350, 351, 353, 365, 433, 440, 441, 455, 492, 497, 500, 554, 585, 593, 594, 608, 610, 612, 614, 617, 620–624, 626, 627, 631, 633, 658, 659, 665, 678, 679, 684
Conspiracy, 176, 181, 182, 184–188, 190, 192, 221, 317, 404, 423, 425, 437, 491, 514
Content moderation, 92–95
Convention on Certain Conventional Weapons, 390
Convergence, 12, 109, 260, 325, 399, 466, 474, 573, 588, 590, 594, 614, 615, 618–620, 644
Convergent methodology, 609, 618–620
Conversational AI, 83, 96, 138, 139, 141, 145, 265
Corporate actors, 191, 195, 287
Corporation, 5, 11, 27, 148, 155, 162, 184, 189, 191, 192, 204, 213, 233, 234, 280, 284, 285, 287, 288, 299, 322, 392, 397, 410, 412, 413, 429, 492, 509, 512, 514, 518, 523, 585, 593, 601, 648, 650, 681
Corruption, xiii, 27, 184, 191, 232, 245, 277, 318, 490, 491, 515, 550, 553, 573, 642
Counterspeech, 119, 120
COVID-19, xviii, 2, 10, 40, 113, 121, 155, 156, 175–195, 273–277, 283, 303, 305, 312, 317, 323, 338, 340, 342, 400, 424, 490, 491, 494, 519, 522, 543, 561, 563, 564, 566, 569, 642, 681, 682
Cowan, Thomas, 317

Credibility, 117, 140, 161, 162, 275, 278, 523
Critical infrastructure, 39, 144, 151, 378, 406, 413, 431, 438, 454, 463, 490, 496, 500, 542, 543, 646
Cryptocurrency, 260, 284, 310, 544, 568, 610
Cuban Missile Crisis, 244
Culture of shame, 425
Cummings, Dominic, 213
Cyberattacks, 14, 39, 115, 116, 305, 358, 401, 408, 409, 411, 423, 431, 463, 543, 568, 610, 611
CyberBRICS, 319–321, 324
Cyberbullying, 318, 425, 434, 518
Cyber-colonization, 455
Cybercrime, 11, 58, 140, 260, 277, 280, 282, 285, 320, 424, 432, 487, 488, 492, 496, 500, 532, 543, 568
Cybercrimes Act of South Africa, 318
Cyber defense, 231, 305, 463, 468, 490
Cyber Kill Chain, 116
Cybersecurity, xii–xiv, xvii, 26, 30, 53, 54, 58, 139, 149, 178, 179, 236, 253, 265, 279, 285, 298, 299, 303, 321–323, 335, 343, 358, 360, 362, 401, 404, 422, 424–426, 431, 432, 462–464, 471, 500, 523, 532, 543, 545, 552, 568, 569, 601, 610, 681
Cyber Security Law of the People's Republic of China, 336, 360
Cyberspace, xii, xx, 15, 158, 161, 252, 283, 336, 360, 361, 424, 426, 456, 458, 462, 463, 492, 497, 584
Cyberspace Administration of China, 154, 336, 343, 347, 359
Cyberwarfare, 387
Cyber weapon, 256

Cyborg, 437, 637
Cyborgization, 15, 161, 632, 637, 662, 680
Czech Republic, xi, xix, 176, 182, 183, 185

D

Dahua Technology, 323
Dark web, 260, 358, 543
DART, Chilean company, 535
Data, 3, 56, 65, 67, 68, 82, 86, 94, 109, 114–120, 122, 123, 148–150, 152–154, 158, 160, 161, 180, 190, 194, 204, 206, 211, 213, 218, 220, 235, 236, 254–257, 261, 263, 265, 274, 276, 277, 279, 282, 284, 300–302, 305, 311, 313, 316, 319–322, 325, 335, 336, 339, 341, 343, 346–349, 355, 357, 360, 362, 364, 386, 390, 392, 398–401, 404, 405, 407–413, 424, 425, 427, 429, 431, 433, 434, 437, 438, 440, 441, 454, 456, 458–461, 463–467, 471, 472, 474–479, 509, 510, 514, 522, 523, 535, 538–541, 543–545, 549, 552, 554, 564, 567–572, 585, 587, 592, 595, 598, 600, 607, 613–616, 620, 621, 624, 627, 633, 647, 650, 680, 681
Data hygiene, 118, 120
DDoS, 82n1, 306, 568
Deception, 5, 14, 55, 140, 355, 507, 508, 511, 513, 514, 523
Decision-making, xii, xvi, 6, 15, 33, 38, 149, 161, 219, 260, 283, 284n1, 287, 300, 383–386, 398, 399, 402, 421, 457, 468, 490, 491, 509, 553, 554, 572, 607,

609, 610, 612, 614, 618–621, 625, 626, 637, 644, 646–648, 662, 665, 679, 682
Deepfake, 3, 6, 9, 11, 14, 24, 31, 32, 48–59, 61, 65–67, 69–71, 150, 189, 261, 262, 266, 276, 281, 287, 298, 307–311, 314, 315, 318, 319, 344, 354–356, 358–362, 364, 398, 400, 403, 404, 407, 408, 413, 425, 432, 454, 494, 495, 497, 500, 508, 515–523, 532, 546, 551, 552, 554, 570, 571, 596, 600, 610
Deepfake puppetry, 50
Deepfake smell, 62
Deep learning, 55, 61, 67, 299, 361, 385, 400, 429, 612, 616
DeepNostalgia application, 494
Deeptrace, 308
Deep video portrait (DVP), 51
Degradation of democratic institutions, 135, 244
Delhi Legislative Assembly, 309
Democratic Party, 313
Democratic Party of Japan, 423
Democratic People's Republic of Korea (DPRK), 433, 434
Denial, 82n1, 240, 306, 520, 640, 642
Deranking, 147, 313, 315
Deterrence, 384, 389, 392, 463, 603, 647
Digital Complaints Committee, 319
Digital divide, 561, 573
Digital imperialism, 455, 478
Digital public goods, 398, 411, 413
Digital revolution, 455, 461
Digital sovereignty, xx, 464, 474, 475, 479, 480, 567
Digital transformation, xx, 299, 324, 475, 547
Disaster Management Act, South Africa, 319

Disinformation, xiii, 3, 10, 11, 32, 48, 49, 52, 53, 55, 69, 71, 82, 85, 86, 110, 115, 134, 145, 146, 159, 183, 185, 187, 189, 191, 192, 195, 252, 261, 273, 278, 279, 298, 308–311, 313, 318, 319, 361, 463, 495, 498, 500, 508, 514, 517, 521, 541, 549–552, 569, 570, 572, 597
Distributed dissent, 82, 82n1
Dominican Republic, 546, 551
DoublePaymer ransomware, 543
Doxing, 263
Drone, 39, 144, 150, 151, 256, 259, 260, 301, 303, 346, 389, 400, 406, 407, 438, 507, 542, 569, 645
Drozd, Alexei, 312
Dual-use technology, 38, 40, 50, 70, 252, 388, 651
Duarte, Jesse, 318
DYMAXION Labs, 535

E

East Japan Railway Company, 429
Ecuador, 539, 543, 546, 549–551
Edelman Trust Barometer, 152, 273
ELIZA, chatbot, 138, 658
Ellis, Evan, 541, 541n3
Emotet, 431
Emotion, 9, 63, 83, 87, 90, 94, 106–112, 114–118, 121, 122, 148, 186, 219, 220, 233, 284, 353, 385, 424, 425, 434, 435, 534, 589, 614, 644, 646
Emotion AI/emotional AI
emotional AI, xiii, xiv, xvi, 108–110, 112, 114–123, 148, 149, 284, 349, 425, 434, 435, 658
Emotional regime, 106, 110–114, 116, 118

Emotion recognition, 106–110, 114, 118, 122
Emotives, 111
Enabling technology, 383
Ethical guidelines, 119
Ethical Specifications of Next-Generation Artificial Intelligence, 343
Ethics, 82, 150, 192, 222–224, 274, 391, 460, 498–500, 515, 610, 623, 624
EU General Data Protection Regulation, GDPR, 466
The Eurasian Economic Union, 239
European Parliament, 4, 153, 185, 189, 467–469, 520, 659
The European Union (The EU), xi, xvii, xx, 2, 4, 13, 91, 153, 157, 182, 213, 234–236, 239, 241, 259, 339, 340, 343, 454, 456, 459–480, 488, 497, 498, 509, 510, 666, 667
Europol, 5, 32, 91, 92, 185, 188, 253, 259–261, 280, 567, 570, 596
Expert Group on the Implementation of AI Principles, 427
Expert systems, 385, 600
Extremism, 9, 13, 32, 82–84, 86, 88–96, 111, 118, 143, 145, 176, 183, 185, 187–191, 236, 257, 265, 423, 425, 493–495, 498, 500, 570, 596, 597
Extremist, 82, 84, 85, 91, 92, 185, 189, 254, 259, 487, 492, 494, 495, 500

F

Facebook, 54, 60, 86, 92–94, 119, 146, 147, 152–154, 158, 183, 204, 211, 213, 235, 236, 265, 309, 347, 357, 405, 433, 460, 476, 494, 497, 508, 515, 522, 544, 547, 549, 585, 587
Facebook Papers, 183, 508
Face re-enactment, 32
Face swap, 32, 50
Facial recognition, 150, 260, 282, 309, 323, 341, 363, 400, 436, 507, 509, 510, 541, 569
Facial re-enactment, 50
Fake news, xiii, 53, 55, 56, 85, 146, 147, 153, 214, 235, 236, 276, 278, 281, 285, 287, 306, 308, 313, 319, 347, 354, 413, 493, 514, 515, 549, 570, 611
Fake people, 59, 425, 437
Far right, 176, 182, 183, 185, 187, 188, 252, 255, 258, 262, 420, 433, 494
Federal Bureau of Investigation (FBI), 3, 84, 188, 359, 515
Federal Criminal Police Office (Bundeskriminalitat), Germany, 490
Federal Service for Supervision of Communications, Information Technology and Mass Media, Roskomnadzor, 154, 315
Federal University of Espírito Santo, 305
Federation Council, Russia, 315
Feedback loops, 83, 386
Feeling, 6, 63, 87, 89, 90, 107, 108, 111, 115, 233, 265, 285, 387, 441, 563, 572, 618, 624, 633, 634, 654
Fields, Anna, 552
Film and Publication Act no. 65, South Africa, 319
5G, 135, 221, 304, 316, 317, 322, 536, 588, 590
Foundation for Advanced Research (FAS), 302, 303

4G, 304, 316
Fourth Industrial Revolution, 303, 320, 321, 639
Fox News, 157, 314
France, xviii, xix, 13, 153, 241, 350, 421, 454, 470–477
Fraud, 3, 32, 57, 58, 141, 261, 264, 267, 276, 282, 287, 307, 310, 325, 346, 354, 543, 544, 549
Frerichs, Lisa, 57
Fully synthetic material, 32
Fundraising, 252, 257

G

GAFAM, 152, 153, 460, 465–466, 468, 472, 475, 476, 478
Gandhi, Rahul, 308
Gartin, Joseph, 545
Gates, Bill, 274, 639
Gato, intelligent agent, 649, 650
Gazprom Neft, 315
GDP, 2, 152, 156, 240, 299, 300, 399, 534, 535, 538, 563, 565
General Data Protection Regulation (GDPR), 466, 478, 509
Generative adversarial network, 59, 437, 514, 551, 635
Genetics, 635–638
Geopolitical balance, 454, 469, 479
Geopolitical competition, 5, 36, 211, 222, 226, 391, 465, 476, 531
Geopolitical order, 456, 459, 479
Geopolitical rivalries, 23, 133, 135, 457, 479, 553
Geopolitics, xviii, xix, 221, 276, 453, 456, 457, 459, 462
Geospatial dominance, 458
Geospatial intelligence, 458
German Research Center for Artificial Intelligence, 489
Germany, xv, 13, 27, 57, 84, 221, 241, 337, 350, 426, 454, 470–477, 487–501, 541, 640, 682

GETTR, 85
Getúlio Vargas Foundation, 305, 321
Global confrontation, 40, 442
Global Cooperation and Training Framework, 422
Globalization, 10, 316, 470, 601, 603, 664
Golden Shield, 356, 357
Goldin, Ian, 29, 316
Google, 85, 137, 147, 152–154, 156, 158, 214, 312, 313, 341, 357, 361, 433, 460, 474–476, 489, 546, 547, 585, 639, 650, 657, 658, 660
Google bomb, 85
Gopal, a voice assistant, 300
Governance Guidelines for Implementation of AI Principles, 427
Governance Principles for Responsible AI, 343
Great Firewall of China, 356
Great power rivalry, 378, 479
G7, 461, 488
G20, 392, 430, 488
Guaidó, Juan, 551
Guatemala, 309, 543, 547, 550
Gulf Cooperation Council (GCC), 563, 563n1, 564, 568
Gutierrez, Camilo, 552

H

Haraway, Donna, 638
Harrari, Yoval, 274
Hate crime, 111, 497
Health security, 178, 179, 184–186, 195
Heteromation, 36
Hexagon Capability Center India, 300
Hezbollah, 259
Hicks, Kathleen, 647
Higher School of Economics, 302, 321

High-tech strategic psychological warfare (HTSPW), 231, 232, 236, 242–246
Hitachi, 429
Hitler, Adolf, 2, 49, 141, 257, 431, 440, 641, 661
Honda, 435
Hong Kong, xv, 12, 58, 338–345, 351, 364
Huawei, 304, 316, 317, 340, 350, 539
Human-centric AI, 427, 460
Human-centric use of AI, 471, 477
Human induction, 385
Hybrid AI, 611, 617, 618
Hybrid intelligence, 631, 653, 683
Hybrid war, 25, 26
  hybrid warfare, 242
Hybrid warfare
  hybrid war, 13, 135, 453

IBM, 63, 152, 158, 299, 475, 568, 635, 648
iFlytek, 338
Ill-defined malicious goal, 614, 618–620
Image, 9, 13, 34, 36, 50–52, 56, 59, 61, 144, 214–216, 257, 260, 265, 275, 300, 314, 319, 338, 341, 345, 347, 348, 351, 355, 358, 361, 421, 424, 436, 437, 441, 489, 511, 516, 519, 520, 593, 610
Impact from AI, 134
Independent Polling System of Society, 318
India, xii, 2, 11, 12, 24, 55, 162, 211, 241, 281, 297, 298, 300–301, 305–319, 322, 397–414, 473, 517, 518, 649, 667
Indian Centre for Development of Advanced Computing, 309
Indian National Association for Software and Services Companies, 322
Indian National Congress, 308, 309
India's Army Training Command, 301
Indoctrination, 83, 84, 90
Influence, xix, 3, 5, 10, 12, 13, 23, 25–27, 29, 39, 40, 49, 62, 63, 66, 69, 86, 108, 110, 112, 116, 133, 134, 136, 139, 142, 149, 154, 160–163, 182, 183, 186, 206, 207, 212, 213, 218, 219, 231, 233, 235, 240, 243, 246, 252, 259, 265, 267, 277, 313, 316, 324, 337, 338, 346, 348, 350, 356, 359, 362, 378, 386, 389, 402, 405, 421, 424, 425, 435, 441, 454, 456, 457, 472, 476, 478, 488, 490, 492, 498, 500, 511, 513, 515, 531, 539, 540, 542, 547, 554, 564, 570, 583, 591–595, 597, 602, 613, 625, 633, 641, 654, 666, 667, 679
Infodemic, 192
Information asymmetry, 381
Information literacy, 11, 178, 186, 189, 192, 195, 286, 288, 357, 571
Information security, xvii, 26, 29, 57, 68, 252, 336, 354, 363, 545, 597, 599, 602
Information Technology (Intermediary Guidelines and Digital Media Ethics Code) Rules, India, 310
Information Technology Act, India, 310, 411
Information warfare, 83, 88, 96, 233, 235, 244, 402, 419, 441, 457, 508
Innopolis University, 302
Innovation BRICS Network (iBRICS Network), 321, 322, 324

Institute for the Integration of Latin America, 534
Integrated Innovation Strategy, Japan, 427
Integration, 12, 30, 138, 245, 298, 324, 338, 343, 392, 400, 422, 428, 550, 572, 653, 662
Intentionality, 388, 631
Inter-American Development Bank, 532, 534, 538
Interconnectedness, 243, 382
International Data Corporation, 204
International humanitarian law, 389
International IT Forum, 8, 320
International Labour Organization (ILO), 541
International law, xv, 26, 39, 70, 191, 192, 224, 226, 325, 363, 388
International Monetary Fund (IMF), 277, 563, 564, 566
International psychological security, ix, xv, 6–8, 11–13, 15, 26, 30, 84, 86, 95, 138, 175–177, 179–186, 188–190, 192, 193, 195, 205, 235, 274–276, 279, 280, 285–288, 325, 354, 377, 453, 454, 456, 458, 459, 462–464, 467, 470, 476, 477, 479, 480, 544, 554, 591, 594, 599
International relations, xi, xiii, xv, xvii, xix, xx, 1, 7, 23, 26, 30, 48, 258, 354, 380, 382, 391, 393, 432, 455, 456, 458, 459, 477, 608, 626
International Standardization Organization (ISO), 301
International system, 6, 30, 70, 234, 381, 454–456, 459, 468, 477, 487
Internet, xii, xiv, xx, 3, 33, 55, 61, 69, 70, 95, 106, 110, 123, 135, 138, 141, 144, 146, 152–154, 158, 182, 183, 185, 191, 204, 205, 207–210, 214, 215, 217, 220, 243, 246, 256, 265, 281, 299, 301, 305–308, 313, 315, 316, 321, 322, 326, 338, 341–343, 347, 348, 353, 355–364, 378, 398, 399, 404, 409–410, 412, 424, 431, 433–435, 457, 462, 476, 499, 508–510, 512, 515, 520, 522, 537, 549–553, 565, 571, 572, 584, 585n1, 595, 601, 611, 652, 658
Intrusive verification regimes, 390
IntSights Cyber Intelligence, 305
Inverse problem-solving, 609, 618, 624, 626
Islamic State, 11, 27, 85, 251, 345, 423, 436
Islamic State in Afghanistan Islamic State in Khorasan, 251
Islamic State in Khorasan Islamic State in Afghanistan, 251
Islamist, 84

J

J-Anon, 423
Japan, xii, xiv, xv, xvii, 13, 152, 237, 241, 340, 344, 355, 400, 419–443, 473, 565, 663
Japanese Society for Artificial Intelligence, 428
Johannesburg Declaration, BRICS, 320
Joint All-Domain Command and Control (JADC2) Implementation Plan, 647

K

Kejriwal, Arvind, 309
Ken, Kange, 545
Khassoggi, Jamal, 85
Killer robots, 437, 511
Kim Jong-un, 314

Klitschko, Vitali, 56, 57
Kurzweil, Ray, 608, 637, 638
Kybernetiq magazine, 436

L

Labour Party, 213
Lancaster, Thomas, 60, 242, 615
Latin America, 14, 240, 299, 305, 531–554, 541n3, 642
LaunchPad project, 429
Legislation, 55, 150, 154, 221–226, 298, 310, 313, 314, 325, 362, 365, 411, 434, 477, 478, 510, 596
Lemoine, Blake, 657
Lenin, Vladimir, 240
Lethal autonomy, 388
Levandowski, Anthony, 658
Liberal Democratic Party, Japan, 423
Liu Duo, 322
Lok Sabha, 211
London, Jack, 643
Lone wolves, 252, 261
Lubcke, Walter, 491

M

Machine learning, 3, 9, 51, 62, 81, 83, 135, 137, 147, 226, 264, 273, 286, 300–303, 346, 386, 398–400, 403, 405, 408, 410, 433, 588, 591, 610, 611
Macri, Mauricio, 547, 551
Maduro, Nicolas, 259, 548
Malicious use of chatbots, 139
Manipulation, 2, 3, 5, 13, 14, 36, 40, 52, 56, 85, 86, 105, 106, 110, 112, 113, 115, 117, 137, 144, 147, 148, 151, 162, 206, 214, 219, 220, 236, 252, 261–263, 265, 276, 283, 287, 310, 311, 313, 315, 318, 320, 323, 342, 344, 350, 361, 401, 405, 408, 413, 422, 424, 440, 454, 468, 487, 494, 496, 511, 513, 514, 520, 521, 532, 547, 550, 552, 554, 569–571, 599, 610, 657, 678
Manturov, Denis, 322
Marcus, Gary, 658
Marwala, Tshilidzi, 303, 318
Mashinini, Nomalanga, 319
Matus, Jonathan, 633
McKinsey Institute, 316, 538
Media, xiii, xiv, xviii, 3, 9, 11, 25, 33, 35, 37, 51, 52, 54, 56, 61, 65, 69, 70, 82, 83, 86, 88, 89, 91–96, 109, 112, 113, 119, 133, 137, 142–144, 147, 149, 150, 153, 157, 175, 176, 183, 185, 186, 188, 191, 192, 195, 207, 213, 215, 219, 235, 242, 253, 256, 258, 259, 261, 265, 273, 275, 278, 283, 286, 288, 298, 306, 308–314, 317, 318, 325, 336, 343, 344, 346, 347, 350, 352, 354, 356, 379, 404, 405, 420, 423, 432, 434, 441, 442, 459, 468, 492–494, 496, 508, 509, 511–516, 518–520, 523, 532, 540, 545, 549, 550, 562, 569–572, 610, 611, 622, 638, 639, 642, 656, 681
Media literacy, 70, 119, 192, 195, 523, 572
Media organizations, 186, 192
Mega-crisis, 175–178, 181–185, 190, 194, 195
M-81, robot, 314
Merrill Lynch, 33, 533, 538
Meta-citizen, 586
Metaverse, 14, 15, 141, 583–603, 587n3, 646
Mexico, 305, 350, 533, 535, 539, 542, 544, 546, 547, 550

Meyerriecks, Dawn, 545
Microsoft, 53, 60, 115, 137, 140, 152, 153, 158, 274, 284, 299, 352, 353, 430, 460, 474–476, 521, 536, 611
Middle East, xvi, 4, 14, 57, 69, 254, 255, 345, 400, 468, 561–574
Military-political warfare, 25
Miller, Geoffrey, 636, 636n1
Mindar, robot, 441
Ministry of Economic Development, Russia, xvi, 315
Ministry of Health and the Ministry of Economic Development, Russia, 315
Ministry of Industry and Information Technology, China, 336, 343
Ministry of Science and Technology of the People's Republic of China, 341
Misinformation, 9, 57, 113, 150, 159, 183, 185, 187, 192, 275, 278, 281, 286, 319, 413, 508, 518, 523, 550, 623
MIT Technology Review, 214
Modeling, 111, 588, 613–615, 618, 619, 621
Modi, Narendra, 211, 308
Moldova, 207
Monopoly, 302, 343, 360, 365, 454, 468, 600
Morales, Evo, 547, 549
Moravec, Hans, 649
Moreno, Lenin, 549
Moscow Institute of Physics and Technology (MIPT), 302, 303
MSNBC, 314
Multimodal, 93, 109, 119, 598
Multipolarity, 467, 468, 479, 480
Musk, Elon, 60, 155, 213, 274, 637, 644

N

National In National Institution for Transforming India, NITI Aayog, 300, 410
National Institution for Transforming India, NITI Aayog, 300, 410, 411
National Technical Research Organisation, India, 311
Nation-states, 176, 181, 191, 192, 195, 462, 592
Natural language processing (NLP), 83, 89, 264, 265, 283, 286, 299, 435, 597, 633
Nazism, 252, 684
NEC, 429
Neuroprosthetically augmented information systems, 68
Neves, Aècio, 305, 306
New Energy and Industrial Technology Development Organization, Japan, 428
Noise bot, 85
Non-state actors, 5, 27, 31, 133, 149, 158, 189, 191, 232, 235, 242, 243, 246, 260, 317, 320, 344, 398, 399, 402, 404, 550, 553, 563, 571, 648, 677
Non-zero-sum game, 386
North Africa, 254, 400
The North Atlantic Treaty Organization (NATO), xv, 157, 234, 239, 456, 461, 463, 464, 467–470, 473, 478–479, 488, 513, 624
Northeast Asia, ix, xiii–xv, 355, 420
Nuclear deterrence, 38, 384
NVIDIA, 59, 60, 152, 429

O

Oleg, bot, 313, 521
Online reputation management, 278

OpenAI, 60, 635, 650
Oxford Internet Institute, 306, 549–551
Oxford University, 33, 262, 316, 379, 468, 538, 638, 651

P

Page, Larry, 639
Panama, 543, 546
Pandemic, xviii, 2, 10, 40, 49, 87, 113, 122, 155, 156, 175–195, 213, 221, 258, 273–277, 283, 305, 312, 323, 340, 342, 350, 400, 491, 522, 523, 531, 532, 534, 535, 543, 544, 553, 561, 563, 564, 566, 567, 573, 642, 681, 682
Paradigm, 83, 193, 208, 210, 213, 215, 226, 381, 453, 469, 534, 554, 613, 614, 624, 647, 665
PARMA, company, 535
Pavlov, Ivan, 64
Peña Nieto, Enrique, 547
Perception management, 39, 49, 51, 52, 106, 109, 110, 112–118, 120–123, 138–139, 160, 398, 550
Personal Data Protection Bill, India, 311
Personal Data Protection Law of the People's Republic of China, 355
Peru, 533–535, 543, 544, 547, 549
Peru's National Engineering University, 535
Petróleos Mexicanos, Pemex, 543
Pharming, 263, 264
Phishing, 61, 88, 110, 114, 116, 140, 189, 263, 264, 266, 276, 282, 284, 285n2, 287, 305, 306, 310, 312, 349, 364, 401, 403, 407, 408, 413, 431, 438, 545, 546
Pindrop, 49, 57, 253, 263, 298, 307

Piñera, Sebastian, 551
Platform technology, 384
Poisoning the data, 149
Political culture, 420
Political stability, 9, 49, 55, 70, 71, 112, 117, 122, 134, 147, 148, 273, 362, 378, 567
Pontes, Marcos, 299
Populism, 240, 491, 532, 534, 541n3, 554
Post-truth, xiii, 420, 512
Pranking, 14, 512, 513
Predictive analytics, 24, 35, 148, 149, 161, 264, 265, 284, 320, 349, 545, 570, 591
Preventing and Combating of Hate Speech Bill, South Africa, 319
Privacy, 48, 235, 255, 276, 277, 312, 320, 323, 337, 361, 364, 379, 406, 407, 411, 413, 436, 466, 509, 510, 522, 544, 612, 642
Prognostic weapon, 35, 149, 320, 399
Propaganda, 3, 7, 14, 49, 52, 60, 83, 84, 89, 91, 110, 134, 145, 148, 183, 233, 244, 252, 256–260, 263–265, 274, 276, 278–281, 287, 306, 313, 318, 345, 398, 420, 425, 434, 436, 454, 468, 493, 513, 514, 522, 523, 551, 569, 571, 572, 592, 596, 597, 678
Property, 156, 232, 239, 319, 401, 542, 587, 589, 657
Psychological operation, 11, 13, 14, 29, 61, 109, 114, 135, 145, 148, 161, 233, 344, 364, 399, 402, 406, 422, 434, 532, 539, 547, 549, 550, 553, 554, 562, 650
Psychological security, ix, xiii, xv, 1, 4–16, 23–26, 28–30, 32, 34, 36, 38–41, 55, 59, 82, 84, 86, 95, 113, 117, 122, 136, 146, 147, 152, 154, 160, 162, 175,

177–181, 183–192, 195, 209, 220, 222–227, 252, 261, 265, 267, 280, 285, 297, 298, 301, 304, 308, 310–313, 316, 318–320, 325, 336–338, 342, 343, 345, 346, 348, 349, 352–354, 363, 364, 399, 401, 402, 406, 410, 414, 420, 422, 425, 430, 432, 442, 443, 488, 492, 493, 495, 497, 500, 532, 537, 544, 584, 591, 599, 608, 610, 622, 626, 645, 677, 680–683
Psychological stability, 118, 595, 599
Psychological warfare, xvii, 5, 10, 11, 13, 14, 25, 36, 39, 52, 54, 70, 147, 159, 161, 162, 231, 232, 244, 274, 281, 314, 315, 317, 350, 351, 420, 442, 453, 508, 512, 514, 523, 539, 542, 545, 607–609, 615, 616, 620, 621, 625, 626, 648, 677, 678, 682
Psychological weapon, 38, 90, 280, 608, 678
Public awareness, 119, 300–301, 361, 519
Public opinion, 32, 48, 83, 110, 147, 207, 236, 283, 359, 405, 419, 491, 496, 500, 507, 522, 569–571
Putin, Vladimir, 48, 147, 157, 302, 314, 495, 518

Q

QAnon, 176, 187, 423
Quantum semantics, 617, 623, 624, 626
Quantum technology, 428
Querdenker, 491, 494, 495

R

Radicalization, 9, 13, 82–84, 87, 89–91, 95, 96, 487, 488, 490–492, 497, 498, 571
Rain, telecom operator, 304, 317
Ramaphosa, Cyril, 303, 316, 318
RAND Corporation, 647
Ransomware, 140, 358, 454, 490, 492, 493, 496, 543, 552, 568
Rashtriya Raksha University, 301
Reality Defender, plugin, 311
RecoMed, 304
Recruitment, xvi, 9, 37, 83, 84, 88, 90, 186, 252, 254–258, 261, 263, 267, 345, 353
Reddit, 48, 94, 403
Reflexive control, 399, 402, 407, 410
Reinforcement learning, 385
Reputation, xvii, xix, 14, 52, 92, 143, 145, 274–279, 281–283, 285, 287, 288, 308, 309, 346, 356, 419, 421, 422, 424, 519, 546, 570
Reserve Bank of India, 310
Responsible AI, 150, 194
Revisionism, 433
Rinna, chatbot, 430, 440
Risks, xviii, 1–5, 7, 10–12, 14, 15, 24, 25, 31, 34, 49, 59, 60, 66, 69, 71, 94, 116, 117, 123, 138, 139, 141, 144, 151, 157, 159, 188, 191, 194, 223, 232, 236–239, 243, 245, 254–258, 260, 261, 266, 274, 276, 277, 279–285, 287, 301, 307, 310, 312, 314, 316, 320, 323, 324, 338, 339, 342, 346, 347, 349, 354, 355, 378–393, 399, 401, 406, 407, 411, 412, 422, 456, 458, 460–465, 467, 468, 470, 473,

476–480, 490, 492, 496, 498, 507, 522, 531, 532, 538, 539, 541, 542, 544, 545, 547, 548, 553, 562, 564, 567, 591, 595, 597, 598, 600, 610, 622, 623, 631, 633, 636–638, 642, 648, 654, 655, 657, 658, 665, 668, 679, 682
Rivero, Gustavo A., 550
Robotics, 35, 68, 93, 149, 241, 260, 266, 314, 322, 339, 342, 429, 438, 439, 509, 608, 622, 643–645, 649, 658, 659, 665, 684
Robotization, 33–35, 426, 430, 538, 637, 643–646, 662, 666, 667, 678
Rosenthal, Yani, 549
Rosseti, 302
Rostelecom, 302
Rousseff, Dilma, 306
R.U. Sirius, 639
Russia, ix, xi, xiii, xv–xix, 2, 8, 11, 14, 23, 34, 35, 48, 67, 92, 139, 143, 147, 151, 152, 154, 156–158, 162, 187, 234–237, 239–242, 277, 297, 298, 301–303, 305–320, 322, 355, 363, 402, 420, 433, 434, 442, 465, 467–469, 474, 476–480, 508, 510, 511, 513, 515, 521, 565, 596, 645, 648, 649, 660, 666, 667
Russian Association of Robotics, 322
Russian Direct Investment Fund, 315
Russian Railways, 302
Russia Today (RT), 147, 313, 433

S

Sajju, Sobha, 309
Sao Paulo Research Foundation, 299
Saudi Arabia, 33, 144, 565, 568, 569

Sberbank, 302, 315
Scenario analysis, 12, 253, 399, 401, 412, 413, 487–488, 532
Schmidt, Eric, 147, 221, 313
Schopenhauer, Arthur, 242
Schwab, Klaus, 186, 221, 639
Schwartau, Winn, 233
SCL Group, 551
SearchInform, 312
Sechenov, Ivan, 64
Self-driving car, 37, 658
Self-learning, 138, 302, 304, 323, 434, 627, 644, 645
Sensory augmentation, 66
Sentiment analysis, 9, 106, 108–110, 114, 120, 122, 264, 405, 406
Shaktikanta Das, 310
Shallowfake, 508, 517, 521
Shoigu, Sergei, 302
Simonyan, Margarita, 147, 313
Singh, Rajnath, 301
Sinha, Pratik, 192, 311
Skoltech University, 302
Slim, Carlos, 639
Smart cities, xvi, 299, 341, 406, 409
Smartphones, 213–215, 217, 220, 313, 339, 353, 355, 357, 509, 510, 585, 590, 633
Smishing, 312, 545
SMS revolution, 207
Social audits, 413
Social credit, 362, 363, 469, 510
Social engineering, 14, 25, 29, 110, 140, 252, 256, 258, 260, 262–266, 274, 280, 282, 285–287, 312, 358, 359, 545, 546, 552–554
Social listening, 31
Socially significant technologies, 33
Social media, xviii, 3, 9, 11, 13, 27, 33, 37, 48, 49, 52, 53, 59, 61, 81–88, 91–96, 105, 106, 109, 110, 112–114, 116, 120,

136–138, 142–144, 146, 150, 153, 154, 182, 183, 209, 211, 215, 217, 257, 258, 261–263, 265, 273, 275, 278–279, 281, 283, 287, 303, 305, 306, 309, 311, 314, 316–318, 344, 346, 348, 351–353, 355, 359, 363, 403–407, 410, 411, 413, 423, 433, 434, 437, 454, 457, 468, 492–494, 496, 508, 515, 518, 532, 545, 550, 552, 569, 595–597, 601, 635, 645
Social polarization, 2, 232, 239, 241, 245, 442
Social responsibility, 16, 183, 189, 193, 275, 287, 612, 654, 668, 684
Society 5.0, 424, 426
Sock puppet, 59, 550
SoftBank, 429, 435
Soft power, xiv, 275, 338, 424
Software robot, 82, 90, 93, 95
Somatosensory system, 63
Sophia (robot), 33
Soros, George, 346, 639
South Africa, 11, 162, 221, 297, 298, 303–319, 624
South African Human Rights Commission, 319
South African Institute of International Affairs, 316
South African Protection of Personal Information Act, 318
South America, 533, 534, 537, 539
Southern Switzerland's Dalle Molle Institute for Artificial Intelligence, 652
South Korea, 3, 55, 56, 147, 234, 340, 355, 422, 425, 437, 473, 533
Sovereign cloud, 474–476, 478
The Soviet Union, 158, 241, 244, 455, 468
Spam, 61, 85, 183, 264, 431, 592
Spam bot, 85

Spatio-temporal geopolitics, 458
Spear phishing, 256, 263, 283, 364, 545, 546
Sputnik, 147, 313, 433
State Bank of India, 312
State Duma of the Russian Federation, 312, 315, 518
State Research Institute of Aviation Systems, GosNIIAS, 303
Strategic autonomy, 465, 467–471, 479, 480
Strategic communications, ix, xv, xix, 7, 84, 87, 95, 118, 120, 238, 279, 533, 551, 624–627, 662, 667
Strategic competition, xx, 344, 378–380, 382, 388, 393, 421
Strategic Council for AI Technology, Japan, 427
Strategic psychological warfare (SPW), 10, 231, 232, 235, 238, 243, 244, 246
Strategic stability, 379, 393, 648
Structural power, 421
Super Artificial Intelligence, 15, 633, 656–660
Sustainable development, 323, 325, 409, 574, 679
Synthetic products in agenda setting, 150

T

Taiwan, xv, 12, 338–345, 347, 351, 352, 364, 422
Taliban, 251, 345
Target audience, 31, 71, 116, 148, 259, 314, 514, 594
Technological revolution, 379
Telegram, 87–89, 91, 92, 94, 154, 256–258
Tele2, 313
Tencent, 152, 153, 341, 342, 350, 352, 353, 359

Terrorism, xvii, 10–12, 27, 37, 186, 188, 251, 253–255, 259–261, 263, 266, 267, 303, 353, 363, 423, 567, 625, 627
Tesla, 155, 281, 637, 644
Text-to-speech and signing, 135
Thiel, Peter, 639, 660
Ticketmaster, 140, 284
TikTok, 154, 262
Tinkoff Bank, 313
Tiwari, Manoj, 309, 311, 516
Toshiba, 429
Toyota, 429
Trading bot, 142, 144
Transhumanism, 638–643
Trolling, 14, 146, 186, 512, 513
Trump, Donald, 54, 85, 86, 92, 145, 187, 211, 213, 236, 240, 313, 314, 340, 346, 356, 423, 513, 514, 518, 681, 682
Trust, 5, 6, 11, 12, 57, 60, 65, 69, 87, 141, 148, 150, 153, 178, 184, 191, 193, 210, 222, 241, 273, 275, 277, 280, 282, 285, 286, 288, 306, 344, 354–356, 362, 363, 377–384, 386, 388, 389, 391–393, 401, 404, 408, 421, 423, 424, 461, 492, 495, 496, 498, 500, 508, 519, 520, 523, 536, 546, 553, 570, 626, 643
Trust deficit, 382, 392
Twitter, 60, 85, 86, 88, 91–94, 119, 137, 139, 141, 144, 146, 149, 154, 213, 257, 305, 306, 308, 313, 353, 404, 430, 433, 495, 518, 547–549
Twitter bomb, 85

U

Uber, 37, 658
Ufa Declaration, BRICS, 320
Ukraine, 2, 40, 48, 54, 156–158, 239, 277, 466, 467, 489, 495, 596
Uncertainty, 6, 28, 35, 113, 121, 122, 186, 261, 288, 379–382, 385, 390, 393, 404, 455, 466, 561, 620, 648, 663
Unemployment, 11, 33, 34, 232, 239–240, 316, 344, 566, 573, 622, 637, 664
UNESCO, xix, 8, 280, 286, 480, 571
Unicorns, 341
United Cyber Caliphate, 256
The United Kingdom, xiv, 58, 60, 86, 213, 241, 242, 306, 340, 350, 426, 473, 474, 489, 516, 518, 636, 640, 642
United Nations, xvii, 33, 57, 157, 158, 160, 162, 185, 266, 280, 409, 513, 565–567, 569, 571, 652
United Nations Internet Governance Forum, 320
The United States, xvii, xix, 2, 10, 12, 14, 24, 49, 54, 57, 69, 84, 88, 115, 142, 143, 152, 156, 158, 159, 176, 186–190, 195, 204, 234–236, 241, 244, 253, 259, 263, 281, 314, 316, 339–341, 343–345, 350, 351, 359, 360, 364, 377, 378, 380–384, 386–388, 391–394, 400, 405, 409, 419–423, 426, 442, 460, 464–470, 472–474, 476–480, 488, 489, 497, 498, 508, 511, 516, 521, 532, 537, 539, 540, 548, 549, 565, 601, 610, 624–626, 638, 640, 647–649, 651, 652, 657, 658, 666, 667, 681–683
Universidad San Pablo, Arequipa, 535
University of Cape Town, 321
University of Hong Kong, 321
University of Johannesburg, 303, 318

University of Pretoria, 304
Unmanned aerial vehicles, 259, 303, 341, 406
Unstable dynamic social equilibrium, (UDSE), 10, 231, 232, 237, 239, 242, 244
U Planner, company, 535
Uruguay, 533, 537
U.S. Army Research Office, 553
U.S. Central Intelligence Agency, 545
U.S. Congress, 313
U.S. Department of Defense, 23, 251, 378, 640, 647
U.S. Department of Homeland Security, 540
US Department of Justice, 314
U.S. Department of State, 512, 540
US Government Accountability Office (GAO), 651
Utrecht University, 637

V

Vaccination, 113, 184
Van Staden, Cobus, 316
Venezuela, 234, 543, 546–548, 550
Video games
    computer games, xiv, 259, 350, 352, 353, 435, 649
Visual and auditory sensory systems, 29
Vkontakte, 143, 315
Voronkov, Vladimir, 57

W

Wargame Research and Development Centre, New Delhi, 301
WeChat, 138, 336, 341, 342, 353, 355, 356
Weizenbaum, Joseph, 658

Wells, Herbert G., 640
Weston A. Price Foundation, 317
WhatsApp, 281, 309, 311, 433, 516, 518, 544, 547, 585
White supremacism, 92, 257
Wolfe, Audra, 244
Woolley, Samuel, 549
World Economic Forum (WEF), xii, 33, 221, 259, 287, 346, 533, 538, 539, 564, 567, 570, 639, 640, 642
Wray, Chris, 261
Wright, Charity, 51, 305

X

Xenophobia, 433
Xiamen Declaration, BRICS, 320
XiaoBing, 352
XiaoIce, 353
Xi Jinping, 346, 351, 392
Xinjiang, 338–345, 363, 364

Y

Yale University, 379, 638, 651
Yandex, 315, 660
Yefremov, Ivan, 664
Yoon Suk-yeol, 3, 55

Z

al-Zawahiri, Ayman, 257, 261–262
Zelensky, Volodimir, 48, 495
Zero-sum game, 566
Zero-sum thinking, 378
Zhang, Sophie, 549
Zhejiang Buddha Technology, 322–323
Zuckerberg, Mark, 153, 236, 639
Zuma, Jacob, 318

Printed in the United States
by Baker & Taylor Publisher Services